Signing of the Preliminary Treaty of Peace in 1782

THE PAPERS OF

Benjamin Franklin

VOLUME 38 *August 16, 1782, through January 20, 1783*

ELLEN R. COHN, *Editor*

JONATHAN R. DULL, *Senior Associate Editor*

KAREN DUVAL, *Associate Editor*

JUDITH M. ADKINS, KATE M. OHNO, AND
MICHAEL SLETCHER, *Assistant Editors*

CLAUDE A. LOPEZ, *Consulting Editor*

JENNIFER M. MACELLARO, *Editorial Assistant*

New Haven and London   YALE UNIVERSITY PRESS, 2006

As indicated in the first volume, this edition was made possible through the vision and generosity of Yale University and the American Philosophical Society and by a substantial donation from Henry R. Luce in the name of Life Magazine. Additional funds were provided by a grant from the Ford Foundation to the National Archives Trust Fund Board. Subsequent support has come from the Andrew W. Mellon Foundation. The Papers of Benjamin Franklin is a beneficiary of the generous and long-standing support of the National Historical Publications and Records Commission under the chairmanship of the Archivist of the United States, and the National Endowment for the Humanities, an independent federal agency. Major underwriting of the present volume has been provided by the Barkley Fund, the Florence Gould Foundation, the Norman and Lyn Lear Foundation, the National Trust for the Humanities, the Packard Humanities Institute, and The Pew Charitable Trusts. We gratefully acknowledge the bequest of Raymond N. Kjellberg, which will continue to sustain our enterprise. We offer particular appreciation to Richard Gilder, Charles and Ann Johnson, Mason Willrich, the Yale Class of 1954, The Pew Charitable Trusts, and Yale University for generous donations that will insure the future of the edition. We are grateful for the generous support of Candace and Stuart Karu, the family and friends of the late Malcolm N. Smith, and the late Ralph Gregory Elliot. Gifts from many other individuals as well as donations from the American Philosophical Society and the Friends of Franklin help to sustain the enterprise. For the assistance of all these organizations and individuals, as well as for the indispensable aid of archivists, librarians, scholars, and collectors of Franklin manuscripts, the editors are most grateful.

Publication of this volume was assisted by a grant from The Pew Charitable Trusts.

Library of Congress catalog card number: 59-12697
International standard book number-13: 978-0-300-10930-6
International standard book number-10: 0-300-10930-X

Printed in the U.S.A.

To

CHARLES AND ANN JOHNSON

with gratitude

Contents

Foreign-language surnames and titles of nobility often run to great length. Our practice with an untitled person is to provide all the Christian names at the first appearance, and then drop them; a chevalier or noble is given the title used at the time, and the full name is provided in the index.

*Denotes a document referred to in annotation.

xviii

CONTENTS

List of Illustrations

xxix

Franklin of September 22. The designs were based on Franklin's proposal of a medal commemorating the victories of Yorktown and Saratoga. The pen and ink sketch by Gibelin (top) is reproduced by courtesy of the Musée national de la Coopération Franco-Américaine, Blérancourt, France, and the Réunion des Musées Nationaux Art Resource, New York. The first of Dupré's two pencil sketches (bottom left) is reproduced by courtesy of the American Philosophical Society. The second (bottom right) is reproduced by courtesy of the Musée des arts décoratifs, Paris.

William Hodgson and Family *facing page 224*

Undated oil portrait of the Hodgson family by Johann Zoffany (1733–1810). The London merchant William Hodgson and his wife, Mary, are shown with six of their nine children who were born between 1749 and 1774. Photograph © National Portrait Gallery, London.

Richard Oswald *facing page 276*

Oil portrait by William Denune, 1749. Private Collection. This portrait of a young, handsome Oswald is the only known likeness produced during his lifetime. Photograph reproduced by courtesy of the Scottish National Portrait Gallery.

The Mitchell Map *facing page 382*

A detail of the northeast section of the 1755 map of North America by John Mitchell, printed by Jefferys & Faden. This sheet was used by the peace commissioners in 1782. It shows a boundary line drawn in red ink by John Jay, labeled "Mr. Oswald's Line." Reproduced by courtesy of the New-York Historical Society.

Benjamin Franklin's Suit of Clothes *facing page 501*

A silk suit of French manufacture that William Temple Franklin sent to Elkanah Watson in response to his request for a suit of Franklin's "Old Cloaths, that never can be of any Service to him." Watson wanted to create a lifelike dummy of Franklin on which he would place the wax head that Patience Wright had sculpted for him; the results are described in our notes on Watson's request to William Temple Franklin, December 25. Watson presented the suit to the Massachusetts Historical Society in 1803. At the time of the donation he wrote that the clothes dated from 1778, and that if the wax head had not been broken some years earlier, he would have donated that as well: *Proc.* of the Mass. Hist. Soc., I, 155. Reproduced from *Benjamin Franklin and His Circle; a Catalogue of an Exhibition at the Metropolitan Museum of Art* (New York, 1936).

Franklin had this work printed with his own types, either on his own press or elsewhere, in late 1782. It was completed by January 8, 1783, when he sent a copy to Mary Hewson; his cover letter is published in this volume. The only copy of this small book known to have survived is in the Franklin Collection, Yale University Library.

Contributors to Volume 38

The ownership of each manuscript, or the location of the particular copy used by the editors of each rare contemporary pamphlet or similar printed work, is indicated where the document appears in the text. The sponsors and editors are deeply grateful to the following institutions and individuals for permission to print or otherwise use in the present volume manuscripts and other materials which they own.

INSTITUTIONS

American Philosophical Society
Archives de la Marine, Vincennes
Archives du Ministère des affaires
    étrangères, Paris
Bibliothèque Nationale
British Museum
John Carter Brown Library
Chapin Library, Williams College
William L. Clements Library
Columbia University Library
Connecticut State Library
Fitzwilliam Museum, Cambridge,
    England
Historical Society of Pennsylvania
Henry E. Huntington Library

Library of Congress
Massachusetts Historical Society
Museo Civico Gaetano Filangieri
National Archives
National Museum, Prague
New-York Historical Society
New York Public Library
Public Record Office
South Carolina Historical Society
United States Naval Academy
    Museum
University of Pennsylvania Library
University of Virginia Library
Yale University Library

INDIVIDUALS

Alice T. Bates, Los Angeles, California
G. T. Mandl-Trust, Nestal, Switzerland
Mrs. Herbert May, Washington, D.C.
D. A. F. H. H. Hartley Russell, on deposit at the Berkshire County
    Record Office

Statement of Methodology

Arrangement of Materials

The documents are printed in chronological sequence according to their dates when these are given, or according to the date of publication in cases of contemporary printed materials. Records such as diaries, journals, and account books that cover substantial periods of time appear according to the dates of their earliest entries. When no date appears on the document itself, one is editorially supplied and an explanation provided. When no day within a month is given, the document is placed at the end of all specifically dated documents of that month; those dated only by year are placed at the end of that year. If no date is given, we use internal and external evidence to assign one whenever possible, providing our explanation in annotation. Documents which cannot be assigned a date more definite than the entire length of Franklin's stay in France (1777–85) will be published at the end of this period. Those for which we are unable to provide even a tentative date will be published at the conclusion of the series.

When two or more documents have the same date, they are arranged in the following order:

1. Those by a group of which Franklin was a member (*e.g.*, the American Commissioners in Paris)
2. Those by Franklin individually
3. Those to a group of which Franklin was a member
4. Those to Franklin individually
5. "Third-party" and unaddressed miscellaneous writings by others than Franklin.

In the first two categories letters are arranged alphabetically by the name of the addressee; in the last three, by the name of the signatory. An exception to this practice occurs when a letter to Franklin and his answer were written on the same day: in such cases the first letter precedes the reply. The same rules apply to documents lacking precise dates printed together at the end of any month or year.

Form of Presentation

The document and its accompanying editorial apparatus are presented in the following order:

1. *Title*. Essays and formal papers are headed by their titles, except in the case of pamphlets with very long titles, when a short form is substituted. Where previous editors supplied a title to a piece that had none, and this title has become familiar, we use it; otherwise we devise a suitable one.

Letters written by Franklin individually are entitled "To" the person or body addressed, as: To John Adams; To John Adams and Arthur Lee; To the Royal Society.

Letters to Franklin individually are entitled "From" the person or body who wrote them, as: From John Adams; From John Adams and Arthur Lee; From the Committee of Secret Correspondence.

Letters of which Franklin was a joint author or joint recipient are titled with the names of all concerned, as: Franklin and Silas Deane to Arthur Lee; Arthur Lee to Franklin and Silas Deane. "Third-party" letters or those by or to a body of which Franklin was a member are titled with the names of both writers and addressees, as: Arthur Lee to John Adams; The American Commissioners to John Paul Jones.

Documents not fitting into any of these categories are given brief descriptive headings, as: Extract from Franklin's Journal.

If the name in the title has been supplied from external evidence it appears in brackets, with a question mark when we are uncertain. If a letter is unsigned, or signed with initials or an alias, but is from a correspondent whose handwriting we know, the name appears without brackets.

2. *Source Identification*. This gives the nature of the printed or manuscript version of the document, and, in the case of a manuscript or a rare printed work, the ownership and location of the original.

Printed sources of three different classes are distinguished. First, a contemporary pamphlet, which is given its full title, place and date of publication, and the location of the copy the editors have used. Second, an essay or letter appearing originally in a *contemporary* publication, which is introduced by the words

"Printed in," followed by the title, date, and inclusive page numbers, if necessary, of the publication. Third, a document, the manuscript or contemporary printed version of which is now lost, but which was printed at a later date, is identified by the words "Reprinted from," followed by the name of the work from which the editors have reproduced it. The following examples illustrate the distinction:

Printed in *The Pennsylvania Gazette*, October 2, 1729.
Reprinted from William Temple Franklin, ed., *Memoirs of the Life and Writings of Benjamin Franklin* . . . (3 vols., 4to, London, 1817–18), II, 244.

The Source Identification of a manuscript consists of a term or symbol (all of which are listed in the Short Title List) indicating the character of the manuscript version, followed by the name of the holder of the manuscript, as: ALS: American Philosophical Society. Because press copies replicate the manuscripts from which they were made, we indicate the character of the original manuscript, as: press copy of L. Since manuscripts belonging to individuals have a tendency to migrate, we indicate the year in which each private owner gave permission to publish, as: Morris Duane, Philadelphia, 1957. When two or more manuscript versions survive, the one listed first in the Source Identification is the one from which we print.

3. An editorial *Headnote* precedes some documents in this edition; it appears between the Source Identification and the actual text. Such a headnote is designed to supply the background of the composition of the document, its relation to events or other writings, and any other information which may be useful to the reader and is not obtainable from the document itself.

4. The *Text* of the document follows the Source Identification, or Headnote, if any. When multiple copies of a document are extant, the editors observe the following order of priority in determining which of the available versions to use in printing a text: ALS or ADS, LS or DS, AL or AD, L or D, and copy. An AL (draft) normally takes precedence over a contemporary copy based on the recipient's copy. If we deviate from the order set forth here, we explain our decision in the annotation. In those instances where multiple texts are available, the texts are collated, and sig-

nificant variations reported in the annotation. In selecting the publication text from among several copies of official French correspondence (*e.g.*, from Vergennes or Sartine) we use the version which is written in the best French, on the presumption that the French ministers used standard eighteenth-century spelling, grammar, and punctuation.

The form of presentation of the texts of letters is as follows: The place and date of composition are set at the top, regardless of their location in the original manuscript.

The signature, set in capitals and small capitals, is placed at the right of the last line of the text if there is room; if not, then on the line below.

Addresses, endorsements, and notations are so labelled and printed at the end of the letter. An endorsement is, to the best of our belief, by the recipient, and a notation by someone else. When the writer of the notation has misread the date or the signature of the correspondent, we let the error stand without comment. Line breaks in addresses are marked by slashes. Different notations are separated by slashes; when they are by different individuals, we so indicate.

5. *Footnotes* to the Heading, Source Identification, Headnote, and Text appear on the pages to which they pertain. References to documents not printed or to be printed in later volumes are by date and repository, as: Jan. 17, 1785, APS.

Method of Textual Reproduction

1. *Spelling* of all words, including proper names, is retained. If it is abnormal enough to obscure the meaning we follow the word immediately with the current spelling in brackets.

2. *Capitalization and Punctuation* are retained. There is such variety in the size of initial letters, often in the same manuscript, that it is sometimes unclear whether the writer intended an upper or lower case letter. In such cases we make a decision on the basis of the correspondent's customary usage. We supply a capital letter when an immediately preceding period, colon, question mark, exclamation point, or dash indicates that a new sentence is intended. If a capital letter clearly indicates the beginning of a new thought, but no mark of punctuation precedes it, we insert a period. If neither punctuation nor capital let-

ter indicates a sentence break, we do not supply them unless their absence renders comprehension of the document nearly impossible. In that case we provide them and so indicate in a footnote.

Dashes were used for a variety of purposes in eighteenth-century personal and public letters. A dash within a sentence, used to indicate a break in thought, is represented as an em dash. A dash that follows a period or serves as a closing mark of punctuation for a sentence is represented as an em dash followed by a space. Occasionally correspondents used long dashes that continue to the end of a line and indicate a significant break in thought. We do not reproduce the dash, but treat it as indicating the start of a new paragraph.

When there is an initial quotation mark or parenthesis, but no closing one, we silently complete the pair.

3. *Contractions and abbreviations* are retained. Abbreviations such as "wd", "honble", "servt", "exclly", are used so frequently in Franklin's correspondence that they are readily comprehensible to the users of these volumes. Abbreviations, particularly of French words, that may be unclear are followed by an expanded version in brackets, as: nre [navire]. Superscript letters are brought down to the line. Where a period or colon is a part of the abbreviation, or indicates that letters were written above the line, we print it at the end of the word, as: 4th. for 4.th. In those few cases where superscript letters brought down to the line result in a confusing abbreviation ("Made" for "Mad^e"), we follow the abbreviation by an expanded version in brackets, as: Made [Madame].

The ampersand by itself and the "&c." are retained. Letters represented by the "y" are printed, as: "the" and "that". The tailed "p" is spelled out, as: "per", "pre", or "pro". Symbols of weights, measures, and money are converted to modern forms, as: *l.t.* instead of Ħ for *livres tournois*.

4. *Omissions, mutilations, and illegible words* are treated as follows:

If we are certain of the reading of letters missing in a word because of a torn or taped manuscript or tightly bound copybook, we supply the letters silently.

If we cannot be sure of the word, or of how the author spelled it, but we can make a reasonable guess, we supply the missing letters in brackets.

When the writer has omitted a word absolutely required for clarity, we insert it in italics within brackets.

5. *Interlineations* by the author are silently incorporated into the text. If they are significant enough to require comment a footnote is provided.

Textual Conventions

/	denotes line break in addresses; separates multiple endorsements and notations.
⟨roman⟩	denotes a résumé of a letter or document.
[*italic*]	editorial insertion explaining something about the manuscript, as: [*one line illegible*]; or supplying a word to make the meaning clear, as: [*to*].
[roman]	editorial insertion clarifying the immediately preceding word or abbreviation; supplies letters missing because of a mutilated manuscript.
(?)	indicates a questionable reading.

Abbreviations and Short Titles

AAE	Archives du Ministère des affaires étrangères.
AD	Autograph document.
Adams Correspondence	Lyman H. Butterfield, Richard A. Ryerson, *et al.*, eds., *Adams Family Correspondence* (7 vols. to date, Cambridge, Mass., 1963–).
Adams Papers	Robert J. Taylor, Gregg L. Lint, *et al.*, eds., *Papers of John Adams* (12 vols. to date, Cambridge, Mass., 1977–).
ADB	*Allgemeine Deutsche Biographie* (56 vols., Berlin, 1967–71).
Adm.	Admiral.
ADS	Autograph document signed.
AL	Autograph letter.
Allen, *Mass. Privateers*	Gardner Weld Allen, ed., *Massachusetts Privateers of the Revolution* ([Cambridge, Mass.], 1927) (Massachusetts Historical Society *Collections*, LXXVII).
Almanach des marchands	*Almanach général des marchands, négocians, armateurs, et fabricans de France et de l'Europe et autres parties du monde* . . . (Paris, 1779).
Almanach royal	*Almanach royal* (91 vols., Paris, 1700–92). Cited by year.
Almanach de Versailles	*Almanach de Versailles* (Versailles, various years). Cited by year.
Alphabetical List of Escaped Prisoners	Alphabetical List of the Americans who having escap'd from the Prisons of England, were furnish'd with Money by the Commissrs. of the U.S. at the Court of France, to return to America.

	A manuscript in the APS, dated 1784, and covering the period January, 1777, to November, 1784.
ALS	Autograph letter signed.
ANB	John A. Garraty and Mark C. Carnes, eds., *American National Biography* (24 vols., New York and Oxford, 1999).
APS	American Philosophical Society.
Archaeol.	Archaeological.
Assn.	Association.
Auphan, "Communications"	P. Auphan, "Les communications entre la France et ses colonies d'Amérique pendant la guerre de l'indépendance Américaine," *Revue Maritime,* new series, no. LXIII and LXIV (1925), 331–48, 497–517.
Autobiog.	Leonard W. Labaree, Ralph L. Ketcham, Helen C. Boatfield, and Helene H. Fineman, eds., *The Autobiography of Benjamin Franklin* (New Haven, 1964).
Bachaumont, *Mémoires secrets*	[Louis Petit de Bachaumont *et al.*], *Mémoires secrets pour servir à l'histoire de la république des lettres en France, depuis MDCCLXII jusqu'à nos jours; ou, Journal d'un observateur . . .* (36 vols. in 12, London, 1784–89). Bachaumont died in 1771. The first six vols. (1762–71) are his; Mathieu-François Pidansat de Mairobert edited them and wrote the next nine (1771–79); the remainder (1779–87) are by Barthélemy-François Mouffle d'Angerville.
Balch, *French in America*	Thomas Balch, *The French in America during the War of Independence of the United States, 1777–1783* (trans. by

Thomas Willing Balch *et al.;* 2 vols., Philadelphia, 1891–95).

BF   Benjamin Franklin.

BF's accounts as commissioner   Those described above, XXIII, 20.

BF's journal of the peace negotiations   Described in XXXVII, 291–346. This refers to the copy in Josiah Flagg's hand with corrections by BF, at the Library of Congress.

BFB   Benjamin Franklin Bache.

BFB's journal   Described above, XXXVII, 682n.

Bigelow, *Works*   John Bigelow, ed., *The Works of Benjamin Franklin* (12 vols., New York and London, 1887–88).

Biographie universelle   *Biographie universelle, ancienne et moderne, ou histoire, par ordre alphabétique, de la vie publique et privée de tous les hommes qui se sont fait remarquer . . .* (85 vols., Paris, 1811–62).

Bodinier   From information kindly furnished us by Cdt. Gilbert Bodinier, Section études, Service historique de l'Armée de Terre, Vincennes.

Bodinier, *Dictionnaire*   Gilbert Bodinier, *Dictionnaire des officiers de l'armée royale qui ont combattu aux États-Unis pendant la guerre d'Indépendance* (Château de Vincennes, 1982).

Bowler, *Logistics*   R. Arthur Bowler, *Logistics and the Failure of the British Army in America, 1775–1783* (Princeton, 1975).

Bradford, *Jones Papers*   James C. Bradford, ed., *The Microfilm Edition of the Papers of John Paul Jones, 1747–1792* (10 reels of microfilm, Alexandria, Va., 1986).

Burke's Peerage   Sir Bernard Burke, *Burke's Genealogical and Heraldic History of the Peerage*

Baronetage and Knightage with War Gazette and Corrigenda (98th ed., London, 1940). References in exceptional cases to other editions are so indicated.

Burnett, *Letters* Edmund C. Burnett, ed., *Letters of Members of the Continental Congress* (8 vols., Washington, 1921–36).

Butterfield, *John Adams Diary* Lyman H. Butterfield *et al.*, eds., *Diary and Autobiography of John Adams* (4 vols., Cambridge, Mass., 1961).

Cash Book BF's accounts described above, XXVI, 3.

Chron. *Chronicle.*

Claghorn, *Naval Officers* Charles E. Claghorn, *Naval Officers of the American Revolution: a Concise Biographical Dictionary* (Metuchen, N.J., and London, 1988).

Clark, *Ben Franklin's Privateers* William Bell Clark, *Ben Franklin's Privateers: a Naval Epic of the American Revolution* (Baton Rouge, 1956).

Clark, *Wickes* William Bell Clark, *Lambert Wickes, Sea Raider and Diplomat: the Story of a Naval Captain of the Revolution* (New Haven and London, 1932).

Clowes, *Royal Navy* William Laird Clowes, *The Royal Navy: a History from the Earliest Times to the Present* (7 vols., Boston and London, 1897–1903).

Cobbett, *Parliamentary History* William Cobbett and Thomas C. Hansard, eds., *The Parliamentary History of England from the Earliest Period to 1803* (36 vols., London, 1806–20).

Col. Column.

Coll. *Collections.*

comp. compiler.

Croÿ, *Journal* Emmanuel, prince de Moeurs et de Solre et duc de Croÿ, *Journal inédit du duc de*

xlii

Croÿ, 1718–1784 (4 vols., Paris, 1906–7).

d.   *denier.*

D   Document unsigned.

DAB   *Dictionary of American Biography.*

DBF   *Dictionnaire de biographie française* (19 vols. to date, Paris, 1933–).

Dictionary of Scientific Biography   Charles C. Gillispie, ed., *Dictionary of Scientific Biography* (18 vols., New York, 1970–90).

Deane Papers   *The Deane Papers, 1774–90* (5 vols.; New-York Historical Society *Collections*, XIX–XXIII, New York, 1887–91).

DF   Deborah Franklin.

Dictionnaire de la noblesse   François-Alexandre Aubert de La Chesnaye-Dubois and M. Badier, *Dictionnaire de la noblesse contenant les généalogies, l'histoire & la chronologie des familles nobles de la France* . . . (3rd ed.; 19 vols., Paris, 1863–76).

Dictionnaire historique   *Dictionnaire historique, critique et bibliographique, contenant les vies des hommes illustres, célèbres ou fameux de tous les pays et de tous les siècles* . . . (30 vols., Paris, 1821–23).

Dictionnaire historique de la Suisse   *Dictionnaire historique & biographique de la Suisse* (7 vols. and supplement, Neuchâtel, 1921–34).

DNB   *Dictionary of National Biography.*

Doniol, *Histoire*   Henri Doniol, *Histoire de la participation de la France à l'établissement des Etats-Unis d'Amérique. Correspondance diplomatique et documents* (5 vols., Paris, 1886–99).

DS   Document signed.

Duane, *Works*   William Duane, ed., *The Works of Dr.*

Benjamin Franklin . . . (6 vols., Philadelphia, 1808–18). Title varies in the several volumes.

Dubourg, *Œuvres*   Jacques Barbeu-Dubourg, ed., *Œuvres de M. Franklin* . . . (2 vols., Paris, 1773).

Dull, *French Navy*   Jonathan R. Dull, *The French Navy and American Independence: a Study of Arms and Diplomacy, 1774–1787* (Princeton, 1975).

Ed.   Edition or editor.

Edler, *Dutch Republic*   Friedrich Edler, *The Dutch Republic and the American Revolution* (*Johns Hopkins University Studies in Historical and Political Science*, ser. XXIX, no. 2; Baltimore, 1911).

Elias and Finch, *Letters of Digges*   Robert H. Elias and Eugene D. Finch, eds., *Letters of Thomas Attwood Digges (1742–1821)* (Columbia, S.C., 1982).

Etat militaire   *Etat militaire de France, pour l'année* . . . (36 vols., Paris, 1758–93). Cited by year.

Exper. and Obser.   *Experiments and Observations on Electricity, made at Philadelphia in America, by Mr. Benjamin Franklin* . . . (London, 1751). Revised and enlarged editions were published in 1754, 1760, 1769, and 1774 with slightly varying titles. In each case the edition cited will be indicated, *e.g.*, *Exper. and Obser.* (1751).

f.   florins.

Fauchille, *Diplomatie française*   Paul Fauchille, *La Diplomatie française et la ligue des neutres de 1780 (1776–1783)* (Paris, 1893).

xliv

Ferguson, *Power of the Purse* — E. James Ferguson, *The Power of the Purse: a History of American Public Finance* . . . (Chapel Hill, N.C., 1961).

Fitzmaurice, *Life of Shelburne* — Edmond George Petty-Fitzmaurice, *Life of William, Earl of Shelburne, Afterwards First Marquess of Lansdowne, with Extracts from His Papers and Correspondence* (3 vols., London, 1875–76).

Fitzpatrick, *Writings of Washington* — John C. Fitzpatrick, ed., *The Writings of George Washington* . . . (39 vols., Washington, D.C., 1931–44).

Ford, *Letters of William Lee* — Worthington Chauncey Ford, ed., *Letters of William Lee, 1766–1783* (3 vols., Brooklyn, N.Y., 1891).

Fortescue, *Correspondence of George Third* — Sir John William Fortescue, ed., *The Correspondence of King George the Third from 1760 to December 1783* . . . (6 vols., London, 1927–28).

France ecclésiastique — *La France ecclésiastique pour l'année* . . . (15 vols., Paris, 1774–90). Cited by year.

Freeman, *Washington* — Douglas S. Freeman (completed by John A. Carroll and Mary W. Ashworth), *George Washington: a Biography* (7 vols., New York, 1948–57).

Gaz. — *Gazette.*

Gaz. de Leyde — *Nouvelles extraordinaires de divers endroits,* commonly known as *Gazette de Leyde.* Each issue is in two parts; we indicate the second as "sup."

Gen. — General.

Geneal. — *Genealogical.*

Gent. Mag. — *The Gentleman's Magazine, and Historical Chronicle.*

Giunta, *Emerging Nation* — Mary A. Giunta, *et al.,* eds., *The Emerging Nation: a Documentary History of*

xlv

	the *Foreign Relations of the United States under the Articles of the Confederation, 1780–1789* (3 vols., Washington, D.C., 1996).
Harlow, *Second British Empire*	Vincent T. Harlow, *The Founding of the Second British Empire, 1763–1793* (2 vols., London and New York, 1952–64).
Hays, *Calendar*	I. Minis Hays, *Calendar of the Papers of Benjamin Franklin in the Library of the American Philosophical Society* (5 vols., Philadelphia, 1908).
Heitman, *Register of Officers*	Francis B. Heitman, *Historical Register of Officers in the War of the Revolution* . . . (Washington, D.C., 1893).
Hillairet, *Rues de Paris*	Jacques Hillairet, pseud. of Auguste A. Coussillan, *Dictionnaire historique des rues de Paris* (2nd ed.; 2 vols., [Paris, 1964]).
Hist.	Historic or Historical.
Hoffman and Albert, eds., *Peace and the Peacemakers*	Ronald Hoffman and Peter J. Albert, eds., *Peace and the Peacemakers: the Treaty of 1783* (Charlottesville, Va., 1986).
Idzerda, *Lafayette Papers*	Stanley J. Idzerda *et al.*, eds., *Lafayette in the Age of the American Revolution: Selected Letters and Papers, 1776–1790* (5 vols. to date, Ithaca, N.Y., and London, 1977–).
JA	John Adams.
JCC	Worthington Chauncey Ford *et al.*, eds., *Journals of the Continental Congress, 1744–1789* (34 vols., Washington, 1904–37).
Jefferson Papers	Julian P. Boyd, Charles T. Cullen, John Catanzariti, Barbara B. Oberg, *et al.*,

eds., *The Papers of Thomas Jefferson* (32 vols. to date, Princeton, 1950–).

Jour. Journal.

JW Jonathan Williams, Jr.

Kaminkow, *Mariners* Marion and Jack Kaminkow, *Mariners of the American Revolution* (Baltimore, 1967).

Klingelhofer, "Matthew Ridley's Diary" Herbert F. Klingelhofer, ed., "Matthew Ridley's Diary during the Peace Negotiations of 1782," *William and Mary Quarterly,* 3rd series, XX (1963), 95– 133.

L Letter unsigned.

Landais, *Memorial* Pierre Landais, *Memorial, to Justify Peter Landai's Conduct during the Late War* (Boston, 1784).

Larousse Pierre Larousse, *Grand Dictionnaire universel du XIXe siècle* . . . (17 vols., Paris, [n.d.]).

Lasseray, *Les Français* André Lasseray, *Les Français sous les treize étoiles, 1775–1783* (2 vols., Paris, 1935).

Laurens Papers Philip M. Hamer, George C. Rogers, Jr., David R. Chestnutt, *et al.,* eds., *The Papers of Henry Laurens* (16 vols. to date, Columbia, S.C., 1968–).

Le Bihan, *Francs-maçons parisiens* Alain Le Bihan, *Francs-maçons parisiens du Grand Orient de France* . . . (Commission d'histoire économique et sociale de la révolution française, *Mémoires et documents,* XIX, Paris, 1966).

Lee Family Papers Paul P. Hoffman, ed., *The Lee Family Papers, 1742–1795* (University of Virginia *Microfilm Publication* No. 1; 8 reels, Charlottesville, Va., 1966).

xlvii

Lewis, *Walpole Correspondence* — Wilmarth S. Lewis *et al.*, eds., *The Yale Edition of Horace Walpole's Correspondence* (48 vols., New Haven, 1939–83).

Lopez, *Lafayette* — Claude A. Lopez, "Benjamin Franklin, Lafayette, and the *Lafayette*," *Proceedings* of the American Philosophical Society CVIII (1964), 181–223.

Lopez, *Mon Cher Papa* — Claude-Anne Lopez, *Mon Cher Papa: Franklin and the Ladies of Paris* (rev. ed., New Haven and London, 1990).

Lopez and Herbert, *The Private Franklin* — Claude-Anne Lopez and Eugenia W. Herbert, *The Private Franklin: the Man and His Family* (New York, 1975).

LS — Letter or letters signed.

l.t. — *livres tournois.*

Lüthy, *Banque protestante* — Herbert Lüthy, *La Banque protestante en France de la Révocation de l'Edit de Nantes à la Révolution* (2 vols., Paris, 1959–61).

Mackesy, *War for America* — Piers Mackesy, *The War for America, 1775–1783* (Cambridge, Mass., 1965).

Madariaga, *Harris's Mission* — Isabel de Madariaga, *Britain, Russia, and the Armed Neutrality of 1780: Sir James Harris's Mission to St. Petersburg during the American Revolution* (New Haven, 1962).

Mag. — *Magazine.*

Mass. Arch. — Massachusetts Archives, State House, Boston.

Mazas, *Ordre de Saint-Louis* — Alexandre Mazas and Théodore Anne, *Histoire de l'ordre royal et militaire de Saint-Louis depuis son institution en 1693 jusqu'en 1830* (2nd ed.; 3 vols., Paris, 1860–61).

Medlin, *Morellet* — Dorothy Medlin, Jean-Claude David,

Paul LeClerc, eds., *Lettres de Morellet* (3 vols., Oxford, 1991–96).

Métra, *Correspondance secrète*   [François Métra *et al.*], *Correspondance secrète, politique & littéraire, ou Mémoires pour servir à l'histoire des cours, des sociétés & de la littérature en France, depuis la mort de Louis XV* (18 vols., London, 1787–90).

Meyer, *Armement nantais*   Jean Meyer, *L'Armement nantais dans la deuxième moitié du XVIIIe siècle* (Paris, 1969).

Meyer, *Noblesse bretonne*   Jean Meyer, *La Noblesse bretonne au XVIIIe siècle* (2 vols., Paris, 1966).

"Mission of Col. Laurens"   "The Mission of Col. John Laurens to Europe in 1781," *The South Carolina Historical and Genealogical Magazine*, I (1900), 13–41, 136–51, 213–22, 311–22; II (1901), 27–43, 108–25.

Morison, *Jones*   Samuel E. Morison, *John Paul Jones: a Sailor's Biography* (Boston and Toronto, 1959).

Morris, *Jay: Peace*   Richard B. Morris *et al.*, eds., *John Jay, the Winning of the Peace: Unpublished Papers, 1780–1784* (New York, Cambridge, London, 1980).

Morris, *Jay: Revolutionary*   Richard B. Morris *et al.*, eds., *John Jay, the Making of a Revolutionary: Unpublished Papers, 1743–1780* (New York, Evanston, San Francisco, 1975).

Morris Papers   E. James Ferguson, John Catanzariti, Mary A. Gallagher, Elizabeth M. Nuxoll, *et al.*, eds., *The Papers of Robert Morris, 1781–1784* (9 vols., Pittsburgh, Pa., 1973–99).

Morton, *Beaumarchais*   Brian N. Morton and Donald C. Spinelli,

xlix

Correspondance	eds., *Beaumarchais Correspondance* (4 vols. to date, Paris, 1969–).
MS, MSS	Manuscript, manuscripts.
Namier and Brooke, *House of Commons*	Sir Lewis Namier and John Brooke, *The History of Parliament. The House of Commons 1754–1790* (3 vols., London and New York, 1964).
Neeser, *Conyngham*	Robert Walden Neeser, ed., *Letters and Papers Relating to the Cruises of Gustavus Conyngham, Captain of the Continental Navy 1777–1779* (New York, 1915).
NNBW	*Nieuw Nederlandsch Biografisch Woordenboek* (10 vols. and index, Amsterdam, 1974).
Nouvelle Biographie	*Nouvelle Biographie générale depuis les temps les plus reculés jusqu'à nos jours* . . . (46 vols., Paris, 1855–66).
p.	pence.
Pa.	Pennsylvania.
Pa. Arch.	Samuel Hazard *et al.*, eds., *Pennsylvania Archives* (9 series, Philadelphia and Harrisburg, 1852–1935).
Palmer, *Loyalists*	Gregory Palmer, ed., *Biographical Sketches of Loyalists of the American Revolution* (Westport, Conn., 1984).
Phil. Trans.	The Royal Society, *Philosophical Transactions*.
PMHB	*Pennsylvania Magazine of History and Biography*.
Price, *France and the Chesapeake*	Jacob M. Price, *France and the Chesapeake: a History of the French Tobacco Monopoly, 1674–1791, and of Its Relationship to the British and American Tobacco Trade* (2 vols., Ann Arbor, Mich., 1973).

1

Proc.	*Proceedings.*
Pub.	*Publications.*
Quérard, *France littéraire*	Joseph Marie Quérard, *La France littéraire, ou Dictionnaire bibliographique des savants, historiens, et gens de lettres de la France, ainsi que des littérateurs étrangers qui ont écrit en français, plus particulièrement pendant les XVIIIe et XIXe siècles* . . . (10 vols., Paris, 1827–64).
Rakove, *Beginnings of National Politics*	Jack N. Rakove, *The Beginnings of National Politics: an Interpretive History of the Continental Congress* (New York, 1979).
RB	Richard Bache.
Repertorium der diplomatischen Vertreter	Ludwig Bittner *et al.*, eds., *Repertorium der diplomatischen Vertreter aller Länder seit dem Westfälischen Frieden (1648)* (3 vols., Oldenburg, etc., 1936–65).
Rev.	*Review.*
Rice and Brown, eds., *Rochambeau's Army*	Howard C. Rice, Jr., and Anne S.K. Brown, eds., *The American Campaigns of Rochambeau's Army, 1780, 1781, 1782, 1783* (2 vols., Princeton and Providence, 1972).
s.	*sou.*
s.	shilling.
Sabine, *Loyalists*	Lorenzo Sabine, *Biographical Sketches of Loyalists of the American Revolution* . . . (2 vols., Boston, 1864).
SB	Sarah Bache.
Schelle, *Œuvres de Turgot*	Gustave Schelle, ed., *Œuvres de Turgot et documents le concernant* (5 vols., Paris, 1913–23).
Schulte Nordholt, *Dutch Republic*	J. W. Schulte Nordholt, *The Dutch Republic and American Independence*

li

	(trans. Herbert M. Rowen; Chapel Hill, N.C., 1982).
Sellers, *Franklin in Portraiture*	Charles C. Sellers, *Benjamin Franklin in Portraiture* (New Haven and London, 1962).
Sibley's Harvard Graduates	John L. Sibley, *Biographical Sketches of Graduates of Harvard University* (17 vols. to date, Cambridge, Mass., 1873–). Continued from Volume IV by Clifford K. Shipton.
Six, *Dictionnaire biographique*	Georges Six, *Dictionnaire biographique des généraux et amiraux français de la Révolution et de l'Empire (1792–1814)* (2 vols., Paris, 1934).
Smith, *Letters*	Paul H. Smith *et al.*, eds., *Letters of Delegates to Congress* (26 vols., Washington, D.C., 1976–2000).
Smyth, *Writings*	Albert H. Smyth, ed., *The Writings of Benjamin Franklin* . . . (10 vols., New York, 1905–7).
Soc.	Society.
Sparks, *Works*	Jared Sparks, ed., *The Works of Benjamin Franklin* . . . (10 vols., Boston, 1836–40).
Stevens, *Facsimiles*	Benjamin F. Stevens, ed., *Facsimiles of Manuscripts in European Archives Relating to America, 1773–1783* (25 vols., London, 1889–98).
Taylor, *J. Q. Adams Diary*	Robert J. Taylor *et al.*, eds., *Diary of John Quincy Adams* (2 vols. to date, Cambridge, Mass., and London, 1981–).
Tourneux, *Correspondence littéraire*	Tourneux, Maurice, *Correspondence littéraire, philosophique et critique par Grimm, Diderot, Raynal, Meister, etc. revue sur les textes originaux comprenant*

	outre ce qui a été publié à diverses épo- ques les fragments supprimés en 1813 par la censure les parties inédites conservées à la Bibliothèque Ducale de Gotha et l'Arsenal à Paris (16 vols., Paris, 1877–82).
Trans.	Translator or translated.
Trans.	*Transactions.*
Van Doren, *Franklin*	Carl Van Doren, *Benjamin Franklin* (New York, 1938).
Van Doren, *Franklin-Mecom*	Carl Van Doren, ed., *The Letters of Benjamin Franklin & Jane Mecom* (American Philosophical Society *Memoirs,* XXVII, Princeton, 1950).
Villiers, *Commerce colonial*	Patrick Villiers, *Le Commerce colonial atlantique et la guerre d'indépendance des Etats-Unis d'Amérique, 1778–1783* (New York, 1977).
W&MQ	*William and Mary Quarterly,* first or third series as indicated.
Ward, *War of the Revolution*	Christopher Ward, *The War of the Revolution* (John R. Alden, ed.; 2 vols., New York, 1952).
Waste Book	BF's accounts described above, XXIII, 19.
WF	William Franklin.
Wharton, *Diplomatic Correspondence*	Francis Wharton, ed., *The Revolutionary Diplomatic Correspondence of the United States* (6 vols., Washington, D.C., 1889).
Willcox, *Portrait of a General*	William B. Willcox, *Portrait of a General: Sir Henry Clinton in the War of Independence* (New York, 1964).
WTF	William Temple Franklin.
WTF, *Memoirs*	William Temple Franklin, ed., *Memoirs of the Life and Writings of Benjamin*

	Franklin, L.L.D., F.R.S., &c . . . (3 vols., 4to, London, 1817–18).
WTF's accounts	Those described above, XXIII, 19.
Yela Utrilla, *España*	Juan F. Yela Utrilla, *España ante la Independencia de los Estados Unidos* (2nd ed.; 2 vols., Lérida, 1925).

Note by the Editors and the Administrative Board

As we noted in volume 23 (pp. xlvi–xlviii), the period of Franklin's mission to France brings with it roughly two and a half times as many documents as those for the other seventy years of his life. In the present volume once again we summarize a portion of his incoming correspondence in collective descriptions; they appear in the index under the following headings: emigrants, would-be; offerers of goods and schemes; favor seekers; consulship seekers.

As we noted in volume 30 (p. lx), Franklin's French secretary Jean L'Air de Lamotte was responsible for keeping the official letterbook. Many of the copies produced by L'Air de Lamotte are severely flawed. They contain errors of spelling, punctuation, and syntax that could not have been present in Franklin's originals. Regrettably, however, these copies are the only extant versions of much of Franklin's official correspondence dating from this period, and we publish them as they stand, pointing out and correcting errors only when they threaten to obscure Franklin's meaning.

A revised statement of textual methodology appeared in volume 28 and is repeated here. The original statement of method is found in the Introduction to the first volume, pp. xxiv–xlvii. The various developments in policy are explained in xv, xxiv; xxi, xxxiv; xxiii, xlvi–xlviii.

In 2005 Edmund S. Morgan expressed a wish to retire as Chairman of the Administrative Board, though to our relief he agreed to continue serving as a member. He joined the Board in 1968, as volume 13 was in preparation, and became Chairman in 1991. No one cares more deeply about the success of this project, nor gives wiser counsel, than he. We accepted his resignation as Chairman with reluctance but with deep appreciation for all his contributions and with gratitude for his continuing guidance.

Two staff members left the project while Volume 38 was in preparation: Judith Adkins, Assistant Editor, and Jennifer Macellaro, Editorial Assistant. We wish them both well.

Introduction

After eight years of bloodshed, the War for American Independence ended on January 20, 1783, with an armistice signed in the office of the French foreign minister Charles Gravier, comte de Vergennes. The five months leading up to that moment, chronicled in this volume, were far from smooth. Franklin had already constructed the basic framework for a peace treaty during negotiations he conducted with Richard Oswald, the British representative, in the spring and early summer of 1782. For the final rounds of negotiations he was joined, in succession, by American peace commissioners John Jay, John Adams, and eventually Henry Laurens. The first two greeted him with frank mistrust; Adams, in fact, was downright hostile. Forging a cooperative and unified team, however, would prove to be the least of Franklin's difficulties.

Franklin had initiated the peace negotiations in March, 1782; the first phase of those negotiations is covered in Volume 37 of this series. During these months he was the sole American negotiator, by default rather than by choice: Adams felt obliged to remain in the Netherlands, where he was trying to arrange a loan; Laurens refused to serve on the peace commission; and Jay—who answered Franklin's summons to Paris—fell ill and could not participate.[1] By the end of July, Franklin had persuaded British prime minister Shelburne to agree to a framework for peace based on recognition of American independence, the curtailment of Canada to its old boundaries (leaving to the United States the Mississippi River as a western boundary), and American access to the Newfoundland fishery.[2]

By August 16, when the present volume begins, Jay had recovered from his illness. Distrusting Shelburne, he vigorously objected to the official commission to treat for peace that Shelburne had just sent to Oswald, because it referred to the Amer-

---

1. Jay resumed public activities on Aug. 3, beginning discussions with Spanish Ambassador Aranda on boundary questions: XXXVII, 733n.
2. XXXVII, 599–601, 686–7.

ican commissioners as representatives of the "thirteen Colonies." Jay refused to allow negotiations to move forward until Parliament explicitly recognized the United States of America.[3] Franklin tried in vain to find a compromise that would allow negotiations to resume.[4] Days later he suffered an acute attack of what was either kidney or bladder stones, which left him housebound and in debilitating pain for over a month. Fearing that he might not survive, he asked Jay to assist him in drawing up a "private Affair"; this, we believe, was a revised will.[5] He also made provision, during this lull in the negotiations, for William Temple Franklin to be appointed official secretary of the commission.[6] To complicate matters further, in early September, Jay and Franklin learned that one of Vergennes' chief assistants, *premier commis* Gérard de Rayneval, had gone to England to consult with Shelburne. Convinced that the French were trying to broker a secret arrangement, Jay dispatched Benjamin Vaughan to England to intercede with Shelburne. Though Jay did not disclose to Franklin the nature of Vaughan's mission, Franklin seems to have been aware of it. In fact, he facilitated the mission by reversing a previous decision and granting a passport to Elkanah Watson, the man who carried Vaughan's confidential letters forewarning the prime minister of his imminent visit.[7] Vaughan asked Shelburne on behalf of the American commissioners to make no agreement with France without consulting them first. This was a needless precaution, since Rayneval's mission was merely to explore the possibilities of serious subsequent negotiations. Jay also told Vaughan, however, to hint to Shelburne that the Americans might not adhere strictly to their instructions from Congress requiring them to act in consultation with France.[8] (Franklin had made such hints, too, but he was careful

---

3. XXXVII, 713n. See also Jay's comments to Oswald at the end of July, reported in Jay to Livingston, Nov. 17 (Giunta, *Emerging Nation*, I, 663–4).

4. See BF to Jay, Aug. 16.

5. See John MacMahon's prescription of Aug. 23 and letter of Aug. 24, William Withering's observations and our editorial note on remedies for the stone (both of which are after Aug. 24), and BF to [Jay], Sept. 17.

6. See WTF's commission, [Oct. 1].

7. See Watson & Cossoul to BF, Aug. 20; Lafayette to BF, Sept. 12.

8. "That it hence appeared to be the obvious interest of Britain immedi-

to keep them vague.)[9] Vaughan also emphasized to Shelburne the critical importance of revising Oswald's commission if the negotiations were to continue.

The British cabinet did revise the language of Oswald's commission in a way that satisfied Jay, by stating that Oswald was negotiating with representatives of the United States. The language was still ambiguous, however. Should negotiations fail, the cabinet could claim that the independence implicitly recognized in the commission was conditional upon their success.[1]

Jay and Oswald formally exchanged commissions at the beginning of October, and the two men began negotiations in Paris, with Jay consulting Franklin periodically at Passy. Jay presented to Oswald a draft treaty on October 5.[2] In the interim, however, Britain's military fortunes had improved dramatically. On September 13 the British had repulsed a massive attack on Gibraltar, leading to a new bellicosity on the part of the British public. The concessions Shelburne had been prepared to make to Franklin were no longer politically viable. This change of mood was clear when the cabinet sent the professional diplomat Henry Strachey to stiffen Oswald's resolve. Strachey arrived in Paris on October 28, two days after John Adams had arrived from the Netherlands. A new round of negotiations began immediately.[3] With Franklin's health improved, the three American peace commissioners worked together. Adams, who suspected Franklin of subservience to the French, was pleasantly

---

ately to cut the Cords, which tied us to France; for that, though we were determined faithfully to fulfill our Treaty and Engagements with this Court, *yet it was a different Thing to be guided by their or our Construction of it.*" Vaughan also was instructed to tell Shelburne that America felt no obligation to continue the war for the sake of Spain: Jay to Livingston, Nov. 17 (Giunta, *Emerging Nation*, I, 668–9). For the peace commissioners' instructions from Congress see XXXV, 166–7.

9. XXXVII, 309n, 320.

1. Home Secretary Thomas Townshend to Edward Thurlow, Lord Thurlow, Sept. 20, quoted in Samuel F. Bemis, *The Diplomacy of the American Revolution* (rev. ed., Bloomington, Ind., 1958), p. 226n. For the commission see Giunta, *Emerging Nation*, I, 582–4.

2. Below, [Oct. 5–7].

3. See the headnotes for JA to BF, Nov. 1, and the Second Draft Treaty, [Nov. 4–7].

surprised during the first negotiating session to find him so willing to agree with Jay and himself on matters of policy and strategy. Franklin, he later wrote, went along with his colleagues "in entire Harmony and Unanimity." Such unity was necessary in the face of the difficult negotiations with Oswald and Strachey. When the commissioners submitted a second draft treaty, they had been forced to retreat from the Canadian borderline they thought they had won. Unable to obtain what today is southern Ontario they left the British government the option of using the St. Lawrence River, the Great Lakes, and their connecting rivers as a border (which the British accepted). Even so, the British cabinet found much of the second draft unacceptable and instructed Strachey and Oswald to obtain better terms. The contested issues were the fisheries, debts owed to British creditors, and most critical, because of its potential political impact, compensation for the Loyalists. The British counterproposal, approved by the King on November 19, called for full amnesty and restitution of the Loyalists' property. Strachey presented this counterproposal to the American commissioners on the morning of November 25.[4]

From November 25 through November 29, Oswald, Strachey, Franklin, Jay, and Adams engaged in intensive negotiations; Laurens joined them on the final day. Adams took the lead on the fisheries article, which was finally settled on November 29. Most of that last day, however, was spent wrangling over the Loyalist question, on which Franklin had the strongest feelings. Discussions were at an impasse until Franklin produced an article he proposed to substitute for Article 5 of the British counterproposal; it reversed the demand, asking for compensation for American patriots who had suffered at the hands of the British.[5]

---

4. The British counterproposal is described under the date of [Nov. 19]. See also Strachey's remarks to the peace commissioners, Nov. 25.

5. BF's proposed Article 5, published under [Nov. 29]. This was a theme BF had been insisting on throughout the negotiations, and which he elaborated upon in a letter addressed to Oswald of Nov. 26, below, which he may have put aside in favor of the shorter and more dramatic "proposed article." In August, he threatened that if a reconciliation did not take place he would produce the schoolbook cataloguing British cruelties that he and Lafayette had started to gather illustrations for (XXIX, 590–3): Vaughan to Shelburne, Aug. 17, 1782, APS.

All four American commissioners then elaborated on the injustices listed in Franklin's article.

The British commissioners dropped their insistence on the issue, and a compromise was forged whereby Congress would recommend to the states that they offer compensation (a recommendation none of them followed).[6] The treaty was reviewed, final compromises were reached, and the commissioners agreed to sign and seal fair copies the following day. That night Strachey wrote to a British official that he was "half dead" from anxiety, and assured his correspondent that this was "the best [peace] that could have been made."[7] Franklin was dressed in black for the signing, since his position at the French court required him to observe a recently declared period of mourning for Princess Charlotte Amalie of Denmark.[8]

The Preliminary Articles of Peace signed on November 30 were conditional upon the other belligerents signing treaties as well. The terms, particularly those relating to the boundaries of the United States, were very generous. Shelburne was willing to make whatever concessions were necessary to obtain what in effect was a separate peace with the United States, thereby putting pressure on Britain's other enemies. For their part, the American peace commissioners, in signing even a provisional agreement, violated at least the spirit if not the letter of their instructions from Congress to "undertake nothing in the Negotiations for Peace or Truce without [French] Knowledge and Concurrence" and to govern themselves "by their Advice and Opinion."[9] This preliminary agreement placed their ally in grave peril. With the French war effort in the Caribbean unraveling, France was more dependent than ever on the American army's holding British troops in New York.

But despite the conditional nature of the November 30 agreement, the American public viewed the war as over.[1] This threat-

6. See the fifth article of the Preliminary Articles of Peace, Nov. 30.
7. See our headnote for BF's proposed Article 5, [Nov. 29].
8. See Séqueville to BF, [Nov. 25].
9. XXXV, 167.
1. William C. Stinchcombe, *The American Revolution and the French Alliance* (Syracuse, 1959), p. 198.

ened the effectiveness of the American army, and placed France under enormous pressure to satisfy Shelburne. Desperate for peace, France already had arranged a complicated set of exchanges by which its other major ally, Spain, would receive Gibraltar and make peace with England; this would permit France to do likewise. The massive concessions to the United States, however, made it untenable for Shelburne to exchange Gibraltar, and the British withdrew their acceptance of the proposal. For the next month and a half France worked to find a compromise which would satisfy Spain and permit an end to the war.[2]

Franklin and his colleagues took no part in these discussions, and they heard little from Vergennes in the weeks following the signing of the provisional agreement with Britain. Of particular concern was whether Louis XVI would grant the major new loan that Franklin had requested at the urging of Congress. Eager to send part of the money to the United States aboard the packet *General Washington,* for which George III had just granted a passport, Franklin wrote Vergennes on December 15 informing him of this opportunity and asking what the response of the court might be. Vergennes shot back an answer, rebuking the peace commissioners for their lack of gratitude to the King.[3] Franklin's famous response of December 17 is generally considered a masterstroke of diplomatic finesse: a weaving together of apologies, reassurances, expressions of gratitude and flattery, and finally, a warning that without further financial assistance the "whole Ediface" that Louis XVI helped construct, "so glorious to his Reign," would collapse.[4] By good fortune, the day before Franklin sent this answer, substantial progress was made in the negotiations between Britain and Spain: Spanish ambassador Aranda decided to accept Florida and Minorca in lieu of Gibraltar.[5] On December 20 Vergennes met with Franklin, ac-

2. Dull, *French Navy,* pp. 297–302, 319–25, 329–35, and see our annotation of BF to Livingston, Dec. 5[–14].

3. To Vergennes, Dec. 15, below; From Vergennes, Dec. 15, below. As noted in our annotation of the latter, Vergennes blamed BF's colleagues.

4. To Vergennes, Dec. 17, below.

5. See our annotation of Vergennes to BF, Dec. 15.

cepted his apology, and announced that France would grant a loan of 6,000,000 *livres tournois*, 600,000 of which would be given immediately to send on the *General Washington*.[6]

It would be another month before the negotiations among Britain, France, and Spain were concluded. The anxiety of the French court is clear from a declaration they drafted on January 2 for the American commissioners to sign, affirming the Americans' continued loyalty and the provisional nature of the preliminary articles. This, we believe, was never shown to the Americans, though both the draft and a fair copy are among the French ministry's papers.[7] Meanwhile, Jay left for a trip to Normandy and Laurens went to Bath. Suddenly, on the evening of Saturday, January 18, Vergennes sent word to Passy that it was "essential" for him to confer with the American commissioners; he summoned them to Versailles the following Monday morning before ten o'clock. As there would be writing to do in both English and French, he requested that Franklin bring his grandson. Franklin's reply, penned at ten o'clock that night, assured Vergennes that they would be punctual.[8]

On the morning of January 20, in Vergennes' office, Franklin, Adams, and William Temple Franklin witnessed Britain sign preliminary treaties with France and Spain. (France and Britain had arranged a provisional agreement on behalf of the Netherlands, though no Dutch representative was present.) Then Franklin and Adams, representing the United States, and Alleyne Fitzherbert, representing Great Britain, affixed their signatures and seals to a declaration of the cessation of hostilities which confirmed the terms of the preliminary articles signed on November 30. Wrote Adams, "Thus was this mighty System terminated with as little Ceremony, and in as short a Time as a Marriage Settlement."[9] The Americans returned to Paris for a celebratory dinner. They could congratulate themselves not only on peace but upon the astonishing terms they had received, terms which

6. See our annotation of BF to Morris, Dec. 23.
7. Draft of a Declaration to be Made by the American Peace Commissioners, Jan. 2, below.
8. Vergennes to BF, Jan. 18; BF to Vergennes, Jan. 18.
9. See below, The American Peace Commissioners: Acceptance of the British Declaration of the Cessation of Hostilities, [Jan. 20].

in outline resembled the "necessary articles" Franklin had presented to Oswald the previous July.[1]

In the weeks following the signing of the preliminary articles, Franklin and Adams drafted additional proposals which they hoped would be incorporated into the definitive version of the treaty. They discussed the issue of reciprocal trade privileges for American and British ships, one of Franklin's former "adviseable articles."[2] Franklin also drafted an article concerning privateering and the law of nations, an adaptation of the ideas he had expressed in a letter to Benjamin Vaughan of July 10, 1782, and in two related essays. He sent this proposed article to Richard Oswald on January 14. It was never incorporated into the definitive peace treaty with Great Britain, but it was included in the 1785 treaty of amity and commerce with Prussia.[3]

While the sporadic peace negotiations dominated Franklin's attention during the months covered by this volume, they did not prevent him from actively pursuing other interests including science and technology. During his illness he sent for a number of scientific works, and received from Priestley his new volume of experiments on air.[4] As he began to recover, Frankin reviewed a manuscript on geology by the abbé Soulavie and wrote an extensive theory of the earth's formation which was later published.[5] As soon as the *Journal de Paris* carried an announcement for an astonishing new invention—self-igniting candles called *bougies phosphoriques*—William Temple Franklin was at the shop, trying to obtain them. Franklin described them in letters to both François Steinsky and Jan Ingenhousz. He also hailed the invention of a deceptively simple device to fight fires—a loop of rope that would carry water up to heights of several stories in a matter of minutes, invented by a French postal worker.[6]

---

1. XXXVII, 598–601.

2. XXXVII, 600; Franklin's Sketch of Articles of Peace, [between Dec. 10 and 13].

3. XXXVII, 608–11, 617–20; Franklin's Proposed Article for the Definitive Treaty, [on or before Dec. 13]; BF to Oswald, Jan. 14.

4. Achille-Guillaume Lebègue de Presle to WTF, Sept. 2, below.

5. To Jean-Louis Giraud Soulavie, Sept. 22; From Soulavie, Oct. 21.

6. Bettaly & Noseda to WTF, Oct. 1; BF to François Steinsky, Nov. 23.

Franklin pursued a number of projects that were both political and deeply personal. He reviewed sketches from two different artists for the *Libertas Americana* medal, commemorating
the victories at Saratoga and Yorktown, and selected a design by
Augustin Dupré.[7] He and La Rochefoucauld began planning
their edition of the American state constitutions.[8] And in the
weeks following the signing of the preliminary articles, he took
a manuscript he had in his possession, an expanded version of
Jacques Barbeu-Dubourg's *Petit Code de la raison humaine*, and
had it printed in Dubourg's memory.[9]

Coincidentally, as the preliminary articles were being finalized, the outline of Franklin's autobiography was making its
way to France. The famous undated letter from Abel James enclosing a copy of those "notes" is published in this volume. We
place it before December 8, the date when Benjamin Vaughan indicated that he had read "the papers which [Franklin's] quaker
American friend lately sent him."[1] Also in this volume, among
the undated documents from 1782, we publish Franklin's "mod-
ernized" version of six verses from the first chapter of the book
of Job.[2] Franklin's playful side is illustrated by his willingness to
send an old suit of clothes to Elkanah Watson, who intended to
create a lifelike dummy using the wax bust of Franklin sculpted
by Patience Wright. With it, Watson fooled a stream of gullible
visitors in both Nantes and London.[3] Franklin in turn would be
intrigued by another hoax, the chess-playing mechanical Turk
that would soon visit Paris with its inventor, Wolfgang von Kempelen. Their arrival was announced in a letter from Rodolphe
Valltravers.[4]

As mentally agile as ever, Franklin was nonetheless shaken by
his illness, and once the negotiations were concluded he began
talking again about returning to America. He longed to see his

7. From Alexandre-Théodore Brongniart, Sept. 22; From Antoine-Alexis-
François Cadet de Vaux, Jan. 13.
8. See our annotation for Regnier to BF, Oct. 12.
9. BF to Mary Hewson, Jan. 8.
1. From Abel James, [before Dec. 8].
2. BF's Proposed New Version of the Bible, [1782 or after].
3. Elkanah Watson, Jr., to WTF, Dec. 25.
4. From Valltravers, Dec. 24.

country and his old friends before he died. As he wrote to Robert Livingston, in a long summary of events that he began on December 5, he was about to enter his seventy-eighth year, fifty years of which had been devoted to public service. "I wish now to be, for the little time I have left, my own Master. If I live to see this Peace concluded, I shall beg leave to remind the Congress of their Promise then to dismiss me." He concluded with the opening line of the *Nunc dimittis*, which he had quoted earlier to William Hodgson: "Now lettest thou thy Servant Depart in Peace, for mine Eyes have seen thy Salvation."[5]

5. BF to Livingston, Dec. 5[–14].

Chronology

August 16, 1782, through January 20, 1783

  1782

August 15 / 16: De Grasse arrives in Paris after release from captivity; Spaniards construct siege works at Gibraltar.

August 16: Oswald meets with Franklin, Jay about Jay's objections to Oswald's commission.

c. August 20: Franklin becomes seriously ill from kidney or bladder stones, is confined to house for about a month.

September 4: Oswald offers American peace commissioners acceptance of Franklin's "necessary articles" as basis for peace.

September 7–*c.* September 24: Gérard de Rayneval's first mission to England.

September 9: Elkanah Watson, Jr., leaves for England with message for Shelburne.

September 10: Franklin, Jay promise Oswald to negotiate if his commission changed; Gérard de Rayneval holds first meeting with Shelburne.

September 11–27: Benjamin Vaughan's first mission to England.

September 13: British repulse attack on Gibraltar.

September 17: Franklin seeks help from Jay in writing his will.

September 28: Congress empowers Franklin to make commercial treaty with Sweden.

October 1: Jay and Oswald exchange commissions, permitting negotiations to resume; Franklin and Jay sign commission for William Temple Franklin as secretary to American peace commission.

October 5–7: First American draft treaty.

October 8: Adams signs commercial treaty with Netherlands.

October 16: Replenishment convoy reaches Gibraltar.

October 17–26: Adams, Thaxter travel to Paris.

October 28: Henry Strachey arrives in Paris.

November 4–7: Second American draft treaty.

November 14–15: Cabinet approves terms for preliminary treaty with United States.

  lxvi

c. November 15–28: Gérard de Rayneval's second mission to England.

November 17–27: Benjamin Vaughan's second mission to England.

November 19: King George III approves counterproposal to second draft treaty.

November 25–29: The American peace commissioners conduct intensive negotiations with Oswald and Strachey.

November 28: Henry Laurens arrives in Paris; the conde de Aranda agrees to cede Minorca to British, Santo Domingo to France, while France agrees to cede Guadeloupe, Dominica to Britain, in exchange for British cession of Gibraltar to Spain.

November 29–*c.* February 15: Gérard de Rayneval's third mission to England.

November 30: Signing of the preliminary peace agreement between Britain, United States.

December 3: Cabinet rejects exchange of Gibraltar.

December 8: Fleet, transports for Jamaica operation leave Brest for Cadiz.

December 11: British agree to offer Minorca, Florida to Spain.

December 14: Green's army takes possession of Charleston.

December 15: Elkanah Watson, Jr., returns to Paris after three-month trip to England.

December 16: Aranda agrees to accept Minorca, Florida in lieu of Gibraltar.

December 20: Vergennes promises BF new loan of 6,000,000 *l.t.*

December 24: Vaudreuil's squadron sails from Boston.

1783

January 7–23: Jay makes trip to Normandy.

January 11: Laurens leaves Paris for London and Bath.

January 20: French, Spaniards sign preliminary agreement with Britain; American peace commissioners agree to cession of arms.

THE PAPERS OF
BENJAMIN FRANKLIN

VOLUME 38

August 16, 1782, through January 20, 1783

Editorial Note on Franklin's Accounts

One new account begins during the period covered by this volume.

XXXI. Jacques Finck's Accounts of Household Expenditures, January 15, 1783–February 1, 1784: University of Pennsylvania Library, 81 pages. Jacques Finck, the new maître d'hôtel, remained in the Passy household until Franklin left France.[1] He submitted two statements each month: an itemized list of groceries and household supplies, and a list of miscellaneous expenses. The collection described here is complete for Finck's first year. Thereafter, the only surviving statements are for early 1785 and will be discussed in the appropriate volume.

Finck's initial contract, published below [before Jan. 1], specified that he would assume the duty of paying the household servants and the tradesmen who provided services. This was a departure from previous practice and, as Finck did not submit their invoices to Franklin, we no longer have records of most of these individuals' names. During the last two weeks of January he paid a water carrier, baker, butcher, laundress, wood merchant (who also split and stacked), blacksmith, and milkman. He had the knives sharpened and the coffeemakers repaired. He purchased new brooms, chamber pots, English candle snuffers, and a polished iron chandelier. The new kitchenware included a waffle iron, four glazed soufflé dishes, 31 molds "tres necessere pour faire la patiserie," and a small copper casserole for his office. The gardener's wife provided four days' housework, and a *porteur* was paid for assistance in moving.

We offer here a summary of entries from previously described accounts that have not found a place elsewhere in our annotation but that provide insights into Franklin's private and public life.[2]

Account XVII (Franklin's Private Accounts with Ferdinand Grand, xxvi, 3) reveals a variety of personal and household transactions. In August and September Franklin loaned a total of 3,000 *l.t.* to Benjamin Vaughan. Vaughan repaid the full amount through Jonathan Williams, Jr.'s account on November 19.[3] Duchemin, the outgoing *maître d'hôtel*,

---

1. For Finck's arrival see his Agreement with BF, [before Jan. 1]. His years of service are reviewed in Lopez, *Mon Cher Papa*, pp. 132–3.

2. The following accounts cover the period of this volume: VI and VII (XXIII, 21), XVII (XXVI, 3), XIX and XXII (XXVIII, 3–4), XXV, XXVII, and XXVIII (XXXII, 3–4), and XXX (XXXVI, 3).

3. BF loaned Vaughan 1,000 *l.t.* on Aug. 29 and the balance on Sept. 11. Vaughan made at least the first of these requests through WTF, explaining that "the purchases I have made call for money faster than I at first intended." Vaughan to WTF, Aug. 29, 1782 (APS).

received monthly payments up through January 16. Mlle Chaumont is paid for unspecified services. The tailor Angenend submitted a bill on October 22 for 968 *l.t.* 5 *s.* 6 *d.*[4] On December 31 Franklin reinvested a dividend from the *Caisse d'escompte* by purchasing an additional share.[5]

Account XXV (Account of Postage and Errands, XXXII, 3). During the period covered by this volume, L'Air de Lamotte kept these records and dispensed the small daily sums; he was reimbursed monthly by Grand from the public account. Apart from the packages and letters for Franklin, there is occasional postage paid for Jay, Barclay, Martha Laurens (in September), Jonathan Williams, Jr. (during his visit to Passy in November), and "Mr. Fox" (on December 28). Jean-Nicolas Bonnefoÿ, the gardener, ran errands to Paris and Versailles; the annual subscription to the *Courier de l'Europe* was renewed; and shears for cutting paper were purchased on October 25. Two books purchased by Temple for the office were delivered. An invoice from bookseller Nyon aîné indicates their titles as "Droit de la Guerre" in two volumes and "Droit naturelle de Wolfe" in three volumes.[6]

Account XXVII (Accounts of the Public Agents in Europe, XXXII, 4), notes an October payment for paper furnished by Cabaret for Franklin's office. Henry Laurens received 20,000 *l.t.* on December 20, on Franklin's order. A courier from Lorient was paid 240 *l.t.* on December 3, and L'Air de Lamotte was reimbursed 288 *l.t.* on December 28 for advancing expenses to a courier going to Lorient.[7]

Account XXX (Franklin's Account with Congress, XXXVI, 3) records Franklin's payment of annual gratuities to the "ministers servants & others at Versailles." On Jan. 15 he advanced "to a poor sailor of the Bonhomme Richard" 10 *l.t.* 16 *s.*

4. That bill has not survived, but an earlier itemized bill submitted by Angenend is in XXXI, 102–4.

5. That purchase, for approximately 3,814 *l.t.*, appears on a list of stock transactions that is part of Account XXII (XXVIII, 4).

6. Livingston had requested Hugo Grotius' *De Jure Belli ac Pacis* in January: XXXVI, 401. Its French title was *Le Droit de la guerre et de la paix.* The second book was most likely Christian von Wolff, *Principes du droit de la nature et des gens . . .* (3 vols., Amsterdam, 1758).

7. This sum may have included the 48 *l.t.* that BF (or his household) paid on Dec. 20 to a certain Grenieux for the account of Jean Quiré, "courier de L'Orient." This receipt, in WTF's hand, is at the APS.

Editorial Note on Promissory Notes

During the months covered by this volume, seven American seamen claiming to have escaped from British prisons, all but one of whose claims seem to have been legitimate, received financial assistance on Franklin's order and signed promissory notes at Passy.[8] They each received the same amount: 120 *l.t.*, or 5 *louis d'or*.

Capt. Samuel Mansfield, who signed a promissory note on Aug. 25, brought Franklin a letter of introduction from Francis Coffyn dated August 21 (below). Thomas Potter[9] and John Smith also applied to Franklin on August 25. Chipman Bangs of Boston[1] and Rufus Hopkins of Providence, both of whom called themselves midshipmen on the *Alliance*, signed promissory notes on December 7. Thomas Cox[2] signed a note on December 18, and Thomas Connoly[3] on January 13, 1783. Connoly carried a letter of introduction from Francis Coffyn dated January 9 (below).

8. These printed promissory notes are at the APS, and all seven men are on the Alphabetical List of Escaped Prisoners. For a history of the printed promissory note forms see XXXI, 497; XXXV, 6; XXXVII, 4. The first three notes described here were from the third printing; the last four were from the second printing.

Account XXVII (XXXII, 4), which lists these payments, also shows that John Allen (who did not sign a promissory note) received 240 *l.t.* on Nov. 26. Allen was probably the Massachusetts native who commanded the *Newbury:* Claghorn, *Naval Officers*, p. 4; Kaminkow, *Mariners*, p. 231.

9. Potter was no escaped prisoner. A former whaleman who served as a midshipman on the *Bonhomme Richard* (XXVII, 653n; XXX, 630), he had just completed a lucrative cruise on the French privateer *Eclipse* where he was first lieutenant under the command of Nathaniel Fanning. Fanning had been his fellow midshipman under John Paul Jones (XXX, 630). Potter challenged Fanning's authority on numerous occasions, and he forced the *Eclipse* back to Dunkirk in mid-August after he had plundered a neutral vessel carrying wealthy French passengers; see our annotation of Fanning to BF, Nov. 23, below.

1. In a 1780 petition Bangs signed as the ship's steward: XXXII, 456.

2. Possibly the commander of the schooner *Franklin*, captured en route from Lorient to the U.S. in late July or early August, 1782, and sent to Plymouth: *Courier de l'Europe*, XII (1782), 77; Claghorn, *Naval Officers*, p. 76.

3. For whom see Francis Coffyn to BF, Jan. 9, 1783, below.

To [John Jay]   ALS: American Philosophical Society

On August 15, Richard Oswald informed Franklin (at Passy) and John Jay (in Paris) that the official copy of his commission to treat for peace had arrived. It was identical in wording to the preliminary version that Shelburne had sent a week earlier. Jay had vigorously objected to that preliminary version on the grounds that it did not explicitly acknowledge the independence of the United States.[4] He reiterated those objections on August 15. Furthermore, since he believed that George III had authorized Lieutenant General Guy Carleton and Rear Admiral Robert Digby, the British commanders in America, to acknowledge American independence in their dealings with Congress, Jay proposed that the King issue a royal patent to that effect. He drafted that patent and brought it to Oswald later that day.[5] On August 16 Oswald, meeting with both Jay and Franklin, promised to send the draft to England. He queried the commissioners, however, on the assertion in the text that Carleton had orders to propose to Congress "Treaties of peace amity and Commerce." Oswald believed this to be a mistake, and Jay admitted that he might have misremembered this detail. Franklin, who had been given extracts of the commanders' instructions, promised to send a duplicate to Jay "in a few Hours."[6] He sent that duplicate under cover of the present letter.

Sir,   Passy, Augt. 16. 1782
    Inclos'd is a true Copy of the Extracts from Gen. Carleton's Instructions given to me by Mr Vaughan from Lord Shelbourn.[7] You will see that the Instruction I mention'd as given to Mr Grenville is acknowledged and recited. Is it not probable therefore that Mr Oswald may have the same? and if he has, and will execute it by

    4. XXXVII, 686, 712n, 713n.
    5. The text is printed in Morris, *Jay: Peace*, pp. 309–10.
    6. Oswald's dispatch of Aug. 15–17, in Morris, *Jay: Peace*, pp. 305–6.
    7. Shelburne wrote to Carleton and Digby that Thomas Grenville, the representative in Paris of Foreign Secretary Charles James Fox, had been authorized to propose independence "in the first Instance." Shelburne had permitted Benjamin Vaughan to copy passages from the letter; Vaughan, without authorization, gave them to BF: XXXVII, 672–4. BF already had rejected such an offer from Grenville: XXXVII, 301, 303, 307–8, 318–22.

making ministorially in Writing the Declaration intended,[8] perhaps the Paper propos'd to be sent to England may in that Case not be necessary. With great Esteem I have the honour to be, Sir, Your most obedient and most humble Servant   B FRANKLIN

Endorsed: Dr. Franklin—16 Augt. 1782 enclosg Ex. of Carltons Instrucs. of 5 June 1782

From William Bell[9]   AL: Historical Society of Pennsylvania

Friday evening 3 oClock [August 16, 1782][1]
Mr. Bells best respects waits on His Excellency Docr. Franklin and begs the Docr. to favour him with a passport to Ostend— Mr. Bell did not set off As he yeasterday intended, but will undoubtedly set off early tomorrow morning—therefore will be thankfull to have the pasport this evening.

Should His Excellency have any commands Mr. Bell will be happy in rendering his Excellency any service in his power.

Docr. Franklin will please to Include Miss Beckwiths name in the pass[2]

Endorsed: Mr Bell & Mademoiselle Beckwith Citoyens de l'Amerique avec leur Domestiques

---

8. Presumably a declaration to the effect that the independence of America would be "the Basis & Preliminary of the Treaty now depending," as Shelburne had promised Oswald in his letter of July 27: XXXVII, 686.

9. A Philadelphia merchant whom Sally Beckwith had met earlier in the summer: XXXVII, 644n.

1. The day (a Friday) when BF granted the passport requested here: XXXVI, 380.

2. Sally Beckwith (XXXVII, 425–6) was en route to America to establish herself as a teacher or milliner. BF gave her a warm letter of recommendation to the Baches (now missing): SB to BF, Jan. 24, 1783 (two letters, APS).

From David Hartley

Reprinted from William Temple Franklin, ed., *Memoirs of the Life and Writings of Benjamin Franklin* . . . (3 vols., 4to, London, 1817–18), II, 394–6.

My Dear Friend,   London, August 16, 1782.

Yours I received by Major Young together with the work of your *veritable philosophe,* which is full of humanity.[3] I was not before that, at a loss where I should have looked for my *veritable philosophe* in the present actual scene of public politics. Your honest, anxious and unremitted endeavours towards the re-establishment of peace, must endear you to your own country, and to all mankind. Whatever may have been transacting in America, (if it can be possible that the suspicions which you mention should become true) viz. to tamper with America for a breach of faith, of which some suspicions seem to be thrown out by the provinces of Maryland and Philadelphia, I can give the strongest testimonies of the constant honour and good faith of your conduct and correspondencies; and my letters to you will bear me equal testimony, that I have never thrown out any dishonourable suggestions to you. When the proposed Congress of your *veritable philosophe* shall meet, neither of us need fear its censures, upon the strictest examination of our correspondence. We will claim the Poet's character of the sincere statesman,

"Who knew no thought but what the world might hear."[4]

In times of suspicion it must be some satisfaction to both of us to know, that no line or word has ever passed between us, but what the governments of Great Britain, France and America might freely peruse as the words of good faith, peace and *sweet reconciliation.*

The resolutions of Maryland and Philadelphia[5] together with

3. BF to Hartley, July 10: XXXVII, 607–8. The *philosophe* was Pierre-André Gargaz, whose treatise on perpetual peace BF printed.

4. "Just of thy word, in ev'ry thought sincere, / Who knew no wish but what the world might hear": "Epitaph On the Monument of the Honble. Robert Digby . . . ," lines 5–6, in Norman Ault, ed., *Alexander Pope: Minor Poems* (London and New Haven, 1954), p. 314.

5. Presumably the resolutions of the Md. House of Delegates and Pa.

8

the slow proceeding of our *plenipotentiaries,* and even the doubt suggested whether they may not be in waiting for events in America, give me much concern. Not being informed to a certainty of the state of the negociation, I have declined any concern with ministry upon the subject of the refugees, &c. My assistance cannot be indispensable upon that topic, but I deem it indispensable to myself, not to be committed in unknown ground, which from the points above mentioned must appear dubious to me. These are the reasons which I gave to the minister for declining.[6] I must at the same time give him the justice of the most absolute and unlimited professions of sincerity for peace. Whatever divisions there may have been, as you say, suspected in the cabinet, there are some of his colleagues still remaining, in whom I have the greatest confidence for sincerity and good intentions. The public prints of this country have stated what are called *shades* of difference as to the mode. Those opinions which are imputed to Mr. Fox are certainly most suitable to my opinions. I am free to confess to you that my wishes would have been to have taken the most decisive ground relating to independence, &c. immediately from the 27th of March last, viz, the accession of the change of ministry.[7] But I agree with you in sentiment; viz. to concur with all the good that offers, when we cannot obtain all the good that we might wish. The situation of my sentiments at present is, an unbiassed neutrality of expectation, as events may justify.

I shall be obliged to you for the earliest communications of any public events in America which may come to Europe, with any public resolutions of Congress or provinces, &c. and all memorials or negociations which may pass between the parties in America. I am very anxious to have the earliest informations to form my opinions upon, and to be prepared accordingly. My

---

Supreme Executive Council which Livingston had sent to BF on May 22 (XXXVII, 399–400).

6. Hartley had been requested, presumably by Shelburne, to assist Secretary of State Townshend: XXXVII, 678n, 679.

7. The late Rockingham government had taken office on March 27. Fox, its foreign secretary, had favored recognizing American independence: XXXVII, 102–3.

utmost endeavours will always be exerted to the blessed work of peace. I am ever, your affectionate   D. HARTLEY.

From ——— Loyseau[8]   ALS: American Philosophical Society

Monsieur   paris Le 16 aoust 1782.

Je viens de Lire des Lettres tres affligeantes de Mr. Le comte de Benyowsky.[9] Il etoit parti dans La Confiance que Le congrés S'empresseroit a lui donner de L'employ, vous Lui aviés remis une Lettre dans Laquelle vous donnés de son caractère et de Ses talens Militaires L'opinion qu'il faut en avoir.[1] Quelle est donc La cause de La conduite du congrés? Permettés moy, Monsieur, d'avoir L'honneur de vous voir et de vous demander Le jour qui vous conviendra le mieux.

Je Suis avec Respect Monsieur votre tres humble et tres obeissant Serviteur.   LOYSEAU
                              Avocat au parlement Rue Ste. anne
                              prés La Rue neuve des petits champs.

Made. La comtesse de Benyowsky[2] est chez moy dans Ce Moment a Se desesperer des inductions que L'on peut tirer contre Son mari de La conduite du Congrès.

Notation: Loyseau 16 aout 1782.

8. This *avocat au parlement* appears in the *Almanach royal* for the years 1777 through 1781, but not in subsequent years. In 1779, he wrote legal briefs for the Alexander brothers which they discussed with BF: XXXI, 242n; Loyseau to BF, Feb. 17, 1783 (APS).

9. On May 29 Congress declined Benyowzky's offer to raise a foreign legion for the United States: XXXVI, 228n; *JCC*, XXII, 308–9.

1. The two extant letters of recommendation from BF discuss only Benyowzky's civilian plans: XXXVI, 228, 230. In fact, BF had dissuaded him from making the journey: XXXVI, 355.

2. XXXVII, 585–6.

From Jonathan Williams, Jr.

LS: American Philosophical Society; copy: Yale University Library

Dear & hond. sir,   Nantes 16th. August 1782

I have lately received a letter from Tristram Dalton Esqr. of Newbury-Port, informing me that you some Time ago advis'd him of having obtain'd orders for payment of a Sum, for the loss sustain'd by the owners of the Brigt. Fair-Play; & that you would deposit it in my hands—[3] Mr. Dalton desires me to give him some information concerning this matter, & I should be much obliged if you would give me some advise that I may communicate to him the information desired—[4] The death of my new-born daughter, & the present debility of Mrs. Williams[5] forbids my adding more than that I am most respectfully & dutifully yours   JONA WILLIAMS J

3. BF's letter to Dalton is missing. Dalton's to JW, describing it, was dated May 15: JW to Dalton, Aug. 15, 1782 (Yale University Library). Dalton was one of the owners of the *Fair Play,* a ship that was mistakenly fired upon and sunk by a Guadeloupe shore battery in early 1779. On the basis of a petition by BF, Louis XVI agreed to accord an indemnity "proportional to the loss": XXVIII, 350; XXIX, 393–4, 486–8, 546. The indemnification of 15,000 *l.t.* ordered by Sartine in 1780, based on the report of a Guadeloupe commission, was a fraction of what the owners claimed, and both they and BF disputed the sum: XXXII, 614–15; XXXIII, 100–2, 175; Tristram Dalton *et al.* to Castries, Feb. 28, 1781 (APS).

4. JW answered Dalton on Sept. 15. From the letters BF exchanged with Castries, copies of which JW enclosed, Dalton would see that the King considered the 15,000 *l.t.* as full indemnification. From BF's letter to JW (now missing), JW learned that the owners wanted the money entrusted to him. Now that he knew of this arrangement, he would try to procure the money "without giving a Receipt which would preclude all future demands." If this plan did not work he would await further instructions. Yale University Library.

5. Mariamne, ill with influenza, gave birth prematurely on Aug. 2. The baby was christened Bethia on Aug. 7 but lived only thirteen days. JW buried her on Aug. 16, the date of the present letter. Mariamne had been too ill to attend the christening, but by mid-August she was out of danger: JW to WTF, Aug. 7, 1782 (APS); JW to William Alexander, July 26, to Williams Moore & Co., Aug. 4, and to Alexander Alexander, Aug. 18, 1782 (Yale University Library); Baptismal Certificate for Bethia Williams, Aug. 7, 1782, Archives de Nantes. The editors are grateful to Joan Challinor for bringing the baptismal certificate to our attention.

His Excelly. B. Franklin Esqr.

Addressed: A Son Excellence / Monsr Franklin / a / Passy / près Paris

Notation: J. Williams 16. Aout 1782.

To Mary Hewson   ALS: Mrs. Herbert May, Washington, D.C. (1963)

My dear good Child,   Passy, Augt. 17. 1782
    I received your kind Letter by Dr Shuttleworth.[6] It always gives me great Pleasure to hear of the Welfare of you and yours. As to my self, I continue as hearty as at my Age could be expected, and as chearful as ever you knew me, hoping ere long to see Peace and my Friends, whose continued Regard for me after so long and so thorough an Acquaintance with me, I esteem among my Honours and Felicities. It is now a Quarter of a Century since our Friendship commenc'd, and tho' we lived much of the time together, it has never been interupted by the smallest Misunderstanding or Coolness.—[7] In this Observation I include your good Mother, from whom I had lately the Pleasure of receiving a few Lines.[8] I embrace you both with the most tender Affection, being ever sincerely yours   B FRANKLIN

From Henry Johnson[9]   ALS: American Philosophical Society

May it please your Excellency   Bordeaux Augt: 17t: 1782
    The Incld: Bills belong to an Industrious Black man who is with me. Shall esteem it a favour if your Excellency would En-

---

6. Her letter of July 19 is in XXXVII, 650–3. For John Shuttleworth see his letter of this date, below.
    7. BF lived with the Stevensons from 1757 to 1762 and again from 1764 to 1775: *Autobiog.*, pp. 306, 308–9, 313.
    8. Margaret Stevenson wrote on July 24: XXXVII, 675–6.
    9. Johnson (XXIII, 338n) now commanded the privateer frigate *Flora*, recently arrived from St. Domingue: XXXVI, 240; John A. McManemin, *Captains of the Continental Navy* (Ho-Ho-Kus, N.J., 1981), p. 212.

dorse or rather accept those Bills & send them to me.— In my last to your Excellency[1] I forgot to mention to you that I took on board the Amazon Prize four Preists, Subjects of the King of Sardinia,[2] who were going as Missionaries to Quebeck. I let them go here. They are still in this Town. I do not Know whether we cannot hold them as British Subjects and Exchange them for four Americans. Your Excellency can best judge of that matter.

I am with much Respect—Your Excellencys Most Obedt: & Most Humble Servant   HENRY JOHNSON

Addressed: A Son Excellence / A Son Excellence Benja: Franklin Ecuyer / Ministre Plenipotentiare pour les / Treize Etats Unies. a la Cour de / Versailles. a Son Hotel / a Passy—

Notations in different hands: Henry Johnson 17. Aout 1782. / Ansd 24 Augt 82[3]

From ——— Puchelberg[4]

ALS: University of Pennsylvania Library

Monsieur,   Versailles 17. Aout 1782.

Il y a près d'un mois que Mrs. schweighauser & dobrée de Nantes m'ont prevenû, que le Congrés ayant pleinement approuvé les fournitures faites par ma maison à l'Orient pour la fregate l'Alliance, Capt. Landais a chargé Votre Excellence de me payer cet objet conformément au Compte des fournitures que j'en ai remis.[5]

---

1. Missing. Johnson anchored at Bordeaux shortly before Aug. 5, when JW wrote to congratulate him on his arrival (Yale University Library).

2. Victor Amadeus III (1726–1796): Larousse.

3. The answer is missing.

4. The Lorient merchant whose firm, Puchelberg & Cie., was involved in outfitting the *Alliance* in June, 1780: XXXIII, 56.

5. See the letters from Schweighauser & Dobrée, June 8 and July 20: XXXVII, 450–1, 657–8. In the latter, the firm asked for BF's intervention since Joshua Johnson, whom Congress had appointed to settle the claim, refused to do so. Contrary to Puchelberg's statement here, the matter at this point was far from settled. BF evidently turned the commission over to Thomas

C'est pourquoi Et comme je me trouve actuellement à Versailles, j'ai l'honneur de prier Votre Excellence, de vouloir bien me faire Savoir l'heure de Sa Commodité, pour être finalement payé d'un Compte qui m'a causé bien des peines.

Comme, au reste, l'equipage de la dite fregate l'Alliance ne discontinue pas à me tourmenter pour la rentrée des fonds de leurs parts des prises Et dont j'ai la procuration en main;[6] je Suplie également Votre Excellence, de me marquer, Si le partage de ces parts de prises aura lieu ou non? Dans ce dernier cas je Serai bien aise d'en prevenir le monde, afin que l'on me laisse tranquille.

J'ai l'honneur d'Etre avec bien du Respect Monsieur, de Votre Excellence le très humble Et très obeissant Serviteur

PUCHELBERG

Notation: Puchelberg 17e Aôut 1782.

Barclay when he arrived at the end of August: XXXVII, 215n; Barclay to BF, Dec. 16, 1783 (AAE).

The dispute grew increasingly complicated and would occupy BF for years. In the summer of 1783, he summarized the early stage as follows: "Capt. Landais taking Possession of the ship [*Alliance*] surreptitiously in the Absence of Capt. Jones, apply'd to one Puchelberg, a Commis of Mr Schweighauser, for some Provisions, who not only *without* Orders either from me or Mr Schweighauser, but *contrary* to express Orders from both, furnished the same, pretending that Landais demanded them in the Name and on Account of the Navy Board of Boston. Payment was afterwards demanded of me, which I refus'd. . . . It was also demanded of his Employer Schweighauser, who it seems refus'd also . . .": BF's Note on Barclay's letter of July 28, 1783 (AAE).

6. In June, 1780, Puchelberg & Cie. had notified BF that they were authorized by the crew to receive and disburse the prize money, and BF had urged the firm to contact Chaumont, who was in charge of the matter: XXXII, 618–19; XXXIII, 18–19.

From John Shuttleworth[7] ALS: University of Pennsylvania Library

Dr Sir   Hotel d'Hambourg Saturday Morn: 17 Augst: 1782.

My Servt. will waite your leisure for the papers you are so good to give me[8] and for any letter or letters you may please to commit to my care.

Permit me once more to acknowledge your very great civillities and to assure you that I shall ever remember them with gratitude I remain Dr Sir Yr most obedt: Servt   J Shuttleworth

Addressed: Doctor Franklin / Plassy

Notation: J. Shuttleworth 17. Augt. 1782.

From Jonathan Williams, Jr. ALS: American Philosophical Society

Dear & hond sir.   Nantes Augt 17. 1782.

I beg Leave to introduce to your particular Notice and Friendship my Friends Mr Nat Barrett and Mr Frazer, the former of these Gentlemen is the son of an old Friend of yours[9] and the Latter is particularly reccommended to me. Mr Barrett has many Letters for you, and I have given him the one you sent to me for Mr Paradise that Gentleman being returned to Paris.[1]

7. The physician who had recently asked BF for a letter of introduction to George Washington. He was on his way to Maryland: XXXVII, 650–3, 745–6.

8. These probably included a letter from BF to Washington (now missing) and a passport (mentioned in Henry Harford to BF, [before June 7, 1783], APS.) Once in New York, Shuttleworth forwarded BF's letter to Washington under cover of his own letter dated Dec. 22 (Library of Congress).

9. The Boston merchant Nathaniel Barrett (1743–1793), son of Deacon John Barrett, had arrived in Lorient from Cuba in early July with a cargo of sugar: *New-England Hist. and Geneal. Register,* XLII (1888), 263; JW to Williams Moore & Co., July 11, 1782 (Yale University Library); Barrett to BF, Sept. 30, below. He was later involved in efforts to open up the whale oil trade with France and became American consul in Rouen. In 1785 JA described him as an experienced merchant of good reputation: *Jefferson Papers,* IX, 73–5.

1. John Paradise, who had intended to go to America, was now en route from Nantes to London: XXXVII, 629–30, 704n. For BF's letters of recommendation for Paradise and William Jones see XXXVII, 630–2.

I am as ever most dutifully and affectionately Yours

JONA WILLIAMS J

Addressed: His Excellency / Doctor Franklin.

Notation: J. Williams Nantes Augt. 17. 1782.

From the Comte de Grasse[2]

LS: Library of Congress

hotel de Modêne,

Monsieur   ruë jacob à Paris le 18. aoust 1782.

J'ai l'honneur de prier Votre Excellence, de vouloir bien m'indiquer le jour et l'heure, ou je pourrais avoir celui de vous Faire ma cour, ayant differentes choses a vous communiquer.[3] Je serais charmé de Faire connoissance avec vous, et de vous as-

---

2. Admiral de Grasse, captured aboard his flagship at the Battle of the Saintes, returned to Paris from London on the night of Aug. 15/16: *Courier de l'Europe* XII (1782), 140. On Aug. 17 he wrote to Vergennes what Shelburne had charged him to communicate: that Shelburne considered American independence a given, that he wanted to be able to work with Vergennes to effect a peace, and that he was prepared to make major concessions to France concerning the West Indies and elsewhere. Jean-Jacques Antier, *L'Amiral de Grasse: Héros de l'Indépendance américaine* (Paris, 1965), pp. 358–9; the letter is summarized in Andrew Stockley, *Britain and France at the Birth of America: the European Powers and the Peace Negotiations of 1782–1783* (Exeter, Eng., 2001), p. 78. Shelburne, unauthorized to make such concessions, gave George III a different account of their conversation. On Aug. 11 he wrote the King that he had conversed with de Grasse the day before, had assured him of the King's disposition for peace and his ministers' sincerity, but that he had not entered into particulars: Fortescue, *Correspondence of George Third*, VI, 99–100.

Shelburne's message was successful at opening serious negotiations with France. Anxious to make peace so as to pursue his domestic agenda, he subsequently played American and French negotiators against each other to obtain it: Harlow, *Second British Empire*, I, 312; John Norris, *Shelburne and Reform* (London and New York, 1963), pp. 171–6, 256–60.

3. This may have included the substance of his conversation with Shelburne, and Vergennes' reaction. On Aug. 18 Vergennes asked de Grasse to reply to Shelburne that Louis XVI was very pleased with the prospects of peace, but could do nothing without first consulting his allies and above all the King of Spain: Antier, *L'Amiral de Grasse*, pp. 359–60.

16

surer de vive voix de la sincerité des sentiments d'Estime et de respect avec lesquels je suis De Votre Excellence Le très humble et très obéissant serviteur.   LE COMTE DE GRASSE

From John Swindell[4]   ALS: American Philosophical Society

Sir,   August 18th. 1782

   I in the most submissive manner beg leave to inform you, our Friends Henry Wilde and party are gone for Londonderry in order to embark for America; and herewith you will receive a full account of my abilities—in Machinery of which in the Cotton Branche & Wollen Manufactories have an inestimable secret;—and they wishing thro' your-means to be accomodated with some of them—for the good of themselves and the united States—and your orders to me are by the orders of Henry Wilde to be forwarded to Mr. Hennessey Merchant Ostend—which will be duly Honord; and as they cannot possably transact buisiness without them they wish them to be expedited as early as possable, the particulars of which they will give you a detail and your immediate answer will confer a lasting obligation on Sir Your most Obedient Humble Servant

                                        JOHN SWINDELL
                                        Engineer Stockport Cheshire

Notations in different hands: Le 18 aoust 1782. Swindell / Recue le 30 août Reple

From Benjamin Vaughan   ALS: American Philosophical Society

My dearest sir,   Paris, Augt. 18, 1782.

   The inclosed[5] I believe is what you wished; and it is of the party's hand writing. His account of himself *may be* natural, and it may be otherwise. But you of course will be the best judge.

---

   4. For this Stockport engineer, who informed on Henry Wyld and his party, see XXXVII, 742–4.
   5. Missing.

On Tuesday morning about 10 o'clock I shall bring the lady we spoke of to visit you, according to your kind permission.— The more I see of her, the more her appearance of virtue, good sense, resolution, & humility, interest me; and the more her story assumes of truth and necessity. I have given Mr Jay all the particulars I know, and shall not repeat them here therefore.

As I shall at all events wait here the return of this courier, if things do not suit for her going out, I will take charge of her back again in some way or other, if her *female* friends here judge it discreet. I am, my dearest sir, with the utmost respect, your affectionate, devoted, and grateful,   Benjn: Vaughan

In haste.

Addressed: A son Excell. Monsr: / Monsr. Franklin, / a Passy.

Notation: Vaughan Augt. 18. 1782.

To Henry Laurens   ALS: Massachusetts Historical Society

Sir,   Passy, Aug. 19. 1782
    I had the honour of receiving yours of the 7th Instant.[6] The Account you give of your bad State of Health alarms your Friends. Mr Oswald informs me, that the Waters of Bath used to recover you effectually.[7] And tho' we[8] are very sensible that if you could get well to America, you might be of great Service to the Publick, yet we think the Hazard is too great, as it may be Winter before you can come upon the Coast, and perhaps at this Juncture you might be equally useful in England. On these Considerations we agreed to advise your Return thither. You will excuse the Freedom we take in so doing, as it proceeds from sincere Regard, and Concern for a Life so valuable. With great

6. XXXVII, 708–10.
7. Laurens, who had declined to join his fellow peace commissioners in Paris, told Oswald he hoped to visit Bath and then travel to America from Falmouth: *Laurens Papers*, XV, 570–2. He had visited Bath earlier in the year: XXXVI, 371, 407, 440.
8. Presumably he means himself and John Jay.

Respect, I have the Honour to be, Sir, Your most obedient &
most humble Servant   B FRANKLIN

Honble H. Laurens Esqr

Endorsed: Benja. Franklin 19th Augt. 1782. Recd. 24th. Answd.
3d. Septemr.

From Joseph Hardy[9]   ALS: Historical Society of Pennsylvania

Honored sir   Nantes 19th August 1782
    Beg leave to inform you that I am one of the unfortunate per-
sons that was captured in the Confederacy Frigate and sent a
prisoner from New York for England but by accident happened
to put into Ireland, where I made my escape & arrived here in
France a few Months past.— I expected to have taken passage
for Philada, in the last vessel that sailed from here; but at the time
of that Vessels sailing an unforeseen circumstance took place
that prevented it.— A Merchant in this City who had a property
of mine in his hands (from which I expected to have defrayed my
expences without calling on a Public Character for assistance)
failed & disappeared with it in his possession.[1] This prevented
my returning to America by that opportunity and obliged me to
call on Mr. Barclay Consl. Genl, for a supply of money, who to
my mortification informs me, that it is not in his power to answer
my demand, but strongly recommended my making application
to your Excellency for relief.— Emboldened by his advice but
more especially by that of the Honble, Mr. H. Laurens, at pres-

    9. Hardy, captain of marines on the *Confederacy,* was captured on April
14, 1781 (XXXV, 434n), and immediately petitioned Congress to remit his
salary to his father: *JCC,* XX, 690; XXI, 840, 884–5, 942–3. He was one of
several prisoners who escaped from Kinsale and made their way to Bordeaux
by March, 1782. JW paid their transportation to Nantes and several months'
board: XXXVII, 58–9, 741–2n. Hardy was back in Philadelphia by May, 1783,
and died in 1813: Claghorn, *Naval Officers; Morris Papers,* VIII, 41; Elizabeth
H. Jervey, "Marriage and Death Notices from the City Gazette and Daily
Advertiser of Charleston, S.C.," *S.C. Hist. Mag.,* XXXVIII (1937), 67–8.
    1. This may have been Pierre Penet, who fled his creditors in July: XXXVII,
640–1, 683–4.

ent in Nantes to request the favor of your Excellency to remit me the sum of Forty Guineas, for which Mr. Laurens has authorized me to mention to you, that he will stand responsible for the punctual return in such manner and time, after my arrival in America, as you shall think proper to mention.— Pray Honor me with an Answer by return of the post. Please to direct to the care of Messrs, Watson & Cassoul Merchts, Nantes.— I hope I shall be able to return to Philada, with Captn All, who will sail shortly. If your Excelly. shou'd have any dispatches or Commands to the Continent, I shall with pleasure as a Public Officer take particular charge of them. I am with deference and all respect Your Excellys most Obt. and devoted Hble Servant

JOSP. HARDY.—

P.S. I bear the rank of Captn, in the Marines of the U.S. of America

His Excelly. B. Franklin Esqr.

From Michel-René Hilliard d'Auberteuil[2]

ALS: American Philosophical Society

Monsieur   Paris ce 19e. aout 1782
    Je remercie votre excellence de m'avoir prêté l'histoire de l'administration de Lord North, je la lis avec soin et avec grand plaisir.[3]
    J'ai à entretenir votre excellence d'un objet diferent. Mr. sobl negotiant et armateur à Bordeaux est à Paris ou il est venu exprès pour solliciter la commission du congrès, pour les fournitures et

---

2. The historian whose second volume of *Essais historiques et politiques* . . . (which BF read in proofs) had just been issued: XXXVII, 132–3 and following.
3. *A View of the History of Great Britain, during the Administration of Lord North, to the Second Session of the Fifteenth Parliament* (London, 1782), the first part of which was entitled *The History of Lord North's Administration*. Hilliard incorporated a partial translation of that work (with deletions and additions to emphasize the history of the American Revolution) in his *Histoire de l'administration de Lord North . . . et de la guerre de l'Amérique Septentrionale, jusqu'à la paix* . . . (2 vols., London, 1784).

marchandises que les états unis font acheter en Guyenne. Comme il m'a connu longtems à St. Domingue où il a fait le commerce avec beaucoup de succês, il a cru que je pouvais le servir dans cette affaire et c'est à moi seul qu'il en a fait confidence. J'ai voulu faire quelques reflexions avant de vous en parler, mais la probité, l'intelligence et la fortune de ce negotiant, me donnant lieu de croire que l'arrangement qu'il propose ne peut être qu'avantageux, je vous demande la permission de vous le presenter.

Il a des capitaux et un credit capables de procurer au Congrès les facilités dont il pourrait avoir besoin et de faire avoir les fournitures à un prix qui n'excederait pas celui que les particuliers obtiennent en payant argent comptant.

Si mercredi matin votre excellence veut bien lui accorder une entrevue je la prie de me le faire savoir.

Je suis avec la plus respectueuse consideration de votre excellence Le tres humble & très Obéissant Serviteur

HILLIARD D'AUBERTEUIL

Notation: Hilliard D'auberteuil Paris 19. Aout 1782.

From William Carmichael[4]   ALS: American Philosophical Society

Dear Sir   Sn. Ildefenso 20th Augt. 1782.

I begin this as I have done several of my former Letters with Advising your Excy that I have drawn on You a bill in favor of Messrs. Estevan Drouilhet & Co. for 2400 Livres Tournois at 90 days after Date, this Sum being the ballance of the Quarters Salary for which you permitted me to draw—[5] The Cte. de Montmorin informs me that the King has been pleased to furnish you lately with further supplies to answer our Demands in Europe—[6] In that case I hope you will have the goodness to think

---

4. Whom Jay had left in Spain as acting chargé d'affaires: Morris, *Jay: Peace,* p. 147.

5. Grand honored this bill and others, for a total of almost 18,000 *l.t.,* on Sept. 15: Account XXVII (XXXII, 4).

6. On July 5, BF received the final installment of a 6,000,000 *l.t.* loan: XXXVI, 650; XXXVII, 635.

of my Wants & to inform me when it will be in your Power to accept drafts for what may be due of my Salary—

This Court is as Dilatory as ever— It is an excellent School for Patience, for which reason I suppose so many Young Ministers are sent hither from Other Countries; if It was only innattentive to our Affairs, We should have still more reason to complain, But I find that All who have business here, even our Allies, are treated Alike by the Ministry, Neither Soothing or Menacing make any Impression; I have seen Memorials in each Stile, which have shared the Same Fate— A Terrible Mortification for those who write & reason well & who love to write & reason— I wait from time to Time on the Count de F.B [Floridablanca] & Mr Del Campo & in a respectful Manner Sollicit their Attention to the Offices passed by Mr Jay, They receive me politely & promise and make Excuses. To shew Resentment without the Ability to gratify it, would be as Idle as it might be prejudicial at this Crisis— The Ct. de Florida Blanca repeated at this Sitio his Invitation to me to dine with the Corps Diplomatique on the Saturday, I have availed Myself of it but once & that on Consequence of the Advice of the French Ambassador & the Ministers requesting me to see him on the Saturdays a half an hour before Dinner— He will probably soon have more to do than Ever, Mr Roda the Minister de gracias y Justicia being dangerously ill, it is said that the King in case of his Death will oblige the Ct de F.B. to accept of that Department Also—[7]

The Depretiation of the paper is now at 10 pr Ct., The Subscription for the Bank of Carlos[8] fills slowly, I beleive not more than 11 millions of Rials have been subscribed—

On the night of the 14th Inst the Beseigers were to make their Approaches on the Land Side agst. Gibraltar, six thousand men of which 1000 are French were to be employed on this Occasion: if discovered by the Beseiged, before they had time to cover themselves, it is probable that it has been a bloody business,[9] The

7. Manuel de Roda, a reformist, served as minister of justice from 1765 until 1783: John Lynch, *Bourbon Spain, 1700–1808* (Oxford, Eng. and Cambridge, Mass., 1989), pp. 252–3, 276, 328.

8. The Banco de San Carlos, the first national bank of Spain, recently founded by François Cabarrus (XXXIV, 352n): Lynch, *Bourbon Spain*, p. 326.

9. Some 10,000 soldiers and 15,000 workmen constructed the siege works

Courier which brings this to your Excy, will also carry an Acct of the Issue of this Affair— 620 bouches de feu are to be employed in this seige.

The Prussian Minister[1] was presented to the King and Royal Family on Sunday last. On Sunday evening he visited the Foreign Ministers chargés des Affaires &c & myself Among the Number, leaving at my Lodgings the following note.

"Le Comte de Nostitz a l'honneur d'informer Monsr Carmichael qu'il a pris ce Matin ces audiences du Roy et de la Famille Royale.   A St. Ildefence le 18 Aout 1782."

I have returned his visit and he appears disposed to live on Good terms with me— I am told that the Empress of Russia has given or is about to give Orders to her Ministers at foreign Courts to treat those of America in the Same manner as they treat Those of Other Nations. I have no Correspondence with Mr Dana, nor with Mr Adams— I have not had the honor to hear from Mr Jay since he left this Country & your last to me was of the 11th of June—[2] I am without Information from Congress, for Mr Livingston refers me to Mr Jays letters.[3] I am without Instructions, altho' I know that late ones have been sent to our Ministers. In short I believe that no person in my character was ever in a more embarassed Situation. I cannot console myself with the reflection, that where little is given, little can be expected, for I receive 1000 pounds Sterling pr. Anm. & I dun your Excy for it as if I merited it by my Services—

I hear that a Mr Fitzherbert has or is to reimplace Mr Greenville,[4] that Mr Oswald treats still with you— That the Ct

---

during the night of Aug. 15 / 16 and were able to avoid detection: Jack Russell, *Gibraltar Besieged, 1779–1783* (London, 1965), pp. 204–5. The main attack on Gibraltar, however, was intended to come on the seaward side, using floating gun batteries: Dull, *French Navy*, p. 307.

1. The new Prussian minister plenipotentiary, Ludwig, Graf von Nostitz: *Repertorium der diplomatischen Vertreter*, III, 340.

2. Missing.

3. *I.e.*, to Livingston's letters to Jay: Livingston to Carmichael, May 1, 1782, in Wharton, *Diplomatic Correspondence*, V, 383–4.

4. Alleyne Fitzherbert now dealt with the French government on Grantham and Shelburne's behalf: XXXVII, 685n. On Aug. 10, Vergennes sent Montmorin a copy of Fitzherbert's letter of credence (AAE).

de Aranda has commenced his Conferences with Mr Jay—[5] I have little hopes from this quarter until a general pacification takes place.

The Fables of yriarte[6] which I sent by Mr Jay to your Excy have occasioned the publication of One against him entitled El Asno Erudito,[7] this has produced an answer in Prose— I shall send copies of each to you by this Courier, if those to whom I have lent them return them in Time— In return I take the Liberty of Intreating You to procure & send me a work published by the Mr Cumberland who resided here some time—[8] The French and Imperial Ambassadors and Many Others are desirous of seeing it & it would be a particular pleasure to me to have it in my power to be the first to gratify their Curiosity— It may be addressed by a Courier to the Ct. de Montmorin— I write to Mr Jay by this Courier on his private Affairs— If there appears Any Intelligence on this Letter Worth his Attention, I beg you to Communicate it to him— You will please to present my Compliments to your Grandson & to believe me ever with high respect and Regard Your Excys. Obliged & Humble Sert.

WM. CARMICHAEL

His Excy. Benjamin Franklin

From William Cheetham   ALS:[9] American Philosophical Society

Most excellent Sir   Newton Moor 20th. August 1782

With defference & respect I presume (thro' the medium of my Friend Henry Wilde) to acquaint you that I am prevented by an unforeseen event of accompanying my Friends to pensilvania,

5. XXXVII, 733n.
6. Tomás de Yriarte (or Iriarte), *Fábulas literarias en verso castellano* (Madrid, 1782).
7. Juan Bautista Pablo Forner y Segarra, *El asno erudito* (Madrid, 1782).
8. Richard Cumberland, *Anecdotes of Eminent Painters in Spain, during the sixteenth and seventeenth centuries* . . . (2 vols., London, 1782). For Cumberland see XXXIII, 86n.
9. Written on the verso of Wyld's letter of introduction, letter (II) of Aug. 12 (XXXVII, 744–5), and labeled as a postscript.

But am resolved to follow (together with a number of other useful & well disposed Artisans) If it should appear from your Answer to the following Queries to be advantageous to us. Will wool that is grown in America suit for making Hats, or is stuff hatting the only branch of that Manufactory carried on there. Is there any quantity of pit Coal got there. But if any thing be asked here that is improper for you to answer, I beg you will forgive the same, & impute it to any other cause than a want of respect for your excelleny & the goverment you represent both of which is held in the highest estimation by your excellencies most obedient humle servant   WILLIAM CHEETHAM

N.B. Directions back

William Cheetham hat maker Nwton Moor Near Ashton underline to the care of George Ashley Manchester

From Jan Ingenhousz   ALS: American Philosophical Society

Dear friend.   Vienna aug. 20th. 1782

I Was very happy in recieving your lettre containing the explication of the stroke of lightning at Cremona, and an other, dated July 4th,[1] which came to hand before yesterday. Recieve my most harty thanks for both these favours and particularly for your kindness of forwarding my lettre to mr. Sam. Wharton and joining to it an admonitory note of your own on my behalf,[2] of

1. The latter has not been located. BF's explanation of the lightning strike at Cremona, a response to Carlo Barletti's pamphlet analyzing the strike, is above, XXXVII, 504–12. The letter enclosing it is in XXXV, 544–51.

2. Ingenhousz is here acknowledging BF's answer of June 21: XXXV, 549–51. BF's "admonitory note" has not been located. For the two letters Ingenhousz wanted BF to forward to Wharton see XXXVII, 212, 468.

BF told Ingenhousz on June 21 that Wharton never wrote to him; that same day Wharton complained to WTF that BF had not answered any of the four letters he had sent from America (only one of which is extant: XXXV, 160). Wharton promised to soon send BF a long letter about American affairs. If it was sent, BF did not receive it: BF to Ingenhousz, May 16, 1783, Library of Congress. Wharton's letter and a copy of it are at the APS; it is published in Smith, *Letters*, XVIII, 597. He remarked that "Cassius" (probably Arthur

which note you tell me to have inclosed a copy, which was left behind as it was not in the lettre. I thank you allso for the Communication of the American News. I doe not give up all hopes of a general congress being held at Vienna, as, besides the affaires to be adjusted between Gr. Brittain and the united states of America, the other European powers have direct or indirect relation with America as a New power starting up all at once. Old treatises between Gr. Brittain and Holland will be annihilated and new ones made and many new regulations must take place between all the European Powers after the tremendous power of that prowd insulary nation will be reduced to a more moderate condition. All those things can not be adjusted so soon, and will require some time to be settled, which, I imagine can't be conveniently done but by convoking a congress.

I am very glad to see, that your wighty political occupations have not yet been able to make you laid aside those pursuites, which were formerly your favourite studies. I hope for the sake of Philosophy, that you will fulfill your desires to pass the evening of life in the pursuit of Nature's laws. I wish I was at liberty to follow you on that Spot, where you will finish your glorious carreer, and where I my self have had the strongest inclination to finish mine: and indeed this thaugt had a great wight with me in resolving to employe a part of my fortune in a way, by which there was a faire prospect of augmenting my Stock so as to make me independent from Europe: and indeed, if I could write to you, what I think upon the times to be expected in this country, you would certainly think it much better for me to live in country of freedom, whose laws are framed by those, who submitt to them, and where no frowns of a monark will ever inspire terror and apprehensions to any man.

Your remarks upon the experiment with the wires seems to be wighty;[3] but when I was to prepare for the repetition of it, I be-

Lee) had not changed his behavior since returning from Europe and reminded BF of his comment about him, "If He cannot find a Quarrel wherever he goes, He will be sure to make One." He also said that Cassius had a "predilection . . . in favor of the adverse party," probably meaning those averse to his and BF's land claims (XXXI, 525–48).

3. See XXXV, 545–6.

gan to make some reflexion [on] your advise to put the hot oil in
motion when the end of the wires are plunged in it; I apprehended from such motion, that the wires beying unequaly dipt
in it by the very motion of the fluid, will contract the more heat
as they will be in contact with more of the heated fluid. I should
think that leaving the hot oil quiet, but sliding the frame, in
which the wires are fastened, slowly over the edge of the vessel
would answer the purpose. The leaving the wires a long while
into the melted wax, till they are thoroughy and equaly heated,
seems to me of great importance, and I will observe this if I repeat the experiment. I thank you for the hint.

I have not yet been able to find a copy of the pamflet of Pere
Barletti on the stroke of lightning at cremona. It is not to be got
here, but I will endeavour to get it from Italy; tho I believe you
have rightly understood the meaning of the author, as I remem-
bre of having run over the performance when I was with you at
passy.[4] I made an extract of what yould wrote about the American Affaires in the letter accompanying the reflexions on pere
Barletti book, and at what you say, that it is the intrest of whole
Europe to prevent a foederal Connexion between Gr. Britain
and the American free states;[5] I joined some reflexions about the
danger to be apprehended for the tranquillity of Europe if so
proud and quarlsom a nation should be again united with North
america so as to have its full support in time of warr and be at no
expenses to keep it in time of peace. I did make use of those reflexions you Communicated to me by reasoning about this affaire.
I gave the paper to the first lord of the bedchamber, who gave it
to the Emperour. He kept it. But I made no extract of you lettre
of July 4th, as you write me the Contents are for my private information. I am much obliged to you for those informations and
will be very glad of knowing from time to time who your Countries affaires goe on: But it is a pity that letters remain such a long
while behind. If a lettre, not to big, was recommended by you to
Count Mercy,[6] he would Send it to me by the ordinary post in his

4. In the winter of 1779/80: XXXI, 140n; XXXII, 342n.
5. XXXV, 551.
6. The comte de Mercy-Argenteau, the Imperial and Austrian ambassador.

pacquet to the court, if no Courier or private court messenger was agoying, which happens once every month, thereabouts at a fixed day.

I write by this oportunity to mr. le Begue, that, if he should find it inconsistent with his affaires, or impossibly by his frequent absence from town to take care of the impression of my book, I should be obliged to him to get A substitute in his room, who could act in the time of absence. I propose mr. le Roy in case of necessity, informing him that I make no doubt but you would employe, in case it should be required, your good offices in begging this favour for me of mr. le Roy.[7]

I am Verry respectfully Dear Sir Your obedient humble servt and affectionate friend   J. INGEN HOUSZ

to his Excellency B. Franklin Minister Plenip. of the united States of America. at Passy.

From Watson & Cossoul   LS: Historical Society of Pennsylvania

Sir   Nantes 20th Augt. 1782

By request of Mr. Laurens we have prevailed on Capt. Hardy to make application thro' your channel for the releif that his necessitys claim, as an unfortunate prisoner in the Service of our Country. As Mr. Laurens inguages himself to become responsible to indemnify you to the Publick, we Sincerely hope you will make the necessary advance as soon as possible. Mr. Laurens will write you on this Subject.[8]

---

7. BF had suggested that Le Roy would be a better choice than Le Bègue de Presle for overseeing the publication of the French translation of Ingenhousz' work: XXXV, 548, 549–50n; XXXVII, 211.

8. We have found no letter from Laurens to BF. Hardy himself wrote BF on Aug. 19, above. BF evidently turned down Hardy's request, prompting Elkanah Watson, Jr., to write WTF on Sept. 6, from Paris, with a plea to reconsider (APS).

Watson had come to Passy on Sept. 5 with the hope of obtaining a passport from BF and traveling to England on the Calais-Dover packet to pursue business concerns. BF initially denied his request and tried to discourage him from risking the trip. Some days later, however, he granted the passport.

We are most respectfully Your Excellency Most Obedt. Sts.
WATSON & COSSOUL

His Excellency Benja. Franklin Esqr. Passy

From Francis Coffyn

ALS: American Philosophical Society

Monsieur   Dunkerque ce 21. aoust 1782.

J'ai l'honneur de vous ecrire la presente, laquelle vous sera remise par Mr. Samuel Mansfield, Capitaine au Service des Etats unis de L'amerique; Lequel a été pris dans le brigantin Rizing States et conduit a Pool en Angletterre, d'ou il s'est Sauvé des prisons, il est arrivé ici manquant d'argent, comme il désire Retourner en sa patrie, je lui ai fourni pour le compte de Votre Excellence une Somme de 72. *l.t.* pour l'aider a payer les frais de sa route.[9]

J'ai l'honneur d'Etre tres respectueusement Monsieur Votre tres humble & tres obéissant Serviteur   F. COFFYN

Addressed: A Son Excellence / M. Bn franklin / Ministre plenipotentiaire des Etats unis / de L'amerique Septentrionale a la cour de / france / a Passi pres Paris

Notation: F Coffyn 21. Aout 1782.

(The form was filled in by WTF on Sept. 7 for travel to Calais or Ostend. APS.) Watson's journal gives the reason for BF's reversal: "I go with strong assurances of personal security, as Mr. Vaughan has plac'd in my charge an important packet for Lord Shelburn, which I stand pledg'd to deliver in person the moment of my arrival in London. I afterwards learn'd it was on account of these dispatches Dr. Franklin yielded his assent": Elkanah Watson Papers, Journal B (1781–1820), New York State Library, Albany, N.Y. For Watson's mission to Shelburne see the headnote to Lafayette's Sept. 12 letter, below. BF also gave Watson letters to deliver to Priestley, Price, and Burke: Winslow C. Watson, ed., *Men and Times of the Revolution; or Memoirs of Elkanah Watson . . .* (New York, 1856), p. 141.

9. Mansfield, captured by the *General Conway,* received assistance from BF on Sept. 25: Editorial Note on Promissory Notes, above; Kaminkow, *Mariners,* p. 238. Coffyn was reimbursed on Sept. 24: Account XXVII (XXXII, 4).

From John MacMahon:[1] Prescription and Directions

(I) Press copy of ADS: Library of Congress; (II) ALS and press copy of ALS: Library of Congress

During the third week of August, Franklin suffered a severe attack of bladder or kidney stones, accompanied by a pain in the hip that extended down his left thigh. The latter problem was generally (and erroneously) attributed to gout.[2] Franklin would be confined to his house for nearly six weeks. During that time, news of his illness spread throughout Europe, some of it false. In Italy officials learned from their diplomats at Versailles that Franklin had suffered a stroke; in England it was reported that he had had a fit of apoplexy.[3]

Elkanah Watson visited Passy on September 5 and was convinced that Franklin was dying. On September 17 Franklin, still in pain from "Gravel & Gout," confessed to John Jay that he feared his situation was more serious than those around him realized, and seems to have asked Jay to draw up a will for him.[4] Five days later he was said to be

1. Although MacMahon and BF had known one another since 1777 (XXV, 4), this prescription is our first evidence of BF consulting MacMahon professionally. Several weeks earlier MacMahon had recommended a treatment for WTF's skin eruptions: MacMahon to WTF, Aug. 4, 1782, APS.

2. Benjamin Vaughan wrote Shelburne on Aug. 24: "Dr. Franklin is very much indisposed this week with gravelly complaints, but to-day is somewhat better. In the warm bath he for some days has voided small stones." Morris, *Jay: Peace*, p. 325. On Aug. 28 Matthew Ridley visited BF and noted that he "had an attack of the Stone and has a little of the Gout": Klingelhofer, "Matthew Ridley's Diary," p. 101. On Sept. 8, Richard Oswald reported that for the last ten days BF had "at first a Gravel in the Kidneys, which is gone off—but he continues very ill of a Rheumatic gout in his legs & thighs, which prevents his getting rest & sleep": Oswald's memorandum to [Shelburne], for which see XXXVII, 678–9n. In January, 1783, BF seems to have thought the hip and thigh pain might be due to sciatica: BF to Mary Hewson, Jan. 8, below.

3. Van Berkenrode, the Dutch ambassador, learned of BF's illness at Versailles on Aug. 25; see his Aug. 26 letter, below. Francesco Favi, the Tuscan chargé d'affaires, and Daniele Delfino, the Venetian minister, reported in their dispatches that BF suffered a stroke: Antonio Pace, *Benjamin Franklin and Italy* (Philadelphia, 1958), p. 118. On Oct. 5, Jeremy Bentham reported having heard from a reliable source in Paris that BF was recovering from "a fit of the apoplexy from a retrograde gout": Timothy L. S. Sprigge et al., eds., *The Correspondence of Jeremy Bentham* (11 vols. to date, London, 1968–), III, 142.

4. Watson's journal entry of Sept. 5 records his alarm: Elkanah Watson

30

"much better," though he would continue to allude to poor health over the next few weeks. By late October, Franklin was able to resume his rounds.[5] The pain in his thigh, however, had rendered him so weak on the left side that he still had difficulty going up and down stairs as late as January.[6]

This was the first major episode of an illness that would eventually become chronic and debilitating. According to the case history which Franklin wrote some years later, the methods he employed during this attack "in order to bring the suppos'd Gout down into the Foot" included "warm Bathing, and a Poultis of Mustard." This treatment caused his foot to swell but did not draw the pain down from the thigh, where it persisted. As for the stone, he remarked that as a young man he had suffered milder attacks but had been free of them for the past fifty years. During this acute episode, he "daily voided Gravel Stones the Size of small Pease, [and] took now and then some Decoctions of Herbs & Roots that were prescribed him by Friends or Physicians. . . ."[7] Among the remedies Franklin tried were the saponaria pills specified in the following prescription, which were to be taken with an herbal decoction described in the accompanying directions.

Were they effective? Unfortunately not, and Franklin discontinued their use. Though he would receive advice and remedies from well-wishers all over England and France,[8] he wrote in his case history that he "persisted . . . in nothing except the Use of Honey at Breakfast instead of or sometimes with Butter on his Bread, he remembering to have heard in the Conversation of Physicians, Honey mentioned as of

---

Papers, Journal No. 5, New York State Library. For BF's own assessment see his letters to David Hartley and John Jay, both dated Sept. 17.

5. Klingelhofer, "Matthew Ridley's Diary," pp. 113, 122–3, where Ridley notes that BF was on the road to Paris on Oct. 28 and dined with Jay on Oct. 30. On Oct. 27, Ridley told JA that BF was still weak, but was now able to sit at table: Butterfield, *John Adams Diary*, III, 37–8. See also BF to Jay, Oct. 9, below.

6. BF to Mary Hewson, Jan. 8, 1783.

7. BF, "Case," [on or before March 1, 1784], APS.

8. Of the many remedies BF received, the only one dating from the period of this volume was sent to M. Brillon on Aug. 29 by a friend responding to what must have been an urgent appeal. The writer assured Brillon that he was sending by express 28 jugs of Griesbach water, famous for curing the stone: Library of Congress. Miscellaneous remedies that the editors have been unable to date are described in the Editorial Note on Remedies for the Stone, [after Aug. 24].

great Service in Gravelly Cases."[9] Eventually the malady subsided, "but observing Sand constantly in his Urine, he continued the use of the Honey to the amount of perhaps a Pound per Week." In spite of this precaution, he had another attack of the stone the following autumn, and chronically thereafter.[1]

[August 23–24, 1782]

I.

ce 23 Aoút

Rx Sapon. medic[2] —— ½ oz.

f. pilul. singul. gran. vi.[3]

pulves. glycir. composs.[4]

d. ad [*illegible*][5]

S.[6] six pilules deux fois par jour   MacMahon

pour son Excellence M. Franklin

9. In 1744 BF explained to his parents why he thought honey might be effective in treating stones: II, 413–14.

1. See George W. Corner and Willard E. Goodwin, "Benjamin Franklin's Bladder Stone," *Journal of the History of Medicine and Allied Sciences*, VIII (1953), 359–77. BF's case history, and the medical opinions of five eminent physicians and surgeons of London to whom it was submitted in July, 1785, are printed there.

2. Saponaria medicinalis. This botanical drug contained saponin, a glucoside found in several species of Saponaria, including s. officinalis or soapwort. A decoction of Saponaria leaves was also used at this time for cases of "visceral obstructions." For the pharmaceutical information in these footnotes and general help in deciphering MacMahon's barely legible prescription, the editors thank Glenn Sonnedecker, professor emeritus, School of Pharmacy, University of Wisconsin-Madison, and director emeritus, American Institute of the History of Pharmacy.

3. Fiant pilulæ singulæ granarum vi., *i.e.*, make each pill to contain six grains.

4. Pulvis glycyrrhizae compositus (compound licorice powder), a widely used product containing senna, glycyrrhiza (licorice), washed sulphur, oil of fennel, and sugar. Professor Sonnedecker believes that while this was often used as a laxative, the pharmacist would have used it *ad lib.* as a flavoring and binder, since no quantity is specified.

5. "D." could stand for "dividatur," instructing the pharmacist to divide the pill mass into a specific number of pills.

6. Signa (write), *i.e.*, direct the patient to take six pills two times per day.

on enverra aussi une demi-once des semences de carotte sauvage
et un verre d'emulsion édulcorée avec une once de syrop de diacode[7]

II.

ce 24 Aout
On fera bouillir une demi-douzaine de sebestes et autant de jujubes, une demi-once de pois chiches, deux gros de semences de
mauve et autant de celle de guimauve dans cinq demi setiers
d'eau, qu'on réduira à une pinte.[8]

Passez la décoction, que Monsieur boira par verrées de temps
en temps dans la journée, il peut en boire un verre une heure
avant les répas, mais il n'en boira que trois heures après le diner.
Les pilules au nombre de six doivent étre prises le matin et le soir;
il boira après les pilules ce matin une tasse de l'infusion de graine
de lin et de carotte sauvage, et après la prise du soir, toute l'é-
mulsion.[9]

7. Diacodion, a syrup made from white opium poppies. This narcotic emulsion was a single dose to be consumed at night; see the directions, below.

An unsigned, undated note in French, written by someone concerned
about this pain medication, is among BF's papers at the Library of Congress.
The writer has been assured that BF is taking only moderate doses of the
"sirop de pavots blancs" (white poppies). Mr. MacMahon knows, as does the
writer, that large doses of narcotics taken internally cause problems for gout
sufferers. He proposes applying to the affected extremity a topical unction of
sweet almond oil mixed with a small amount of camphor. If this does not ease
the pain sufficiently, one could add to the unction eight drops of liquid lau-
danum. This can be applied two to three times per 24–hour period.

8. These ingredients, not listed on the prescription above, are: sebesten
plums, jujubes, chick peas, and seeds of the mallow and marsh-mallow
plants. A demi-setier was equivalent to eight Parisian pints.

9. The infusion of flax seeds and the seeds of wild carrot was a diuretic,
often prescribed for the stone; see the Editorial Note on Remedies for the
Stone. See also Corner and Goodwin, "Benjamin Franklin's Bladder Stone,"
p. 368. The emulsion, containing an opiate, is described at the end of MacMahon's prescription, above.

Benjamin Vaughan sought independent confirmation of MacMahon's recommended treatment from two Englishmen in Paris, presumably physicians.
He sent their opinions to WTF on Aug. 26 (APS). W. Lisle and Mr. Hume concurred that the prescription was what an English physician might have ordered: the soap pills were a good medicine and active at the dose prescribed;
the opiate taken in an emulsion at night was established practice; and while

Demain après chaque prise de six pilules il boira un verre de la tisane ci-dessus. Mc. M

From Margaret Stewart
ALS: American Philosophical Society

London 23 August 82

I was honored with Your Excellency's; Letter of June 13;[1] which I shou'd; have answered, imidiatly but waited to Send You the doz; Copies, of My Brothers wrok, You did me, the honor to write for; but I have been so distressed by an expencive Law Suit; & a long illness that I have Not have it in my power to get them printed;[2] as I am no Stranger to You benevolence; beg, You will; recommend the Work to Some of Your freinds here at the Price You paid thro; Madame Frensh;[3] to enable me to Print fivty Copies; which will be no More trouble than Twelve; besides I have had Some Subsribed for; I beg pardon; for the trouble I have been under the necessity of giving You; Excellency; & am with due Respect Your Much obliged Most humble Servant

M STEWART

P.S. I hope to have an enswere as soon as possible

Addressed: A Son Excellence / Dr Franklin Passy / Pres de Paris

---

neither marsh-mallow nor mallow would be used in England, the ingredients were mucilaginous and the decoction appeared to be adapted to the complaint. Vaughan wished his inquiry to remain confidential "lest Dr. McMahon might feel hurt at it." Vaughan also solicited the opinion of Dr. William Withering in England; Withering's response is résuméd below, [after Aug. 24].

1. Not found, but probably a reply to her letter of April 26: XXXVII, 229–30.

2. For John Stewart's *The Senator's Remembrancer* and his sister's legal troubles see XXXV, 636; XXXVI, 410n, and the references cited there.

3. In 1771, BF paid one guinea per set to Katherine French, who had first sent him the work: XVIII, 35–7.

From the Comte de Vergennes

Draft:[4] Archives du Ministère des affaires étrangères; copy, press copy of copy, and transcript: National Archives

à Versailles le 23. aout 1782.

J'ai reçu, M, la lettre que vous m'avez fait l'honneur de mecrire le 9 de ce mois, ainsi que le mémoire qui y étoit joint.[5] J'ai communiqué cette piéce à M. le Mis. de Castries, et je ne doute pas que ce Ministre ne prenne en considération la demande qu'elle renferme autant que les Circonstances le permettront. Nous nous occupons, M, des moyens de faire prospérer le commerce qui s'est établi entre la france et les Etats-unis, et nous ne négligerons rien pour remplir cet objet à la satisfaction commune des deux Pays. Le Congrès faciliteroit beaucoup notre travail s'il vouloit bien nous communiquer ses idées et ses vües à cet égard, et je vous en fais la demande avec d'autant plus de confiance, que je suis persuadé que cette assemblée desire autant que nous d'établir d'une maniere avantageuse et solide les relations de commerce entre la france et l'Amerique.

M. Franklin

From Jonathan Williams, Jr.

ALS: Historical Society of Pennsylvania; copy: Yale University Library

Dear & hond sir.   Nantes Augt. 23. 1782.

I beg leave to solicit your kindness in forwarding the inclosed to the Marquis de Castries and to add a Line in addition to my Request.[6] You will see it is no Favour out of the common Line I therefore ask without hesitation.

---

4. In the hand of Joseph-Mathias Gérard de Rayneval, the *premier commis* who dealt with American affairs. An English translation is printed in Wharton, *Diplomatic Correspondence*, V, 671–2.

5. Robert Morris' "State of American Commerce," which BF had forwarded on Aug. 9 (XXXVII, 714). It asked, among other things, for the help of two French ships of the line and ten frigates: *Morris Papers*, V, 151–2.

6. JW's letter, dated Aug. 23, informed Castries that he had established the mercantile firm of Williams, Moore & Co. at Lorient. He requested that the

If I had 100 Tons of the public Stores here I could put them on board the Cato & land them in Boston or some neighbouring Port according to Circumstances. It is strange that we need depend on french Transports when there are now at least 10 American ships well armed & none will go away full.[7]

I did not inform you of the Birth of my Daughter because I never reckoned her as an Aquisition and she is now as if she had never been.[8] Mrs Williams is yet very poorly, but I hope not dangerous. I am as ever Yours most dutifully & affectionately

JONA WILLIAMS J

His Excellency Doctor Franklin.

To Vergennes

L:[9] Archives du Ministère des affaires étrangères

Passy 24 Augt 1782.

Mr Franklin presents his respectful Compliments to Monsieur le Comte de Vergennes. He has search'd for the Boston Paper, in which mention is made of 4000 Troops being embarked at New-

---

firm be allowed to store their goods in French warehouses at Lorient, just as the Dutch East India Company did, on the basis of America's having status as a most favored nation. He also requested that Castries write to the port commandant at Lorient granting permission for the firm to use a French dry dock in order to copper the bottom of one of their ships. Yale University Library. BF forwarded the letter to Castries on Aug. 31, below.

7. The previous February BF had asked JW to arrange for shipping these stores warehoused at Brest, supplies for the American army that were replacements for those captured aboard the *Marquis de Lafayette* and *Rusé*. JW had been unable to persuade any American captain at Nantes to risk sailing to Brest for the consignment. BF turned to the French for help, which they gave reluctantly. Some of the supplies were sent aboard three French ships, which subsequently were forced into Rochefort. American merchants now volunteered to take the stores. In June JW suggested using the *Cato:* XXXVI, 546, 556, 685–6; XXXVII, 71–2n; JW to Robeson, June 6 and 26, 1782 (Yale University Library). For the problems encountered by the French, see Palteau de Veimerange to BF, Sept. 6; BF to Castries, Sept. 7, below.

8. Bethia had died a week earlier: JW to BF, Aug. 16, above.

9. In WTF's hand.

1. A note in the margin, in French, indicates that the newspaper was dated June 6. This now-missing account may have been the source for an undated

York, but cannot now find it.[1] Thinks it may be in the Hands of M. le Marquis de la Fayette, and that it was dated about the Beginning of July. He sends inclosed a Copy of two Articles relating to an Embarkation intended. In a Letter he received from an intelligent Person at Warwick in Rhodeisland dated June 25.[2] it is said, "We have been lately surprised with considerable Fleets appearing as if they intended to re-possess Rhode island, but they passed by after three or four Days."

From their passing by Rhodeisland, Mr F. imagined they were gone to re-inforce Halifax, or Newfoundland and Quebec.

From Gaetano Filangieri[3]

Translation of ALS in Italian:[4] Historical Society of Pennsylvania

Most respectable Sir,　　　　　　　Naples, August 24, 1782

Your precious gift has finally reached me after many months, and I consider it one of the greatest prizes I received for my

---

memoir written by the French naval ministry stating that 4,000 British troops might be sent from New York to the West Indies: Dull, *French Navy*, p. 308n. The only related rumor we have located is in the June 10 issue of the *Boston Gazette, and the Country Journal*, reporting that a convoy of 20 sail escorted by two frigates was in Long Island Sound and speculating that there could be 1,500 or 2,000 troops (or refugees) aboard.

2. From Jane Mecom: XXXVII, 549.

3. This is the first extant letter between BF and Filangieri (1752–1788), one of the leading writers of the Italian Enlightenment and a disciple of Montesquieu. His master work, *La scienza della legislazione*, was to have comprised seven books covering different aspects of the law. Filangieri completed only four of the projected seven (some of which were divided into multiple volumes) before his untimely death. Books I and II, one volume each, were published in Naples in 1780. The first covered general rules of the science of legislation. Book II, political and economic laws, compared, as did Montesquieu's *Esprit des lois*, the laws, political institutions, and economic policies of various ancient and modern states. Filangieri was a fervent advocate of free trade but feared the economic consequences of American independence: Marcello Maestro, *Gaetano Filangieri and His Science of Legislation* (Philadelphia, 1976); Antonio Pace, *Benjamin Franklin and Italy* (Philadelphia, 1958), pp. 139, 147–66; Franco Venturi, *The End of the Old Regime in Europe, 1776–1789: the Great States of the West*, trans. R. Burr Litchfield (Princeton, 1991), pp. 25–32.

4. Prepared by the late Robert S. Lopez, Sterling Professor of History,

work. Your graciousness would have provoked a feeling of vanity in me had it not been prevented by my knowledge of the generosity of your soul. To show you my gratitude, I sent a few copies of my work to Signor Pio, Embassy Secretary in Paris of the Court of Naples[5] and I asked him to give you a copy in my name—[6] also to beg you to accept a few more, should you be inclined to give them to some friends.

I have almost completed the third book, the one dealing with criminal law. It will take up two volumes, one of which is concerned with the procedural system, and the other with the penal code. The novelty of my ideas on both objects frightens me. In a century during which so much has been written and thought about everything that has to do with public prosperity, it is quite easy to see originality as akin to strangeness. This thought disturbs me and sometimes even oppresses me. In order to surmount that feeling, I keep repeating to myself: "If you had merely repeated the ideas of other people, what benefit could humanity have expected from your writings? If my ideas are strange, they will be rejected and in that case humanity will not suffer any damage; but if, while novel, they are also reasonable,

---

Yale University. The Italian original is printed in Pace, *Benjamin Franklin and Italy*, pp. 398–9 and in Eugenio Lo Sardo, ed., *Il mondo nuovo e le virtù civili: L'epistolario di Gaetano Filangieri (1772–1785)* (Naples, 1999), pp. 231–2.

5. On Sept. 11, 1781, Luigi Pio wrote Filangieri that he had loaned BF the first two volumes of *La scienza della legislazione*. In exchange, BF gave Pio "a large quarto edition of his essays on scientific experiments." BF reads Italian slowly, Pio said, but understands it well, and found Filangieri's theories "presented with the utmost clarity and precision." BF asked Pio to tell the author that he was eagerly awaiting the volumes dealing with criminal legislation, "because they will be of special interest to his nation, still needing to be enlightened on this subject." Pio wrote again on Sept. 23, 1781, saying that BF had asked him to forward to Filangieri some of his "political publications." Maestro, *Gaetano Filangieri*, p. 26. The gift may have been *Political, Miscellaneous, and Philosophical Pieces* (XXXI, 210–18).

Pio was chargé d'affaires of the court of the Two Sicilies (Naples and Sicily) at the French court from April, 1781, until August, 1783: *Repertorium der diplomatischen Vertreter*, III, 423.

6. These two volumes, inscribed "From S. Pio" and signed by BF, are in the Loganian Library at the Library Company of Philadelphia: Edwin Wolf 2nd, catalogue of books and pamphlets in BF's library (XXXVI, 331n).

applicable and opportune, if they manage to diminish the suffering of a single person, if they result in preventing just one injustice, shouldn't you applaud yourself for having spoken out, shouldn't you regret to have kept your ideas secret because of a cowardly feeling of doubt and of fear of seeing those ideas condemned and ridiculed?"

Such is the reasoning that propelled me to pursue my enterprise with all possible vigor. As I have said, I am almost at the end and you, respectable man and remarkable being, will be the first to judge it, you who struggling against men and against the gods, snatched the lightning from Jupiter and the scepter from tyrants. Once I receive your opinion on this part of my work, I shall tell you about a personal project.[7] You, who can ensure my happiness and make me an instrument of use to my fellow men, please allow me to hide a secret that I shall reveal to you when I have obtained your promise not to communicate it to anybody.

I kiss your hand with the respect inspired by your talents and your virtues, and I subscribe myself Your truly devoted servant

IL CAVALIER GAETANO FILANGIERI

William Withering's "On Calculus Complaints": Résumé

Printed in William Withering, *The Miscellaneous Tracts of the Late William Withering; to Which is Prefixed a Memoir of His Life, Character, and Writings* (2 vols., London, 1822), II, 478–84.

When Franklin fell ill, Benjamin Vaughan (then in Paris) sought medical advice from the eminent British physician William Withering,[8] whose areas of research included "human calculi" or stones. Wither-

7. See Filangieri's letter below, Dec. 2.
8. Withering was a physician, botanist, and mineralogist who moved to Birmingham in 1775 and became chief physician to the Birmingham General Hospital. A friend of Priestley's (see XXXVI, 238n), he was a member of the Lunar Society and was active in the Society for Promoting the Abolition of the Slave Trade. *DNB.*
Vaughan also sought advice from two Englishmen in Paris; see the annotation of MacMahon's prescription and directions, Aug. 23–24.

ing's reply is missing, but Franklin later described it as "a very ingenious & judicious Letter (as it appear'd to me) written by you on the
Subject of calculous Complaints & the Remedies that had been propos'd for them."[9] Withering's "On Calculous Complaints," dated
1782 and published in a posthumous collection of his works, is in the
form of an essay but was obviously drawn from this letter. We summarize it here, as Withering's editor reported that the doctor wrote
this overview of the stone and its treatments "in compliance with the
wishes of Dr. F. and his friends." In his reply to Vaughan, Withering
also invited Franklin to send him an account of his case so that he
might be able to recommend a specific course of treatment. Franklin
waited until another acute attack of the stone in early 1784 to take
Withering up on this offer.[1]

⟨[after Aug. 24, 1782]:[2] Believing the stone to be composed of
"calcareous earth, fixed air, and some animal gluten," many doctors had reasoned that the glue holding the particles together
might be dissolved by soap lye, lime water, and "caustic vegetable alkali." These methods proved ineffectual. Other research
suggested that stones might be dissolved by "fixed air," or car-
bon dioxide. Physicians whom Withering respected had their
patients drink large quantities of "fixed air water." This produced so many successes that Withering tried injecting fixed air
directly into the bladder. His technique was not painful to the patients but the results were mixed, and Withering eventually realized that fixed air was not a cure. He then undertook a series of
rigorous chemical analyses on a variety of stones, and concluded
that "not one of them contained a single particle of calcareous
earth; nor would it be easy to demonstrate that they contain any
earth at all." Convinced that "mistaken principles had led us to
erroneous practice," he was currently trying to determine a better method of treatment based on "attentive observation of nature and from facts supported upon the basis of large experience," which would of course take time. Withering concluded
with a section on his observations and recent hypotheses. These

9. BF to Withering, March 1, 1784, APS.
1. BF to Withering, cited above.
2. The date Vaughan wrote Shelburne about BF's attack of the stone. He
may have sent his letter to Withering at the same time. See the annotation of
MacMahon's prescription and directions, Aug. 23–24.

included the firm belief that a "sudden check to the perspiration" is certain to induce an attack.⟩

Editorial Note on Remedies for the Stone

Franklin received dozens of remedies for the stone during his stay in France, from friends and strangers alike. Most were unsolicited and many are undated. We have determined that most of the undated remedies were sent in response to later episodes; they will be noted in future volumes. The rest we describe here at their earliest possible date, following Franklin's first attack. All of them are in French.[3]

Don Adroyon, a Spanish marine officer, spells French phonetically in a nearly illegible hand. Being at Passy, he has heard about Franklin's health, and like all honest men he is concerned. He understands that a certain substance (possibly calomellas) from South America is a powerful agent against the stone.

Two pages survive of what may have been a longer letter from the duc de Chaulnes. He hates consulting doctors but relies on one named Guenand, who is sensible and has had excellent apothecary training. Just that morning Guenand gave him a very good and simple remedy for the stone, to which, Vaughan tells him, Franklin is susceptible. It is soap lye diluted in water, which one should inject into the bladder through a catheter in the urethra. Would Franklin like Chaulnes to send the doctor to him?

Guerin, *médécin du roy*, writes that mineral water from Griesbach in Alsace is renowned for its effectiveness in all maladies of the kidneys and bladder, especially the gravel. It is this property that gave the town its name, since "gries" in French is "gravelle." As with all mineral water, one should begin treatment by drinking two or three glasses daily, gradually increasing the number to ten or twelve. Continue this for two or three weeks, or more, if it is having a good effect. The waters of Contreville in Lorraine are also reputed to be beneficial in the same maladies.

A Bordeaux merchant named Vincent has heard about Franklin's acute attack of the stone from John Bondfield. Bondfield, who knows that Vincent possesses a remedy, has asked him to send it. The cure is

---

3. Unless otherwise noted, all these documents are at the Library of Congress.

infallible, but is a secret. Vincent offers to forward the remedy and instructions for its use, but solemnly asks that Franklin divulge the secret to no one.

The remaining miscellaneous remedies were written on separate sheets in unknown hands. "Recette contre les Coliques Néphrétiques" contains instructions for making a decoction of rhubarb, sugar, and cream of tartar. "Remède contre le Calcul et la Gravelle" recommends a plant that is just beginning to come to the notice of the Faculty of Medicine: the nettle. An infusion of steeped nettles has marvelous diuretic properties. A brief note entitled "Une infusion à jeun de *l'uva ursi*" notes that the bearberry has been used with success in Switzerland, and was recently introduced to Paris and London. Mr. Nairne of the Royal Society has found it effective. "Remede éprouvé contre les pierres calculs et graviers de la Vessie"[4] was obtained from a seventy-eight-year-old man who claims to have been cured by it, and whose "Observation" follows the remedy. The ingredients are: a pinch of pellitory, a pinch of white nettle flowers, a pinch of linseed, and an ounce of elm shoots, boiled together in sufficient water to result in one pint of liquid. The patient is to drink a pint in the morning, on an empty stomach, for three consecutive days. After two days' pause, the remedy may be repeated if necessary.

From Mattheus Lestevenon van Berkenrode

AL: American Philosophical Society

paris ce 26 Aout. 82.
L'Ambassadeur de Hollande, aiant appris hier a Versailles, que Monsieur Francklin se trouve incommodé, fait demander des Nouvelles de Sa Santé, et a L'honneur de L'assurer de Ses tres humbles civilités.[5]

Notation: L'Ambassadeur de Hollande.

4. This remedy is at the APS.
5. For BF's illness see MacMahon's prescription of Aug. 23.

From De Grasse

AL: American Philosophical Society

Paris le 26. aoust 1782.

Le Comte de Grasse á l'honneur de souhaiter le bonjour á son Excellence le Docteur franklin; il le prie de vouloir bien prendre lecture de la lettre ci jointe[6] et se charger de la Faire parvenir á M. le Président du Congrês, dont il ignore le nom.[7]

Notation: Le C. de Grasse 26. Aout 1782.

From William Hodgson

ALS: Historical Society of Pennsylvania

Dear sir   London 26 August 1782

Not having any thing particular to Communicate I have deferred too long paying my tribute of thanks for the Civilities I recd from you during my short stay at Paris—[8] I saw the Minister[9] soon after my Return, who was much upon the *Fish* to know why I paid you a Visit, I turned it off, by saying we had a long Acc't to settle & that I flatterred myself my Visit had not been alltogether fruitless as I had endeavoured & I hoped with some Success, to convince you that his Lordship was fully resolved to grant American Independence, of the Truth of which most Men

---

6. The letter, dated Aug. 25, was written on behalf of Capt. Charles Asgill, the British officer awaiting execution in America (XXXVII, 432n). De Grasse solicits clemency and justice for Asgill as repayment for the good treatment he received in England, particularly by Asgill's family. It would be unjust to punish an innocent man for the conduct of one of his colleagues. De Grasse asks this as a personal favor, invoking his own "foibles services" to the United States. This letter is still among BF's papers at the APS.

7. John Hanson was elected president on Nov. 5, 1781, the day after de Grasse sailed from the Chesapeake: XXXVI, 10n; *JCC*, XXI, 1100.

8. Hodgson seems to have been in Paris from late July through at least the first week of August, during which time he settled his 1782 accounts through July 26 (XXXVI, 605–6n), and was paid by Ferdinand Grand on Aug. 1: Account XXVII (XXXII, 4). On July 31 Vaughan mentioned in a letter to Shelburne that he would ask Hodgson to carry his letters, and on Aug. 6 Vaughan reported to Shelburne that he, Hodgson, and Bancroft had discussed the possibility of America making a separate peace; both letters are at the APS.

9. Shelburne, with whom Hodgson had conferred in mid-July about the peace negotiations: XXXVII, 653–5.

entertained great Doubts, he said I did right—& that alltho the Commission for that purpose had not been expedited, yet the Copy had, & the Commission itself shou'd be sent as soon as the Chancellor returned to Town, all which I hope will be carried into execution—[1] If in the course of this Business any thing shou'd occurr which may require a fuller Conversation with his Lordship than perhaps can be obtained from the Gentleman at Paris, I shall be happy in being employed & you may depend upon my Zeal & discretion & you will oblige me much by a hint of Information how things go on.

I have sent the 4 Boxes of pepper Mint drops to Shelburne house which I hope you will receive Safe[2] & I have made application for another Cartel Vessell to carry what American Prisoners have been collected since the last Sailed—with those who were left behind sick the No. is about 130[3]—& I am promised that they shall be sent away as soon as a Vessell can be procured for the purpose— If you have any Dispatches to send I can forward them by some of the Officers that go & perhaps it may be a safe & eligible mode of Conveyance— I have given Directions to Mr Wren[4] to pay a weekly allowance to the Prisoners 1 s., to Officers & 6 p. to Men. I am with the greatest Respect Dr sir Yours most sincerely WILLIAM HODGSON

I wrote to Digges pursuant to what we settled but he has not given any Answer, nor do I expect he will—

1. The official copy of Oswald's commission was sent on Aug. 10: Morris, *Jay: Peace*, p. 286n.

2. These were for Gérard de Rayneval; see XXXVII, 31n, and BF to Rayneval, Sept. 4.

3. There still were 157 American prisoners at Forton and Mill on Aug. 28: Sheldon S. Cohen, *Yankee Sailors in British Gaols: Prisoners of War at Forton and Mill, 1777–1783* (Newark, Del., and London, 1995), p. 204.

4. Rev. Thomas Wren, who assisted American prisoners at Forton Prison, Portsmouth: XXV, 416–17n.

From John Wright

ALS: Historical Society of Pennsylvania

Esteemed Friend   London 26th of 8th mo (Augst.) 1782

Having just heard of an Opportunity of conveying a letter I am unwilling to let it slip without acknowledging the rect. of thy very kind & acceptable favr. dated May 8[5] which afforded me much pleasure on many accots. particularly to observe that old Time who is silently making depredations upon the mental & bodily powers of all other mortals seem to have passed by the habitation of my good old friend leaving him in full possession of all the Vigor of youth whilst accompanied with the mature judgment of Age. May he not Call Yet of many Years and may we live to see an End of all strife a fair firm & honourable peace That the Christian World so Called might become so far Christian at least as to learn War no more.

I was also pleased to find thou hadst no Concern with our neighbours but surprised at their Conduct towards thee. Am perswaded it was not with T:Cs. approbation thou knowest he is more a man of Science than business. He sufferd. him self to be over ruled in the Conduct of that House more than seemed Consistant with his good sense & manly spirit on other occasions.[6]

A very hansome subscription has been set on foot & a large sum raised to purchase annuities sufficient for what may be Called a genteel support & he has taken a Small house at Southgate to which he is retired with his wife, Before they went thither they spent a few weeks with us at Camberwell & seemed to bear their misfortune with becoming fortitude Yet not without sensibly feeling the situation he was fallen into with all its painful Circumstances. He spoke of thee with respect but not a word of the transaction thou mentions nor did I mention it to him.

---

5. Not found. It was probably a response to Wright's letter of April 4: XXXVII, 174–6.

6. In his letter of April 4 (cited above), Wright reported on the bankruptcy of BF's bankers Brown, Collinson & Tritton, one of whose partners was BF's old friend Thomas Collinson ("T.C."). BF's last extant letter to the firm is in XXXI, 360. Wright's own banking firm was located nearby on Lombard Street: F. G. Hilton Price, *A Handbook of London Bankers . . .* (1876; reprint, New York, 1970), pp. 20, 125.

Hearing the other day that thy old Landlady & her Daughter[7] live in Kensington Square I went yesterday to see them. The old Lady I think looks full as well as she did 7. or 8 years ago which I noticed. She said seeing me painted her up. However I found her much heartier & better than I expected her Daughter appeared to be very well & in good spirits with her three Children about her. If I can be of any Use in handing thy letters of friendship to them it will give me pleasure.

It afforded me great satisfaction to observe that thou hoped for a restoration of Peace & good will between the two Countries. I know of none so capable of Contributing to the accomplishment of so desirable so blessed a work. I should rejoice to see it & particularly to see thee again which with the renewal of our old Connection I should esteem a great favr. And notwithstand the great loss we & may I not say the world has sustained by the death of the Marquis of Rockingham & the alterations which followed Yet I hope but perhaps it is only the hope of Ignorance Still I would fain flatter myself that when the present Naval campain is over a General peace will be seriously thought of & set about in earnest and if all sides are willing surely it may be effected.

I thank thee for thy kind good wishes for me & our House & am with great Esteem Dear Friend Thine very respectfully

JOHN WRIGHT

My partner Smith[8] is married a second time and is now at Brighthelmstone with his wife & family but think theres no Chance of increase

Dr. Benjamin Franklin Passy

Addressed: Dr. / Benjamin Franklin

Notation: J. Wright, London 26. August 1782.

7. Margaret Stevenson and Mary Hewson.
8. Thomas Smith: XI, 179n.

From Félix Vicq d'Azyr

LS: American Philosophical Society

Monsieur, [before August 27, 1782]

J'ai l'honneur de Vous adresser quelques Billets d'invitation pour la seance publique de la société Royale de médecine, qui aura lieu le 27 de ce mois et dont elle Vous prie de Vouloir bien disposer. La Compagnie espére que Vous Voudrez bien honorer cette assemblée de Votre présence.[9]

Je serai en mon particulier infiniment flatté, si nous avons le bonheur de Vous posséder à cette séance. J'y ferai la lecture de l'Eloge du Célebre M. foterghill dont j'ai appris, depuis peu de jours, que Vous êtiez l'ami. Entre autres matériaux qui m'ont été adressés pour servir à la redaction de cet éloge, j'ai reçu celui qui en a été fait par M Thompson.[1] Si Vous aviez quelques anecdotes particulieres relatives à M foterghill Je Vous prie de Vouloir bien me les Communiquer, Je m'empresserai d'en faire usage.[2]

Je suis avec respect Monsieur Votre tres humble et très obeissant serviteur. VICQ DAZYR

M franklin

Notation: Vic-d'azir

9. The meeting was held on Aug. 27 at 4:30 p.m. at the Louvre. Vicq d'Azyr read his eulogy (mentioned below) near the end of the session: *Jour. de Paris*, issues of Aug. 27, 28, and 30, 1782.

1. In May David Barclay had sent BF two tributes to Fothergill, who died on Dec. 26, 1780: XXXVII, 423. One of them may have been Gilbert Thompson's *Memoirs of the Life and a View of the Character of the Late Dr. Fothergill* (London, 1782). Thompson, a close friend of Fothergill's, was also a physician: *ODNB*.

2. Vicq d'Azyr's eulogy was printed in the *Histoire de la Société royale de médecine* (10 vols., Paris, 1779–[90]), IV (1785), 50–84. It says that he drew information from tributes published by Fothergill's fellow physicians Gilbert Thompson, John Elliot, William Hird, and John C. Lettsom, and owed the greatest debt to Lettsom: *Histoire*, p. 52. Lettsom had earlier asked BF for anecdotes about Fothergill: XXXV, 479.

To Pierre Colomb

LS:[3] American Philosophical Society

Passy le 27 Août 1782.

J'ai reçu, Monsieur, les deux Lettres que vous m'avez fait l'honneur de m'écrire le 19 du mois dernier et le 19 du courant pour m'engager à vous procurer votre échange, ainsi que les moyens de retourner en Amerique rejoindre vos drapeaux.[4] Je suis bien faché, Monsieur, de me trouver dans l'impossibilité absolue de vous accorder ce que vous me demandez. Les Échanges se font en Amerique et ces Sortes d'Affaires ne me regardent aucunement; et quant à votre seconde demande elle n'est pas plus dans mon pouvoir que la premiere, n'ayant point d'ordres de fournir aux officiers les moyens de retourner en Amerique, ni d'argent entre les mains pour cet éffet. Je n'ai pas de reponse plus satisfaisante à vous donner au Sujet de vos appointements, J'ignore entierement quelles sont les Regles qu'on suit en Amerique dans ces occasions.[5]

J'ai l'honneur d'être, Monsieur, votre très humble et tres obeissant Serviteur./. B FRANKLIN

Mr. Colombe

Addressed: A Monsieur / Monsieur Colombe Major de / Dragons au Service des Etats / Unis de l'Amerique Septentrionale / à Nîmes./.

3. In the hand of L'Air de Lamotte, who may have drafted it using the outline of a reply that BF wrote on Colomb's July 19 appeal (XXXVII, 648–50).

4. Colomb's Aug. 19 letter (APS) was an urgent restatement of his first appeal.

5. Although Colomb did not return to America, his military career was not over. He joined the Paris National Guard in July, 1789, and rose to the rank of general of brigade before retiring for health reasons in 1794: Bodinier, *Dictionnaire;* Six, *Dictionnaire biographique.*

From Juliana Ritchie[6]

ALS: American Philosophical Society

Sir.   Cambray. August 27th. 1782.

I have the honor to thank you in all sincerity—for your great politeness in answering my letter—[7] My poor suffering heart will ever retain a just sence of what I owe to your good nature & kind condesention in *that proof* of your pardoning my intrusions. Nothing but my state of anxiety—cou'd have induced me to break thro' all rules of decoram, by impertinently addressing you sir—on that subject. The event proves—that the report I heard of my poor husbands death, was but too well grounded. Letters are arrived—that confirms the truth of that *circumstance* which is a most severe stroke to me, I *feel it* deeply. My Father, & Family—insist upon my returning to Them, & I am now preparing to bid an adieu to this Country, as soon as possible, & hope to be ready to sett off for London in about ten days—or a fortnight from this date. It wou'd give me great pleasure—to be able to render to you any service in England—either by Conveying *Letters* or papers—or any thing—that you may do me the honor to Commit to my care, you may depend upon any Commission being most faithfully Executed. Any thing will come safe that is addressed to me at Cambray—before I leave the place.

I have now sir to wish you a Continuence of health, & the full enjoyment of every other Blessing that this wretched life can afford. A speedy & happy Issue to those measures that have so long detain'd you here in Care & Anxiety—that you may return in Peace & quietness to your own home, & there long enjoy the heart felt satisfaction—that must ever result from conscious Virtue like yours. When ever you see your daughter, do not forget to remember me affectionately to Her. My heart is still tied to Philadelphia—and many Dr. old friends there tho' I must now bid them an Eternal adieu,—as I shall *do*—hence *forward*,—to every care that respects this life in *which* I have had a

6. This is the last extant letter between BF and Ritchie, an Englishwoman and one-time Philadelphia resident who had lived primarily in France since 1775: XXIII, 162–3.

7. Her latest previous extant letter to BF was dated Dec. 8, 1781 (XXXVI, 225–6); we have not found a reply.

49

large portion of bitter drafts to swallow; but I hope they are finished, as they have left me without any *stings* from *self reproach,* & I hope, from *that* of any *others.*

I have the honor to be with great esteem sir your obliged & obt. humble servt.   J. RITCHIE

Mr. Franklin.

Addressed: A Monsieur / Monsieur Franklin / Ministre Plenipotentiare / des Etats-Unis de L'Amerique / en son Hotel / a / Paris.

Notation: J. Ritchi—Cambray Augt 27. 1782.

To Caleb Whitefoord   ALS: Fitzwilliam Museum, Cambridge

Passy, Augt. 29. 82

If you know any thing of the Character of *J. Miller* late Printer of the London Evening Post, as to his Honesty, Sobriety, Industry, &c. you will oblige me by communicating it.[8] Yours affectionately,   B FRANKLIN

8. BF knew John Miller as the former printer of the *London Evening Post;* see XXIV, 45n, and Lucyle Werkmeister, *The London Daily Press, 1772–1792* (Lincoln, Nebr., 1963), p. 113. More recently Miller was the printer of the *London Courant, Westminster Chronicle, and Daily Advertiser.* His anti-government views had earned him a series of prosecutions for libel. In November, 1781, he was sentenced to one year in prison and fined £100 for reprinting an accusation that Russian Minister Ivan Simolin was a stockjobber: Werkmeister, *London Daily Press,* pp. 125–6; Solomon Lutnick, *The American Revolution and the British Press, 1775–1783* (Columbia, Mo., 1967), p. 179. Six months later he announced his release from prison and his reappointment as printer of that paper: *London Courant,* May 20, 1782. For reasons that remain mysterious, his name was dropped from the colophon after May 27.

Miller sailed to the United States from Ostend at the end of 1782, seeking asylum. He must have sought a letter of recommendation from BF, though we have no evidence that he received one. He did carry a letter from Henry Laurens, whom he had apparently met in prison, and was assisted in his journey by William Bell (who wrote to BF on [Aug. 16], above). He settled in South Carolina, where he established two newspapers and served as the state printer: *Morris Papers,* VII, 315–16n; *Laurens Papers,* XVI, 3–4.

Addressed: A Monsieur / Monsieur Whitefoord / Hotel d'Orleans, Rue des / petits Augustins / à Paris

Joseph Wright[9] to William Temple Franklin

ALS: American Philosophical Society

Dear Sir   [*c.* August 29, 1782][1]

I found at my return to Paris yesterday, that I am oblidged to be detained a Week longer, as every place was taken both in the Dilligence and Cabriole and there being no other Conveyance before then—and as I receiv'd your Packet this Morning perhaps your letter to Mr. Williams may require an immediate conveyance.— I return my sincere thanks for this continued instance of your grandfathers kindness— I could wish my situation here had put it in my Power to shew you that I had a sence of the friendship, I have received from him and yourself, but I find I have only more favours to ask— I could Wish he would give me leave to make another Copy of his Picture either in small or Large— As I wish to make a Present of to Mrs Beech or whatever Person he should think fit, the last I did, Mr Whitford has been pleased to take from me, I am fearful to ask, as I

9. The artist who had painted several oil portraits of BF during the summer of 1782: XXXVI, 223n; XXXVII, frontispiece, xxvii, 626–7n, 692. By early August Wright was trying to secure a passage to America; WTF tried to help him find a ship and the means. Elkanah Watson arranged for free passage on the *Argo,* a vessel Watson & Cossoul were outfitting at the time. The bond they cosigned with owner and commander Samuel R. Trevitt on Aug. 7 was forwarded to Passy by JW on Aug. 31: XXXVII, 668, 699; JW to WTF, Aug. 7 and 31 (APS); Winslow C. Watson, *Men and Times of the Revolution; or Memoirs of Elkanah Watson . . .* (New York, 1857), p. 138.

1. The day Wright expected to leave Paris for Nantes. According to John Jay, who gave him letters for America, Wright thought he would leave on Aug. 29 ("last Thursday") but revised that to the following Thursday, Sept. 5. Also on Aug. 29, Wright received a payment from Ferdinand Grand for the portrait BF gave Hodgson: Jay to Livingston, Sept. 4, 1782, quoted in Monroe H. Fabian, *Joseph Wright, American Artist, 1756–1793* (Washington, D.C., 1985), pp. 37–8; XXXVII, 626n.

consider I may be in some Measure troublesome, and he must be tired of Seeing me so Constantly.

I remain Sr Sincerely Yours   JOSEPH WRIGHT.

I had a great notion of Making it the Size of My Mothers, or the other little one you Saw, as it will be Portable, and yet sufficiently worked to keep the Likeness.[2]

Addressed: A Monsieur / Monsieur Franklin—fils / a Passy

Endorsed: Joseph Wright Août.—

From Benjamin Franklin Bache

ALS: American Philosophical Society

Mon cher grand Papa   Geneve ce 30 Aoust 1782

Je vous ècris ne voulant pas perdre courage de ce que vous ne m'ècrivez pas il y a longtems que je n'ai eu de vos nouvelles, les dernieres que J'ai eu etoient par Mr Pigott.[3] Je vous prierai si vous ne pouvez m'ècrire a cause de vos affaires de me faire ècrire un mot par Mon cousin car Mr Marignac et moi Sommes fort en peine ne recevant point de vos nouvelles. Mr de Marignac m'a acheté le livre dont je vous avois parlé regardant vôtre silence comme vôtre consentement[4] je vais Si vous le Souhaitez vous faire la description des auteurs que j'explique dans la classe ou je suis. Telemaque; Terence, Saluste, les catilinaires de Ciceron, le Lucien, Auteur Grecque, le testament qui est aussi un auteur grecque nous aprenons les Vers de Virgile et nous L'expliquons et nous aprenons de la gammaire grecque. La ville est a present en assez bon ordre nous avons commencé la classe il y a quelques Semaines. Vous mavez Priez de vous envoyer des dessins mais je ne puis a present je vous en enverrai bientôt par Mr Papillion directeur de la messagerie et qui va tous les mois a Paris il vous en à deja apportés Mr Me de Marignac et Jo-

2. Two small portraits of BF are known to be in private hands, though their origins are obscure and neither has been located: Sellers, *Franklin in Portraiture,* p. 426; Fabian, *Joseph Wright,* p. 89.

3. Robert Pigott had visited Paris the previous winter: XXXVI, 92, 322–3.

4. *Le Voyageur françois,* a multivolume compilation of travel writings: XXXVI, 597n; XXXVII, 682–3.

honnot vous presentent bien leurs respects faites mes compliments a mon cousin et priez le de m'excuser si je ne peux lui ecrire je n'ai guere de tems a moi, faites mes amities a cockran. Je vous prie de m'informer quand les Morrices viendront.[5] Mr Marignac vous ayant demandè dans une de ses lettres si vous vouliez qu'il vous envoya mon compte et Celui de Johonnot, et, n'ayant point reçu de reponse m'a priè de vous le demander.

Je Suis mon cher Grand Papa Votre très affectioné et très obeissant Petit fils   B FRANKLIN BACHE

Addressed: A Monsieur / Monsieur Franklin Ministre / Plenipotentiaire des etats unis damerique / auprès de Sa Majesté très chretienne. / adrésée a Mr Grand Banquier / Rue Montmart / A Paris

Notation: B. Franklin Bache 30 Août 1782—

To the Marquis de Castries

ALS: Archives de la Marine

Sir   Passy Augt. 31. 1782

If there is nothing improper in the Requests made by Mr Williams in the enclos'd Letter, I beg leave to recommend them to your Excellency's favourable Attention.[6] With great Respect, I am, Sir, Your Excellency's most obedient and most humble Servant   B FRANKLIN

Marquis de Castries

Notation: R [Repondu] le 8. 7bre. 1782. / [audela ?] 1er 7bre v. la f. du même jour et la lettre ecrite à M Clouet

5. Robert Morris' sons Robert Jr. and Thomas: XXXVI, 80–1n.

6. BF enclosed JW's Aug. 23 appeal to Castries, described in our annotation of JW to BF, Aug. 23. The present letter and its enclosure were submitted to Castries with a memorandum (in an unknown hand and dated only September, 1782) summarizing their contents and advising Castries that if he intended to grant permission, he should sign the two letters attached. One was to BF, the other to M. Clouet (commissary at Lorient: XXXVI, 629n). Notations on the memorandum, which is at the Archives de la Marine, indicate that Castries approved the request and answered BF on Sept. 8. The notations on the present letter confirm this information. BF sent a copy of the Sept. 8 letter (now missing) to JW, who forwarded it to Williams, Moore & Co. in Lorient on Sept. 14 (Yale University Library).

From Jean-Baptiste Le Roy   ALS: American Philosophical Society

Jeudy matin [after August, 1782?][7]

Arrivé hier au Soir Mon Illustre Docteur J'envoye Savoir de vos
nouvelles. J'espere bien que vos douleurs de Goutte Se Sont bien
calmées. J'ai recu un billet du Musée de M. Court de Gébelin où
l'on me presse fort de vous engager à y venir aujourdhui où il y
aura une assemblèe publique et des choses qui pourront vous interesser. Je Serois bien enchanté Si votre santé vous permettoit
de ceder à Ces Sollicitations. Vous savez combien Je vous suis
passionnément attaché pour la vie   Le Roy

M. Le Dr. Franklin

Wine Cellar Inventory[8]   D:[9] American Philosophical Society

Etat du vin au 1er. Sept. 1782	[September 1–30, 1782] Nombre des Bouteilles	[*Total consumed*]
Bierre de Paris	{ 83	20
	18	

7. This is the earliest possible date, as BF's severe attack of what he thought
was gout in August, 1782, was the first episode since his introduction to Court
de Gébelin's musée in May, 1781 (XXXV, 32, 36).

8. Unlike the inventory we published in XXVIII, 455–6, this chart of the
"Depense journaliere du Vin pendant le mois de 7bre. 1782" was filled in.
The state of the cellar was noted in the lefthand column; days of the month
were written across the top, and the number of bottles consumed per day was
marked. A final column indicated the total number of bottles consumed. We
print here the figures from the first and last columns. As the chart shows (see
illustration on the facing page), the household generally consumed one bottle of *vin ordinaire* per day, except for Sundays, when BF entertained.

The only other surviving inventory is for December, 1782. It shows a very
different pattern. As of Dec. 3, the daily bottle of ordinary table wine was
replaced by a bottle of red champagne. (At the beginning of December, 212
bottles of "Champagne rouge" and 190 of "champagne blanc" were listed.)
No Sunday dinners are evident. The only days on which more than one bottle was consumed were Dec. 12 and 13, when there was an assortment of red
and white champagne, Parisian and English beer, madeira, and Bordeaux.
The December inventory, also kept by L'Air de Lamotte, is at the Hist. Soc.
of Pa.

9. In L'Air de Lamotte's hand.

54

Chart of Daily Wine Consumption for the Month of September, 1782

vin de Champ. mouss.[1]	24	
Cidre	138	
Eau de Vie d'andaye	24	
Vin ordinaire	153.	41
Vin de madere	216½	9
Champ non mouss.	119	
Bordeaux rouge	127	11
Vin de Cherry	157	
Bierre d'angre.[2]	{ 67	4
	{ 35	
Rum	4	
Champe. Couleur de Rose	140	

Notation: Wine in Septr. 82

From Charles Grant, Vicomte de Vaux[3]

ALS: University of Pennsylvania Library

Monsieur   ce 2. 7bre. 1782

Serois-je asses malheureux pour que mes projets, qui m'avoient paru si honestes et faits pour estre goustés par vous, eussent pu

1. Champagne mousseux (sparkling).
2. English beer.
3. Grant (b. 1749) began investing in privateers in 1777. He sustained heavy losses on all his ships, including the two whose disappearance prompted him to write BF in 1778: XXVI, 507–8n. In the summer of 1782 he drafted a memoir proposing that Congress reimburse him for his losses by ceding him unclaimed fertile land in a favorable region, perhaps along the Connecticut River or in Virginia along the banks of the "ohohio," where he and his people would establish a colony. We earlier speculated that this memoir was addressed to Chaumont, since he was the one who answered it (XXVI, 508n), but it is clear that Grant wanted Lafayette to deliver it to Congress: BF's copy (which bears a notation by L'Air de Lamotte) ends with an expression of faith in Lafayette's intervention with some unspecified member of Congress whose name was left blank, as though Grant hoped that BF would fill it in. Another draft of this memoir, addressed "au congrès amériquain," is in the Vaux Papers at the University of Michigan; see John Weatherford, "The Vicomte de Vaux: Would-be Canadian," *Ontario History,* XLVII (1955), 49–51.
Chaumont answered Grant on July 18, possibly at BF's direction. He did

55

vous déplaire, et que vous ne les jugiés pas dignes d'une reponse.
J'y serois d'autant plus sensible, monsieur, que j'ay fondé sur
cela m'est plus douçes esperançes. J'ay perdu une partië considerable de ma fortune a m'interesser dans les affaires des ameri-
quains, et j'espere y trouver un dedomagement, surtout des injustices des hommes, ainsi que des moyens d'y travailler librement
a faire le bien. Je perdrois cependant tout espoir, si je n'obtients
pas vottre appuy. Si vous ne voulés pas monsieur, me repondre
par ecrit, voudrés vous bien m'accorder une audience a ce sujet?
J'ay l'honeur d'estre avec respect Monsieur vottre tres humble et
tres obeissant serviteur   LE VTE. DE VAUX-GRANT

Notation: Le Vicomte de Vaux 2. 7bre. 1782.

From Matthew Ridley

AL: American Philosophical Society; copy: Massachusetts Historical
Society

Monday Morning Sept. 2d. 1782.
Mr. Ridley has the honor to present his respects to Mr. Franklin.— The inclosed obligation was Sent Mr Ridley by Mr. Johnson for the purpose of procuring a Letter of Marque for a Vessel at Nantes— As Mr. Johnson is very pressing with Mr. Ridley
to forward it, he will think himself obliged to Mr. Franklin if he
will Send it to his Apartments so soon as possible.[4]

Mr. Ridley sincerely hopes Mr. Franklin is better than when
he had the Honor of Seeing him yesterday.

---

not know when Lafayette would depart, and did not think that Lafayette had
met with BF since Grant had done so. In any case, Grant's request to Congress
was impossible. Congress had no authority to issue land grants on behalf of
individual states. As for the vicomte's titles and recommendations, there was
no place in the universe where they would be of less use; talent and valor were
the highest recommendations in America. Yale University Library.

4. The bond, dated Aug. 26 (APS), is for the brigantine *Resolution*, 12,
owned by Nathaniel Allen of Edenton, N.C. It is for the sum of 20,000 Spanish milled dollars and is signed by the ship's captain, Stephen Carpenter, as
well as by Joshua Johnson and a Nathan Kelso.

Mr. R left some Bills of Exchange for acceptance which he would be glad could be forwarded at same time.[5]

Achille-Guillaume Lebègue de Presle to William Temple Franklin

ALS: American Philosophical Society

Paris ce 2, 7bre 82

A la reception de votre lettre, Monsieur, je me suïs assuré d'un Exemplaire de L'ouvrage de m Cavallo sur les Airs,[6] que j'avois conseillé a un libraire de faire venir. Il est chez moi et vous pourrez le faire prendre quand vous souhaiteres. Jai aussi recu dernierement les planches qui manquoient a un magnifique ouvrage qu'on vend 25 guinées a Londres que mr fothergil m'a envoyé successivement pour le faire passer a la bibliotheque de Philadelphie par le bon office de mr votre grand pere.[7] En outre jai recu le dernier vol de Priestley, en present pour mr franklin de la part de L'auteur;[8] enfin deux autres livres de mr Letsom[9] presents de L'auteur.

5. Doubtless the 28 bills sent on Aug. 20. Ridley sent another 41 bills on Sept. 24: XXXVII, 278n. On Oct. 1 Ridley wrote WTF thanking him for returning the 41 bills, sending him two more, and accepting a dinner invitation from BF for the following Friday (APS). This letter is in the hand of Ridley's secretary Nicolas Darcel (XXXVII, 278n).

6. Tiberius Cavallo, F.R.S., *A Treatise on the nature and properties of Air, and other Permanently Elastic Fluids: to which is prefixed an introduction to chymistry* (London, 1781).

7. John Miller, *Illustratio Systematis sexualis Linnaei* (London, 1777). The three-volume work, which included over 200 plates, was a gift from Fothergill: XXXVII, 151.

8. Though it was published the previous year, Priestley may have sent the second volume of *Experiments and Observations . . . on Air* (London, 1781), which he had promised to send BF. The presentation copy is in the Yale University Library: XXXIV, 197n. In 1782, an expanded, second edition in two volumes was issued of *Disquisitions relating to Matter and Spirit . . .* (XXV, 281), and a second edition was issued of *A Free Discussion of the Doctrines of Materialism and Philosophical Necessity, in a Correspondence between Dr. Price and Dr. Priestley . . .*, both at Birmingham.

9. John Coakley Lettsom. To our knowledge, the only writings of his published in 1782 were *Some Account of the Late John Fothergill* (XXXV, 479n) and the letter he wrote to Dr. William Hawes that was printed in Hawes's work on influenza, *An address to the King and Parliament . . .* (London, 1782).

Je comptois aller rendre mes devoirs incessamen a son Excellence et lui porter ces divers effets mais comme elle desire avoir au plutot le Cavallo et que vous venez frequement en ville, vous pourries faire prendre le tout a la fois; d'autant plus qu'il seroit difficile de porter a pied les plantes qui sont *Carta Maxima*,[1] sans les gater. Si vous voulez bien Monsieur me prevenir de Lheure a peu prés ou vous envoyeries, je me trouverai chez moi: je desirerois que ce fut avant vendredi, parceque je pars ce jour la des le matin pour la campagne.

L'ouvrage de Cavallo coute 24 *l.t.*
et les frais des autres objets 36 *l.t.*

Jai lhonneur d'etre avec L'estime et la consideration la plus parfaite Monsieur votre tres humb tres obeist. serviteur

LEBEGUE DE PRESLE

Addressed: A Monsieur / Monsieur franklin / Le fils / a Passy / Banlieue de Paris

Notation: Le Begue de Presle Paris 2. 7bre. 1782.

To Robert R. Livingston

Incomplete LS with complete press copy,[2] LS with incomplete press copy, copy, and transcript: National Archives

Sir,   Passy, September 3d. 1782.

I have just received your No. 13 dated the 23d June.[3] The Accounts of the general Sentiments of our People, respecting Propositions from England, and the Rejoicings on the Birth of the Dauphin, give Pleasure here; and it affords me much Satisfaction to find the Conduct of Congress, approved by all that hear or speak of it, and to see all the Marks of a constantly growing Regard for us and Confidence in us among those in whom such Sentiments are most to be desired.

---

1. The plates to Miller's *Illustratio* were printed *in folio*.
2. This LS in WTF's hand is missing the final page, which we supply from the press copy. The other LS and copy are in the hand of L'Air de Lamotte.
3. XXXVII, 517–19.

I hope the Affair of Capt. Asgill was settled as it ought to be, by the Punishment of Lippincut. Applications have been made here to obtain Letters in favour of the Young Gentleman. Inclosed I send you a Copy of the answer I gave to that made to me.[4]

I had before acquainted M. Tousard that his Pension would be paid in America, and there only, it being unreasonable to expect that the Congress should open a Pay Office in every Part of the World where Pensioners should chuse to reside. I shall communicate to him that part of your Letter.

You wish to know what Allowance I make to my Private Secretary. My Grandson, William T. Franklin, came over with me, served me as private Secretary during the Time of the Commissioners; and no Secretary to the Commission arriving, tho' we had been made to expect one, he did Business for us all, and this without any Allowance for his Services, tho' both Mr Lee and Mr Deane at times mention'd it to me as a thing proper to be done, and a Justice due to him. When I became appointed sole Minister here, and the whole Business which the Commissioners had before divided with me, came into my Hands, I was obliged to exact more Service from him, and he was indeed by being so long in the Business, become capable of doing more. At length in the beginning of the Year 1781 when he became of Age,[5] considering his constant close Attention to the Duties requir'd of him, and his having thereby miss'd the Opportunity of studying the Law for which he had been intended, I determined to make him some Compensation for the time past, & fix some appointment for the time to come 'till the Pleasure of Congress respecting him

---

4. XXXVII, 687–8; see also de Grasse to BF, Aug. 26. Asgill's fate became a *cause célèbre* in France, especially after Lady Asgill petitioned Vergennes to write a personal appeal to George Washington. Vergennes did so on July 29, enclosing Lady Asgill's letter and pleading as "a tender father . . . in favor of a mother and family in tears." Vergennes' letter and its enclosure are printed (the former in translation) in Wharton, *Diplomatic Correspondence*, V, 634–6. The dramatic story, ending in young Asgill's pardon, was widely reported in the European press and would later be fictionalized in a novel and on the stage: Tourneux, *Correspondance littéraire*, XIV, 97–103.

5. BF consistently maintained that WTF was born in 1760. See XXII, 67n, for a discussion of his year of birth.

should be known. I accordingly settled an Acct with him, allowing him from the beginning of Decr 1776 to the End of 1777 the Sum of 3400 Livres, and for the Year 1778, the Sum of 4000 Livres, for 1779 4,800 Livres and for 1780, 6,000 Livres.— Since that Time I have allow'd him at the Rate of 300 Louis per Annum, being what I saw had been allow'd by Congress to the Secretary of Mr. William Lee,[6] who could not have had, I imagine, a fourth Part of the Business to go through; since my Secretary, besides the Writing and Copying the Papers relative to my Common Ministerial Transactions, has had all those occassioned by my acting in the various Employments of Judge of Admiralty, Consul, Purchaser of Goods for the Publick &ca &ca. besides that of Acceptor of the Congress Bills, a Business that requires being always at home, Bills coming by Post from different Ports & Countries, and often requiring immediate Answers whether good or not: and to that End it being necessary to examine them by the Books exactly kept of all preceding Acceptations, in order to detect double Presentations which happen very frequently; the great Number of these Bills make almost sufficient Business for one Person; and the Confinement they occasion is such, that we cannot allow ourselves a Days Excursion into the Country, and the Want of Exercise has hurt our Healths in several Instances. The Congress pay much larger Salaries to some Secretaries who I believe deserve them;[7] but not more than my Grandson does the comparatively small one I have allow'd to him, his Fidelity, Exactitude, and Address in transacting Business, being really what one could wish in such an Officer, and the genteel Appearance a young Gentleman in his Station obliges him to make, requiring at least such an Income. I do not mention the extraordinary Business that has been imposed upon us in this Embassy as a Foundation for demanding higher Salaries than others. I never sollicited for a Publick Office either for myself or any Relation, yet I never refused one that I was capable of executing, when public Service was in question, and I never bar-

6. Samuel Stockton (XXII, 198n): *JCC*, XVIII, 926–7. A *louis* was equal to 24 *l.t.*

7. Jay's secretary, William Carmichael, and JA's secretary, Francis Dana, had been voted salaries of £1,000 (nearly 24,000 *l.t.*) apiece: XXX, 543.

gain'd for Salary but contented myself with whatever my Constituents were pleased to allow me. The Congress will therefore consider every Article charg'd in my Account distinct from the Salary originally voted, not as what I presume to insist upon, but as what I propose only, for their Consideration and they will allow what they think proper. You desire an accurate Estimate of those contingent Expenses. I enclose Copies of two Letters which pass'd between Mr. Adams and me on the Subject,[8] and show the Articles of which they consist. Their Amount in different Years may be found in my Accts., except the Article of House Rent which has never yet been settled; M. de Chaumont our Landlord having originally proposed to leave it 'till the End of the War, and then to accept for it a Piece of American Land from the Congress, such as they might judge equivalent.[9] If the Congress did intend all contingent Charges whatever to be included in the Salary, and do not think proper to pay on the whole so much, in that Case I would humbly suggest that the saving may be most conveniently made by a Diminution of the Salary, leaving Contingencies to be charged; because they may necessarily be very different in different Years and in different Courts. I have been the more diffuse on this Subject, as your Letter gave occasion for it, and it is probably the last time I shall mention it. Be pleased to present my dutiful Respects to Congress, assure them of my best Services, and believe me to be with sincere Esteem, Sir, Your Excellency's, most obedient & most humble Servant.

B FRANKLIN

P.S. As you will probably lay this Letter before Congress, I take the Liberty of joining to it, an Extract of my Letter to the President of the 12th. March 1781,[1] & of repeating my Request therein contained relative to my Grandson.— I inclose likewise Extracts of Letters from Messieurs Jay and Lawrens, which both

8. Probably those printed in xxxv, 145–6, 558.

9. Chaumont now wanted BF to pay rent, including retroactive payments: xxxvii, 220, 224, 280, 605.

1. xxxiv, 446–8 (from "I must now" to "Favour to me"), which is included with the transcript of the present letter.

show the Regard those Gentlemen have for him, and their Desire of his being noticed by the Congress.[2] Sept 3d. 1782.   BF

Honble. Robt. R. Livingston Esqr.

From Isaac All

ALS: American Philosophical Society

Dear Sir   Nantes 3d September 1782

I did myself the honour of writing to you on my arrival in this Country thirteen Months ago per Mr. Price, Inclosing a Packet from Mr. Samuel Wharton, since when I have not had the pleasure to hear from you.[3] I have now to inform you, that I have with much pain and trouble got a fine Ship built, capable of Carrying Twenty Nine pound Cannon, but at present shall only Mount Sixteen, which are Worked under Cover or what we Call Close Quarters. I hope I shall be ready to Sail in four or five Weeks, and shall think my self happy to execute any Commands you may think proper to trust me with.[4]

Among the Articles necessary for Ships, which are Scarce at this place, is Anchors, and hearing there are in Mr. Dobre's hands Several at your disposal,[5] I take the liberty to pray you will, (If the public Service will permitt) let me have Two or three of them. My Friends here, Messrs. David Gallwey & Co.[6] will either pay for them, or Replace them, with the first Anchors that can be got. If you Can Comply with this Request, and give me a

2. These were extracts from John Jay's letters to the President of Congress of April 21 and 25, 1781 (Morris, *Jay: Peace*, pp. 65–6; Wharton, *Diplomatic Correspondence*, IV, 388), and from John Laurens' June 9, 1781, letter to BF (XXXV, 140–1). These extracts are included in the transcript of the present letter.

3. XXXV, 338–9.

4. The ship was the *Prince de Liège:* JW to Bullock & Baynton, Aug. 28, 1782 (Yale University Library). She did not sail for America until mid-April, 1783: *Morris Papers*, VII, 625n.

5. See XXXVII, 450–1.

6. For David Gallwey and his brother Andrew see XXXII, 478–9. This is the first mention in BF's papers of the company as such.

line Signifying the Same, You Will Oblige Dear Sir, Your Affectionate And Very humbl. Servt.   ISAAC ALL

Addressed: A Monsieur / Monsieur Le Docteur / Fran

Notations: Isaac all. 3 Sept. 1782. / [*In William Temple Franklin's hand:*] Ansd. 8 Do.

From Thomas Barclay   ALS: American Philosophical Society

Sir   Paris 3 Sepr. 1782

I have return'd to Mr. Franklin the Papers relative to the Consular powers which he was so obliging as to send Me;[7] and as he desired I wou'd Make My observations thereon, I shall trouble Your Excellency with a few lines relative to the third Article—[8] was My opinion to have any weight, it shou'd be that the Consuls and Vice Consuls were left at liberty to Carry on what Commerce they pleased, and if any alteration Cou'd be made in that article, there are some reasons, that I think have a good deal of weight with them, why it shou'd be done; but I dare say they have already been duly Considerd by Congress. I submit it to Your Excellency, whether, though at this time it May be proper to prevent the Consul or Vice Consuls from trading, it wou'd Not be better to do it by Instructions than by a Convention from which Congress will Not have the power of receding, even if the Interdiction shou'd prove inconvenient— The other articles appear to me very proper for the Establishment of the Consulate on a proper footing, Nor do I know any thing that Can be added on the subject.

I have the honour to be with the greatest respect Sir Your Most Obed Most Huml Servant   THOS BARCLAY

7. On Sept. 3, Barclay wrote WTF to thank him for his letter of Sept. 1 (now missing), which enclosed a copy of Congress' draft convention relative to consular functions and privileges (for which see XXXVI, 484–5). APS.

8. The third article of the draft reads, "Consuls and vice consuls shall be subjects or citizens of the power appointing them, and interdicted from all traffick or commerce for their own or another's benefit." *JCC*, XXII, 48.

His Excellency Benjn. Franklin Esqre

Notation: Thos. Barclay 3 Sept. 1782.

From Henry Laurens

ALS: American Philosophical Society

Sir.   Nantes 3d. September 1782.

I thank you very sincerely for the kind attention to my health & welfare signified in your favor of the 19th. Ult. My acknowledgements are also due for your condescensions to my Son lately at Passy.[9]

I am waiting now for permission to re-enter England & to embark at Falmouth for New York with a Passport for proceeding thence to Philadelphia which I have hopes of receiving in a few days. Certainly it is due to the United States from Great Britain to set me down in safety in my own Country in return for the safe delivery of Lord Cornwallis at his own House in London,[1] it would be unjust to expose me to the danger of a second Capture, perhaps to restraint & plunder together with aggravated expences from being carried far out of my Road. As there is no room to doubt my obtaining the expected Permission, I must further trouble you with a request to procure & transmit as early as possible the necessary Passport for leaving this Kingdom for myself & family my Son two Daughters & a Domestic.

If I can be serviceable to you here in England or elsewhere I intreat you Sir to lay your Commands on me, to be assured of my best endeavors to execute them & of the Esteem & Regard with which I have the honor to be Sir Your most Obedient servant   HENRY LAURENS.

His Excellency Benjamin Franklin Esquire Passy.

Addressed: His Excellency / Benjamin Franklin Esquire / Min-

---

9. Henry Laurens, Jr., was at Passy on Aug. 28: XXXVII, 708–9; Klingelhofer, "Matthew Ridley's Diary," p. 101.

1. After BF discharged Cornwallis from his parole, the British general was presented to the King and Queen and resumed his seat in the House of Lords: XXXVII, 565.

ister Plenepotentiary from / the United States of America &c &c / Passy.

Notation: H. Laurens 3 7bre. 1782.

To Joseph-Mathias Gérard de Rayneval

ALS: Archives du Ministère des affaires étrangères

Sir,   Passy, Sept. 4. 1782

With this you will receive the Boxes you desired of Mint Drops.[2] They came by Mr Oswald's Courier, who arrived this Morning. He has been with me,[3] and tells me he has a Letter from Mr Secry. Townsend, acquainting him, that the King has consented to declare the Independence of America, authorizing him to make it the first Article in the Treaty, in which he is now ready to proceed.[4] I hope Mr Jay will agree to this.

The Royal George, a Ship of 100 Guns, Admiral Kempenfeldt being on board, sank a few days since at Spithead, as she lay at Anchor. She had 700 Men on board, and went down so suddenly, that 400 of them, with the Admiral himself, were drowned in her.[5]

---

2. See Hodgson's Aug. 26 letter.

3. That is, Oswald. BF asked whether Oswald had an answer to the Americans' desire for "a previous Declaration of their Independence before a commencement of Treaty": Oswald to Townshend, Sept. 10, in Morris, *Jay: Peace,* p. 351.

4. Townshend to Oswald, Sept. 1, in Giunta, *Emerging Nation,* I, 545–7. The letter also authorized Oswald to offer BF's necessary articles (XXXVII, 599–600), with the understanding that the Canadian boundary be confined to pre-1774 limits, and that the fishing rights not include the right to dry fish on the Newfoundland coast, as BF did not specifically request it. If these terms were accepted, and the American commissioners insisted on it, Oswald could (as a "very last resort") inform them that the King would recommend to Parliament that it acknowledge American independence apart from the treaty negotiations. The cabinet had submitted these terms to the King on Aug. 29: Fortescue, *Correspondence of George Third,* VI, 118; see also Godfrey Davies and Marion Tinling, "The Independence of America: Six Unpublished Items on the Treaty in 1782–83," *Huntington Library Quarterly,* XII (1948–49), 213–14; Harlow, *Second British Empire,* I, 274–6.

5. Some 900 people were drowned when the *Royal George* sank on Aug.

I have the honour to be, with great Regard, Sir, Your most obedient humble Servant   B FRANKLIN

The Death of the King's youngest Son[6] is given as the Reason of the Delay of the Courier.

M. de Raynevall.

To John Jay[7]

Reprinted from William Temple Franklin, ed., *Memoirs of the Life and Writings of Benjamin Franklin* . . . (3 vols., 4to, London, 1817–18), II, 396.

Dear Sir,   Passy, Sept. 4, 1782.

Mr. Oswald's courier being returned, with directions to him, to make the independence of America the first article in the treaty, I would wait on you if I could, to discourse on the subject: but as I cannot, I wish to see you here this evening, if not inconvenient to you.[8] With great esteem, I have the honour to be, dear Sir, your most obedient and most humble servant,

B. FRANKLIN.

29: David Syrett, *The Royal Navy in European Waters during the American Revolutionary War* (Columbia, S.C., 1998), p. 161. For Kempenfeldt see XXXVI, 557n.

6. Prince Alfred died on Aug. 26, one month shy of his second birthday: E. B. Fryde *et al.*, eds., *Handbook of British Chronology* (3rd ed., London, 1986), p. 47.

7. BF penned this letter at the end of his meeting with Richard Oswald (for which see the preceding document), and asked Oswald to deliver it: Morris, *Jay: Peace*, p. 351. The previous week BF and Jay, anticipating the eventual negotiations, instructed Oswald to procure from London "a compleat Sett of the last & largest Edition of N. American Maps": Oswald to Shelburne, Aug. 27, 1782, PRO. The editors are grateful to Ed Dahl, formerly the Early Cartography Specialist of the National Archives of Canada, for this reference and for general help on the maps used in the negotiations.

8. BF was still too ill to travel.

From Charles-Guillaume-Frédéric Dumas

ALS: American Philosophical Society

Monsieur   La haie 4e. Sept. 1782

Je profite du départ de Mr. Brantsen, nomé Minre. Plenipo: de cette Rep., pour aller, dans un parfait Concert avec les Ministres de la Cour de Fce. & ceux des autres Puissances en guerre avec la Gde. Brete., traiter des Préliminaires d'une paix générale conjointement avec Mr. l'Ambr. de Berkenrode,—[9] pour vous faire passer l'incluse, laquelle ayant lue, vous voudrez bien avoir la bonté d'acheminer cachetée.[1] J'aurai l'honneur de vous écrire un de ces premiers jours sous le Couvert de Mr. F. Grand. En attendant, j'espere que mes précédentes, par la voie de Couriers de Mr. l'Ambassadeur vous sont parvenues en leur temps, que vous jouissez d'une parfaite santé, & que vous honorez toujours de votre bienveillance particuliere, celui qui ne cesse de s'en rendre digne par l'attachement respectueux avec lequel il est pour toujours Monsieur Votre très-humble & très obéissant serviteur[2]

DUMAS

Passy à Son Exc. M. B. Franklin

Addressed: à Son Excellence / Monsieur Franklin, Ministre / Plenipo: des Etats-Unis d'Amérique / à Passy près Paris

Notation: Dumas 4. 7bre. 1782.

---

9. Gerard Brantsen (1734–1809) had been an Arnhem burgomaster. He arrived in Paris on Sept. 10: La Vauguyon to Vergennes, Aug. 13 (AAE); Berkenrode to Vergennes, Sept. 11 (AAE); *NNBW,* VII, 195; Schulte Nordholt, *Dutch Republic,* p. 198; *Repertorium der diplomatischen Vertreter,* III, 263.

1. Presumably Dumas was sending his Aug. 16–19 letter to Livingston. He may also have forwarded a copy of JA's Sept. 4 letter to Livingston: Wharton, *Diplomatic Correspondence,* V, 662, 685–93.

2. On Sept. 12, WTF acknowledged receipt of this letter on behalf of his grandfather, who for the last three weeks had been "much indisposed with the Gravel & an attendant severe Pain in his Thigh" (Yale University Library). He also sent Dumas an extract from BF's June 25 letter to Livingston recommending Dumas to Congress (XXXVII, 539).

From Henry Grand

AL: University of Pennsylvania Library

Monday morn. [before September 5, 1782][3]

Mr. Grand's most respectfull Compliments wait on Doctor Franklin & begs to be informed whether he approves being debitted of £55: for a former Invoice of Books of Messrs. Hohlenfeld & Embser at strasbourg & 9: for a late one from the same.[4]

Mr. Grand also craves the favour of an order for the £200 stg he sent to Mr. Wm. Hodgson in London the 18th of last April for American Prisoners.[5]

Addressed: A Monsieur / Monsieur le Docteur / Franklin / a Passy—

Notations in different hands: Grand / Grand

From Robert R. Livingston

Two LS and L:[6] University of Pennsylvania Library; AL (draft): New-York Historical Society; transcript: National Archives

Sir   Philadelphia 5th. September 1782

Having written to you lately,[7] I should not again trouble you so soon were it not necessary to remind you, that your last letter is dated in March, since which there have been frequent arrivals from France— and since which too we have reason to beleive, the most interesting events have taken place in Europe— We learn from private letters and common fame, that Mr Adams was received by the United Provinces in his public Character on the 19th. of April,[8] we have yet no accounts of this interesting event,

3. The date on which the 9 *l.t.* payment mentioned in the first paragraph was debited to BF's private account with Henry's father, Ferdinand: Account XVII (XXVI, 3).

4. For these books see XXXVI, 387–8, 433; XXXVII, 347.

5. For this payment see XXXVI, 440n.

6. According to a notation on the transcript the original was sent by the packet *Washington,* the duplicate by the ship *Nonsuch,* and the triplicate by the ship *Heer Adams.* Several passages of this letter, indicated in the annotation below, were written in cipher. BF deciphered those sections on the LS.

7. His last extant letter was written on Aug. 9: XXXVII, 717–9.

8. See XXXVII, 199.

or the measures he has pursued to accomplish our other objects in Holland since.— Mr Laurens it is said has been liberated, has travelled to Holland and to France—has entered upon the execution of his trust, but has left us to gather events so interesting to him and to us, from private letters and the public prints— Mr Jay tells us on the 14th. of May, that he is about to sett out for Paris and that he presumes Doctor Franklin has assigned the reasons for this step—[9] Doctor Franklin has told us nothing. As to Mr. Dana if it were not for the necessity of drawing Bills in his favour, we should hardly be acquainted with his existance—[1] It is commonly said that Republics are better informed than monarchs of the State of their foreign Affairs, and that they insist upon a greater degree of vigilance and punctuality in their Ministers— We on the contrary seem to have adopted a new system, the ignorance in which we are kept of every interesting event renders it impossible for the Sovereign to instruct their servants, and of course forms them into an Independent privy Council for the direction of their Affairs without their advise or concurrence— I can hardly express to you what I feel on this occasion, I blush when I meet a member of Congress who enquires into what is passing in Europe— When the General applies to me for advises on the same subject which must regulate his movements, I am compelled to inform him that we have no intelligence but what he has seen in the Papers, the following is an extract of his last letter to me. "But how does it happen that all our information of what is transacting in Europe should come thro' indirect Channels or from the Enemy?—or does this question proceed from my unacquaintedness with facts?"[2] But let me dismiss a subject which gives me so much pain, in the hope that we shall in future have no farther cause of Complaint.

Since the evacuation of Savannah the Enemy have by the general Orders contained in the enclosed papers announced the pro-

9. Wharton, *Diplomatic Correspondence*, v, 417.

1. Dana, the minister designate to the Russian court, wrote to Livingston from St. Petersburg this very day: Wharton, *Diplomatic Correspondence*, v, 700–2.

2. Washington to Livingston, Aug. 14: Fitzpatrick, *Writings of Washington*, XXV, 16–17.

posed evacuation of Charles town,[3] we are in daily expectation of hearing therefore that tranquility is restored to the Southern States—several circumstances lead us to suppose, that they entertain thoughts of abandoning New York some time this fall—you only can inform us whether this step has been taken in consequence of any expectation they entertain of a general peace—or with a view to pursue the system which the present administration appear to have adopted, when they so loudly reprobated the American War,— And whether by withdrawing their Troops from hence, they only mean to collect their force and direct it against our Allies.—[4] This Knowledge would render such an alteration in our system necessary, that it affords us new reasons for regretting our want of information on these important points.

The Marquis de Vaudruiel has unfortunately lost the Magnifique sunk by running on a rock in the harbour of Boston, where he is now with the remainder of his Fleet consisting of twelve sail of the Line except 3 refiting at Portsmouth—[5] This has enabled Congress to shew their attention to his most Christian Majesty, and their wish to promote his interests as far as their circumstances will permit by presenting him the America of 74. Guns—enclosed is their resolve on that subject, and the answer given by the Minister of France, the Ship is in such a state that she may with diligence be fitted for Sea in about two Months, and from the accounts I hear of her, she will I beleive prove a fine Ship—[6] The General is collecting the Army. The last division

3. On Aug. 7, the Loyalists of Charleston were issued general orders to prepare for evacuation. Savannah had been evacuated in July: Richard K. Showman *et al.*, eds., *The Papers of General Nathanael Greene* (12 vols. to date, Chapel Hill and London, 1976–), XI, 439, 490n. The enclosures are missing.

4. The intention of the Rockingham government from its beginning had been to send part of its forces from North America to the West Indies: Mackesy, *War for America*, p. 474. Shelburne, the new prime minister, had no plans to change that strategy, although he hoped to end the war before the strategy was implemented.

5. XXXVII, 715n.

6. On Sept. 3, Congress resolved to present the *America*, 74, to La Luzerne as a replacement for the *Magnifique*: *JCC*, XXIII, 543. (BF's endorsed copy of this resolution is at the University of Pa. Library; another copy is at the APS.) The following day La Luzerne sent Congress his thanks on behalf of

of the french Troops marched from hence this morning, when collected they will I presume repair to their old post at the white Plains, and perhaps endeavour to accelerate the departure of the Enemy.[7]

I am sorry you did not pursue your first design and enlarge in your letter upon the subjects which you imagined would be discussed in the negotiation for a peace,[8] it might have changed our sentiments, and altered our views in some points—two things are of great moment to us, one of which at least would meet with no difficulty if France and England understand their true interest— I mean the West India trade, and the right to cut log wood and Mahogany—without a free admission of all kinds of provisions into the Islands our agriculture will suffer extremely, this evil will be severely felt at first, and when it remedies itself which it will do in time it must be at the expence of the nations that share our commerce— It will lessen the consumption of foreign sugars, encrease the supplies which the poorer People among us draw from the maple &c. and by reducing the price of provisions and rendering the cultivation of lands less profitable make a proportionable encrease of our own manufactures, and lessen our dependence upon Europe— This will in some measure I must confess check our population, and so far I regard it as an evil— The Merchants and Farmers if secluded at a peace, from the advantages which this commerce gave them while connected with England[9] will consider themselves as loosers by the War and pine again for the Fleshpots of egypt.— A variety of Arguments on this subject arising as well from the general interests of

---

the King and promised to notify Vaudreuil (National Archives). He did so on Sept. 5: *Courier de l'Europe*, XII (1782), 333. The *America* was launched on Nov. 5, but served in the French Navy only until 1786: Morison, *Jones*, pp. 327–9.

7. Rochambeau's army halted near White Plains on its march north from Philadelphia (to which it had come from Virginia). After a month's stay along the Hudson, it left for Boston in late October. In December, it embarked for the West Indies: Rice and Brown, eds., *Rochambeau's Army*, I, 76–85, 162–70; II, 183–93.

8. See XXXVI, 671; XXXVII, 70–1.

9. From here to the end of the sentence was in cipher. The reference to the fleshpots of Egypt is based on Exodus 16:3.

france, as from her political connection with us, might be urged to shew the wisdom of adopting the same liberal sentiments on this point, which has of late distinguished her on so many others— But if She should not be able to overcome her ancient prejudices, I beleive they will be found to have less influence on the british whom you will press earnestly on this head, besides the general interest of the Kingdom, there is with them a powerful west India interest to plead in behalf of a free importation of provisions into their Islands— If I mistake not the present wishes of the Nation, as well as the professions of Administration lead to every measure which may wear away our present resentments, strengthen the connection between us, and them. The opposition between their views and those of France on this Subject will give you greate advantage in your negotiations—[1] The log wood trade we have some claim to from our continued exercise of the right.— Nor can England pretend to exclude us from it without invalidating her own title, which stands upon the same ground— If Spain admits the right in England[2] she gains nothing by excluding us, since in proportion as She diminishes our commerce in that article she encreases that of Britain, other manufacturing nations are interested in exciting a competition between us at their markets.— When you write to me be pleased to be very particular in your relation of every step which leads to a negotiation, as every thing of this kind must be interesting.

I ought before I conclude to inform you that[3] the Collection of Taxes owing to the decay of Commerce the loss of labour by the War & a variety of other Causes has fallen extreamly short of our Expectations & that every Exertion whether your negotiation terminate in a Peace or whether War is continued will be necessary to procure a Loan from France, agreable to your former instructions.

I have the honor to be, Sir with great Respect & Esteem your most obedt. humble Servant   Robt R Livingston

1. This sentence was enciphered.
2. Logwood, used in dyeing cloth, came from Spanish Central America. British rights to cut and export it were affirmed in the 1763 Treaty of Paris: Fred L. Israel, ed., *Major Peace Treaties of Modern History, 1648–1967* (4 vols., New York, Toronto, and London, 1967), I, 314.
3. From here to "France" was enciphered.

No. 16.

His Excellency Benj: Franklin

Endorsed: No 16. Mr Secry. Livingston Sept 5. 1782 Sundry Informations Points of Treaty, &c Necessity of Money—

Notation: (By C. [cipher] No 4.)

From Richard Oswald

Copies: Public Record Office (three), William L. Clements Library, Library of Congress

Sir,   Paris 5th September 1782.

In consequence of the Notice I have just now had from Mr Jay of Your Desire of an Extract from my last Letter from His Majesty's Secretary of State, regarding the proposed Treaty on the Subject of American Affairs, & my Authority in relation thereto, I take the liberty to send the same inclosed,[4] which together with the Powers contained in the Commission which I had the Honor of laying before You & Mr Jay I am hopeful will satisfy You of the Willingness & sincere Desire of His Majesty to give You entire Content on that important Subject.

This Extract I shou'd have sent You before now, if I had thought You wished to have it, before I had the Honor of waiting on You myself, which was only delayed, until I cou'd be in-

---

4. Townshend's letter to Oswald of Sept. 1, for which see BF to Gérard de Rayneval, Sept. 4, above. The extract comprises part of the first sentence, expressing the King's approval of Oswald's communicating to the American commissioners the fourth article of his July 31 instructions, and the second sentence, expressing the hope that the commissioners "will not entertain a doubt of His Majesty's determination to exercise, in the fullest extent, the powers with which the act of parliament hath invested him, by granting to America, full, complete, and unconditional independence, in the most explicit manner, as an article of treaty." The extract (filed with copies of the present letter at the Public Record Office and Library of Congress) is published in WTF, *Memoirs*, II, 396–7.

formed by Mr Jay, that You was well enough to see me upon Business.[5]

I heartily wish for a perfect re-establishment of Your Health & am with sincere Regard & Esteem Sir &[6]   R: O.

Copy

Notations: Copy of a Letter from Mr Oswald to Dr Franklin inclosing an Extract from Mr Secretary Townshend's Letter 5th September 1782. / In Mr Oswald's Letter of 10th Septr 1782.

From Edward Bridgen   ALS: Historical Society of Pennsylvania

Dear Sir   Sepr: 6 1782

I am just requested to pass through your hands the inclosed to Mr Jay I therefore hope for your pardon for the liberty I take it goes round by Antwerp and Consequently its arrival will be later than by the Usual conveyance Which, I am informed, will not be material; will you do me the favour to present my most respectful compliments to that Gentleman, as a Meritorious Man whom I have the pleasure to know only by Character.[7]

I have been much engaged lately in the *copper* buisness; in which I flatter myself to have been not useless, when that Matter may come under consideration. Will you, My Dear Sir, permit me to send you my thoughts on that Subject?[8] It is late, and I am hurried at present and therefore shall hastily conclude myself with all veneration and respect Dr Sir Yr: most Affect Friend

E B

5. Oswald kept away from Passy for fear of disturbing BF: Oswald to Townshend, Sept. 10, in Morris, *Jay: Peace*, p. 353.

6. Fragments of two brief notes that Oswald wrote to BF around this time are filed together at the Library of Congress. One of them is dated Sept. 7, 1782, and alludes to something "which came by Mr. Fitzherbts . . . which he forgot to forward." The other, whose date is missing, mentions newspapers he received and that "Mr Townshend ackno . . . Letters of the 8th."

7. BF forwarded the letter to Jay on Sept. 17, below.

8. BF and Bridgen first corresponded in 1779 about the latter's plan to supply blank copper rounds to America for coinage: XXX, 355–6, 429–31; XXXI, 129–30. For Bridgen's thoughts see his letter of Oct. 23.

Addressed: A Monsieur / Monsr: Franklin / a Passeè / Pres / Paris

From Samuel Cooper

AL: American Philosophical Society

My dear Sir,   Boston N.E. Septr. 6th. 1782.

In a Letter I wrote you a few Weeks past, giving some general Account of our Affairs, I mentioned my Kinsman William Cooper, and Mr Leverett, who I then thought were Prisoners in England, since which they with many others of our Countrymen have happily arrived here.[9]

I have been suspicious that our late severe Disappointment in the West Indies by the Defeat of the Count de Grasse would encourage the Court of London to continue the War by insisting on inadmissible Terms of Peace. If this should be the Case it would be perhaps as unwise as it is contrary to all the former declared Principles of the new British Ministry. For notwithstanding this Disappointment the Cause of the Allies still stands upon high Ground. Savanna is already evacuated and there are strong Appearances that Charlestown will soon follow. The Refugees and American Levies in N. York are in great Confusion and Distress upon being notified by Sr. Guy Carleton that the Court of London was disposed to acknowledge the Independence of America as a Basis of Peace.[1] At present we are at a Loss what Judgment to form of the real Intentions of that Court. If it means to continue the War it must intend to employ it's Forces now on this Continent, or at least a great part of them, in some other Quarter, perhaps in the West Indies; and yet we have a recent Report that fresh Troops are arrived at Hallifax from Britain.[2]

9. See Cooper's letter of June 15: XXXVII, 480–3. Hundreds of American prisoners were shipped home from England in late June and early July. Cartels arrived in Massachusetts on Aug. 11, 14, and 21: Sheldon S. Cohen, *Yankee Sailors in British Gaols: Prisoners of War at Forton and Mill, 1777–1783* (Newark, Del., and London, 1995), pp. 202–3; *The Continental Journal, and Weekly Advertiser,* Aug. 15 and 29, 1782.

1. See XXXVII, 674n, 717.

2. George Washington had learned that the *Warwick,* 50, was escorting

The Marquiss de Vaudruiel with 13 Ships of the Line and several Frigates lately arrived here from the West Indies to repair. I cannot easily describe to you the mutual Tokens of Respect and Friendship that have passed between the Marquiss & his Officers and the Government and principal Inhabitants of this Common Wealth. Every Thing has appeared in the true Spirit of the Alliance, to promote the Purposes this Visit of the Fleet must contribute not a little. Unluckily a few days ago the Magnifique of 74 Guns in changing her Station run a Ground, and we fear is lost. Immediately it was the Cry of every Body, let the 74 Gun Ship ready to be launched at Portsmouth be offerr'd to the King by Congress, to supply the Place of the Magnifique. We are but one of the 13 States, and we know not the Views and Engagements of Congress respecting that Ship; but I never knew a Proposal made with more Warmth of Friendship than this appeared to be done here by every Rank of men; upon which Account as it was peculiarly pleasing to me, I thought it worth mentioning to you.

General Washington has taken every Care to afford the Marquiss de Vaudrueil the best and most early Intelligence. A Day or two ago an Express arrived from the General acquainting the Marquiss that an English Fleet had arrived from the W. Indies near the Chesapeek of 25 Sail of the Line, and this Morning another Express was received that came with uncommon Dispatch upon the same Subject.[3] Proper Measures have been taken, and

---

five transport ships carrying 1,500 to 2,000 troops from New York to Halifax: Washington to the marquis de Vaudreuil, Sept. 3, in Fitzpatrick, *Writings of Washington*, xxv, 115–6.

3. That particular dispatch has not been located, though Washington forwarded some intelligence on Aug. 27. On Sept. 3, he told Vaudreuil that he had no information on the arrival of the fleet. On Sept. 4, he reported that ten ships of the line had been spotted off the New York coast. By Sept. 8 he had learned that a fleet from the West Indies, commanded by Adm. Pigot, was off Sandy Hook with 22 ships of the line: Fitzpatrick, *Writings of Washington*, xxv, 115–6, 125–6, 128–9; Washington to Vaudreuil, Sept. 8, 1782, Library of Congress. In fact Adm. Hugh Pigot's detachment of 25 ships of the line had anchored on Sept. 5: W. M. James, *The British Navy in Adversity: a Study of the War of American Independence* (London, New York, and Toronto, 1926), p. 360; Robert Beatson, *Naval and Military Memoirs of Great Britain from 1727 to 1783* (6 vols., London, 1804), vi, 346–7.

the Governor accompanied the Marquiss down the Harbour this Morning to accelerate with the Aid of our People all proper Precautions.

Mr Temple has of late been much offended with me for not acknowledging before a Committee of the Genl. Court, that I knew and advised to his last Going to England and to Lord North's Closet with a professed View to oppose the Representations of Galloway, &c &c, when I never did advise to it, nor ever thought it a justifiable or prudent Measure.—[4] My Sermon on the Taking of Quebec the last War was sneeringly advertised for, with a manifest Design to bring into View what I had formerly said of the French Nation.[5] The Advertisement was supposed to be from Mr T. tho carried to the Press by a Nathan Blodget, formerly Purser to the Alliance Frigate, who on his Return from France discovered, I am told, great Prejudices against you,[6] and has lately been an Intimate of Mr T. He has since embarqued again for that Country. Judge Sullivan,[7] a most respectable Character took some Notice of the Advertisement in the public Papers. This brought on a Controversy in Print, in which I would take no part, and which has risen high.[8] Mr T. claims great Merit for procuring and sending to this Country Hutchinson's Letters at the Expence of all he held under the British Crown. To this Mr Sullivan opposes your Advertisement in a London Paper respecting the Letters,[9] and a printed Letter

4. Cooper had already informed BF about his disagreement with John Temple: XXXVII, 660–1.

5. Cooper's *A Sermon . . . Upon Occasion of the Reduction of Quebec* (1759) denounced France as an enemy to America's religion and liberties. An unnamed "Delegate of Congress" advertised in the *Continental Journal* of July 11, 1782, that he was seeking copies and would pay double the publication price. The incident is described in Charles W. Akers, *The Divine Politician: Samuel Cooper and the American Revolution in Boston* (Boston, 1982), pp. 333, 422.

6. In 1780 BF had refused the requests of Blodget and others aboard the *Alliance* for back pay, prize money, and the reinstatement of Capt. Pierre Landais: XXXII, 243–4, 454–6, 488–91, 492–3.

7. James Sullivan, a Mass. legislator and supreme court justice: *DAB*.

8. This played out in numerous Boston newspapers, especially the *Continental Journal* from mid-July through early September: Akers, *The Divine Politician*, pp. 333–4, 422.

9. For BF's statement claiming responsibility see XX, 513–16.

of Mr. T. in which he declares solemnly he had no Concern directly or indirectly in procuring or sending them. As I have ever been disposed to be friendly to Mr T. his Behavior in this whole Matter has been unkind to me as well as injurious to himself.

I cannot omit mentioning the Situation of Mr Jonathan Amory, formerly a noted Merchant of this Town, and who left us at the opening of the War, and went to England, and afterwards at Newport took an Oath of Allegiance to the British King, but has long wished and applied for Leave to return to his native Country, from which he is now excluded by Law. He is a Gentleman of an amiable private Character, and has never taken an active part against his Country. He resides at Brussells, where should the Conferences for Peace open he will wait on you and state his Case and his Views. I am sure you will be ready to serve him as far as public Propriety and Safety will admit. From the Importunity of his Friends I could not forbear making this Mention of him.[1]

I am extremely obliged to you for all your kind Attention to my Grandson; and am sorry to hear of the Disturbances in Geneva; I have the Satisfaction to find by a Letter from him to his Father that he was safe out of the City. Col. Johonnot arrived fortunately two months past at Baltimore, where his Affairs, as he writes, wore an agreeable Aspect. I expect to see him in Boston every Moment.[2]

1. Cooper is referring to John Amory (1728–1805), not Jonathan (1726–1797), his brother and business partner. John sailed to London with his wife in late April, 1775, leaving their ten children behind. Her illness prolonged their stay, and after her death in April, 1777, he returned to America, landing in New York where he was obliged to swear an oath of allegiance to the crown. The Boston authorities subsequently examined him, and upon his refusal to swear allegiance to the United States, banished him from Massachusetts. He returned to Europe, where he continued to assist his brother in mercantile ventures. On Sept. 2, 1782, hearing that peace was imminent, Jonathan advised him to seek BF's help and informed him that Cooper promised to write this plea. We have no indication that John contacted BF, but he returned to Rhode Island in the spring of 1783: Gertrude E. Meredith, *The Descendants of Hugh Amory, 1605–1805* (London, 1901), pp. 203, 216–37, 239–43.

2. Samuel Cooper Johonnot probably joined BFB at the country home of their schoolmaster's brother: XXXVII, 123–4, 139, 682–3. Johonnot's father,

With every Sentiment of Respect and Affection Your old
Friend

From ——— Mesny   ALS: University of Pennsylvania Library

Monsieur   Paris le 6. 7bre. 1782. / .

En 1778. Vous eutes la bonté de Vous charger d'envoyer en
Amerique cent exemplaires de l'ouvrage de Mr. de la faye, et de
me promettre de m'en faire payer icy le prix, aprés que la Vente
en seroit faitte.[3] J'ai eu l'honneur de Vous en demander des nouvelles il y a environ 15 jours, et aujourdhui je prends la liberté de
vous retourner vôtre propre lettre pour vous en rappeller le
Soüvenir, Vous priant de vouloir bien me la renvoyer.[4]

J'ay l'honneur d'etre avec un trés profond respect Monsieur
Votre trés humble et trés obeissant serviteur   Mesny.

maison de l'epicier au coin des rues du bacq et de Verneuil

Endorsed: answer'd Sept. 11

Notation: Mesny 6. 7bre. 1782

Col. Gabriel Johonnot, had returned from France after a year's absence:
xxxvii, 483.

3. Mesny had supplied BF with 50 copies each ("brochés," or sewn in paper wrappers) of La Faye's two works on ancient Roman methods of construction and the composition of Roman limes and mortars. The first, *Recherches sur la préparation que les Romains donnoient à la chaux . . .* was issued
in 1777, and the sequel, *Mémoire pour servir de suite aux Recherches . . .* , was
issued in May, 1778: xxiv, 65; xxvi, 514. The former appears on BF's List of
Books: xxxvi, 333. The two works were subsequently reissued in one volume under the half-title *Recherches et Mémoire sur la manière de bâtir des An-
ciens.*

4. BF did not return his May 20, 1778 letter, which remains among his papers: xxvi, 514.

From Gabriel-Claude Palteau de Veimerange

LS: American Philosophical Society; copy:[5] Archives de la Marine

Monsieur, Paris le 6. Septembre 1782

Vôtre Excellence a été informé qu'il a été embarqué à Brest, dans le courant des mois d'Avril et May derniers, sur les Navires L'*Achille,* Le *Maurice* et la *Marie-Therèse,* divers Effets et Marchandises pour le service des Etats unis de l'Amérique Septentrionnale, dont j'ai eû l'honneur de vous faire remettre les Etats détaillés.[6] Ces Navires sont partis de Brest à la fin de mai; ils ont fait une relache à Rochefort d'où les Circonstances n'ont pas permis jusques à present qu'ils pûssent partir.

Je suis informé que le Capitaine L'Eguillon commandant le Navire La *Marie-Therèse,* demande que l'on fasse décharger l'Entrepont de son Bâtiment y soupconnant de l'avarie. Vôtre Excellence sentira facilement que cette Opération ne peut se faire sans occasionner une dépense assés considérable, dont je n'ai pas crû devoir prendre sur moi de faire faire l'avance. Je ne puis au surplus que vous informer de l'Etat des choses, àfin de vous mettre en Etat de prendre le parti que vous jugerés le plus convenable.

J'ai l'honneur d'être avec une très respectueuse Considération, Monsieur, de Vôtre Excellence, Le très humble et très Obéissant Serviteur   VEIMERANGE

M. Franklin, Ministre Plenipotre. des Etats unis. A Passy.

Notation: Veimerange 6. 7bre 1782

---

5. In L'Air de Lamotte's hand.
6. These lists are missing. Palteau de Veimerange had begun collecting these stores a year earlier, and helped find ships to transport them: XXXV, 509–10; XXXVI, 685–6; see also our annotation of JW to BF, Aug. 23, above.

From Vicq d'Azyr

LS: Historical Society of Pennsylvania

Monsieur.   6 7bre. 1782.

La société Royale de médecine à laquelle j'ai Communiqué le Billet qui m'a été ecrit en Votre nom, a été d'autant plus fachée, d'etre privée de la satisfaction de Vous posséder à sa séance publique que c'est une indisposition qui en a été la Cause.[7] Elle m'a chargé de Vous témoigner toute la part qu'elle y prend et elle desire bien sincèrement qu'elle n'ait point de suites facheuses.

Je joins ici le programe des prix proposés dans son assemblée publique et un exemplaire des réflexions qu'elle a publiées Sur une maladie epidémique qui Vient de Regner dans le haut Languedoc.[8]

Je Suis avec le plus profond Respect Monsieur Votre très humble et très obeissant serviteur   VICQ DAZYR

M franklin

Notation: Vic d'Azir 6. 7bre. 1782.

To Castries

Copy: Archives de la Marine

Mr.   a Passy 7. 7bre. 1782.

J'ay l'honneur de transmettre à V. E. la copie d'une lettre que je viens de recevoir de M. de Veimerange au sujet des avaries arrivées à un des Batiments de transports chargés des munitions destinées pour les Etats unis de l'amerique.[9] Je pense qu'il est a propos que Votre Gouvernement ayant eté chargé jusqu'a present de ces sortes d'affaires, continue à les diriger, et je prie en consequence, V. E. de vouloir bien donner à Rochefort les ordres

---

7. Vicq's letter of invitation to BF is above, [before Aug. 27]. BF's reply has not been found.

8. The proposed prizes were reported in the *Jour. de Paris*, Aug. 28. Jean-Noël Hallé read a paper on the epidemic in Languedoc and Roussillon: *Jour. de Paris*, Aug. 30. Vicq probably enclosed "Réflexions sur la Nature & Traitement de la maladie qui regne dans le Haut-Languedoc," the published version of a paper read at the June 4 meeting of the society. For the epidemic and this paper see XXXVII, 490–1.

9. Palteau de Veimerange's letter of Sept. 6, above.

relatifs à ces objets dont les Etats Unis qui sont deja en compte ouvert, doivent supporter la depense.

Je prends aussi la liberté de rappeller à V. E. que faute de Batiments, il reste à Brest une grande quantité de munitions dont les Etats Unis ont un besoin très pressant. Je me flatte que V. E. ne perdra pas cet objet de vuë et qu'elle donnera les ordres necessaires pour les faire embarquer lorsque l'occasion favorable s'en presentera.

Je suis avec beaucoup de respect Mr De V. E. Le très obeissant et très humble serviteur   signé FRANKLIN

To Richard Oswald

Copies: Public Record Office (three),[1] William L. Clements Library, Library of Congress

Sir   Passy 8th Septr. 1782

I have receivd the honour of yours dated the 5th. Instant, inclosing an Extract of a Letter to you from the Rt. Hon: Thos. Townshend, one of his Majesty's principal Secretaries of State, wherein your Conduct in communicating to us the 4th Article of your Instructions appears to have been approved of by his Majesty.[2]

I suppose therefore that there is no Impropriety in my requesting a Copy of that Instruction; And if you see none, I wish to receive it from you; hoping it may be of use in removing some of the Difficulties that obstruct our proceeding.[3]

---

1. We print from the copy made by Caleb Whitefoord, forwarded by Oswald to Townshend on Sept. 10. All other extant copies were made from this one.

2. Article 4 of Oswald's July 31 instructions (which BF had not yet seen) reads, "In case you find the American Commissioners are not at liberty to treat on any terms short of Independence, You are to declare to them that You have Our Authority to make that Concession; Our earnest Wish for Peace disposing Us to purchase it at the Price of acceding to the complete Independence of the Thirteen States, namely New Hampshire &c.": Giunta, *Emerging Nation*, 1, 482.

3. The chief obstruction to the negotiations was Jay's continued objection

With great & Sincere Esteem I am Sir Your most obedt. &c. &c.   signd B. FRANKLIN

To Richd. Oswald Esqr.

/ Copy /

Notation by Richard Oswald: In consequence of the above I waited of the Doctr and delivered him a Copy of the 4th Article abovementd, Signed by me, as in my Letter of this date 10th Sepr[4]   RO

---

to Oswald's commission. On Sept. 9, Jay finally told Oswald that he would accept (pending BF's approval) an alteration in the language of that commission, rather than an express acknowledgement of independence. He drafted a sentence specifying that Oswald would be treating with "the thirteen United States of America": Morris, *Jay: Peace,* p. 349. (A copy in Oswald's hand is among BF's papers at the Library of Congress.) He also drafted a letter to Oswald explaining his reasons and indicating his willingness to proceed with negotiations if the commission were altered: Morris, *Jay: Peace,* pp. 350–1.

Jay consulted BF at Passy on the evening of Sept. 9 and again the following morning. BF advised against sending the letter, which he thought too strong. Jay concurred, and on Sept. 10 Oswald forwarded to Townshend Jay's proposed alteration of the commission without Jay's letter of explanation. The following day, however, Oswald convinced Jay to give him a copy of that letter for private use. Without BF's knowledge, Oswald forwarded the letter with his dispatch to Shelburne dated Sept. 11. See Morris, *Jay: Peace,* pp. 351–9.

4. Oswald was reluctant to give BF a copy but finally did so. Oswald wrote Townshend on Sept. 11 that BF checked it for accuracy, laid it aside, and said "very kindly, that the only use he proposed to make of it, was, that, in case they took any liberties, for the sake of removing difficulties, not expressly specified in their Instructions, he might have this paper in his hands to shew": Morris, *Jay: Peace,* p. 355. Oswald also reported that Jay and BF had agreed to proceed with negotiations if Oswald received a new commission empowering him to treat with "the Thirteen United States of America" and listing the states by name. Unless this new commission was sent, negotiations would cease immediately. Oswald wrote the same admonition to Shelburne on Sept. 11, urging haste. Morris, *Jay: Peace,* pp. 355–7, 357–9.

To Vergennes   LS:[5] Archives du Ministère des affaires étrangères

Sir,   Passy, 8th. Sepr: 1782

Mr Barclay who will have the honour of delivering you this, will have that of laying before your Excellency his Commission from the Congress of the United States of America, appointing him their Consul General in France.[6] Mr. Barclay being about to enter on his Consular Functions, I request your Excellency would in the usual manner, authenticate & make known his Appointment; that in the exercise thereof he may meet with no Molestation or Impediment, but on the contrary receive that Countenance & Assistance he may stand in need of.

With great Respect, I have the Honour to be, Sir Your Excellency's most obedient & most humble Servant.   B Franklin

[His] Exy. [?] Ct. de Vergennes. &ca—

Endorsed: M. de R[7]

To Joseph Banks

LS:[8] British Library; AL (draft) and copy: Library of Congress

Dear Sir,   Passy, Sept. 9. 1782.

I have just received the very kind friendly Letter you were so good as to write to me by Dr. Bonssonnet [Broussonet].[9] Be assured that I long earnestly for a Return of those peaceful Times, when I could sit down in sweet Society with my English philosophic Friends, communicating to each other new Discoveries, and proposing Improvements of old ones, all tending to extend

5. In WTF's hand.
6. *JCC*, xx, 735–6. Barclay presented his commission to Vergennes on Sept. 12: Klingelhofer, "Matthew Ridley's Diary," p. 104.
7. Rayneval (*i.e.*, Gérard de Rayneval), who handled Vergennes' American correspondence.
8. In the hand of L'Air de Lamotte.
9. L'Air de Lamotte misread BF's draft, which correctly spelled the name. Banks's letter of recommendation for the French doctor and scientist is above, xxxvii, 716–17. We have silently corrected several other copying errors.

the Power of Man over Matter, avert or diminish the Evils he is subject to, or augment the Number of his Enjoyments. Much more happy should I be thus employ'd in your most desirable Company, than in that of all the Grandees of the Earth projecting Plans of Mischief, however necessary they may be supposed for obtaining greater Good.

I am glad to learn by the Dr. that your great Work goes on. I admire your Magnanimity in the Undertaking, and the Perseverance with which you have prosecuted it.

I join with you most perfectly in the charming Wish you so well express, "That such Measures may be taken by both Parties as may tend to the Elevation of both rather than the Destruction of either." If anything has happen'd endangering one of them, my Comfort is that I endeavour'd earnestly to prevent it, and gave honest faithful Advice which if it had been regarded would have been effectual. And still if proper Means are us'd to produce not only a Peace but what is much more interesting, a thorough Reconciliation, a few Years may heal the Wounds that have been made in our Happiness, & produce a Degree of Prosperity of which at present we can hardly form a Conception.

With great & sincere Esteem & Respect, I am Dear Sir, Your most obedient & most humble Servant   B FRANKLIN

Sir Joseph Banks.

From Lamarque, Fabre & Cie.[1]

ALS:[2] University of Pennsylvania Library

Monseigneur   Paris ce 10e. Septbre. 1782.

Pour prouver à Votre Excellence qu'elle a daigné honorer de ses bontés de Négociants honnêtes qu'un événément inattendu avoit mis dans la détresse & affecté la délicatesse, nous prenons

1. A merchant firm from which Alexander Gillon had purchased uniforms shipped aboard the *South Carolina:* XXXI, 51–2; XXXV, 462–3, 463–4, 644.

2. In the hand of Lamarque, who wrote to L'Air de Lamotte the following day asking him to intercede with BF (University of Pa. Library).

la liberté, Monseigneur, de remettre à Votre Excellence un Etat des sommes que nous avons payé par le secours que nous a procuré M Gillon qui forme la moitié de ce que nous devions.[3]

Comme ce commodore nous a écrit de la havane, suivant la copie de sa lettre que nous avons l'honneur de mettre sous les yeux de Votre Excellence, que s'il trouvoit de lettres de change à la havane pour solder notre compte avec l'Etat de la Caroline du sud, il nous en féroit passer ou qu'à defaut à son arrivée a Philadelphie il nous en enverroit,[4] nous avons l'honneur de vous supplier, Monseigneur de vouloir par une suite de votre bienfaisance & de l'intérêt que vous aves bien voulu prendre à notre triste position, écrire à Mr. amelot pour que ce Ministre ait la complaisance de vouloir faire renouveller pour un an notre arret de surséance qui est sur le point d'expirer,[5] de lui reccomander notre requête présentée à cet éfflet dont nous n'attendrons certainement pas l'expiration pour nous libérer, si M Gillon nous paye ce qui forme ce que nous restons devoir, ou si d'autres rentrées nous en facilitent les moyens.

Notre gratitude, Monseigneur, sera des plus vives & par notre zèle à remplir le surplus de nos engagements nous reconnoitrons la faveur de Votre Excellence.

Nous sommes avec un très profond respect Monseigneur Vos très humbles & trés Obéissants Serviteurs   LAMARQUE FABRE

Rue St. Bon.

Notation: La Marque Fabre, Paris 10. Septr. 1782.

3. The enclosed "Etat des sommes" detailed sixteen payments for a total of 25,000 *l.t.*

4. Gillon's letter was dated Jan. 24, 1782: University of Pa. Library. For his failed attempt to land at British-occupied Charleston, which he explained in this letter, see XXXVII, 135–6.

5. Secretary of State Antoine-Jean Amelot de Chaillou had helped the firm obtain the *arrêt* the year before: XXXV, 462–3, 463–4. This is the firm's last extant letter to BF. In 1788 they were still trying to collect the debt: *Jefferson Papers*, XII, 633–4.

From Henry Laurens

ALS: American Philosophical Society; AL (draft): University of South Carolina Library

Sir.   Nantes 10th. septemr. 1782.

I had the honor of addressing you under the 3d Inst. requesting you to procure & transmit a Passport for myself & family to go out of this Kingdom into England—this Morning I am advised from London that the proper document of leave to re-enter the latter, had been obtained & would be forwarded to Mr. Ginett[6] at Versailles.[7] I shall therefore begin my journey within eight & forty hours, but my strength will not admit of rapid traveling; if you shall not have sent on the Passport before this waits on you, be pleased to direct it to me at the House of Monsr. Pierre Bernard Calais, where it will overtake me. I beg leave to repeat the offers of my best services & the assurances of being with great Esteem & Respect Sir. Your most Obedient & most humble servant[8]   HENRY LAURENS

His Excellency Benjamin Franklin Esquire Passy.

Addressed: His Excellency / Benjamin Franklin Esquire / Minister Plenepotentiary / from the United States of America / &c &c / Passy.

Notation: Henry Laurens 10 Sept. 1782.

---

6. Edmond-Charles-Edouard Genet: XXXVI, 228n.

7. Laurens' request had been approved by the King, and Townshend arranged for the passport. Laurens received it on Sept. 18: *Laurens Papers,* XV, 604.

8. WTF sent the passport on Sept. 14, with a note written on behalf of BF who was "much indispos'd with the Gout and Gravel": N.Y. Public Library. Laurens answered WTF from Calais on Sept. 19 that he had received it: APS. See also *Laurens Papers,* XV, 604n.

From Jonathan Williams, Jr.   ALS: American Philosophical Society

Dear & hond sir   Nantes Sept. 10. 1782

I recvd the Catalogue of the Marquis de la Fayettes Cargo only last Night—and I now return it with marks & a note on the other side which I hope may answer your Purpose.[9]

I have been very uneasy on accot of your Illness but a Letter from Billy this morning has relieved me,[1] & I hope by the Time you receive this you will be perfectly recovered.

I am as ever most dutifully & affecy Yours   JONA WILLIAMS J

Mrs Williams is much better but yet weak.—[2] Mumford has the Fever & ague—besides I have my man Servant my Wifes maid & my Bookeeper all sick, with my hands more full of Business than usual, this must apologise for my brevity. I am as before.

JWJ

Note.—

I have examined the Catalogue of the sale of the Marquis de la Fayette, and marked *Public* against those Goods I shipped on the public Accot.

Where I have marked against Totals I mean all to be public, whether the Detail be marked or not. Such as I think are private property I have marked *not public* in the Summary & X in the Detail.

There were a few Goods shipped on Freight with my Knowledge and a List was sent to Congress, but as the marks are not preserved I cannot tell exactly which they are. I believe however they did not amount to ⅛ the quantity which appear in the List

9. We have no record of when BF sent JW this set of London auction catalogues (XXXVII, 498n), which William Hodgson had sent to him in July. They provide a nearly complete inventory of the captured *Marquis de Lafayette* and reveal a large quantity of goods shipped on private account (counter to the charter, which was to carry military supplies for Congress). In his effort to understand the shipping terms for the vessel and to determine who was responsible for loading the illegitimate cargo, BF evidently asked JW to review the catalogues and mark the items that he had authorized. See XXXVII, 473–5, 497–500, 648.

1. JW wrote to WTF on Aug. 31, expressing concern about BF's health (APS). WTF noted on that letter that he replied on Sept. 8.

2. See JW to BF, Aug. 16, above.

marked X.;—and of the Wine, Salt, Brandy, Cordials Ancho-
vies, Oil, Medecines Crockery Ware preserved Fruit &c I was
kept Ignorant. They were shipped without my knowledge &
Consent except 45 Cases containing about 2250 Bottles of Claret. So that in these articles alone the ship had the Bulk of about
125 hhds 60 Cases & 110 Boxes.

To Baron Grantham[3]

AL (draft): Library of Congress

My Lord   Passy, Sept. 11. 1782

A long & severe Indisposition has delay'd my acknowledging
the Receipt of the Letter your Lordship did me the Honour of
Writing to me by Mr Fitzherbert:—[4]

You do me Justice in believing that I agree with you in
earnestly Wishing the Establishment of an honourable and lasting Peace; and I am happy to be assur'd by your Lordship, that
it is the real System of the Ministers with whom you are Co-
operating.— I know it to be the sincere Desire of the United
States; and With such Dispositions on both sides, there is reason
to hope that the good Work in its Progress will meet with little
Difficulty. A small one has occur'd in the Commencement, with
which Mr Oswald will acquaint you. I flatter myself that means
will be found on your part for removing it, and my best Endeavours in removing subsequent ones, (if any should arise)
may be firmly rely'd on.—

I had the Honour of being known to your Lordship's Father.[5]
On several Occasions he manifested a Regard for me, and a
Confidence in me.— I shall be happy if my Conduct in the pre-
sent important Business may procure me the same Rank in the
Esteem of his worthy Successor.

I am, with sincere Respect, My Lord, Your Lordship's

3. British secretary of state for foreign affairs: XXXVII, 684–5n. He had less
influence over the peace negotiations than did Prime Minister Shelburne,
who directed them personally.

4. XXXVII, 684–5.

5. Sir Thomas Robinson, 1st Baron Grantham: XII, 220n.

To Mesny
ALS: American Philosophical Society

Sir,   Passy, Sept. 11. 1782

I have received two Letters from you relating to some Books you put into my Hands some years since to be sent to America.[6] A severe Indisposition has prevented my answering sooner. I sent one of the Bundles to Nantes, to be forwarded by some Ship from thence; and having never heard that the Books arrived, I suppose the Ship was lost or taken. I was thereby discouraged from sending the other, till a Peace should make the Communication between the two Countries more secure, and it remains with me ready to be delivered to your Order. And as you mention your having an urgent Occasion for the Money, I will at the same time, to end the Affair, and do you Service, pay for the Bundle that is lost.[7] I have the honour to be, Sir, Your most obedient and most humble Servant   B Franklin

M. Mesny.

Addressed: A Monsieur / Monsieur Mesny / Maison de l'Epicier au Coin des Rues / du Bacq & de Verneuil.— / à Paris—

From ———— St. Clair[8]
ALS: American Philosophical Society

Dunkerque Prison Roial ce 11eme. Septembre 1782

J'ai ete favorisé d'une lettre de Monsieur Joly qui m'a fait part d'une conversation qu'il a eu l'honeur d'avoir avec votre Excellence a mon sujet.[9] Les mesures que le Prince De Robecq prenait pour mon elargissement m'a fait croire qu'il etait inutile d'importuner votre Excellence davantage a cet egard: mais une lettre daté du Burau de la guerre dont on m'a fait part fait mention, que la seule chose qui avait empéché ma liberté etait que le Ministre

---

6. See Mesny's letter of Sept. 6.

7. Mesny was paid 75 *l.t.* on Sept. 15: Account XVII (XXVI, 3), entry of Sept. 16.

8. A marine who had served on the *South Carolina*. For his first appeals to WTF (July 5) and BF (July 26), see XXXVII, 680–2.

9. Joly delivered St. Clair's earlier letter to BF.

avait voulu prendre des eclaircissemens d'une autre coté ce qui m'a fort etonné vu que les seules eclaircissemens qu'il peut avoir etoit en arrettant Le Capitaine Du Doggerbank (Corsaire Hollandais) pour lequel je suis soupconné si mal a propos d'avoir voulu lever de monde en France. Sitot que je recus la nouvelle de l'arrivée de ce Corsaire au Havre de Grace j'en donnais avis a Monsieur De Cheaulieu[1] qui envoya prendra ma Declaration mais malgré que ledit Batiment a resté quelque tems au Havre de grace et ensuite a relaché a Morlaix on n'a fait aucune perquisition a ce sujet. Ce Batiment a été depuis pris par l'ennemi.[2] J'ai fait tout mon possible pour que le Ministre fut amplement instruit et si le succes n'a pas repondu a mes vues j'espere qu'on me fera la justice que d'avouer que J'ai fait tous mes efforts, ce que je n'aurais pas surement fait si j'avais été coupable, vu que le Capitaine Dudit navire etant arretté a mon instigation n'aurait pas manqué de faire tout ce qu'il aurait pu pour me perdre. Je conjure votre Excellence de vouloir bien faire cette exposition a Monsieur Le Marquis de Segur et je suis fermement persuadé qu'il mettra fin a une detention qui a deja duré trois mois et m'a entierement ruiné etant une perte pecuniaire pour moi de dix-sept-cens livres. J'aurais l'honneur de vous rendre mes devoirs à Passy immediatement a ma sortie. Dans la ferme persuasion de vos bonnes offices je reste De votre Excellence Le tres humble et tres respectueux Serviteur[3]   ST CLAIR DE ROSLIN

A son Excellence B. Franklin

1. Chaulieu, the commandant at Dunkirk: xxx, 396.
2. The *Dogger-Banck*, 20, commanded by James Pile, was captured by H.M.S. *Vengeance* on Aug. 9: *Courier de l'Europe*, XII (1782), 117.
3. St. Clair wrote to WTF the same day. He complains that he has received no answer to his earlier letter, explains that his circumstances are dire, and begs WTF to intervene with BF. APS.

The Marquis de Lafayette's Note Containing
Vergennes' Proposal   AD and copy:[4] Library of Congress

Vergennes had advised the American commissioners against delaying negotiations over the issue of Oswald's commission. As he wrote to La Luzerne, in politics one should yield on form when satisfied with the substance.[5] Franklin agreed. When Jay continued to object, Vergennes and Lafayette proposed to him a solution that might expedite matters: having Oswald write a letter to the American commissioners stating that he was treating with them as representatives of an independent nation. The present memorandum, in Lafayette's hand, is undoubtedly the draft of this statement, that Vergennes wanted Franklin (who was still too ill to travel) to read.

Jay deeply distrusted Vergennes and refused to consider this compromise. He suggested to Franklin that they state their objections in writing and request from Vergennes a written response. Franklin agreed, and Jay drafted a letter of colossal length. It was still under Franklin's consideration when it was rendered moot by the arrival of Oswald's new commission.[6]

4. The copy is by WTF, with corrections by BF.

5. XXXVII, 714n; Vergennes to La Luzerne, Sept. 7, in Giunta, *Emerging Nation*, I, 559. His advice to the commissioners seems to have been based on an undated set of "Reflections" (AAE) that recommended that BF and Jay compromise "to facilitate the opening of the peace negotiations," and observed that "form can be yielded when the substance is assured": "Reflections on Richard Oswald's Commission," translated in Giunta, *Emerging Nation*, I, 473–5.

6. Jay's recapitulation of these events, and the text of his unsent letter to Vergennes, are in a Nov. 17 letter to Livingston: Wharton, *Diplomatic Correspondence*, VI, 21, 32–44. He also explained Vergennes' and BF's positions in a Sept. 18 letter to Livingston, saying that BF "believes [the French court] mean nothing in their proceedings but what is friendly, fair, and honorable": *ibid.*, V, 740. Matthew Ridley noted on Sept. 13 that BF "still thinks Vergennes means well — in short he is inclined to have every confidence in him." (Klingelhofer, "Matthew Ridley's Diary," p. 106.) Oswald, in a Sept. 8 note to Shelburne partially quoted in XXXVII, 678–9n, observed that BF was not blinded by his attachment to the French: "Considering how long he has lived here, & how he has been caressed, it must require a great Share of resolution not to feel the effects of it even in matters of business yet upon the whole I must still say I have neither seen or heard of anything that can make me doubt of his Sincerity nor of his Attatchment to his Friends." Oswald also noted how ill BF had been, marvelling that despite the severe pain from gout that affected his legs and thighs and prevented him from sleeping, "yet he kept

[September 11, 1782?][7]
In Case a letter is Received from M. Oswald Count de Vergennes proposes to have this Sentence.

Que d'après les Instructions et les pouvoirs dont il est Muni, il traitera avec les plenipotentiares Americains dans leur Qualité de plenipotentiaires des Etats Unis, et que l'article premier du traité preliminaire portera la Renonciation la plus Expresse de tous les Droits et pretensions que le Roy et la Couronne d'anglettere ont formé ou pu former dans Aucun tems Sur les territoires Composant la Souveraineté des Etats Unis.

From Williams, Moore & Co.[8]

ALS:[9] Historical Society of Pennsylvania

L'Orient 11th. Septr. 1782

We beg leave to trouble your excellency respecting the departure of three Privateers—the Revolution, Buccaneer, & Cicero, the Property of Messrs Cabots of Beverly.[1] These Vessells have lain long in Port, stopped by the Orders of the Commandant,[2] & were sinking a very large Sum to the Owners, perhaps more than they Could well bear, having from 100 to 130 Men in each Ves-

---

me talking of the business I came upon in the kindest way I would have wished."

7. A day when Jay and Lafayette planned to go to Versailles to discuss "les Scrupules qui Embarassent Notre Negotiation": Idzerda, *Lafayette Papers,* V, 54–5, 367–8. Two days earlier Jay had agreed that an alteration in Oswald's commission would be an adequate acknowledgement of independence; see BF to Oswald, Sept. 8.

8. The Lorient firm formed in May by JW and James and Philip Moore: XXXVII, 245–6n.

9. In the hand of James Moore.

1. These three ships, owned by John and Andrew Cabot, were commanded by Stephen Webb, Jesse Fearson, and Hugh Hill, respectively. The *Revolution* and the *Buccaneer* had been sending prizes into French ports since early summer. The *Cicero,* coming from the West Indies, arrived in Lorient in August: XXXV, 590n; XXXVII, 556, 567–8; Claghorn, *Naval Officers,* p. 106; JW to John and Andrew Cabot, Sept. 30, 1782 (Yale University Library).

2. Antoine-Jean-Marie Thévenard.

sell.— A few Days ago from repeated Sollicitations they procured Liberty to go to the Isle of Groix; We have heard with Orders to remain 'till the departure of the fleet. This fleet has been
long in Port, & many favourable Winds for the departure of the
Privateers have passed, without their having permission to
Sail—this Morning we are told they departed, & have likewise
been informed a Frigate went after them. We are sorry they went
off without Liberty—& neither knew of their Promise to the
Commandant, or of their Sailing—till this Evening. We are
Confident the Captns. meant neither to slight the Port or give
Offence, but were actuated from the regard due to their Owners
Interest. In Justice to the Captains & Ourselves we think it prudent to intimate the Affair—that if any representation is made,
or Accident Occur— Your excellency may receive every Information We Can give Remaining With the greatest Respect Your
excellencys most obedient & devoted Servants

WILLIAMS MOORE & CO

From Francis Dana   Copy:[3] Massachusetts Historical Society

Sir.   St: Petersbourg Septr: 2/12 1782[4]

Mr: Livingston in a letter of the 22d. of May last, which I have
lately received, writes me, "Your salary will in future be paid
here, where your Agent will vest it in bills on Doctor Franklin
quarterly, upon whom you will draw accordingly. I shall consider myself as Agent for all our foreign Ministers, and transact
the business accordingly for you, unless you shou'd choose to
appoint some other."[5] As I do not know whether he has in pur-

3. In Dana's hand. The bottom of this letter has been clipped, leaving only
the left margin. Visible are the initial words of two lines; "His" and "Minis[ter]."

4. We publish under the New Style date, Sept. 12, rather than the Old Style
date, Sept. 2. One of these dates is in error, as the difference between the Old
Style or Julian calendar used in Russia and the New Style or Gregorian calendar used in western Europe was, at this time, eleven days. Dana did receive
mail on Sept. 12: Taylor, *J. Q. Adams Diary*, 1, 146.

5. Wharton, *Diplomatic Correspondence*, v, 436.

suance of this new arrangement already transmitted any bills to you, I shall continue to take up money as it may become due to me, and I may have occasion for it, of Messrs. Strahlborn & Wolff upon Mr: Grand's letter of Credit as before,[6] untill I can be informed of the fact. I pray you to acquaint me as soon as may be, whether you have received any bills of Mr: Livingston on my account, & what amount for a quarter: and whether the course we are now in is to be changed, and bills to be drawn by me directly upon you according to the method he has proposed. In this case it will be necessary I shou'd be informed of the periods he has fixed for the payments, so as my receipts here, or my drafts may conform to them— I shall in a short time take up at once a considerable sum of Messrs: Strahlborn & Wolff upon Mr: Grand's last letter of credit, upon which I have not yet taken up any thing. I shall keep within my old rule never to take up any before it becomes due.

Things remain here as to us in their old state. This Court seems not disposed to take any step which wou'd be offlensive to the Court of London. Nothing is therefore to be expected untill that Court shall have agreed to consider the United-States as an Independant Power. Many will have it here that you are far advanced in that matter, and that you will give us peace in the course of next Winter. You wou'd much oblige me by the communication of any intelligence upon these points which it may be prudent to make— I beg you to present my best regards to Mr: Jay who we are told is with you.

I am, Sir, with the greatest Esteem & Respect, your obedient humble Servant

Doctr: Franklin

6. See XXXV, 53–4, 677; XXXVI, 35–6; XXXVII, 354.

From Lafayette

ALS: Historical Society of Pennsylvania

In the present letter Lafayette confirms that Vergennes secretly sent
Gérard de Rayneval to England for a meeting with Shelburne. Jay had
heard this news on September 9, the day he and Oswald were forging
a compromise about the language of Oswald's commission.[7] Suspecting that the purpose of Rayneval's mission was to arrange a peace with
France at America's expense, Jay immediately asked Benjamin
Vaughan to go to Shelburne's estate at Bowood and argue the American case, even instructing him to hint broadly at the possibility of a separate peace.[8] Vaughan dashed off a note to Shelburne asking him not to
make any decisions about France until he received further word. He entrusted the note to Elkanah Watson, Jr., who was leaving that day for
England carrying a passport from Franklin.[9] Vaughan wrote Shelburne
a longer letter on September 11, alerting him to his own imminent departure, warning him of the Americans' concern about Rayneval's
agenda, and again asking him to delay making any arrangements with
Rayneval. Vaughan also warned that unless the language of Oswald's
commission were changed, the negotiations would fail.[1]

Jay did not tell Franklin about his conference with Vaughan because, as he later explained to Livingston, he knew that Franklin did
not share his suspicions about Vergennes.[2] This is not to say, however,

7. Jay's source was Matthew Ridley: Klingelhofer, "Matthew Ridley's Diary," p. 104. For the compromise reached on Sept. 9 see our annotation of BF
to Oswald, Sept. 8.

8. Jay recounted his instructions to Vaughan in a Nov. 17 letter to Livingston: Wharton, *Diplomatic Correspondence*, VI, 29–32.

9. Vaughan to Shelburne, Sept. 9, in Morris, *Jay: Peace*, p. 338. For Watson's passport see the annotation of Watson & Cossoul to BF, Aug. 20. The
merchant arrived in London on Sept. 14 and immediately waited on Shelburne
"with the important dispatches committed to my charge by Mr. Vaughan." He
spent a half hour conversing with the prime minister about "American affairs
and about his old friend Dr. Franklin." According to Watson's journal, he was
hailed in the London papers as a "messenger of peace" and introduced to the
leading members of the House of Commons: Journal B, Elkanah Watson Papers, New York State Library. Watson later annotated his passport with a description of his mission, "the most interesting moment of my Life."

1. Morris, *Jay: Peace*, pp. 338–40. Throughout his stay in France, Vaughan
carried on a regular, confidential correspondence with Shelburne; Vaughan's
own copies of those letters, including this one, are at the APS.

2. Wharton, *Diplomatic Correspondence*, VI, 29–32; Klingelhofer, "Matthew Ridley's Diary," p. 104. See also Vergennes' memorandum under the
date of Sept. 11.

that Franklin was ignorant of Vaughan's mission. The ostensible reason for Vaughan's trip was personal (his wife was pregnant) and the Franklin household gave him a list of items to procure in England.[3] More to the point, Franklin reversed his decision about granting Elkanah Watson a passport because, according to Watson, he knew the merchant would carry to Shelburne Vaughan's urgent message. Vaughan must have let Franklin know that he intended to call on Shelburne, if only to underscore the necessity of revising Oswald's commission.[4] It is difficult to believe that Vaughan was capable of keeping secrets from a man he so idolized, and whose approval he so keenly sought. If Franklin ever knew that Jay had given Vaughan specific instructions designed to counteract Rayneval's perceived mischief, however, he certainly never let on to Jay.

Dear Sir   Paris September the 12h 1782

Inclosed I Have the Honor to send You a Letter that Relates to our Continental Stores,[5] and When I am able to Get the Account of them You Have Seemed to Desire, I will immediately Communicate it to Your Excellency— I fear the Army is in want, and of Course Am Particularly interested in their safe and speedy Departure—if You Approuve of it, I will wait Upon M. de Castries, and from Him know Every Particular About the Convoy.[6]

By a Very Good Information, tho Not Ministerial, I Have found that Mr. Reyneval Has Been truly intended to Go, or perhaps is Gone, in which I Confess I Have Been Mistaken— Having at once Put two Questions to Count de Vergennes it Appears He Answered But one of them, But Had I sooner Received Your Letter I Would Have Been More Pointed in My Enquiries with that Minister.[7]

---

3. Vaughan to BF, Sept. 23, below.

4. Vaughan's letter cited immediately above, written on the eve of his return, takes for granted that BF knew that he would be carrying to Paris the new sealed commission for Oswald.

5. From Palteau de Veimerange; see BF's response to Lafayette of the following day.

6. Apparently a long-delayed French convoy for the Chesapeake, which finally was canceled in November: XXXVI, 546n, 557–8; XXXVII, 71n.

7. Gérard de Rayneval was sent to meet with Shelburne in order to verify the British prime minister's intentions, as reported by de Grasse; see de Grasse to BF, Aug. 18. Louis XVI approved the meeting on Sept. 5. Rayneval

Upon Recollection, I Cannot Help thinking Mr. jay Had some Notion of My knowing Mr. Rayneval's Departure, and Having with You some Reserve about it which it was But Proper to Return— When I thought of it, it Made me smile, and As it was the 11th september I Might Have spoke to Him pretty Much the same way As Scipio did to the Romans Upon a Mistaken Notion of theirs.[8]

Be pleased, My Good friend, to Let Me know How You do, and Accept the tender Assurances of the High Respect and Warm Attachement I Have the Honor to Be With Your obedient hbe sert and devoted friend   LAFAYETTE

Notation: Mr. La Fayette

---

left Paris two days later, arrived in London on Sept. 10, and began discussions at Bowood, Shelburne's estate, on Sept. 13. Over the next week Shelburne convinced Rayneval that he was prepared to work with Vergennes not only in making peace but also in resisting Russian expansion against the Turks, a prime concern of the French foreign minister. The Rayneval mission thus laid the foundation for serious negotiations between Britain and France: Dull, *French Navy,* pp. 302–7; Jonathan R. Dull, "Vergennes, Rayneval, and the Diplomacy of Trust," Hoffman and Albert, eds., *Peace and the Peacemakers,* pp. 113–20; Harlow, *Founding of the Second British Empire,* I, 329–42; Andrew Stockley, *Britain and France at the Birth of America: the European Powers and the Peace Negotiations of 1782–1783* (Exeter, 2001), pp. 98–103. The minutes Rayneval took of his meetings with Shelburne are in Doniol, *Histoire,* V, 603–26.

BF's now-missing letter must have inquired about the Rayneval mission, which Vergennes was trying to keep quiet. According to Ridley, Rayneval himself had told Jay only that he would be absent for several days: Klingelhofer, "Matthew Ridley's Diary," pp. 104, 112; Morris, *Jay: Peace,* p. 330.

8. Sept. 11 was the anniversary of Lafayette's being wounded at Brandywine in 1777. Scipio the Elder, when accused of crimes against Rome, answered by reminding his accusers that it was the anniversary of his victory over Hannibal: Idzerda, *Lafayette Papers,* V, 56n.

From Mary Maccatter and Amy Kelly[9]

ALS:[1] American Philosophical Society

Sr   Dunkirk 7ber 12th 1782

We they undernamed, do take the liberty of acquainting your honour of the distress, and Situation of our husbands, whose names are Captain Edward Maccatter Captain John Kelly alias Grumbly, they had the misfortune of being Captured, the former was taken to London, the latter to Dublin, each of them has a property in the hands of a John Torris, who was armateer of the Vessels they commanded, to their Great disadvantage, as he is a man that deals very unjustly with his partners or the people that are concerned with him in this town, and has it more in his power to cheat us,[2] Maccatter was condemned to die, but I think (under God) it was by your Interest or Some Other friend, at Paris that he was respited, and I am now informed he got the Kings pardon, and likewise Mr Ryan who was equally condemned,[3] but notwithstanding, he Still wants Some money to help him out of London, this Torris Says he Owes Maccatter very little money, and cannot pay it, as he Says, he did not receive the price of the prizes they took, which were a vast many and very Valuable, but this is only a false and Villainous excuse, as we are informed, now depending on your humanity and the charitable character you bear, you wd be pleased to speak to

---

9. Mary Maccatter was the wife of Edward "Macatter" (xxx, 130–1), who in fact was Edward Wilde. He had commanded the privateer *Black Princess* and, as his wife says here, was captured, convicted of piracy, and later pardoned; see xxxvi, 548–9. Amy Kelly's husband John, alias Jean Grumlé, was captain of the privateer *Chardon*, 20, and then the *Anti-Briton*, 22: Henri Malo, *Les Derniers Corsaires: Dunkerque (1715–1815)* (Paris, 1925), pp. 122, 130, 152, 274. Kelly had served with Maccatter aboard Luke Ryan's smuggling cutter, the *Friendship:* Clark, *Ben Franklin's Privateers*, p. 5.

1. In Maccatter's hand.

2. Torris and Macatter had been business partners before Macatter in 1779 took command of Torris' *Black Princess:* xxx, 273, 328; Donald A. Petrie, "The Piracy Trial of Luke Ryan," *American Neptune*, LV (1995), 186.

3. On May 14, 1782, Ryan and Macatter were condemned to be hanged. The day before the scheduled execution the King issued a respite (after the intervention of Shelburne and the cabinet). Both men received a full pardon on March 2, 1783: Petrie, "Piracy Trial," pp. 197–9.

Some of your friends at Court, about our circumstances, and that they Shd Send Orders to the Judges of the Admiralities in the different ports or harbors they Sent the prizes into, to prepare their liquidations or get them ready as Soon as they can, as this Torris Says if he got the liquidations that he wd Settle with every body he has dealings with, but he thinks the longer he is from paying this money the more he will have to himself, as there is a great many in want and distress in this town, who have been in his employment, not in this town only but in English prison at present, and Sent to America and will not give one farthing to assist them, he expects they Shd go again to Sea, and wd be either killed or taken and be Sent to America, as they mostly are Americans there are Some of them oblidged to leave their letters of Attorney with people here for want of being paid their due, and then he can Say, they owed him what he pleases to Say, as he Said when my husband Maccatter And Captain Ryan were greatly in his debt at the time he expected they were executed, this is the Sort of a man that Torris is, to which I can get three or four hundred people to Subscribe their names, besides Several Merchants of good characters, Sr it is great necessity that Oblidges us, to trouble you, as it will be as meritorious a thing as can be expected from any Gentleman, as it will serve a vast many distressed people, along with our poor husbands, ourselves and Six children I Mary Maccatter have four, and Amy Kelly alias Grumby two, this Torris has at the risqu and hazard of our husbands lives, and many more besides appeared on change, after paying the Great debts he owed and made a purchase of land, to the value of thirty thousand pounds sterling, and Several houses, and has Sent Some Ships to the West indies laden with Merchantdizes, and Says he cannot pay a poor starving family what is lawfully due to them, it wd take Severall pages to mention how this knave intended to treat us, as being stangers and of the weaker Sex, memory cannot retain or tongue express the deceit of this ungratefull man, who does not care what becomes of our husbands if he could keep what they acquired, we hope youill take to consideration our condition, if the liquidations Shd come he can have no farther excuse, Edward Maccatter had the honour to know and Speak Several times to Mgr de Castries, who knows perfectly well the great quantites of prizes

and ransoms taken by him and Kelly, we found a gentleman here that would make him Shew his acompts, if the liquidations were here, in complying with our requests, you shall for ever have the prayers and good wishes of a vast many, and in particular of your humble petitioners   MARY MACCATTER
AMY KELLY ALIAS GRUMLY

P.S. the pleaces or towns they have sent the prizes into are Brest Lorieant Morlaix Cherbourgh Baiyone I hope youill Send your answer to this when you Speak to your friends to the white hart to the care of Mr Williamson, for either of us

Notation: Macater Mary Dunkerque 12 Sept. 1782.

To Lafayette[4]   Press copy of ALS: Historical Society of Pennsylvania

Dear Sir,   Passy, Sept. 13. 1782.
I am oblig'd to you for communicating M. de Viemerange's Letter, which I return. I wish you would continue your Application to the Marquis de Castries to provide Means for the Embarkation of the Goods: It is impossible for me to do it.—
I believe Mr Jay did not suspect your knowing of Mr Rayneval's Departure; he only wonder'd that you did not know it.
I am oblig'd by your kind Enquiries. I have had a bad Night, but at present have some Ease. Your natural Activity will always preserve you from the cruel Disorders that arise from too little Excercise. God give you good Health & long Life for the Advantage of our two Countries.—
With the greatest Esteem & Affection, I am, Your most obedient and most humble Servant   B FRANKLIN

P.S. I congratulate you on the Improvement of your Hand-writing since yesterday. It is more legible than Mr Viemerange's—

M. le Marquis de la Fayette

4. In answer to Lafayette's of the previous day, above.

From Robert R. Livingston

LS and L:[5] University of Pennsylvania Library; AL (draft): New-York Historical Society; copy and transcript: National Archives

Sir,   Philadelphia, 13th[−14] Septr. 1782

I have nothing to add to mine of the 5th instant, but to congratulate you on the safe arrival of two Vessels from Holland, having on board the goods left by Commodore Gillon,[6] & to present you in the name of Mr Paine with three copies of a late work of his, addressed to the Abbé Raynal, in which he takes notice of some of the many errors with which this work abounds—[7] The Abbé has a fine imagination, & he indulges it— The enclosed resolution contains an important fact which I am using every means to ascertain, but from the ill Success I have hitherto met with in every similar attempt I am fearful that it will be very long before I can effect it.[8]

5. Sent by the packet *Washington*. The duplicate, listed here as an L, was signed for Livingston by a secretary (University of Pa. Library) and sent by the ship *Nonsuch*, and the now-missing triplicate by the ship *Heer Adams*. The National Archives copy and transcript, both of which are misdated Sept. 12, list the conveyances.

6. One of these vessels, the *Heer Adams*, arrived on the evening of Sept. 10, bringing goods worth £22,677 sterling: *Morris Papers*, VI, 351, 371–3; Smith, *Letters*, XIX, 149. The other probably was the neutral ship mentioned by Barclay as being bound for Philadelphia: XXXVII, 494.

7. Paine's *Letter Addressed to the Abbe Raynal, on the Affairs of North-America: in which the Mistakes in the Abbe's Account of the Revolution of America are Corrected and Cleared Up*, which was dated Aug. 21 and published in early September: Philip S. Foner, ed., *The Complete Writings of Thomas Paine* (2 vols., New York, 1945), II, 211–63, 1211n; Charles Evans et al., comps., *American Bibliography* . . . (14 vols., Chicago and Worcester, 1903–59), VI, 179 (no. 17651).

8. Livingston enclosed (as one item) the related resolutions of Sept. 10. The first instructed him to compile accurate figures of "the slaves and other property which have been carried off or destroyed in the course of the war by the enemy," and to transmit this information to the peace commissioners. The second instructed him, "in the meantime," to inform the commissioners that "many thousands of slaves and other property to a very great amount have been carried off or destroyed by the enemy." *JCC*, XXIII, 562–3. Livingston's enclosure is now missing, though L'Air de Lamotte copied it into the legation letterbooks of the peace negotiations. BF enclosed a copy in his letter to Oswald, Nov. 26, below.

102

I have the honor to be, Sir with great respect & esteem Your most obt. humble Servt.   ROBT R LIVINGSTON

No. 17

His Excellency Benjamin Franklin

Sir,[9]

Since writing the above, I have received the enclosed resolutions of Congress— I have already anticipated all that can be said upon the subject of the last—[1] The[2] Melancholy Tale of our Necessitys Is sufficiently known to you. It has been too often repeated to need reiteration. The SuperIntdt. who writes from an empty treasury amidst perpetual duns will speake most feelingly. In short Money must be had at any rate whether we have Peace or War.}[3] France haveing all ready done much for us & it not being probable that we shall extend our demands beyond the present she may think it wise not to let us open accounts with a new banker since the debtor is always more or less under obligations to the Creditor.

9. This postscript must have been added on Sept. 14, the date of the congressional resolutions it discusses.

1. There were three resolutions of Sept. 14. The first informed all American ministers in Europe that Robert Morris would henceforth be in charge of managing all funds obtained in Europe. The second indicated that "a sum not exceeding four millions of dollars, exclusive of the money which Mr. Adams may obtain by the loan now negotiating in Holland, be borrowed in Europe on the faith of the United States of America, and applied towards defraying the expences . . . for carrying on the war." The third instructed BF to communicate that resolution to Louis XVI, along with assurances of gratitude and an explanation of the necessity of a new application to him: *JCC*, XXIII, 576–9.

Individual copies of the latter two resolutions are with BF's papers at the Hist. Soc. of Pa. He endorsed the first, "More Money to be borrowed." He endorsed the second, "Necessity of the Application for more Money." Robert Morris enclosed copies of these resolutions in his letter of Sept. 27, appending the latest resolution of Sept. 23. BF endorsed that sheet, "Money! Money!" (University of Pa. Library.)

2. The remainder of this paragraph is in cipher, except for a few scattered words. We print BF's decipher.

3. BF had L'Air de Lamotte copy the text of this postscript down to the brace (which he added). He sent that extract to Vergennes on Nov. 8.

I have the honor to be sir With great respect & esteem Your most obt humble servt. ROBT. R LIVINGSTON

No. 18

Endorsements: No 17 & 18 Mr Secry. Livingston Sept. 13. 1782— Abbé Raynal's Work— Extreme Want of Money / No 4[4]

From Jonathan Nesbitt   ALS: American Philosophical Society

Sir   L'Orient Septr. 13: 1782

I take the liberty to request that your Excellency will furnish me with a Commission, to Command a *Letter of Marque*, for Captain Thomas Bell,[5] formerly Commander of the Luzerne, now of the Renette, bound from this Port to Philadelphia;— I must likewise trouble your Excellency for Copy of the Instructions, and Bond that is given on receiving a Commission, the latter of which shall be immediately return'd you in form.

I have the honor to remain wth. the highest respect. Your Excellencys most Obedt. & very humble Servt. JONATN: NESBITT

His Excellency Benjn: Franklin Esqr

Addressed: Son Excellence / Benjn. Franklin / Ministre plenipotentiaire des / Etats unis de L'Amerique / a Passy / pres Paris

Notation: Jona. Nesbitt L'Orient Sept. 13. 1782.

From ——— Bouchet   ALS: American Philosophical Society

Monsieur   Paris Le samedi, 14e 7bre 1782

Je reçois une lettre de Mademoiselle Aléxandre, de St Germain, qui me charge de vous demander un paquet, contenant un corps, des Souliers &a, pour Madame Williams, de Nantes.[6]

---

4. A reference to Cipher No. 4: XXXVI, 262.

5. Nesbitt had been instrumental in obtaining Bell's exchange at the beginning of 1782: XXXVI, 377.

6. William Alexander's three unmarried daughters, Bethia, Christine, and

Si vous ne lui avez pas encore fait passer ces objets, je vous prie, Monsieur, de vouloir bien me les envoyer. J'ai l'honneur de vous inviter à y joindre tout ce qui peut vous obliger: je serai enchanté de m'en charger & de vous rendre service. Je pars Lundi pour Nantes, ou je me rends dans deux ou trois jours: ma voiture est commode & je peux y placer bien des choses sans me gêner.

Je suis avec un profond respect Monsieur Votre très humble & très Obéissant serviteur BOUCHET
Logé à L'hotel du nom de Jesus
rue de la comédie italienne

Notations in different hands: Bouchet 14. 7bre. 1782. / Repd—

From John MacMahon: Prescription and Directions

(I) Press copy of ADS: Library of Congress; (II) ALS and press copy of ALS: Library of Congress

I.

ce 14 septbre. [1782?][7]
Huit paquets de sel de Glauber,[8] chacun d'une demi-once.
Six prises de pilules de Starkey,[9] chacune de quatre graines.
Pour son Excellence M. Franklin   Mc. M

[*In William Temple Franklin's hand:*] De plus Une once d'Emulsion, edulcorée avec une Once de Syrop de Diacode[1]

Jane, lived with him at Saint-Germain-en-Laye: XXIX, 534n. Their sister Mariamne Williams was recuperating from the birth and untimely death of her second daughter: JW to BF, Aug. 23 and Sept. 10.

7. Though BF was ill in subsequent autumns, his suffering in mid-September, 1782, was particularly acute. We therefore suspect that this prescription was a follow-up on MacMahon's prescription of Aug. 23–24, above. For BF's own concern over his situation at this time see his letters to Lafayette, Sept. 13 and 17; to Hartley, Sept. 17; and to Jay, Sept. 17.

8. Sodium sulphate, which was used as a cathartic and a diuretic, and introduced by the German physician and chemist Johann Rudolph Glauber of Amsterdam *c.* 1650: J. Worth Estes, *Dictionary of Protopharmacology: Therapeutic Practices, 1700–1850* (Canton, Mass., 1990), pp. 90, 205.

9. An opiate devised by George Starkey in London in the seventeenth century: *ibid.*, p. 182.

1. A narcotic which MacMahon also prescribed in August.

II.

sept. the 14th. [1782?]

An ounce of wild succory roots[2] is to be boiled in a quart of water, during seven or eight minutes.

Strain the decoction and dissolve in it one of the packets of salt.

This is to be drank every morning fasting, by glasses of a quarter of an hour's distance between each glass.

One of Starkey's pills is to be taken every night.

They are a little laxative and anodyne. Mc. M.

From Jonathan Williams, Jr. Copy: Yale University Library

Dr & Hond Sir Nantes Sept 14 1782

Mr Louis Tardy informs me that he could obtain an advantageous protection for his Brother who is lately gone to St Domingo if you would kindly signify a favourable opinion of him.[3] I therefore do not hesitate to assure you that the person in question Mr Gabriel Tardy has been near 5 years with me and I can with truth declare him to be an honest, industrious & intelligent young man possessing the strickest principles of Probity honour and Morality. I am as ever most dutifully and affectionately

His Excellency Doctor Franklin Passy

2. Or chicory; a cathartic or intestinal tonic: Estes, *Dictionary,* p. 47.

3. BF must have met Gabriel Tardy when JW sent him to Passy in June with a letter of introduction: XXXVII, 516–17. He left Nantes for the West Indies the following month: XXXVII, 670. He was the brother of the Paris merchant Louis Tardy (XXIX, 260): JW to Louis Tardy, Jan. 14, 1781 (Yale University Library).

From John Carroll[4]

AL: American Philosophical Society

Sep 15. 1782

The Revd. Mr. John Carroll whom Docr. Franklin may remember by the Campn. into Canada presents his comps. & requests the Docr. to do him the favor to forward the inlosd Letter for Liege[5] by post— His care is requested of the other to forward when a favourable oppy offers—

Addressed: His Excelly / Docr Franklin / Passy / near / Paris— / to be Sent under Cover by Mr Livingston

From Henry Wyld

ALS: Historical Society of Pennsylvania

Most Excellent sir,   Londonderry 15th. sepr. 1782

Yours on the 31st. April duly came to hand with those inclosed, addressed to M.——— E——— C[6] our London friend, I desire to be forgiven respecting forms, all I have to say, is that on our arrival at L,Derry we were apprehended and committed to Goal,[7] we are now liberated upon giving security for our ap-

---

4. The Catholic priest who accompanied his cousin Charles Carroll, Samuel Chase, and BF on their mission to Canada in 1776: XXII, 380, 431–2n. Since then John Carroll had been living on his mother's plantation at Rock Creek, Maryland, and serving local congregations: Annabelle M. Melville, *John Carroll of Baltimore: Founder of the American Catholic Hierarchy* (New York, 1955), pp. 54–5.

5. Carroll attended the academy at Liège in the late 1750s and was ordained there a decade later. He maintained a keen interest in the school and individuals associated with it: Thomas O'Brien Hanley, ed., *The John Carroll Papers* (3 vols., Notre Dame, Ind., and London, 1976), I, xlvi, 63, 65.

6. Edmund Clegg.

7. The group was betrayed by John Swindell, who turned informer in early August; see XXXVII, 742–3. On Sept. 12 Swindell wrote directly to the mayor of Londonderry with an updated version of intelligence he had already disclosed to Whitehall: Wyld would be carrying BF's passport and recommendation concealed either in the binding of his bible, in the lining of his boot, or in a cavity in the head of his crutch. On Sept. 14 he added that William Schofield, "being a weak man in his intellects," would likely turn evidence, and that Mr. Wood, who had arranged for their ship, had fled soon after the emigrants were seized. PRO.

pearance when called for, what the End may be I cannot say, but our determinations are still the same 'tho frustrated at present,[8] and in hopes of meriting a Continuance of your Friendship on future Occations, am Your excellency's Most obedient humble servant   HENRY WYLD

Addressed: Mr. Ferdinand Grand Mercht. / Paris

Notation: Henry Wyld 15 Sept. 1782.

From Samuel Beall[9]

Two ALS and copy:[1] American Philosophical Society

Sir: Williamsburg Sept. 16. 1782
    At the desire of Mrs. Evans, I have taken the liberty of troubling you with the inclosed letters, and bills of Exchange for sev-

---

8. David Young of Londonderry posted bail for the prisoners, and they were released in two days. The legal charges against them were eventually dropped when it was determined that their desire to emigrate to Pennsylvania did not constitute smuggling industrial secrets to a foreign nation: Young to Edward Newenham, Dec. 13, 1782, APS; and see Robert Glen, "Industrial Wayfarers: Benjamin Franklin and a Case of Machine Smuggling in the 1780s," *Business History*, XXIII (1981), 316, 324. The men were soon hired by Robert Brooke for his newly established textile manufactory in Prosperous, near Dublin. According to British intelligence, the emigrants surrendered to Brooke BF's passport and recommendation (which had eluded the officers' searches, and which are now missing): Lord Lieut. Temple to Thomas Townshend, Sept. 25 [1783, *i.e.* 1782], British Library.
    9. A merchant based in Williamsburg: "Personal Notices from the Virginia Gazette," *W&MQ*, 1st ser., XII (1903), 26.
    This letter concerns BF's involvement with Ann Hudson de Lavau (also called "Loviel" and "Loviet"), who first sought his assistance in August, 1781; see XXXV, 376–7, where our overview of the story does not take note of the present letter. She must have applied to him again in early October, 1782, before he received the present letter, as he issued her a passport for Rochefort on Oct. 3 from whence he expected her to sail to America: XXXVI, 380.
    1. The two ALS differ slightly in wording. The copy (which is of the ALS we publish) is in BF's hand, and is attested by him as a true copy. BF also copied one of the marriage certificates that Lavau's mother sent from Virginia (APS). It differs from the one cited in the note below in that two additional witnesses are listed. BF may have copied these documents for Lenoir, whom he had asked to intercede in this affair: XXXV, 376–7.

enty two dollars, for Mrs. Loviel her daughter. You will see by her letters, which I am desired to send open to you, that she is very desirous of getting her daughter back to Virginia, and I have engaged that I will pay her passage on her arrival, which you may depend I will do to the commander of any Vessel that will receive Her.—[2] I have the honor to be, sr. Your mo Ob st

SAMUEL BEALL

Addressed:[3] The Honble / Benjamin Franklin Esqr. / Minister Plenipotentiary / from the United States of / America to the Court of France, / at, Paris.

From William Bell

ALS: Historical Society of Pennsylvania

Dear Sir   Ostend September 16th 1782

Agreable to my promise, I here Inform you that I shall (wind & Weather permitting) sail for Philadelphia the 1th of next Month—[4] Should you have any commands that may be in my

---

2. Ann Hudson de Lavau had written two letters to her mother, Ann Evans, presumably in early summer, detailing her misfortunes and mentioning BF's assistance. Evans and a close family friend hastily wrote the answers that Beall forwarded. They both assured her that they could prove she was married, and they urged her to return home immediately. Evans sent a certificate attesting to her daughter's marriage to Charles Loviet in May, 1780 (promising to send two others by different conveyances), and enclosed care of BF a bill of exchange to pay the passage home. The friend's letter further explained that Evans was herself extremely ill: Ann Evans to Ann Loviet [Lavau], July 24, [1782], with a Sept. 20 postscript by James Anthony; Christiana Vaughan to Loviet [Lavau], July 24, 1782; certificate by Anglican clergyman Thomas Price, July 22, 1782; all at the APS.

Two sets of these letters were sent to BF (covered by Beall's two ALS), as was explained to Lavau by another family friend. Evans had originally sent copies to BF by mistake, and then sent the originals at the first opportunity: Rosette Broomfield to [Ann Hudson de Lavau], undated, APS. BF forwarded one set to Lavau on Aug. 10, 1783.

3. On the address sheet of the second ALS is written the following name and address: "Saudot Graveur rue de la Tannerie maison de M. Belmont". Saudot came to Passy in December; see Pierres to BF, Dec. 14.

4. Bell arrived in Philadelphia by Jan. 20, and established himself as a grocer: *Morris Papers*, VII, 325; *Laurens Papers*, XVI, 1n. Sally Beckwith, who had

power to execute, and will let me have them in time, they will merit my utmost attention; as it will at all times give me great Pleasure to shew you my Gratitude— I have nothing new to Communicate worth your notice having no late letters from Philadelphia—my best wishes attend you, and am Dear Sir, your most Obt. Huble Servt. WILLIAM BELL

His Excellency Benjamin Franklin Esqr.

From Samuel Courtauld II

ALS: Historical Society of Pennsylvania

Sir   Paris 16 sepr. 1782

I always flatter'd myself that the recommendations I had the honor to deliver you on my Arrival here, were such, as might have secur'd me your Confidence,[5] but am sorry to find they seem to have produc'd the Contrary Effect— I am totally Ignorant of the cause, being confident I have acted with Propriety:

Least you shou'd be tempted to think I might make an ungenerous use of the kind letter of Introduction you gave me for Mr. Franklyn your Son in Law[6] I here take the liberty of Returning it:

I have the honor to be Sir Your most Obedient & most humble Servt.   SAML. COURTAULD

---

been traveling with him, must have sailed on the same ship as she arrived in Philadelphia around the same time: SB to BF, Jan. 24, 1783 (two letters, APS).

5. For Courtauld and the letters he brought BF from Richard Price and Benjamin Vaughan in early 1782 see XXXVI, 406n.

6. He must mean RB. The letter has not been found, but Courtauld, who earlier signed an oath of allegiance to the United States and received a passport from BF, did eventually immigrate to Philadelphia, where he became a merchant and married Sarah Norris Wharton: XXXVI, 406n; XXXVII, 132n; Anne H. Wharton, "The Wharton Family," *PMHB*, II (1878), 211.

From Antoine-Nicholas Servin,[7] with Franklin's Note
for a Reply
ALS: Historical Society of Pennsylvania

Monsieur Le Docteur   a Dieppe 16 7bre. 1782

Je viens de faire imprimer a Basle un ouvrage Sur La Législation Criminelle Auquel le Celebre Monsieur Iselin a joint des observations de Sa façon.[8] Je Vous prie de permettre Que mon Libraire Vous en adresse un Exemplaire par la poste. C'est un hommage Que je dois a un des plus Grands hommes d'etat et des Scavans Les plus distingués de l'univers. J'ose Esperer Que Vous ne le refuserez pas et que Vous y Verrez un gage de La haute Estime et du respect profond Avec lequel je Suis De votre Excellence Monsieur Le Docteur Le trés humble & trés obéissant Serviteur   SERVIN

avocat au parl. de Rouen

Endorsed: That I should be glad to see the Work mention'd, being curious of every Thing on that important Subject. That I shall esteem the Present propos'd as a great Honour, & be much oblig'd by it hoping it may [*be*] of Service to our new States in America &c. &c[9]

Notation: Servin 16. 7bre. 1782.

7. Servin (1746–1811) was a well-regarded lawyer at Rouen and the author of *Histoire de la ville de Rouen . . .* (2 vols., Rouen, 1775). His works on jurisprudence included the study mentioned in the present letter and *Manuel de jurisprudence naturelle* (Paris, 1784): Larousse; Quérard, *France littéraire.*

8. Though completed in 1778, *De la législation criminelle* (Basel, 1782) was twice refused publication and distribution in France because of its articles on incest and crimes against nature, among others. Servin's friend Isaac Iselin (1728–1782), jurisconsult, co-founder of the Société helvétique, and author of several philosophical works, had the work published at Basel and appended his own *Considérations générales sur les loix et sur les tribunaux:* Quérard, *France littéraire; Nouvelle biographie* under Servin; Larousse under Iselin.

9. The letter BF sketched here, now missing, was dated Nov. 16: Servin to BF, Jan. 13, below.

To David Hartley   LS:[1] Yale University Library

My dear Friend,   Passy, Sept. 17. 1782.

Since those acknowledg'd in my last, I have received your Several Favours of Aug. 16. 20. & 26.[2] I have been a long time afflicted with the Gravel & Gout, which have much indispos'd me for writing: I am even now in Pain, but will not longer delay some answer.

I did not perfectly comprehend the Nature of your Appointment respecting the Refugees, and I suppos'd you would in a Subsequent Letter explain it: But as I now find you have declin'd the Service[3] such Explanation is become unnecessary.

I did receive the Paper you enquire about intitled *Preliminaries* and dated May 1782.[4] but it was from you, and I know nothing of their having been communicated to this Court. The third Proposition "that in Case the Negociation between great Britain and the Allies of America should not succeed, but War continue between them, America should act, and be treated as a Neutral Nation," appear'd at first Sight inadmissible being contrary to our Treaty— The Truce seems not to have been desired by any of the Parties.

With regard to the Iron Plates, your Arguments in the Letter to Count Sarsefield seem to me conclusive. Iron Plates horizontally placed will have no farther Effect towards inviting the Lightning as Conductors, than in Proportion to their Thickness. If placed vertically indeed it would be in proportion to their Height. There is a new Book printed this Year at Strasbourg entitled, *Moyens de preserver les Édifices d'Incendies, et d'empecher le Progrès des Flammes, par M. Piroux*.[5] There are some good Things in it. If you cannot find it at London, I will send it to you.

1. In L'Air de Lamotte's hand.
2. Only the letter of Aug. 16 is extant. BF's last known letter to Hartley is dated July 10: XXXVII, 607–8.
3. See Hartley's Aug. 16 letter.
4. XXXVII, 369–70.
5. Piroux, an architect at Nancy, had won a prize for this memoir from the Académie royale de Nancy in 1781. It was published at Strasbourg in 1782: Quérard, *France littéraire*.

With unalterable Esteem and affection, I am, my dear Friend, ever Yours   B FRANKLIN

David Hartley Esqe.

Addressed: To / David Hartley Esqr. / M. P. Golden Square / London

Endorsed: D F Sept 17 1782

To [John Jay][6]   ALS: American Philosophical Society

Dear Sir,   Passy, Sept. 17. 1782
   I have just receiv'd the Enclos'd from Mr E. Bridgen of London. Please to return me his Letter.
   I long to finish my private Affair you are so good as to assist me in, & shall be glad to receive the additional Provisions you intended, that I may copy the whole, for I think my present Situation more hazardous than those about me seem to imagine.[7]
   With sincere Esteem, I am, Dear Sir, Your most obedient humble Servant   B FRANKLIN

From Lafayette   ALS: University of Pennsylvania Library

My dear Sir   Paris Septembre 17h 1782
   Every Child of Mine that Comes to Light is a Small Addition to the Number of American Citizens— I Have the pleasure to inform You that, tho she Was But Seven Month Advanced, Mde

6. Identified on the basis of Bridgen's enclosure, mentioned in the first sentence, which was addressed to Jay. See Bridgen to BF, Sept. 6.
   7. In light of BF's fears about his health, we believe that he had asked Jay to help him revise his will. Though there are no further allusions to this "private affair" during the period the men were in France, after they returned to America BF asked Jay to send him a copy of his will, since Jay was the only person "on this Side the Water" who had one: BF to Jay, Aug. 24, 1786, in Smyth, *Writings,* IX, 537–8. Elkanah Watson also feared that BF was dying; see the headnote to MacMahon's prescription and directions, Aug. 23.

de Lafayette Has this Morning Become Mother of a daughter Who However delicate in his Begining Enjoys a perfect Health, and I Hope Will Soon grow Equal to the Heartiest Children.

This Reminds me of our Noble Revolution, into Which We Were forced sooner than it ought to Have Been Begun— But our Strength Came on Very fast, and Upon the whole I think We did *at least* as Well as Any other people.

They Ask'd me What Name My daughter is to Have— I want to present Her as an offering to My Western Country— And As there is a good *Sainte* By the Name of Virginie, I Was thinking if it Was not presuming too Much to Let Her Bear a Name Similar to that of one of the United States.[8]

With the Highest Regard and Most Lively Affection I Have the Honor to be My dear Sir Your obedient Humble Servant

LAFAYETTE

forgive the Hand writing, But I am in Hurry[9]

His Excellency M. franklin

Notation: La Fayette. Sept. 17. 1782

To Lafayette   Press copy of ALS: University of Pennsylvania Library

Dear Sir   Passy, Sept. 17. 1782

I continue to suffer from this cruel Gout: But in the midst of my Pain the News of Made [Madame] de la Fayette's safe Delivery, and your Acquisition of a Daughter gives me Pleasure.

In naming our Children I think you do well to begin with the most antient State. And as we cannot have too many of so good a Race, I hope you & Me. de la Fayette will go thro' the Thir-

8. Marie-Antoinette-Virginie du Motier de Lafayette (1782–1849) was the fourth and last child of the marquis and marquise: Idzerda, *Lafayette Papers,* I, xliv; v, 457.

9. BF also received from Lafayette a birth announcement, handwritten by a secretary and dated Sept. 17 (APS). Lafayette's apology about his handwriting (which is no worse here than usual) refers to BF's quip on Sept. 13, above.

teen. But as that may be in the [common?] Way too severe a Task for her delicate Frame, and Children of Seven Months may become as Strong as those of Nine, I consent to the Abridgement of Two Months for each; and I wish her to spend the Twenty-six Months so gained, in perfect Ease, Health & Pleasure.

While you are proceeding, I hope our States will some of them new-name themselves. Miss Virginia, Miss Carolina, & Miss Georgiana will sound prettily enough for the Girls; but Massachusetts & Connecticut, are too harsh even for the Boys, unless they were to be Savages.[1]

That God may bless you in the Event of this Day as in every other, prays Your affectionate Friend & Servant   B FRANKLIN

From Castries[2]

Copy: Archives de la Marine

Paris ce 17 7bre. 1782.

Vos preposés, Monsieur, ont été chargés jusqu'a ce moment de traiter par Eux memes les objets qui regardent Le service des Etats unis de L'amerique, cette disposition doit etre suivie relativement au batiment qui Se trouve a rochefort et qui parait Exiger des reparations. Il en est de meme pour Les munitions qui sont deposées a Brest. Le gouvernement ne peut Se charger de vous procurer les moyens de les faire transporter, mais il Se pretera volontiers a vous accorder toutes Les facilités qui dependront de lui pour applanir Les difficultés qui pourraient Se rencontrer dans vos Expeditions. Je donne en consequence des ordres a rochefort pour qu'on favorise les demandes de vos preposés autant que Les moyens du port seront dans le cas d'y Satisfaire sans nuire au service du roy.

Jai &

1. The birth of Lafayette's daughter and the essence of the present response were reported in Bachaumont, *Mémoires secrets*, where BF was said to have doubts about the names "M. Connecticut ou Mlle. Massa-Chusset's Bay": XXI, 125–6.

2. In answer to BF's Sept. 7 letter.

de la main du Mtre. [Ministre] je donne en conséquence des ordres a Rochefort Nantes et L'orient. / .

M. franklin.

From Francis Xavier Schwediauer[3]

AL: American Philosophical Society

17th. Septemb. 1782. chez Mr. Folliart Apothicaire Ruë St. Dominique Fauxbourg St. Germain. Dr. Schwediauer Physician from Vienna and fellow-traveler of Dr. Ingenhousz in his last journey to England,[4] now coming from London, presents his respectful Compliments to Dr. B. Franklin, and wishes the Satisfaction of being acquainted with the Dr., especially as he is able to communicate to him, a plan of a code of penal laws, which might be agreable to him to See, and which might prove a very useful one to any nation who is interested to possess a code of that Kind, founded on the only right principle, The *Principle* of utility of the community.[5] Tho' this

3. The Austrian-born physician, scientist, and philosopher (1748–1824) who settled in London in the mid-1770s. He practiced medicine in both London and Edinburgh. In 1783 he presented "An Account of Ambergrise" to the Royal Society: *Phil. Trans.*, LXXIII (1783), 226–41. He translated works on medical and scientific subjects, published studies of venereal disease, and wrote a series of political and philosophical pieces that were compiled in *The Philosophical Dictionary . . .* (4 vols., London and Edinburgh, 1786): *ADB;* Larousse under Schwediauer and Swediaur; Quérard, *France littéraire.*

4. In 1778: XXVI, 67–70, 625.

5. This was Jeremy Bentham's introduction to a never-completed penal code which defined his political and ethical theory of utility. After meeting Schwediauer in 1778 and learning of his distinguished acquaintances, Bentham determined to use him as a means to introduce his ideas abroad. Schwediauer's friendship with Ingenhousz would provide Bentham a "ladder by which my Code . . . might be hoisted up to Franklin. Code might do for America when settled." Bentham had the introduction printed in 1780 and at that time drafted letters to sovereigns and ministers of various nations: Timothy L. S. Sprigge *et al.*, eds., *The Correspondence of Jeremy Bentham* (11 vols. to date, London, 1968–), I, xxviii–xxxi; II, 179–80, 182–3, 414n, 416–18. Bentham's draft letter to BF is above, XXXII, 236, where we explain that BF never commented on the introduction, and that Bentham eventually published it in 1789.

code is not yet published, Dr. S. has leave to communicate it to Dr. F., and will wait on him any day and hour agreable to the Dr.[6]

Addressed: à Monsieur / Monsieur Le Docteur Franklin / Bassy

Notation: Dr. Schwediauer 17. Sept. 1782.

From Robert R. Livingston

Three LS and L:[7] University of Pennsylvania Library; AL (draft): New-York Historical Society; transcript: National Archives

Sir   Philadelphia 18th. Septr. 1782

Just after closing my dispatches, I was favoured with yours of April and the 25th. & 29th. of June—[8] The ships that brought them were so unfortunate as to be chased into the Delaware by a superior force— The Eagle was driven a shore and sunk— The Papers and Money were however hapily saved, and part of the Crew, but Captain Latouch not having been since heard of is supposed to be taken— The other ship has arrived safe with all the Passengers of both Ships.[9]

6. Schwediauer wrote Ingenhousz on Oct. 1 that he had seen BF, who was suffering some lameness: Julius Wiesner, *Jan Ingen-housz, Sein Leben und sein Wirken als Naturforscher und Arzt* (Vienna, 1905), p. 227. He reported to Bentham in mid-September that BF had nearly recovered from his acute attack of the gout: Sprigge *et al., The Correspondence of Bentham,* III, 142.

7. We publish the first LS, whose enciphered passage (discussed below) was deciphered by WTF. The other two LS (neither of which was deciphered) are both marked "triplicate," and the L is marked "duplicate." According to the transcript the present text was carried by the packet *Washington,* while the duplicate was carried by the ship *Nonsuch.*

8. Livingston was confused about the date of the April letter; in his draft, he first wrote "25" but amended that to "18th." The duplicate retains the first date, while the triplicates contain the second. BF's only extant letters to Livingston in April are dated April 8 and 12 (XXXVII, 112–14, 137–9). The June letters are in XXXVII, 535–9, 565–7.

9. The frigates *Aigle* and *Gloire* crossed the Atlantic together: XXXVII, 539–40n. The captain of the former, Louis-René-Madeleine Le Vassor de La Touche (XXVII, 78n; XXXIII, 151n), was taken prisoner to New York and then to England: Six, *Dictionnaire biographique;* G. Rutherford, "The Case of M. de la Touche," *Mariner's Mirror,* XXXIV (1948), 34–41. Most of the 70 barrels of specie (a total of 1,000,000 *l.t.*) carried by the *Aigle* were saved: Lee

As I am just about to leave town for a short time, I will not touch upon the important subjects mentioned in your Letters, which will on account of my abssence be committed to a special Committee—[1] I would only observe to you, that the Resolution in my last shews the sense of Congress on the subject of money matters[2] and will urge you to follow their Instructions at all Events: on their success depends being able to go on, if the War continues or to set down in Peace if Peace should come. An Army is not to be disbanded without Money nor is Money to be got in a Country distressed as ours is untill we have had a little breathing spel.

You will see by the anexed Resolutions, that Congress have refused to accept Mr Laurens's resignation, and that they have made some alteration in your powers—[3] I send the paper which contain the little news we have, and am Sir with great Respect and Esteem your most obed. humble Servant,

ROBT R LIVINGSTON

His Excellency Benjamin Franklin

No. 19.

Kennett, *The French Forces in America, 1780–1783* (Westport, Conn., and London, 1977), p. 67. See also *Gaz. de Leyde,* Nov. 15, 1782 (sup.).

1. In his June 25 letter, BF had mentioned Sweden's desire for a commercial treaty with the United States (XXXVII, 538). A congressional committee consisting of Arthur Lee, Ralph Izard, and James Duane considered the proposal, and on Sept. 19 Congress approved the idea and appointed the same delegates to draft a treaty, commission, and instructions: XXXVII, 567n.

2. The resolution, ordering BF to obtain a new loan of $4,000,000, was enclosed with Livingston's letter of Sept. 13, above. The remainder of this paragraph was encoded, and WTF noted next to his decipher "C. No 4." We silently correct from the draft one minor deciphering mistake.

3. The enclosed resolutions were passed on Sept. 17. The first responded to Laurens' letter of May 30, 1782, informing him that "his services in the execution of that trust [serving as peace commissioner] cannot be dispensed with." The second instructed BF, JA, Jay and Laurens to "punctually attend and assist in the negotiations for peace," and that "upon receiving information of the time and place appointed for opening the negotiations, [they were] immediately to give notice thereof to the rest that may be in Europe, in order that each may have a seasonable opportunity to take part in the trust reposed by the said commission, and earnestly enjoined by this act." *JCC,* XXIII, 584, 585.

Endorsed: No 19 Mr Secry. Livingston Sept. 18. 1782 Extreme Occasion for Money

From Philippe-Denis Pierres ᴌs: American Philosophical Society

Monsieur,   Paris, 18 7bre. 1782.

J'ai l'honneur de vous adresser un Exemplaire du Manuel d'Épictete en Grec que je viens d'Imprimer. Cet Exemplaire est tiré Sur le Papier que vous avez bien voulu me donner.[4] J'aurois desiré pouvoir vous le présenter relié; mais j'aurois craint que l'Impression n'eut maculé.

J'y joins, Monsieur, 4 Exemplaires imprimés Sur papier ordinaire. Je vous prie d'en donner un à Monsieur votre fils, & les trois autres aux personnes auxquelles ils pourront faire plaisir.

Je Suis avec respect, Monsieur, Votre très humble & très obéissant serviteur,   Pɪᴇʀʀᴇs
Impr. Ordre. du Roi.

M. franklin.

Notation: Pierres, Paris 18. 7bre. 1782.

To Pierres   ᴌs:[5] Alice T. Bates, Los Angeles, California (1956)

Passy le 20 sept. 1782.

J'ai reçu, Monsieur, avec la Lettre que vous m'avez fait l'honneur de m'ecrire, les 5 Exemplaires du Manuel d'Epictete en Grec, que vous avez eu la bonté de m'envoyer pour mes Amis et moi. Agréez je vous prie mes Remerciemens sinceres, pour ces Beautés Typographiques. On ne sauroit rendre un plus bel hommage à un Auteur: Epictete est ainsi rendu doublement immortel.

---

4. ʙғ had given Pierres a quantity of wove paper imported from England: xxxv, 635. This latest work was the diminutive *Épicteti Enchiridion*, ed. J.-B. Le Febvre de Villebrune (Paris, 1782), in 18°. In 1783 Pierres printed the same Greek text with a French translation.

5. In the hand of ᴡᴛғ.

J'ai l'honneur d'etre très parfaitement, Monsieur, votre très humble et très obeisant Serviteur.   B FRANKLIN

M. Pierres.

Addressed: A Monsieur / Monsieur Pierres, Imprimeur / Ordinaire du Roi, / rue St. Jacques

From Amelia Barry

ALS: American Philosophical Society

My Dear Sir,   Pisa 20th 7bre 1782
    Docr. Burrows, the Gentleman who will have the honor to present you this letter, is one of the few friends to whom I am under infinite obligations. During his residence in Tuscany, I have found united in his Person, the character of a skilful Phisician, and a most sincere Friend: To my lasting regret, he is going with his family, to England; should he meet with any obstacle at Paris, in the prosecution of his journey, I earnestly entreat your powerful exertions in his favor; and every attention you may shew Docr. Burrows I shall consider as most immediately extended to me. He will give you my revered paternal Friend, my news & I am sure your benevolent heart will sympathize in the misfortunes[6] of Most Dear Sir, Your grateful, affecate. & devoted   A. BARRY

His Excellency B. Franklin Esqr.[7]

Endorsed: 20 Sept. 82

Notation: A Barry 20 Sepr. 82

---

6. The death of her husband, who left her penniless: XXXVI, 207–8.
7. Barry folded this letter inside an address sheet from a letter she had received at the "Piaza St. Nicola Pisa." That sheet is now crowded with other names and addresses written by visitors to Passy. Burrows must have written his when he left this letter for BF: "Doctr. Burrows / Rue Gilt Cœur / Hotel de [*blank*] / vis a vis Le Commissaire / du coté de la rue St. Andre des Arts." The Baron de Hermelin, whom BF recommended to Livingston on Nov. 7 (below), wrote: "Samuel Gustaf Hermelin Conseiller des Mines in suede". Coulougnac (for whom see our annotation of BF to Morris, Dec. 14) wrote: "Coulougnac rüe des deux Boules hotel des Bourdonnois p une lettre de reccomandation au sujet d'une Creance de 85 mille Livres sur l'etat de Virginie".

From Samuel Cooper Johonnot

ALS: American Philosophical Society

Respected Sir   Geneva 20 Sep. 1782

Your Letter of the 11t Inst. Which put an End to your long Silence gave Me great Pleasure, but at the same Time I am surpriz'd at not receiving any News from America since the 3d February.[8] However I must take Patience. We are All well here & hope that is the Case with You,— I am perfectly sensible of the good Advice You give Me in your Letter, I shall make every Effort to persuade You that it is not lost upon Me,—. I am perfectly contented with my present Situation, & in wishing You every Blessing You can enjoy I subscribe Myself with the greates Respect & Gratitude Your Most humble & obedient Servant

                                    SAMUEL COOPER JOHONNOT.

N.B. Mr. Pigott present his respectful Compliments to You, & would write but He thinks He would not take up your precious Time.[9]— S. C J.

His Excellency Doctor Franklin.

Addressed: To His / Excellency Benjamin Franklin Esqr. / Passy / near / Paris

From Lafayette

AL: American Philosophical Society

                    Paris Saturday Evening [September 21, 1782?]

I am Very sorry, My Dear sir, I Have not the Pleasure to Wait Upon You this Evening— But Mr. jay Called at Half Past Eight and told me He Had Considered of the Affair Now in Question, And Before Any thing Was Determined He Wants to Have A

8. The last extant letter from BF is above, Jan. 25: XXXVI, 478. In that letter, as in the missing one here mentioned, BF forwarded letters from Boston and offered advice.

9. According to BFB's journal (XXXVII, 682n), he and Johonnot had dined with Robert Pigott (an "anglais fort riche") twice at his estate just outside Geneva, on Aug. 25 and on Sept. 8. On both occasions Benjamin Webb and his son Charles were present (XXXVI, 321–2).

long Conversation With You— He Will be at Passy to Morrow
Morning—[1] for My Part I see You Will not of Course Give me
Any Commands to Count de Vergennes, and Will therefore
Confine Myself to a Conversation Upon General terms—late as
it is I will Not trouble You, and Wish you a Better Night[2]—to
Morrow Evening I will do Myself the Honor to Pay My Respects
to You.

From Jonathan Williams, Jr.

ALS: American Philosophical Society

Dear & hond sir.   Nantes Sept. 21. 1782
    The Bearer of this Mr Natl Nelson is the son of a particular
Friend of mine now here, & his Object is a Visit to the other parts
of his Family in Ireland. This young Gentleman lately arrived
from Philadelphia whither he will probably return after having
seen his Friends & reestablished his Health, which is another
motive for his present Journey.
    I beg sir you will please to grant Mr Nelson the necessary
Passport and your notice & Civility to him during his stay will
much oblige Dear & hond sir Your dutifull & affece Kinsman[3]
                                            JONA WILLIAMS J.
His Excelly Doctor Franklin.

1. It may be that the "Affair Now in Question" concerned Rayneval's mission to England, for which see our headnote on Lafayette to BF, Sept. 12. According to Matthew Ridley, on Sept. 21 Jay and Lafayette had a long and testy discussion about why Rayneval was sent. The next day, Sunday, Jay went to Passy but Lafayette went to Versailles to see Vergennes, who (Lafayette claimed) told him for the first time that Rayneval was to see Shelburne. Vergennes was surprised that Jay knew about it, since he had only told two or three people: Klingelhofer, "Matthew Ridley's Diary," pp. 111–12.
    The "Affair" might also be the ongoing question of Oswald's commission. On Sept. 21 Ridley also wrote, "Dr. Franklin is not for Standing out for the previous acknowledgement of Independancy etc. and says it is a pity to keep 3 or 4 millions of People in War for the sake of Form etc."
    2. Ridley noted on Sept. 22 that BF was "much better": *ibid.*, p. 113.
    3. To the left of the signature, someone has sketched the profile of a man's head.

Notation: Jona. Williams Sept. 21st. 1782

To Jean-Louis Giraud Soulavie[4]

Copy, signed:[5] Historical Society of Pennsylvania; copies: American Philosophical Society (two), Indiana University

Sir   Passy. Sepr. 22d. 1782

I return the Papers with some corrections.[6] I did not[7] find Coal mines under the Calcareous rock in Derbyshire. I only remarked that at the lowest Part of that rocky Mountain which was in sight, there were Oyster Shells mixed with the Stone; & part of the high County of Derby being probably as much above the level

---

4. This letter was eventually published as "Conjectures concerning the formation of the Earth, &c. in a letter from Dr. B. Franklin, to the Abbé Soulavie": APS *Trans.*, III (1793), 1–5. BF gave it and several other pieces to the APS in 1788, after offering them first to the American Academy of Arts and Sciences in 1786 (BF to JW, Jan. 27, 1786, Yale University Library).

5. In the hand of Samuel Vaughan, Jr., and probably made in 1786 when he and BF were both in Philadelphia, and BF was organizing his papers. BF numbered the copy and wrote the explanatory note at the end; it is now in the William Smith Papers. The two copies at the APS are in the Benjamin Vaughan Papers; BFB wrote the first one, and Benjamin Vaughan copied BFB's version. BF made one emendation to BFB's copy (indicated in annotation below), and endorsed it, "Letter to M L'Abbé Soulavie, on some Parts of the Theory of the Earth." Vaughan turned that endorsement into a title. The copy at Indiana University is among JW's papers and is in the hand of L'Air de Lamotte. There is also a French translation by the abbé de La Roche at the Institut de France.

6. Soulavie had sent BF an account (now lost) of what he had understood BF to say about the earth's formation during an earlier conversation about geology and politics. He hoped to insert BF's views in vol. 5 of his *Histoire naturelle de la France méridionale*, which was already in press: XXXVII, 384–5; and see Soulavie's answer to the present letter, Oct. 21. The publication of vol. 5 was delayed until 1784 and did not, in the end, include BF's geological observations. Soulavie did mention them, however, in an account of their conversation which he published in 1801. The section of that published "conversation" that deals with geology, incorporating BF's views as expressed in the present letter, is in XXXV, 356–7.

7. On the copy made by BFB, BF here inserted the phrase "as you suppose." Benjamin Vaughan, copying BFB, followed suit. This insertion does not appear in the other copies or in the APS publication.

of the Sea, as the Coal Mines of Whitehaven were below, it seemed a proof that there had been a great Bouleversement in the Surface of that Island some part of it having been depressed under the Sea, & other Parts which had been under it being raised above it. Such Changes in the superficial Parts of the Globe seemed to me unlikely to happen if the Earth were solid to the Center. I therefore imagined that the internal parts might be a fluid more dense, & of greater specific gravity than any of the Solids we are acquainted with; which therefore might swim in or upon that Fluid. Thus the surface of the Globe would be a Shell, capable of being broken & disordered by the violent movements of the fluid on which it rested. And, as Air has been compressed by Art so as to be twice as dense as Water, in which case if such Air & Water could be contained in a strong glass Vessel, the Air would be seen to take the lowest place & the Water to float above & upon it; & as we know not yet the degree of Density to which Air may be compressed, & M. Amontons calculated, that its Density encreasing as it approached the Center in the same proportion as above the Surface it would at the depth of [*blank in MS*] Leagues be heavier than Gold,[8] possibly the Dense Fluid occupying the internal Parts of the Globe might be Air compressed. And as the force of Expansion in dense Air when heated is in proportion to its density; this central air might afford another Agent to move the Surface; as well as be of use in keeping alive the central fires:— Tho' as you observe the sudden Rarefaction of Water coming into Contact with those fires, may be an Agent sufficiently strong for that purpose, when acting between the incumbent Earth & the fluid on which it rests.

If one might indulge Imagination in supposing how such a Globe was formed, I should conceive, that all the Elements in separate Particles being originally mixed in confusion & occupying a great Space they would as soon as the Almighty Fiat or-

---

8. Guillaume Amontons (1663–1705) found that at 19 leagues air would equal gold in density: "Sur le nouveau thermometre de M. Amontons," *Histoire de l'Académie royale des sciences* for 1703, pp. 7–8. The blank space in BF's letter was preserved in all copies and in the APS publication. The abbé de La Roche, in his French translation (noted above), filled in the blank with the number 7.

dained Gravity or the mutual Attraction of certain Parts, & the mutual repulsion of other Parts to exist all move towards their common Center: That the Air being a fluid whose Parts repel each other, though drawn to the Common Center by their Gravity, would be densest towards the Center & rarer as more remote; consequently all Matter lighter than the central Parts of that Air, & immersed in it, would recede from the Center & rise till they arrived at the region of the Air which was of the same specific Gravity with themselves, where they would rest; while other Matter, mixed with the lighter Air would descend & the two meeting would form the Shell of the first Earth leaving the upper Atmosphere nearly clear. The original Movement of the Parts towards their common Center would[9] form a Whirl there; which would continue in the turning of the new formed Globe upon its Axis & the greatest Diameter of the Shell would be in its Equator. If by any Accident afterwards the Axis should be changed, the dense internal Fluid by altering its form must burst the Shell & throw all its Substance into the confusion in which we find it. I will not trouble you at present with my fancies concerning the manner of forming the rest of our System. Superior Beings smile at our theories & at our presumption in making them. I will just mention that your observation on the Ferruginous Nature of the Lava which is thrown out from the Depths of our Volcanoes gave me great pleasure. It has long been a supposition of mine that the Iron contained in the substance of the Globe has made it capable of becoming, as it is, a Great Magnet. That the Fluid of magnetism exists perhaps in all space; so that there is a Magnetical North & South of the Universe as well as of this Globe, & that if it were possible for a man to fly from Star to Star he might govern his course by the Compass. That it was by the Power of this general Magnetism this Globe became a particular Magnet. In soft or hot Iron the fluid of Magnetism is naturally diffused equally— When within the influence of a Magnet, it is drawn to one end of the Iron, made denser there & rarer at the other. While the Iron continues soft & hot it is only a temporary Magnet: If it cools or grows hard in

9. All other versions have "naturally" here.

that situation, it becomes a permanent one, the Magnetic fluid not easily resuming its Equilibrium. Perhaps it may be owing to the permanent Magnetism of this Globe, which it had not at first, that its Axis is at the present kept parallel to itself, & not liable to the changes it formerly suffered, which occasioned the Rupture of its Shell, the submersion & Emersions of its Lands & the confusions of its Seasons. The present Polar & equatorial Diameters differing from each other near ten Leagues. It is easy to conceive in case some Power should shift the Axis gradually, & place it in the present Equator, & make the New Equator pass through the present Poles, what a sinking of the Waters would happen in the present equatorial regions, & what a rising in the present polar Regions; so that vast tracts would be discovered that now are under Water, & others covered that now are dry, the Water rising & sinking in the different Extreams near five Leagues. Such an operation as this, possibly, occasioned much of Europe, & among the rest this Mountain of Passy on which I live, & which is composed of Limestone Rock & Seashells, to be abandoned by the Sea & to change its antient Climate, which seems to have been a hot One. The Globe being now become a permanent Magnet we are perhaps safe from any future change of its Axis. But we are still subject to the Accidents on the Surface which are occasioned by a Wave in the internal ponderous Fluid; & such a Wave is produced by the sudden violent Explosion you mention happening from the Junction of Water & fire under the Earth, which not only lifts the incumbent Earth that is over the Explosion, but impressing with the same force the fluid under it, creates a Wave that may run a thousand Leagues, lifting & thereby shaking successively all the countries under which it passes.[1] I know not whether I have expressed myself so clearly,

---

1. The translation by the abbé de La Roche added here the following sentence: "C'est du moins l'effet que m'ont dit avoir éprouvé des tremblemens de terres les personnes éclairées que j'ai consultées et qui se sont trouvées dans les cas de les observer Sur le continent de l'Europe et de l'amerique." In the margin next to "les personnes" La Roche added "M. Olavides." Pablo Antonio José de Olavide y Jáuregui (1725–1803), a Spanish statesman born in Peru, had witnessed the devastating earthquake of 1749 at Lima. He had been living in France since 1780. Javier Abués Villa et al., eds., Gran Enciclopedia de España (17 vols. to date, Zaragoza, 1990–); Larousse.

as not to get out of your Sight in these Reveries.— If they occasion any new enquiries & produce a better Hypothesis they will not be quite useless. You see I have given a loose to the Imagination, but I approve much more your Method of philosophizing, which proceeds upon actual Observation, makes a collection of facts, & concludes no farther than those facts will warrant. In my present circumstances, that mode of studying the Nature of the Globe is out of my Power & therefore I have permitted myself to wander a little in the wilds of fancy. With great Esteem I have the honor to be Sir &c,   B FRANKLIN

PS. I have heard that Chemists can by their art decompose Stone & Wood, extracting a considerable Quantity of Water from the one & Air from the other. It seems natural to conclude from this that Water & Air were ingredients in the original Composition. For Men cannot make new Matter of any kind. In the same manner may we not suppose, that when we consume Combustibles of all kinds, & produce Heat or light, we do not create that Heat or light; we only decompose a Substance which received it originally as a part of its composition? Heat may thus be considered as originally in a fluid State but attracted by organized Bodies in their growth, becomes a part of the Solid. Besides this, I can conceive that in the first Assemblage of the Particles of which this Earth is composed, each brought its Portion of the loose heat that had been connected with it, & the whole when pressed together produced the Internal fire which still subsists.

[*In Franklin's hand:*] Letter to Abbé Soulavie occasioned by his sending me some Notes he had taken of what I had said to him in Conversation on the Theory of the Earth. I wrote it to set him right in some Points wherein he had mistaken my Meaning.

No 1

From Alexandre-Théodore Brongniart[2]

ALS: American Philosophical Society

Monsieur   Ce dimanche 22. 7bre 1782

J'ai enfin obtenu du Sculpteur dont j'avois eu L'honneur de Vous parler, deux esquisses de Medailles assez grandes. J'ai priè aussi un peintre de Mes amis de dessiner Le meme sujet et je Crois qu'il y a bien Reussi.[3] Quel jour Voulez Vous, Monsieur, que Nous[4] allions a Passi pour avoir L'honneur de Vous presenter les ouvrages. Ou Si Vos affaires Vous appeloient a paris et que Vous Voulussiez Vous donner la peine de venir chez Moi Vous y trouveriez tout Reuni en me prevenant La veille. Mais la Seule grace que j'aye a Vous Demander C'est de Ne Vous gener nullement, trop heureux Si je puis avoir Secondé Vos idées.[5]

---

2. A member of the Académie royale d'architecture since 1781, Brongniart (1739–1815) was one of the most prominent architects in Paris. He had designed *hôtels* for the duc d'Orléans and the prince de Condé, and would later design the Père-Lachaise Cemetery and the Paris Bourse. *DBF;* Jane Turner, ed., *The Dictionary of Art* (34 vols., New York, 1996); *Almanach royal* for 1783, p. 523. Brongniart's brother Antoine-Louis had written BF in 1778: XXVI, 253.

3. Once BF received Livingston's encouragement to have a medal struck commemorating the victories of Yorktown and Saratoga, he wasted little time in searching for an artist to execute his design; see XXXVI, 644; XXXVII, 432, 732. He evidently employed Brongniart to serve as his agent. The two artists from whom Brongniart had obtained sketches were Augustin Dupré and Esprit-Antoine Gibelin. Dupré (1748–1833) was a goldsmith and medalist who was well known as an engraver of arms; in 1791 he would replace Duvivier as the chief engraver of the Paris Mint. Gibelin (1739–1813) was known primarily as a painter and muralist, and had executed important commissions for several public buildings including at least one that Brongniart designed; see the *DBF* and *The Dictionary of Art* for both artists. Despite the claim by Dupré's biographers that he and BF were friends, we have found no evidence that they were previously acquainted.

4. Brongniart was probably accompanied by Cadet de Vaux; see Cadet's letter of Jan. 13.

5. BF's original idea, conceived just after Yorktown, was to depict the infant Hercules in his cradle strangling two serpents, while Minerva as nurse, representing France, sat by with her spear and helmet: XXXVI, 644. As the sketches demonstrate, the conception had evolved by the time the artists were given their instructions. In all three sketches Minerva is actively defending the infant against an attacking leopard, representing England.

Preliminary Sketches for the Libertas Americana Medal

J'ai L'honneur d'etre avec Les Sentimens Les plus Respectueux Monsieur Votre tres humble et obeissant Serviteur
BRONGNIART
architecte du Roi Rue st Marc.

Notation: Brognard 22 7bre. 1782.

From Jonathan Shipley ALS: American Philosophical Society

My dear Sir   Chilbolton Sep: 22d [1782]

What excuse can I make for delaying to answer so kind so wise so delightful a Letter as I recievd from my ever honour'd Friend two Months ago?[6] I spent the Summer at my Diocese,[7] where I heard but little & could find no channel of correspondence. The Consequences of Ld Rockinghams Death[8] I doubt not, were sooner & more circumstantially known to You than to me: but I must still deny myself all reflections upon matters of that sort, tho I believe that no freindly communication of sentiments would be less likely to injure England or America than our own. You flatter my whole family extreamly in your kind remembrance of the too few & too short Visits, that formerly made us all so happy. I entirely agree with You in your Ideas of the high value We ought to set upon our Daughters. There is something in their little Habits of Kindness & Attention, which even

---

Gibelin placed a crown on the leopard's head, while Dupré situated Hercules on his father's shield rather than in a cradle. BF selected Dupré to engrave the dies.

For the history of the infant Hercules emblem see Winfried Schleiner, "The Infant Hercules: Franklin's Design for a Medal Commemorating American Liberty," *Eighteenth-Century Studies,* X (1976–77), 235–44. See also Lester C. Olson, *Benjamin Franklin's Vision of American Community: a Study in Rhetorical Iconology* (Columbia, S.C., 2004), pp. 147–55; Carl Zigrosser, "The Medallic Sketches of Augustin Dupré in American Collections," APS *Proc.,* CI (1957), 535–50.

6. It was actually three months ago: XXXVII, 457–8.

7. Shipley was the bishop of St. Asaph, an Anglican diocese in northern Wales.

8. Prime Minister Rockingham, Shelburne's predecessor, died on July 1: XXXVII, 598.

Friendship cannot supply. & I feel their use more advantageous to me every day, as the cares & infirmities of old Age come on; Sollicitæ lenimen dulce Senectæ.[9] I heartily wish You enjoyd this domestick happiness in as large a Family as mine. Your Breed is worth preserving. But if You should return, as We wish & You flatter us, with all your Merit & Honours to be more lov'd admird & valued than ever by your Friends in this Country, I promise at least that whenever You please You shall have your share & I believe the greatest share of the Kindness & Attention of my four Daughters. Did I ever tell You that one of them as She was reading Xenophon's Account of Socrates to her Mother, cried out, Mamma, Socrates talks just like Dr. Franklin.[1] But alas! the Happiness of seeing You again is what I hardly dare to hope for.

You are kind in expressing your Wishes for my Preferment, which however appears to me much less probable than to every body else.[2] I find it more easy to agree in condemning the late Ministry than in approving all the measures of the present; & after so long enjoying the pleasure of acting upon principle, I am determind not to part with it. That Pleasure & my Friendship & Veneration, for You will be some of the last & best feelings of my Heart.

I am, Dr Sir, Your ever affectionate   J St Asaph

9. The sweet consolation of old age: Ovid, *Metamorphoses*, VI, 500–1.

1. Shipley is referring to his daughter Georgiana who, when reading about Socrates in 1777, herself wrote to BF that she found many similarities between the two philosophers: XXIII, 305. Xenophon's *The Memorable Things of Socrates* was a work that BF consciously adopted as a model: *Autobiog.*, p. 64.

2. In June, Horace Walpole had predicted, erroneously, that Shipley would obtain the bishopric of Salisbury: Lewis, *Walpole Correspondence*, XXXIII, 338.

From Jonathan Nesbitt   ALS: American Philosophical Society

Sir   L'Orient Septbr. 23me. 1782
    The Captains Cain, Josiah & Deale, of the Ships St. James,
Lady Washington, & Queen of France, arrived in this port the
19th. Inst &, have communicated to me the Contents of a Letter
they have had the honor to address Your Excellency this day.[3]
These Gentlemen have from the first of the American War, engag'd their lives and Fortune in the Contest,[4] & I am convinced
in every respect prefer the publick Interest to their own. I therefore take the liberty in the warmest manner to second their request being well convinced that Your compliance therewith will
conduce to the Publick good.
    I have the honor to remain with Respect Your Excellency's
Most humble Servt.   JONATN: NESBITT

His Excellency Benj: Franklin Esqr. Passey

Addressed: His Excellency / Benjn: Franklin Esq / at / Passey
/ near / Paris

Notation: J. Nesbit 23 Sept 1782.

---

    3. The letter is missing. Alexander Cain, James Josiah, and Richard Dale
brought into Lorient the three prizes *Luxford, Lyon,* and *Will.* They wanted
instructions for what to do with the 90 prisoners: Nesbitt to WTF, Sept. 20,
1782 (APS).
    4. Dale (1756–1826) had served since 1776 in the Continental navy and
was an officer on the *Bonhomme Richard.* He had been imprisoned by the
British four times during the course of the war: xxx, 631; Gregory B. Keen,
"The Descendants of Jöran Kyn, the Founder of Upland," *PMHB,* IV
(1880), 495–500. Josiah (1751–1820), who on this cruise was part-owner of
both the *Queen of France* and the *Washington,* had also served in the Continental navy: William Bell Clark, "James Josiah, Master Mariner," *PMHB,*
LXXIX (1955), pp. 452–84. Cain (b. *c.* 1750) was part owner of the *St. James*
and had previously commanded several other privateers. For the maritime
careers and investments of all three see Claghorn, *Naval Officers;* William
Bell Clark *et al.,* eds., *Naval Documents of the American Revolution* (11 vols.
to date, Washington, D.C., 1964–), I, 1361; and Charles Henry Lincoln,
comp., *Naval Records of the American Revolution, 1775–1785* (Washington,
D.C., 1906).

From Benjamin Vaughan[5] ALS: Historical Society of Pennsylvania

Totteridge, Herts [Hertsfordshire],

My dearest sir,   Septr. 23rd, 1782.

Lest by some accident I should miss the opportunity of travelling with the courier, I sit down just to tell you that I am prepared to depart the instant I hear the commission is sealed,[6] which by the Chancellor having been at Buxton[7] has been for some days delayed.

I have got together the different articles committed to my care to procure, and shall not be long upon the road.[8]

I hope your health is better. Lord Shelburne has insisted on my bringing you a medicine to prevent a return of your complaints.[9] I beg my best regards to your son; and am, my dearest sir, your ever devoted, grateful, & affectionate

BENJN: VAUGHAN

5. Vaughan had left for England on Sept. 11; see Lafayette to BF, Sept. 12. He spent his final week in Totteridge with his pregnant wife Sarah: Craig C. Murray, "Benjamin Vaughan (1751–1835): the Life of an Anglo-American Intellectual" (unpublished Ph.D. diss., Columbia University, 1989), p. 107.

6. Vaughan was awaiting the sealed copy of Oswald's revised commission, which was drafted by Townshend on Sept. 19, presented to the cabinet that same day, and approved by the King on Sept. 21. The commission was sealed and ready on Sept. 24: Giunta, *Emerging Nation*, I, 582–4, 589; Fortescue, *Correspondence of George Third*, VI, 135; Morris, *Jay: Peace*, pp. 360–2. It incorporated the compromise that Jay and Oswald had agreed upon, altering one sentence to state that Oswald would be negotiating with representatives "of the Thirteen United States of America," listed by name; see our annotation of BF to Oswald, Sept. 8. As Independence would still be the first article of the treaty, however, the British could continue to regard it as conditional upon the conclusion of that treaty; see Harlow, *Second British Empire*, I, 285–7. Copies of the commission are in BF's and JA's legation letterbooks at the Library of Congress and the Mass. Hist. Soc.

7. During the autumn of 1782 Lord Chancellor Thurlow took the waters at Buxton: Robert Gore-Brown, *Chancellor Thurlow: the Life and Times of an XVIIIth Century Lawyer* (London, 1953), p. 206.

8. Vaughan returned to Paris on the morning of Sept. 27. He immediately wrote to WTF, telling him that WF was in England, that as soon as his luggage was recovered he would "give a good account of the commissions he was favored with from Passy," and that he would delay his visit until after Oswald had had a chance to confer with BF. APS.

9. This may have been "Adams's Solvent for the Stone," which Shelburne

Notation: Vaughan Septr. 23. 1782.

From Richard Oswald

Copies:[1] National Archives, Library of Congress (two), Massachusetts Historical Society; transcript: National Archives

Sir,   Paris 24. Sept. 1782

Having received by a Courier just now arrived, a Letter from Mr. Secy Townshend, in answer to mine which went by the Messenger dispatched from hence on the 12th.[2] I take this Opportunity of Mr. Whitefoord, to send you a Copy of it. I hope he will bring good Accounts of your Health, which I sincerely wish & am Your Excellency's most obedt humble Servant

(signed) RICHD. OSWALD.

Copy of a Letter from Richard Oswald Esqr to Benjamin Franklin Esqr.

---

later said he had recommended to BF via Vaughan: the marquess of Lansdowne (Shelburne) to BF, [Dec.] 11, [1784], Library of Congress. Vaughan had reported to Shelburne BF's problems with stones as soon as they began: Morris, *Jay: Peace,* p. 325.

1. We publish the one in WTF's hand. All the copies include the enclosure.
2. Oswald's messenger carried letters to Townshend of Sept. 10 and 11, for which see our annotation of BF to Oswald, Sept. 8. Townshend's answer, dated Sept. 20, announced that it had been agreed "to make the alteration in the Commission proposed to you by Mr. Jay": Giunta, *Emerging Nation,* 1, 585–6.

From the Board of Trustees of Dartmouth College[3]

ALS: University of Pennsylvania Library

Sir   University of Dartmouth September 24th. 1782

We could wish to avoid any seeming indelicacy in a matter, that respects your Excellency, by communicating an idea of the repeated and increasing joys, which are handed from breast to breast among the citizens of the empire of this western world— But permit us, Sir, to render a tribute of praise, that Providence has been propitious to honor our nation, and imbellish the present age, with the genius of philosophy, united with the virtues of a patriot, and the talents of a statesman.

From your known character we fondly perswade ourselves, Sir, that, while successfully attentive to the most interesting arts of national government, your mind is inspired with a love of other things, which are productive of happiness to mankind— We might mention particularly that extensive department, the cultivation of knowledge, and unbiassed virtue.

With these views, Sir, permit us to recommend to your particular attention and patronage the honorable John Wheelock Esquire, the worthy president of this institution; (accompanied by Mr. James Wheelock) and the design, which is the object of his attention.[4]

---

3. Dartmouth College was on the verge of financial collapse. Unable to raise funds in America, the trustees decided to seek assistance in France and the Netherlands. At their Sept. 20 meeting they elected their young president John Wheelock to make the trip with his brother James as companion and assistant. (At the same meeting they conferred an honorary degree upon JA.) The two men left Hanover on Nov. 1 and traveled to Philadelphia hoping to find passage to Europe; finding the Delaware blockaded, they went north to Boston and sailed for France on Jan. 3. Along the way they gathered letters of recommendation from eminent public officials (including George Washington) and personal friends of BF, which will be published or summarized below. The present letter is the official introduction from the college itself. See Leon B. Richardson, *History of Dartmouth College* (2 vols., Hanover, N.H., 1932), I, 205; Dick Hoefnagel, "Benjamin Franklin and the Wheelocks," Dartmouth College Library *Bulletin*, new ser., XXXI (1990), pp. 12–19.

4. John Wheelock (1754–1817), after serving in the Continental army, replaced his late father, Eleazar Wheelock (XIV, 219n), as president of Dartmouth College in October, 1779. James (1759–1835) was the youngest of

We beg leave to say, that the institution, founded on the most catholic and liberal basis, is unrestrained by the barrs of bigotry, and calculated for the furtherance of extensive knowledge and humanity; as your Excellency may see by the tenor of the recommendation herewith forwarded from his Excellency, the President, and the members of Congress; and others, the most eminent characters in these United States.[5]

In so usefull and benevolent a cause permit us, Sir, to solicit the favor of your friendship and influence, as a patron of learning, and of mankind.

We beg only to add our sincere wish, that you may long live to enjoy all that personal felicity, which is meritted by the greatest services to society, and the republic of letters.

We have the honor to be with the greatest respect, Sir, your Excellencys most obliged, obedient, and humble servants, Signed by order of the board of Trustees

BEZA WOODWARD[6]
Secretary

His Excellency Benjamin Franklin LLD &c &c &c

Eleazar Wheelock's eleven children: *ANB* under Eleazar and John Wheelock; Richardson, *History of Dartmouth College*, 1, 204; James D. McCallum, *Eleazar Wheelock: Founder of Dartmouth College* (Hanover, N.H., 1939), pp. 63n, 151–66.

5. Wheelock carried a large document on parchment that outlined the college's circumstances and recommended that assistance be sought in the United States and Europe. The document was probably drawn up in March, 1781, and it was signed by 39 prominent Americans between December, 1781, and November, 1782. George Washington was one of the first to sign, followed by other army generals; other signatories included Benjamin Lincoln, Robert Morris, Robert Livingston, presidents and governors of states, and delegates to Congress. An additional resolution was added on Sept. 20, 1782, authorizing John Wheelock to make this particular journey. A facsimile and transcription of the document is in Hoefnagel, "Benjamin Franklin and the Wheelocks," pp. 14–17.

6. Bezaleel Woodward (1745–1804) had served as president pro tempore after the death in April, 1779, of Eleazar Wheelock. He had held various positions at Wheelock's schools since 1766 and in 1772 married Wheelock's daughter Mary. He served as acting president of Dartmouth while John Wheelock was abroad: Franklin B. Dexter, *Biographical Sketches of the Graduates of Yale College . . .* (6 vols., New York, 1885–1912), III, 89–92; Richardson, *History of Dartmouth College*, 1, 15n, 101.

From Le Roy: Two Letters

(I) ALS: University of Pennsylvania Library; (II) AL: American Philosophical Society

I.

Wednesday morning [on or after September 25,[7] 1782]
I have read with great pleasure my Dear Doctor your ingenious Hypothesis about the cause of the extraordinary Motions of the Earth and certainly if one may Suppose The air at liberty in the internal part of the Earth and to be compressed by the internal atmosphere its density may be vastly great. I do not doubt but you have read Dr Halley's Hypothesis of an internal Globe moving in this part internal and pretending that the Surface of That *Enveloppe* was luminous or shining so that there might be there a new world of inhabitants.[8] I am very glad to find that I had the Same Idea with you of the whole Earth's being a magnet by the ferrugenious parts of which it is composed for it is what I writ in a paper for the Academy Long-time ago for I was but a very young man at that time. Your Idea of a magnetism General that extends through The whole Universe is really very grand and very curious and Seems to have many presumptions in its favour.— I do not know whether you will approve of some small alterations I have made in the translation of M De La Mothe.[9]

Accept My Dear Doctor of my Best compliments.   LE ROY

Addressed: a Monsieur / Monsieur Franklin

Notation: Le Roy.

---

7. The first Wednesday after Sept. 22, the date of BF's letter to Soulavie, which Le Roy is here discussing.

8. Halley postulated a globe suspended in the middle of the earth to explain the four magnetic poles. He conjectured that this globe might be somehow illuminated and capable of sustaining life: Edmond Halley, "An Account of the cause of the Change of the Variation of the Magnetical Needle, with an Hypothesis of the Structure of the Internal parts of the Earth," *Phil. Trans.*, XVI (1691), 563–78.

9. We have found no record of this translation by L'Air de Lamotte.

II.

[on or after September 25, 1782]
Mille Pardons mon cher et Illustre Docteur Si vous n'avez pas eu cette note sur la Condensation de l'air ce matin.

M. Boyle[1] a trouvé le moyen de rendre l'air 13 fois plus dense en le comprimant; d'autres pretendent lavoir réduit a un volume 60 fois plus petit. M. Hales l'a rendu 38 fois plus dense à l'aide d'une presse mais en faisant geler de l'eau dans une grande boule de fer il a réduit l'air en un volume 1828[2] fois plus petit.

Cependant M. Halley assure dans les Trans Philosophiques en conséquence d'expèriences faites à Londres et d'autres faites dans Lancienne Académie *Del Cimento*[3] qu'on peut en toute Sureté décider quil n'y a pas de force capable de reduire L'air a la 800me partie de Son volume Sur la surface de la terre cependant M. Amontons de notre Académie Soutient qu'il n'y a point de bornes à la Condensation de Lair et que ces bornes ne peuvent ètre que celles de Nos moyens.

A cette Occasion il est bon d'observer que M. Halley étant anterieur de nombre d'années à M. Hales et que ce dernier connoissant les Expèriences de L'autre et ce qu'il a ècrit il n'auroit pas avancé ce quil a avancé Sil ne l'avoit observé dans ses expèriences Etant un homme très exact d'ailleurs.

Voila Mon Illustre Docteur un extrait de ce que j'ai trouvé de

1. This paragraph and the one that follows are excerpted from Mathurin-Jacques Brisson, *Dictionnaire raisonné de physique* (2 vols., Paris, 1781), I, 145–6. They are taken from two contiguous paragraphs in the long entry on Air, and constitute the "extrait" from "Le Dictionnaire de Physique" to which Le Roy alludes later in the letter. Three of the four scientists mentioned in these paragraphs are Robert Boyle (1627–91), Stephen Hales (1677–1761), and Edmond Halley (1656?–1743), of the Royal Society. Guillaume Amontons of the Académie des sciences is identified in our annotation of BF to Soulavie, Sept. 22.

2. Le Roy mistranscribed this number; it should read 1838.

3. The Accademia del Cimento was established at Florence in 1657, and was the first organization dedicated exclusively to the making of scientific experiments. Its one publication was *Saggi di naturali esperienze* (Florence, 1667), translated into English in 1684. Incomplete French translations appeared in 1754 and 1755: W. E. Knowles Middleton, *The Experimenters; a Study of the Accademia del Cimento* (Baltimore and London, [1971]), pp. 1, 347–54.

mieux dans Le Dictionnaire de Physique qui a pris la Substance de celui de Muschenbroek.[4]

Je vous proposerois a game of Chess Si je n'attendois une Dame qui vient voir quelques experiences d'Electricité mais je crois qu'elle s'en ira vers les huit heures. Si cette heure n'est pas indüe Je suis à vos ordres.

Je vous écrivois ceci Mon Illustre Docteur hier précisément Lorsque cette Dame entroit. Je n'ai pu vous envoyer mon domestique et elle est restée par des contre tems que j'ai éprouvés dans mes expériences et vraiment Singuliers jusqu'a neuf heures du soir. J'ai craint que vous ne fussiez couché.

Je vous renvoye Le Mercure.

Addressed: A Monsieur / Monsieur Franklin / &c &c &c

From Benjamin Lincoln

LS: American Philosophical Society; copy: Archives du Ministère des affaires étrangères

Sir   War Office September 25. 1782

Congress has ordered me to prepare and lay before them a State of the pay Rations and Subsistence of the Officers and Men in the Armies of the different powers in Europe—as these often vary I have no means of procuring the necessary information with accuracy from any books I have seen— I am under the necessity therefore of requesting that your Excellency would be so good as to procure and forward to me the state of the pay Rations and Subsistance of the Officers and Men in the Service of france Spain and the Emperor of Germany.

The State of matters here your Excellency will receive from the Secretary of foreign affairs— I cannot however avoid men-

4. The relevant work by Petrus van Musschenbroek was *Cours de physique expérimentale et mathématique* (3 vols., Paris, 1769), translated from the Latin by Sigaud de La Fond. In his chapter on air, Musschenbroek discussed the findings of Boyle, Hales, and Halley; he credited Halley (which Brisson's entry did not), for claiming to have reduced air to a volume 60 times smaller: *Cours de physique . . .*, III,142.

tioning to you that we have now a better Army in the field than we have had at any time before—since the War, they are well clothed and are in high discipline—[5] Count Rochambeau a few days since was polite enough on seeing the American Troops to compliment the Commander in Chief with having a Prussian Army.[6]

The Troops of His most Christian Majesty are joining the Main Army on the Hudson—[7] I should be wanting in duty and must deny myself a particular pleasure did I not assure you that the order and regularity uniformly observed by this Army, and the chearfulness with which they have fought and bled in our Cause has endeared them to the people of America and they are held in esteem not merely by the thread of policy but by the permanent band of sincere friendship—there is the greatest harmony between the Troops of the two Armies and no other Contest but what arises from the Spirit of the Soldier and what ought to be considered an honourable pursuit—to excell in the field and in acts of politeness and generosity.

I have the honor to be, with perfect respect and Esteem, Your Excellency's most obedt. humble servant   B LINCOLN

His Excellency Benjamin Franklin Esquire.

Endorsed: Gen. Lincoln to BF. Sept. 25. 1782

5. Only a week later, however, Washington complained to Lincoln of the "discontents which . . . prevail universally throughout the army": *Morris Papers*, VI, 478n.

6. Rochambeau reviewed Washington's army on Sept. 22. He is rumored to have told Washington, "You must have signed an alliance with the king of Prussia. These troops are Prussians": Rice and Brown, eds., *Rochambeau's Army*, I, 78, 166; Lee Kennett, *The French Forces in America, 1780–1783* (Westport, Conn., and London, 1977), p. 162. The comparison, although flattering, was obvious: the American army was drilled in the Prussian manner and like the Prussian army wore blue uniforms.

7. Its stay was temporary; see Livingston to BF, Sept. 5.

From Robert Morris: Two Letters[8]

(I) LS: Yale University Library, Historical Society of Pennsylvania, American Philosophical Society; copy: Library of Congress; (II) LS: Yale University Library, Independence National Historical Park, Historical Society of Pennsylvania, American Philosophical Society; copy: Library of Congress

I.

Sir   Office of Finance 25th September 1782.

I do myself the Honor to enclose for your Perusal Acts of Congress of the twenty seventh of November and third of December 1781 and the fourteenth and twenty third Instant.[9] In Consequence I have to request that all Bills hitherto drawn by Authority of Congress be paid and the Accounts of those Transactions closed. After this is done, and I hope and believe that while I am writing this Letter it may have been already accomplished you will be freed from the Torment and Perplexity of attending to Money Matters. I am persuaded that this Consideration will be highly pleasing to you as such Things must necessarily interfere with your more important Attentions.

I have long since requested the Secretary of foreign Affairs to desire you would appoint an Agent or Attorney here to receive and remit your Salary which will be paid Quarterly,[1] in the mean Time it is paid to him for your Use. As to any contingent Expences which may arise I shall readily make the necessary Advances upon Mr. Livingston's Application. These Arrangements will I hope be both useful and agreable to you.

I am Sir with perfect Respect Your Excellency's most obedient & humble Servant   ROBT MORRIS

His Excellency Benjamin Franklin—

---

8. Letter (I) was sent to BF, JA, and Jay. Morris' letterbook copy (Library of Congress) lists the names of all three recipients and is labeled "Circular." See also *Morris Papers*, VI, 432n.

9. These acts gave Morris authority over American funds in Europe. For the 1781 acts see XXXVI, 128n, 192n, 502. The September, 1782, acts are in *JCC*, XXIII, 575–6, 594–5. The latter specifically forbade Thomas Barclay from drawing any funds on the account of the United States without prior authorization from Morris or Congress.

1. BF had already asked Morris to be his agent: XXXVII, 738.

Endorsed: Office of Finance Sept. 25. 1782

II.

Sir   Office of Finance 25th. September 1782.

In my Letter of the 27th of November last I requested your Excellency to cause Purchases to be made of certain Articles contained in an Invoice exhibited to me from the War Office.[2] The Difficulties which have hitherto attended every Purchase and Shipment of Goods on public Account and other Circumstances have determined me to obtain all future Supplies by Contracts here, and therefore I am to request that no future Purchases may be made. I have directed Mr. Barclay to send out whatever may have been already purchased on public Account.[3]

With perfect Respect I have the Honor to be Sir Your most obedient & humble Servant   Robt Morris

His Excellency Benjamin Franklin Esqr.

Endorsed: Office of Finance Sept. 25. 1782

To Robert R. Livingston

Two ls,[4] press copies of each ls, and transcript: National Archives

Sir,   Passy, Sept. 26. 1782.

I have just received your No. 15. dated the 9th of August, which mentions your not having heard from me since March.[5] I have however written sundry Letters, viz. of Apl. 8th. & 12th. June 25th & 29th, Augt 12th and Sept. 3d, and sent Copies of the same, which I hope cannot all have miscarried.[6]

The Negotiations for Peace have hitherto amounted to little more than mutual Professions of sincere Desires, &ca. being obstructed by the Want of due form in the English Commissions

2. The articles were mainly clothing for the American Army: xxxvi, 147–8, 154; *Morris Papers,* iii, 289–90.

3. In a letter to Barclay dated Sept. 25, which also enclosed the 1782 congressional acts cited above: *Morris Papers,* vi, 431.

4. Both in wtf's hand. The one we do not reproduce is marked "3d copy."

5. xxxvii, 717–19.

6. All are published above.

appointing their Plenipotentiaries. The Objections made to those for treating with France, Spain & Holland were first removed; and by the inclosed it seems that our Objections to that for treating with us will now be removed also; so that we expect to begin in a few Days our Negociations.[7] But there are so many Interests to be consider'd and settled in a Peace between 5 different Nations, that it will be well not to flatter ourselves with a very speedy Conclusion. I mention'd in a former Letter my having communicated to Count de Vergennes the State of American Commerce which you sent me, and my having urged its Consideration, &ca.[8] Enclosed is a Copy of a Letter received from that Minister on the Subject.[9]

The Copy of General Carleton's Letter, and the Bills of Exchange, which you mention as inclos'd, do not appear.— I hope soon to have a better Opportunity of writing, when I shall be fuller.

With great Esteem, I have the honour to be, Sir, Your most obedient & most humble Servant.   B FRANKLIN

Honble. Robt. R. Livingston Esqr.

Endorsed: From Doctor Franklin Passy 26th. Septr. 1782.

To Robert Morris: Extract[1]   Extract:[2] National Archives

Sepr. 26th. 1782

By letters from the Commissioners formerly, if you have them in your office it may appear to you that the Farmers general,

7. BF enclosed Oswald's letter of Sept. 24 and its enclosure, from Townshend.

8. BF to Livingston, Aug. 12: XXXVII, 730.

9. Vergennes to BF, Aug. 23, above.

1. Made from a now-missing letter that probably was a response to Morris to BF, July 1 (XXXVII, 568–72). BF sent at least two copies of this letter, which evidently stated that he was enclosing a copy of his July 16 contract with Vergennes (XXXVII, 633–9). The first arrived by Dec. 27, when it was read to Congress. As Morris informed BF on Jan. 13 (below), the enclosure was missing. The second version to arrive did include the contract: Morris to BF, Jan. 19 (below); and see *Morris Papers,* VI, 440n.

2. In the hand of Arthur Lee.

soon after our arrival here, advancd us a million upon a contract for furnishing them with 5000 hhd. [hogshead] of tobacco which were to have been deliverd by Christmas 1778. Only three cargoes, on that account have been receivd by them. I have settled with them & given my acknowlegmt. of the debt due to them.[3]

From Robert Morris: Two Letters

(I) Two LS: American Philosophical Society; copies: Library of Congress, Archives du Ministère des affaires étrangères; (II) LS: American Philosophical Society, Yale University Library, Historical Society of Pennsylvania; copy: Library of Congress

I.

Sir,   Office of Finance 27th Septemr. 1782
I have the Honor to enclose the Copy of Acts of Congress of the fourteenth and twenty third Instant,[4] together with the Copy of my Letter of the thirtieth of July covering the Estimates for the Year 1783.[5] These Estimates are not yet finally decided on. By the Act of the fourteenth you are (as you perceive) instructed to communicate the Resolution for borrowing four Millions of

---

3. The tobacco received by the Farmers General was worth only 153,229 *l.t.* 5 *s.* 7 *d.*, according to a Nov. 17, 1781, statement signed by BF and five farmers general (XXXVI, 145n), a copy of which may have been enclosed (see *Morris Papers*, VIII, 345). The remainder of the 1,000,000 *l.t.* apparently was never repaid: Price, *France and the Chesapeake*, II, 715. The contract with the Farmers General was signed on March 24, 1777: XXIII, 514–17.

4. For the congressional resolution of Sept. 14 directing BF to borrow another four million dollars from France see the postscript of Livingston to BF, Sept. 13. The Sept. 23 resolution (*JCC*, XXIII, 595–6) states that BF should be informed that his letters to Livingston and Morris dated June 25 were received, and that "notwithstanding the information contained in those letters," he should attempt to raise the loan specified in the Sept. 14 resolution. BF's letters argued against seeking any further assistance from France: XXXVII, 535–9, 539–44.

5. This letter was addressed to John Hanson, president of Congress, and proposed borrowing four million dollars to reduce the deficit faced by Congress: *Morris Papers*, VI, 91–103. BF's endorsed copy is at the APS.

Dollars to his most Christian Majesty,—and first to assure His Majesty of the high Sense which the United States in Congress assembled entertain of his Friendship and generous Exertions; secondly their Reliance on a Continuance of them; and thirdly the Necessity of applying to his Majesty on the present Occasion. From this, and even more particularly from the Act of the twenty third, you will see that it is the wish of Congress to obtain this Money from or by Means of the King. After the decisive Expressions contained in these Resolutions of the Sense of our Sovereign, I am sure that it is unnecessary for me to attempt any Thing like Argument to induce your Exertions. I shall therefore rather confine myself to giving Information.

The grateful Sense of the King's Exertions which has so warmly impressed your Bosom, operates with undiminished Force upon Congress; and, what is of more Importance in a Country like ours, has the strongest Influence upon the whole Whig Interest of America. I have no Doubt but the King's Minister here has given his Court regular Information on this and every other Subject of equal Importance, and therefore any general Assurances on your Part will be complimentary and in some Degree superfluous. But there is a Kind of Knowledge not easily attainable by Foreigners in any Country, particularly on such a Matter as the present. It is not amiss therefore that I should convey it to you, and your good Sense will apply it in the most proper Manner. You (of all Men in the World) are not now to learn that the sower english Prejudice against every Thing french had taken deep Root in the Minds of America. It could not have been expected that this should be obliterated in a Moment: But by Degrees almost every Trace of it has been effaced. The Conduct of Britain has weaned us from our Attachments, and those very Attachments have been transferred in a great Measure to France. Whatever Remains of monarchical Disposition exist are disposing themselves fast to a Connection with the french Monarchy: For the british Adherents begin to feel the Pangs of a deep Despair; which must generate as deep Aversion. The british Army here felt the national Haughtiness encreased by the Contempt which as Englishmen they could not but feel for those who had combined against the Freedom of their own Country. Every Part of their Conduct therefore towards the Tories while they flattered themselves with Victory shewed how much they despised their American Friends. Now that a Reverse of Fortune has brought on a little Consideration, they find a total Seperation from this Country unavoidable: They must feel for the Fate of their Country; they must therefore hate, but they must respect us too, while their own Adherents are both detested and despised. Treated thus like common Prostitutes it is not in Human Nature so much to forgive as not to feel in Return. Since General Carleton's Arrival,[6] or rather since the Change of Ministers, the British have shewn that their Intention is, if possible, to conciliate the Rulers of America, and by the Influence of a common Language and similar Laws, with the Force of ancient Habits and mutual Friendships not yet forgotten, not only to renew again the commercial Intercourse, but to substitute a new federal Connection to their ancient Sovereignty and Dominion.

The Assurance therefore which Congress has directed you to make must not be considered in the Number of those idle Compliments which are the common Currency or small Change of a Court. It is an Assurance important, because it is founded in Truth; and more important still, because it is dictated by the Affections of a whole People. If I may venture an Opinion still farther, it is principally important, because of the critical Situation of Things.— The sudden Change of Britain from Vengeance and War to Kindness and Conciliation, must have Effects, and those Effects, whether they be Contempt or Affection, will depend less perhaps on them than upon Others. It cannot be doubted that they will ring all the Changes upon their usual Theme of gallic Ambition. They will naturally insinuate the Idea that France will neglect us when we have served her Purposes, and it would be very strange if they did not find some Converts among that Class of People who would sacrifice to present Ease, every future Consideration. What I have said will I am confident put your Mind into the Train of Reflections which arise out of our Situation; and you will draw the proper Conclusions and make a proper Application of them.

6. Sir Guy Carleton, the newly appointed commander-in-chief of the British forces in North America, arrived in New York on May 5: XXXVII, 399n.

Congress have directed you further to express to the King their Reliance on a Continuance of his Friendship and Exertions. I have no Doubt that a full Beleif of this Reliance will be easily inculcated. Indeed I rather apprehend that we shall be considered as relying too much on France, or in other Words doing too little for ourselves. There can be no sort of Doubt that a mighty good Argument may be raised on the usual Position that the Nation which will not help itself does not merit the Aid of Others, and it would be easy to tell us that we must put our own Shoulders to the Wheel before we call upon Hercules. In short if the Application be refused or evaded, Nothing can be easier than to assign very good Reasons why it is done. But you have very justly remarked in one of your Letters that it is possible to get the better in Argument, and to get Nothing else.[7] So it might be here. True Sagacity consists in making proper Distinctions, and true Wisdom in taking Determinations according to those Distinctions. Twenty Years hence when Time and Habit have settled and compleated the federal Constitution of America Congress will not think of relying on any other than that Being to whose Justice they appealed at the Commencement of their Opposition. But there is a Period in the Progress of Things, a Crisis between the Ardor of Enthusiasm and the Authority of Laws, when much Skill and Management are necessary to those who are charged with administering the Affairs of a Nation. I have already taken Occasion to observe that the present Moment is rendered particularly critical by the Conduct of the Enemy, and I would add here (if I dared even in Idea to seperate Congress from those they represent) that now above all other Times Congress must rely on the Exertions of their Ally. This Sentiment would open to his Majesty's Ministers many Reflections the least of which has a material Connection with the Interests of his Kingdom: But an Argument of no little Weight is that which applies itself directly to the Bosom of a young and generous Prince, who would be greatly wounded to see that Temple, dedicated to Humanity, which he has taken so much Pains to rear, fall at once into Ruins by a Remission of the last Cares which are

7. XXXVI, 673.

requisite for giving Solidity to the Structure. I think I might add that there are some Occasions on which a good Heart is the best Counsellor.

The third Topic which Congress have directed you to dwell upon is the Necessity of their present Applications, and it is this which falls most particularly within my Department; for I doubt not that every Sentiment on the other Objects has been most forcibly inculcated by the Minister of Foreign Affairs. I might write Volumes on our Necessities and not convey to you so accurate an Idea as by the Relation of a single Fact which you may see in the Public News Papers. It is that the Requisitions of last October for eight Millions had produced on the first Day of this Month only One hundred and twenty five thousand Dollars.[8] You are so perfectly a Master of every Thing which relates to Calculation that I need not state any Thing of our Expences. You know also what were our Resources beyond Taxation and therefore you have every Material for forming an accurate Idea of our Distresses. The Smallness of the Sum which has been paid will doubtless astonish you, and it is only by Conversation or a long History that you could see why it has been no greater. The People are undoubtedly able to pay, but they have easily persuaded themselves into a Conviction of their own Inability, and in a Government like ours the Beleif creates the Thing. The Modes of laying and levying Taxes are vicious in the Extreme: The Faults can be demonstrated, but would it not be a new Thing under the Sun that People should obey the Voice of Reason? Experience of the Evil is always a Preliminary to Amendment, and is frequently unable to effect it. Many who see the Right-road and approve of it, continue to follow the wrong road because it leads to Popularity. The Love of Popularity is our endemial Disease and can only be checked by a Change of Seasons. When the

8. For the requisitions see xxxvi, 135–6, 141. By the end of June, 1782, only Rhode Island, New Jersey, and Pennsylvania had contributed to the treasury, for a total of approximately $30,000. Massachusetts and Connecticut began contributing in July, followed by Maryland in either August or September. By the end of September, according to Morris' quarterly accounts, the total was approximately $185,000: *Morris Papers,* IX, 895–902; *Boston Gaz.,* issues of Sept. 2 and 16, 1782.

People have had dear Experience of the Consequences of not being taxed, they will probably work the proper Amendment; but our Necessities in the Interim are not the less severe. To tell America in such a Situation that she should reform her interior Administration would be very good Advice; but to neglect affording her Aid, and thereby to lose the capital Objects of the War, would be very bad Conduct. The Necessity of the present Application for Money arises from the Necessity of drawing by Degrees the Bands of Authority together, establishing the Power of Government over a People impatient of Control, and confirming the federal Union of the several States, by correcting Defects in the general Constitution. In a Word it arises from the Necessity of doing that infinite Variety of Things which are to be done in an infant Government placed in such delicate Circumstances that the People must be woed and won to do their Duty to themselves and pursue their own Interests. This Application also becomes the more necessary in order to obviate the Efforts of that british Faction which the Enemy are now attempting to excite among us. Hitherto indeed they have been unsuccessful unless perhaps with a very few Men who are under the Influence of disappointed Ambition; but much Care will be required when their Plans are brought to greater Maturity. The savage Inroads on our Frontiers have kept up the general Horror of Britain. The great Captures made on our Coasts have also rather enraged than Otherwise, tho such Captures have always the twofold Operation of making People wish for Peace as well as for Revenge. But when the Enemy shall quit our Coasts (and they have already stopped the Inroads of their savage Allies) if the People are urged at once to pay heavy unusual Taxes, it may draw forth and give weight to Arguments which the boldest Emissaries would not at present hazard the Use of.

I have already observed that Congress wish to obtain this Money either from or by Means of the King. The most cautious Prudence will justify us in confiding to the Wisdom of his Ministers the Portrait of our Situation. But it might not be very wise to explain to Others those Reasons for the Application which lie so deep in the Nature of Things as easily to escape superficial Observers. I shall enclose a Copy of this Letter to Mr. Adams, and you will find herein a Copy of what I say to him on the Subject.——[9] I hope the Court will take such Measures as to render any Efforts on his Part unnecessary. But you and he must decide on what is best for your Country. I must trouble you still farther on this Subject with the Mention of what you will indeed collect from a cursory Reading of the Resolutions—that Congress have the strongest Reason for their Procedure when they direct your utmost Endeavors to effect this Loan, notwithstanding the Information contained in your Letters.[1] If the War is to be carried on this Aid is indispensible, and when obtained will enable us to act powerfully in the Prosecution of it. If a Peace takes place it is still necessary, and as it is the last request which we shall then have Occasion to make I cannot think that it will be refused. In a Word, Sir, we must have it.— With perfect Respect I have the Honor to be, Sir, Your Excellency's most obedient & humble Servant ROBT MORRIS.

His Excellency Benjamin Franklin Esquire.

II.

Sir   Office of Finance 27th September 1782.

By my Letter of this Date you will be informed of the Intention of Congress to provide for a principal Part of the Expenditures of the Year 1783 by Loan. I expect that you will be able to obtain the four Millions of Dollars either from the Court of France or by their Assistance. I wish an immediate Disposition of a Part in the following Manner. That the Court of Spain should give Orders for the Shipment of a Million of Dollars at the Havanna free of Duties, and to be convoyed by One or more

9. Morris to JA, Sept. 27: *Morris Papers,* VI, 443. BF's endorsed copy is at the APS.

1. When BF sent Vergennes a copy of this letter on Nov. 8, below, he enclosed the following explanation (in WTF's hand and entitled, "Note by B.F."): "The Information here alluded to, was, that the last Loan of six Millions was accompanied with the most explicit Declarations to me, that no more was to be expected, or could possibly be granted; and that if I accepted Bills to a greater Amount, I must seek Assistance elsewhere for the Payment of them, as it could not be furnish'd here. I also mentioned all the particulars to the Kings Goodness to us in the Contract by which our Debt was settled; and intreated that I might not be forced to disoblige so kind a Friend by new and reiterated Demands." AAE.

Ships of the Line to an American Port; the Money to be paid to them during the Year in Europe.[2] I wish this Order may be so expedited as that Captain Barney in the Washington, by whom this Letter goes, may carry it out to the Havanna, and receive the Money, which will by that Means arrive Sometime during the Winter, and of Course will, I expect, come safely as well as seasonably. I wish that half a Million Dollars may be paid to Messrs. Le Couteulx and Company as soon as possible, to enable them to execute my Orders as to a particular Negociation wch: I commit to them.[3] Whatever else of the Money is obtained in France, will of Course be paid to Mr. Grand, subject to my Order. If any Part of the Money be negociated in Holland, it will be, I suppose, proper to leave it in the Hands of those who negociate the Loan, subject to my farther Disposition.

I am, Sir, Your most obedient & humble Servant

ROBT MORRIS

His Excellency Benjamin Franklin Esqr.

(Duplicate.)

Endorsed: Office of Finance Septr. 27. 1782 Disposition of the 4 Milln. of Dollars, if obtained.

2. For Morris' attempts at importing specie from Havana see *Morris Papers*, VI, 425–6n.

3. This negotiation was intended to make the proceeds from the Dutch loan of 1782 available at Havana: *Morris Papers*, VI, 424–7, 452–3.

From the Continental Congress: Commission and Instructions[4]

(I) and (II) Two copies and draft:[5] National Archives

I.

[September 28, 1782]

The United States in Congress Assembled— To all who shall see these presents send Greeting—

It having been represented to Congress by their Minister Plenipoy: at the Court of Versailles, that the King of Sweden has signified by his Ambassador at that Court to our said Minister, his desire to enter into a treaty with the United States in Congress Assembled,[6] and We being willing to promote the same, for establishing harmony & good intercourse between the Citizens of the United States, and the Subjects of the said King Know Ye therefore that we confiding in the integrity, prudence and ability of the honorable Benjn. Franklin Esq have nominated, constituted & appointed and by these Presents do nominate, constitute and appoint the said Benjamin Franklin our Minister Plenipotentiary, giving him full Powers general and Special to act in that Quality; to confer, treat, agree & conclude with the Person or Persons vested with equal Powers by the said King, of and concerning a Treaty of Amity & Commerce between the

---

4. Authorizing BF to negotiate a commercial treaty with Sweden, these were drafted by the congressional committee of Arthur Lee, Ralph Izard, and James Duane (for which see the annotation of Livingston to BF, Sept. 18). The committee also drafted the proposed treaty, which they enclosed. BF received the dispatches by Nov. 14, when he so informed Swedish Ambassador Creutz: Amandus Johnson, *Swedish Contributions to American Freedom, 1776–1783* (2 vols., Philadelphia, 1953–57), I, 575.

5. The draft of the proposed American-Swedish commercial treaty is filed with the draft of these two documents. The basic text was that of the proposed treaty with Holland, with "King of Sweden" substituted in the relevant places, articles 2 and 3 combined into one rewritten article 2, and the subsequent articles lightly edited. The text, with emendations shown, is in *JCC*, XXIII, 610–21. The drafts of the commission and instructions are in *ibid.*, 621–4.

6. BF had informed Livingston of the Swedish ambassador's approach to him in a letter of June 25: XXXVII, 204–5, 312, 538.

United States in Congress Assembled, and the King of Sweden, and whatever shall be so agreed & concluded for us and in our Name to sign and thereupon to make such Treaty, Conventions & Agreements as he shall judge conformable to the ends we have in view; hereby promising in good faith that we will accept, ratify & execute whatever shall be agreed, concluded & signed by our said Minister: And Whereas it may so happen that our aforesaid Minister may die or be otherwise incapacitated to execute this Commission We do in that case by these presents Constitute and appoint the honble. John Adams our Minister Plenipotentiary for the purpose aforesaid. And in case of his Death or incapacity We appoint the honorable John Jay our Minister Plenipotentiary for the purpose aforesaid. And in case of his Death or incapacity also We do appoint the honble. Henry Laurens our Minister Plenipotentiary for the purpose aforesaid, with all the Powers herein before Delegated to the honble. Benjn. Franklin.

In Testimony whereof we have caused the Seal of the United States of America to be affixed to these Presents.[7] Witness His Excellency John Hanson Esq. President of the United States in Congress Assembled the twenty Eighth Day of September in the Year of our Lord one thousand seven hundred and Eighty two—and of our Sovereignty and Independence the seventh.

Form of Commission to B. Franklin for negotiating Treaty with Sweden & Instructions.—

II.

[September 28, 1782]

1.

You are to negotiate & conclude the proposed treaty of Amity & Commerce with the Person or Persons that shall be appointed by his Swedish Majesty, at Paris, and not elsewhere, unless some

7. Since July 4, 1776, when BF, JA, and Jefferson were appointed by Congress to design the Great Seal (XXII, 562–3), there had been a succession of unsuccessful proposals. Congress approved Charles Thomson's design on June 20, 1782. The die was completed by Sept. 16, when the seal was impressed for the first time on an official document. Richard S. Patterson and Richardson Dougall, *The Eagle and the Shield: a History of the Great Seal of the United States* (Washington, D.C., 1976), pp. 83–7, 122–8, 138–9.

other place should be fixed on for negotiating a General Peace, in which case you may negociate and Conclude it at the same Place.

2.

As we shall be better able to Judge by experience, What Commercial Regulations will be most beneficial for the Citizens & Subjects of the Contracting Powers; it is our desire that the treaty be made for twelve Years only.

3.

It is possible that the 4th Article in the Plan of a treaty may be objected to on the part of the King of Sweden as unequal he having more Ships of War than the United States & not being engaged in any War which may render protection necessary to the Ships of his Subjects. He may also apprehend that the giving Protection to our Vessels may involve him in a War with Great Britain. To this it may be answered, that the 15th Article is as unequally in favor of Sweden, giving her the benefit of the carrying Trade, which cannot be enjoyed by the Citizens of the United States. Therefore the one Article may be set against the other. But as the direct & essential object of the treaty is to obtain the Recognition of our Independency by another European power— You are instructed not to adhere to the 4th Article so as to prevent the conclusion of the Treaty. Upon the same principle You may also use Your discretion in extending the Term of the Treaty to twenty Years but no farther.

You are also at liberty in case it be found necessary to recede from the stipulation proposed in the 9th Article that whatever shall be found laden by the Subjects & Inhabitants of either party on any Ship belonging to the Enemies of the other shall be subject to Confiscation.[8]

8. The fourth article called for the King of Sweden to protect American ships trading with Sweden. The fifteenth article stipulated the principle of "free ships, free goods," except for contraband, giving Swedish ships the right to trade with America's enemies in case of war without fear of American warships or privateers. The ninth article authorized confiscation of each other's goods and merchandise, if they were captured aboard an enemy's ship: *JCC*, XXIII, 612–13, 616, 618–19.

From Charles Grant

ALS: Historical Society of Pennsylvania

Sir   paris Street anjou st. honoré 28—7bre. 1782:

I am extreamly oblidg'd to you for the Book you was so Kind as to lend me, it has much contributed to augmente my desir to go next spring to america,[9] I only wish to find means to be usefull either in the field of war, either as citizen of the world, and particularly as an admirer of the laws who established *security* in general, and conserve *liberty* : with them a considerable new soil wich offers immense ressources to a lover of agriculture. There the objets of my wishes, for which I shall continue to ask, sir, your Kind good offices and protection, begging youl be persuaded of the true sentiments of veneration and respect with which I have the honour to be sir Your most obedient and humble servant [*illegible*]   VTE. DE VAUX-GRANT.

From William Grey

ALS: Historical Society of Pennsylvania

May it please your Excellency   Bourdeaux 28 Sptr. 1782

Owing to the fate of war I had the misfortune of being captured in the Ship Amazon a Transport in his Majestys service that I commanded bound from London to Quebec, by Cpt. Johnson of the Ship Flora and brought to this place a prisinor.[1]

I request that you will pardon my presumtion in writing to your Excellency humbly beging my parole for England for any

---

9. The book was probably Crèvecœur's *Letters from an American Farmer*, which the author sent BF in July: XXXVII, 628.

Grant remained in France until 1790, when he fled to Scotland and sought the assistance of the British Grants. He supported himself by writing on various subjects, and tried to organize the emigration to Canada of French royalists living in Britain: John Weatherford, "The Vicomte de Vaux: Would-be Canadian," *Ontario History*, XLVII (1955), 51–7. He also publicized his difficulties in two pamphlets: *Appendix to the State of the Case of Major-General Charles Grant, Viscount de Vaux, . . .* (London, [1806?]) and *A Statement of the Circumstances concerning Major-General Charles Viscount Grant de Vaux* (London, 1812).

1. Henry Johnson brought his prizes into Bordeaux in early August: Johnson to BF, Aug. 17, above; John Davies *et al.* to BF, Oct. 26, below; *Courier de l'Europe*, XII (1782), 119.

limitted time, any security that your Excellency will be pleas'd
to demand will be given that I will procure an American of equal
rank his liberty or return to this place a prisinor within the time
prescrib'd and youl will greatly Oblidge your Excellency's Most
Humble & Obdt. Servant   WILLIAM GREY

From Robert Morris

LS:[2] American Philosophical Society; copies: Library of Congress, Archives du Ministère des affaires étrangères

Sir,   Philadelphia. 28 Sept. 1782

In my Letter of yesterday, I have dwelt on the resolutions of
Congress, in the manner requir'd by my duty as their Servant. I
will now add a few hints, as Your friend. Your Enemies industriously publish that your age & indolence have unabled you for
your station, that a Sense of obligation to France Seals your lips
when you should ask their aid, & that (whatever your friends
may say to the contrary) both your connections & Influence at
Court are extremely feeble. I need not tell you that Messieurs Lee
& company are among the foremost who make these assertions,
& many others not worth mention, I should not have given you
the pain of reading even these but that (as you will see from the
resolution of the twenty third instant) Congress have believed
your grateful sensibilities might render you unwilling to apply
with all that warmth which the sense of their Necessities con-
vinces them is necessary. In addition to the general reflection
how envy has pursued superior merit in all Ages, You will draw
a farther consolation from this, that many who censure you are
well disposed to cast like censure on France, & would fain describe her as acting only the part of self interest, without a wishe
to render us effectual aid. You will I am sure attribute what I now
say to a friendly desire of apprizing you of things useful for you

2. The body of the letter is entirely in cipher, and was deciphered by L'Air
de Lamotte. The Library of Congress copy is from Morris' letterbook; it too
is in cipher. The copy at the AAE, in English and in WTF's hand, was sent by
BF to Vergennes on Nov. 8.

to know, & you will so act, as to convince every man that your exertions are what I verily believe them to be.

I am Sir, Your most obedient Servant   ROBT MORRIS

His Excellency Benjm. Franklin Esqre.

1st

Endorsed: Mr Morris Officer of Finance Sept. 28. 1782 on Personal or private Affairs

Notation:[3] (By C No. 4)

From Thomas Barclay   LS: American Philosophical Society

Sir   Brest 30th. Seper. 1782

Upon my arrival here I waited on the Count De Hector and delivered him a letter which the Marquis de Castres gave me, in which he requested that I might receive all the assistance necessary to enable me to pursue Such Measures as I Should think proper in Expditing the American Supplies from hence, and on this Occasion I received every assurance on the part of the Count that I could wish. Here the matter must rest for the present, for there is not a Vessell now in this harbour, unemployed, that is fit for so Important a business; and I trust we Shall not here be in the Situation I was in at Holland, of dividing the goods by various Conveyances some of which were not very desirable ones.[4] Mr. Franklin[5] was so Kind as to give me a hint about the manner in which the Vessells were to be ingaged, and refered me to the Marquis de la Fayette with whom I had several Conversations, and who was so good as to promise that if any farther in-

3. In WTF's hand. The cipher was actually No. 3, which Morris used in letters to BF the previous spring: XXXV, 266n; XXXVII, 119n, 163n, 426n; *Morris Papers*, VI, 456.

4. Before attempting to ship the military supplies at Brest, Barclay had sent supplies to America from Amsterdam and Ostend via various ships: XXXVII, 493–4, 560–1, 641–4, 739–41. His bills from those transactions continued to be paid by Grand throughout the fall; he was reimbursed nearly 165,000 *l.t.* between Aug. 19 and Dec. 12: Account XXVII (XXXII, 4).

5. WTF. In a letter of Sept. 30, Barclay thanked him for recommending that he see Lafayette (APS).

terpossition of the Marquis de Castres was wanting, I Shou'd have it, and his idea was that the Business was to be done at the expence of the Court of France. It was Never my Intention to Interfer farther than to urge the Shipments on, as fast as I Cou'd, and I Supposed that the presence of a Servant of Congress, whose peculiar duty it is to attend the forwarding the Supplies, might be a Means of attaining an object of so much Consequence. Yet Still, if it can not be done in the line we wish your Excellency will Considere whether Some other Cannot be pursued— There are two Vessells at Nantes which I am told wou'd Suit, but when I conversed with the Owner of them, he did not Seem willing to engage them. However when I get there I Shall See farther about them, the Ships st. James, Washington and Queen of France are at L'Orient in 34 days from Philadelphia—[6] The St. James is a very fine Ship of 20 Nine pound Cannon, and would be Suitable for our purpose, were the goods at L'Orient I am pritty Certain a part might be Ship'd by her at a reasonable freight payable in America, but I do not think it wou'd be by any means proper to remove any of them as long as there is a probability of the Court of France Sending them. I need not give you any farther trouble at present—after Seeing my family[7] a few days at L'Orient I Shall proceed to Nantes, and if any thing occurs to your Excellency on this or any other Subject to which you think my attention Necessary I Shall be glad of your Communicating it, I need not, to you Sir, say how Indispensibly Necessary it is that the Supplies shou'd be got out in time for the Next Campaign, and I am in hopes Some way or other may be fallen on, I very Sincerely wish you a Speedy recovery from your Indisposition and remain with great respect Sir, Your Most Obed. and Most Huml Serv.   THOS BARCLAY

His Excellency Benjn. Franklin Esqe.

Notation: T. Barclay Brest 30h. Septr. 1782

6. See Nesbitt to BF, Sept. 23.

7. Barclay had been accompanied to Europe by his wife and their three children: XXXV, 559n.

From Nathaniel Barrett

ALS: Historical Society of Pennsylvania

Sir,   L'Orient sept 30 1782

I was renderd very unhappy just now to be informd by my friends Messrs Cumming & Maccarty, that they had recd a Letter from Monsr. Jolley de fleury Minr. of Finance handing them a Determination respecting a Cargo of sugars which I brot with me from the Havanna in the Briga. Genl Galvez.[8]

These sugars being the product of Cape Francois I took in at the Havanna, being apprehensive of a difficulty attending the Importation of those of foreign Growth, & in full Confidence that evry Indulgence would be granted & no greater Duties woud be requird of me, as an Inhabitant of the American Colonies than of a Subject of this Kingdom coming directly from Hispaniola.

The whole matter has been layd before the farmer Genl—by Mr Vincen, banker, of Paris—[9] & Encouragement was given that No more Duties would be requird than on sugars direct from the Cape— In Consequence of wch. I have laid in a Cargo for my Brig & She is now ready for sailing, but if the whole Duties as on foreign Sugars is insisted on it will take more than one third of the sugars to pay them—& must ruin my Voyage.

I have therefore most earnestly to request your Excellency's Interposition with the Minister in whose Department this Matter rests that Leave might be granted to ship off to some foreign friendly port, the whole of these sugars which thro' Ignorance of the Customs of this Country I have brought into it—freed from the Duties which are demanded which will greatly alleviate my Distress. I beg the favour of a Line from you on the subject as soon as possible that I may not be detaind here so long as to ruin myself & those who are concernd with me.[1]

8. For the *General Galvez* see XXXVII, 693.

9. Louis Vincens fils was Cuming & Macarty's banker. The farmers general in charge of the tax assessment for Lorient were Louis-Adrien Prévost d'Arlincourt (XXXVI, 41n) and Paul-Pierre de Kolly (d. 1793): Lüthy, *Banque protestante*, II, 700; *Almanach royal* for 1782, p. 556; Yves Durand, *Les Fermiers généraux au XVIIIe siècle* (rev. ed., Paris, 1996), p. 651.

1. John Jay took charge of trying to secure the waiver for the cargo of sugar during BF's illness: Morris, *Jay: Peace*, p. 369n. Jay received a letter

Acknowledging my Obligations for the Civilities recd at passy I remain with the utmost Respect Your Excellencys most obd hum servt.   NATHL BARRETT

His Excelly B Franklin Esqr. Passy

From Robert Morris

LS: American Philosophical Society, Yale University Library, Historical Society of Pennsylvania; copy: Library of Congress

Sir,   Office of Finance 30th September 1782

I have received and already acknowledged your Letters of the 9th January, two of the 28th January, those of the 30th January, 4th March 9th March and 30th March. The Acknowledgement of the three last was by mine of the first of July. I am now to acknowledge yours of the eighth of April and twenty fifth of June. I have written to you since the Ninth of March (which you acknowledge the Receipt of in yours of the twenty fifth of June) on the twenty second and twenty third of March, on the seventeenth of April, on the seventeeth, and twice on the eighteenth and twenty third of May, also on the twenty ninth of May, twenty sixth of June, first and fifth of July.[2]

It is in some Respects fortunate that our Stores were not shipped, because, as you observe,[3] they might have been taken; but I hope they are now on the Way, for if they are to lie in France at a heavy Expence of Storage &c while we suffer for the Want, it will be even worse than if they were taken. You will find by the Letters which are to go with this, that Mr. Barclay is prohibited from making any more Purchases on Account of the United States.[4] I confess that I disapprove of those he has made: for the Purchase of unnecessary Things, *because they are cheap,*

---

identical to the present one; a French translation of that letter, in L'Air de Lamotte's hand, is among BF's papers at the APS.

2. With the exception of Morris' letter of March 9, which has not been found, all these letters are above.

3. See BF to Morris, June 25: XXXVII, 540.

4. See Morris' second letter of Sept. 25.

appears to be a very great Extravagance. We want Money as much as any Thing else, and the World must form a strange Idea of our Management, if, while we are begging to borrow, we leave vast Magazines of Cloathing to rot at Brest, and purchase Others to be shipped from Holland. I have said Nothing on this Subject to Mr. Barclay, because the Thing, having been done, could not be undone, and because the pointed Resolutions of Congress on the Subject will prevent any more such Operations.[5] What I have now said however will, I hope, lead you to urge on him the Necessity of making immediate Shipments of all the Stores in Europe. A Merchant does not sustain the total Loss of his Goods by their Detention, but the Public do. The Service of the Year must be accomplished within the Year by such Means as the Year affords. The Detention of our Goods has obliged me to purchase Cloathing and other Articles at a great Expence, while those very Things were lying about at different Places in Europe. I am sure that any Demand made for Money on our Part must appear extraordinary, while we shew so great Negligence of the Property we possess. The Funds, therefore, which were obtained for the Year 1781, are not only rendered useless during that Year, but so far pernicious as that the Disposition of them will naturally influence a Dimunition of the Grants made for the Year 1782.

You mention in yours of the twenty fifth of June, that you would send enclosed the Account of the Replacing of the Fayette's Cargo, if it could be copied in Season. As it did not arrive, I shall expect it by the next Opportunity.

I have received Mr. Grand's Accounts, which are not stated in the Manner I wish; and in Consequence I have written to him by this Opportunity to alter them.[6] I have desired him to give your Account Credit for every Livre received previous to the current Year, including therein the Loan of 10.000.000 *l.t.* in Holland, tho a Part of it may not have been received until this Year. I have

5. Those resolutions are described in annotation to Morris' first letter of Sept. 25.
6. *Morris Papers*, VI, 457–8.

desired him to debit your Account for every Expenditure made by your Order, which will include all your Acceptances of Bills &c, and of Course Mr. De Beaumarchais' Bills, if they shall have been paid.[7] Finally, I have desired him to carry the Balance of your Account to mine, in which he is to credit all Monies received for the current Year: for Instance the six Millions (and the other six, if they are obtained) together with such Monies as may come to his Hands from the Loan opened for the United States by Messrs Willink Stapherst &c.—

I did expect to have had some Kind of Adjustment made by this Time of Captain Gillon's Affair, but Congress referred much of it to a Committee with whom it has long slept; but I have informed Mr. Gillon that I must have a Settlement, and at present I wait a little for the Determination of Congress.—[8]

You mention to me that the Interest on the 10,000.000 *l.t.* Dutch Loan is payable at Paris annually on the fifth of November at four per Cent.[9] I must request you to send me the particular Details on this Subject, such as who it is payable to, and by whom, that I may make proper Arrangements for a punctual Performance, so as not to incur unnecessary Expence. I presume that the first Year's Interest may be discharged before this reaches you; but at any Rate I enclose a Letter to Mr. Grand,[1] to prevent any ill Consequences which might arise from a Deficiency of Payment.

I informed you in mine of the first of July, that Congress had resolved to appoint a Commissioner to settle the public Accounts in Europe: This is not done, but they have reconsidered and committed the Resolution. Where the Thing will end I do

7. BF paid Beaumarchais' bills on June 25: XXXVII, 735n.

8. The committee finally delivered its report on the detention of goods purchased in Holland on Nov. 1. Congress dismissed its censure of Gillon, suggesting that if Morris wished to pursue the charges against him, he take it up with the state of South Carolina: *JCC*, XXIII, 700–6; *Morris Papers*, IV, 344–5n and VI, 397–8n; James A. Lewis, *Neptune's Militia: the Frigate* South Carolina *during the American Revolution* (Kent, Ohio, and London, 1999), p. 81.

9. XXXVII, 542–3.

1. Authorizing him to pay the interest: *Morris Papers*, VI, 467.

not know. I think however that eventually they must send over some Person for the Purpose.[2]

The Appearances of Peace have been materially disserviceable to us here, and general Cautions on the Subject from Europe, and the most pointed Applications from the public Officers, will not prevent that Lethargy which the very Name of Peace extends thro' all the States. I hope Measures will be taken by our public Ministers in Europe to prevent the People from falling into the Snares which the Enemy has laid. Undue Security in Opinion is generally very hurtful in Effect; and I dread the Consequences of it here if the War is to be carried on, which is not improbable.

I am, Sir, Your most obedient & humble Servant,

ROBT MORRIS

His Excellency Benjamin Franklin Esquire.

Endorsed: Office of Finance Sept. 30. 1782 Various Subjects

To Thomas Pownall: Extract[3]

Press copy of copy: Library of Congress

[September, 1782]

The Box you committed to the Care of Mr Bridgen was duly sent by him, & received at Ostend; but in its way from thence hither it has miscarried.[4] I am taking pains to find out what is become

2. XXXVII, 569. A committee was assigned on July 29 to reconsider, in consultation with Morris, the appointment and the comissioner's instructions. The committee delivered its report to Congress on Sept. 3, and it was not adopted until Nov. 18: *Morris Papers*, v, 128–9n; vi, 209n, 254–9.

3. These paragraphs, which we believe to be in BFB's hand, were written at the top of a letter BF wrote to Pownall on March 1, 1785. Alluding to the extract, which he said came from a letter he wrote Pownall in September, 1782, BF said that a key piece of information was incorrect. The box had not been received at Ostend. It had been placed on board a ship and had been taken by mistake to the West Indies, where it had lain for several years. It had only just been delivered.

4. The box contained 187 copies (sewn and unsewn) of Pownall's *A Topographical Description . . . of North America . . .* and the annexed reissue of Lewis Evans' *General Map of the Middle British Colonies in America:* XXXI, 302; XXXVII, 370–2, 583.

of it. I hope it is not irrecoverably lost. Tho I have lost other things before which were coming to me, and think the Carriage between Ostend & Paris is by no means a safe Conveyance.

I had in May last received Almon's Account which you sent me.[5] There are several Articles in it that appear to me monstrously extravagant. But I suppose there is no Remedy. His whole Charge amounts to £300..11..0; and he gives Credit for Cash received by the Sale £312.16.0.— There is then a Ballance remaining for Mrs Barry of £12..5..0, which I hope you have received, or will receive from him.— The Copies delivered in, ballance the Number; but they by no means discharge any part of that Sum, being all charged and paid for in the Account.

From Benjamin Putnam[6]   ALS: Historical Society of Pennsylvania

Hon'd Sir,   Bordeax Sept. 1782—

While I beg Permission to inform you of my extreem Mortification for so long & unexpected Detention at this Place, unfortunately occasioned by a violent Attact of Fever, which, tho' declining, will for some days render me unable to Journey, 'tis with equal regret for the common Good and Anxiety for your personal Health I hear of your Excellency's Indisposition— wishing for your Excellency, an entire Restoration & long enjoyment of perfect health.

Am with sentiments of great Respect Your Excellency's most Obedient & humble Servant   BENJAMIN PUTNAM.

His Excy Doct Franklin

---

5. See XXXVII, 370–1.
6. Putnam had written BF while en route to France; he wanted to consult in person about two prizes in which he had an interest: XXXVII, 478.

The American Peace Commissioners: Commission for William Temple Franklin

DS:[7] Yale University Library; copies: Library of Congress (two), American Philosophical Society, Massachusetts Historical Society

The present document, penned by William Temple Franklin on October 1, was most likely signed by Franklin the same day. It was eventually signed by all the peace commissioners, but not without hesitation (on the part of John Jay) and outright hostility (on the part of John Adams). Its history reflects not so much the other commissioners' feelings about Temple as their relationship to his grandfather.

In January, 1782, Jay had reassured Franklin that he would support the appointment of Temple as secretary of the peace commission.[8] Franklin brought up the subject again in mid-September, suggesting to Jay that they fill in a commission for secretary with Temple's name. The negotiations were at that time stalemated over the wording of Oswald's commission, and Franklin and Jay disagreed about whom they could trust and how best to proceed. Why, then, draw up this document? Franklin may have been motivated by his ill-health; in mid-September he was suffering such acute pain from bladder or kidney stones that he feared for his life. Evidence suggests that Jay was helping Franklin revise his will at this time,[9] and despite private misgivings he obliged Franklin in this request. On September 18 Jay told Ridley that the secretary's commission had been filled in, and that the document was in Temple's possession.[1]

Oswald's revised commission arrived on September 27, allowing negotiations to resume. On October 1, Oswald and Jay exchanged copies of their respective commissions; Franklin, not well enough to make the trip into Paris, was not present.[2] That exchange of commissions is mentioned in the present document. According to Matthew Ridley's diary, that same day Franklin sent Temple to meet with Jay and urge him to begin drafting the preliminaries. He also, according to Ridley, suggested that Temple's commission as secretary "might be

---

7. In WTF's hand.
8. XXXVI, 497.
9. BF to [Jay], Sept. 17.
1. Klingelhofer, "Matthew Ridley's Diary," p. 109.
2. Oswald described the Oct. 1 exchange of commissions with Jay in a letter to Townshend dated Oct. 2, saying the Americans were "entirely satisfied": Morris, *Jay: Peace*, p. 372.

filled up." We suspect that Franklin sent Temple to Paris with the fair copy of this commission in hand, signed and sealed by Franklin, in order for Jay to sign it. Jay deferred, having told Ridley that he did not see that there would be enough work to employ a secretary. "Indeed," wrote Ridley, "it is plain [Jay] wishes he had not made the promise."[3] We have no evidence of when Jay did affix his signature to Temple's commission, but we assume that it must have been fairly soon thereafter, probably when he next visited Passy. Before signing he evidently made Temple swear an oath he had composed. That oath, in Jay's hand, is among Franklin's papers at the American Philosophical Society.[4]

The other two peace commissioners added their signatures long after they joined their colleagues in Paris. Henry Laurens arrived on November 28, just in time for the final peace negotiations. His health had so deteriorated by early January that he determined to return to Bath. He signed the present commission on January 10, the day before leaving Paris.[5]

The day after Laurens signed, Temple brought the commission to John Adams. Rather than getting a signature, he received a lecture. Adams was furious and, in his own words, "considered myself as directly affronted in this Affair." Considering that Congress had originally appointed him as sole peace commissioner, and that he had been named "at the head of the new Commission," he thought he should have had a say in the selection of a secretary. But "without saying or writing a Word to me, Dr. Franklin had wrote to Mr. Jay at Madrid and obtained a Promise from him." He told Temple that "I thought my self Ill treated in this as in many other Things. That it was not from any disrespect to him, Mr. W.T.F., that I declined it."[6] It was not until after the Definitive Treaty was signed nearly nine months later that Adams added his name to the bottom of this commission.

3. Klingelhofer, "Matthew Ridley's Diary," p. 117.

4. It reads: "I Wm. T. Franklin do swear on the holy Evangelists of amighty god that I will faithfully do the Duties of Secretary to the Commissioners appointed by the United States of America in Congress assembled, for negociating and concluding Peace with Great Britain So help me God."

5. *Laurens Papers*, XVI, xlv.

6. Butterfield, *John Adams Diary*, III, 102–3. JA learned of WTF's commission as soon as he arrived in Paris in late October: *ibid.*, p. 38. Though he told WTF that he thought John Thaxter had the most right to the position, he also admitted that he would have recommended another name. This was most likely Edmund Jenings, whom JA had recommended in an Aug. 15 letter to Laurens: Wharton, *Diplomatic Correspondence*, v, 662; Butterfield, *John Adams Diary*, III, 103n.

[October 1, 1782]

To ALL TO WHOM these Presents shall come, Benjamin Franklin & John Jay send GREETING.

WHEREAS the United States of America in Congress assembled did on the 15th June in the Year of our Lord 1781. appoint and constitute the said Benjamin Franklin and John Jay, & John Adams, Henry Lawrens and Thomas Jefferson Esquires, and the Majority of them, and of such of them as should assemble for the Purpose, their Commissioners & Plenipotentiaries to treat of and conclude Peace in their Behalf.[7] AND WHEREAS the said United States in Congress assembled, did on the 26th. June in the Year of our Lord 1781. appoint Mr. Francis Dana, untill he could proceed to the Court of Petersburgh, either in a Public or Private Capacity to be Secretary to the said Plenipotentiaries for negociating a Peace with Great Britain,[8] And in case Mr Dana should have proceeded or thereafter proceed to Petersburgh or to any Part of the Dominions of the Empress of Russia, the Ministers appointed by the Said Act of Congress of the 15th of June 1781. or a Majority of such of them as should assemble, should be & thereby were authoris'd to appoint a Secretary to their Commission, and that he be entitled to receive in Proportion to his Time of Service, the Salary of one thousand Pounds Sterling per Annum allow'd to Mr. Dana.[9] AND WHEREAS His Britannic Majesty hath issued a Commission dated the 21 Sept. 1782 to Richard Oswald Esquire to treat of and conclude Peace with any Commissioners or Persons vested with equal Powers by and on the Part of the thirteen United States of America.[1] AND WHEREAS the said Richard Oswald is at Paris, ready to execute his said Commission, and hath exchanged with the said Benjamin Franklin & John Jay, Copies of their respective Commissions, and enter'd on the Business of the same, Whereby the Appointment of a Secretary to the American Commission hath

7. XXXV, 161–7.

8. XXXV, 298n, 299.

9. *JCC,* xx, 699. WTF did not receive this salary until 1784, long after the peace treaty was signed. £1,000 was worth approximately 24,000 *l.t.* He did continue to draw 300 *louis* (7,200 *l.t.*) per year as BF's secretary: BF to Livingston, Sept. 3, above; Account XXVII (XXXII, 4).

1. See Vaughan to BF, Sept. 23.

become necessary. And the said Mr Dana now being at Petersburgh, the Right of appointing such Secretary hath in pursuance of the afore recited Act of Congress, devolved on the said Commissioners and on the Majority of them and of such of them as have assembled for the Purpose of executing their said Commission. AND WHEREAS Mr. Jefferson one of the said Commissioners hath not come to Europe, and Mr. Lawrens, another of them, hath declined to accept the said Office,[2] and Mr Adams another of them is at the Hague, so that, the said Benjamin Franklin and John Jay are the only Commissioners now assembled to execute the said Commission.

Now Know Ye that they reposing special Trust and Confidence in the Ability & Integrity of William T. Franklin Esqre. to perform and fulfil the Duties of Secretary to their said Commission have appointed and constituted And by these Presents do appoint and constitute the said William T. Franklin, Secretary to the said Commission. In Witness whereof the said Benjamin Franklin & John Jay have hereunto set their Hands and Seals this first Day of October in the Year of our Lord one thousand seven hundred and Eighty two and in the seventh Year of the Independence of the said United States.

[seal]   B. FRANKLIN
[seal]   JOHN JAY

[seal]   Approved on my part Mr. Franklin having acted with propriety as Secretary to the Commission from the time of my arrival here. Paris 10th January 1783.
             HENRY LAURENS.

[seal]   Approved on my part, Mr Franklin having acted with Propriety as Secretary to the Commission from the Time of my arrival here. Paris 8 Septr 1783
             JOHN ADAMS.

2. XXXVII, 377–8.

Franklin: Discharge of Captain Fage's Parole[3]

Three copies:[4] Public Record Office; ALS (draft) and copy: Library of Congress

Passy, Oct 1st. 1782.

Being informed by Richard Oswald, Esqr., Minister Plenipotentiary. from His Britannic Majesty to treat here of Peace, that General Conway[5] desires much to have an English Officer, Capt. Fage of the Artillery, absolved of his Parole, having occasion for his Service as Aid de Camp; and Application being made to me for obtaining such Discharge: And being farther of Opinion that it will be pleasing to Congress that General Conway should be obliged in that Respect. I do hereby, as far as in my Power may lie, absolve the Parole of the said Capt. Fage; but on this Condition, that an Order be obtained for the Discharge of some Officer of equal Rank, who being a Prisoner to the English in America, shall be named by the Congress or by General Washington for that Purpose;[6] and that three Copies of such Order be transmitted to me.

(L. S.)   (signed) B. FRANKLIN
                                 Minister Plenipotentiary from the
                                 United States of America at the
                                 Court of France

Notations: Discharge by Dr. Franklin of Capt. Fages Parole 1st. Octr. 1782 / Copy

---

3. Edward Fage had served with Benedict Arnold in Virginia in 1781 and presumably was captured with Cornwallis: *A List of the General and Field Officers, As they Rank in the Army* . . . (London, 1777), p. 203; K. G. Davies, ed., *Documents of the American Revolution, 1770–1783 (Colonial Office Series)* (21 vols., Shannon and Dublin, Ire., 1972–81), XIX, 248; XX, 143.

4. We publish one of the copies made from the now-missing ALS, in preference to BF's sketchy draft. A note at the PRO (FO27 / 2) indicates that this discharge was enclosed in Oswald's letter to Townshend, Oct. 2.

5. Henry Seymour Conway (XII, 209n) was appointed commander-in-chief of the British army in March, 1782: *DNB.*

6. On Oct. 23, Home Secretary Townshend ordered Gen. Carleton to release an American prisoner of equal rank: Davies, *Documents,* XIX, 339.

From Benjamin Franklin Bache

ALS: American Philosophical Society

Mon cher Grand   Geneve Ce 1er Octobre 1782

J'ai Reçue votre lettre du 10 Septembre[7] elle m'a fait un très grand Plaisir parcequ'elle a mit fin a vôtre long silence car j'etois en peine de vous n'ayant point de vos nouvelles. J'ai regardé vôtre silence à Legard des livres dont je vous ai parlé[8] comme vôtre Consentement et comme Mr Marignac craignoit qu'on ne les vendit il les a acheté. Je suis très faché que Cockran aye été en amerique parceque je ne pourrois pas avoir aussi souvent de ses nouvelles[9] mais j'espere pourtant den avoir quelque fois par vôtre moyen, Je suis très etonné de n'avoir point de nouvelles dAmerique depuis si longtems. Mr de Marignac m'a payé une lettre de Change comme vous l'en avez prié par votre lettre du 25 Janvier je vous l'envoye pour que vous en jugiez.[1] Nous allons être Bientôt dans les Congès des Vendanges qui durent un mois mais nous ne restrons pas sans rien faire; dabord avant que de commencer Les Congès le maître nous donne une tahe [tâche] a faire et l'on montre cet ouvrage a la fin des congés[2] et outre cela nous aurons un maitre de latin et un autre de dessin— et le maître du colege donnent une leçon qui dure une heure par jour et je fais mon journal je traduis le Joseph andrews que vous m'avez envoyé. Mr Pigott vous fait bien ses compliments demême que Me Cramer Mr et Me de Marignac vous presentent bien leurs respects.

Je Suis Mon cher grand Papa Votre très humble et très obeissant fils   B Franklin Bache

7. Not found.

8. See his letter above, Aug. 30.

9. Cochran must have sailed in late summer. He left Nantes for Lorient in mid-August: JW to Williams, Moore & Co., Aug. 17, 1782 (Yale University Library).

1. As the notation indicates, BFB enclosed two copies of the bill in his handwriting. This was the condition BF had set for crediting an earlier bill: XXXVI, 477, 597.

2. On Oct. 5, the first day of the vintage holiday, BFB observed in his journal that "il ne faut pas croire que lon ne donne rien a faire au contraire si l'on vouloit bien faire ses Taches l'on travalleroit plus que quand ce n'est pas congé."

Me Serre me Prie de vous demander si les lettres quelle vous a envoyées pour envoyer au Docteur Cooper son arrivées[3] vous me ferez le Plaisir de men dire un mot dans vôtre 1ere Lettre

Docteur Franklin

Addressed: A Monsieur / Monsieur Franklin ministre plenipoten / des etats unis d'amerique auprès de sa majesté / très chetienne addresée a mr. Grand Banquier / Rue Mont Martre / A Paris

Notation: B.F.B. to Dr. Franklin. Geneva, Oct. 1. '82, with 2 drafts of bills of Exchange in B.F.B.'s hand-writing

From Richard Bache

ALS: American Philosophical Society

Dear & Hond: Sir   Philadelphia October 1st. 1782.

We were happy in hearing from you by the Eagle Frigate;[4] you honored me likewise by her with an Introduction to the Prince De Broglii & Count De Segur; these Gentlemen set off immediately for Camp, but as probably they will spend the Winter here, I hope to have an opportunity of shewing them every Civility in my Power—the latter strikes me, as a very amiable young Gentleman.[5]

You request to know Ben's age, he was thirteen last 12th. August— I am afraid the disturbances at Geneva will prevent for some time his progress in his Studies, I find by his Letters, he is quite the Frenchman, but I flatter myself he will soon recover his English.[6]

In looking over some of your papers I find a Note from William Pritchard, who went to Canada with you, for ten Guineas,

3. Doubtless forwarded by Marignac that February: XXXVI, 555.

4. BF's letter was dated June 26, 1782: XXXVII, 550.

5. For de Broglie and Ségur, and BF's letters of introduction, see XXXVII, 88n, 109–10.

6. The armed unrest of the preceding spring had interrupted BFB's schooling for several months, but classes resumed in early August: XXXVII, 123, 139, 682. BF forwarded letters from BFB on June 26. SB worried that if BFB did not recover his English, he would be unable to converse with her: SB to BFB, Oct. 1, 1782 (Musée de Blérancourt).

he is now married & settled here, upon my applying to him, he did not at first recollect that he had given any such Note, but afterwards said he did recollect it, & that he had paid you the Money, but that he had no receipt to shew— I should be glad to know whither you remember its being paid.[7]

I am informed your Friends I-z—d & L—[8] continue their old game of trumping up charges & insinuations against you, they never can forgive your being such a Favorite at the Court of France—they may grin—but I trust they cannot bite.

Sally and the Children are perfectly well, Debby, a sweet little Girl, is a year old this day, her Mother has just weaned her— You have our joint Love & Duty, we beg also to be remembered to Ben.

I am ever Dear Sir Your affectionate son   RICH: BACHE

Dr. Franklin

Addressed: His Excellency / Doctor Franklin / Passy.

From Sarah Bache   ALS: American Philosophical Society

My dear Papa   Philadelphia October 1st. 1782

I should think it wrong to let any opportunity slip without informing you of the Welfare of my little Family, they are well and lovely the Youngest, one Year old this day, and as an infant she is perfect, I have just weaned her, Willy a fine tall straight Lad, this week he began to go to dancing School, Betsy and Lous go to my Old Madam Marsh, how happy should I be to see you surrounded by them, but that's a thought I must put a stop to—[9]

It is something remarkable that we have not had six hours rain at a time since the twenty fifth of may, the People in the Coun-

---

7. For this printer, who had sought assistance from BF in 1776, see XXII, 472–3; XXVII, 605.

8. Ralph Izard and Arthur Lee.

9. The youngest child was Deborah. William was nine years old, Elizabeth five, and Louis almost three: I, lxiii–lxiv. SB previously mentioned her old schoolteacher Nancy Marsh (Mash) in XXXV, 610.

try have something in reality to complain of there will be little or no Buckwheat or Turnips—

William has wrote to you and his Brother[1] he still goes to the Acadimy which has had its name changed to the University, the French Acdimy is where he goes every other evening to learn to dance— Betsy is too Young to go yet.

The Mr Barckly and his Lady who are with you in France are the same who receiv'd me and treated me with so much hospitality when the British turnd us out, little Betsy was not two weeks old when we made the second move from Mr Duffields to Mr Barcklys where the whole Family was three months, Mrs Meaze and Mrs Barckly were to me as two Sisters, when she saild I had lain in with Deby but a day or two and they would not let me write, since which I have mentioned her in several letters but know not wether or not you receiv'd them, I am sure as an American if she comes to Parris you will notice her but I wish you to look on her as one of my best Frends, and one whom I am under obligations to that I could never repay, I mean both for never was a better hearted nor a more hospitable man in the World than Mr Barckly—[2]

Mr Bache will write, the Children join in duty with Your Afectionate and dutifull Daughter[3]   S BACHE

Addressed: Doctor Franklin

1. These letters to BF and BFB have not been found.

2. Fleeing Philadelphia in the autumn of 1777, the Baches stayed for ten days at Edward Duffield's and then removed to Thomas and Mary Barclay's country seat. The Baches also stayed with the Meases, most likely the family of James Mease: XXXI, 20n; XXXII, 337; XXXV, 559.

The Barclays departed for France in October, 1781, and were in Paris by early December: XXXV, 346n; XXXVI, 55, 201.

3. On the same day, both SB and RB wrote to WTF (APS). SB had been faithfully collecting the squirrel skins that local boys were procuring, and promised to send them soon. She also sent news of WF, and reassured WTF that he ought not to believe what the Philadelphia press wrote about him. Above all, she wrote, her affection for both WF and WTF was as strong as ever, and she "should despise the Person who could not make a distinction between a Political difference and a Family one."

From Robert Morris

LS:[4] American Philosophical Society (two), Syracuse University Library; copy: Library of Congress

Sir,—   Office of Finance 1st October 1782—

In my Letter of the twenty seventh of September last I express my Wish "that the Court of Spain should give Orders for the Shipment of a Million of Dollars at the Havanna free of Duties, and *to be convoyed by One or more Ships of the Line* to an American Port, &c." Upon farther Reflection I am induced to believe that the Court of Spain will not readily go into the whole of this Arrangement; for altho they may & probably will agree to so much of it as will procure them an Equivalent in France for the Million Dollars to be shipped from the Havanna, yet there are Reasons to doubt whether they will convoy the Washington hither. I wish you therefore (should you meet with Difficulties in that Quarter) to apply to the Court for such Convoy. I wish it may consist of a Ship of the Line, because none but Frigates will cruize on this Coast during the Winter, and therefore One Ship of the Line will afford more Protection than two or three Frigates. However this will depend entirely on the Convenience or Inconvenience which may attend the Business. I shall communicate both this Letter and that of the twenty seventh to the Chevalier de la Luzerne,[5] on whose Representations I rely much, as well for procuring the Aid asked for, as for accomplishing the necessary Arrangements after it is procured.

I am, Sir, Your most obedient & humble Servant

ROBT MORRIS

His Excellency Benjamin Franklin Esqr.—

Endorsed: Office of Finance Oct. 1. 1782

4. We publish the one endorsed by BF.
5. See *Morris Papers,* VI, 476–7.

From Caleb Whitefoord and Richard Oswald

AL:[6] American Philosophical Society

Paris 1st October [1782]

Mr Whiteford & Mr Oswald present their best respects to Doctr Franklin & will do themselves the honour to wait of him to Dinner on Friday next.[7]

Mr Oswald begs leave to Send the Letter he mentioned Respecting Capt Blair,[8] & will call on the Doctr to morrow in hopes of having a favourable answer to General Conways Request.[9] Mr Fitzherbert is to dispatch a Courier to morrow night, who will carry the Doctors Commands on that head or any other.

Upon looking back upon Mr Hyndmans Letter I observe Capt Blair was an Officer of one of our Regiments

Notation: Mr. Whiteforth & Mr. Oswald

Addressed: A Monsieur / Monsieur Franklin / a Passy

Bettally & Noseda[1] to William Temple Franklin

ALS: American Philosophical Society

This document concerns an invention that Jean-François Pilatre de Rozier had described and announced for sale in the previous day's

---

6. In Oswald's hand.

7. The following Friday was Oct. 4, on which day Oswald and Whitefoord dined at Passy with BF, John and Sarah Jay, Edward Bancroft, Matthew Ridley, and others: Klingelhofer, "Matthew Ridley's Diary," p. 117.

8. The letter is missing, but it probably concerned George Blair of Virginia, a Scot who had emigrated in 1762 and in 1775 joined Lord Dunmore's Loyalist corps. He was commissioned captain of the Guides and Pioneers in 1779 and was captured aboard H.M.S. *Romulus* in 1781: Palmer, *Loyalists,* p. 71; Evan Nepean to ———, Nov. 23, 1782 (APS).

9. See BF's discharge of Capt. Fage's parole, Oct. 1, above.

1. Noseda, a maker and dealer of scientific instruments whose shop was on the rue Saint-Honoré (XXXIV, 4n), was at this time working with a partner about whom we know little. The pair signed themselves "physiciens, rue St. Honoré" in a Nov. 6 letter to the *Jour. de Paris.*

Journal de Paris: bougies phosphoriques, or self-igniting candles.[2] A precursor to matches, *bougies phosphoriques* were the first instruments capable of generating a flame without the arduous use of flint and tinder. The public response was overwhelming, and manufacturers had trouble meeting the demand. As the present document indicates, when Temple inquired about buying *bougies phosphoriques* from Bettaly & Noseda, dealers in scientific instruments, they had only one left, and Pilatre de Rozier—their supplier—had none. The following day Pilatre de Rozier published a statement begging the public to be patient: his stock was depleted and he was waiting for more. He apologized for the manufacturing defects in the first batch of *bougies phosphoriques,* announced a price reduction on future sales, and promised compensation—either in cash refunds or in additional candles—to those who had purchased candles at the higher price.[3]

The inventor, referred to as an anonymous "amateur" in Pilatre de Rozier's article, was Louis Peyla of Turin, who made his first successful *bougies phosphoriques* in 1779. News of his invention reached France in 1782 through the pamphlet of one comte de Challant, who claimed to have made significant improvements.[4] Peyla's own memoir establishing himself as the inventor and describing his manufacturing technique was published in the October, 1782, issue of the *Journal de physique.* His *bougies,* hermetically sealed in close-fitting glass tubes, were reed-thin wax tapers, four to five inches long, whose wicks were infused with a mixture of phosphorus and sulfur. The glass tubes were scored in the middle where they were to be snapped open. The user would warm the wick end of the tube, break off the opposite end, and quickly extract the candle from its casing. If the atmosphere was dry and the air not too damp, the candle would ignite spontaneously and burn long enough to light several other candles or a lamp in the dark.[5]

Many people began making *bougies phosphoriques* and improving

2. "Bougies phosphoriques, inflammables par le contact de l'air; par M. Pilâtre de Rozier," *Jour. de Paris,* Sept. 30, 1782. Though the author had neither invented them nor made them, he marketed them, and his name quickly became associated with the widely discussed invention: Métra, *Correspondence secrète,* XIII, 298–9. For Pilatre de Rozier (1754–1786), whose name is more commonly associated with balloon flights, see the *Dictionary of Scientific Biography.*

3. *Jour. de Paris,* Oct. 2, 1782.

4. Le comte de Challant, *Procédé pour obtenir les bougies inflammables au simple contact de l'air* (Turin, 1782). Pilatre de Rozier cited this pamphlet in his Sept. 30 article.

5. *Jour. de physique,* XX, 312–16.

the technique. In his initial *Journal de Paris* article Pilatre de Rozier wrote that he himself had suggested improvements to the two manufacturers who sold them at the Musée.[6] Bettally & Noseda, finding that their customers complained of low success rates, soon began selling *bougies phosphoriques* of their own manufacture. In a November 6 letter to the *Journal de Paris* they explained that they had learned the secret of a successful phosphorus mixture. Their *bougies* worked in any weather, even in below-freezing temperatures. They also addressed the recently published complaint of a user who had suffered severe burns when excess phosphorus spilled onto his hands. That was due to poor manufacturing, they explained; in their own candles, not a speck of phosphorus could possibly escape.

Franklin was so impressed with these devices that he included *bougies phosphoriques* among the recent scientific developments he described to François Steinsky and Jan Ingenhousz.[7] When Thomas Jefferson arrived in Paris in 1784, he was likewise amazed by these "phosphoretic matches" and planned to send some to America. He later learned that they were already being sold in Philadelphia.[8]

Monsieur   Paris ce pre. octobre 1782

Nous nous trasportame á L'instans che Mr. Desrosierre pour avoirs Des Bougie Fosforique. Il nen avait pas de Fait. Nous en avons eut un que Nous vous envoions vous aure Soin Pour en voir Leffet De Le Casser á Lá Marque du papier e Lescouer aussi tot il S'enflamerá.

Demain Nous en aurons D'autre. Si vous avez ocasion D'envoier Nous en Remeterons La Douzaine.

En atendent L'honeur Des vous ordre Nous Avont Celui Detre parfaittement

Monsieur Votres heumble Serviteur   BETTALLY & NOSEDA

Addressed: A Monsieur / Monsieur Franklin Le Fils / A Passÿ

Notation: Bettaly & Noseda 1er. Oct. 1782

6. The Musée de Monsieur was a scientific library and laboratory open by subscription to scholars and amateurs. Pilatre de Rozier was its director. He described his improvements in a memoir that was published posthumously in Alexandre Tournon, *La Vie et les mémoires de Pilatre de Rozier, écrits par lui-même* ... (Paris, 1786), pp. 92–7.

7. BF to Steinsky, Nov. 23 (below); Ingenhousz to BF, Jan. 28, 1783 (APS).

8. Howard C. Rice, *Thomas Jefferson's Paris* (Princeton, 1976), pp. 22–3; *Jefferson Papers,* VII, 504–5, 514–15, 518; VIII, 16.

From Ingenhousz   ALS: American Philosophical Society

Dear Friend.   Vienna octob. 2. 1782.
    I got at last an account of Pere Barletti's pamphlet in an ital-
ian journal et will peruse it for the farther elucidation of the
notes you was so good as to send me.[9] Mr. le Begue acquaintd me
that you begin to make experiments with air.[1] I am glad of it. But
have you laid aside the reflexions you were making two or 3 years
ago on fire places principaly in relation to the new fire place
which has the forme of a vase or urne?[2] which contrivance has
much affinity with the furnase of the chemists, which they called
very properly *furnus acapnus,* which last word from the greek
Χάπνος smook, the α privatiuum[3] makes it signifie *a furnace
which give no smoak.* Let us not loose your doctrins. Every thing
coming now from you gets an additional importance. The affaire
of chimnies is but little understood, as philosophers have not
much inquired on this, so useful, subject.
    I have not yet recieved neither the Pensylvania almanack nor
the American Newspapers. Doe not forget the admonitory note

    9. See Ingenhousz' letter of Aug. 20, above, for this and subsequent allu-
sions.
    1. Our only evidence of these experiments is the August correspondence
between WTF and Rouland, nephew and protégé of Joseph-Aignan Sigaud
de La Fond, about purchasing a vat with which to produce "dephlogisticated
air" or oxygen. Rouland was a demonstrator in experimental physics at the
University of Paris and had for many years assisted his uncle in the courses
offered at Sigaud de La Fond's renowned *cabinet de physique.* Rouland inherited the *cabinet* when his uncle retired in 1782.
    Rouland initially sent WTF prices for two kinds of vats that could be made
according to his uncle's descriptions (undated, APS). On Aug. 30 Rouland
corrected the prices he had previously quoted, which were far too low. A vat
of the size WTF ordered would cost 57 *l.t.;* varnished and decorated with gold
fleurons (as was the one WTF had seen in the *cabinet*), it would cost an additional 24 *l.t.* APS. For Rouland see *Jour. de Paris,* Oct. 25, 1782; and Jean Tor-
lais, "La Physique expérimentale," in René Taton, ed., *Enseignement et diffusion des sciences en France au XVIIIe siècle* (Paris, 1964), pp. 630–1, 637,
640; *Dictionary of Scientific Biography.*
    2. BF had actually planned to publish his scheme ten years earlier, but never
got beyond having an engraving made of his design. He had copies of that
engraving with him in Passy, and undoubtedly showed it to Ingenhousz during his most recent visit: XXXII, 342n; XXXV, 8–9.
    3. *Privantium, i.e.,* the initial "a" reverses the meaning of the word.

to mr. Wharton, which you forgot to put in you last, tho you mentioned I would find it inclosed: thus you will likely find it on your table— I have not recieved a single word of Dr. Bankroft, tho I begged him as well as mr. Coffyn to acquaint me with the Mercantil transactions Concerning me more than himself. Indeed such behaviour can not but give me some apprehension about his caracter. I have neither any farther intelligence from Mr. Coffyn since I wrote you about it. I trust your admonition will have effect on mr. Sam. wharton and his Son.[4]

This lettre will be delivred to you by mr. *Brantzen* new Duch Minister for making peace. This Gentleman will very willingly and expiditiously transmit to me any lettre, Amer. Newspaper or other parcels of papers, which you will put into his hand. He will transmit them to Count Wassenaer Duch envoye here at Vienna, whose friend I am. Thus we have twoo channels open for correspondence.[5]

A few days ago Sir Robert Murray Keith[6] did send a message to Count Wassenaer with the most agreable (for Sir Rob.) and equaly important news that 7 of the 13 American Provinces submitted to the English Gouvernment, and that the rest would soon follow their exemple. This message was immediately dispersed thro all the town and is still kept up with the same confidence. But it does not goe down by every one, and for my part I can not believe a word of it; as it would be the most shamefull cowardly and unpararelleld treacherous behaviour of them towards themselfs and their alleys.[7] Count Wassenaer however,

4. Ingenhousz had addressed his June 12 letter to Wharton or, in his absence, his son Samuel Lewis Wharton, merchant in Philadelphia. We summarize that letter in XXXVII, 468n; for the son (1759–1788), see Anne H. Wharton, "The Wharton Family," *PMHB*, II (1878), 212.

5. Brantsen forwarded the present letter on Oct. 15; see his letter to BF of that date, below. Carel Georg van Wassenaer tot Wassenaer was minister to the imperial court from early 1782 until Nov. 11, 1784: *Repertorium der diplomatischen Vertreter*, III, 261–2.

6. The British ambassador to Austria: XXIII, 324n.

7. The *Gaz. de Leyde*, Sept. 20, sup., likewise asserted that recent rumors concerning American disunity were "absurd." Only the British, the article said, could be so gullible as to believe these stories, which originated with American Loyalists. The paper included a text that the editors believed had started the stories.

how [who] is a warm defender of the American cause, was so much affected by the news, tho he could not quite believe it, that he beggs me very much to ask from you whether there was any foundation for such rapports. If you have no oportunity of seing Mr. Brantzen him self, you may only send your letters or parcels by the penny post to his hotel, and he will punctualy transmit him to count wassenaer for me.

I Continue to make new and important discoveries on vegetables. I now have discovered the organ it self of the leaves, by which the production of dephlogisticated air is transacted— I hope you have allready seen the burning of wires.[8] I have burned wires even thicker than the sample you will find inclosed. The show of the burning of Such thick piece is wonderfully magnificent and would inspire a terror in those who are not convinced there is no danger at all in the experiment. I believe there is a possibility of burning the blade of a Sword, in one of the Greates Glas vessels filled with fine dephlogisticated air.

I was much pleased to be informed by mr. Tourton & Baur[9] that you are quite recovred from an indisposition, of which our newspapers made mention. As there will be now a Congres for peace, I hope it will be at Vienna.

Doe not forget your old friend. Bestow now and than a moment of you leasure time on him, and believe him to be respectfully Your obedient obliging Serv. and affectionate friend

J. INGEN HOUSZ

to his Exc. Benj. Franklin ministre Plenip. of the united states of America at Paris

Addressed: a Son Excellence / Mr. Benj. Franklin Ministre / Plenipotentiaire des Etats unies / de l'Amerique / a Passy

Endorsed: Oct. 2. 82

8. Described in Ingenhousz' Dec. 8, 1781 letter: XXXVI, 221.

9. The Parisian banking firm who had agreed to serve as intermediaries in Ingenhousz' correspondence with BF: XXXV, 98.

From Rolland frères

ALS: University of Pennsylvania Library

Monsieur   Marseille Ce 2e. 8bre. 1782

Le Navire Wolf[1] appartenant au port d'Edenton et Commandé par le Capne. Sam Butler chargé de 138. boucauds de Tabac de la Virginie et quélqúes Milliers de Merin [merrain]; est arrivé dans Ce port depuis quélqúes jours, ce Capne. qui N'avait aucune Connaissance dans Ce paÿs a bien Voulû s'adresser à Nous, et comme les Administrateurs de la ferme Généralle ne luy ont offert que 60 *l.t.* le quintal de Son Tabac poids de marctare d'usage,[2] nous allons le faire Mettre en entrepôt et pour en rendre la Vente plus avantageuse et Exiter la Concurence; Nous en avons donné avis à nos correspondants des principalles Villes d'Italie & de piemont ou Cette marchandise pourait Convenir, afin de donner de L'emulation aux administrat. de la ferme Généralle. Ce Navire etant armé en Guerre et Marchandise et ayant un Equipage Nombreux: Nous avons Compté au capne. l'argent qu'il Nous a demandé pour faire faire a Son Vaisseau les reparations Utiles et Nous luy fournirons Egalement tout Celuy dont il aura besoin pour accellerer son retour Sans Nuire A sa Vente, et par ce Moïen Eviter un trop long sejour qu'un Nombreux Equipage rendrait fort dispendieux.

Nous sommes tres flâtté: Monsieur, que le premier Navire des Etats unis arrivé dans Ce port nous soit adressé et Nous procure l'occasion de presenter nos homages au liberateur de L'Amerique, et à l'auteur de la plus heureuse révolution que le Globe ait Jamais Eprouvé; Nous avons une fabrique de draps tres Considerable dans le languedoc, et Nous Nous Estimerons heureux si nous pouvions être de quélqúe utilité pour Cet Objet et pour tout autre a Votre Excellance et à sa Nation.

Nous Avons L'honneur de Vous adresser Monsieur, une

---

1. The Virginia ship *Wolf*, carrying 16 cannon and a crew of 60, was commissioned on May 10, 1782: Charles H. Lincoln, comp., *Naval Records of the American Revolution, 1775–1788* (Washington, D.C., 1906), p. 494; É. M. Sanchez-Saavedra, *A Guide to Virginia Military Organizations in the American Revolution, 1774–1787* (Richmond, Va., 1978), p. 172.

2. The price of American leaf peaked in early 1782, sometimes exceeding 125 *l.t.* per quintal, but when the supply increased, the price dropped: Price, *France and the Chesapeake*, II, 721, 723, 728.

lettre du Capne. Sam Butler,[3] son Navire est tres bon Voillier, il y a un Excellent Equipage, et il parait homme à Tirer de l'un et de l'autre toutes les ressources dont il peuvent être susceptible, ainsi si Votre Excellance avait quélqúe chose à faire passer en Amerique, Nous Croyons qu'elle pourrait l'en Charger avec dautant plus de Confiance que les risques dans la Mediterannée et aux detroits Sont actuellement bien Moindres qu'à la sortie des ports du Ponant.

Nous sommes avec un tres profond respect De Votre Excellance Les Tres humbles Et Tres Obeissant Serviteurs

ROLLAND FRERES &CE

Notation: Rolland & freres 2. Octr. 1782.

From Georgiana Shipley   ALS: American Philosophical Society

My dear Sir,   Chilbolton Octber the 2d 1782

Altho: you will very lately have heard from my father,[4] I have too much pride as well as pleasure in the correspondence to relinquish my part of it; the difficulty of finding a safe conveyance for my letter can alone induce me to be silent.

We had the pleasure of breakfasting with Dr Priestley on our return out of Wales, he has an exceeding pretty house 1 mile from Birmingham & appears as happy & comfortable as possible, he is pleased with his situation & lives chiefly with a society of ingenious sensible men who reside at Birmingham;[5] but I believe his happiness proceeds from that cheerful temper of mind, which inclines him to see only *la belle jambe,*[6] & which is the greatest blessing any one can possess. Our good friend Doctor

---

3. Butler's letter is dated Sept. 30. It is published in XXXV, 540–1, where we misread the year as 1781.

4. Jonathan Shipley wrote on Sept. 22, above.

5. The Lunar Society, an informal group of scientists, industrialists, and intellectuals who met monthly and shared an interest in the pure and applied sciences: Jenny Uglow, *The Lunar Men: the Friends Who Made the Future, 1730–1810* (London, 2002).

6. An allusion to "La Belle et la Mauvaise Jambe," which BF had sent her: XXXIV, 41–6; XXXV, 33.

Price has had an ugly accident from a kick of a horse on his an-
kle-bone. This has confined him a considerable time & deprived
us of the pleasure of seeing him at Chilbolton—we expect Mr
Jones next week, from him I hope to hear many satisfactory particulars of our much honor'd & esteemed friend, whom he so
lately has had the happiness of visiting. I do not find Lord Shelburne has decided, whether he shall remain in England or be employed in a judicial capacity in the East-indies, I own, I wish the
former, as I am of opinion Lord Shelburne can not do wiser, than
strengthen himself by the assistance of such men—[7] as for politics, you possibly at Paris may know more of the measures intended to be pursued, than we do at Chilboton, where we live extremely retired & hear little of what passes dessous les Cartes.[8]
I see, by the papers, the arrival of Gov: Franklin,[9] had he been
deserving of [*torn:* you?], how happy should we have been to
have shewn him every mark of friendship & regard, [as] it is, I
feel angry he should bear a name, I have long learned to love and
respect.

Although I have declared my intention of not relinquishing
the correspondence, I see no good excuse for engaging more of
your time, than is sufficient to assure you, how highly we continue to think of our good Doctor Franklin & with how much

7. William Jones arrived in England on Sept. 9 and for several weeks
awaited Shelburne's commands. When none were forthcoming he arranged
a visit to Chilbolton, where he courted Georgiana's older sister Anna.
Garland Cannon, *The Life and Mind of Oriental Jones: Sir William Jones,
the Father of Modern Linguistics* (Cambridge, New York, and Port Chester,
N.Y., 1990), pp. 179–83. For Jones's visit to BF in the summer of 1782 and his
aborted plan to sail for America with John Paradise see XXXVII, 529–30, 704–
5. See also Jones to BF, Nov. 15, below.
8. The "underside of cards" as they lie face down when dealt; an expression meaning that she lacks privileged information.
9. WF was widely blamed for the murder of Joshua Huddy, for which see
XXXVII, 432n, 482n. Moreover, his Board of Associated Loyalists was in danger of dissolution by Gen. Guy Carleton. Bitter and disillusioned, he sailed
from New York on the *Roebuck* on Aug. 18 and arrived in London on Sept.
24: *The London Courant, and Daily Advertiser*, Sept. 25, 1782; Sheila L.
Skemp, *William Franklin: Son of a Patriot, Servant of a King* (New York and
Oxford, 1990), pp. 257–65; Milton M. Klein and Ronald W. Howard, eds.,
*The Twilight of British Rule in Revolutionary America: the New York Letter
Book of General James Robertson, 1780–1783* (Cooperstown, 1983), p. 258n.

warmth and sincerety we pray for that happy day, which shall restore you to England & to those friends, who have long known the misfortune of losing a society so dear to them. Adieu, my dear Sir, & believe me with great respect Your affecate & obliged

G: SHIPLEY.

Addressed: Dr Franklin

From Johann Rodolph Valltravers

ALS: American Philosophical Society

Sir! From Vienna, in Austria, Octr. 2d. 1782.

None of the five Letters, which I had the Honor to write to Your Excellency in the Year 1778, from Switzerland, having been so happy, to meet with the Favor of a Reply: I could not know, how to account for My Misfortune.—[1]

Having since that Time left my native Country, to sollicit in person in Germany, several Sums due to me, from several Courts, as well as Persons, expended in their Service, and Commissions, whilst in England, and France:[2] I forbore to trouble Yr. Excy. any further, as my Letters were then more exposed than ever, to be intercepted; alltho' I much wished to impart many valuable Intelligences, in suport of yr. great Cause, the reasonable Liberties of Mankind.

Monsr. Lieuthaud, a dramatic french Author,[3] and well versed in french and german Literature, on his present Return to Paris, being so obliging, as to take particular Charge of this Letter, and to afford me a long wished for opportunity, of conveÿing a Renewal of mÿ sincere Respects, with a Tender of every good office in mÿ Power, to your worthy self, in Safety: I once more venture to beg ÿour kind Acceptance thereof.

All Attempts, both by Law, and by my humble Petitions and

1. Valltravers had actually written seven times during 1778. BF was ignoring him; see XXIII, 610–11.

2. For his financial difficulties see XXVII, 555–6.

3. Doubtless the dramatist Rauquil-Lieutaud, whose work was produced in Paris in 1783: Tourneux, *Correspondance littéraire*, XIII, 432; XIV, 18–19, 424.

Remonstrances, to recover my sacrificed Propertÿ, from these german Vulturs, proving all vain: I now prepare for a Journey to Venice, towards the latter End of this Month, where I shall be happy, to recieve the Honor of yr. Excellcy's. Commands, under Cover of his christian Majs. Minister, Monsr. le Presidt. de Vergennes, Brother to the King's Minister at Versailles, my old Patron, when ambassador in Switzerland.[4] Or, if ÿr. Excy. had anÿ Commands for this Place, previous to my leaving it, theÿ might still reach me in Time, conveÿed for me, to Baron Fichtl,[5] Agent for the holÿ roman Empire, at Vienna.

If your Exccy. thinks, I might be usefull to his Constituents, in Sounding the general Dispostion of the Venitian State, towards the free States of America; in bringing that respectable Common Wealth over to the Suport, Independence and Prosperity of their new-born Sister-Republick beÿond the Atlantik; in forwarding an early Connection, Friendship, Trade, and defensive Alliance between both; or in raising at, least, Some, under Hand, pecuniary Assistance, of Cash, Shipping, and Merchandise, if over-awed bÿ Great-Britain: Yr. Exccy's. Instructions on these Objects shall be received with Joy, managed with Prudence and Discretion, and obeÿed with Punctuality, Zeal, Fidelitÿ and Dispatch.——

Mr. Jas. Creassey (Surveÿor, lately returned from the East-Indies, with heavy Complaints against the Brittish Companÿ's Depredations and the Treachery & Tÿranny of their Servants;) having made me a Cession of Part of his Lands, in the North-Part of the Province of New-York, along the Mohawk River; and being promised a Similar Cession in Georgia, from Genl. Oglethorpe:[6] I consider mÿself as a Fellow-Citizen of ÿours, in the new World, and am not a litle proud of that Honor.——

A Tour made thro' Hungaria, a most fertile Country, ill-peopled, wretched, and ill-cultivated, from the slavish Condition of

4. Jean Gravier, marquis de Vergennes (XXIV, 551n), the brother of the French foreign minister, was French ambassador in Venice from 1779 to 1784, following a posting in Switzerland: *Repertorium der diplomatischen Vertreter,* III, 137, 143.

5. Probably Johann Baptist von Fichtl: *Repertorium der diplomatischen Vertreter,* III, 512.

6. James Oglethorpe (*DNB*) was the founder of Georgia.

184

theirs Husbandmen, has convinced me more & more that legal & equal Liberty alone, is the Soul of Industrÿ, Diligence, Wealth & Happiness.

I am with everlasting Veneration, Gratitude and Attachment, Sir! Your Excellence's Most devoted hble. Servt.

RODH. VALLTRAVERS.

P.S. yr. friend, Dr. Ingenhuÿs, continues well, & indefatigable in his instructive Labors.—

William Temple Franklin to Robert R. Livingston

ALS and transcript: National Archives

Sir,   Passy, 2 Oct. 1782.

I am directed by my Grandfather[7] to forward you the inclosed Papers, which were put into his Hands by the Ambassador from Portugal, and to request you would take them into Considera-tion.—[8]

With great Respect, I have the honour to be, Sir, Your most obedient & most humble Sert.—   W. T. FRANKLIN

The honble R. R. Livingston Esqr.

7. Oswald reported to Townshend on Oct. 2 that BF was still unwell and not able to travel: Giunta, *Emerging Nation*, I, 594.

8. The papers were English translations of a shipping manifest from Limerick for a cargo of butter and beef, and documents establishing that the vessel *Nossa Senhora da Soledade Saõ Miguel é Almas* was owned by Capt. Manoel Joze Gomes da Costa of the Portuguese port of Faro, and Miguel do O' of nearby Olhaõ. The vessel had been captured by an American ship and sent to Boston: Wharton, *Diplomatic Correspondence*, VI, 344. Seven months earlier BF had called Livingston's attention to a longstanding complaint of Ambassador Sousa de Coutinho about the seizure of another Portuguese ship: XXXVI, 644.

From Benjamin Franklin Bache

ALS: American Philosophical Society

Mon cher grand Papa,   [on or after October 3, 1782][9]

J'ai reçu Par Mr Griffiths la lettre de mon cousin du 18 Septembre avec le livre que vous avez eu la bonté de m'énvoyér.[1] J'en ferai un bon usage et je veux en apprendre plusieurs Morceaux me conseille de faire je vous envoye vôtre portrait fait de ma main d'après la gravure que vous m'avez envoyé la paix ne se fait pas et c'est ce qui me fait beaucoup de peine mais j'espere que quand elle sera faite vous viendrez a Genêve comme vous me l'avez promis[2] il y a bien longtems que je n'ai eu des nouvelles de mes parents c'est pour quoi j'en attends tous les jours mais c'est en vain vous me ferez plaisir de m'apprendre les principales nouvelles dans vôtre premiere lettre (car a Geneve on en apprend guere que des fausses) ou par mon cousin a qui vous ferez bien mes Compliments.

Je suis Mon cher Grand Papa Vôtre très humble et très Obeissant Petit Fils   BENJAMIN FRANKLIN BACHE

Addressed: A Monsieur / Monsieur Franklin Ministre / Plenipotentiaire des états unis / dAmerique auprès de sa majésté / très chretienne / A Passy près Paris

9. The day BFB reported in his journal that Samuel Griffitts (XXXV, 246n) had arrived with a letter and package for him.

1. Possibly William Enfield's *The Speaker: or, miscellaneous pieces* (XXXVI, 288n), which BFB mentioned having received in a March 30, 1783, letter (APS).

2. Before civil unrest broke out at Geneva in the spring of 1781, BF had planned to visit BFB there: XXXIV, 140, 486n.

From Sir Edward Newenham[3]

ALS: University of Pennsylvania Library

Sir, Paris Thursday Evenig [October 3, 10, or 17, 1782][4]

I have the honor to Enclose for your Excellencys perusal the Speches of Mr. Fox &c &c which I am well assured are Genuine—

The London paper of the 1st Instant, has done me the honor of mentioning that I Breakfasted with Mr Laurens—

The same paper contains the Important resolutions of the most respectable Volunteer Corps against the raising of the fensibles, & the very proper Contempt they shewed Mr Dobbs, upon his *treachery* in accepting of so disgracefull a Commission;[5]

3. Newenham, who in July had requested a passport to visit France with his wife, three of his children, and three servants (XXXVII, 627–8), delayed his departure until September. He left England sometime after Sept. 24, the day when both Henry Laurens (whom he visited, as he says below) and WF arrived in London. (Laurens' date of arrival is recorded in *Laurens Papers*, XV, xlv, 26.) Upon hearing that WF had arrived, Newenham wrote him that he would soon be leaving for Paris, and would be glad to carry a message to BF. We have no indication that WF responded, but Newenham must have brought BF a copy of that letter (undated); it is at the University of Pa. Library and bears a notation by L'Air de Lamotte. For the context of Newenham's trip, see James Kelly, *Sir Edward Newenham MP, 1734–1814: Defender of the Protestant Constitution* (Dublin, 2004), pp. 180–4.

A fragment of Newenham's journal of this trip survives (National Archives of Canada). It begins with Oct. 11, halfway through the family's stay in Paris. That first section, up through Oct. 19, their last full day in the city, is published in Dixon Wecter, "Benjamin Franklin and an Irish 'Enthusiast,'" *Huntington Library Quarterly*, IV (1940–41), 215–19. BF and Jay included them in many dinners and social events; BF showed Newenham his "Electrical Apparatus" and supposedly discussed with him territorial concessions made by Britain.

4. The three Thursdays between Oct. 1, a date mentioned in the present letter, and Oct. 20, the day the Newenhams left Paris.

5. The Volunteers, established in Ireland through local initiative after regular troops were withdrawn to fight the Revolution, defended property, enforced law and order, and championed several political causes, including legislative independence (secured earlier in 1782). Fencible regiments were proposed during the summer of 1782 to restore military power to the government. Many Volunteers perceived them as rivals, but some prominent Volunteers, including Francis Dobbs (1750–1811), accepted commissions in the new regiments. A lawyer, writer, and future member of Ireland's Parlia-

Each resolution is Copyed from that of my Corps—[6]
I have the Honor, to be, with Every sentiment of Respect &
Esteem your Excellencys most Obt: & most Hbl: Sert

EDWARD NEWENHAM

Notation: Newenhay

From the Comtesse de Ponteney

ALS: American Philosophical Society

Monsieur   paris 3. 8bre. 1782
Jait Eü lhonneur il Lia quatre ans de diner avec vous la veille
de mon depart pour Litaillie rue du Bacq chez Mr. de la faye.[7] Je
suis de retourd depuis plusiers semaines. Le 12 du Mois passé jeü
lhoneur de remettre a la Reine une lettre que la Reine de Naple[8]

---

ment, Dobbs had played a leading role in the push for legislative independence. S. J. Connolly, *The Oxford Companion to Irish History* (Oxford
and New York, 1998), pp. 151, 581; Maurice R. O'Connell, *Irish Politics and
Social Conflict in the Age of the American Revolution* (Philadelphia, 1965),
pp. 325–38; Edith M. Johnston-Liik, ed., *History of the Irish Parliament,
1692–1800* (6 vols., Belfast, 2002), IV, 67–8; P. D. H. Smyth, "The Volunteers and Parliament, 1779–84," in *Penal Era and Golden Age: Essays in Irish
History, 1690–1800*, ed. Thomas Bartlett and D. W. Hayton (Belfast, 1979),
pp. 122–4.

    Four resolutions opposing the fencibles, three from Volunteer units and
one from Dobbs's own County Armagh, appeared in the Oct. 1 edition of
The Morning Post, and Daily Advertiser (though the reference to Laurens did
not). The resolution from the Ulster Regiment declares that a self-justifying
statement from Dobbs "deserves no particular answer from the Delegates of
Ulster—he may collect the sense of that body from the universal odium in
which the measure he defends is held."

    6. Newenham was the colonel of Dublin's Liberty Volunteers, who had
successfully pressured him to renounce Dobbs. Dobbs had recently listed
Newenham as a fellow opponent of attempting to force Britain to formally
renounce any claim of legislating for Ireland: Kelly, *Newenham*, pp. 149,
177–9.

    7. Julien-Pierre de La Faye, the treasurer for military pensions, had
warmly recommended Mme de Ponteney's husband to BF in 1777 as a source
of military supplies and continued to promote the couple's interests: XXIV,
550; XXV, 47n; XXVI, 581; XXVII, 55–6.

    8. The Queen of Naples was Marie-Antoinette's older sister Marie-Car-
oline (1752–1814): Larousse.

luy a Ecrit an ma faveurs. Je suis obligee dailler demain Vendredy a la muette[9] et Comme jignore le tams que je serois obligee
dattendre je desireroit savoir Monsieur si sans vous aincomoder
vous voulies me permettre dattendre chez vous le tams que je
seres dans le Cas dattandre la reponse de S.M. qui Mautorisse(?).
Jen serois dautant plus charmee que jorois locasion de vous renouveller les sentiments respectueux avec la quelle jait lhoneur
detre Monsieur Votre tres humble et tres obeisente servante

LA COMTESSE DE PONTENEY
rue du Bacq hotel de Nevers.

Notation: La Ctesse. de Ponteney 3 8bre. 1782.

From Vergennes

L (draft):[1] Archives du Ministère des affaires étrangères; two copies and
transcript: National Archives

A Vlles le 3. 8bre 1782.

J'ai l'honneur, M. de vous renvoyer la patente par laquelle le Sr.
Thomas Barclay a êté nommé Consul des Etats unis pour resider
en france, et j'y joins l'exequatur qui lui est necessaire pour le-
gitimer Ses fonctions.[2] Je dois vous prevenir que cette derniere
piece doit etre revetue de l'attache de M. l'amiral[3] avant d'etre
enregistrée Soit au Greffe de l'amirauté de l'Orient ou le Sr. Barclay compte fixer Son Sejour, Soit à ceux des autres Ports du
Royaume ou des raisons de commerce exigeroient Sa presence.

M. franklin

9. The royal château at the entrance to the bois de Boulogne on the Passy
side. The court was in residence there for two months while the King's
three-year-old daughter, Marie-Thérèse-Charlotte, was inoculated against
smallpox: Bachaumont, *Mémoires secrets,* XXI, 106–7; Mathurin-François-
Adolphe de Lescure, ed., *Correspondance secrète inédite sur Louis XVI, Marie-
Antoinette: La cour et la ville de 1777 à 1792* (2 vols., Paris, 1866), I, 509; *Almanach royal* for 1782, p. 33.

1. In the hand of Gérard de Rayneval.

2. Barclay had presented his commission to Vergennes on Sept. 12; see BF
to Vergennes, Sept. 8.

3. The duc de Penthièvre, *amiral de France,* who concerned himself chiefly
with judicial matters.

From the Comte de Mercy-Argenteau[4]

AL: American Philosophical Society

Le 4 8bre. 1782

L'ambassadeur de LEmpereur aura grand soin de faire parvenir Le Paquet adressé a Mr d'Ingenhouse, que Monsieur Franklin Lui a fait l'honneur de lui envoÿer,[5] il a celui de lui offrir ses hommages tres humbles.

Notation: de l'Empereur. 4. Oct. 1782

Preliminary Articles of Peace: First Draft Treaty[6]

Incomplete copy and copy:[7] National Archives; copies: Massachusetts Historical Society (three), Public Record Office[8]; four transcripts: National Archives

[October 5–7, 1782]
Articles agreed upon, by & between Richard Oswald Esqr. the Commissioner of his Britannic Majesty for treating of Peace

4. The ambassador of the Holy Roman Empire, who had forwarded books and letters to Jan Ingenhousz from BF and others: XXXIV, 123; XXXV, 549; XXXVII, 468.

5. The packet may have been from Ingenhousz' friend Dr. Schwediauer, who introduced himself to BF on Sept. 17, above.

6. Jay and Oswald began discussing the preliminary articles once they exchanged commissions on Oct. 1; see the headnote to WTF's commission, Oct. 1, above. BF was not well enough to attend their sessions in Paris, though they consulted him at Passy. John Jay wrote this draft with BF's approval and delivered it to Oswald on Oct. 5. Oswald was optimistic about a speedy conclusion; when sending the draft to Townshend, he suggested that if it were acceptable "in the main," he should be trusted to negotiate whatever small changes were desired and authorized to sign the treaty: Oswald to Townshend, Oct. 2, 7, and 8, 1782, in Morris, *Jay: Peace,* pp. 372–8, 384, 388. BF hosted a dinner at Passy on Oct. 4 for Oswald and others; see our annotation of Oswald and Whitefoord to BF, Oct. 1.

7. The incomplete copy (missing the end of the final paragraph) is in L'Air de Lamotte's hand and is most likely the version that BF sent Livingston on Dec. 5. We print that text, supplying the final section from the other copy at the National Archives, which was undoubtedly made from the version BF sent.

8. In Oswald's hand. Oswald sent this copy to Townshend on Oct. 8; it is printed in Morris, *Jay: Peace,* pp. 389–92.

with the Commissioners of the United States of America, on the behalf of his said Majesty on the one part, and Benjn. Franklin, John Jay [*blank*]⁹ of the Commissioners of the said States for treating of Peace with the Commissioner of his said Majesty on their behalf, on the other part. To be inserted in, & to constitute the Treaty of Peace propos'd to be concluded between the Crown of Great Britain and the said United States. But which Treaty is not to be concluded, untill his Britannic Majesty shall have agreed to the Terms of Peace between France and Britain, proposed or accepted by his most Christian Majesty; and shall be ready to conclude with him such Treaty accordingly. It being the Duty and Intention of the United States, not to desert their ally, but faithfully and in all things to abide by, and fulfil their Engagements with his most Christian Majesty.

Whereas reciprocal Advantages & mutual Convenience are found by Experience, to form the only permanent Foundation of Peace and Friendship between States, it is agreed to frame the Articles of the proposed Treaty, on such Principles of liberal equality and Reciprocity, as that partial Advantages (those seeds of Discord) being excluded, such a beneficial & satisfactory intercourse between the two Countries may be established, as to promise & secure to both the Blessings of perpetual Peace & Harmony.

I.

His Britannic Majesty acknowledges the said United States viz, Newhampshire, Massachusetts Bay, Rhode Island & Providence Plantations, Connecticut, New York, New Jersey, Pensylvania, Delaware, Mariland, Virginia, North Carolina, South Carolina and Georgia, to be free, Sovereign & independent States; That he treats with them as such; and for himself his Heirs & Successors relinquishes all Claims to the Government Propriety and territorial Rights of the same, and every part thereof. And that all Disputes which might arise in future on the Subject of the Boundaries of the said United States, may be pre-

---

9. Left blank for the insertion of JA's name, should he arrive in time for the final negotiations.

vented, it is hereby agreed and declared, that the following are, and shall remain to be their Boundaries, Viz:

The said States are bounded *North,* by a Line to be drawn from the Northwest Angle of Nova Scotia, along the high Lands which divide those Rivers which empty themselves into the River St. Laurence, from those which fall into the Atlantic Ocean, to the northernmost head of Connecticut River, thence down allong the Middle of that River, to the forty fifth Degree of North Latitude, and thence due west in the Latitude forty five Degrees North from the equator, to the Northwestermost Side of the River St. Lawrence, or Cadaraquii; thence straight to the South End of the Lake *Nipissing,* and thence Streight to the Source of the River Mississippi:[1] *West,* by a line to be drawn along the Middle of the River Mississipi from its Source, to where the said Line shall intersect the thirty first Degree of North Latitude. *South* by a Line to be drawn due east from the termination of the Line last mentioned, in the latitude of thirty one Degrees North of the Equator to the Middle of the River appalachicola or Catahouchi, thence along the middle thereof to its Junction with the flint River; thence Straight to the head of St. Mary's River; and thence down along the middle of St. Mary's River to the Atlantic Ocean. And *East,* by a Line to be drawn along the middle of St. John's River, from its Source, to its Mouth in the Bay of Fundy; comprehending all Islands within twenty Leagues of any Part of the Shores of the United States, and lying between Lines to be drawn due East from the points where the aforesaid Boundaries between Nova Scotia on the one Part, and East Florida on the other, shall respectively touch the Bay of Fundy and the Atlantic Ocean.

(2)

From and immediately after the Conclusion of the proposed Treaty, there shall be a firm and perpetual Peace, between his Britannic Majesty and the said States; and between the Subjects of the One & the Citizens of the other. Wherefore all Hostilities both by Sea and Land, shall then immediately cease; All Pris-

1. This border would have given the United States a major portion of what now is the province of Ontario.

oners on both Sides shall be set at Liberty; and his Britannic Majesty shall forthwith and without causing any Destruction withdraw all his Armies Garrisons and Fleets from the said United States and from every post, Place & Harbour within the same; leaving in all Fortifications the American Artillery that may be therein. And shall also order and cause all Archives, Records, Deeds and Papers belonging to either of the said States or their Citizens, which in the Course of the War may have fallen in to the hands of his officers, to be forthwith restored and delivered to the proper States and Persons to whom they belong.

3

That the Subjects of his Britannic Majesty and People of the said United States, shall continue to enjoy unmolested the Right to take fish of every kind, on the Banks of Newfoundland and other Places where the Inhabitants of both Countries used formerly, Viz: before the last War between France and Britain, to fish; and also to dry & cure the same, at the accustomed places, whether belonging to his said Majesty, or to the United States: And his Britannic Majesty, and the said United States will extend equal Priviledges and Hospitality to each other's Fishermen, as to their own.

4.

That the Navigation of the River Mississipi from its Source to the Ocean shall for ever remain free & open, and that both there and in all Rivers, Harbours, Lakes, Ports and Places, belonging to his Britannic Majesty, or to the United States, in any Part of the World, the Merchants and Merchant Ships of the one and the other shall be received, treated and protected like the Merchants and Merchant Ships of the Sovereign of the Country. That is to say, the British Merchants & Merchants Ships[2] on the one hand, shall enjoy in the United States & in all Places belonging to them, the same Protection & commercial Priviledges, & be liable only to the same Charges & Duties, as their own Merchants & Merchant Ships. And on the other hand, the Merchants

2. From this point to the end is reprinted from the other National Archives copy.

& Merchant Ships of the United States shall enjoy in all Places belonging to his Britannic Majesty, the same Protection & commercial Priviledges & be liable only to the same Charges & Duties as British Merchants & Merchant Ship Saving always to the chartered trading Companies of Great Britain, such exclusive Use & Trade of their respective Posts & Establishments as neither the other subjects of Great Britain, nor any the most favoured Nation participates in.

N.B.[3] Mr. Oswald objecting to the Eastern Boundary of the United States as described in the first Article it was agreed to substitute the following vizt.

East by Nova Scotia the true Line between which & the United States shall be settled by Commissioners as soon as conveniently may be after the War.

3. On the morning of Oct. 7 Oswald expressed to Jay his reservations about the Nova Scotia boundaries as delineated in Article 1. According to Oswald, Jay was "willing to Sett that matter to rights, so as the Massachusetts Government shall have no more of that Coast, than they had before the War. He took his directions from maps, and they are not distinct, nor do they agree in this matter. This is in the mean time referred, to be afterwards properly adjusted." Oswald also asked Jay about the issue of drying fish on Newfoundland, which had not been included in BF's necessary articles. Jay said he "put them into the Treaty to avoid an Appearance of unneighborly distinctions," feeling certain there was room enough for the British, Americans, and the French, but Oswald sensed that Jay seemed willing to negotiate the point. Jay suggested that once the British government had approved the treaty and it had been signed, a copy could be sent to Gen. Carleton so that he and Gen. Washington could settle a convention for the evacuation of the British garrisons in America. Jay then left to consult with BF about the boundary and about their writing to Washington in advance: Oswald to Townshend, Oct. 7, in Morris, *Jay: Peace,* pp. 384–6.

Jay met again with Oswald that evening. BF "could not determine as to the Boundary Line between Nova Scotia and Massachusetts Bay, and thought it was best to leave it to be Settled by an express Commission for that purpose, after the War, and accordingly added a Minute of that Clause to the enclosed Treaty, to Stand as a part of it when Signed." BF also argued against the American commissioners' writing to Washington, feeling confident that once Washington saw a signed copy of the treaty he would immediately come to an agreement with Carleton about the matter: Oswald to Townshend, Oct. 8, in Morris, *Jay: Peace,* pp. 387–8. Oswald enclosed a copy of the preliminary articles under cover of the letter just cited, urging that he be granted orders to sign it.

From Laurent Josselin and Other Applicants for
Emigration   L: University of Pennsylvania Library

Many of the applicants for emigration during the period covered by this volume claim solid technical skills or commercial experience which they hope to exploit in some fashion in America.[4] Laurent Josselin, whose letter is printed below, is an expert surveyor and civil architect.

On November 27, M. des Rosières writes from the château de Vincennes on behalf of a poor young man named Minet. The year before, when Franklin supposedly was seeking journeyman printers to send to "l'imprimerie de Philadelphie," Minet had applied. He is educated, very intelligent, and has wit, talent, and a readiness to work. Would Franklin send him to America anyway, either to Philadelphia or elsewhere, as he could do almost anything? Des Rosières is a chevalier de Saint-Louis and former captain of students at the Ecole militaire.[5]

N. Leleu l'aîné, an Amiens merchant who had aided American prisoners in May,[6] writes on November 29 on behalf of an unnamed young man, 30 years old, who is sensible, intelligent, and a veteran of several commercial firms. The young man hopes to establish his own firm in America once he has familiarized himself with that country. He has not the means to pay his way, but is persuaded that with Franklin's protection he will secure free passage on a French or American vessel.[7]

Also unable to pay for a voyage to America, Pierre and Jean-Baptiste Payen have arrived in Paris with letters of recommendation for several persons of note. They are manufacturers at the royal drapery at Sedan, like their father, Pierre.[8] Convinced that peace is soon to come, they wish to contribute to the commercial rebuilding of the young nation by establishing a drapery there or engaging in some kind of enterprise, including military service if Franklin cannot help them otherwise. Their three-and-a-half-page letter is undated, but the sev-

---

4. Except where indicated the documents in this group are in French and located at the APS.

5. He is probably the Desrozières mentioned in Mazas, *Ordre de Saint-Louis*, I, 480. Attached to each of the four companies of students at the Ecole militaire were a first and a second captain. There were also two supernumerary second captains: *Almanach royal* for 1775, p. 137.

6. See XXXVII, 273, 276–7.

7. Leleu attached a now-missing plea from the young man's family.

8. The father is listed in the *Almanach des marchands*, p. 447.

eral allusions to the coming peace suggest that it was written sometime in 1782.

On January 7, Damboix fils writes on behalf of his group of five or six young people, all from honest and modest families, who want to go to Boston and wish Franklin to tell them if Congress will extend its protection to them. They all have received good educations and they lead simple, quiet lives. If in his letter he has sinned against etiquette, Damboix adds in a postscript, Franklin should please excuse his youth and inexperience.

The last to write, on January 16, is M. Penide, a silk merchant of Lyon. He and two companions want to establish a silk factory in America where, he has been assured, the soil is highly suited to the mulberry and will allow this branch of commerce to flourish. He is experienced in raising silkworms as well as finishing the silk. His companions have each their own expertise: one in dyeing wool and silk, and the other in drawing and engraving designs for silk and cotton fabrics. They desire Franklin's assessment of their project and his protection for their passage.

[on or before October 5, 1782][9]
A Son Excellence Monsieur franklin, Ambassadeur des Etats-Unis de l'Amérique, auprès de la Cour de france.

Le sr. Laurent Josselin, Natif de Compiégne, Agé de 30. Ans; cy devant employé dans l'arsenal du Roi de Marseille; Géométre Juré pour la Provence, professant l'Architecture Civile, et ayant des connoissances Elémentaires de celle Militaire; ayant perdu son Emploi par la vente que le Roi à faitte de Son Arsenal dans cette dite Ville,[1] a été compris dans la réforme générale des Su-

---

9. The day Vicq d'Azyr wrote to BF forwarding Josselin's petition. Vicq recommended the young man as one who burned to make himself useful in the country that owed a large part of its liberty to BF. People of merit had vouched for Josselin's worth and honesty, and Vicq thought him deserving, too, and hoped that BF would help him. University of Pa. Library.

One of these people of merit was the painter Claude-Joseph Vernet (XXIV, 491n), who on Sept. 25 wrote Mme Brillon asking her to recommend Josselin to BF. Vernet had learned about his talents from a friend in Marseille. As a civil and military architect, Josselin could be useful in America given "Les circonstances ou nous sommes." University of Pa. Library.

1. The Arsenal des Galères, closed in 1748 when Louis XV abolished the galley corps as a separate naval service, had resumed operations on a small scale in 1762. Early in 1781, it was decided to close the arsenal and sell the land to the city of Marseille. The one remaining galley was sent to Toulon:

jets qui y étoient employés. Quoiqu'il pût continuer son Etat de Géométre et d'Architecte dans ladite Province de laquelle il a obtenu des lettres d'exercice d'après un Examen qu'il a subi Sur diverses branches des Mathématiques; Il préféreroit cependant pour plus d'extension et pratiquer davantage passer au Service des Etats-unis de l'Amérique. Avant de quitter sa Patrie il désireroit avoir quelqu'espoir bien fondé d'être employé dans ces contrées: ce dont il n'en douteroit point s'il étoit assez heureux pour y aborder Sous les auspices d'un homme que Sa Patrie respecte autant que les Pays Étrangers. Il peut être employé à la suite des Armées; et très utilement dans la Levée des Cartes et Plans, dans lesquels Seroit joints la description Topographique des Lieux &c.

Il a aussi des Connoissances de la Méchanique et de l'hydraulique, tant théorique que pratique.

L'objet de Ses désirs, est de Se rendre utile chés un peuple assez fortuné, pour ne dépendre que des Loix qu'il a reçues des mains des sages./.

From Robert Morris

LS: American Philosophical Society; copy: Library of Congress

Sir   Office of Finance 5th. October 1782.

I have the Pleasure to enclose you the Copy of an Act of Congress of the ninth of September last.[2] I shall make no Comments on this Act which as it relieves you from farther Trouble and Anxiety on the Subject it relates to will I am sure be agreable.

Raoul Busquet, *Histoire de Marseille* (rev. ed., Paris and Marseille, 1998), pp. 260–1; Charles Carrière, *Négociants marseillais au XVIIIe siècle* (2 vols., Marseille, 1973), I, 164, 166.

2. The resolution ordered Morris to forbid loan office commissioners from issuing bills of exchange on American ministers in Europe to pay the interest on loan office certificates: *JCC*, XXIII, 553–5. Congress had earlier placed limits on such bills of exchange: XXXV, 379n. BF endorsed one of his copies "Resolution of Congress Sept 9. 1782 No more Interest Bills to be issued": University of Pa. Library. Other copies are at the APS and the Hist. Soc. of Pa.

I am Sir Your Excellency's most obedient & humble Servant
ROBT MORRIS

His Excellency Doctor Franklin.

Endorsed: Office of Finance Oct 5. 1782

From Samuel Powel Griffitts[3]

ALS: Historical Society of Pennsylvania

Honoured Sir,   Lyons October 6th. 1782.

I arrived here Yesterday from Geneva, where I left young Mr. Bache very well the Day before. He, as well as his School-Mate, Mr. Johnnot were very happy to hear from you: They both appear to be contented with their Situation & what is more Monsieur Marignac seems very well satisfied with their Conduct—[4] He treats them as Friends, & they repay him with Respect and Attention— The City is at present very still & free from Disorders.

Mr. Mayo joins with me in Compliments and best Wishes for your Health—[5] We should both be very happy to hear of its being perfectly re-established— With the greatest Respect & Consideration, I remain Your much obliged hble. Servant
SAML. POWEL GRIFFITTS

His Excelly. Doctor Franklin

3. After having spent a year in Paris to continue his medical studies, Griffitts (XXXV, 246–7) was on his way to the University of Montpellier, where he attended a course of lectures. (He wrote WTF from Montpellier on Oct. 31; APS.) In 1783 he took courses at the University of Edinburgh and returned to Philadelphia the following year: Gouverneur Emerson, *Biographical Memoir of Dr. Samuel Powel Griffitts* (Philadelphia, 1827), pp. 7–8; Whitfield J. Bell, Jr., "Philadelphia Medical Students in Europe, 1750–1800," *PMHB*, LXVII (1943), 1, 15, 24.

4. The day Griffitts arrived BFB took him to the bell tower of the Cathedral of St. Peter to view the city. The following day he and Johnnot met Griffitts for lunch and accompanied him partway to meet the coach to Lyon: BFB's journal for Oct. 3 and 4 (APS).

5. Joseph Mayo, a contemporary of WTF's, had been traveling around Europe for about a year: XXXV, 375n, 649. On Aug. 8, he wrote WTF from Dijon that he expected soon to go to Besançon or Lyon (APS).

From Jane Mecom

ALS: University of Pennsylvania Library

Ever Dear Brother   Warwick Rhoad Island octr 6—1782

I hear Freequently of the Arival of Vesals From France to all Parts of America but not won Scrape of a Pen has your Sister Recived from you two-years & half Past.[6] Thank God I hear of you by others that you are in Health and spirits, Sill Labouring in the way of Duty for our poor Country; and that is a comfort to me, but I can't help wishing, tho I have all most given over Expecting, a Leter from you; I have however acording to your Desier in a former leter keept on writing[7] tho I recved no Ansure, & want to comunicate to you my fealings at times, some times the Sorrows I am Exercised with, but mor Frequently my Gratitude for the comfortable Circumstances that have atended my Old Age throw your means, which I Reflect on as the Foundation of all under God. But as no Temporal Injoyment is Permanent I have mett a Severe Lose in the Death of my Grandaughter, her temper, and Sentements, were so agreable to me & she was so Tender of me on all Ocations, I have wrot you wons Since her Death[8] & so many times before I cant Sopose they have all miscarried,—if this should Reach you do let me know from your own Hand you have not Loste the Affection you Used to have for me and it will be a comfortable soport under my Present Berevement.

I am still with the children and Husband of the Deceas'd who behaves wery Affectionatly to me, & wishes my continuance with them, and I know nothing to the conterary at present but where Ever I may be your Leters would find me Directed to Cousen Williams's or Goverener Greenes.[9] I beleve your Publick Business is Fatigueing anouf, but I hope you have some time for Relaxation & that your Life and Health will be Preserved till you see an End to those Dreadfull Wars.

6. BF's most recent letter, now missing, was written in March, 1780: XXXVII, 495n.

7. Perhaps his request in 1779 that she not let the uncertainty of the mail discourage her: XXIX, 357.

8. Jane Flagg Greene died in April, 1782. Mecom had written twice since then: XXXVII, 495–6, 548–9.

9. Jonathan Williams, Sr., and William Greene.

I have not had a Line from Mr Bache or cousen sally these two years Past, I have no Idea of the cause I have wrote to them twice in the time.[1]

Thus far I had wrot when I rec'd a Leter from cousen Williams Informing me He was going to France & wish'd to be the Barrer of a Leter from me to you, Glad as I am to have it go by won who I know will Deliver it saif if he gits there I can't be Reconciled to his going till the War is over for my own sake as well as His & his Famelies, he has allways been a valeuable Friend to me, I shall mis Him very much in His Absence I dont know the Person that can suply his Place & would do it so Respectfully & affectionatly. But Pope says Submit in this & Evry other Sphere, Secure to be as Bles'd as thou canst bare,[2] that sentence has been often a humbling to me to vew my self to be of so weak & low a mind that could bare so litle besides croses & afflictions.

My Friend the Governers wife has wrot you several times[3] & has had no Ansure I am sorry If the Politeness of the French Ladies Lessen your old American acquaintaince in your Esteeme this you will Excuse from your Ever affectionate sister.

JANE MECOM

His Excellency Dr Franklin

Addressed: His Excellency Benjamin Franklin Esqr / at Pasy / In / France

From William Lee

ALS: Historical Society of Pennsylvania; copies: Virginia Historical Society (three), University of Virginia Library

Sir.   Bruxelles 7 Oct. 1782.

I have the Honor to send you herewith, Copy of a Letter from Mr. Robt. R. Livingston Secretary of Congress for Foreign Af-

1. For their most recent known correspondence see XXXIV, 202n, 425n.
2. Mecom closely paraphrases Alexander Pope's *Essay on Man*, Epistle I, lines 285–6.
3. Catharine Greene had written in May and June: XXXVII, 285–7, 545.

fairs—of the 18th. of July last, & of an order of Congress of the 2d. of the same Month, to which be pleased to refer.[4]

As you inform'd me in you Letter of the 25th of August last, that you had a copy of the order of Congress of the 12th. of Septr. 1781. ascertaining the Ballance due to me, to be Forty two thousand, one hundred & eigty nine Livres, with 6 per Ct. per an. Interest from that time 'till paid,[5] I have only to observe that the Interest for 19 Months added to the principal debt amounts to Forty six thousand one hundred & ninety six Livres, nineteen sols; for which sum I have this day drawn on you the following Bills payable to my own order the 12th. of April next, viz one for £12000 [*i.e.* 12,000 *l.t.*]— one for £12000 [*i.e.* 12,000 *l.t.*]— one for £12000— & one for £10196.19s. [*i.e.* 10,196 *l.t.* 19 *s.*]

These Bills will be presented to you for acceptance with which I hope you will honor them, as I have drawn them at so long a date, in order to accommodate you in the most convenient manner; but if you choose to pay the money at a shorter Period, be pleased to signify your wishes in a letter to me, sent to the care of Mr. Grand in Paris, that I may give him orders to receive it.

I am most Respectfully Sir Your most Obedt. & most Hble Servt. W: LEE.

Turn Over if you Please

His Excellency, Benjamen Franklin Esq. at Passy.

Endorsements: W Lee Esqe / Answer'd 21st.

Notation: Wm. Lee 7. Octr. 1782

4. Livingston's July 18 letter to Lee (Wharton, *Diplomatic Correspondence*, v, 610) enclosed the July 2 resolution (*JCC*, XXII, 369) that ordered him to inform Lee that he should apply to BF for the money due him. Lee copied both on the verso.

5. BF's Aug. 25 letter is missing. The 1781 congressional order was sent to BF by Robert Morris (XXXVI, 155), but BF responded to Morris that he "could not prudently" pay Lee: XXXVII, 736. For Lee's earlier requests for payment see XXXVII, 595.

From Robert Morris: Three Letters[6]

(I) LS: American Philosophical Society; (II) LS: American Philosophical Society, Independence National Historical Park; copy: Library of Congress; (III) LS: American Philosophical Society (two), Syracuse University Library; L (draft): Yale University Library; copies: Archives du Ministère des affaires étrangères,[7] Library of Congress

I.

Sir   Marine Office 7th. October 1782.—

This Letter will be delivered to you by Joshua Barney Esqr. a Lieutenant in the Navy of the United States, and now commanding the Packet Ship Washington.[8] This young Gentleman is an Active, gallant Officer, who has already behaved very well on many Occasions, and I recommend him to your particular Notice and Attention from the Conviction that his Conduct will do Honor to those by whom he is patronized and introduced.

I am Sir Your most obedient & humble Servant

ROBT MORRIS

His Excellency Benjamin Franklin Esqr.

Endorsed: Marine Office Oct. 7. 1782

II.

Sir   Office of Finance 7th. October 1782.

Captain Barney having been detained until this Day and it being probable that he will not arrive in Europe so early as I expected I am very doubtful whether it would be proper to send him to the Havanna but think it would be better he should return immediately hither because it is likely that the Negotiation I proposed[9] will consume more time than he can spare. His Ship is small but she sails remarkably well and will therefore give us a good Chance of being well informed of the Situation of our Af-

6. The first letter was also sent to JA, John Jay, Lafayette, and William Carmichael: *Morris Papers,* VI, 522.

7. BF sent this deciphered copy to Vergennes on Nov. 8 (below). It is in L'Air de Lamotte's hand.

8. Barney also carried Morris' letters to BF of Sept. 25, 27, 28, and 30 and Oct. 1 and 5: *Morris Papers,* VI, 518n.

9. In his second letter of Sept. 27, above.

fairs. If there is likely to be any Delay or Difficulty in the Havanna Plan it will be best that you endeavor to obtain the Shipment of a considerable Sum in Europe on Board some of the King's frigates.[1] At any Rate we must have Money and I think you may venture fifty thousand Crowns by this Vessel. You will see that Capt. Barney is put under your Directions and is to wait your Instructions but I must at the same time inform you that Congress have directed his Ship to be purchased and sent to France[2] among other Things for the Purpose of obtaining a better Communication with their Servants and more frequent and accurate Intelligence from Europe you will see therefore the Propriety of dispatching her as speedily as possible and I think we may probably fall upon ways & Means to afford you frequent Opportunities of writing with a great Chance of Security.

I am Sir your most obedient and humble Servant

ROBT MORRIS

His Excellency Benjamin Franklin Esqr.

Endorsed: Office of Finance Oct. 7. 1782

III.

Dear Sir   Office of Finance 7th October 1782

In a Letter of the second Instant which I have just now received from the Head Quarters of the American Army is the following Paragraph—[3] In short, my dear Sir, the Want of Money gives rise to so many complaints and uneaseinesses, that without a portion of it, I fear the infection will spread from Officer to Soldier. It is most vexatious to see the parade of the states upon every occasion; They declare in the most pompous manner that they will never make peace but upon their own terms, and yet call upon them for the support of the war, and you may as well call upon the dead. If they persist in their present accursed system, I do not see but they must accept Peace upon any terms.

I am Sir your most obedient Servant   ROBT MORRIS

---

1. For the latest version of the Havana plan see Morris' letter of Oct. 1.
2. In a resolution of Aug. 29: *JCC,* XXIII, 537.
3. The rest of this paragraph is in cipher. We print the interlinear decipher by L'Air de Lamotte, corrected by WTF.

P.S. I would have sent the whole Letter from which this is extracted but I have not time to put it in Cypher

His Excellency Benjn. Franklin Esqr.

Endorsed: Office of Finance Oct. 7. 1782 Letter from Head Quarters decyphered

Notation:[4] (By C. No 4.)

From Jonathan Nesbitt   ALS: American Philosophical Society

Sir   L'Orient Octor: 7th: 1782

I receiv'd in course the honor of your Excellencys Letter of the 30th Ulto: inclosing one for the Captains Cain Josiah & Deale, which I have deliver'd them.— They are extremely sensible of your Excellencys attention to their request, & beg that you will accept of their most sincere thanks.— Inclosed, I have the honor to transmit you a Letter from them.—[5] I likewise take the Liberty to trouble you with Seven pices relative to the Prize Ship the Lion which I request you will examine, & order every thing necessary to be done, to accelerate her speedy Condemnation.—[6]

There are now three American Ships of Force in this Road, that will Sail for Philadelphia between the 15th. & 20th Inst.

---

4. In WTF's hand. The cipher used here is the same as the one used in Morris' letter of Sept. 28; see our annotation there.

5. All three of these letters are missing, but see Nesbitt's previous letter of Sept. 23.

6. BF signed and sent to the Judges of the Admiralty of Vannes a certificate condemning the *Lyon,* Capt. Mungo Wright, captured on Sept. 13 en route from Bristol to Guinea: Archives départementales de Morbihan. (For these certificates, printed at Passy, see XXX, 361; XXXVII, 582n.) The cargo was reported to be gunpowder and dry goods for the slave trade, worth as much as 900,000 *l.t.: Courier de l'Europe,* XII (1782), 242.

Ships' papers were customarily returned along with the prize condemnation certificate. One of the *Lyon*'s documents is still among BF's papers, however: a London Customs House certificate dated July 23, 1782 (University of Pa. Library).

Any Dispatches that your Excellency may have to send shall be taken the utmost care of.

I have the honor to remain with the utmost respect. Sir! Your most hble & Obedient Servant   JONATN: NESBITT

His Excellency Benja: Franklin Esqr.

Notation: J. Nesbit 7. Oct. 1782.

From Patience Wright   ALS: American Philosophical Society

Honored Sir   London octobr 7th 1782

With most Sincere Distress of mind I herd last from France You was ill and Since not had the good news of your Recovery I beg Mr Thare[7] the Barer of this may give me the Early Inteligence of your helth and wellfare— My hopes are Placd high on your life health and Situation— May almighty Ruler of Kings give you the blessing of long life is the Prayer of dr Sir your Estemd Friend and very humbl Serv   PATIENCE WRIGHT

my Dear Wm.[8]

with dificulty am Silent I Returnd from Bath when the Spirit of the times made it very Entertaining being Company from all Parts &c. would to god you was their with *others* now on their way to that blessed Water

mrs Wright Respectful Complents To Doctr Bancroft to hold him Self Ready to meet us:

Addressed: His Exelency B Franklin Esqr / Passy France / (per Mr Thayer.)

Notation: Wright Oct 7. 1782.

7. Former chaplain John Thayer: xxxv, 127n.
8. Presumably she means WTF. Around this time, Wright wrote him a separate letter (undated), expressing alarm at reports of BF's health, mentioning the N.Y. Loyalists' petition to the King, and conveying the regards of several friends. APS.

From Thomas Barclay

LS:[9] American Philosophical Society

Sir   Brest 8th. October 1782

I had the honour of addressing your Excellency the 30th. Past, Since which I have taken as much Information Concerning the probability of Sending the Supplies forward at the expence of the Court of France as I could, and I do not find that there is the least. The Intendant Informs me that the want of Transports for the Kings Service is So great that Gouverment Cannot afford the least assistance to America,[1] beyond that of furnishing men for any vessells we can engage in the Service, or Shipping the goods for us round to L'Orient without any Expence. I think it probable that if the goods were there, various Shipments might be made (of part of them) by different Vessells bound to Philadelphia &c. at a reasonable freight payable in America. If you Shou'd approve of this Method I will order Such of them round as I can agree for by the Ship st. James, washington and Queen of France all of which Vessells are now at L'Orient. The Ship Baltimore and Brigantine Nancy are now taking in Salt here for Cheseapeak Bay the former is a stout vessell of about 270 Ton, will Sail I believe very well, Mount 8 Twelve pound Caronades, and four Swivills, the Brigantine is about 180 Ton unarmed except Sufficient to Keep off Boats in Cheseapeak Bay. If you Chuse it about 100 Ton of the Supplies may be put on board the Ship and about 50 Ton on board the Brigantine the freight paid at the usual rate in America. I should think it right to put Some of the Blanketts on board each Vessell, and if you approve of it I will return from L'Orient and See it done, or give the Necessary Instructions about it, but it will be Necessary for me to have your Excellencys determination by return of Post addressed to me at L'Orient, as both Vessells will go as soon as they are loaded without waiting for Convoy.[2]

---

9. Barclay wrote the dateline, the complimentary close after "respect," the internal address, and the postscript.

1. A large convoy had to be assembled in Brest to take troops to Cadiz for use in an invasion of Jamaica, should peace talks fail. The convoy sailed on Dec. 8: Dull, *French Navy,* pp. 318–19.

2. Barclay shipped 7,000 blankets aboard the *Baltimore;* she ran aground off a Maryland inlet, but her cargo was saved: *Morris Papers,* VII, 372, 401,

There is also a Brigantine Cutter here that will be fitted for Sea in about a Month, by whom 100 Ton of Goods may be Shipped to Philadelphia, She will be unarmed except a few Swivills, but I believe She is Noted for being a fast Sailling Vessell. It were to be wished that the Supplies, expecially if there is a prospect of an other Campaign in America, Could be sent by more Suitable Conveyances, but indeed I See not the Smallest chance of Succeeding other ways, without the Command of Finances which Seem to be out of reach— I was once in hopes of procuring a Frigate which lyes here, but after being in Suspence Some days, I found it could not be done. There is a Ship at L'Orient of 500 Ton, and the Frigate Flora of Some what Greater dimention lyes at Bordeaux, Either of these Vessells I believe might be got to come here for about 200 livs. per Ton, if you wou'd accept bills for the freight at 3. 6, 9, & 12 Months after the bills of Lading were Signed. I have the pleasure to Inform your Excellency that Captain Grinnell arrived at Boston in 40(?) days from Amsterdam with about 2500 suits of the Cloathing which I Shipped and as Smedley Sail'd at the Same time I hope we Shall Soon hear that he is arrived also—[3] I Sincerely wish that this will find you perfectly restored to your health, bing with great respect Sir Your Excellencys Most Obed Huml Servant

THOS BARCLAY

Inclosed I send you two printed paragraphs from a Boston Newspaper of Sepr. 9th

His Excellency Benjamin Franklin Esqre

Notation: T: Barclay. Brest 8th. October 1782

---

474. We do not know if Barclay used the *Nancy,* which may have been the Pa. brigantine, Peter Young master: Charles H. Lincoln, comp., *Naval Records of the American Revolution, 1775–1788* (Washington, D.C., 1906), p. 400.

3. Moses Grinnell was captain of the *Sukey,* Samuel Smedley of the *Heer Adams:* XXXVII, 134–5n, 560.

From the Chevalier de Kéralio

ALS: American Philosophical Society

Forbach, le 8e. 8bre. 1782.

Après cinq mois de course et de travaux,[4] monsieur et respectable ami, je suis arrivé avant-hier chès nôtre céleste amie,[5] et déja nous nous sommes beaucoup entretenus de vous; inquiets de votre santé qui a été altérée pendant l'été dernier, nous supplions monsieur votre petit fils de nous en donner des nouvelles: recevés en même temps le tendre hommage de la Dame du chateau, et de ma part celui de la profonde Vénération que je me ferai toujours gloire d'avoir pour Vous.

Vous connoissés mon patriotisme et mon attachement à la Cause commune: aussi ai-je bien souffert des facheuses nouvelles que j'ai apprises depuis mon départ de paris; mais je n'en espere pas moins qu'enfin le jour de la paix dont nous commençons à voir l'aurore éclairera les deux mondes.

J'ai appris avec grand plaisir que trois navires américains arrivés de philadelphie à l'orient,[6] avoient amené deux prises dont une estimée 600,000 *l.t.* Les piqures répétées font de grandes blessures.

Je ne cesserai d'être avec l'attachement le plus inviolable et le plus tendre respect, monsieur et digne ami, votre très humble et très obéissant serviteur   LE CHR. DE KERALIO

Mille et mille amitiés, S'il vous plait, à Mr. votre petit fils: notre amie qui lui dit mille belles choses lui enverra incessamment Un paquet pour son fils[7] et le prie d'avance de l'expédier pour L'amérique, quand l'occasion se présentera.

---

4. During which he inspected the military school at Brienne and conversed with the young Napoleon Bonaparte, who announced his desire to devote his life to science and possibly to present a general theory of electricity: Frank McLynn, *Napoleon: a Biography* (London, 1997), pp. 20–1.

5. Marianne Camasse, comtesse de Forbach and duchesse douairière de Deux-Ponts: xxv, 413n; Lopez, *Mon Cher Papa*, pp. 192–4.

6. The *St. James*, *Washington*, and *Queen of France*.

7. Comte Christian de Forbach de Deux-Ponts (xxviii, 539), the commander of the regiment of Deux-Ponts, currently stationed near the Hudson with Rochambeau's other troops: Rice and Brown, eds., *Rochambeau's Army*, I, 167n.

Notation: Le Chr. de Keralio Forbac le 8. Oct 1782.

From Henry Wyld   ALS: University of Pennsylvania Library

Most excellent sir   Londonderry Oct. 8th. 1782
    We have all got our Bonds discharged, but with a great deal
of trouble and expence, we still wish to persevere in the first design, but our Circumstances being greatly impared we shall not
be able to proceed directly, yet as there are hopes of a more free
passage through a Peace which we conclude by our Prints not to
be far off we wish early to arrive at Philadelphia, and in hopes of
you giving us the most early inteligence that possible can be relied upon, and if consistent afording us a passage in one of your
Country vessels I am for self and Co. your Excellencys Most
obedient servant   HENRY WYLD

P.S. I desire you will forwd. the inclosed to the Person to whom
it is addressed, and I will write to you shortly desiring your reply[8]

Addressed: Mr. Ferdinand Grand / Mercht. / Paris

Notation: H. Wyld. 8 Oct. 1782

To John and Sarah Jay   L:[9] Columbia University Library

                                    Passy 9. Oct. 1782.
Dr. Franklin regrets exceedingly that his Health does not permit
him the honour & Pleasure of waiting upon Mr. & Mrs. Jay, according to their obliging Invitation.— He hopes Mr. & Mrs. Jay
will condescend to indemnify him for the Loss he sustains, by
honouring him with their Company at Dinner on Saturday

---

8. This is the last extant letter from Wyld, and we have no evidence of a
reply.
9. In the hand of WTF.

next.—[1] The Dr. would be happy to see Mr. Murowe[2] at the same time.

Endorsed: From Doctr Franklin 9 Octr. 1782

From Anthony Kennan   ALS: Historical Society of Pennsylvania

Bourdoux 9[–12]th. October 1782

I the subscriber your Excellencies most Humble Pettioner, an American Subject, my place of residence, when at home, is in Orange County North Carolina, where I have resided for a number of years past, till Cornwallis, attacked General Green at Guilford Court House,[3] then I went out to the West Indies, with a small property on my own Accot.; and traded among the French West India Islands, but very unfortunately, a little time before St. Kitts was Captured by the French, on my passage from Bassterre Guardaloupe, bound for St Thomas, I was taken by a Privateer and carried into St. Kitts, when I lost every thing in my possesion, even my wearing Apperal and remained a prisioner, till Count De Boulia[4] Governor of Martinico took that Island, After which I went down to Cape Francois where I entered on board a French Mercht. Ship bound for this port to do a little business in the writting way, Just for a support, and my wages being very small which is now all expended. And no American

1. Oct. 12. Jay's diary records that Sir Edward Newenham, his wife, their eldest son, and two of their daughters also attended the dinner: Morris, *Jay: Peace*, p. 447. Newenham's journal mentioned that Lafayette was there; he described it as "a plain but good Dinner, dressed a la mode de Anglais," with "various and Delicious" wines. That day BF showed Newenham his electrical apparatus, and the Newenhams and Jays stayed for a 9 p.m. supper: Dixon Wecter, "Benjamin Franklin and an Irish 'Enthusiast'," *Huntington Library Quarterly*, IV (1940–41), 216.

2. John's nephew, Peter Jay Munro: XXX, 555–6n; XXXVII, 288.

3. On March 15, 1781: XXXV, 79n.

4. Francois-Claude-Amour, marquis de Bouillé, the governor general of the Windward Islands, commanded the troops that captured St. Christopher (St. Kitts) in mid-February, 1782: XXXVII, 70n; W. M. James, *The British Navy in Adversity: a Study of the War of American Independence* (London, New York, and Toronto, 1926), pp. 322, 326–7.

Ships here that will sail for those some months to come, having little or no Cash to support me, and few wearing Apperal, quite a Stranger, no friends nor Acquaintances, Therefor I am under the real necessity of giving your Excellenci, this trouble, and Pray's your Excellenci out of your great goodness, would be pleased to render me Some Assistance in my present distress, without which I must unavoidably suffer in this Strange, Country, your Excellence's immeidately, ordering me whatever you'll please to see proper will for ever Oblige, Your Excellencis, most humble pettioner   ANTHONY KENNAN

I purpose taking the first oppty, for America, that Offers, for Philadelphia Maryland. Virginia, or North Carolina

Bourdoux 12th. October
I have omitted a few lines which ——— Pray Turn Over to [read?]. ——— I am at present quite out of Cash, and has been, for some days past, but very lucky meeting with one Mr. De Pass living opposite the Augustin whom I am inform'd has been always a very good friend to the Distressd Americ[ans] tho: a man of a large family, and has but little property, for my own part I must say so with great propriety, he uses me very kindly, and can, have no Expectations from me, in the least, without your Excellences pleases immeidately to Order me some Assistance, when I may have it in my Power to return him payment for his, Expence & trouble wt. me. I most humbly pray your Excellence will be Pleas'd to order me some reliefe from my Present unhappy situation, which will Oblige your Excellence's most humble Pettioner[5]   ANTHONY KENNAN

To His Excellence Benjamin Franklin Esqr.

---

5. Kennan sent a near-duplicate of this letter on Oct. 21, expressing his gratitude to "Depass," who had now loaned him clothing. Hist. Soc. of Pa. M. Depas in Bordeaux was reimbursed for boarding American prisoners and providing medical assistance in October, 1781: Account XXVII (XXXII, 4).

From Williams, Moore & Co.

LS:[6] University of Pennsylvania Library

Monsieur   L'orient le 9. 8bre. 1782.

Le Corsaire ameriquain Le Ciceron, Capitaine hill a nôtre consignation, est arrivé ce matin en ce port avec deux prises venant de la Jamaique; Sur une desquelles ce Sont trouvés Le lieutenant en pied & 29 hommes de L'Equipage du Vau. du Roy Le Romely, qui avoient été Sauvés par Cette prise Lorsque le Général Gaÿes qui le Commandoit, avoit Jugé a propos dy mettre Le feu,[7] quoiquil ne nous paroit pas Juste que cet officier et les hommes de l'equipage sauvés du dit Vaisseau, Soyent regardés Comme prisonniers, nous n'avons pas ausé prendre Sur nous de leur donner leur Liberté Sans auparavant avoir reçu vos ordres a ce Sujet.

Nous avons Lhonneur dêtre avec Respect Monsieur Vos très humbles & très obeissants serviteurs[8]   WILLIAMS MOORE & CO

6. Signed by James Moore.

7. The officer and crew had been rescued from Rear Adm. Thomas Graves's flagship, H.M.S. *Ramillies,* when that vessel, five other ships of the line, and the convoy they were escorting from Jamaica to the British Isles encountered a hurricane off Newfoundland. Many ships were lost. The crew of the *Ramillies* was distributed among several of the merchant ships in the convoy before orders were given to set the sinking ship on fire. On Oct. 3 three American privateers, the *Cicero, Revolution,* and *Buccaneer,* captured four of the convoy's merchantmen and sent them to Lorient consigned to Williams, Moore & Co. The four prizes were the *Arundel, Two Brothers, Hope,* and *Jamaica;* we do not know which two the *Cicero* escorted. John A. Tilley, *The British Navy and the American Revolution* (Columbia, S.C., 1987), p. 274; Robert Beatson, *Naval and Military Memoirs of Great Britain from 1727 to 1783* (6 vols., London, 1804), V, 496–526; *Courier de l'Europe* XII (1782), 237, 250–1.

8. On the day the present letter was written, BF signed a prize condemnation form for the *Commerce,* Capt. "Maktier" (McTier, McTeer), en route from Liverpool to St. John's, Newfoundland, which was taken by the *Buccaneer* on Sept. 19. The form was filled out by WTF and addressed to the Judges of the Admiralty of Vannes (Dossiers des Prises, 9 B 183, Archives départementales de Morbihan). The prize was brought into Lorient at the end of September and consigned to Williams, Moore & Co.; their letter requesting BF's adjudication is missing. JW to John and Andrew Cabot, and to Williams, Moore & Co., Sept. 30, 1782 (both at Yale University Library); *Courier de l'Europe,* XII (1782), 215.

Notation: Williams Moore 9. Octr. 1782.

From the Baron d'Arendt[9] AL: Historical Society of Pennsylvania

Jeudi [October 10, 1782]

Baron Arendt, qui est arrivé icy de L'amerique par Londres & la Nouvelle York, ayant eù le malheur d'avoir été pris par Les Anglois[1] souhaite avoir l'honneur d'assurer ses respects a Son Excellence Mr. Le Docteur Franklin pour Lui remettre une Lettre de La part du Mr Robert Morris, et se presentera demain le Vendredi chés Lui vers Le Midi.[2]

Le Baron a joint a cette Lettre quelques gazettes de Londres.[3]

9. Identified in XXXVII, 33–4, where Robert Morris asks BF to honor a certificate promising the balance of d'Arendt's back pay for military service in America. Morris' letter and its enclosure are the subject of the present letter.

1. Morris reported d'Arendt's capture in early June: XXXVII, 461.

2. D'Arendt may have called at Passy the following day, but BF saw him on Sunday, Oct. 13. On that day, d'Arendt signed a receipt written by BF stating that he had received from BF an order on Ferdinand Grand for 14,986 *l.t.* 18 *s.*, the equivalent of the dollar amount specified in the certificate. D'Arendt also signed an identical statement written by WTF on the verso of the certificate itself: XXXVII, 33n. Grand paid him the following day: Account XXVII (XXXII, 4).

Later on Oct. 13, however, back in Paris, d'Arendt wrote BF that he was owed interest on the period between when the certificate was issued and when he received payment; 6% for six months amounted to $90 or 450 *l.t.* (Hist. Soc. of Pa.). BF evidently refused, lacking Morris' authorization. On Nov. 15, writing from Frankfort (undoubtedly Frankfurt am Main), d'Arendt indicated that if Morris approved this payment, BF should remit the sum to Prussian Ambassador Goltz (University of Pa. Library). Morris refused to do so: *Morris Papers,* VII, 750.

3. D'Arendt's only other extant letter, dated "Lundi matin" from Paris (Oct. 14), was addressed to WTF, whom he hoped would oblige him by doing certain favors with which he did not want to trouble BF. He sent $170, or 850 *l.t.*, to repay a bill of exchange drawn in New York on a George Jay; he was sorry not to have mentioned this the day before (APS).

From Jonathan Williams, Jr.

ALS: Historical Society of Pennsylvania; copy: Yale University Library

Dear & hond sir.   Nantes Octr. 10. 1782

Onboard of one of the prizes lately arrived at L'Orient to the address of my House Williams Moore & Co, are part of the Crew of his Brittanic Majestys ship Ramilies which sunk at sea. One of them being an Officer has desired to know if he & his Comrades are to be prisoners of War or not, having fallen into our Hands in consequence of a Misfortune seperate from those of War.[4] I request you to give directions to W M. & Co how to proceed in this Business, and if there is any Cartel established, so as an equal number of our Countrymen may be had in return, it would be well to send over all the prisoners we have in Nantes & L'Orient, which I suppose together amounts to a considerable Number.

I hope you are perfectly recovered and am with the most perfect Respect Your dutifull & affectionate Kinsman

JONA WILLIAMS J

His Excellency Doctor Franklin.

From Henry Johnson

ALS: Historical Society of Pennsylvania

May it please your Excellency   Bordeaux 11th Octor: 1782

I Take the liberty to Inclo: you a letter from some Americans who are taken out of some Merchant Ships. and sent off to serve his Majesty the King of France.[5] On Receipt of the letter I waited on the Commissary General here. respecting the matter. He told me as they had served in the Merchant Ships. and got great Run money. that they ought to serve the King. he and I differ'd in our opinions. I told him I should write you on the Subject— This is not the only thing that is fell under my Eye since I left Boston. At the Cape[6] they serve them the same. And what between the French & English we have not a Sailor left in New England. Sev-

---

4. See Williams, Moore & Co., Oct. 9, above.
5. Missing.
6. Cap Français, St. Domingue.

eral fine Vessels have been Obliged to lay by for want of men— I do not Know what I shall do myself for men. as I cannot take out a Frenchman with me.— For want of an Agent at Cape François we suffer every thing in fact— Our Vessels who carry in any prisoners there. give them up to the French Commissary they are Exchanged for Frenchmen. while our people lay in the Jamaica Prisons till they are starved. then Hunger compells them to go on board a British Ship. So that not One out of ten that are taken & carried to Jamaica ever return. this you may depend on to be a fact. While I lay at the Cape I took upon me to take out of Vessels of different nations Numbers of Americans. who were compell'd to serve by some means or other— A Danish frigate had taken the Liberty to press Seven in the Island of St Thomas's[7] some of them I got. So that we are Kick'd about by every Raschally nation that pleases. I could heartily wish that a Deputy Consul was settled here. that we might have some degree of Justice shown us. I hope it will not be long ere that takes place.— I perhaps have taken more upon me. than I ought to have done. but as a Subject of the United States of America. it makes my blood boil whenever I see things of this Kind Take place, and I cannot help speaking.

I Inclo: your Excellency likewise a Bill for Thirty dollars. shall be much Obliged to you, if you would endorse it and forward it. I am with the greatest Respect Your Excellencys Most Obedt: & Most Huml Servt   HENRY JOHNSON

Endorsed: answer'd 22d

From Cuming & Macarty ALS:[8] American Philosophical Society

Sir   [before October 12, 1782]

Permit us to request your Excelleny to Transmitt us the Necessary Order's, for the Sale of the Two Prizes, mention'd in the Papers herewith Inclose'd—[9]

---

7. St. Thomas was a Danish colony.
8. Probably in William Macarty's hand.
9. These were doubtless the *Luxford* and *Will*, two of the three prizes cap-

We are very Respectfully your Excellency's Most Obedient and Very Humble Servts. CUMING & MACARTY

Notation: Cuming & Maccarty

From ———— Regnier ALS: American Philosophical Society

Monsieur, Paris le 12 Octobre 1782.

Pendant que je m'occupois à ramasser et à mettre en ordre la suite des Constitutions des Etats-unis de l'Amerique[1] j'ai appris que M. le Duc de la Rochefoucault s'amusoit à traduire le Recueil imprimé par ordre du Congrès.[2] Ce Seigneur, auquel j'ai eu l'honneur de presenter mon premier volume, et à qui j'ai fait voir ce que j'avois déja ramassé pour former le Second, a eu la bonté de me dire qu'il comptoit remettre à votre Excellence, vers la st. Martin, sa traduction, et qu'il verroit avec plaisir publier la suite de cette sage Législation.[3]

---

tured by the privateers *St. James, Washington,* and *Queen of France* and brought into Lorient; see the annotation of Jonathan Nesbitt to BF, Sept. 23. BF signed condemnation certificates for both prizes on Oct. 12: the *Luxford,* Capt. William Payne, en route from Bristol to Newfoundland, was taken on Sept. 10; the *Will,* Capt. Abraham Buttermer, en route from Cork to Charleston, was taken on Aug. 27. Archives départementales de Morbihan.

An undated memorandum by BF, listing this basic information about the two ships and evaluating each as a "Good Prize" consigned to Cuming & McCarty, is at the University of Pa. Library. WTF filled out the forms.

Jonathan Nesbitt sent papers relative to the third prize, the *Lyon,* on Oct. 7 (above).

1. In 1778 Regnier published *Recueil des loix constitutives des colonies angloises, confédérées sous la dénomination d'Etats-Unis* . . . , which he dedicated to BF: XXVI, 529–30; XXVII, 200n. We have found no record of a sequel being published or of any further letters to BF from Regnier.

2. *The Constitutions of the Several Independent States of America* . . . (Philadelphia, 1781) also contained the Declaration of Independence, the Articles of Confederation, and the English versions of the Treaty of Alliance and Treaty of Amity and Commerce between the United States and France. Two hundred copies were printed, as Congress had ordered: *JCC,* XVIII, 1217; XXI, 1200–1; Charles Evans *et al.,* comps., *American Bibliography* (14 vols., Chicago and Worcester, Mass., 1903–59), VI, 149.

3. This is the earliest mention of La Rochefoucauld's translating for BF the

Les pieces que Votre Excellence ainsi que M. Jay ont bien voulu me communiquer, et celles que j'ai recueilli avec Soin dans les Journaux, pourroient former un Second Volume considerable et interessant; mais désirant completter a present cette collection et la publier dans le meilleur Ordre possible, je Supplie Votre Excellence de vouloir bien me permettre de tirer copie des pieces qui pourroient me manquer et de Soumettre à Sa Sagesse et à ses lumieres l'Ordre et le plan que je me propose de donner à ce Recueil.

Daignés recevoir avec bonté l'hommage du respectueux dévouement avec lequel je Suis, Monsieur, Votre tres humble et tres obeissant Serviteur   Regnier
hôtel de la Guette, rue du four fauxbourg st. Germain

M. Franklin, Ministre plénipotentiaire des Etats-unis.

Endorsed: Regner 12 Oct. 1782

To Gérard de Rayneval

ALS: Archives du Ministère des affaires étrangères; copies: Library of Congress (two), Massachusetts Historical Society

Sir   Passy, Oct. 13. 1782.
With this you will receive the Copy you desired of Mr Oswald's Commission.[4]

I request your kind Care in forwarding the enclos'd Letter to Spain, by your first Courier.

---

state constitutions and other founding documents. In the spring of 1783 BF arranged for Philippe-Denis Pierres to print these translations in both ordinary and deluxe editions, under the title *Constitutions des treize Etats-Unis de l'Amérique.* The Feast of St. Martin was Nov. 11: *Almanach Royal* for 1782, p. 28.

4. Vergennes had still not seen the commission by the following day, when he complained to La Luzerne that BF and Jay were keeping from him all news of their negotiations with Oswald, including showing him a copy of Oswald's full powers: Giunta, *Emerging Nation,* 1, 617. According to Ridley's account, BF also wanted to send Vergennes a copy of the preliminary articles (above, Oct. 5–7), but Jay insisted on silence because the French had "communicated to us none of their Secrets": Klingelhofer, "Matthew Ridley's Diary," pp. 117–18 (entries of Oct. 2 and 5).

I have the honour to be with sincere Esteem & Attachment Sir
Your most obedient and most humble Servant   B Franklin

M. de Rayneval

From Anne-Louise Boivin d'Hardancourt Brillon de Jouy

ALS: American Philosophical Society

ce 13 octobre a la thuillerie [1782][5]

Comment estes vous mon bon papa? Jamais il ne m'en a tant
coutté de m'éloigner de vous, chaques soirs il me semble que
vous seriés bien aise de me voir, et chaques soirs je pense a vous;
lundi 21 j'irai vous retrouver, j'espere qu'alors vous serés bien
Sur vos jambes et que le thé du mercredi samedi, et celui du dimanche matin reprendront tout leur lustre. Je vous mennerai *la
bonne évésque*,[6] mon gros mari nous fera rire, nos enfans rirons
ensemble le grand voisin[7] pérsiflera, les abbés la roche et morelét
mangeront tout le beure, mde grand son aimable niéce et Mr
grand[8] ne nuirons pas a la societé, le pére pagin jouera dieu
d'amour sur le violon, moi la marche au piano,[9] vous petits
oiseaux sur l'harmonica, óh mon ami voyons dans l'avenir de
belles et bonnes jambes pour vous, et ne pensons plus a la mau-

5. The year is established by her reference to "lundi 21," which occurred
in October only once during BF's stay in France. Mme Brillon writes from
the country house of her mother, Marie Martin d'Hardancourt: XXXV, 124n.

6. Probably poking fun at BF's difficulty with genders, Mme Brillon refers
in this and future letters to "la bonne évesque," who, in one undated letter,
is said to be returning to Corsica (APS). Pierre Peineau du Verdier (1721–
1787) was consecrated bishop of Mariana and Accia, in Corsica, in April,
1782: Armand Jean, *Les Evêques et les archevêques de France depuis 1682
jusqu'à 1801* (Paris, 1891), under "Peineau."

7. Le Veillard.

8. Marie Silvestre and Ferdinand Grand, with their niece Marie Labhard
(XXIV, 400n; her first name is established in Lüthy, *Banque protestante*, II,
341).

9. Two compositions by Mme Brillon: the romance "Viens m'aider ô dieu
d'amour" and the "Marche des insurgents." See XXXIV, 237n; XXXVI, 241n;
Bruce Gustafson, "Madame Brillon et son salon," *Revue de Musicologie*
LXXXV (1999), 313.

vaise qui vous a tant pérsecuté; aprés le mal on jouit mieux du bien, la vie est semée de l'un et de l'autre qu'elle varient sans cesse, ce qu'elle ne peut empêcher d'estre égalle, uniforme, c'est ma tendrésse pour vous, que les tems, les lieux, les évenemens n'altéreront jamais:

Ma mére et toute ma famille se rappéllent a votre souvenir:

J'ai eu de vos nouvélles par le voisin, mais il m'en faut absolument de vous:

Addressed: A Monsieur / Monsieur Franklin / A Passy

To Robert R. Livingston   LS[1] and transcript: National Archives

Sir,   Passy, Oct. 14. 1782.

I have but just received Information of this Opportunity,[2] and have only time allow'd to write a few Lines.

In my last of the 26th. past I mentioned that the Negociation for Peace had been obstructed by the Want of due Form in the English Commissions appointing their Plenipotentiaries. In that for treating with us, the Mentioning our States by their public Name had been avoided, which we objecting to, another is come of which I send a Copy inclosed. We have now made several preliminary Propositions, which the English Minister, Mr. Oswald has approved & sent to his Court.[3] He thinks they will be approved there; but I have some Doubts. In a few Days however the answer expected will determine.[4] By the first of these Arti-

1. In L'Air de Lamotte's hand, except for the last seven words of the complimentary close, which are in BF's hand.

2. Probably provided by Duportail, who carried an Oct. 13 letter from Jay to Livingston: Wharton, *Diplomatic Correspondence,* v, 809.

3. For Oswald's new commission see Vaughan to BF, Sept. 23. The preliminary articles are above, [Oct. 5–7].

4. On Oct. 17 the cabinet directed that Oswald be notified, either in writing or by personal messenger, that the terms he had agreed to were unacceptable. They insisted that the Nova Scotia boundaries be expanded; that Oswald state the King's "Right to the Back Country and urge it as a means of providing for the Refugees" (a condition the King was willing to revoke if the Americans made adequate provisions for those refugees); that the

cles the King of Great Britain renounces for himself and Successors all Claim and Pretension to Dominion or Territory within the thirteen United States; and the Boundaries are described as in our Instructions; except that the Line between Nova Scotia & New-England is to be settled by Commissioners after the Peace. By another Article the Fishery in the American Seas is to be freely exercis'd by the Americans wherever they might formerly exercise it while united with Great Britain.[5] By another, the Citizens and Subjects of each Nation are to enjoy the same Protection & Privileges in each others Ports and Countries, re-

---

Americans' claim to dry fish on the shores of Newfoundland be rejected; that the right to navigation on the Mississippi be accepted but the rest of the fourth article be referred to a Treaty of Commerce, where it would be more appropriate; and that Oswald should "strongly" urge that pre-war debts be repaid to British merchants: Fortescue, *Correspondence of George Third*, VI, 143–4. These terms, less generous than what Shelburne had been prepared to offer, were likely strengthened after the news arrived in London on Sept. 30 that the British fortress at Gibraltar had repulsed a major Spanish attack: Jack Russell, *Gibraltar Besieged, 1779–1783* ([London, 1965]), pp. 229–56; Harlow, *Second British Empire*, I, 287–9.

5. The first and third articles of the draft treaty. For Jay the questions of borders and fishing rights involved contestation with Spain and France as well as Britain. His futile discussions with Aranda over the competing territorial claims of Spain and the United States east of the Mississippi River led him to encourage Britain to retake West Florida from Spain. Luckily for the United States, Britain rejected the offer, which could have had dire consequences for later American history: Morris, *Jay: Peace*, pp. 268–83, 362–3, 368, 372–82, 394–5; Jonathan R. Dull, *A Diplomatic History of the American Revolution* (New Haven and London, 1985), p. 149. Gérard de Rayneval's attempts to mediate the dispute helped convince Jay that France was hostile to American interests. He was further convinced by a letter from François Barbé de Marbois, the French *chargé d'affaires* in Philadelphia, which had been intercepted by the British and leaked to Jay in mid-September. In it Marbois opposed American claims to Newfoundland fishing rights. Jay immediately sent a copy of this letter to Livingston. BF was less alarmed. According to Matthew Ridley, BF "affect[ed] not to see the drift" of the letter, surmised that Marbois was acting out of his own "zeal," and refused to believe that Vergennes had given him any encouragement: Giunta, *Emerging Nation*, I, 313–16, 581–2, 612; Klingelhofer, "Matthew Ridley's Diary," pp. 107–8.

Vergennes did think the American land claims extravagant, and was concerned lest they cause the American negotiations to fail and hence end the chance of a general peace: Vergennes to La Luzerne, Oct. 14, in Giunta, *Emerging Nation*, I, 616.

specting Commerce, Duties &c. that are enjoy'd by native Subjects. The Articles are drawn up very fully by Mr. Jay; who I suppose sends you a Copy. If not it will go by the next Opportunity.[6] If these Articles are agreed to, I apprehend little Difficulty in the rest. Something has been mention'd about the Refugees and English Debts; but not insisted on, as we declar'd at once that whatever Confiscations had been made in America, being in Virtue of the Laws of particular States, the Congress had no Authority to repeal those Laws, and therefore could give us none to stipulate for such Repeal.

I have been honour'd with the Receipt of your Letters No. 14 & 15.[7] I have also received two Letters from Mr. L R. Morris both dated the 6th. of July and one dated the 10th. of August[8] inclosing Bills for

68,290. Livres

71,380

9,756

In all 149,426. Livres

being intended for the Payment of Ministers Salaries for the two first Quarters of this Year. But as these Bills came so late that all those Salaries were already paid, I shall make no use of the Bills,

6. On Oct. 13 Jay wrote Livingston that he would not communicate details until he found an American to carry his letter: Wharton, *Diplomatic Correspondence*, V, 809.

7. Livingston's letters of July 5 and Aug. 9: XXXVII, 580–1, 717–19.

8. The confusion BF expresses in this paragraph stems from the new arrangements Congress was making for paying its ministers in Europe. Having learned in April that France would no longer pay these salaries and would only recognize bills sent from America, Congress passed a resolution on May 29 that Robert Morris would pay the ministers' salaries. It revised those instructions on June 5, returning the authority to Livingston: as of August, Livingston would receive money from the Treasury, purchase bills of exchange on European bankers, and send those bills to the ministers and their secretaries. This arrangement would hold until such time as the ministers appointed agents in Philadelphia: *Morris Papers*, V, 128. Lewis R. Morris was one of Livingston's undersecretaries. Although his three letters mentioned here by BF are missing, we know that in July he sent a bill or bills for 68,290 *l.t.* drawn on Robert Morris (Morris to Ferdinand Grand, July 6: *Morris Papers*, V, 542; VI, 164–5), whereas the August bill for 71, 380 *l.t.* was drawn on Livingston (who also wrote about it to BF; see XXXVII, 718).

but lay them by till farther Orders. And the Salaries of different Ministers not having all the same Times of falling due, as they had different Commencements, I purpose to get all their Accounts settled & reduced to the same Period, and send you the State of them; that you may be clear in future Orders. I see in one of the Estimates sent me that a Quarter's Salary of a Minister is reckoned at 14,583 Livres; in the other it is reckon'd 16,667 livres. And the Bill for 9756 Livres is mentioned, as intended to pay a Ballance due on the Remittance of the 68,290. Livres.[9] Being unacquainted with the State of your Exchanges I do not well comprehend this, and therefore leave the whole for the present as I have said above. Permit me only to hint for your Consideration, whether it may not be well hereafter to omit Mention of Sterling in our Appointments, since we have severed from the Country to which that Denomination of Money is peculiar; and also to order the Payment of your Ministers in such a Manner that they may know exactly what they are to receive, & not be subject to the Fluctuations of Exchange. If it is that which occasions the Difference between 14,583 for the first Quarter, & 16,667 for the second, it is considerable. I think we have no right to any Advantage by the Exchange, nor should we be liable to any Loss from it. Hitherto we have taken 15,000 Livres for a Quarter (subject however to the Allowance or Disallowance of Congress) which is lower than the Medium between those two Extreams.

The different Accounts given of Lord Shelburne's Character with respect to Sincerity, induced the Ministry here to send over M. de Rayneval, Secretary of the Council,[1] to converse with

9. Livingston here noted in the margin: "N.B: This not merely to pay a ballance but an excess on acct. of contingencies."

The estimates BF mentions may have been in the missing letters from Lewis Morris. BF drew on Grand for 14,583 *l.t.* on Aug. 1: Account XXVII (XXXII, 4). Lewis Morris sent him a bill of exchange for 16,666 *l.t.* on Nov. 11, below, which he did not cash. The former was calculated at an exchange rate of 5.25 *l.t.* per specie dollar, and the latter at 6 *l.t.* per specie dollar. (Robert Morris had converted BF's annual salary of £2,500 to 11,111 $^{10}\!/_{90}$ specie dollars: *Morris Papers*, V, 127.)

1. Gérard de Rayneval was *secrétaire du Conseil d'état:* Jean-Pierre Samoyault, *Les Bureaux du secrétariat d'état des affaires étrangères sous Louis XV: Administration, personnel* (Paris, 1971), p. 289.

him, and endeavour to form by that Means a more perfect Judgment of what was to be expected from the Negociation. He was five or Six Days in England, saw all the Ministers, and return'd quite satisfy'd that they are sincerely desirous of Peace; so that the Negociations now go on, with some Prospect of Success.[2] But the Court & People of England are very changeable. A little Turn of Fortune in their Favour sometimes turns their Heads; and I shall not think a speedy Peace to be depended on till I see the Treaties signed.

I am obliged to finish. With great Esteem I have the honour to be, Sir, Your most obedient and most humble Servant

B Franklin

Honble. Robt. R Livingston Esqe.

Endorsed: Letter 14 Oct 1782 Doct Franklin so far as relates to the mode of paying the salaries of Ministers referred to Mr Osgood Mr Rutledge Mr Wharton Dec. 27. 1782[3]

To Robert Morris: Extract[4]

Extract:[5] National Archives

Ocr. 14th. 1782

The three millions you mention previous to 1778 were two of them given & the third was an Advance on a Contract with the Farmers general of tobacco.[6]

2. For Rayneval's mission to England see Lafayette to BF, Sept. 12.

3. Another section of the letter was referred to a congressional committee consisting of delegates James Madison, John Rutledge, Abraham Clark, Alexander Hamilton, and Samuel Osgood. Their report, issued on Dec. 31 (*JCC*, XXIII, 838), led to the congressional resolution sent by Livingston on Jan. 2, 1783 (below).

4. Excerpted from a now-missing letter probably written in response to Morris' letter of July 1 (XXXVII, 568–72). An extract of BF's earlier response is above, Sept. 26.

5. In Arthur Lee's hand.

6. During 1777 the commissioners received 1,000,000 *l.t.* from the farmers general (see BF to Morris, Sept. 26) and four grants, each of 500,000 *l.t.*, from the French government. These were paid in January, April, July, and October: XXIII, 198–9, 468; XXIV, 561; XXV, 40–1.

From the Abbés Chalut and Arnoux

AL:[7] American Philosophical Society

Paris 14 8bre 1782

Les abbés de Chalut et Arnoux assurent de leur amitié leur respectable ami. Ils lui envoyent quatre lettres de recommandation pour M. le Chevalier Neuvenham.[8] Ils sont à ses ordres dans toutes les choses qui dependront deux.

Mille amitiés au cher petit fils.

From William Hodgson

ALS: American Philosophical Society

Dear sir   London 14 Oct 1782

I have recd your two favors of the 25th & 30th Ultimo,[9] it rejoices me much to hear you are getting the better of your late Complaints, the World cannot afford to part with you yet— You must not sing the Nunc Dimittis,[1] untill you have compleated that great & glorious work which is to teach future Kings & Ministers that the Liberties & propertys of Mankind are not to be trifled with for their sport & Amusements.

By this Conveyance you will receive another Box of pepper Mint Drops each parcell cost 8 *s.*— the whole of course 16 *s.*[2]

---

7. In the hand of Guillaume Arnoux. The first names of Arnoux and Jean Chalut have been supplied to us by Philippe Alasseur: Archives nationales, Minutier central, étude XVIII, 903, Sept. 3, 1792, and étude v, 2 (46), Sept. 11, 1787.

8. Sir Edward Newenham. In an Oct. 13 letter to WTF, Newenham requested that BF either write or procure for him letters of introduction to friends in Lyon, Marseille, Toulon, and the Iles d'Hyères, where he and his family planned a stay of some months. Newenham also asked for advice on a matter of court etiquette: would it be proper for him, a stranger, to invite the marquis de Lafayette to dinner, an honor he would dearly like to mention on his return to Ireland? APS.

9. Not found.

1. From the opening line of the canticle of Simeon ("Now lettest thou [thy servant] depart"): Luke 2:29.

2. The peppermint drops were for Gérard de Rayneval; see BF's Sept. 4 letter to him.

William Hodgson and Family

I have been at the Secretarys Office relative to the Exchange of Americans here for those you furnish me a List of that are carried into LOrient—[3] I was told that your request shou'd be complyed with & that as soon as a Vessell cou'd be got ready the Americans here shou'd be sent to LOrient I believe that there are about 120 prisoners here at present[4] most of the persons you enquire after went in the last Cartells to America Capt Houston[5] has left Forton without Leave Mr Wren[6] had recommended him to me before I recd your Letter & I advanced him £10 10 s. on his Bill on Messrs Cummins & Macartny of LOrient (at my own Risque) & I now inclose you the said Bill to gether with a Letter which I have written to the above Gentlemen, wherein I request the favor of them to give me some Information in a matter in which I am interested,[7] if you will be so obliging as to second my request to them I shall esteem it a favor.

If the above Bill in LOrient is honored you will please to apply the whole or what part you please to Mr Wright for the Picture,[8] which when proper Opportunity offerrs, I am expecting, I thank you for your hint about publick Affairs—I cannot see that the French Minister will be warranted in continuing the War, for Interests foreign to the Original Dispute with you & your Affairs once agreed upon I woud hope other lesser Matters will be adjusted, not but to be sure it will be a work of some Time, I shall depend upon your Kindness for future necessary Information of the progress of Things.

I have nothing new to inform you of— You woud no doubt be surprised at reading Carlton & Digbys Letter because you woud see that they therein mention certain propositions &

3. Some 90 prisoners had recently arrived at Lorient; see our annotation of Nesbitt's Sept. 23 letter.

4. The Commissioners for Sick and Wounded Seamen reported on Oct. 16 that there still were 284 American detainees: Sheldon S. Cohen, *Yankee Sailors in British Gaols: Prisoners of War at Forton and Mill, 1777–1783* (Newark, Del., and London, 1995), p. 204.

5. Probably Capt. Thomas Houston of Pennsylvania, formerly captain of the captured brigantine *McClenachan:* Claghorn, *Naval Officers,* p. 157.

6. Rev. Thomas Wren.

7. We have not found the enclosures.

8. Joseph Wright's portrait of BF: XXXVII, xxvii, 626–7n, 692n.

Terms relative to the Exchange of Prisoners that have not the least Foundation in point of Fact.[9] Where the Blunder lies is difficult to say, but the Minister was much hurt at it, I am with the greatest Respect & Esteem Dr sr your most obliged & Hble Servt   WILLIAM HODGSON

Addressed: To / His Excellency / Benj Franklin Esqr / á Passy

To John Adams

LS:[1] Massachusetts Historical Society

Sir   Passy, 15 Oct. 1782.

A long and painful Illness has prevented my corresponding with your Excellency regularly, but I paid the Bill you drew upon me and advised me of in your last Letter.[2]

Mr Jay has I believe acquainted you with the Obstructions our Peace Negociations have met with, and that they are at length removed.[3] By the next Courier expected from London, we may be able perhaps to form some Judgment of the Probability of Success, so far as relates to our Part of the Peace. How likely the other Powers are to settle their Pretensions, I can not yet learn. In the mean time America is gradually growing more easy, by the Enemy's Evacuation of their Posts; as you will see by some Intelligence I enclose.[4]

I have had the Happiness formerly to help your Excellency in

9. Livingston had promised to send this to BF in his letter of Aug. 9, but apparently did not: XXXVII, 717; BF to Livingston, Sept. 26, above.

1. In WTF's hand except for the last six words of the complimentary close, which are in BF's hand.

2. The last extant letter from JA regarding his salary payment was June 10: XXXVII, 458–9.

3. Jay informed JA on Sept. 28 of the arrival of Oswald's new commission and expressed his hope that he would see his colleague very soon: Morris, *Jay: Peace*, p. 367. On Oct. 17 JA left for Paris from The Hague: Butterfield, *John Adams Diary*, III, 29.

4. Perhaps this refers to the British evacuation of Savannah on July 11: Richard K. Showman *et al.*, eds., *The Papers of General Nathanael Greene* (12 vols. to date, Chapel Hill and London, 1976–), XI, 439. Benjamin Vaughan had conveyed a false report of the evacuation of Charleston, which he learned from Henry Laurens: Vaughan to WTF, Aug. 26, 1782 (APS).

the Discharge of the Public Demands upon you.[5] I am now obliged to recur to you for the same kind of Assistance. Notice has been given me that the Interest of the Ten Millions borrow'd in Holland under the Guarantee of this Court becomes due the 5th. of next Month.[6] My Funds here are all engaged by Bills accepted and expected. I must therefore request that you will undertake the Payment of that Interest, which at 4 per Cent amounts to about 400,000 Livres Tournois.

With great Respect, I have the honour to be, Sir Your Excellency's Most obedient and most humble Servant   B Franklin

His Exy. J. Adams Esqr.

Endorsed: Dr Franklin 15 Oct. 1782

From Gerard Brantsen[7]   AL: University of Pennsylvania Library

Paris ce 15. d'octobre 1782.
Mr. de Brantsen, Ministre Plenipotentiaire de LL. HH. PP.[8] les Etats Generaúx des Provinces Únies des Pays bas a l'honneúr d'assurér Mr. Franklin de ses tres humbles civilités et de lui envoÿer ci jointe úne lettre dú Professeúr Ingen-Hoúz, qu'il a reçue hier dans son paqúet de Vienne.[9] Il lui offre en même temps ses services poúr faire parvenir en sureté la reponse a Mr. d'Ingen-Hoúz.

Notation: Brantsen 15. Oct. 1782.

5. See, for example, XXXIV, 567–8.
6. BF's July 16 contract with Vergennes obligated Congress to pay this interest to France, which would pay it to the Dutch creditors: XXXVII, 638.
7. Who was introduced by Dumas on Sept. 4, above. Although he had been in Paris since Sept. 10, Brantsen did not present his diplomatic credentials until Nov. 3. He informed BF of his reception at court in a brief letter dated only November, 1782 (APS); the event was also reported in the *Gaȝ. de Leyde,* Nov. 15, sup.
8. Leurs Hautes Puissances, an honorific title given to the States General of the Netherlands.
9. Ingenhousz to BF, Oct. 2, above.

From Joshua Preble[1]

ALS: American Philosophical Society

Hond. Sir.   Tenterton October th16 1782

Haveing the Misfortune to be Capturd by the Intriped of Sixty four Guns in the Ship Called the Retaliation Merchantmen my father in Law the Principle Owner Liveing at Newbury Port his Name is Stephen Cross[2] Esqr Hond Sir I am on my Parole of Honour and Should beg the favour of your Kind assistance in Supplying me with ten or twelve Pounds Sir I will Give my Honour that I will remit it to you as Soon as I get my Self Exchang'd and would Pay you what Intrest you think Propper I was Capt of the Ship and Sir My Drawing on you was by my Fathers Desire If incase I was Carried into England my Own father Lives at Falmth Casco Bay in the State of Massachusetts in New England his Name Is Jedediah Preble Esq He is one of the Council at Boston.

Sir I am Your Most Obedient Humble Servant

JOSHUA PREBLE

Addressed: Honrd Doctor Frankling Esq / at / Paris in France

Notation: J Hall

From Girardot, Haller & Cie.

LS:[3] American Philosophical Society

Monsieur   Paris Le 18. 8bre 1782

Nous avons Lhonneur de vous presenter mr Housberg chef d'une manufacture de fonte de fer a qui nous donnâmes il y a

---

1. Preble (1759–1803) had served on privateers since at least 1778. His father, whom he mentions below, was Brig. Gen. Jedidiah Preble (1707–1784), one of the wealthiest citizens of Falmouth (now Portland, Me.): George Henry Preble, "Brigadier General Jedidiah Preble.—1707–1784," *New England Hist. & Geneal. Register,* XXII (1868), 405–19; Massachusetts Office of the Secretary of State, *Massachusetts Soldiers and Sailors of the Revolutionary War* (17 vols., Boston, 1896–1908), XII, 732–3.

2. Preble was married to Hannah Cross: Allen, *Mass. Privateers,* p. 259; Preble, "Brigadier General Jedidiah Preble," p. 419. The ship *Retaliation,* 10, received a commission on Feb. 21, 1782, under the command of Samuel Rice.

3. In the hand of Jean Girardot de Marigny.

Trois ans une Lettre d'introduction auprès de vous Monsieur.[4] Nous Serons charmés si Les propositions quil a vous faire peuvent vous Etre agreables c'est dans cette vue que nous nous sommes prêtes à L'instance de mr housberg.

Nous avons Lhonneur d'être avec La consideration La plus distinguée Monsieur Vos très humbles & très obeissants Serviteurs   GIRARDOT HALLER ET CO

Mr Le Docteur francklin à Passy

Notation: Girardot & Haller 18. 8bre. 1782.

From Francis Hopkinson

ALS: Yale University Library

My dear sir.   Philade. Octr. 18th: 1782

It is very long since I have had the Satisfaction of a Line from you. This I attribute to the great Uncertainty of Opportunities. The last Letter I received from you mentioned an Electrical Battery, which you said was in the Hands of Mr. Coombe.[5] I have at last got the Battery you mention, & found five of the Bottles broke. The Rest are in good Order. All your Philosophical Apparatus in my hands hath been carefully preserved, & shall at any Time be delivered in good Condition to your's or Mr. Bache's Order, to whom I have given a Receipt for every Article I have borrowed. The Use of them has afforded much Amusement & some Instruction to me for which I heartily thank you.— I wrote to you some Time ago requesting you would enter me as a Subscriber to an Encyclopædia now publishing at Paris;[6] as I understand the Price will not be very great I am desirous of having it— I leave this to your Discretion.—

I enclose for your Amusement a Piece I wrote to save the Trees of this City from being all cut down agreeably to a Law passed for that purpose. This together with some Petitions, saved the Trees & the Law was repealed.[7] I thought a Piece like this a

4. Not found.
5. See XXXV, 473.
6. XXXVII, 240–1.
7. In April, 1782, the Pa. Assembly passed a law ordering the removal of

more rational Trifle than the abusive paragraphs which fill our Papers—in which I assure you I have no Part.

I have only Room to request my respectful Regards to Mr. Jay if yet in paris, & also to Mr. Adams— And to assure you (for which I have always Room in my Heart be the paper as scanty as it may) that I am ever your affectionate friend & very humble servant   F. HOPKINSON

Addressed: Honourable / Doctor Franklin / at Passey / near *Paris*

Endorsed: Mr Hopkinson Oct. 18. 1782 With a Paper in favour of the Trees.

Notation: Hopkinson, Phila. Octr. 18. 1782.

From the Comtesse d'Houdetot

L: American Philosophical Society

a Sanois le 18. 8bre.[8] 1782

Mde. la Cesse D'houdetot qui a L'honneur D'offrir Mille tendres Complimens a Monsieur franklin Le prie De Vouloir Bien faire passer surement Ce paquet En Amerique. Il apartient a Mr. St. Jean de Crevecœur a qui il a deja Bien Voulû Rendre Ce Service a Sa Consideration.[9] Ce Mr. De St. Jean Est aussy En peine De Scavoir Sy Mr. franklin a Recu Et agreés un Livre quil a Eû l'honneur De Luy Envoyer sur Les troubles Et Les Desastres De L'Amerique.[1] Madame D'houdetot Espere que La Santé De Monsieur franklin Est Bonne. Elle Le prie D'Agréer L'assurance

---

all the trees in the streets, lanes, and alleys of Philadelphia. Hopkinson responded by publishing a fable on the utility of trees, citing Priestley and Ingenhousz: "To the Printers," signed "Silvester", in *Pa. Gaẓ.*, Aug. 21, 1782. The Assembly repealed the law on Aug. 29: *Pa. Gaẓ.*, Sept. 4, 1782; George Everett Hastings, *The Life and Works of Francis Hopkinson* (Chicago, 1926), pp. 374–5.

8. The month could also be read as "9bre."

9. See XXXVII, 75.

1. Crèvecœur's *Letters from an American Farmer* was delivered to BF in mid-July: XXXVII, 628–9.

De Son tendre attachement. L'adresse De Mr. De Crevecœur De St. Jean Est Chez Mr. De Lile Lieutenant general Du Baillage a Caen.[2]

Notation: Mde. la Comtesse d'Houdetot.

From George Washington

ALS: American Philosophical Society; LS (draft): Library of Congress

Sir,　　　　Head Qrs. State of New York 18th. Octr. 1782.

I have been honored with two favors of Your Excellency— one presented by the Count de Segur, of the 2d. of April—the other delivered by the Prince de Broglie of the 8th.—both which were rendered doubly agreeable, by the pleasure I had in receiving them from the hands of two such amiable & accomplished Young Gentlemen.—[3]

Independent of my esteem for your Excellency—be assured Sir, that my respect & regard for the French Nation at large, to whom this Country is under so great obligations—as well as the favourable impressions I have conceived for these particular Characters, will secure my warmest attention to the persons of these distinguished young Noblemen.

I am much obliged by the political information which you have taken the trouble to convey to me—but feel myself much embarrassed in my wish to make you a return in kind.— At the first of the Season the expectations of America were much raised, in consequence of the change of the British Ministry & the measures of Parliament.— But events have shewn, that these hopes have risen too high— The Death of the Marqs. of Rockingham, the advancement of the Earl of Shelburn, and the delays of Negociation, have given us very different impressions from those we at first conceived— We now begin again to reflect upon the persevering obstinacy of the King, the Wickedness of his Ministry, & the haughty pride of the Nation, which

---

2. Crèvecœur's relative; see XXXVII, 694n.
3. BF's letters introduced Ségur and de Broglie: XXXVII, 87–9, 115–16.

ideas recall to our Minds, very disagreeable prospects—and a probable continuance of our prest. troubles.

The Military operations of the Campaign, are drawing to a close, without any important events on this side the Water unless the evacuation of Charlestown, which is generally expected, but not yet known to me, should take place and form a paragraph in the page of this years history.[4]

The British Fleet from the West Indies, still continues in New York— I have not been able yet to decide on the Enemy's intentions there— It is generally thought that a detachment of their Troops will sail with them when the Fleet returns to the West Indies, where it is conjectured their efforts for the Winter, will be prosecuted with vigor.[5]

I have the honor to be. with great esteem & Regard Sir Yr. Excelly's Most Obt Se   GO: WASHINGTON

His Excelly. Doctr. Franklin. Minister at the Ct. of France.

Duplicate

From Jonathan Williams, Jr.

ALS: Historical Society of Pennsylvania

Dear & hond sir   L'Orient Octor. 18. 1782

I came hither on the Business of our House having 5 rich Jamaica prizes to our address, with upwards of 2000 hhd Sugar & 400 hhds Rum. The Alliance is just arrived with 4 more,[6] & she

---

4. The British evacuation of Charleston was delayed until Dec. 14 because of the shortage of transports: David Syrett, *Shipping and the American War, 1775–83: a Study of British Transport Organization* (London, 1970), pp. 231–8; Richard K. Showman *et al.*, eds., *The Papers of General Nathanael Greene* (12 vols. to date, Chapel Hill and London, 1976–), XII, 291–2n, 303–4n.

5. A portion of Pigot's fleet sailed from New York for the Caribbean on Oct. 24, the remainder a month later: W. M. James, *The British Navy in Adversity: a Study of the War of American Independence* (London, New York, and Toronto, 1926), pp. 360–1.

6. All four of the prizes taken by the *Alliance*, Capt. John Barry, had been part of the storm-damaged Jamaica convoy (for which see Williams, Moore

has sent 5 into America, two have got into Nantes so we know of 16 taken; I have another privateer which I hourly expect will bring in 2 or 3 more.— I have advice from my Father of the Reception of Johonnotts & Warrens Bills, but no accot of the payment yet.—[7] I shall carry Mrs Williams to her Friends to pass the Winter, for I fear her Health will never be perfectly established at Nantes,[8] I hope at same Time to pay my Duty to you and to see you much better than I hear you have been. I am most dutifully & affectionately ever Yours.   JONA WILLIAMS J

Addressed: a son Excellence / M. Le Docteur Franklin / Ministre americain / en son Hotel / A Passy prés / Paris.

Notation: J. Williams, Oct. 18. 1782

From James Mathews   ALS: Historical Society of Pennsylvania

Belone [Boulogne] the 19 day of October 1782
Sir I have taken this oppertunity of wrighting These few lines to let you know the sewerahson [situation?] that i am in i belong to a meracahn ship belonging To the congres my ship left me behind i had the Misfortune of looseing my Cloathes the ship Left me at haver de grass and i went down to belone for to get a shipe and the comeserey Wou'ld not let me pass without a pass port

---

& Co. to BF, Oct. 9, above). BF signed prize condemnation forms for them on Nov. 24. The forms, filled out by WTF and addressed to the Judges of the Admiralty at Lorient, indicate that the *Britannia* and the *Anna* were captured on Sept. 23, the *Commerce* on Sept. 25, and the *Kingston* on Sept. 28: Archives départementales de Morbihan. For Barry's cruise see William Bell Clark, *Gallant John Barry, 1745–1803: the Story of a Naval Hero of Two Wars* (New York, 1938), pp. 271–6.

7. For these bills see XXXVII, 12n.

8. Mariamne had recovered from a serious case of influenza that induced an early delivery and the subsequent loss of her baby (see above, JW to BF, Aug. 16), but had recently developed dropsy (edema) and continued in a depression. The Williamses left for St. Germain, where Mariamne's family lived, on Oct. 26: [Samuel White] to Williams, Moore & Co., Oct. 28, 1782, and to Jonathan Williams, Sr., Oct. 30, 1782 (both at the Yale University Library).

ware Can i get pass and i have no bodey for to get one from. The comeserey put me in preson he gives me bread Aand waghter He has forst me to go on board of A loger [lugger] belonging to the king wich i doant like. I want to sare [serve] no other nesion [nation] but the one. The loger is cald the belone comanded by Captain banstable:[9] she is going to breast. I hope your honir will let me free. If you please to dereck the letter for brest— We espect to sale frome belone a thusday or On wednesday i have no frends to helpe me if you Doant i have not a farthing to helpe me. I have no Cloathes and no friends at present. Bread and waghter is verey low diat for a man. I hope you will helpe me i belong to boston.

I am your most humble sarvant   JAMES MATHEWS

From Pierre Penet[1]

ALS: American Philosophical Society

Belft. [Belfort] 20. 8bre. 1782

Si jai tardé dinformer Son Exélance du malheur qui m'est Survenu dans le momen ou je devais my attendre le moins c'est que javois espoire de pouvoir remédier a une événement occationné par la mechansté et chalousie cruel de gens qui depuis que je Suis dans les affaires de L'amerique ont chergé a me nuire.

Je representerés Seulement a votre Exelance que le Sujet qui ma obligé de Suspandre mes payements et me retirer afin de nêtre pas exposé a la volonté et méchansté de partie de mes créantiers viens d'une lettre de change que javois reçu en payement pour Solde de mes avances d'un vaisseaux armée que j'ai fais construire a Nantes pour compte de la maison Stiven Houper et Co. de Nieuberyport,[2] cette maison ma remis des Effets pour mes

---

9. Lieutenant de frégate Pierre-Jean Vanstabel (1744–1797) of Dunkirk, who would become one of the most famous admirals of the French Revolution: Christian de La Jonquière, comp., *Les Marins français sous Louis XVI* . . . (Issy-les-Moulineaux, France, 1996), p. 286; Larousse.

1. Penet had not written in almost a year, as far as we know. For part of the time he had been in hiding from his creditors: xxxv, 667–8, 674–5; xxxvii, 640–1, 683–4.

2. The ship built for Stephen Hooper was the *Vengeance:* xxxv, 329n.

avancés Sur L'espagne que j'ai fais passer a mon chargé d'affaires a Paris, cet homme vient a mourir a laissé des enfans mineur il fut nommé un éxécuteur testamanthére le quèl ayant pris connoissance des affaires du défun, a trouvé que de tous les Effets que je lui avois fait passer, un Seule d'environs 10 mille livres tournois na point été accepté ny payé. Sans autre forme obtient Santance contre moi l'envoit a un chargé de procuration a Nantes gens de mes Enemis qui la garterent pendant quinze-jours attendant linstans que je Suis absans, font une dessante dans ma maison avec quatre husier Sans prevenir ny Comis, ni Domestiques, font Saisire méttent arét Sur mes Effets et laissent une garde. Ce qui fut connu dans la place et au Loins, de maniere que tous ceux aux quèls j'avois à faire tant pour les Etats que par-ticuliers, Croyant que je devois des Sommes imances ont obtenu Santance et meussent fait arrêter Si je n'avois pris le partie de me retirer.

Je Suis occupé àprendre des arrengements pour que mes créantiers maccordent du terme pour leurs remboursements qui tous Seront Satisfait avec les intéréts même de leurs avances, les propositions que je leurs fais Sont fontée Sur lEquité nayant já-mais eu dautres principes. Mais mes Enemis et chaloux font lin-possible pour me contrarier, et faire Echouer mes propositions.

Je Suplie donc Son Exlance et j'ai déjas occation de lui dé-moigner ma reconnoissance dans le Compte qu'elle à rendüe a ceux qui Sont venü aux informations chés elle de vouloir bien me Continuer Ces bontés, et protecxions, ce Serat rendre la plus haute justice au plus inosans des hommes et a celui qui dans Son Etat C'est le plus Distingué dans les affaires qui lui ont été confié tant des Etats unies, que de la Nation, et particuliers dont il à les plus grandes preuves et temoigniages. Cy joint une lettre, de la quelle je prie Son Exelance de vouloir bien prandre connois-sance, elle voirat que dans touttes les circonstances je me Suis comporté en homme D'honneur.[3]

3. The enclosure may have been a copy of a memoir from the chevalier d'Artus, whose address Penet uses below; see XXXVII, 640–1n. Among BF's papers at the APS also is a Dec. 5, 1781[–June 12, 1782] letter from Stephen Hooper & Co. to Penet, expressing gratitude to him. The postscript reported the capture of the *Vengeance* while sailing to Virginia. APS.

J'ai fais un mêmoir qui doit avoir Eté presenté au Ministre à fain qu'il m'obtienne de la bonté du Roy un Saufe Conduit pour par moi même regler mes affaires.

Si prés de Son Èxelance on venoit aux informations je Soumet tout a Sa justice, et ne Cesserai de faire des voeux au Seigneur pour la conservation des jours de Votre Exelance Le très humble et très Obeissant Serviteur   P. PENET./.

adressé a Belfort en Alsace ches Mr Dartus chevalier de St louis, qui me fairat parvenire les lettres de Son Exelance, Si elle me ren-voy la lettre cy incluse./.

Endorsed: Penet

To William Lee

> Copies: University of Virginia Library,[4] Virginia Historical Society (two)

Sir.   Passy Octr. 21st. 1782.

I receiv'd the Letter you did me the Honor of writing to me the 7th. instt., inclosing a copy of an order of Congress with a copy of a Letter to you from Mr. Secretary Livingston, & informing me, that you had in consequence drawn on me for £46196..19 [*i.e.*, 46,196 *l.t.* 19 *s*] payle. to your order the 12th. April next. This is to acquaint you that I have accepted the said Bills hoping to have by that time Funds in my hands for payment: But as that is uncertain, I confide that you will not hazard the credit of congress by indorsing any of them to others, 'till you have heard from me that I am likely to be in Cash, of which you shall be inform'd in the month of January next. I have the Honor &c—   (Sign'd) B. FRANKLIN.

Honble. Wm. Lee Esq.—Bruxelles

(Copy) No 2

---

4. In William Lee's hand. See our annotation of Lee's reply, Nov. 12.

From Deacon M. Auer,[5] with Franklin's Note for a Reply

ALS: American Philosophical Society

Monseigneur!

Ebingen pres de Bahlingen en Wurtemberg, le 21 obr: 1782.

Rien n'est plus genereux, que l'Action, que Vous venez de faire, Monseigneur! La pauvre Veuve Hoeklin se croit heureuse. Elle a reçu un Billet que Son Excellence, Votre Beaufils aye accepté 200 Pound de Mons. Schneider a Germantown. Mons. Richard Bache a ecrit lui meme.[6] Mais a cette heure nous sommes en peine. Permettez donc, je Vous supplie, de Vous demander a) par quel Moyen nous pourrions recevoir cette Somme et b)combien elle soit selon notre Argent.

Nous nous addressons directement a Votre Excellence, parceque je n'ai de confience, qu'en elle. Daignez donc jetter les yeux Sur la Veuve. Le grand Dieu recompensera tout, il Vous comblera de toute Sorte de Bonheur devant Son Trone. Je suis avec un parfait devouement et une Veneration profonde Monseigneur, de Votre Excellence tres humble Valet,

M. Auer,
Pasteur.

Notation: Auer. 21 Oct. 1782.

[*In Franklin's hand:*] That I have receiv'd from Mr Bache [*blank in MS*] Livres which lies in the Hands of Mr Frederic Grand Banker in Paris from whom it may be drawn by Mrs Hoeklin in such manner as she shall be advis'd.[7]

---

5. Auer had been corresponding with BF on behalf of the widow Höklin since the summer of 1779: XXX, 189–90; XXXV, 275n, 280.

6. Christian Schneider had written BF on April 3, enclosing a letter for the widow, his sister-in-law, and a copy of RB's April 2 receipt: XXXVII, 90.

7. XXXVII, 576–7. BF's reply was evidently not received; de Thun wrote on Auer's behalf on Dec. 14, below.

From [Christophe-Claire] Danyel de Kervégan *et al.*[8]

ALS: Historical Society of Pennsylvania

Monsieur,   Nantes 21. Octobre 1782./.

Le Régisseur des Octrois de cette Ville veut contraindre les Négocians de L'amérique Septentrionale établis à Nantes, à lui payer, sur les Tabacs qui leur sont adressés *vingt sols par quintal comme droguerie,* au lieu de *trois sols par fardeau de 150* livres pesant *comme marchandise prohibée;* Il s'est élevé un procès à ce sujet, parcequ'il se trouve une contradiction manifeste dans les articles 13 et 22. de L'arrêt du Conseil du 14. 9bre. 1741. qui fixe ces deux perceptions.

Pour faire terminer plus promptement cette contestation, nous avons adressé au Ministre des finances, une Requête que nous présentons au Roi et à son Conseil, tendante à ordonner que les Tabacs soyent rangés dans L'art. 13, et assujetis à *trois sols* seulement comme *marchandises prohibées.*

Nous nous sommes faits un devoir de venir au secours de ces Négocians et de les favoriser autant qu'il nous a été possible: outre l'inclination naturelle qui nous y porte, nous ne vous dissimulerons point, Monsieur, que l'intérêt particulier du Commerce de cette Place, nous y a aussi engagés.

Si d'un côté Messieurs vos Compatriotes trouvent beaucoup d'avantages et de facilités à demeurer en cette Ville, à cause de la bonne foi avec laquelle on y traite les affaires, la commodité de la Loire et la proximité de la mer; d'un autre, ils ne doivent point y être plus maltraités qu'ailleurs. Or il n'est dû aucuns droits Sur les Tabacs ni à L'orient, Bordeaux, La Rochelle ni au havre.

Nous espérons que ces considérations et celles qu'il vous plaira d'y ajouter, vous porteront, Monsieur, à faire toutes les réprésentations et les démarches que vous jugerez convenables, pour faire affranchir les Négocians, Sujets des Etats unis de L'amérique, qui résident ici, du droit de vingt sols par quintal sur

---

8. Judge and consuls at Nantes, as they sign themselves. Christophe-Claire Danyel de Kervégan was mayor of Nantes in 1789–91 and 1797. Mosneron, Geslin, and Plumard de Rieux were all prominent mercantile families: Paul Bois, ed., *Histoire de Nantes* (Toulouse, 1977), pp. 251, 463; Yvonne Arnous Rivière, *Nantes et ses messieurs les Arnous* (Chabris, [1994]), p. 128; Meyer, *Armement Nantais,* pp. 45, 103n, 185.

les Tabacs, aux offres qu'ils font de payer celui de *trois sols* par fardeau, comme *marchandises prohibées.*

Nous sommes avec un profond Respect, Monsieur, Vos très-humbles et très-obéïssants Serviteurs, Les Juge et Consuls de Nantes. /.   DANYEL DE KERVEGAN

                MOSNERON L'AINÉ

                GESLIN

                PLUMARD DE RIEUX

Mr. franklin, Ambassadeur des Etats unis de l'amérique septentrionale. à *la Cour de france.*

From Soulavie   LS: University of Pennsylvania Library

Monsieur   paris ce 21 8bre 1782

J'ai Lu avec un plaisir extreme vos raisonnemens très profonds[9] qui caracterisent le Beau genie de leur auteur et à moins que je ne reçoive des ordres contraires, je me ferai un grand honneur de les inserer dans mon tome 5 qui S'imprime,[1] avec les Memoires que Vous M'avez promis de me renvoyer, & qui ont besoin d'etre corrigés. Alors Mon Volume aura un Merite ina-

---

9. BF's letter of Sept. 22.

1. Soulavie intended his *Histoire naturelle de la France méridionale* to comprise two divisions: Part I was "mineraux" (geology) and Part II would concern plants and animals. The four volumes he had published so far were all on geology, and these had provoked the abbé Augustin de Barruel to attack him for contradicting the Biblical account of creation. Though vol. 5 of the "mineraux" series was in press, as Soulavie here tells BF, it was not published until 1784. He blamed the two-year delay on the death of his cartographer (as he explained in the "avis aux souscripteurs"), but that did not explain why the second section of the text was only printed in 1784. Soulavie may have delayed publication because of the ongoing religious controversy, which threatened to block his clerical advancement. When vol. 5 was finally issued, the latter section included a "profession of faith" which attempted to reconcile his theories with Biblical truth. Soulavie left out all mentions of BF and his theory of the formation of the earth.

The dispute between Soulavie and the abbé Barruel is the subject of Léon Aufrère, *Soulavie et son secret* (Paris, 1952). An analysis of the 1782 and 1784 portions of vol. 5 of *Histoire naturelle . . .*, with the "profession of faith" quoted, is on pp. 113–20, 158–64. See also Albin Mazon, *Histoire de Soulavie . . .* (2 vols., Paris, 1893), I, 32–5.

preciable. Je demeure dans la rue des Vieilles thuileries à Lhotel de Mr. L'evêque de Bayeux[2] ou j'ai un Logement.

Voila une place Vacante à L'academie des Sciences;[3] il Se presente Mrs. fontaine, Avit, Descemet personnes ignorées du public;[4] je N'ai personne, Monsieur, pour me porter dans ce Corps, je ne Connois qu'un peu M. le Roi parcequ'il fut nommé Comissaire de l'edition que j'ai donnée des œuvres de Mr. Hamilton.[5]

Je Vous devrai donc, illustre philosophe, cet avantage Si Votre bonté peut vous porter à Vous interresser pour Moi, Vous êtes de cette academie, Vous êtes lié avec tous Ses membres et avec M. Amelot[6] qui est le ministre dans le departement de qui Se trouve L'academie.

2. Joseph-Dominique de Cheylus: xxxv, 361n.

3. The Academy was organized by scientific disciplines, and, within each discipline, by a prescribed hierarchy. Membership at all levels was limited, and the death of a senior member allowed for promotions and the induction of a new member at the lowest rank, *adjoint*. Henri-Louis Duhamel du Monceau died in August, creating a vacancy in botany. See Roger Hahn, *The Anatomy of a Scientific Institution* . . . (Berkeley, Los Angeles, and London, 1971), pp. 78–9, 99, and for Duhamel du Monceau, *Dictionary of Scientific Biography; Index biographique des membres et correspondants de l'Académie des sciences de 1666 à 1939* (Paris, 1939), p. 148.

4. Botanist René Louiche Desfontaines (Des Fontaines) (1750–1833), recently named *docteur régent* in the Faculty of Medicine, was admitted to the Academy on March 2, 1783, as *adjoint botaniste surnuméraire*. He later became professor of botany at the Jardin royal: *DBF; Index biographique* . . ., p. 136; *Almanach royal* for 1783, p. 483.

We have not identified Avit. Jean Descemet (1732–1810), *docteur régent* in the Faculty of Medicine and royal censor, made contributions in botany and medicine: *DBF; Almanach royal* for 1782, pp. 477, 487.

5. BF's friend Jean-Baptiste Le Roy was a *pensionnaire ordinaire* and thus in a position to vote in the election of new members: *Almanach royal* for 1782, p. 502; Hahn, *The Anatomy of a Scientific Institution*, pp. 129–33. He was evidently on the committee that evaluated the French edition of Sir William Hamilton's works, *Œuvres complètes de M. le chevalier Hamilton* . . . (Paris, 1781), which dealt with volcanoes in Italy and contained 158 pages of commentary by Soulavie that emphasized the importance of direct observation in the natural sciences. That edition was published in December, 1782, and carried the approbation of the Academy. Albin Mazon, *Histoire de Soulavie* . . . (2 vols., Paris, 1893), II, 117–18; Pahin de La Blancherie's *Nouvelles de la république* . . . , issue of Dec. 11, 1782.

6. Amelot de Chaillou had been president of the Academy in 1779: XXIX, 285n.

Aucun de Ceux qui Se presentent N'a autant travaillé que moi pour L'academie: je n'ai publié aucun Volume sans Son approbation, et j'ai lû huit memoires differens. L'esprit de L'academie est de recevoir des adjoints jeunes & zelés et qui N'ont d'autre occupation que les Sciences. Et Comme C'est la classe dhistoire naturelle et surtout des plantes je dois presenter dans peu de tems mon tome I des Vegetaux dont j'ai eu Lhonneur de Vous entretenir.[7]

Si Sans Vous Compromettre, Sans Vous gener, Vous pouvez me rendre ce Service, je ne l'oublierai jamais de la vie, je M'abandonne à Vos bontés avec toute la Confiance.

Je suis avec un profond respect Monsieur Votre très humble et très obeissant Serviteur   LABBÉ SOULAVIE

rue des Vieilles thuileries hotel de M. lévêque de Bayeux

Notation: Solavie 21. Oct 1782

From Williams, Moore & Co.

LS:[8] University of Pennsylvania Library

L'orient le 21. 8bre. 1782.

Nous avons l'honneur de vous remettre cy joint les procédures des mis en Regle par L'amirauté de Vannes, ausy que La Reconnoissance de Monr Le Commandant de nôtre port des prisonniers que nous lui avons Livrés.[9]

Nous Sommes avec Respect Monsieur Vos trés humbles & trés obeissants Serviteurs   WILLIAMS MOORE & CO

Endorsed: Williams & Moore 21. Octr. 1782.

7. Soulavie's *Histoire naturelle de la France méridionale* was published with the approbation of the Académie des sciences, but as we noted above, he had not yet published any of the volumes on botany. Part II of the series, entitled "Les Végétaux," was (as he says here) in progress; vol. I was published in 1783, bound with vol. 6 of "Minéraux." Soulavie never was elected to the Academy.

8. Signed by James Moore.

9. Both enclosures are missing.

From Jacques-François Crespin[1]

L:[2] American Philosophical Society

Monseigneur   Dunkerque ce 22 8bre 1782

Votre reponse du douze aoust 1781 dont vous avez honoré M Epidorge faisoit beaucoup ésperer aux pauvres infortunés du corsaire La revange commandé par le capitaine coningham d'une prompte recette de leurs dû,[3] mais dépuis n'en ayant recu aucune nouvelle cela leur fait perdre toute esperance. Il est bien douloureux pour des pauvres gens qui ne possedent au monde que ce qu'ils ont si Legitimement gagnés dans laditte course a la Sueur de Leurs corps et au peril de Leurs Vie pour se solliciter eux et Leurs famille Se voir Si Longt tems ménés ces infortunés. Jusqu'a present ont trouvés des personnes qui ont bien Voulu Leurs avancer de quoi Se procurer leurs alimens necessaires pour Vivre mais ces personnes fatigués de promesses Sans effet ne veuillent plus rien leur avancer. Vous voyez D'après cela sans ressource D'autres que le fruit de Leurs travaux ils se verront contraints à se trouver Dans La rue Si on ne les payent. J'ose vous persuader monseigneur que la Lanteur de L'armateur après avoir fait de Si belles prises a payer son Equipage Surprend beaucoup les messieurs de la marine de Dunkerque. Cés infortunés implorent Votre pitié vous priant de solliciter Mr. richard bache a leurs faire rentrer leurs fond c'est ce quils attendent de Votre bonté ils ne cesseront Jamais D'adresser des vœux au ciel pour la conservation De vos Jours Si precieux. Ils esperent que vous daignerez leurs accorder une reponse et Sont avec le plus grand respect Monseigneur Votre très humble et très obeissant serviteur   CREPIN

---

1. Whose name we formerly read as Crispin. He was a member of the prize crew of the *Northampton*, a 1777 prize of Gustavus Conyngham's *Revenge*, which was retaken by the British. After being released from captivity the twenty members of the prize crew sought back wages and prize money: XXXIV, 367–8, 379n.

2. The letter and signature are in the same secretarial hand, which omitted the "s" in Crespin's name.

3. BF had promised his assistance, but we have no record of his writing on the prize crew's behalf: XXXV, 353.

Si vous daignez honorer d'une reponse Je vous Supplie D'adresser La Lettre a Mr. alicherie commissaire au bureau des classes de la marine de dunkerque./.[4]

Addressed: A Monsieur / Monsieur franklin plenipotentiaire / des Etats reunis de L'amerique / Septentrionnalle a passy prés / paris / A Passy

Notation: Crepin 22 Oct. 1782.

From Edward Bridgen   ALS: Historical Society of Pennsylvania

London Octr 23 1782

I was much obliged by the honour of your Excellency's favour of the 25th: of last Month[5] which did not arrive until the 9th. Currant.

I feel myself much indebted to you My Dr: Sir for the kind interest you have taken in my affairs in No: Carolina:[6] I fancy nothing will now be done until a Peace is made, which is not far off. On this Account I now beg leave to trouble your Excellency, with the Proposals, formerly hinted at, respcting the Copper Coinage for the United States, which if you Sir approve, I beg you would have the goodness to forward to Congress by the first good Opportunity.[7]

I think the proposals are advantageous to the States, however if, upon enquiry, the buisness can be done more advantgeously

4. Crespin repeated this plea (with minor wording variations) on Dec. 27, this time in his own hand, signing "Jacques francois Crespin est les Compagions."

5. Not found.

6. BF wrote the governor of North Carolina to request that Bridgen's confiscated land and slaves be restored: XXXVII, 703.

7. Bridgen enclosed the proposal that he had alluded to on Sept. 6, above. Dated Oct. 23, it was a copy of what he and his partner John Waller had presented to Henry Laurens in May, 1782, and were now offering to Congress "through the hands of Benjamin Franklin Esqr." They proposed to supply Congress with round copper blanks of any size or, alternately, to mill and strike copper coins according to whatever drawings Congress might supply (National Archives). See also *Laurens Papers,* XV, 512n.

in any other Country (for I am certain that it cannot here) I have nothing more to say, but that I should be happy to be in posession of Some of the first coin.

I have a Seperate paper on the Subject of the Designs, which I shall take the liberty to Trouble you with the next good opportunity I have, which I hope will be soon; but at present I have not time to transcribe it.

I also have receiv'd a letter from Mr Bowens respecting the Case of Books & Maps Sent by the Governor to your Excellency; giving me an Acct that the Capt: had lost the Case, and requesting to know its Value?[8] I accordingly wrote to the Govr: immediately, to know its Value, but have receiv'd as yet no Answer: therefore must request Sir that you would send Mr Bowens of what Value the Case was?

I have the honour to be with great respect and Esteem Your Excellency's much obliged & Obedt Servt   EDWARD BRIDGEN

His Excellency Benjn: Franklin Esqr

From Thomas Townshend

Two copies and draft: Public Record Office; copies: Library of Congress, William L. Clements Library

Sir,   Whitehall, 23d. October 1782.

As Mr. Strachey is going from hence to Paris with some particulars for Mr Oswald, which were not to be easily explained in Writing, I take the liberty of introducing him to your acquaintance, though I am not sure, that he is not already a little known to you.[9]

8. Thomas Pownall sent the case of books and maps to Bridgen, who was to forward it to BF through François Bowens: XXXVII, 371. See also BF to Pownall, [September, 1782].

9. Henry Strachey, whom BF had met in 1776, was now Townshend's undersecretary: XXII, 598–9; Namier and Brooke, *House of Commons*, III, 487–9. He was sent to work with Oswald in the negotiations, and delivered to Oswald the cabinet's Oct. 17 instructions (for which see our annotation of BF to Livingston, Oct. 14). Shelburne's notes of verbal instructions for Strachey and his letter of introduction of Strachey to Oswald, are in Giunta, *Emerg-*

The confidential Situation in which he stands with me, makes me particularly desirous of presenting him to you.

I believe, Sir, I am enough known to you for you to believe me when I say that there has not been from the beginning a single Person more averse to the unhappy War, or who wishes more earnestly than I do for a return of Peace and mutual Amity between Great Britain & America.

I am &ca.   T: TOWNSHEND

Doctor Franklin

From Gérard de Rayneval   Partial AL: Library of Congress

[before October 24, 1782][1]

... [sous] les yeux de M. le Cte. de Vergennes.

Je desirerois fort, Monsieur, davoir un entretien avec vous et M. Jay, et vous m'obligeriez si vous vouliez me recevoir et me donner à diner avec lui jeudy prochain. J'attendrai votre réponse.

J'ai l'honneur dêtre avec un

M franklin

---

ing Nation, 1, 619–20, 623. He arrived in Paris on Oct. 28: Morris, *Jay: Peace,* p. 450.

1. On Oct. 24, a Thursday, Jay dined with BF at Passy and was surprised to find Rayneval there. (Afterwards BF explained to him that Rayneval had sent word that he would dine at Passy that day and would be glad to meet Jay there as well.) Rayneval asked them about their negotiations with Oswald, particularly on the questions of the Canadian border and the fisheries, and contested the American demands: Jay's diary entry of Oct. 24, in Morris, *Jay: Peace,* pp. 449–50.

From Jean de Neufville & fils

ALS: Historical Society of Pennsylvania

Sir   Amsterdam 24th October 1782

Not being honour'd with any of yr. Excellency's Letters since the 1st. of July when we dated our last respects to you,[2] the Subject of the present will be only on 4 small Continental bills remitted us here by our friend Wm. Foster Esqr. of Boston[3] and Wch our Banker Sir John Lambert return'd us for want of their being endorss'd by R R Livingston Esqr. to whose order they are made pble. for 18 Dollrs. each,[4] on observing the same to Mr. Foster, he thought proper to lay before your Excellcy. the reason for it, Which you will find by the enclosed which he desired us to forward,[5] adding further that he being possessed of the other Setts he is Willing to give his guarantee, that none of the same shall be presented for payment. It were we Suppose Needless to Offer our own guarantee as an additionl. Security otherway that for our part we shall act therein as may be deem'd Necessary. Being With great respect your Excellency Most Obedt. Humble Servants   JOHN DE NEUFVILLE SON.

PS May we be permitted to enclose a letter for His Excy. Mr. adams just rec'd from petersburg[6]

His Excellency Doctr. Franklin— Minister plenipotentiary for the United States of America, at the Court of Versailles

2. XXXVII, 572–3.

3. Probably the William Foster recommended in July by Thomas Cushing: XXXVII, 694–5.

4. For Sir John Lambert see XIX, 189n; XXX, 556n. Among BF's papers at the APS is an undated letter from Neufville & fils giving a list of bills the firm had endorsed to Lambert.

5. Missing.

6. Possibly from his son John Quincy, who wrote on Sept. 6: *Adams Correspondence*, IV, 378.

From Edward Bridgen

ALS: Historical Society of Pennsylvania

London Octr 25 1782

Two days ago I troubled your Excellency with my proposals abt. the Copper[7] thro: the hands of Mr Hamilton requesting that they might be forwarded by the first good opportunity since which I have consulted with a friend who advises that they lay by in your hands before they are sent as being premature and if taken may lead the proposers into difficulties. I must own that I am not so apprehensive, but I submit to better Judgment.

In that letter I requested that you would forthwith send to Mr Bowens the Value of the Case shipp'd for you by me from the Governor as the Capt: has lost it and Mr Bowen wants the particulars that he may recover the Amount.

I was informed that you have lately been Ill. I hope you are now perfectly recovered which I shall be happy to hear of.

God Bless and protect your Excellency is the hearty prayer of My Dr Sir Yr: faithful & Affect. EDWD: BRIDGEN

His Excellency Benj Franklin Esqr

Notation: Edwrd. Bridgen London 25. Octr. 1782.

From Richard Bache

ALS: American Philosophical Society

Dear & Hond: Sir Philadelphia Octr. 26th, 1782

The other day Sally and myself had the pleasure of writing you per packet—[8] I have only to add that we continue in good Health, and in the enjoyment of many Blessings—you have our best Love & Affections, & constant Wishes & Prayers for your health & Happiness— I am ever Dear Sir Your dutiful & Affectionate Son RICH: BACHE

You will receive herewith some more News papers.

---

7. His letter of Oct. 23.

8. Their most recent extant letters are dated Oct. 1, above, and probably went by the packet *General Washington,* which sailed on Oct. 8: *Morris Papers,* VI, 518n.

Addressed: His Excellency / Dr. Benjamin Franklin / Passy.

From John Davies and David Gavin

ALS:[9] University of Pennsylvania Library

Sir   Chateau Dua [Du Hâ][1] Bourdeaux 26th. Octr. 1782

It is with much concern that we find ourselves reduced to the necessity of beging leave to lay before your Excellency the real state of our situation; which is that of being private Citizens and subjects of Great Britain, taken prisoners at Sea on Board the Snow Industery[2] John Brown master, on our passage from the Island of Antigua to Britain, by the private ship of War Flora, Henry Johnson Esqr. Commander, belonging to Boston, who brought us into France and Lodged us in this Prison on the 3d August last, where we still are without any prospect of releasement, as no Agent appears to be vested with Authority at this place, either from their Honours the Congress, or your Excellency for taking cognisance of prisoners here belonging to the United States of America.

We therefore most humbly beg leave that your Excellency will be pleased to take our case (as private passengers) into your consideration, and either be pleased to grant us such indulgincies as are allowed to passengers taken by other Powers now at War, or else signify to us in what manner we are to be considered.

If we are to remain prisoners in France untill we are regularly Exchanged, a knowledge of the time when that will take place would even afford us some small consolation.

But we are in hopes from what has lately been reported concerning the state of the American War, that your Excellency may

---

9. In the hand of John Davies.

1. Its military commander is listed in the *Etat militaire* for 1782, p. 44. A departmental prison was later constructed on this site: Larousse, under Bordeaux.

2. The *Industry* was captured on June 28: *Courier de l'Europe,* XII (1782), 151.

very unblameably grant us our liberty, on the same terms as other Independent powers now at War with Britain.

We have the Honour to be your Excellencys Most Obedient & Most Humble Servants JOHN DAVIES

DAVID GAVIN

An Orphan Child not four years old whose Father was also a passenger but died in this Prison and left in our Care to be carried home to his relations in Britain } George Lewis March X his mark

Addressed: To / His Excellency / Dr. Franklin / American Ambassador / at / Paris

Notation: Gavin 26. Oct. 1782.

From Henry Johnson   ALS: Historical Society of Pennsylvania

May it please your Excellency.   Bordeaux Octor: 26th: 1782.

Sometime since by request of Capt: William Gray late of the Amazon, a prisoner of mine,[3] I wrote Mr: Barclay to Know whether Capt: Gray could have his parole to go to England. Mr: Barclay Returned me for answer that it lay with your Excellency, but he did not doubt that it would be effected by writing to you.

If your Excellency would be Kind as to permit it, it will lay me under great Obligations, as Capt: Gray has some bussiness of Consequence to settle in England, and keeping him here, will be a very great loss to him. I am with the greatest Respect Your Excellencys Most Obedient & Most Humle: Servant

HENRY JOHNSON

Addressed: Son Excellence / Son Excellence Benja: Franklin Esqr / Ministre Plenipotentiare / à Son Hotel / Passy

Endorsed: H. Johnson Octr. 26. 1782

3. See William Grey's own letter of Sept. 28, above.

From James Jay   ALS: Historical Society of Pennsylvania

Sir   Hague Octobr. 27. 1782.
    The restriction I was subjected to by my parole,—not go to
France—, determined me not even to write to any person in that
kingdom, till I should be exchanged. The officiousness however
of some persons in London, in converting me into a Messenger
of peace from Congress, inclined me, for very obvious reasons,
to break through the restraint I had imposed upon myself, and
to give you an account of my captivity: but on a little reflection,
I could not but think that such a step would be a work of
supererogation.[4]
    Agreeably to the determination I have just mentioned, I
thought of transacting the business of my exchange with Mr.
Adams. As that Gentleman is now also in France, and I of course
stand in the same situation with regard to you both, I take the liberty to write to you on the subject: flattering myself that both of
you will do every thing in your power to expedite my exchange.
Mr. Townshend, the Secretary of State, consents to accept of a
Lieutt. Colo. for me; and that either Colo. Tarlton or Colo. Dundas, both of whom were taken at York Town, may be the man.[5]
I beg Your Excellency will take the matter into your consideration, and favour me with your determination upon it as soon as
possible. I remain, with great respect, Your Excellys Most Obt.
& humble Servt: JAMES JAY.

P.S. please to direct for me to the care of Monsr: Dumas.—

His Excelly. Benjn: Franklin Esqr.

Notation: James Jay Hague; Octr. 27. 1782.

    4. In fact, Jay had arranged for his own capture and had put himself for-
ward as a peacemaker. Having aroused Shelburne's suspicions, he abandoned this project and left England: Morris, *Jay: Peace,* pp. 251–2.
    5. Banastre Tarleton had been defeated at the Battle of Cowpens: XXXIV,
302n. Thomas Dundas (1750–1794) later became a general: *DNB.*

From Robert Morris

LS:[6] Historical Society of Pennsylvania, Yale University Library, American Philosophical Society; copy: Library of Congress

Sir   Office of Finance 27th October 1782.

I do myself the Honor to enclose the Copy of a Paper transmitted to me by the Governor of Virginia.[7] The Cloathing there mentioned is a Part of those Supplies for the State of Virginia which the Court of France have charged to the United States. You will recollect the Discussions on this Subject.[8] It is with a sincere Desire to remove every disagreeable Trace of them that I have agreed to a Proposition made me by the Governor of Virginia in his Letter dated in Council Chamber the twenty third of September last[9] of which the following is an Extract—

"The Regulations you have entered into for Cloathing the continental Army will render useless to the State a quantity of Necessaries now in France furnished by his most christian Majesty, as the Terms we have them on (which I have before transmitted to you) are such as will make the Payment easy to the United States we shall be obliged to you to take them off our Hands, and take the Debt so far as they go on the States. You have a Copy of the Invoice inclosed by which you will see that they will be useful and necessary for the Army which will I hope induce you to oblige the State." The Enclosure referred to is that above mentioned—

I make no Doubt that the Court will chuse to consider the

6. One of the LS was probably carried by the *Nonsuch: Morris Papers,* VI, 668n.

7. The enclosure was an extract from the invoice of supplies needed for the defense of Virginia, which had been delivered to La Luzerne on Feb. 17, 1781. The extract enclosed with the LS at the APS lists the date as Feb. 11, 1781, while the one published in *Morris Papers,* VI, 534, gives the date as Feb. 17, 1782.

8. Morris had corresponded with BF about this matter the previous November, when he protested France's plan to debit the United States for debts incurred by the individual states: XXXVI, 154, 673.

9. Gov. Benjamin Harrison's letter is in *Morris Papers,* VI, 420–1. Morris agreed to the proposal in his reply to Harrison of Oct. 23. On the same date as the present letter Morris instructed Thomas Barclay to send over the goods on account of the United States: *Morris Papers,* VI, 650–1, 667.

whole of these Supplies as advanced on the Credit of the United States, and therefore there is so much the less Objection to taking a Part of the Goods. As for the Remainder I think it better for Congress to adjust the Matter with Virginia than to plague the Kings Ministers with Altercations about it.—

I am Sir Your most obedient & humble Servant

ROBT MORRIS

His Excellency Benjamin Franklin Esquire.

1st.

Endorsed: Office of Finance Oct. 27. 1782 Proposition from Virginia, to take Cloathing

From Ezekiel Edwards[1]   ALS: Historical Society of Pennsylvania

Sir,   Paris Octr. 28th. 1782.

Sometime to morrow Morning I expect to set off for Nantes, and will have the pleasure to wait on your Excellency for any dispatches you may wish to Have forwarded— There is a Schooner at that place ready for Sea with the first wind, bound to Virginia—

I am most respectfully Your Excellency's Obedt. Hhble. Servt.   EZEKIEL EDWARDS

Hotel d'York

His Excellency B. Franklin Esqr.

1. A Philadelphia merchant who was a director of the Library Company, 1775–78: Herbert C. Bell, "The West India Trade Before the American Revolution," *American Historical Review*, XXII (1916–17), 284n; George M. Abbot, *A Short History of the Library Company of Philadelphia* . . . (Philadelphia, 1913), p. 27.

From David Hartley[2]

ALS: Library of Congress

My Dear friend   London Oct 29 1782

I am very sorry to hear of your illness, but I hope that one of your Complaints the Gout will after you have paid off the Score give you a renewed lease of health and strength. As to the *Gravel* I presume you know very well that the Sope boiler's ley (wch must be nearly the same in all Countries) is a specific. It is so likewise for the *Stone* but that is a very difficult distemper to deal with.[3] But for the Gravel the relief is speedy, and after that a few drops taken every day in milk is a certain preventive.

I thank you for your answer respecting the fire plates &c. I have transmitted it to Count Sarsfield & the Duc de Vauguyon. I shall be much obliged to you if you will be so good as to send me the work wch you mention viz *Moyens de preserver les Edifices dincendies &c par M Piroux.*

I cannot agree that the 3d article of the *preliminaries dated May 1782* can be contrary to any treaty because it was proposed to have been made to the Court of *France.* I just say this one word because I wd not lie under the suspicion of suggesting a single idea contrary to good faith. *Multum interest quando* QUO MODO *et a* QUO *quid fiat.*[4] Take this in two senses both respecting the persons *From whom* and *To whom.*— God bless you. Pray let me hear of your health.

Your ever affecte   D H.

Addressed: To Dr Franklin. &c / Passy / near Paris

---

2. In answer to BF's of Sept. 17, above.

3. Just before leaving France BF looked into the use of soapboiler's lye to treat stones: BF to Caleb Whitefoord, May 19, 1785, in W. A. S. Hewins, ed., *The Whitefoord Papers . . .* (Oxford, 1898), p. 197.

4. "It is very important to determine when, in what way, and by whom this is done."

From James Pearce[5]

ALS: American Philosophical Society

Sir   London 29 Oct. 1782

I call'd on Mrs Stevenson and Mrs. Hewson at Kensington this Day— Mrs. Stevenson is in so poor a way that they dont think she will live long. Mrs. Hewson informed me that you had been so kind as to enquire after me in the last letter that she received from you—[6] I am very sorry to send you the melancholy news of my Dear Wife's Death. She died 22 Oct 1781 and has Left me four Dear Children—[7] I have tried every thing in my power to maintain them in as comfortable a maner as I could—but am now at a very great loss what to do for them, being out of all kind of imployment, through a great many misfortuines. Govener Pownel[8] who is my good friend, and Mrs. Hewson have advise'd me to write to you, they thinking, that it might be in your power to be of great service to me and my Dear Children and that you might point out to me some plan for my advantage—if you can, and will be so kind as to think of me, I should esteem it a very great favour, if their is nothing that would be of any service to me in France under your care—prehaps you can point out something for me in America— I should be very ready and willing to imbrace either, I hope your goodness of heart will think of me, as my present maner of living is very retched, if it should be agreable that I should come to France should be glad if you would recomend to me how I am to get to you from I am Sir your most obedient Humble Servant   JAS. PEARCE

Mr. Jas. Pearce at Mrs. Robt. Pearce's No 83 Lower East Smithfield London

I should be glad of an answer as soon as posible if convinent to you

Addressed: To / His Excellancy / Benj. Franklin Esqr / Minester Plenepotentiary / from the States of America / &c &c &c / at Passey France

---

5. The farmer who married Sarah Franklin, BF's first cousin twice removed: XIX, 395n.

6. XXXVII, 625.

7. BF had already learned of her death; see XXXVII, 625, 675.

8. Thomas Pownall.

From John Barry

ALS: Historical Society of Pennsylvania; copy: Library of Congress

Sir,   L Orient Octo. 31. 1782

Having nothing to Communicate to your Excellency of any consequence but my Arrival here,[9] and that Mr. Barclay promised me he would anounce— I therefore thought it would be only Troubling your Excellency to write, as I was at that time in Expectation of being to Sea before an Answer Could Come from Paris— some Necessaries being wanting to the Ship has detained her Longer than I expected— Lieut. Barney of the Continental Ship General Washington being just arrived here & who Informs me he is Immediately under your Excellencys Particular Orders, as She was built on purpose for a Cruizer, and of Course will Carry but Little Goods, she will be of Little or no service on that head— If you mean her to go on a Cruize, I think you would render Great service to the United States to order her out with the Alliance.[1]

I have the Honor to be Sir, Your Excellencys Most Obedt. Humble Servt.   JOHN BARRY

His Excellency Benja. Franklin Esqr.

Addressed: His Excellency / Benja. Franklin Esqr. / Passey / pre / Paris

Endorsed: J. Barry L'Orient 31. 1782.

9. The *Alliance,* Barry's frigate, arrived from New London on Oct. 17. For her cruise, which began on Aug. 4, see *Morris Papers,* VI, 625–6; William Bell Clark, *Gallant John Barry, 1745–1803: the Story of a Naval Hero of Two Wars* (New York, 1938), pp. 270–7.

1. The copy here adds, "who will sail in about Ten Days." Barry became ill and did not sail until Dec. 9, arriving in Martinique on Jan. 8: Clark, *Barry,* pp. 278–89. This is his last extant letter to BF.

From Maxwell Garthshore[2]

ALS: Historical Society of Pennsylvania

Hotel de Modene Rue Jacob.—
Sir   Thursday's night 31 October *1782*.
Having formerly the honour to be a little known to you, I presume to address you in the Cause of Humanity.—

The eldest Son & Heir of the late Mr. Pollhill Member for Southwark, who had the honour to be known to you, is with His Lady now in this Hotel, on His way to Nice, for the recovery of His Health, which the Climate of Paris seems very unfavourable to.—[3] He is taught to beleive the obtaining a Passport for leaving France is absoly. necessary, & that there is some difficulty in getting one. On this account He & I proposed Ourselves the Honour of waiting on, & requesting your kind Asistance tomorrow, but hearing your Health was not good, & Mr. Pollhill being very unfitt to take any unnecessary fatigue, we thought it more respectfull first to address you in this way, to know if we might take the liberty to call on you at Passy, and if you can asist us in this matter, which is of consequence to Mr. Pollhill's Health to get expeded speedily.— Our Friends Sr. John & the Chevalier Lambert,[4] have kindly promised their Endeavours but say they have found it difficult, we can hardly beleive it would be so to you—

I have the honour to remain Sir Yr. most respectfull & Obedt. Humble Servant   MAXWELL GARTHSHORE
                          of St. Martin's Lane London—

2. A prominent London physician and fellow of the Royal Society (*DNB*).

3. Nathaniel Polhill, the son of tobacco merchant Nathaniel Polhill, M.P., who died on Aug. 29, 1782. The younger Polhill did reach the south of France, but he died before the year was out: Namier and Brooke, *House of Commons*, III, 306; *Gent. Mag.*, LII (1782), 206, 407, 598.

4. Sir John Lambert (XIX, 189n; XXX, 556n) and the chevalier Jean-François Lambert were both Paris bankers and possibly related: Lüthy, *Banque protestante*, II, 319–20.

Our Company consists of
Nathaniel Pollhill Esqr.
Mrs. Pollhill[5]
Miss Montague
Maxwell Garthshore
One Female Domestic
One Valet de Chambre
One Avant Courier my Servt.

P.S. As this Morng. turns out frosty & cold, I doubt much if Mr.
Pollhill dare venture abroad.

Notation: Garthshore 31. Octr. 1782

From John Adams AL (draft): Massachusetts Historical Society

John Adams arrived in Paris on the evening of Saturday, October 26,
after a ten-day journey from The Hague. The first person he sought
out the following morning was Matthew Ridley. Ridley gave him general information on the state of the negotiations, and filled him in on
Franklin's health: the Doctor was still weak and had ceased his custom
of hosting Sunday dinners at Passy, but was beginning to be able to sit
at table. The one piece of news that infuriated Adams was the discovery that William Temple Franklin had been appointed secretary of the
commission. He confided in his diary that he thought Jay "honest" and
Temple "malicious." "F[ranklin]'s cunning," he continued, "will be to
divide Us. To this End he will provoke, he will insinuate, he will in-
trigue, he will maneuvre. My Curiosity will at least be employed, in
observing his Invention and his Artifice."[6]

On Monday, October 28, Adams had a three-hour conference with
Jay, during which he "spoke freely what he thought of Dr. Franklin."[7]
On the evening of the following day he finally called on Franklin at
Passy.[8] According to his diary, he told Franklin "without Reserve my

5. Ursula Maitland Polhill, daughter of Ebenezer Maitland: John G. Nich-
ols, ed., *The Topographer and Genealogist* (3 vols., London, 1846–58), I, 192.
6. Butterfield, *John Adams Diary*, III, 37–9.
7. Morris, *Jay: Peace*, p. 450.
8. Matthew Ridley claimed to have persuaded JA to make the trip. JA was
evidently full of excuses. He said that "after the usage he had received from

Opinion of the Policy of this Court, and of the Principles, Wisdom and Firmness with which Mr. Jay had conducted the Negotiation in his Sickness and my Absence, and that I was determined to support Mr. Jay to the Utmost of my Power in the pursuit of the same System." Franklin, he continued, "heard me patiently but said nothing."[9]

Adams' diary entry quoted above was written at the end of November, after the final articles were approved. While thus admitting to his initial distrust of Franklin, he went on to praise his colleague's conduct during the negotiations themselves. The entry continues:

> The first Conference We had afterwards with Mr. Oswald, in considering one Point and another, Dr. Franklin turned to Mr. Jay and said, I am of your Opinion and will go on with these Gentlemen in the Business without consulting this Court. He has accordingly met Us in most of our Conferences and has gone on with Us, in entire Harmony and Unanimity, throughout, and has been able and usefull, both by his Sagacity and his Reputation in the Whole Negotiation.

One of the times Franklin was useful to Adams was when, in the early stages of the negotiations, Adams sought firsthand information about the fisheries and suggested consulting Jonathan Williams, Jr. Franklin promised to ask Williams, who at that moment was on his way to Paris. Williams called on Adams and recommended that they consult his new business partner Maj. Samuel White, a "master of the subject," whom he had left in charge of his affairs in Nantes. On November 8 White sent Williams (care of Franklin) a three-page letter describing in detail the New England fishing trade off Newfoundland, Cape Sable, and the Magdalen Islands. The American commissioners used this account in their discussions with the British.[1]

[BF] he could not bear to go near him"; he also said that BF should make the first move and call on him in Paris. (Ridley explained that "the last comer always paid the first visit.") JA reluctantly agreed to go to Passy, but only because "I [Ridley] would have it so": Klingelhofer, "Matthew Ridley's Diary," p. 123; also quoted in Butterfield, *John Adams Diary*, III, 40.

9. Butterfield, *John Adams Diary*, III, 82.

1. Butterfield, *John Adams Diary*, III, 83; JW to WTF, Dec. 5, 1782 (APS). According to White's account, Marblehead exported to Spain 100,000 quintals of dried fish per year, at £12 per quintal; this, he wrote, "made all our Remittances to England for all New England." An equal amount of fish was traded in the West Indies for rum, sugar, cotton, molasses, cocoa, coffee, and

Sir   Paris November 1. 1782
    In answer to the Letter, your Excellency did me, the Honour
to write me on the 15 of October, a Copy of which you delivered me Yesterday at Mr Oswalds[2] the original not being received, I have only to Say that there is Money enough in the
Hands of Messieurs Wilhem and Jan Willink, Nicholas and Jacob Van Staphorst and De la Lande and Fynji, of Amsterdam,[3]
to discharge the Interest of the Ten Million of Guilders borrowed in Holland by the King of France under the Warranty of
the States General, if it is expected and insisted that Congress
should pay it.
    But the Question is, who shall order it to be paid.— I dont
think myself authorized, by any Powers I have to dispose of that
Money. Congress have only impowerd me to borrow the Money,
and deposit it in the Hands of Bankers, to be drawn out by Congress. And I have advised and requested, that assembly, to draw
the whole, without leaving me the Power to dispose of any Part
of it, beyond my own Salary, a little assistance to our distressed
Countrymen, escaped from British Prisons, and a few trifling
Charges that necessarily arise.[4]
    There is also another Difficulty in the Way at present.— By

---

indigo. Boston's 43 distilleries also made rum from the molasses, and the city
made tremendous profits by exporting it. Hist. Soc. of Pa.
    For White (b. 1744) see Philip Chadwick Foster Smith, ed., *The Journals
of Ashley Bowen (1728–1813) of Marblehead* (2 vols., Salem, 1973), II, 684;
Perley Derby, comp., *The Descendants of Thomas White, of Marblehead and
Mark Haskell, of Beverly, Massachusetts* . . . (Boston, 1872), p. 21. White arrived in Nantes around Aug. 11 with a letter of introduction to JW from
Jonathan Williams, Sr. (June 17, 1782, Hist. Soc. of Pa.).
    2. The commissioners met daily and dined together during these negoti-
ations. On Oct. 30 they were at Jay's; on Oct. 31, at Oswald's: Butterfield,
John Adams Diary, III, 40.
    3. The bankers with whom JA had contracted: JA to Livingston, July 5
(Wharton, *Diplomatic Correspondence*, V, 594–5). For De la Lande & Fynje
see XXV, 700–1n. The new Dutch loan was for 5,000,000 f., but, as JA told
Morris on Nov. 6, less than 2,000,000 had been received to date: *Morris Papers*, VII, 21. Note that "florins" and "guilders" are interchangeable terms,
about 44 f. being worth 100 l.t. (XXXVI, 190n).
    4. JA recommended to Livingston on July 5 that Congress ascertain the
amount available before drawing on him: Wharton, *Diplomatic Correspondence*, V, 594.

the Contract, the Money is not to be paid, untill a Ratification arrives from Congress. A Quintuplicate of the Contract went by Captain Grinnell who is arrived at Boston[5] so that We may expect a Ratification and too probably Draughts for the whole Money by the first ship.[6]

It is therefore impossible for me to engage, absolutely to pay it, untill We hear farther from Congress.[7] But upon the Arrival of the Ratification, if no Contrary orders arrive with it, and your Excellency and Mr Jay advise me to do it, I will direct, if I can, or at least I will desire the Houses who now have the Money to pay it, if insisted on by this Court, which I hope however will be thought better of.

I have the Honour to be

His Excellency B. Franklin Esq.

From Cuming & Macarty   ALS:[8] American Philosophical Society

Sir   L'Orient November 1st. 1782

We are honour'd with your Letter of 26th. October Covering Mr. Hodgsons Letter and Captn. Houstons Bill on us for Ten Guineas.—[9] We shall procure the information Mr. Hodgson desires, for the next post.— We return you Captn. Houstons Bill accepted by us payable at Mr. Vincens Banquer in Paris.— Captns. Cain and Josiah are out of Town but shall deliver your Letter to Captn. Deal.—

5. Barclay also reported Grinnell's arrival: above, Oct. 8.

6. On Sept. 14 Congress ratified JA's contracts with his bankers: *JCC*, XXIII, 579–80. As JA predicted, the money was needed by Congress; see Morris to BF, Sept. 27 and Morris to JA of the same date (*Morris Papers*, VI, 443).

7. JA's refusal left BF in considerable difficulty. On Nov. 6 Grand told JA that after paying the interest on the old 10,000,000 *l.t.* loan BF's account would be in arrears 1,000,000 *l.t.* On the morning of Nov. 7, JA consulted with BF who said "he was preparing a Memorial to the King as Strong as he could pen, but could not foresee what would be his Success": JA to Morris, Nov. 7, in *Morris Papers*, VII, 23. That memorial was BF's letter to Vergennes, Nov. 8, requesting a loan of $4,000,000 (below).

8. Probably in William Macarty's hand.

9. BF's Oct. 26 letter is missing. Hodgson's letter is dated Oct. 14, above.

We are happy to find our distress'd friends so near releaf.—[1]
We are with great respect Your Excellencys Most Obedt. & most
huml. servts.   CUMING & MACARTY

Notation: Cuming & Maccarty 1st. Novr. 1782.

From Jonathan Williams, Jr.

ALS: University of Pennsylvania Library

Dear & hond sir   St Germain Nov. 1. 1782.
    I arrived here last evening, with Mrs Williams, she is not well
enough to be left immediately or I should have paid my Duty to
you in Person. I beg Billy will let me know by a Line how you
are, & I hope in a few days to be able to see you, in the mean time
I remain as ever Your dutifull & affectionate Kinsman
                                                          J WILLIAMS J

Addressed: A monsieur / Monsieur Franklin / ministre plenipotentiare / des Etats unis de l'amerique / en son Hotel A Passy
/ pres Paris.

Notation: J. Williams 1. Nov. 1782.

Philip Mazzei to the American Peace Commissioners

ALS: Historical Society of Pennsylvania

Gentlemen,   Hague, 2. Novr. 1782.
    What I am going to mention to your Excellencies will, I hope,
apologize for the liberty I take of addressing myself to you. In
January 79. I was appointed by the Government of Virginia to
go to Europe to transact there some business of importance for
the State.[2] I was taken prisoner in coming, & did not recover my
liberty 'till Novr. the same year. I arrived at Paris the Spring fol-

---

1. Hodgson had probably notified Cuming & Macarty about the imminent
prisoner exchange; see Hodgson to BF, Oct. 14.
2. To obtain a loan: XXXI, 247–8n.

lowing, & consulted His Excellency Dr. Franklin, to whom I had the honour of having been long personally known, according to the written Instructions I had recd. from the Executive.[3] Not to trouble your Excellencies with a long detail of particulars, which are no ways necessary, I shall only inform you that after a variety of disappointments, proceeding from the miscarriage & neglect of sending papers from Virginia,[4] probably occasioned by the confusions there, & from other causes, such as the non payment of bills drawn in my favour by order of the State, I find myself reduced to the necessity of requesting your assistance to enable me to go to my family in France, & from thence with them to America.[5] In consequence of the disappointments I met with, I disposed of a little estate in Tuscany to defray the expences I was necessarily obliged to incur. This supply has long been expended. A stranger as I am in this Country, & trusting to meet with Mr. Adams, & to receive his assistance & advice, I am at a loss how to raise money on my own credit, or on the property I have in Virginia. The favour therefore which I am to request of your Excellencies is, that you would furnish me, either on the credit of the State, or my own, with a sufficient sum for the purpose above-mentioned, or that you would recommend me to some person who is able & willing to advance me that sum on either of those credits. I am further induced to make & to urge this request, because I am induced to believe, from the last letter I recd. from Government, that it is imagined there, that I have recd. the money which was appointed for me, & of course I can have no expectations from home. Permit me to beg the favour of

3. Upon his arrival in France, BF refused to advance him money: XXXI, 247–9, 285, 414–15.

4. When he was captured en route to Europe, Mazzei destroyed his commission and instructions. The duplicates, sent by Jefferson to France, were not forwarded to Mazzei in Italy for nearly a year, owing largely to BF's neglect: XXXIII, 147; XXXV, 101–2, 330, 345, 369–70; XXXVI, 104.

5. The Va. assembly revoked his powers on Jan. 31, 1782. Mazzei received notification from Gov. Benjamin Harrison by Sept. 6, when he answered that he would leave as soon as possible. He would have been successful, he added, had his papers arrived earlier: Margherita Marchione et al., eds., *Philip Mazzei: Selected Writings and Correspondence* (3 vols., Prato, Italy, 1983), I, 331–2, 367, 378–9.

an answer directed to me *che\(George Henrie Lÿsson dans la grande Cour de l'Empereur á Amsterdam*, & to have the honour of signing myself most respectfully, Gentlemen, your Excellencies most Humble & most Obedient Servant PHILIP MAZZEI

Their Excellencies Dr. Ben: Franklin, John Adams, & John Jay, Ministers Pl. &c.

Notation: Philip Mazzei, 29bre. 1779.

From Francis Dana

Copy:[6] Massachusetts Historical Society

St: Petersbourg Octr. 22d. 1782. OS.

Sir [*i.e.*, November 2, 1782][7]

As it may be proper you shou'd be acquainted with the contents of the enclosed letter to Mr: Morris,[8] I take the liberty to send it to you open, and to request you, after you have read it, to close it and to forward it by the earliest opportunity.

I am, Sir, with much respect and esteem, your most obedient humble Servant

His Excellency Benja: Franklin Esqr: Minister Plenipotentiary &c

Preliminary Articles of Peace: Second Draft Treaty

D[9] and copy: Massachusetts Historical Society; two D and copy: Public Record Office; transcript: National Archives

As new American and British negotiators were converging on Paris, Franklin's isolation in Passy posed certain inconveniences. John

6. A letterbook copy in Dana's hand.
7. We print this letter under its date in the New Style, or Gregorian, calendar rather than the Old Style, or Julian, calendar still used in Russia.
8. Dated a day earlier, it was a covering letter for (and explanation of) Dana's financial account with Congress.
9. In the hand of Caleb Whitefoord with emendations by John Jay. This

Adams arrived on October 26 but, as he initially refused to call on Franklin, the latter was evidently unaware of his arrival until Matthew Ridley mentioned it to him three days later. Surprised at Franklin's ignorance, Ridley returned to Paris from Passy and persuaded Adams to call on his colleague that evening, October 29. Although Ridley believed that Adams did so only because of his insistence, Adams must have recognized that he could no longer delay a conversation.[1] Henry Strachey had just arrived from London, and a new round of negotiations was already under way.

Strachey arrived in Paris on the afternoon of October 28, bearing new instructions for Oswald. The two men spent that evening conferring. The following morning, October 29, Oswald called on Jay and proposed as a western boundary a longitude line east of the Mississippi. Jay flatly refused. Oswald then brought Strachey to meet Jay, and Adams joined them. The British negotiators laid out their government's objections to the first draft treaty, and engaged in general discussions about the points to be included in a revised version.[2] Oswald then took Strachey to Passy, where they had a similar conversation with Franklin. All three American commissioners arranged to meet the following morning at eleven o'clock at Oswald's quarters "to examine Maps & papers." They would then dine together at Jay's.[3] From the morning of October 30 through the evening of November 4 the commissioners met steadily, rotating the location of their meetings and dining at one another's residences.[4]

---

was the American commissioners' retained copy; Oswald's (virtually identical) is at the PRO.

1. Ridley wrote on Oct. 29, "Went in the morning to see Dr. Franklin— did not know of Mr. Adams arrival": Klingelhofer, "Matthew Ridley's Diary," p. 123. Reporting his subsequent conversation with JA, Ridley (who seemed unaware of the diplomatic conversations that had taken place that day) wrote that JA reluctantly agreed to call on BF as a personal favor; see the headnote and annotation to JA's Nov. 1 letter, above.

2. Oswald to Shelburne, Oct. 29, in Giunta, *Emerging Nation*, 1, 629; Jay's diary for Oct. 29, in Morris, *Jay: Peace*, pp. 450–1.

3. Oswald to Shelburne, Oct. 29, in Giunta, *Emerging Nation*, 1, 629. Strachey's impressions of the day's events were mixed. "It is impossible, from the general conversation held with each of these gentlemen, to judge what will be the result; and hitherto I can only venture to say, that it appears as if we shall gain some ground. . . . But I fear it will be several (I hope not many) days before matters come to a conclusion." Strachey to Townshend, Oct. 29, quoted in George William Featherstonhaugh, *Historical Sketch of the Negotiations at Paris in 1782, from Inedited Documents . . .* (London, 1842).

4. They dined at Passy on Nov. 1, at JA's residence at the Hôtel du Roi on

Oswald's new instructions were accompanied by stern rebukes from Shelburne for having been too accommodating in the previous discussions. He was to insist on extending the Nova Scotia boundary as far as possible, preferably to include the province of Maine; to assert Britain's right to "the Back Country," receding from that position only if the United States made "a just provision for the Refugees"; to argue against the Americans' right to dry fish on Newfoundland; to omit all of the fourth article of the first draft treaty except for the freedom of navigation, referring the rest to a treaty of commerce; and to strongly urge "the Discharge of Debts due to British Merchants before the War."[5] Although Oswald was told that Strachey's role was to help him negotiate boundaries, Strachey's oral and written instructions actually authorized him to negotiate all the issues that Oswald had been apprised of. He was to press for as much land as possible, in order to bargain for compensation for the Loyalists. He was to argue for all the back lands accorded by the Proclamation of 1763, for the Canadian boundary established by the Quebec Act, and for a boundary of Nova Scotia that included, if possible, the entire province of Maine, or at the "very least" up to Penobscot. If the Americans refused, he could accept the boundaries proposed in the first draft treaty. The Loyalists were "of great importance," he was told, "but the Debts require the Most Serious Attention." Above all, it "must appear authentically" that he had fought for those two constituencies, the Loyalists and the merchants. Beyond that, he was authorized to accept, if necessary, the terms of the first draft treaty except for two items that were "totally inadmissible": the right to dry fish on Newfoundland,

---

Nov. 2, and again in Paris on Nov. 3: Butterfield, *John Adams Diary*, III, 40–4.

5. Minute of the Cabinet, Oct. 17, 1782, Fortescue, *Correspondence of George Third*, VI, 143–4. In his Oct. 21 letter to Oswald, Shelburne expressed amazement at how easily Oswald had capitulated to the Americans, especially on the issues of boundaries and the fishery, and stated that Oswald's way of negotiating was "diametrically opposite to our Interests in the present moment." He stressed the importance of the new negotiating points, and explained that the merchants owed money before 1775 were "some of our most considerable Merchants, who are full of apprehensions, & are making daily applications to Government." On Oct. 23 Shelburne wrote Oswald to introduce Strachey, whom he said would "explain the Boundary's and the authentic Documents, which were only to be found here . . .": Giunta, *Emerging Nation*, I, 620–2, 623. By "authentic Documents" Shelburne may have meant the documentation brought by Mr. Roberts, discussed below.

and the section of the fourth article regarding free trade. He was also instructed to "urge just boundaries of West Florida."[6]

Joining the initial phase of the negotiations was William Roberts, whom Adams later described as "the oldest clerk in the board of trade and plantations." Roberts had been entrusted with huge volumes of the board's manuscript records, intended to support the British claim to the province of Maine. Adams was able to counter these claims with an arsenal of records and documents that he had brought from America, all of which proved that the legislature of Massachusetts Bay had "laid out counties, incorporated towns, granted lands, and regulated every thing from the date of the charter in the Province of Maine." Before Adams finished reading his evidence, he saw the opposition melt. "Although they did not expressly acknowledge their error," he wrote, "the subject subsided and we heard little more concerning it. The clerk, with his records, soon returned to England."[7]

The boundary between Maine and Nova Scotia was finally clarified, at least theoretically, after prolonged discussions over whether Britain could push as far as the Penobscot River. In the previous round of negotiations Jay and Franklin had postulated (without conviction) that Maine extended as far north as the St. John River. When Oswald objected, Franklin recommended that they leave the question to a future commission, a suggestion that Oswald incorporated in a postscript to the first draft treaty. The commissioners' uncertainty was due to both a lack of documentation and the variety of conflicting maps available to them, all of which were inaccurate.[8] One of the maps they rejected in this second round of negotiations, sent from England at Shelburne's request on October 28, was accompanied by a cover letter explaining that it had been made by the "well accredited" geographer Herman Moll and "published at a time when . . . there were no immediate disputes concerning limits."[9] In fact, this wildly inaccurate

6. Giunta, *Emerging Nation*, 1, 619–20; Morris, *Jay: Peace*, pp. 395–6.

7. Charles Francis Adams, *The Works of John Adams* (10 vols., Boston, 1856), 1, 668–9. See also JA to Livingston, Oct. 31, 1782, in Giunta, *Emerging Nation*, 1, 630–1. William Roberts served as a clerk from 1765 to December, 1781, when he became deputy secretary. This position was abolished in May, 1782: J. C. Sainty, comp., *Officials of the Boards of Trade, 1660–1870* (London, 1974), p. 113.

8. The American commissioners had asked Oswald to send for North American maps as early as Aug. 27; see BF to Jay, Sept. 4.

9. Townshend to Oswald, Oct. 28, 1782, PRO, communicated to the editors by Ed Dahl and printed in George William Featherstonhaugh, *Historical Sketch of the Negotiations at Paris in 1782, from Inedited Documents . . .*

map of North America, made *circa* 1715, showed no delineation at all between "New Scotland" and "New England," gave a confused picture of the rivers in question, and, incidentally, still showed California as an island. The arrival of Adams, and the decision to be guided exclusively by the 1755 Mitchell map,[1] helped the Americans solidify their stance.

The Mitchell map showed Nova Scotia bounded by a river west of the St. John, labeled the "St. Croix." This name conformed to the documentation Adams had brought with him.[2] Even though none of the commissioners was sure which river was meant by "St. Croix," they wrote the name into the second draft treaty.

Adams also took the lead on another issue that had been problematic in the first treaty negotiations. This time he did not clarify an uncertainty but suggested a concession that Jay and Franklin had not yielded. He expressed his views to Oswald and Strachey during their first meeting on the morning of October 29, even before he had met with Franklin. His idea, which greatly pleased the British, was that compensation for the Loyalists and America's repayment of debts incurred before the war were two separate issues and had to be considered independent of each other. He discussed this with Franklin on the evening of October 29, and Franklin explained his and Jay's position: that neither they nor the Congress had the authority to make such decisions. According to Adams' account, he persuaded his colleagues to agree that Congress should recommend to the States "to open their Courts of Justice for the Recovery of all just Debts." Jay drafted the article, and the commissioners and Strachey agreed to it on November 3.[3]

Franklin was not present on November 4, when Adams, Jay, Oswald, and Strachey finalized the article about the fisheries and completed a version of the second draft treaty. They worked from 11 A.M. to 11 P.M., breaking for dinner at 3 P.M. with a group of Frenchmen and Americans including Temple Franklin. Adams and Jay finally con-

---

(London, 1842), pp. 20–1. For a discussion of the maps used in the negotiations see Morris, *Jay: Peace*, pp. 382–4.

1. See the American Peace Commissioners to Livingston, Dec. 14, below. For the Mitchell map see IV, 319n.

2. JA explained to Vergennes that the grant of Nova Scotia issued by James I to Sir William Alexander "bounded it on the River St. Croix." He had copies of this grant in Latin, French, and English: Butterfield, *John Adams Diary*, III, 48; JA to Livingston, Nov. 11, 1782, in Giunta, *Emerging Nation*, I, 656.

3. Butterfield, *John Adams Diary*, III, 43–4.

ceded the right to dry fish on Newfoundland, but obtained drying rights on a group of uninhabited islands and unsettled bays of Nova Scotia. According to Oswald, Franklin had pushed for specifying that fishing rights would extend to the Gulf of St. Lawrence, pointing out that the Americans would spend their profits from the fishery in buying British manufactures. He also, undoubtedly after realizing that drying rights on Newfoundland would never be granted, allowed that it might not be proper "to have a mixture of their people with ours for Drying on Newfoundland," but "Supposed there would be no Inconveniency in throwing onshore their Fish for a few days on an Unsettled Beach, Bay or Harbor, on the Coast of Nova Scotia." Moreover, he said, drying rights would be exercised only occasionally, and even then the fish would be only partially dried and salted, leaving the women and children to complete the curing when the fishermen returned.[4] The Americans also retained the right to fish wherever they had previously done so. Adams drafted the fisheries article.[5]

Having failed to secure compensation for the Loyalists, Oswald and Strachey both wrote letters to the American commissioners insisting on how strenuously they had argued the point. These letters, both drafted by Strachey, are below, November 4 and 5. Strachey told Townshend that they had been written "in the view of having an authentic Proof that every Effort had been used, agreeably to my Instructions from Lord Shelburne, upon a Point wherein the national Honor is so deeply concerned."[6]

Strachey left Paris on November 5, carrying the new draft treaty and a copy of the Mitchell map, on which the American commissioners had drawn two different proposed boundary lines, either one of which they would accept. The boundary described in the text of the draft treaty was the commissioners' second proposal; according to Strachey, it was copied into the draft because it was shorter. The first proposal, which was sent to Townshend on a separate sheet,[7] was the option selected by the British, and it appears *verbatim* in the final draft treaty.

Two days after Strachey's departure, Jay reviewed the draft treaties

4. Oswald's Observations on the Article of the Fishery, in Morris, *Jay: Peace,* p. 416.

5. Butterfield, *John Adams Diary,* III, 45–6.

6. Strachey to Townshend, Nov. 8, in Morris, *Jay: Peace,* pp. 400, 414.

7. *Ibid.,* pp. 413, 415–16. Strachey wrote to Evan Nepean that this copy of the first proposal was the only one: Strachey to Nepean, Nov. 9, 1782, PRO, communicated by Ed Dahl.

with Oswald and entered several changes on both their versions. These changes are noted below, and Oswald sent an account of them to Strachey. Hoping that this draft would be approved and a fair copy sent back for signatures, Oswald advised Strachey that based on Jay's "precision," he "would advise that there should not be the least Alteration, not a single Word, different from the Drafts."[8]

When the process was finished, each set of negotiators expressed surprise at the intransigence of the other. Oswald "did not expect to find Mr. Jay so uncommonly Stiff and particular about these matters." Strachey commented that "these Americans are the greatest Quibblers I ever knew." Adams characterized Strachey as "artfull and insinuating. . . .He pushes and presses every Point as far as it can possibly go." He was more positive about Oswald, "a wise & good man" who, "if untrammeled, would soon settle all."[9]

As this round of negotiations progressed, the Americans' sense of inevitable triumph was expressed by a fable Franklin told of the Eagle and the Cat. The day before the present draft was settled, Adams inscribed the fable in his diary thus:

An Eagle scaling over a Farmers Yard espied a Creature, that he thought an Hair [a hare]. He pounced upon him and took him up. In the Air the Cat seized him by the Neck with her Teeth and round the Body with her fore and hind Claws. The Eagle finding Herself scratched and pressed, bids the Cat let go and fall down. No says the Cat: I won't let go and fall, you shall stoop and set me down.

This fable delighted the French. Jean-Louis Aubert, signing himself "L. A.," gave Franklin a French verse translation. He added a final couplet containing something akin to a moral: the British Eagle never touched the American Cat again in her life.[1]

---

8. Morris, *Jay: Peace*, p. 418.

9. Oswald to Strachey, Nov. 8, 1782, in Morris, *Jay: Peace*, p. 418; Strachey to Townshend, Nov. 8, in Giunta, *Emerging Nation*, 1, 654; Butterfield, *John Adams Diary*, III, 46; JA to Livingston, Nov. 6, in Giunta, *Emerging Nation*, 1, 639–40.

1. Butterfield, *John Adams Diary*, III, 45; "L'Aigle et le Chat, fable allégorique de M. Franklin, mise en vers par M. L. A**." "L. A." also translated into French verse BF's fable of "Le Lionceau et la Dogue," and gave BF an original verse fable, "Le Chardonneret et l'Aigle." All three MSS are undated and at the APS. The Eagle and the Cat, and the Lion and the Dog, which appeared in *The Public Advertiser* in 1770, are above, XVII, 3.

[November 4–7, 1782][2]
Articles agreed upon by and between Richard Oswald Esquire the Commissioner of His Britannic Majesty, for treating of Peace with the Commissioners of the United States of America, on behalf of His said Majesty, on the one part. And Benjamin Franklin, John Jay and John Adams, three of the Commissioners of the said States for treating of Peace with the Commissioner of His said Majesty, on their behalf, on the other part. To be inserted in, and to constitute the Treaty of Peace, proposed to be concluded between the Crown of Great Britain and the Said United States: But which Treaty is not to be concluded untill His Britannic Majesty shall have agreed to the terms of a Peace between France and Britain, proposed or accepted of by His most Christian Majesty, and Shall be ready to conclude with him, Such Treaty accordingly; it being the duty and Intention of the United States not to desert their Ally, but faithfully, and in all things, to abide by and fulfill their Engagements with His most Christian Majesty.

Whereas reciprocal advantages and mutual Convenience are found by experience to form the only permanent foundation of Peace and Friendship between States, It is agreed to form the Articles of the proposed Treaty on Such principles of liberal equality and reciprocity as that partial advantages, (those Seeds of discord) being excluded, Such a beneficial and Satisfactory Intercourse between the two Countries may be established as to promise and Secure to both, perpetual Peace and Harmony.

His Britannic Majesty acknowledges the Said United States Viz New Hampshire, Masachusetts Bay, Rhode Island and Providence plantations, Connecticut, New York, New Jersey, Pensylvania, Delaware, Maryland, Virginia, North Carolina, South Carolina and Georgia, to be free, Sovereign and Independent States. That He treats with them as Such; and for himself, his Heirs and Successors relinquishes all Claims to the Government Propriety and Territorial Rights of the Same, and every part thereof and that all disputes which might arise in future on the

2. The text was largely finalized on the night of Nov. 4, but Jay, in Oswald's presence, entered several changes (noted below) on Nov. 7: Oswald to Strachey, Nov. 8 (Morris, *Jay: Peace*, pp. 417–18).

Subject of the Boundaries of the Said United States may be prevented, It is hereby agreed and declared that the following are and Shall remain to be their Boundaries. Viz.

From the Northwest Angle of Nova Scotia being that Angle which is formed by a Line drawn due North from the Source of St. Croix River[3] to the High-Lands which divide the Rivers which empty themselves into the River St Laurence from those which fall into the Atlantic Ocean, and along the said High Lands, to the Northwestern head of Connecticut River, thence down along the midle of that River to the Forty fifth Degree of North Latitude,[4] following the said Latitude untill it strikes the River Missisippi. Thence by a Line to be drawn along the midle of said River Missisippi untill it shall intersect the Northern most part of the Thirty first Degree of Latitude North of the Equator. South, by a Line to be drawn due East from the termination of the Line last mentioned in the Latitude of Thirty one Degrees, to the midle of the River Apalachicola or Catahouchi [Chattahoochee], thence along the midle thereof to its junction

3. This was a source of future contention because it was unclear whether the "St. Croix River" meant the Magaguadivic River or the Schoodiac River, which both emptied into Passamaquoddy Bay but whose sources lay a considerable distance apart: Richard B. Morris, *The Peacemakers: the Great Powers and American Independence* (New York, Evanston, and London, 1965), pp. 363–4; Francis M. Carroll, *A Good and Wise Measure: the Search for the Canadian-American Boundary, 1783–1842* (Toronto, 2001), pp. 3–6, 15–19. Strachey admitted that this article was contrary to his instructions and complained that the commissioners refused not only to compromise but even to accept the appointment of commissaries to settle where the St. Croix really was: Strachey to Townshend, Nov. 8 (Morris, *Jay: Peace*, p. 413).

4. This is the point at which the two alternative boundaries diverged. The American commissioners gave the British government the option of choosing instead the Great Lakes and connecting rivers as a border between the United States and Canada. Strachey forwarded the proposed alternative boundary to Townshend on Nov. 8; see our note above. The British accepted this alternative proposal, thereby retaining what today is southern Ontario rather than the northern portions of present-day Michigan, Wisconsin, and Minnesota. It remains unclear why the commissioners retreated from BF's earlier insistence on America's obtaining this portion of Canada, a point already conceded by Shelburne (XXXVII, 600, 686). For a full discussion see Bradford Perkins, "The Peace of Paris: Patterns and Legacies," in Hoffman and Albert, eds., *Peace and the Peacemakers*, pp. 207–14.

271

with the Flint River, thence Strait to the head of St Marys River, and thence down along the midle of St Marys River to the Atlantic Ocean. East by a Line from the Mouth of said St Marys River to the Mouth of the River St Croix in the Bay of Fundy, and by a Line drawn through the midle of Said River to its Source, and from its Source directly North to the aforesaid High Lands which divide the Rivers which fall into the Atlantic Ocean from those which empty themselves into the River St Laurence, Comprehending all Islands within twenty Leagues of any part of the shores of the United States, and lying between Lines to be drawn due East, from the points where the aforesaid Boundaries of St Croix River and St Marys River shall respectively touch the Bay of Fundy and the Atlantic Ocean.[5]

It is agreed that all such Loyalists or Refugees as well as all such British Merchants or other Subjects as may be resident in any of the United States at the time of the Evacuation thereof by the Arms and Garrisons of His Britannic Majesty shall be allowed Six Months thereafter to remove to any part of the World And also at their election to dispose of, within the Said Term, or to carry with them, their Goods and Effects. And it is understood that the Said States shall extend Such farther favour to the Said Merchants and Such Amnesty and Clemency to the Said Refu-

5. Here Jay deleted, "Excepting always Such Islands as are now or heretofore have belonged to the Colony of Nova Scotia or have been within the Limits thereof." Oswald thought the deletion to be pointless: Oswald to Stachey, Nov. 8 (Morris, *Jay: Peace,* p. 418). Jay also deleted the following paragraph which would have moved the border of western Florida north from its present location to its location in the 1763 Treaty of Paris, whatever the disposition of Florida in the final British treaty with Spain (which had captured the area during the present war): "Upon a further Consideration of the just Limits and Boundaries of the Province of West Florida, it is agreed that its Northern Boundary shall extend from the Said Thirty first Degree of Latitude to a Line to be drawn due East from the place where the River Yasous [Yazoo] falls into the River Mississippi and along the Said Line due East to the River Apalachicola." Jay did not, however, delete the heretofore redundant separate article at the end of the treaty, which would move the border to the north should the British be in possession or be put in possession of the area. Jay even adjusted the language of that article: Morris, *Jay: Peace,* pp. 417–18.

gees as their respective Circumstances and the Dictates of Justice and humanity may render just and reasonable; and particularly that Amnesty & Indemnity be granted to all such of the said Refugees as may be unaffected by Acts Judgements or Prosecutions actually pass'd or commenced a month previous to such Evacuation.

That the Subjects of his Britannic Majesty and the People of the said United States shall continue to enjoy unmolested, the Right to take Fish of every kind on all the Banks of Newfoundland; also in the Gulph of St. Laurence and all other places where the Inhabitants of both Countries used at any time heretofore to fish; And also to dry and cure their Fish on the Shores of the Isle of Sables, Cape Sables, and the Shores of any of the unsettled Bays, Harbours or Creeks of Nova Scotia, and of the Magdalene Islands. And his Britannic Majesty, and the said United States will extend equal Priviledges & Hospitality to each others fishermen as to their own.

Whereas certain of the United States excited thereto by the unnecessary Destruction of private Property have confiscated all Debts due from their Citizens to British Subjects; and also in certain Instances Lands belonging to the latter.

And whereas it is just that private Contracts made between Individuals of the two Countries before the War, should be faithfully executed, and as the Confiscation of the said Lands may have a Latitude not justifiable by the Law of Nations— It is agreed that British Creditors shall notwithstanding meet with no lawfull Impediment to recovering the full Value, or Sterling amount of such bona fide Debts as were contracted before the year 1775. And also that Congress will recommend to the said States so to correct (if necessary,) their said Acts respecting the Confiscation of Lands in America belonging to real British Subjects, as to render the said Acts consistent with perfect Justice & Equity.[6] As to the Cession made of certain Lands in Georgia, by a number of Indians there, on the first June 1773, for the purpose

6. The version carried by Strachey began a new paragraph at this point. Strachey wrote Townshend on Nov. 8 that this section consisted of "Points which have been obstinately fought for": Morris, *Jay: Peace,* p. 414.

of paying the Debts due from them to a number of Traders—
The American Commissioners say, that the State of Georgia is
alone competent to consider & decide on the same: for that it being a matter of internal Police, with which neither Congress nor
their Commissioners are authorised to interfere, it must of necessity be referred to the Discretion & Justice of that State, who
without doubt will be disposed to do, what may be just & reasonable on the Subject.[7]

Similar Reasons & Considerations constrain the Commissioners to give the like answer to the Case of Mr. Penn's Family.[8]

From, and immediately after the Conclusion of the proposed
Treaty, there shall be a firm & perpetual Peace between his
Majesty & the said States; & between the Subjects of the one, &
the Citizens of the other. Wherefore, all Hostilities, both by Sea
& Land shall then immediately cease: All Prisoners on both sides
shall be set at Liberty: And his Britannic Majesty shall forthwith,
and without causing any Destruction, withdraw all his Armies,
Garrisons & Fleets from the said United States, and from every
Port, Place, and Harbour within the same; leaving in all Fortifications the American Artillery that may be therein: And shall
also order and cause all Archives, Records, Deeds and Papers,
belonging to any of the said States, or their Citizens, which in
the Course of the War may have fallen into the hands of his
Officers, to be forthwith restored and deliver'd to the proper
States & persons to whom they belong.

That the Navigation of the River Missisippi from its Source
to the Ocean, shall for ever remain free and open.

7. Strachey believed this paragraph "too indecisive" for the treaty: Strachey to Townshend, Nov. 8 (Morris, *Jay: Peace*, p. 412). At a congress held
at Augusta in June, 1773, the Creeks and Cherokees ceded more than
2,100,000 acres, the so-called New Purchase. Claims of corruption, however, led to litigation which was not resolved until the middle of the following century: John R. Alden, *John Stuart and the Southern Colonial Frontier . . .*
(Ann Arbor and London, 1944), pp. 304–5.

8. See Juliana Penn to BF, Nov. 23.

Separate Article.[9]
It is hereby understood and agreed that in case Great Britain at the Conclusion of the present War shall be[1] or be put in possession of West Florida, the Line of north Boundary, between the said province & the United States, shall be a Line drawn from the mouth of the River Yassous, where it unites with the Mississippi, due East to the River Appalachicola and thence along the middle of that River to its junction with the Flynt River.

Articles of New Treaty

Compared with the Copy carried home by Mr Strachey by him & RO 5th Novr 1782

To Thomas Townshend

ALS: Public Record Office; copies: Library of Congress (three), Public Record Office (three), William L. Clements Library, Massachusetts Historical Society

Sir,   Passy, Nov. 4. 1782
I received the Letter you did me the honour of writing to me by Mr Strachey,[2] and am much pleas'd with the Opportunity it has given me of renewing and encreasing my Acquaintance with a Gentleman of so amiable and deserving a Character.

I know you were ever averse to the Measures that brought on this unhappy War.[3] I have therefore no doubt of the Sincerity of your Wishes for a Return of Peace. Mine are equally earnest. Nothing therefore, except the Beginning of the War, has given

9. This article was the work of Richard Oswald and John Jay: Morris, *Jay: Peace*, p. 368. By implicitly encouraging the British to recapture West Florida from Spain, Jay disregarded the indispensable contribution to American independence made by Spain's diverting a large share of Britain's naval efforts. He also ignored the danger of replacing a weak neighbor to the south of the United States by one that was strong, militarily and economically.

1. Jay changed this word from "recover".

2. Above, Oct. 23.

3. Townshend, like BF, had worked for the repeal of the Stamp Act. In 1774 he called for repealing the Tea Act and by the following year had joined the Opposition: Namier and Brooke, *House of Commons*, III, 554.

me more Concern than to learn at the Conclusion of our Conferences, that it is not likely to be soon ended. Be assured no Endeavours on my part would be wanting to remove any Difficulties that may have arisen; or even if the Peace were made, to
procure afterwards any Changes in the Treaty that might tend to
render it more perfect, and the Peace more durable. But we who
are here at so great a Distance from our Constituents, have not
the Possibility of obtaining in a few Days fresh Instructions, as
is the Case with your Negociators, and are therefore oblig'd to
insist on what is conformable to those we have, and at the same
time appears to us just and reasonable.

   With great Esteem and Respect, I have the honour to be, Sir,
Your most obedient and most humble Servant   B Franklin

Rt. honble. T. Townsend. Esqr.

Richard Oswald to the American Peace Commissioners[4]

ALS and five copies: Public Record Office; LS: Massachusetts Historical
Society; copies: William L. Clements Library (two), Library of Congress, National Archives (two), North Carolina State Division of
Archives and History; press copy of copy: Library of Congress; transcript: National Archives

Gentlemen   Paris 4th Novemr 1782
   You may remember that from the very beginning of our
Negotiation for Settling a Peace between Great Britain and
America, I insisted that you Should positively Stipulate for a
Restoration of the Property of all those Persons, under the de-
nomination of Loyalists or Refugees, who have taken part with
Great Britain in the present War. Or, if the said property had
been resold, and passed into Such variety of hands as to render
the Restoration impracticable (which you asserted to be the case
in many instances) you Should Stipulate for a Compensation or
Indemnification to those Persons, adequate to their losses. & To
these Propositions you Said you could not accede. Mr Strachey,

---

   4. This letter was drafted by Strachey; see the headnote to the Preliminary
Articles of Peace: Second Draft Treaty, [Nov. 4–7].

Richard Oswald

Since his arrival at Paris, has most Strenuously joined me in insisting upon the Said Restitution, Compensation, or Indemnification, and in laying before you every Argument in favour of those Demands, founded upon national Honor, and upon the true principles of Justice.[5]

These Demands you must have understood to extend, not only to all Persons of the abovementiond description, who have fled to Europe, but likeways to all those who may be now in any parts of North America, dwelling under the protection of His Majestys Arms or otherwise.

We have also insisted upon a mutual Stipulation for a general Amnesty on both Sides, comprehending thereby an Enlargement of all Persons, who, on account of Offences committed, or Supposed to be Committed, Since the commencement of Hostilities, may be now in Confinement; and for an immediate repossession of their Properties, and peaceable enjoyment thereof, under the Government of the United States. To this you have not hitherto given a particular or direct Answer.

It is however incumbent upon me, as Commissioner of the King of Great Britain, to repeat those Several Demands;[6] and, without going over those Arguments upon paper, (which we have so often urged in Conversation) to press your immediate attention to these Subjects; and to urge you to enter into proper Stipulations for the Restitution, Compensation and Amnesty beforementioned, before we proceed further in this Negotiation. I have the honour to be Gentlemen Your most obedient Humble Servant   RICHARD OSWALD

To Benjamin Franklin, John Jay and John Adams, Esquires Commissioners from the Thirteen United States of America, for treating of Peace between the Said States and the King of Great Britain

5. JA later wrote, "Dr. F. is very staunch against the Tories, more decided a great deal on this Point than Mr. Jay or my self": Butterfield, *John Adams Diary*, III, 77. See also BF to Livingston, Dec. 5.

6. On May 23, Shelburne had instructed Oswald, "An establishment for the Loyalists must always be upon Mr. Oswald's mind, as it is uppermost in Lord Shelburne's": Fitzmaurice, *Life of Shelburne*, II, 137.

Notations: Letter from Mr Oswald To the American Commissrs— / In Mr. Oswald's 6h & 7h Novr. 1782

Henry Strachey to the American Peace Commissioners

ALS (draft) and three copies:[7] Public Record Office; copies: William L. Clements Library, Library of Congress (two), Massachusetts Historical Society (two)

Gentlemen, Paris Novr. 5th. 1782.

Knowing the Expectation of the King's Ministers, that a full Indemnity shall be provided for the whole Body of Refugees, either by a Restitution of their Property, or by some stipulated Compensation for their Losses, and being confident, as I have repeatedly assured You, that your Refusal upon this Point will be the great Obstacle to a Conclusion and Ratification of that Peace which is meant as a solid, perfect, permanent, Reconciliation and ReUnion between Great Britain and America, I am unwilling to leave Paris, without once more submitting the Matter to Your Consideration. It affects equally, in my Opinion, the Honor and the Humanity of Your Country, and of ours. How far You will be justified in risking every favorite Object of America, by contending against those Principles, is for You to determine. Independence, and a more than reasonable Possession of Territory, seem to be within Your Reach. Will You suffer them to be outweighed by the Gratification of Resentment against Individuals? I venture to assert that such a conduct hath no parallel in the History of civilized Nations.

I am under the necessity of setting out by Two o'Clock today.[8] If the time is too short for your Reconsideration, and final

7. This text, including all Strachey's emendations, is in Morris, *Jay: Peace*, pp. 405–6.

8. Strachey left Paris with the proposed peace articles that afternoon. Traveling 16–18 hours per day on bad roads he reached Calais on Nov. 8. Writing to Townshend from there he predicted on the basis of conversations with JA and Jay that the commissioners would accept restitution or compensation for the refugees if it were made a *sine qua non* (especially if an exception were made for a few individuals against whom the commissioners were

Determination, of this Important point, I shall hope that you will enable Mr. Oswald to dispatch a Messenger after me, who may be with me before Morning at Chantilly, where I propose sleeping tonight, or who may overtake me before I arrive in London, with a satisfactory Answer to this Letter— I have the honour to be, Gentlemen, Your most obedt. and most humble Servt.

H STRACHEY

Draft of Mr Strachey's Letter to the American Commissioners— 5th. Novr. 1782—

(No. 6)

In Mr. Strachey's 8th Novr. 1782.

From the Marquis de Ségur

AL: Library of Congress

Versailles le 5. 9bre 1782.

M de Ségur a L'honneur de faire à Monsieur franklin ses Remerciments du soin quil a bien voulu prendre de Lui faire adresser Les depeches de L'amerique septle. qui lui sont parvenues pour Lui;[9] il le prie en même tems dagréer ses sinceres Compliments./.

---

particularly irritated). He admitted, however, that Oswald did not agree: Morris, *Jay: Peace*, pp. 406, 411–17.

9. These had been brought by Capt. Joshua Barney of the packet *General Washington;* he arrived in Paris on Nov. 5: Barney to BF, [Nov. 6], and BF to Morris, Dec. 14, below.

From Benjamin Vaughan[1]

ALS: Library of Congress

Tuesday afternoon.
My dearest sir,   [November 5, 1782, or later?][2]

I find that I can go off with convenience very early on Thursday morning; and therefore if agreeable, should wish you to give me your letter for Mr: T: T: *tomorrow evening,* as it may furnish with me with a probable occasion of speaking to that gentleman about certain affairs. Mr: H:'s letter may come under *cover to me* by a courier.— The very moment a certain event happens, I will indubitably take the *journey* I talked of, in order to communicate with my friend.

You will be kind enough to direct that a pass-port may be prepared, in order to save time, should my young friend[3] be absent when I call tomorrow at Passy.

I must now, my dearest, dearest sir, by every tie in the world beseech you not to think of residing in any other house than

---

1. We publish this undated document at its earliest possible date, and can only speculate about the meaning of some of Vaughan's obscure references. If "T.T." in the first sentence is Thomas Townshend, then Vaughan could be offering to carry BF's Nov. 4 letter to him—the only letter BF ever wrote Townshend, to the best of our knowledge. "Mr. H," in that case, could be William Hodgson, to whom BF also wrote on Nov. 4. (That letter is missing, but Hodgson alludes to it in his reply of Nov. 14.) The "journey" is undoubtedly a visit to Shelburne, but the "certain event" that would precede it is a matter of speculation. On Nov. 4, Vaughan wrote to Shelburne that BF seemed "doubtful whether he shall have any occasion or not to use me," and that the two agreed that Vaughan should probably stay in Paris "till we hear the ultimatum of the British Court" (postscript of Vaughan to Shelburne, Nov. 1, 1782, APS). If Vaughan had decided to stay until the Cabinet evaluated the second draft treaty (which is what he in fact did), then his making departure plans on Nov. 5 seems unlikely. On the other hand, he was anxious to be with his wife, who was nearing the end of her pregnancy. He may well have rethought what he and BF had discussed on Nov. 4, and considered leaving earlier for personal reasons. (Sarah Vaughan gave birth to a daughter, Harriet, on Nov. 11: Morris, *Jay: Peace,* p. 422n.) The "certain event" could be either the British government's decision, or the birth of his child; either way, Vaughan seems to be suggesting in this letter that he would still be available for a conference with Shelburne.

2. The first Tuesday after Nov. 4, the date of BF's only extant letter to Thomas Townshend.

3. WTF (to whom Vaughan refers below as BF's son).

mine, were you to reside in London for a thousand "fortnights." We have room & servants & victuals & *quiet* enough; and there are two country houses for you besides, and a good woman who will strive to make every thing in the world comfortable to you.— And we have not only this convenience for you, but for your son, whose situation elsewhere would give us the greatest uneasiness.— Our chief *friends* you know are or may be in common; and your son, for his part, will be like a brother with us.

I am, my dearest sir, your *ever* devoted, affecte: & grateful[4]

BENJN VAUGHAN

The American Peace Commissioners to Henry Strachey

LS and three copies: Public Record Office; copies: National Archives (three),[5] Library of Congress (three), Massachusetts Historical Society, William L. Clements Library; transcript: National Archives

Sir,   Paris 6th. November 1782.

We have been honoured with your Favor of the 5th. Instant, and as our Answer to a Letter We recieved from Mr. Oswald on the same subject contains our unanimous Sentiments respecting it, We take the Liberty of referring you to the enclosed Copy of that Answer.[6]

We have the honor to be, Sir your most obedient Servants

JOHN ADAMS
B FRANKLIN
JOHN JAY.

4. Vaughan did not leave Paris for his second mission to England on a Thursday, as this letter would indicate, but on Sunday, Nov. 17. The previous day, Oswald learned that the British government had rejected the second draft treaty. Oswald urged Jay to go to England to speak to the Ministry, but Jay refused. Vaughan volunteered for the mission, as he had already determined to go "on Account of the critical State of his Family" (according to JA). Vaughan was briefed by both Oswald and the American commissioners, procured a passport from BF, and left at noon the next day: Morris, *Jay: Peace*, pp. 422–4; Butterfield, *John Adams Diary*, III, 57–8. He returned on Nov. 27; see his letter of that date, below.

5. All three are in JA's hand.

6. American Peace Commissioners to Oswald, Nov. 7, below.

H Strachey Esqr

Notations: Letter from the American Commissioners to Mr Strachey 6 Novr 1782 / In Mr. Oswald's 6 & 7 Novemr. 1782.

To Vergennes

ʟs:[7] Archives du Ministère des affaires étrangères; ᴀʟ (draft): Library of Congress

Sir,   Passy Novr. 6. 1782.
   I wonder much that your Excellency has received no Letters by our Packet Boat. There were some for M. De Castries & M. de Segur. I enclose what News I have which is not in the News papers. Those will have informed you of the Unhappy Loss of the Eagle, and saving of the Money &ca.[8]
   I am with great Respect Sir, Your Excellency's most obedient & most humble Sert.   B FRANKLIN

His Exy le Cte. de Vergennes.

Notation: M. De R.[9]

From Joshua Barney   ᴀʟ: American Philosophical Society

Paris Wednesday Octr. [*i.e.*, November 6][1] 82
Capn. Barney has the honor of assuring his Excelly. Doctr.

---

   7. In ᴡᴛꜰ's hand.
   8. The packet boat was the *General Washington;* see Joshua Barney to ʙꜰ, Nov. 6. For the loss of the *Aigle* see Livingston to ʙꜰ, Sept. 18.
   9. Rayneval.
   1. The day after Barney arrived in Paris with dispatches for ʙꜰ from Robert Morris and a letter of introduction from Morris dated Oct. 7 (above). He brought the dispatches immediately to Passy, where ʙꜰ insisted that he stay to dinner "en famille," made him "fight all his battles o'er again," promised to present him to the court at Versailles, and treated him with "paternal kindness and familiarity": Mary C. Barney, ed., *A Biographical Memoir of the Late Commodore Joshua Barney* . . . (Boston, 1832), pp. 135–6. Barney's packet, the *General Washington*, took only about three weeks to sail from the

Franklin of his most respectfull Comps. & wth. pleasure accepts his polite invitation to dinner on Saturday next[2]

Addressed: A Son Excellence / Monsieur Le Doctr. Franklin / ministre Plenipotentiare / des Etats Units de / L'Amerique en / son hotel / a Passy

From François-Louis Bayard[3]

ALS: University of Pennsylvania Library

Monsieur   Ce 6 9bre. 1782

J'ai Lhonneur de vous prier de faire mettre votre Légalisation au bas de la Procuration cy incluse, elle a pour objet la Suite des malheureuses expeditions que j'ai fait d'après mon traitté avec les Etats de Georgie,[4] on m'assure Monsieur que cette Procuration pourroit être contestée en Amerique Si vous n'aviéz La bonté d'y Donner cette Sanction; Comme la personne qui S'en charge part demain, je vous Supplie de me Renvoyer par le Porteur cette Piece revetüe de Cette formalité. Si je nétois assés in-

---

Delaware to Lorient: BF to Morris, Dec. 14, below; *Morris Papers*, VI, 518n and VII, 20; Klingelhofer, "Matthew Ridley's Diary," pp. 124–5.

2. Matthew Ridley also was invited to this Nov. 9 dinner and sent a one-line acceptance to BF on Nov. 6 (APS). According to his diary the guests included JA, John and Sarah Jay, JW, and Dorcas Montgomery: Klingelhofer, "Matthew Ridley's Diary," p. 126. BF had been to Versailles that morning and discussed with Vergennes the need for a new French loan; see his Nov. 8 letter to Vergennes, below. BF discussed Vergennes' reaction with JA when the latter came to dine. He also reinforced the message that Lafayette had just given JA, that Vergennes "took it amiss" that JA had not yet been to Versailles to meet with him: Butterfield, *John Adams Diary,* III, 47.

3. Principal in the firm of Garson, Bayard & Cie. They had been engaged by La Plaigne to furnish military supplies and troop transport for the state of Georgia: XXIII, 225; XXV, 234n, 631–2; XXIX, 232n.

4. Georgia had refused to accept the goods that the firm shipped in 1778 because of financial difficulties. The firm had been trying to get payment ever since. Now that the British troops had left Georgia and the state was once again under American control, Bayard was again pressing his claim: Robert R. Crout, "Pierre-Emmanuel de la Plaigne and Georgia's Quest for French Aid during the War of Independence," *Ga. Hist. Quarterly,* LX (1976), 180–2.

disposé j'aurais Lhonneur de vous presenter cette Requêtte que j'espere vous voudréz bien admettre.—

Je Suis avec Respect Monsieur Votre très humble et très obeissant Serviteur BAYARD

fournisseur des Troupes du Roi
Porte st. honnore

Notations: Bayard 9. Nov. 1782 / [*In William Temple Franklin's hand:*] Ben Wm. Betsey Louis Deborah

From Chalut and Arnoux   AL:[5] American Philosophical Society

Paris 6. 9bre 1782

Les abbés de Chalut et Arnoux ont lhonneur d'assurer Monsieur franklin de leur attachement respectueux, et de lui demander s'il n'y auroit point d'indiscretion de le prier de leur preter les deux premiers Volumes des memoires de la Chine.[6] Si leur respectable ami peut leur rendre ce Service, les deux abbés Le prient de le leur faire sçavoir, et ils feront prendre chez lui les deux volumes qu'ils demandent, qu'ils lui enverront après Les avoir lû et ils lui en demanderont la suite.

Les amitiés des deux abbés a M. le petit fils.

Addressed: A Monsieur / Monsieur franklin Ministre / Plenipotentiaire des Etats / unis d'Amerique / à Passy

5. In Arnoux's hand.
6. Probably the ongoing publication, by multiple authors, of *Mémoires concernant . . . des chinois* (1776–1814). BF purchased six volumes in 1780: XXXIII, 5. This may be the same series that BF promised to loan on another occasion: an undated note in an unknown hand, among his papers at the APS, reads: "Les Mémoires sur la Chine, que Monsieur Franklin veut bien me prêter."

284

From Williams, Moore & Co.

LS:[7] Historical Society of Pennsylvania

Honnorable Monsieur   a L'orient le 6 9bre. *1782.*

Nous avons L'honneur de vous remettre Sous ce ply Les procedures de lamirauté de nôtre ville, des deux prises anglaises les deux freres, & Larundell, faites par Le corsaire ameriquain La Révolution,[8] nous vous Suplions de vouloir Bien nous honorer de leur Condamnation le plutôt quil vous Sera possible, pour de suitte acceleree La vente.

Nous Sommes avec un profond Respect honnorable Monsieur Vos trés humbles & trés obeissants Serviteurs

WILLIAMS MOORE & CO

The American Peace Commissioners to Richard Oswald

LS[9] and three copies: Public Record Office; AL (draft):[1] Massachusetts Historical Society; copies: William L. Clements Library, Library of Congress (three), Massachusetts Historical Society (three), National Archives, North Carolina State Division of Archives and History; press copy of copy: Library of Congress; transcript: National Archives

Sir.   Paris 7th. November 1782.

In answer to the letter you did us the honor to write on the 4th. inst. we beg leave to repeat what we often said in conversation, viz. that the Restoration of such of the Estates of Refugees, as have been confiscated, is impracticable; because they were confiscated by Laws of particular States, &, in many instances, have passed by legal titles, through several hands. Besides, Sir, as this is a matter evidently appertaining to the internal Polity of the

---

7. Signed by James Moore.

8. The *Two Brothers* and the *Arundel* were two of the four prizes taken by the *Revolution, Cicero,* and *Buccaneer* on Oct. 3; see Williams, Moore & Co. to BF, Oct. 9. The enclosures are missing.

9. In the hand of JA's secretary Charles Storer (1761–1829), for whom see *Adams Correspondence,* V, ix–x.

1. In JA's hand, as is the copy at the National Archives.

separate States, the Congress, by the nature of our Constitution, have no authority to interfere with it—

As to your demand of Compensation to these Persons, we forbear enumerating our Reasons for thinking it ill founded. In the moment of conciliatory Overtures, it would not be proper to call certain Scenes into view, over which, a variety of Considerations should induce both Parties, at present to draw a veil. Permit us therefore only to repeat, that we cannot stipulate for such Compensation, unless, on your part, it be agreed to make retribution to our Citizens for the heavy Losses they have sustained by the *unnecessary* Destruction of their private Property—

We have already agreed to an amnesty more extensive than Justice required, and full as extensive as Humanity could demand. We can therefore only repeat, that it cannot be extended further—

We should be sorry if the absolute Impossibility of our complying further with your Propositions on this head, should induce Great-Britain to continue the War for the sake of those, who caused & prolonged it; but, if that should be the Case, we hope that the utmost Latitude will not be again given to its rigours—

Whatever may be the Issue of this Negotiation, be assured Sir, that we shall always acknowledge the liberal, manly, and candid manner, in which you have conducted it; and that We shall remain, with the warmest Sentiments of Esteem and Regard, Your Most Obedt: humble: Servants.   JOHN ADAMS.

B FRANKLIN

JOHN JAY

To Richard Oswald Esqr. his Britannic Majesty's Commissioner for treating of Peace with the Commissioners of the United States of America

Notation: Letter from the Commissioners To Mr Oswald in Mr. Oswald's 6 & 7 Novemr. 1782[2] 7 Novr 1782

---

2. The covering letter was Oswald to Townshend, Nov. 6–7, 1782 (Morris, *Jay: Peace*, pp. 406–10), which notes that the present letter was delivered by Jay at noon on Nov. 7.

To Robert R. Livingston   ALS and transcript: National Archives

Sir   Passy, Nov. 7. 1782

The Baron de Kermelin,[3] a Swedish Gentleman of Distinction, recommended strongly to me by his Excellency the Ambassador of that Nation to *this Court*,[4] as a Person highly esteemed in *his own*, purposes a Journey thro' North America, to view its natural Productions, acquaint himself with its Commerce, and acquire such Information as may be useful to his Country, in the Communication and Connection of Interests that seems to be growing and possibly may soon become considerable between the two Nations. I therefore beg leave to introduce him to you, and request that you would present him to the President of Congress, and to such other Persons as you shall think may be useful to him in his Views; and I recommend him earnestly to those Civilities which you have a Pleasure in showing to Strangers of Merit.

With great Esteem I have the honour to be Sir, Your most obedient & most humble Servant[5]   B FRANKLIN

R. R. Livingston Esqe

3. BF misspelled the name. Baron Samuel Gustaf Hermelin (1744–1820), an expert on mining, was sponsored by the Swedish College of Mines in the spring of 1782 to visit various European countries and study their mines and iron industry. King Gustavus III gave him secret instructions to investigate the economic and political situation in the United States, providing him with credentials to serve as Swedish envoy if Congress appointed a minister to Stockholm (which it did not). Hermelin did not keep secret the fact that he carried credentials; Philadelphia correspondents reported it in June, 1783 and again in June, 1784. In July, 1784, Hermelin visited Connecticut. After returning to Sweden he wrote a report on mining in America, and in 1785 he was elected a foreign member of the APS: *Svenskt Biografiskt Lexikon* (28 vols. to date, Stockholm, 1918–); Amandus Johnson, *Swedish Contributions to American Freedom, 1776–1783* (2 vols., Philadelphia, 1953–57), I, 580–1; *Jefferson Papers*, VI, 276; Smith, *Letters*, XXI, 699; *PMHB*, XXXIX (1915), 244; Franklin B. Dexter, ed., *The Literary Diary of Ezra Stiles . . .* (3 vols., New York, 1901), III, 129; Samuel Gustaf Hermelin, *Report about the Mines in the United States of America, 1783*, trans. and ed. Amandus Johnson (Philadelphia, 1931), pp. 10–13; Adolph B. Benson, *Sweden and the American Revolution* (New Haven, 1926), pp. 47–8n; APS *Trans.*, II (1786), xxvii.

4. Graf von Creutz.

5. Hermelin carried with him to America two other letters of recommen-

From Claude-Mammès Pahin de Champlain de La Blancherie

AL: American Philosophical Society

ce 7 9bre 1782.—hôtel de Villayer rue st andré des arcs. M. De la Blancherie arrivant d'hollande accablé d'occupations,[6] n'a que le tems de faire présenter son respect á Monsieur Le Docteur franklin, et de le supplier de vouloir bien lui faire procurer l'Extrait mortuaire de M. De Troye, Lieutenant dans la Légion de Palaski mort à Charles-Town (dans la lettre de sa famille on écrit *Chartouin*) à l'hôpital de la d. [ditte] Ville et enterré dans la Vieille Eglise anglicane le 21 décembre 1779.[7] Ses parens se sont adressés à M. De La Blancherie pour l'obtenir: il auroit aussi beaucoup d'obligation à Son Ex. Si Elle pouvoit lui faire avoir aussi l'adresse de M. Adams.[8]

Notation: De La Blancherie 7. Nov. 1782.

---

dation from BF that we have located, dated Nov. 2. Nearly identical in wording to this one, but without the request to recommend him to the president of Congress, both letters addressed the unnamed recipient as "Your Excellency." One was to Gov. Jonathan Trumbull (Conn. Hist. Soc.; the notation indicates that it was received on July 23, 1784), and the other (Hist. Soc. of Pa.) was most likely addressed to the President of the Pa. Supreme Executive Council, William Moore. Both are in L'Air de Lamotte's hand and signed by BF.

6. La Blancherie had spent September and October traveling in Flanders and Holland. Before leaving, he offered to his associates in the Agence générale de correspondance pour les sciences et les arts to undertake research in the sciences and the arts during his travels: *Nouvelles de la république des lettres et des arts* for Aug. 21. He was preparing now to hold open house on the following two Saturdays for those eager to have answers to their queries: *Jour. de Paris* for Nov. 7.

7. François-Antoine de Troye was commissioned in October, 1778, to commence June 1 of that year: List of Officers, Oct. 4, 1778 (National Archives); Heitman, *Register of Officers*, p. 152. Lt. Charles Roth, a fellow officer in Pulaski's Legion, wrote Congress in June, 1782, that de Troye had died of illness (National Archives).

8. JA moved into apartments in the Hôtel du Roi in the Place du Carrousel soon after he arrived in Paris on Oct. 26: Butterfield, *John Adams Diary,* III, 39n, 41.

From the Baron Samuel Gustaf Hermelin[9]

AL: American Philosophical Society

[after November 7, 1782]

Le Baron de Hermelin pour prendre congé de son Excellce, devant partir demain l'Apres diné, et il aura l'honneur demain au matin de faire sa visite chez son Excellence.[1]

To Vergennes

LS:[2] Archives du Ministère des affaires étrangères; copy: Library of Congress

Sir,   Passy, Novr 8th 1782.

The Congress disregarding the Proposals made by Sir Guy Carleton,[3] and determined to continue the War with Vigour, 'till a Peace can be obtained, satisfactory as well to the King as to themselves; (as will appear by their Resolves hereto annex'd) but being disabled by the great Deficiency in their Taxes arising from various temporary Causes, have found it absolutely necessary to borrow another Sum in Europe, which they have accordingly directed me to endeavour by all means possible. The Necessity of this Measure is so clearly express'd, in the Letter of Mr. Morris their Financier, and Mr Livingston their Secretary, which are subjoined, that there is little Occasion for any Remarks of mine;[4] I shall therefore only observe that from what

9. Whom BF recommended to Robert R. Livingston on Nov. 7, above.

1. BF was not at home when he called. WTF penned an apology below Hermelin's note: "M. Franklin est bien faché d'etre obligé d'aller ce Matin a Paris pour Affaire,—Il a l'honneur de souhaiter un bon Voyage a M. le Baron." WTF later added, "This Baron is the Gentleman introduced by the Swedish Ambassador." At some time Hermelin wrote his name on the address sheet of Amelia Barry's Sept. 20 letter, above.

2. In WTF's hand.

3. The proposal to recognize American independence immediately. After Congress refused to communicate with him, Carleton sent it to George Washington: XXXVII, 399n, 674n, 717n.

4. BF sent Vergennes extracts from Livingston's postscript to his letter of Sept. 13 (with the enclosed Sept. 14 congressional resolution directing that

pass'd in some of the last Conferences we had with the English Negociators here, I apprehend Peace to be still at a Distance and that another Campaign can scarcely be avoided; our Enemies being well informed of our present Distresses for want of Money & conceiving great Hopes that we shall no where find a Supply. The Congress on this important Occasion have therefore sent a Packet Boat[5] express with their Orders to me to implore the Aid of his Majesty, our Friend & Father which I hereby do most earnestly from a full Conviction that unless the Loan is obtain'd, our Army can neither be kept up nor safely disbanded.

With the greatest Respect, I am, Sir, Your Excellency's most obedient & most humble Servant.[6]   B FRANKLIN

His Exy. Ct. de Vergennes.

From David Hartley   ALS: Library of Congress

My Dear friend   London Nov 8 1782

I beg leave to recommend to your attention the enclosed case of Mr James Nassau Colleton. I do it the more readily because it seems to me to be an equitable claim and because I think every example of compliance on any side with claims of equity and justice will at some time or other emerge in the general account of benevolence & conciliation. Mrs Margaret Colleton whose letter is enclosed left her title about three years ago to the present owner of the title Mr. Colleton who is fourscore years of age

---

BF borrow $4,000,000 from France), and from Livingston's letter of Sept. 18. He also sent copies of Lincoln's letter of Sept. 25, Morris' first letter of Sept. 27 (with an explanatory note and the congressional resolution of Sept. 23 enclosed by Morris), Morris' letter of Sept. 28, and Morris' third letter of Oct. 7. All these are above; the enclosed copies are at the AAE. BF also enclosed copies of a Sept. 27 letter from Morris to JA (*Morris Papers*, VI, 443) and of an Oct. 3 congressional resolution (*JCC*, XXIII, 632–7) promising not to listen to British peace proposals without consulting France: *Morris Papers*, VI, 451n.

5. The *General Washington*, commanded by Joshua Barney.

6. When BF presented this memorial, Vergennes promised to have it translated and laid before the King. He warned, however, that it would meet with many difficulties: Butterfield, *John Adams Diary*, III, 47.

with the reversion to Mr J. N. Colleton whose memorial recites the rest.[7] He is a young man under 30 years of age. I have known his family some years and have been requested by a common friend to recommend the case to your patronage. I shall be very happy to hear from you, more especially if you can say three things to me, first that you will not think me a trespasser upon your goodness in this present recommendation, secondly that you are yourself well in heart and health, and lastly, that Peace may not be far distant.

Your ever Affecte   D H.

Addressed: To Dr Franklin / &c &c &c

From Vicq d'Azyr

LS: American Philosophical Society

Monsieur.   8. 9bre. 1782

Je Suis chargé d'ecrire l'Eloge de feu M Pringle[8] pour être Lu dans notre Prochaine séance Publique; sachant que Vous etiez

---

7. The matter concerned family property in South Carolina that had been confiscated by the state legislature. Margaret Colleton was the widow of Sir John Snell Colleton, a descendant of one of the eight original proprietors of Carolina. The letter from her that Hartley enclosed was an appeal from London dated July 13, 1778, and addressed to Robert Raper and Francis Kinloch of Charleston (the former a lawyer, the latter a future delegate to Congress: *Laurens Papers,* I, 38n; XV, 286n). Her husband had died 12 years earlier; she was 76 years old, and she was unable to make the voyage to file a claim on her estates, the Wadboo Barony and the Mephshew Plantations. Her income from those estates ceased in 1775, which was a great hardship to her. James Nassau Colleton, a cousin of Margaret Colleton's husband, evidently wrote his memorial to BF (undated) at Hartley's suggestion. He had inherited the property upon Margaret's death in 1779. In the memorial he offered to make over possession of the property if he were permitted to reside on it. In 1784 the S.C. legislature granted him the proceeds of the sale of the properties: *Laurens Papers,* IV, 339–40n; Henry A. M. Smith, ed., "The Colleton Family in South Carolina," *S.C. Gen. and Hist. Mag.,* I (1900), 332–3; Charles M. Andrews, *The Colonial Period of American History* (4 vols., New Haven, London, and Oxford, 1934–38), III, 183; *Gent. Mag.,* LXXXV, part I (1815), 183.

8. Sir John Pringle, the distinguished Scottish physician and BF's longtime friend, died on Jan. 18: XXXVI, 407n.

l'ami de cet illustre Médecin, Je Vous prie de Vouloir bien me faire part des Anecdotes intéressantes dont Vous pourriez avoir connaissance relativement à sa Vie, afin de me mettre à portée de Louer sa mémoire le plus dignement qu'il me sera Possible.[9]

Je Suis avec Respect Monsieur Votre trés humble et très obeissant serviteur   VICQ DAZYR

M franklin.

Si Vous aviez quelques ouvrages de M Pringle, Je Vous serais obligé de Vouloir bien Me les Communiquer.

Notation: Vicq d'azir 8. 9bre. 1782.

From Robert R. Livingston

Three LS: University of Pennsylvania Library; transcript:[1] National Archives

Dear Sir,   Philadelphia, 9th. Novr. 1782

Mr Steward[2] informing me that he shall set out to morrow for Paris— He will be the bearer of this, & duplicates of my last Letters— Want of time will prevent my sending Mr Jay duplicates of the resolutions formerly enclosed to him, which will be the more unnecessary, as you will communicate those you receive with this, if my former Letters containing them have not reached him.

We are much flattered by the proposals of Sweden,[3] and feel

9. Vicq d'Azyr did not deliver his eulogy of Pringle until the public meeting of the Société de médecine on Aug. 26, 1783: Vicq d'Azyr to BF, Aug. 21, 1783 (APS).

Among BF's papers at the Library of Congress is a copy in L'Air de Lamotte's hand of another eulogy of Pringle. This was composed by Condorcet for the Académie des sciences, and was published in the *Histoire de l'Académie royale des sciences* for 1782 (Paris, 1785), pp. 57–68.

1. Which indicates that the original LS was carried by the ship *Heer Adams,* the "2plicate" was carried by Col. [Matthias] Ogden, and the "3plicate" was carried by the packet *Washington.*

2. The other two LS and the transcript say "Stewart." He may have been the man introduced by RB on Nov. 27, below.

3. Congress had already drafted a treaty; see our annotation of Livingston's Sept. 18 letter, and the Sept. 28 commission and instructions for BF.

all the force of it's minister's observation— Every new acknowledgement lays the foundation of others, & familiarizes
Great Britain with the idea of acknowledging us as sovereign
and Independent— I feel some pleasure too in thinking that you
are to be the instrument of procuring us a new connection, &
beg leave to remind you of another which calls for your attention, tho' it Seems to have been forgot in the hurry of business I
mean that with the states of Barbary— The good dispositions
of the Court of France towards us & the enlarged policy by which
their measures are actuated, together with the coolness that at
present subsists between the Emperor of Morocco & Great Britain, (if we are well informed) seems to point out this as the favorable moment for making ourselves known to them—[4] As Mr.
Jay is now with you, I wish you would consult upon the means
of bringing this about, so that we may not be shut out of the
Mediterranean in future.

I know you will start a very obvious objection— But as this
can only be removed by your influence where you now are, we
rely upon you for the means as well as for the manner of treating. I have not thought it necessary to say any thing to Congress
on this subject, nor shall I till you give me hopes that something
may be done in it.

The only political object of a general nature that has been
touched upon in Congress since my last is the exchange of prisoners which seems at present to be as far as ever from being
effected. The propositions on the side of the Enemy were to exchange seamen for soldiers, they having no soldiers in their
hands— That the soldiers so exchanged should not serve for one
year against the *United states*— That the sailors ought to go into
immediate service— That the ballance of soldiers in our hands
should be given up at a stipulated price.

Congress rejected this proposal as unequal—as letting loose
a force which might be employed against our Allies in the West
Indies, as making no provision for the payment of the large bal-

4. Congress already had instructed BF to communicate, if he had no objections, its desire for a commercial treaty with the Emperor of Morocco:
XXXIV, 84. In the Treaty of Amity and Commerce, France had agreed to provide the United States its good offices with the Barbary States: XXV, 602–3.

lance due to us for the maintenance of prisoners. They farther required that General Carleton explicitly declare that the powers he gives to his Commissioners for negotiating an exchange are derived from the King of Great Britain so that any engagement for the payment of the debt they have incurred may be considered as binding on the nation—with respect to Mr Laurens, they come to no decided opinion, the Committee to whom it was referred reporting, That

"With respect to the information contained in the Extract of Sir Guy Carleton & Admiral Digby's Letter of the 2d of August *That after Mr. Laurens was discharged, he declared that he considered Lord Cornwallis as free from his parole, your Committee conceive it sufficient to observe that no intimation having been received of such a fact except from the said Extract, & Congress having given no directions* for that purpose, the consideration thereof would in their opinion be premature, & ought therefore to be deferred"—[5]

Since which tho' Letters have been received from Mr Laurens, they have come to no resolution, unless their direction to him to proceed in the business of his mission,[6] may be considered as Such—

General Carleton has sent out the trial of Lippencot, which admits the murder of Huddy, but justifies Lippencut, under an irregular Order of the Board of refugees— So paltry a palliation of so black a crime would not have been admitted, & Capt. Asgill would certainly have paid the forfeit for the injustice of his Countrymen, had not the interposition of their Majesties prevented— The letter from the Count de Vergennes is made the ground work of the resolution passed on that subject— I shall transmit you the resolve—[7] I suppose I need not tell you

5. *JCC*, XXIII, 555–8. Congress had taken further action to regulate prisoner exchanges; see Hodgson to BF, Dec. 12.

6. See Livingston's Sept. 18 letter.

7. The resolve of Nov. 7 freeing Capt. Asgill at the request of Vergennes (for which see de Grasse's Aug. 26 letter): *JCC*, XXIII, 715. Capt. Richard Lippincot was acquitted by a British court martial of having murdered Joshua Huddy after he claimed that the hanging of Huddy was sanctioned by WF, president of the Board of Associated Loyalists: Freeman, *Washington*, V, 419–20; Sheila Skemp, *William Franklin: Son of a Patriot, Servant of a King* (New York and Oxford, 1990), pp. 256–64.

that the Enemy contrived to get off the Eagle & to carry her to New York— You will find in the enclosed papers a very polite Letter from Capt. Elphinstone—[8] it is easier to be so in words than deed among the British— Digby has refused to permit him to comply with his engagements, at least so far as his share of the prize is concerned, & insists upon dividing the baggage of the Officers, & sharing the eight shirt, the eight pairs of breeches &c— On the 4th inst. Mr. Boudinot was elected President in the room of Mr Hanson—[9] Mr Lewis Morris will enclose bills purchased here at 6s 3d [*i.e.* p.] for five Livers for the amount of your last quarter's salary, ending the first of October.[1]

I have the honor to be sir, with perfect esteem & respect, Your most obt humble servt.   ROBT R LIVINGSTON

Honble. B. Franklin LLD.

No. 20

From Jonathan Trumbull[2]   ALS: American Philosophical Society

Sir   Lebanon 9th. Novemr—1782

You will doubtless recollect the circumstances of the first institution of the University of Dartmouth in the State of New-Hampshire.

That the late venerable Dr Wheelock was indefatigable in his endeavours to civilise and chritianise the indian natives, and to promote humanity, literature, and piety, and for that end sought and obtained benefactions in London; and carried forward the

8. Capt. George Keith Elphinstone of the *Warwick*, 50, captured the *Aigle*, which ran aground: *DNB*. The enclosure is missing.

9. *JCC*, XXIII, 708. A copy of the announcement is with BF's papers at the APS. BF had known Elias Boudinot, Jr., as a child: X, 174n; Morris, *Jay: Peace*, pp. 714–16.

1. See Morris' Nov. 11 letter to BF.

2. For background on this letter see the Board of Trustees of Dartmouth College to BF, Sept. 24. Eleazar Wheelock had lived in Lebanon, Conn., Trumbull's home, when he ran Moor's Charity School, a free school for Indians (1754–70). James Axtell, *The Invasion Within: the Contest of Cultures in Colonial North America* (New York and Oxford, 1985), pp. 204–13.

undertaking with success, and to public utility, until the present contest between the two countries put an end to his receiving any further helps from thence, before the great work was ripenned to Maturity.

The Doctor's worthy son the honorable John Wheelock Esqr is now the President, and in imitation of his father's Virtues, and to bring to perfection the institution so happily begun and prospered, is intrusted and authorised by its Trustees to sollicit benefactions in France and Holland to compleat that laudable beneficial & liberal undertaking.— I wish him success, and do recommend him and design to your notice, assistance and patronage.

With every sentiment of Esteem & Consideration I have the honor to be Your Excellency's most obedient hble Servant

JONTH; TRUMBULL

His Excellency Benja. Franklin L L D.

Notation: Trumbul Mr. John 9 Nov. 1782.

To Vergennes   ALS: Archives du Ministère des affaires étrangères

Sir   Passy, Nov. 10. 1782

I have examined the Captain if it might not be possible that he had left your Excellys. Letters in his Ship.[3] He says that he certainly had no others for you than the Pacquets he delivered: But that there came with him as a Passenger, a Mr Forest, who was a Commis he thinks in the Office of the Secretary of the French Minister,[4] and who left him at L'Orient to come to Paris by way of Nantes; saying that he had Letters to deliver to you, & should

---

3. The captain was Joshua Barney. Vergennes was waiting for letters from La Luzerne before making a decision on BF's Nov. 8 request for additional financial aid: Lafayette to BF, [on or before Nov. 22], below.

4. Antoine-René-Charles-Mathurin de La Forest (1756–1846): *Morris Papers,* VI, 517n; *DBF;* Abraham P. Nasatir and Gary E. Monell, eds., *French Consuls in the United States: a Calendar of Their Correspondence in the Archives Nationales* (Washington, 1967), pp. 560–1.

be at Paris within twelve Hours after the Captain. I am, with Respect, Sir, Your most obedt humb. Servt   B Franklin

M. le Comte de Vergennes

Notation: M de R[5]

From Jean-Pierre Duplan[6]   AL: American Philosophical Society

Monsieur   Lausanne le 10e. Novembre 1782.

Le 11e. fevrier *1778*-, vous nous avés honoré de vôtre souscription pour un Exempl: de nôtre Enciclopedie 8° de 36 Volumes de discours & 3 vol: de planches, sur le prospectus que nous Eumes l'honeur de vous mettre sous les yeux; Vous daignattes Monsieur encourager nôtre entreprise de Vôtre aprobation, et de l'esperance que vous ne vous borneriés pas à ce Seul Exemplaire.

Aujourd'hui nous avons pris la liberté de vous rapeller de vôtre Engagement & de vos promesses, et nous vous prions Monsieur, de le faire prendre chès Monsr Dassy D'arpajan Docteur en Medecine à Fontainebleau près Paris, auquel nous avons fait parvenir successivement vos Volumes;

Et comme il ÿ a plus d'une année que Nous avons achevé l'Impression de cet Ouvrage, et qu'une partie des Volumes doit vous avoir eté livré Monsieur depuis longtems Nous prenons la liberté de vous prier de donner un instant d'attention a la chose afin que vous ayés les 39 Volumes qui forment le complet de la Souscription;

Il nous reviendra Monsieur pour le prix de cette Enciclopedie, 225 *l.t.* de france

a raison de 36 Vol: de discours à 5 *l.t.* £ 180
3 de planche a 15 *l.t.*   45
qui est le prix de la Souscription £ 225—.

---

5. Rayneval.
6. Co-director of the Société Typographique de Lausanne. For background on this letter see XXVII, 594–5. In our headnote there, we quoted the total subscription price as £225 (based on the present letter), neglecting to specify that the £ sign in this case stands for *livres tournois*.

Lorsque vous aurés recu tous les Volumes a Satisfaction, vous aurés la bonté Monsieur de faire payer à Mr. Grand n Banqr. à Paris ruë Montmartre, le montant de la Somme c'y contre, au moyen de laquelle ce sera chose consomée.

D'aignés Monsieur vous rapeller dans l'occasion, que nous en avons encore un nombre de la seconde Edition, conforme à vôtre Exempl. et que vous avés eû la bonté de nous encourager dans cette Entreprise.

Permettés nous Monsieur de vous offrir le respect le plus profond, avec lequel nous avons l'honneur d'étre Vos trés humbles et trés Obeissants serviteurs Monsieur

LA SOCIETÉ TYPOGRAPHIQUE DE LAUSANNE EN SUISSE

Notation: La Société Typographique de Lausane, 10 Nov. 1782.

From Edward Bancroft   ALS: American Philosophical Society

Dear Sir   Passy Monday Evening [November 11, 1782?][7]

Mr. Walpole has this evening appointed to go to Seve [Sevres] tomorrow, to see the Manufactory there, & to Dine with me on his return; & as I Know he would be very glad to have the pleasure of meeting you, I beg Leave to Sollicit the honour of your, & your Grandson's Company to a plain Dinner at 3 O'Clock, if you are disengaged, if not, I shall hope for that honor another day.[8]

I am with the utmost respect & Devotion Dear Sir Your most Humble & affectionate Servant   EDWD. BANCROFT

Addressed: A Monsieur / Monsr. Franklin / Ministre Plenipotentiaire &c / &c &c / a Passy

Notation: Bancrof Edwd.

---

7. The Monday preceding Nov. 14, 1782, when we know that Thomas Walpole and his son, Thomas Walpole, Jr. (XXV, 273), were in Paris. On that day they attended a dinner hosted by Bancroft that also included Jay, Vaughan, and Ridley: Klingelhofer, "Matthew Ridley's Diary," p. 129.

8. Bancroft also wrote on an unspecified Saturday morning to WTF, inviting him and BF to dine that day with Walpole and his son (APS).

From Lewis R. Morris[9]   ALS: University of Pennsylvania Library

Sir   Office for Foreign Affairs 11th. November 1782

Enclosed you have a Bill of Exchange on Monsieur Grande for the amount of your Salary from the first of July to the thirtieth September; this Bill has been purchased at the same price as those already remitted vizt. six shillings and three pence currency for five Livres—[1]

As Mr Livingston stands charged in the Treasury Books for all monies remitted for your Salary, let me request your receipt.

We are still ignorant of the allowance you make your private Secretary, and the contingent Expences of your Office— Mr Livingston is desireous to be informed of these expences, with a state of your account, that they may be settled and the ballance remitted.

I have the honor to be sir with the highest Respect your most obedient humble servt   L R Morris

Received from the Superintendant of Finance for Salary due Doctor Franklin from the first day of July 1782. to the thirtieth of September following . . .   2,777.68 Dolls[2]

Exchange 6 / 3 Currency for 5 Livres—

$$\frac{16666\ l.t.\ 13\ s:}{16666\ l.t.\ 19\ s:\ \text{D}\ 2,777.68}$$

The Honble Benjn. Franklin

---

9. Lewis Richard Morris (1760–1825), a nephew of Gouverneur Morris. He and Pierre-Etienne Du Ponceau (XXXVI, 581–2n) were undersecretaries to Robert R. Livingston: *DAB;* George Dangerfield, *Chancellor Robert R. Livingston of New York, 1746–1813* (New York, 1960), p. 145.

1. For background on the recent bills of exchange for BF's salary see BF to Livingston, Oct. 14. Morris purchased this bill of exchange using Pennsylvania pounds, at the same rate of exchange that RB received in July: XXXVII, 576–7. One Pennsylvania pound was worth 16 *l.t.*, whereas the British pound sterling was worth about 24 *l.t.*

2. This is a quarter of BF's annual salary of £2,500, which Congress had approved for BF as minister plenipotentiary (XXX, 543) and did not alter when giving him collateral duty as peace commissioner. Morris here computes the amount in specie dollars, at 4 s. 6 p. in British currency per dollar: *Morris Papers,* V, 127.

From William Lee

ALS:[3] University of Virginia Library; two copies: Virginia Historical Society

Sir.   Bruxelles Novr. 12. 1782

I have had the Honour of receiving your Letter of the 20th. of last Month,[4] informing me that you had accepted my several bills amounting to Forty six thousand one hundred & ninety six Livres Nineteen Sols payle. the 12th. of April next, and you add: *"I confide that you will not hazard the credit of Congress, by indorsing any of them to others—'till You have heard from me that I am likely to be in Cash."*

This does not surprize me as coming from Doctor Franklin, especially when I have in my hands, the following extract from his Letter of the 30th. of March last to the superintendant of Finance, who had order'd him twelve months ago to pay this money, viz—"no demand has been made on me by Mr. Wm. Lee, *I do not know where he is.*"[5] At that moment Doctr. Franklin knew where I was, as well as any Man existing, who had not his eyes on me.

I know Sir that the money has been already lodged in your hands for the specific purpose of paying the debt due to me, which you have hitherto unjustly withheld, consequently, *the credit of Congress,* is at present out of the question, with respect to me, in this business; Therefore I am compell'd to inform you, that I am not in any manner disposed to be triffled with any longer, & that you must take care to pay the Bills punctually which you have accepted.[6]

I have the Honor to be, with proper Respect, Sir &c.

Sign'd— W. LEE

His Excellency Doctr. Benja. Franklin at Passy

(Copy.)

---

3. Retained by Lee as a copy. Among his several notations is the following: "Copies of Letters from Wm Lee to Dr Franklin, Nov. 12th. 1782 / Enclosing a previous one of Oct 7th 1782 / His reply of Oct 21st. 1782." There is no further extant correspondence between the two.

4. Oct. 21, above.

5. XXXVII, 72.

6. Lee was paid on April 12, 1783: Account XXVII (XXXII, 4).

From Sir Edward Newenham

ALS: American Philosophical Society

Sir   Marsailles[7] 12[-13] Novr: 1782

As I have some fears that the British Janus does not intend fair by the Kingdom of Ireland in the expected or depending Treaty of Peace, I hope Your Excellency will pardon my Zeal for my Country, by my most Earnestly entreating to Know, if Ireland is (as it ought of Right to be) particularily mentioned; if it be not, & peace should be finaly concluded, my fears Induce me to think, that our Trade & Commerce may suffer considerable & lasting Injuries—

I have wrote a public Letter to THE MEN of Ireland advising them to demand of their King, that their Kingdom be particuliarily mentioned & acknowledged by all the Belligerent Powers, but I have delayed sending it, untill I have the honor of your Answer, which I mean to use with the most confidential Respect and mention my Authority— My Letter is intended to be published in Every paper in Ireland, & it will finaly finish the fensibles—

All this Family join me in sincerest respects you & best regards to your Grandson—

I have the Honor, to be, with Every sentiment of respect your Excellencys most Obedt: and most obliged Humble Sert

EDWARD NEWENHAM

PS— That the Tenor of my address may appear to yr Excellency, I have the honor to Send a Copy of it—[8]

7. Newenham and his family arrived in Marseille on Nov. 8; see the following document.

8. The enclosed address "To The People of Ireland," dated Nov. 13, acknowledges the recent honor and advantages won by the Irish people (for which see XXXVII, 537) but warns that vigilance and unanimity would soon be required to secure Ireland's commercial rights. Newenham reports that the peace treaty under consideration does not mention "our Kingdom." He asks the people to demand Ireland's inclusion in every relevant article, to protect Irish commerce from the influences of ministers and English factors. Newenham wrote WTF on Jan. 2, 1783, that he was waiting for a response before taking further action (APS). We have no indication that BF ever responded, and the address seems not to have reached Ireland: James Kelly, *Sir Edward Newenham MP, 1734–1814: Defender of the Protestant Constitution* (Dublin, 2004), p. 183.

Addressed: Marsailles / To / His Excellency Dr. Franklin / Minister Plenipotentiary from / the United States of America / Passy / Paris

Notation: Newenham 12 Novr. 1782.

From Sir Edward Newenham

ALS: American Philosophical Society

Sir   Marsailles 13 Novr 1782

I should have done myself the Honor of writing to your Excellency before this, but waited for my Letters, in hopes of having some Irish Politics to acquaint you of, but have not received any thing very interesting, except, that Lord Temple is more assiduous and more prodigal in offers to Corrupt the Parliament than any of his Predecessors, and the British Ministry are determined to push the raising of 5000 fensibles—[9]

After a most agreable tour through Different parts of this Kingdom, we arrived here on Fryday; we came by water from Lyons to Avignion—

We were unlucky at Lyons, at not having any acquaintance, and all your friends for whom we had Letters, were absent from the City & not Expected to return for some time;[1]

---

9. George Nugent-Temple-Grenville, Earl Temple (XXXVII, 299n), was appointed lord-lieutenant of Ireland on July 31, 1782, and assumed his duties in September in Dublin, remaining only until the following June: *DNB;* Maurice R. O'Connell, *Irish Politics and Social Conflict in the Age of the American Revolution* (Philadelphia, 1965), pp. 358–361. Temple ignored Newenham's offer of cooperation: James Kelly, *Sir Edward Newenham MP, 1734–1814: Defender of the Protestant Constitution* (Dublin, 2004), pp. 179–80.

1. Among the people they had hoped to see was M. Fay de Sathonnay, commandant of Lyon, to whom the abbés Arnoux and Chalut had evidently written (see their letter of Oct. 14). Fay de Sathonnay wrote to the abbés on Oct. 31 from his château at Sathonnay, outside Lyon, saying that he hoped to find Newenham when he returned to Lyon after the Feast of St. Martin, Nov. 11. The abbés forwarded his letter to BF on Nov. 4; both letters are at the APS. BF and WTF dined with the abbés on Nov. 12, in company with JA, Chalut de Vérin, Ferdinand Grand, and others: Butterfield, *John Adams Diary,* III, 53–4.

Here we are settled for one month, but the Ladies wish to retire to the Town of Hieres [Hyères], where the Climate is warmer & living much Cheaper, but I could not appear, but in an Awkward situation near the Town of Toulon, except your Excellency could procure me Letters of Introduction to the Commander there,[2] which you may rely upon, shall never be disgraced nor betrayed by me or any of my family; I am told that I could get a Chateau near Hieres for very moderate terms—

Enclosed I have the honor to send you a Letter for your Perusal, and if approved of, you will please to sail it & send it to the post—

My Pen cannot describe the warm respect which Lady Newenham, my Son & I have for your Excellency & your Grandson; it might possibly be Equalled, but cannot be excelled; it is a Respect formed by the purest motives and of the most permanent Nature, as it has originated from an Impartial and Critical observation on the Principles and Conduct of those Concerned in the Important Transactions between America & Britain, and when I can convey to Ireland the Valuable Present of your bust, by some Bourdeaux Vessel bound to Dublin, Posterity shall know our sentiments, as I shall have many Models made with proper Inscriptions for the Pedestal—

That your Excellency & your worthy Grandson may enjoy perfect health & happiness, & that the states of America may hand down the firmest and most Soverign Independance to their latest Posterity is the most fervent Prayer of Sir your most Obliged and most Obt: Humble Sert   EDWARD NEWENHAM

PS— Could it be done with Propriety, I wish my respects Could be presented to his Excellency the Count de Vergennes for the Letter he honoured me with to the Marquiss of Pilleu—[3] all my family Join in sincere respects & Esteem—

2. Newenham worried that his "Constant appearance in the Uniform of an Irish Volunteer, might be misinterpreted," unless he had proper introductions: Newenham to WTF, Oct. 13, 1782 (APS). The naval commandant at Toulon was Louis de Fabry de Fabrègues (1715–1794): *DBF;* [Didier Neuville], *État sommaire des archives de la marine antérieures à la Révolution* (Paris, 1898), p. 135n.

3. Through Lafayette's offices, Newenham obtained letters of introduc-

Addressed: To / His Excellency Dr: Franklin— / Passy / near / Paris

Endorsed: Sir E Newenham

Notation: Newenhan 13 Novr. 1782.

From Vergennes: Two Letters

(I) and (II) copies: Archives du Ministère des affaires étrangères

I.

A Vlles. [Versailles] le 13. 9bre. 1782.
J'ai l'honneur de vous prevenir M. que la Cour de Londres ayant fait proposer au Roi de consentir au retablissement de la communication entre Douvres et Calais, S.M. a fait expedier 4 passeports pour un pareil nombre de Batimens Anglois destinés à remplir cet objet.[4] Je vous prie en consequence M. de ne pas differer à donner les ordres que vous croirez necessaires pour que les armateurs et Corsaires Sujets des Etats unis respectent les Batimens Anglois qui se trouveront munis d'un passeport du Roi.

M. franklin

II.

A Vlles. [Versailles] le 13. 9bre. 1782.
J'ai l'honneur, M. de vous envoyer la copie d'une lettre que j'ai recue de M. le Mis. de Castries.[5] Vous y verrez les raisons qui

---

tion from Vergennes to the governors of Toulon, Brest, and Marseille. (Vergennes had done a similar favor in 1779: XXIX, 471.) Toussaint-Alphonse de Fortia, marquis de Piles (or Pilles), was governor of Marseille, and he and his family socialized with the Newenhams during their stay: Newenham's journal, 1782 (National Archives of Canada); Dixon Wecter, "Benjamin Franklin and an Irish 'Enthusiast'," *Huntington Library Quarterly,* IV (1940–41), 216–17; *Dictionnaire de la noblesse,* VIII, 386; *DBF* under Fortia de Piles; *Etat militaire* for 1782, p. 37.

4. On the same day, Vergennes wrote Dutch Minister van Berkenrode about the new arrangements (AAE). The Harwich packet recently had been captured by a privateer: La Vauguyon to Vergennes, Nov. 8 (AAE).

5. Not found.

l'empechent de Se prêter à la demande que vous avez faite de quelques Batiments pour le transport d'un millier de Tonneaux d'effets necessaires à l'armée americaine.[6]

M. franklin

From William Hodgson

ALS: American Philosophical Society

Dear Sir   London 14 Novr. 1782

I duly reced your favor of the 4th.[7] & am much obliged to you for writing to L'Orient, from whence I have not yet heard—it gives me much Concern that our great Folks here neglect their Business so much, they did absolutely agree with me three months ago. To send away the Prisoners *immediately,* I have been teizing Nepean[8] the Under Secretary to Mr Townshend, every week since, to fullfill the agreement, this week he has again solemnly assured me that as soon as a Ship can be provided they shall all go the No. per last Acc't about 240—& he excuses himself for the delay, by alledging Goverment have no Ships to spare for this Service—not many days ago I was sent to from the Secretarys Office to desire I wou'd propose to you to exchange Lt. Col: Tarleton for two Captains of American Privateers— Tarleton, as I understand, was one of the Prisoners at York Town I promised to mention it to you but at the Same Time observed that as they had hitherto absolutely refused to acknowledge any rank in Americans taken & brought into this Country, but treated all as common Men, I did not see how they coud expect it unless they wou'd alter their own Conduct— You will however please to give your Reply to this proposition—as I strongly suspect, no less a person than the Heir Apparent has interposed at the request of a Beautifull Lady, whose favors are occasionally bestowed both on him & the Lt Col.[9] Mr Laurens is returned

6. Shipping was scarce because of the huge convoy being assembled to take troops from Brest to Cadiz for eventual use against Jamaica.

7. BF's response to Hodgson's letter of Oct. 14 is missing.

8. Undersecretary of State Evan Nepean (XXXVII, 124n).

9. The "Beautifull lady" must be Mary Robinson, a former mistress of both Lt. Col. Banastre Tarleton and George, Prince of Wales: *DNB.*

from Bath—renouncing, as I understand, his design of returning to America & intending I have reason to believe for Paris.[1] I
am sorry that the old Affair does not go on better, there seems to
be Cooks in plenty, I fancy our great Man will tatér le poux[2] du
Parlement avant que de determiner finalement—most truly &
Sincerly I remain yrs   WILLIAM HODGSON

Addressed: To / His Excellency / Benj. Franklin Esqr / Passy

From Sir Edward Newenham

ALS: American Philosophical Society

Sir   Marsailles 14 Novr: 1782
    Last post I had the Honor of writing to your Excellency in re-
gard to Irelands being mentioned in the intended treaty between
the Belligerent powers;[3] Permit me, now, to acquaint your Excellency, that I have seen my most Worthy and respectable friend
Mr John Christopher Hornbostel (Partner with Mr: Folsh, the
swedish Consul) who was on former occasions & has lately been
of Infinite Service to me & my family; We have Gratitude & *wish
to serve him.*
    He is the Gentleman whom I mentiond to your Excellency,
whose Early (4 years agoe) attachment to the Interest of the
United States, whose Character & Principles point him out as a
proper Person to be appointed Chief Consul, for Provence and
Languedoc, on the part of America—[4]

---

1. Laurens had just received at Bath an order from Congress to join the
other peace commissioners. He wrote JA on Nov. 12, announcing his intention to comply: *Laurens Papers,* XVI, 55.
    2. "Tâter le pouls" ("take the pulse").
    3. See his letter of Nov. 12[–13].
    4. In 1778 Jean-Christophe Hornbostel had written BF seeking a consul-
ship in Marseille: XXVI, 212, where we mistranscribed his partner's name as
"Fölich". At that time, his partner was the Swedish consul Henri-Jacques
Fölsch. Beginning in 1781, the consulship was held by Fölsch's son, François-
Philippe: Charles Carrière, *Négociants marseillais au XVIIIe siècle* (2 vols.,
Marseille, 1973), II, 733, 1082; *Almanach royal* for 1780, p. 256, for 1781,
p. 264, and for 1782, p. 268. The younger Fölsch courted Newenham's daugh-

Should your Excellency favor him by so honourable an Employment, I shall most Gratefully acknowledge this addition to the many favors you have conferred upon me, and I am confident the United States will find the Greatest Integrity & Satisfaction in his Conduct—

My Family join me in the sincerest respects to you & your Grandson—

I have the Honor, to be, with the warmest respect your Excellencys most obt: and most Humble. sert[5]

EDWARD NEWENHAM

Notation: Newenham 14 Novr. 1782.

From Charles-Joseph Panckoucke[6]

AL: American Philosophical Society

14. 9bre. 1782.

Panckoucke Présente tous Ses respects à monsieur francklin, et Lui envoye La Lettre cy jointe.[7]

M. franklin à passÿ.

---

ter Margaretta despite her father's objections, and the couple was married at the beginning of January, 1783. Newenham then left for Italy with the rest of his family, a trip for which he sought and received from WTF a new set of introductions: Newenham's journal, 1782 (National Archives of Canada); James Kelly, *Sir Edward Newenham MP, 1734–1814: Defender of the Protestant Constitution* (Dublin, 2004), pp. 183, 300; Newenham to WTF, Dec. 8 and 30, 1782, and Jan. 2[–5], 1783. Newenham had also written to WTF on Nov. 17 that two of his mares in Ireland were in foal; he had promised one of the offspring to Lafayette, and he offered the other to WTF. All these letters are at the APS.

5. Newenham reiterated his request for a consulship for Hornbostel before leaving Marseille: Newenham to WTF, Jan. 2[–5], 1783, APS.

6. This is the only extant letter from Panckoucke, the leading Parisian bookseller and publisher. For a biography see George B. Watts, "Charles Joseph Panckoucke, 'l'Atlas de la librairie française,'" *Studies on Voltaire and the Eighteenth Century,* LXVIII (Geneva, 1969), 67–205.

7. Panckoucke enclosed a Nov. 12 letter he had received from Etienne-Alexandre-Jacques Anisson-Duperron, son of the director of the Imprimerie royale (XXVI, 519) and himself the director-designate: much as Anis-

To Vergennes LS:[8] Archives du Ministère des affaires étrangères

Sir, Passy 15. November 1782.

I received the Letter you did me the honour of writing to me the 13th. Inst, and I loose no time in forwarding to your Excellency the Orders you desire for the 4 English Vessels destined to pass between Dover and Calais;[9] tho' I am persuaded the Passports they are furnished with from his most Christian majesty; would have been sufficient Protection to them, against all Vessels belonging to the United States.

With great Respect I am, Sir, Your Excellency's most obedient and most humble Servant B FRANKLIN

Mr. Le Cte. De Vergennes.

Endorsed: M. Hennin[1]

---

son was flattered by BF's interest, he was not willing to show his printing press until it was perfected. As Panckoucke knew, it was still under construction. As soon as it was finished, he would be honored to show it to BF. APS.

Anisson and others were trying to improve both the pressure of the standard wooden printing press and the size of its platen so that folio sheets could be printed in one pass rather than two. He presented his new press to the Academy of Sciences in 1783, and in 1785 published an illustrated account, *Premier mémoire sur l'impression en lettres, suivi de la description d'une nouvelle presse exécutée pour le service du roi; et publié par ordre du gouvernement.* His design influenced François-Ambroise Didot (XXXVI, 193), whose second "improved" press was markedly similar to Anisson's, and the two men quarreled about who had invented the modifications: *DBF;* André Jammes, *Les Didots: Trois siècles de typographie & de bibliophilie, 1698–1998* (Paris, 1998), pp. 11–13; Bibliothèque nationale, *L'Art du livre à l'imprimerie nationale des origines à nos jours* (Paris, 1951), pp. 17, 80, 89.

8. In L'Air de Lamotte's hand.

9. Below, Nov. 16.

1. Gérard de Rayneval departed a second time for England on or soon after Nov. 15, and on Nov. 20 he began new meetings with Shelburne in hopes of finding a way for the Spaniards to obtain Gibraltar, so they would accept peace: Doniol, *Histoire,* v, 211–22; Dull, *French Navy,* pp. 321–2; Morris, *Jay: Peace,* pp. 481, 483. In his absence, letters normally assigned to him for drafting a reply were given to his fellow *premier commis,* Pierre-Michel Hennin (XXX, 164n).

From Benjamin Franklin Bache

ALS: American Philosophical Society

Dear Grand Papa   Geneva 15 9ber 1782

I wrote this pacquet as soon as possible Because My Cousin told me that there was an opportunity of sending them and as Mama Desires it all in english I wrote them with much of dificulty by that means I hope to make some Progress in the english language.[2]

I hope you have received the picture and the letter I sent you.[3]

I shoud be very happy if I had my parents with me but for only that I am quite unhappy, My life is uniforme, I get up at half after 7, I brekfast to 8, from 8 to 11 I am in class[4] at 11 I have a Latin Lesson to 12, from 12 to 1 I Dine and learn By heart a Lesson that our Regent gives'us, from 1 to 3 I go to class, from 3 to 5 I do a task luncheon and do a theme, from 5 to 6 I have an'other latin Lesson from 6 to 7 I translate Joseph andrews and write my Journal from 7[5] I do my Drawing lesson to 8, and, then, I sup and go to bed. That is the work I do the Monday the tuesday and friday; the Wednesday and Saturday I have no drawing master almost every thursday and Sunday I go too Me [Mme] Cramer's[6] if I don't go, the thursday I arrainge my things write my Journal, and translate.

I am My Dear Grand Papa Your most Dutiful and affectionate Son   B. FRANKLIN B.

Johonnot presents his respects to you and desires yo would send his letters

---

2. BFB had sent his parents a letter in English around the new year (APS), but had not written BF in English since October, 1779: XXX, 586–7. His subsequent letters are all in English.

3. Dated [on or after Oct. 3], above.

4. Classes had resumed on Monday, Nov. 4, after a month off for the vintage holiday; see BFB's letter of Oct. 1.

5. BFB averaged seven entries a month from August through December. On Dec. 5, his final entry for the year, he resolved: "Je compte ne rien faire que patiner dans mes moments de récreation cest pourqoi je veux oublier entièrement Mon journal jusqu'a l'année Prochaine."

6. As he had been doing since the early days of his stay in Geneva: XXXV, 73.

Mr Cramer de Lon the son presents also his respects to you.[7]

Addressed: To / Doctor Franklin / a Passy

From Castries

Copy: Archives de la Marine

A vlles. [Versailles] le 15 9bre. 1782.

Je vois, Monsieur, par ce que M Le Cte. d'hector Commandant la Marine à Brest, me marque, qu'il a prevenu le Commre. des Guerres chargé des Effets des Etats Unis de l'Amerique,[8] qu'il doit les tenir prêts a etre embarqués et qu'il lui sera fourni des moyens pour les faire passer à l'orient, et à Rochefort; mais comme M le Cte. d'hector estime qu'il est necessaire que vous fassiez connoitre s'il n'y a pas de choix à faire dans les quantités et dans les qualités, je vous prie de me mettre en etat d'informer ce commandant de ce qui doit étre observé à cet egard.

J'ai l'honneur d'être avec une parfaite consideration, Monsieur, votre &c.

M franklin

From William Jones

ALS: American Philosophical Society

Lamb Building Temple. 15 Nov. 1782.

My dear and respected Friend,

I should have hastened, if an earlier opportunity had presented itself, to impart to you a piece of intelligence, which, I flatter myself, will give you pleasure. My profile will, I hope, have the honour of being hung up in your apartment with those of a family, whom you love and revere, and by whom you are loved and revered with the greatest cordiality. My connexion with the excellent bishop of St. Asaph, by my marriage with his eldest daughter (of whom I have heard you speak with approbation) is now settled, and will take place as soon as we can be

---

7. Jean-François Cramer: XXXVI, 233n; XXXVII, 683.
8. Palteau de Veimerange.

united with a prudent attention to our worldly interests, and to the highest of all interests, our independence.[9] I consider it as the pride and triumph of my life, that I am received with open arms into a family, which you and I have always known to contain a rare assemblage of publick and private virtues. We were always talking of you in Hampshire, and longing to enjoy again your sweet society: sometimes we were charmed with tidings, that you were coming with an olive wreath to England; at other times we were afflicted with reports of your labouring under a painful illness. I hope to be relieved to-day from that affliction, as I dine with Mr. Hodgson, who, I hope, has heard from you lately. Your friends of the club[1] will heartily join in drinking your health and wishing you among them. I will request Mr. H. to transmit to you the letters, which you had the kindness to write for poor Paradise and myself, and which a variety of accidents prevented my sending to you from Nantz or leaving with your nephew.[2] Mr. Paradise, whom, when I wrote to you last, I did not suppose capable of his excessive weakness,[3] assures all his friends, that You and Mr. Jay told him there was no kind of necessity for his going to Virginia in obedience to the act of assembly, but that his property is in safety and in good hands. I fear he deceived himself, but heartily wish that he understood you right: he could not have better authority. He is certainly described particularly and by design in a special clause of the act, which clause itself was inserted through indulgence in consequence of his letters sent in

9. Georgiana Shipley had sent silhouettes of her family at BF's request; see XXXVII, 455, 458. William Jones proposed marriage to Anna Maria Shipley on Oct. 25: Georgiana Shipley to BF, Oct. 2, above; Garland Cannon, *The Life and Mind of Oriental Jones: Sir William Jones, the Father of Modern Linguistics* (Cambridge, New York, and Port Chester, N.Y., 1990), p. 182.

1. The Club of Thirteen: XXXV, 46n.

2. Letters to Bowdoin, Jefferson, and Livingston on behalf of Jones and Paradise: XXXVII, 630, 630–1, 631–2.

3. Jones's latest letter was dated Aug. 5: XXXVII, 704–5. He wrote numerous friends to justify his desertion of Paradise by denigrating him: Cannon, *Oriental Jones,* p. 180; Archibald B. Shepperson, *John Paradise and Lucy Ludwell of London and Williamsburg* (Richmond, 1942), p. 177. Paradise returned to London rather than traveling to Virginia to prevent his wife's estates being sequestered: XXXV, 26n; XXXVI, 655n; XXXVII, 704n.

your dispatches.[4] "Good will to men and peace on earth" is my anxious prayer; and that you may enjoy the fruit of all your glorious toil and revisit your friends with full splendor and dignity is the fervent wish, of, my dear Sir, Your much obliged and faithful Servant   W. JONES.

P.S. Georgiana is engaged to a young man named Hare.[5] May she be happy!

To All Captains and Commanders of American Vessels

DS:[6] American Philosophical Society, Biblioteca Estense of Modena, Italy

[November 16, 1782]

To all Captains and Commanders of Vessels of War,
Privateers and Letters of Marque
belonging to the United States of America

His most Christian Majesty having consented to the Proposition of the Court of London for renewing the Communication between Dover and Calais, and having to that Effect granted Pass-ports for a like Number of English Vessels, to fulfil that Object— And his Minister for Foreign Affairs having by a Letter to us of the thirteenth Instant, requested, We would give immediate Orders to all Subjects of the United States of America to respect the Vessels thus protected by the Pass-ports of his most Christian Majesty:

---

4. Although Paradise (who had claimed Greek rather than British citizenship) was not exempted by name, the courts of inquisition discontinued their hearings into his wife's estates: Shepperson, *Paradise,* pp. 147–9.

5. Jonathan Shipley opposed her marriage to the author Francis Hare-Naylor, which did not occur until 1784: XVIII, 200n. Hare-Naylor (1753–1815) was a member of the circle of Georgiana's cousin, Georgiana Cavendish, duchess of Devonshire: *DNB* under Hare-Naylor.

6. Both DS are in L'Air de Lamotte's hand, and the right margins of both are trimmed. The two vary slightly in wording. We have supplied the missing word endings on the APS copy based on our reading of the second version.

We therefore the Minister Plenipotentiary of the sd. United States at the Court of France hereby request you to let all such Vessels pass & repass according to the tenor of their Pass-ports, without any Molestation or Hindrance.

Given at Passy this 16th. Day of November 1782.

B FRANKLIN

From William Carmichael   ALS: American Philosophical Society

Sir   Madrid 16 Novr. 1782

Mr Jays acquaintance with the Ct. de Rechteren[7] who does me the honor to ask an Introduction to your Excy might preclude the necessity of the present Address, If I had not a strong desire of convincing the Count of my sense of his Civilities and of my connection with you— I might from your Long Silence conclude that he will owe much more to his own merit than to my Introduction, if the Strong desire that I have always Manifested to be regarded Amongst the Number of your Friends & the proofs that I have heretofore recd of your Indulgence did not flatter me, that in this Instance your Reception of the Person whom I have the honor to present to you, will not fail to Convince him that you regard me still Among the number of Your Excys. Obliged Friends & Humble Serts   WM. CARMICHAEL

His Excy Benjm. Franklin

Notation: Carmichael 16 Nov. 1782.

7. Jacob Godefroy (or Godfried), graaf van Rechteren (1736–1831), was the Dutch envoy to Spain from 1773 to 1793: *Repertorium der diplomatischen Vertreter*, III, 269; *NNBW*, v, 567–8.

From Johann Thaddeus de Ehet and Other Consulship Seekers

The expectation that the independence of the United States would soon be recognized by all the powers of Europe caused many to anticipate the need for agents to represent American commercial and other interests in Europe. On November 16, Johann Thaddeus de Ehet wrote in German from Augsburg, offering his services. Franklin wrote on the letter: "Mr Grand is requested to procure a Translation of this Letter, or at least some Account of its purport." We publish below the French summary that Franklin received.[8]

On December 7, the abbé Bertholon, writing from the Hôtel des invalides in Paris and signing himself as a member of numerous academies and a professor of experimental physics, renews his acquaintance with Franklin[9] for the purpose of recommending a man he knows well, Pierre Galibert, a merchant from Beziers. Galibert has experience in foreign trade and is extremely trustworthy. Bertholon undoubtedly forwarded an undated petition from Galibert, who describes himself as a merchant of Sète and proposes himself as a consul from that port. He asks Franklin to consider the advantages of Sète over Bordeaux: the wines and brandies are not subject to the heavy duties of Bordeaux, and there is ready access to both the woolens of Languedoc and the silks of Lyon. He puts himself forward as the man to teach the American captains the customs of the country and to direct them in their mercantile affairs.[1]

André [Andrew] Chester writes an undated memoir (presumably in December), in hopes of being named consul at Marseille. The son of an immigrant from Derby, England, he is 42 years old and since August, 1778, has been the official English translator for the Admiralty of Marseille.[2] Recently, when the first American ship appeared at that

8. All the documents discussed in this headnote are at the APS and are in French unless otherwise noted.

9. Bertholon had written on lightning rods and the aurora borealis: xxv, 668–9; xxviii, 190.

1. Both letters are at the Hist. Soc. of Pa. A Galibert fils at Beziers specialized in wines and brandies: *Almanach des marchands*, p. 97.

2. During the first year of his appointment, Chester assisted William Kentisbear, an American imprisoned at Marseille: xxviii, 87. Chester was also partner in the mercantile firm of Chester & Duff: Charles Carrière, *Négociants marseillais au XVIIIe siècle* (2 vols., Marseille, 1973), II, 743.

port, Chester was named to fill the role of consul, there being no duly appointed official for the young nation.[3] His training and experience qualify him for the position of consul, and he attaches testimonials from high officials at Marseille: Pléville Le Pelley, naval commandant at Marseille; Gaudemar, an admiralty official; Bertin, commissary of the port; and the marquis de Miran, commandant of Provence.[4]

Cavelier fils, a merchant and former city official at Dieppe,[5] is keen to promote the port at Dieppe where many ships are being built. The rates for transporting goods from Picardy, Normandy, and other provinces to Dieppe are low, and the considerable commerce derived from the local saltworks has secured to the city trade links throughout the kingdom. With the coming peace, the city's large tobacco manufactory offers a wealth of opportunities to American merchants who can exchange American tobacco for local dry goods and all that the nearby market of Paris can supply. Cavelier begs the American minister to appoint him consul at Dieppe. Mr. Deane, an American residing in the Dieppe suburbs to whom Franklin administered the oath of allegiance, has promised to speak to Franklin of Cavelier's helpfulness in lodging troops there in 1780. Both the comte Dethianges, lieutenant

3. The first American ship to arrive in Marseille was the *Wolf*, Capt. Samuel Butler, on Sept. 16, 1782. See Butler's letter to BF, mistakenly printed under Sept. 30, 1781: XXXV, 540–1. In a letter to BF of Oct. 2, above, the firm of Rolland frères claims to have been nominated by the captain of the *Wolf* to act on behalf of its owners.

4. Chester enclosed these testimonials, signed in mid-December, and the undated memoir, described above, in a letter of Jan. 1, 1783, to a M. Chevalier at Paris. Evidently the packet did not reach BF for two months, when Jacques-Philippe Grattepain, *dit* Morizot (1754–1823), *avocat au Parlement* and Lafayette's treasurer and estate manager, forwarded Chester's memoir and testimonials: Morizot to BF, March 8, 1783 (APS); Jean Fromageot, *Jacques Philippe Grattepain dit Morizot: Procureur Général et Spécial des Biens du Marquis de La Fayette et de plusieurs nobles familles, Député de l'Aube au Corps Législatif et Vigneron Militant (Arthonnay 1754—Balnot sur Laignes 1823)* (Tonnerre, 1982), pp. 1, 4–6, 8–9.

Chester addressed a second undated memoir to BF in which he restated his desire to be named consul. He made no mention of the earlier memoir, but said that he has been the interpreter at the Marseille admiralty for five years (APS).

5. Cavelier and his father are listed in the *Almanach des marchands*, p. 175, as agents of the city saltworks. Although his letter is not dated, an allusion to a future peace suggests that Cavelier wrote sometime in 1782.

general in the royal army,[6] and the abbé Marie, professor of mathematics,[7] can testify to his suitability for the consulship.

Jacques Chapel writes on January 9 from Valenciennes, where he has a batiste factory. He thanks Franklin for his willingness, at the marquis de Castries' behest, to assist him in forming ties with American commercial houses in the United States and in Europe.[8] His wife, who will present this letter, will deliver notices he has had printed describing the articles he can supply and giving directions for placing orders. Will Franklin also support his candidacy as American agent for the coastal area between Calais and Ostend? he asks in conclusion.

Writing from her mother-in-law's address, rue Chapon in the Marais, on January 16, Mme Mandat de Fraguier[9] recommends for the post of consul at Lyon a man of merit, the sieur Nivière, who has been recommended to her by the abbé Rojat. She encloses the abbé's letter to her and sends greetings from her husband.

On January 20, Jean-Guillaume (Johann Wilhelm) Backhaus, a doctor of law, writes from Hanover to offer his services in public as well as commercial affairs.[1] Planning to move to Hamburg, he encloses a four-page memoir describing the advantages to the United States of having a consular presence in that city, where all the princes and states of Europe are represented. He himself is a former representative of the duchy of Holstein, and can draw on his negotiating

6. Probably Amable-Gaspard, vicomte and later comte de Thianges: *Almanach royal* for 1782, p. 152, and for 1787, p. 157; Mazas, *Ordre de Saint-Louis*, I, 449n; II, 257, 440. A different comte de Thianges, *maître de la garde-robe* to the comte d'Artois, is listed in the *Almanach royal* for 1782, p. 131.

7. Joseph-François Marie (1738–1801) was professor of mathematics at the Collège Mazarin and in 1782 was named preceptor to the sons of the comte d'Artois: Mlle M. Locoarret and Mme Ter-Menassian, "Les Universités," in *Enseignement et diffusion des sciences en France au XVIIIe siècle*, ed. René Taton *et al.* (Paris, 1964), pp. 145, 743.

8. Chapel's letter to BF of Sept. 7, 1784, states that he had given BF a letter of support from Castries (APS).

9. Marie-Françoise-Félicité Mandat de Fraguier (b. 1742). She was married to Nicolas-Ambroise (Ambroise-Nicolas), marquis de Fraguier (1724–1795), son of the marquise de Saint-Auban by her first husband, Martin Fraguier, seigneur de Tigery (b. 1683), president of the Chambre des comptes: XXXVI, 257n, 282n; *DBF* under Fraguier; *Dictionnaire de la noblesse*, VIII, 522–3; XIII, 108.

1. In 1790, Backhaus published at Hamburg a treatise on the preferential rights of creditors: Johann Christian Koppe, *Lexicon der ... juristischen Schriftsteller* (Leipzig, 1793); Johann Heinrich Stepf, *Gallerie aller juridischen Autoren . . .* (4 vols., Leipzig, 1820–25).

experience and his contacts in several Courts of Europe as well as with most of the artisans and manufacturers of Germany. He intends to associate with one of the most reliable commercial houses of Hamburg to ensure the best service to the Americans. Finally, he offers to serve as the intermediary for all mail from America to be distributed in Germany, and he is willing to forward to America letters from merchants and manufacturers of Germany and northern Europe.[2]

French summary and ALS:[3] American Philosophical Society

[November 16, 1782]

Mr Jno. Thaddeus de Ehet à Augsbourg, conseiller à la Chambre pour l'Inspection des Comptes, profite de l'Epoque où l'Indépendance des Etats unis d'Amérique est reconnue par l'Angleterre, & où elle ne doit pas tarder à l'etre par les autres puissances de l'Europe, en particulier par la Diete de l'Empire, pour réitérer Sa prière à Monsieur le Docteur Franklin, au Sujet de la Correspondence que les Etats unis ne manqueront pas d'avoir avec les principales villes d'Allemagne, & lui offre Ses Services pour les matières de Politique, Commerce & Jurisprudence qui pourront les intéresser à Augsbourg.

C'est le but de Sa longue lettre ègalement mal ècrite & mal orthographiée.

From Luigi Pio   AL: American Philosophical Society

à Paris ce 16. Nove. 1782.
Hôtel de Montmorency chaussée d'Antin. / .

M. de Pio, chargé des affaires de la Cour de Naples, a l'honneur de faire bien des complimens à Monsieur Franklin, Ministre Plénipotentiaire des Etats-unis de l'amerique septentrionale, et de Le prier de lui dire, si dans le tems il a reçu une Lettre de Mr. *Filangieri* de Naples, L'Auteur de *l'Essai sur la Legislation.*[4] Il en

---

2. Backhaus sent this letter care of *premier commis* Edmond-Charles-Edouard Genet: Backhaus to BF, March 8, 1783 (Hist. Soc. of Pa.).

3. The French summary, in an unknown hand, was made at BF's request (as explained in the headnote) from a three-and-a-half-page ALS in German.

4. See Filangieri to BF, Aug. 24.

est inquiet, d'autant plus que Mr. Filangeri ne désire pas mieux que de meriter l'estime, et les bontés du plus grand Philosophe du nouveau monde, et qui merite bien de l'être de celui-ci qu'il a eclairé et qu'il eclaire, toujours.

M. de Pio prie Mr. franklin de lui faire l'honneur d'un mot de reponse.

Notation: Mr. Pio Paris 16 Novr. 1782

From Richard Price   ALS: American Philosophical Society

My Dear Friend   Newington-Green Nov: 18th: 1782

I have for Some time been intending and wishing to write to you; and I now embrace with great pleasure the opportunity of doing this which offers itself by Mr Laurens, now in deep affliction occasioned by the loss of his Son,[5] but happily restored in some measure to health after his long and hard and cruel confinemt: in the Tower. He is, I understand, going on an important commission to *Paris,* to wch: may God grant Success. One of the chief obstacles to Peace is, I hope, now removed by the acknowledgmt: of the independence of America. After many doubts and fears during the course of this war I now See with unspeakable Satisfaction this object Secured, new constitutions of Governmt: favourable to liberty civil and religious established in America, and a refuge there provided for the friends of truth and humanity. This is the consummation of the present contest wch: has been all along the object of my anxious wishes; and, I hope, I may now rejoyce with you on having lived to it. I am Sensible, however, that it is not yet certain how the present negotiations will terminate. God forbid that thro' the pride of this country there Should be a continuation of the war. Could my wishes have had any influence, our new ministers upon the first change would have immediately acknowledged the inde-

5. Col. John Laurens was killed on Aug. 27, 1782, in a skirmish with the British at Chehaw Neck, near Charleston. His father learned of his death in a Nov. 6 letter from JA: John Vaughan to WTF, [Oct.] 10, 1782 (APS); *Laurens Papers,* XV, 605; XVI, 52–3, 55–6; Gregory D. Massey, *John Laurens and the American Revolution* (Columbia, S.C., 2000), pp. 226–31.

pendence of America, and on this ground open'd a negotiation for a *general* peace and made Such concessions as would most probably have brought it about before this time. I have allways deliver'd my Sentimts: freely to Ld Shelburne on these Subjects. We have differ'd much in our opinions about them, but our friendship has continued. I am sorry to observe so much distrust prevailing with respect to him, and I hope he will prove it to be groundless by restoring to this country the blessings of peace and using the power he now possesses to establish oeconomy in our finances and to produce Such a reformation in our Parliament as Shall make it a *real* representation instead of Such a mockery and nusance as it is at present.

I learnt with much pain Some time ago from Dr Hamilton[6] that you were ill of the gout and Stone, but I have been lately informed that you are recover'd. May your life be preserved, and crowned with every enjoymt: that can make the remainder of it happy. I am getting fast after you into the evening of life. Soon the night will Shut in upon us; but, I trust, we Shall See light again and be raised up to enjoy the happiness of brighter days in better regions. This, I don't doubt, will be the lot of all the virtuous and worthy— I have lost within a few months about half a Score of my acquaintance and friends. Such is the consequence of advancing far in the journey of life. One fellow-traveller drops after another till at last we are left to travel alone. I thank God my wife is continued to me; and She desires me to present her best respects to you— We are often talking of you at the little Society of whigs at the London-Coffee-house. We are proud of Still numbering you among our members; and I now begin to flatter myself with the hope, that the time may not be far distant when the return of peace may bring you among us once more.— In a little time I Shall probably write to you again in order to introduce to your notice a Gentleman, one of our club chosen

6. Most likely Dr. William Hamilton (1758–1807), an Irish physician who received his M.D. from the University of Edinburgh (1779) and was a member of the Coffee House Philosophical Society: T. H. Levere and G. L'E. Turner, eds., *Discussing Chemistry and Steam: the Minutes of a Coffee House Philosophical Society, 1780–1787* (Oxford, 2002), pp. 11, 23, 45–6. In previous volumes, we identified him as the Irish naturalist of the same name: XXIX, 99n; XXXII, 301n; XXXIV, 198n.

Since you left us, who is going to leave this kingdom and to Settle for life with his fortune in America.[7] Thither probably, when this contest is over, will many be flocking from all Europe.

Dr Priestley is warmly engaged in his litterary and philosophical pursuits. He has lately discover'd that the *Phlogiston* of the Chymists is the Same with inflammable air; but of this and his other discoveries he will himself probably give you an account.[8] There is in the press a new work of his about wch: he has taken great pains and from wch. I expect much instruction, entitled A *history of the corruptions of Christianity*—[9] I am just now writing about loans, the finances and the public debts; but without the hope of doing much good. I have been for these two years employ'd in preparing a new edition of my Treatise on Annuities, Assurances of lives, population &c. As this work has been well received and this is the 4th: Edition of it I have been anxious about making it as complete as possible. I have enlarged it to two volumes and one half of it will be new. Some time or other this winter I hope to be able to desire your acceptance of a copy.—[1] I received Some months ago a very kind letter from you[2] which indeed made me very happy. I hope you will continue to favour me with your correspondence. We may now, as you have observed, write more freely to one another. With the most affectionate regard I am, my Dear Friend, ever yours

RICHD: PRICE

The inclosed letter from Miss Georgiana Shipley[3] was Sent me Several weeks ago from *Chilbolton* (where the Bishop's family now is) to be deliver'd to the Gentleman mentioned in this let-

7. Archibald Redford, whom Price introduced in his next letter to BF, March 10, 1783 (Yale University Library). Redford, a supporter of the American cause, had been educated as a dissenting clergyman and later joined the Club of Honest Whigs: Adair Crawford to Benjamin Vaughan, [c. March 11, 1783] (APS).

8. Priestley had given BF an account of this experiment on June 24: XXXVII, 532–3.

9. XXXVI, 238n.

1. *Observations on Reversionary Payments* ... (2 vols., 4th ed., London, 1783).

2. XXXVII, 472–3.

3. Georgiana Shipley to BF, Oct. 2, above.

ter, and who I then thot: would have been going soon for *Paris*. But this gentleman (Mr Retford) delaying his journey[4] the letter has been kept by me, and is now Sent by Mr Laurens.

A match is agree'd upon between Miss Shipley (the eldest Single Sister) and Mr Jones, *once* the close and intimate friend of Mr Paradise but now unhappily Separated by a quarrel. Miss Georgiana also, I hrd is engaged.[5] The Seal of her letter was broken by accident, but it has never been open'd.

British Counterproposal to the Second Draft Treaty: Selected Articles

Copy:[6] Massachusetts Historical Society

When Henry Strachey arrived in London on November 10, the British Cabinet was summoned to review the second draft treaty.[7] Shelburne urged the members to come to a "provisional agreement" with America. The King reluctantly agreed to accept independence, rationalizing that "knavery seems to be so much the striking feature of [America's] Inhabitants that it may not in the end be an evil that they become Aliens to this Kingdom."[8]

The Cabinet first met on November 11 and continued deliberations on November 14 and 15, drafting and unanimously approving this counterproposal, which the Americans could either "take or leave." Townshend delivered the proposal to the King on the evening of November 19. That night George III approved it out of "necessity not conviction."[9]

4. Redford did not leave until at least the following March: Price to BF, March 10, 1783, Yale University Library.

5. For both engagements see William Jones to BF, Nov. 15.

6. In JA's hand. He introduced the copy with the following note: "Monday, Nov. 25. 1782. The Three Commissioners Adams, Franklin and Jay, met at Mr Oswalds Lodgings at the Hotel de Muscovie, and after Some Conferences, Mr Oswald delivered them the following Articles, as fresh Proposals of the British Ministry, Sent by Mr Stratchey, vizt." The full text is in Wharton, *Diplomatic Correspondence*, VI, 74–7.

7. For Strachey's arrival see Fortescue, *Correspondence of George Third*, VI, 153–4. The second draft treaty, [Nov. 4–7], is above.

8. Fortescue, *Correspondence of George Third*, VI, 153, 154.

9. Fortescue, *Correspondence of George Third*, VI, 155–7; Harlow, *Second British Empire*, I, 293–4; Richard B. Morris, *The Peacemakers: the Great Pow-*

The British counterproposal retained almost *verbatim* several sections of the second draft treaty; other sections were substantially revised. Many of the paragraphs were rearranged, and the whole was divided into numbered articles. That order and numbering system was retained in the final version of the Preliminary Articles, published below under November 30. We describe here the overall proposal and print below only those articles that the British substantially revised from the second draft treaty and that would be revised again for the final version of the Preliminary Articles, so that readers may examine the evolution of the commissioners' language.

The first three paragraphs of the counterproposal were substantially unchanged, and in fact were carried over from the first draft treaty as agreed to by Jay, Franklin, and Oswald in early October.[1] The third paragraph, naming the states, constituted Article 1, as it had in the first draft treaty.

Article 2, setting the boundaries of the United States, copied the "lakes and rivers line" option given to the British by the American commissioners along with the second draft treaty. Though the British hoped that Strachey would achieve a more favorable boundary, this article was retained *verbatim* in the Preliminary Articles.

Article 7 declared a cessation of hostilities and was almost identical to Article 2 of the first draft treaty, whose language was carried over to the second draft.[2]

Article 8, about free navigation of the Mississippi River, was adopted from the second draft treaty with the addition of a final phrase of clarification.[3]

---

ers and American Independence (New York, Evanston, and London, 1965), pp. 367–8.

1. The one exception was the removal of two words at the end of the first paragraph of Article 1. The British changed "the following are, and shall remain to be their Boundaries" to "the following are and shall be their Boundaries". This change was retained in the final version of the Preliminary Articles.

2. There were two differences. The first clause of the article was dropped, so that the sentence began, "There Shall be a firm and perpetual Peace . . ." Secondly, the promise that the King would withdraw all his armies from American soil "forthwith" was changed to "with all convenient Speed." The American commissioners later agreed to these changes.

3. The British added that navigation would be free and open "to the Subjects of Great Britain and Citizens of the United States." The American commissioners agreed to this change.

The Separate Article was changed from the second draft treaty in two ways. The counterproposal's version ended with the phrase "due East to the River Apalachicola," thereby deleting the reference to the northern border of West Florida as extending to the junction of that river with the Flint (Flynt) River. This change, which left this portion of the border implied, was retained in the Preliminary Articles. The counterproposal also changed the word "Conclusion" (referring to the war) to "End." The Preliminary Articles retained the word "Conclusion."

We publish below the texts of Articles 3 through 6, which addressed the most contentious issues of the negotiations: fisheries, debts owed to British creditors, and the treatment of Loyalists. Townshend told the King that Articles 4, 5, and 6 were the ones that Oswald must insist on; the others were subject to negotiation.[4] It was Strachey, not Oswald, who explained the British positions on these issues when he presented this counterproposal to the American commissioners on November 25. His remarks are published below, under that date.

[November 19, 1782][5]

Article 3.[6]

The Citizens of The Said United States Shall have *the Liberty* of taking Fish of every Kind on all the Banks of Newfoundland, and also in the Gulph of St. Laurence; and also to dry and cure their Fish on the Shores of the Isle of Sables and on the Shores of any of the unsettled Bays, Harbours, and Creeks of the Magdalene Islands, in the Gulph of St Laurence, So long as Such Bays, Harbours and Creeks Shall continue and remain unsettled; on Condition that the Citizens of the Said United States do not exercise the Fishery, but at the Distance of three Leagues from all the Coasts, belonging to Great Britain, as well those of the

4. Fortescue, *Correspondence of George Third*, VI, 156–7.
5. The date on which George III approved this proposal.
6. By substituting "Liberty" for "Right," eliminating Nova Scotia as a location for drying fish, and denying inshore fishing, the Cabinet drastically altered the Americans' article. Shelburne told Oswald that this was to guard against "the Bickerings of Fishermen," citing his adherence to the principle that BF had advocated at the outset of negotiations, "the necessity of laying the Foundation of permanent Peace": Shelburne to Oswald, Nov. 23 (Giunta, *Emerging Nation*, I, 682). Strachey also emphasized this motive in his Nov. 25 remarks to the commissioners (below).

Continent as those of the Islands Situated in the Gulph of St Laurence. And as to what relates to the Fishery on the Coasts of the Island of Cape Breton out of the Said Gulph, the Citizens of the Said United States, Shall not be permitted to exercise the Said Fishery, but at the Distance of fifteen Leagues from the Coasts of the Island of Cape Breton.

Article 4.

It is agreed that the British Creditors Shall meet with no lawful Impediment to the Recovery of the full Value in Sterling Money of Such bona fide Debts as were contracted by any Persons who are Citizens of the Said United States before the Year 1775.

Article 5.[7]

It is agreed that Restitution Shall be made of all Estates, Rights and Properties in America, which have been confiscated during the War.

Article 6.

There Shall be a full and entire Amnesty of all Acts and Offences, which have been or may be Supposed to have been committed on either Side by reason of the War, and in the Course thereof; and no one shall hereafter Suffer in Life or Person, or be deprived of his Property, for the Part he may have taken therein. All Persons, in Confinement on that Account, Shall immediately on the Ratification of the Treaty in America,

7. In his Nov. 23 letter to Oswald cited above, Shelburne claimed that the articles relating to the Loyalists (Articles 5 and 6) were not motivated by interest. "'Tis a higher Principle—This Country is not reduc'd to Terms of *Humiliation*, and certainly will not suffer them from America." Shelburne knew, however, that when Parliament reconvened, the approval of the treaty and the survival of his government depended on the Americans agreeing to articles protecting the interests of the Loyalists. Shelburne went on to admit as much to Oswald: "If Ministers through Timidity or Indolence could be induc'd to give way; I am persuaded the Nation would rise to do itself Justice, & to recover it's wounded Honor." Strachey told the American commissioners on Nov. 25 that Article 5 was the "the grand Point upon which a final Settlement depends."

be set at Liberty: all Prosecutions which may be depending in Consequence of any of the said Offences, Shall cease, and no fresh Prosecutions Shall at any time hereafter be commenced thereupon.

From the Baron d'Espagnac[8]

AL: University of Pennsylvania Library

aux Invalides le 19. 9bre. 1782.

Le Baron d'Espagnac prie Monsieur de francklin d'agréer Ses Excuses et Ses Regrets de L'Impossibilité où il Se trouve de se rendre a L'honneur de Son invitation Jeudy prochain vingt un du Courant, lui étant Survenu depuis Dimanche dernier des Coliques d'Entrailles qui ne lui permettent d'aller manger nulle part; dès que Sa Santé Sera rétablie, Il aura L'honneur d'aller demander à Diner à Monsieur de francklin et de lui renouveller les hommages de Ses Sentimens de dévouement et de Respect.

Notations: Le Baron d'Espagnac / [*in William Temple Franklin's hand:*] Partie remise

From David Hartley

ALS: Library of Congress

My Dear friend London Nov 19 1782

I take the opportunity of Mr Laurens going to Paris[9] to transmitt one line to you, only to express to you my constant & affec-

---

8. Jean-Baptiste-Joseph d'Amarzit de Sahuguet, baron d'Espagnac (1713–1783), *maréchal de camp*, adjoint governor of the Hôtel royal des invalides, and author of several works on the art of warfare: *DBF;* Quérard, *France littéraire*. It was he who hosted the 1778 meal at the Invalides where Parmentier's potato bread was served to a group of high government officials and academicians: XXVII, 578; Bachaumont, *Mémoires secrets,* XII, 155. Later, at the opening ceremonies for the Ecole gratuite de boulangerie, Cadet de Vaux praised him for the changes introduced at the military hospital's bakery: *Jour. de Paris,* June 11, 1780. The baron died on Feb. 28, 1783, and the *Jour. de Paris* ran a 3½-page obituary in the March 21 sup.

9. Laurens left for Paris on Nov. 20: *Laurens Papers,* XVI, xlv.

tionate remembrance of you, in your public character, & as a private friend; And my sincerest wishes for your personal health & happiness, and for success to all your pacific Counsels. The report wch prevails at present on this side of the water, is, that the negotiators at Paris have made some considerable progress towards pacification. Such news wd be acceptable to every country in the world. I shall be very glad to hear from you with any information upon that subject wch it may be proper for you to give; because many of the documents wch have appeared in public require explanation. I am anxious in the cause of peace. You will allways find me persevering in those pacific principles wch have hitherto been the guide of my thoughts and conduct. It was at one time proposed to me, that I shd have been employed in the negotiation.[1] It seemed at that time to be so near the point, that I was requested to keep myself in readiness at the shortest notice. However that proposition passed off. I am ready to confess to you, that such an office wd have been most acceptable to me; And doubly so to have conspired with you in the common of humanity and peace. Your ever affecte   D H.

From Mathew Carey[2]   AL: American Philosophical Society

This brief undated note, Carey's first extant letter to Franklin and the only one we know that either man sent the other during the year Carey lived in France and worked for Franklin as a printer, has bedeviled the editors of these papers since we first considered publishing it in Volume 31. The dating of this letter hinges on when Carey was actually in France. The evidence is contradictory.

In his *Autobiography,* Carey states that he fled Ireland in 1779 to escape prosecution for publishing *The Urgent Necessity of an Immediate Repeal of the Whole Penal Code . . .* , a seditious pamphlet. Once in Paris he was introduced to Franklin, who engaged him for several

1. See his Aug. 16 letter.
2. The Dublin-born printer, publisher, and economist (1760–1839), who emigrated to the United States in 1784 and settled in Philadelphia. He renewed his acquaintance with BF after the latter's return to Philadelphia, and Carey printed several of BF's writings in his *American Museum. DAB.*

months as a printer. When Franklin had no further use for him, he found employment printing English books for Didot le jeune. He was in France for a total of twelve months, he writes, before returning to Dublin. During his stay at Passy, he claims, the French were contemplating an invasion of Ireland, and Lafayette consulted him on the Irish political situation.[3]

Carey's chronology does not correspond altogether to the evidence. His pamphlet could not have been issued in 1779; it refers to the current year as 1781, and there is strong evidence to suggest that it was issued in November of that year.[4] A year later, anecdotes about Carey's odd behavior were circulating in France. A letter sent to William Temple Franklin on November 20, 1782, identifies Carey as Franklin's former printer and says that he was currently an English instructor in Pontlevoy, a position that Franklin may have helped him obtain.[5] By January, 1783, Carey had reportedly left Paris, owing Chaumont's son 12 francs.[6] The evidence is strong, therefore, that Carey arrived in France around December, 1781, and returned to Dublin approximately one year later.

Were it not for Carey's description of his conversation with Lafayette, we would assume that he had simply misremembered the year of his French visit. But the French only contemplated invading Ireland for a brief time, abandoning those plans in early 1779; Lafayette's plans to invade Ireland, which Franklin enthusiastically endorsed, were also made that year.[7] On the other hand, Lafayette—

---

3. *Autobiography of Mathew Carey,* pub. in *The New-England Magazine,* V (1833), 407–9.

4. We are grateful to James Green of the Library Company of Philadelphia, who looked at the Library Company's copy of the pamphlet for us, discovered an advertisement bound in that copy which said that the pamphlet would be published on "Monday next, the 12th Inst.," and provided strong evidence that the publication was set for Nov. 12, 1781. Indeed, on Nov. 11, 1781, a group of Roman Catholics submitted to the press a vigorous protest against a seditious pamphlet that was advertised for publication the following day, and Pat Wogan, whose name appeared on the advertisement as selling the pamphlet, published a renouncement of his involvement: *The Dublin Journal,* issue of Nov. 17–20, 1781.

5. Jacques Le Ray de Chaumont to WTF, Nov. 20, 1782, APS; XXXVI, 694n.

6. Jacques Le Ray de Chaumont to WTF, January, 1783, APS.

7. The French government abandoned the idea of a full-scale invasion of Ireland in February, 1779, just as Lafayette was returning to France: Dull, *French Navy,* pp. 134–7; Idzerda, *Lafayette Papers,* II, xxxviii. Lafayette, however, was involved in planning a raid on Ireland later in the year: XXIX, 185–6n.

who had gone to America in the meantime—returned to Paris in January, 1782, and stayed until December. We can only conclude that Carey met Lafayette in 1782 but mischaracterized their conversation. The marquis may well have asked Carey about the state of Irish politics, but we doubt that he was discussing any active plans for an invasion.

[before November 20, 1782][8]
If his Excellency shall at any time have any job, however trifling, Carey requests he will send a line directed to him at M. Didot's,[9] Rue Pavee, St. Andre as Carey shall ever esteem it a favor to do every thing in his power for his benefactor.

Addressed: His Excellency / Benjamin Franklin

From Vergennes

Copy: Archives du Ministère des affaires étrangères; transcript: National Archives

à Versailles le 20. 9bre: 1782.

J'ai l'honneur, M. de vous adresser la copie du memoire qui m'a êté presenté par le Sr. Louis Anty marchand a Nantes, ainsy que de la note dont il l'a accompagné.[1] Vous y verrez l'exposé des pertes que lui ont occasionné Ses liaisons de commerce avec le Sr. Penet Agent general de l'Etat de Virginie. La fortune de ce marchand de Nantes Se trouve entierement renversée par les en-

8. As explained in the headnote, the date on which Carey was called BF's former printer. Carey worked for Didot after leaving BF's employ.

9. François-Ambroise Didot, called Didot l'aîné (XXXVI, 193), moved from the quai des Augustins when he established a typefoundry: A.-M. Lottin, *Catalogue chronologique des libraires et des libraires-imprimeurs de Paris* (Paris, 1789), p. 243 of second pagination; *DBF; Almanach des marchands*, p. 369.

1. Anty's note and memoir to Vergennes asked him to intercede with BF in trying to get reimbursed for the 92,352 *l.t.* 12 *s.* 7 *d.* owed him by Penet, who had absconded. A merchant for more than 30 years, Anty had overextended himself and was now ruined. A copy of the memoir is filed with the present letter at the AAE. A transcript of the memoir likewise accompanies the transcript of the present letter at the National Archives; both items are translated into English and are filed among papers sent by BF.

gagements qu'il a pris en faveur du Sr. Penet et par la rigueur des poursuites auxquelles l'expose la fuite de celui cy. Toute la ressource du Sr. Anty est donc M. dans les bons offices que vous voudrez bien lui rendre auprès de l'Etat de Virginie afin de lui procurer la justice qu'il est en droit de reclamer contre Son debiteur infidele.[2]

M. franklin

Lafayette to the American Peace Commissioners

ALS: Newberry Library; transcript: New York Public Library

Gentlemen   Paris November the 21st 1782

Since the Early Period When I Had the Happiness to Be Adopted Among the sons of America, I Ever Made it My Point to do that Which I thought Would prove Useful to Her Cause or Agreable to Her Citizens. After We Had Long Stood By ourselves, France did join in our Quarrell, and So Soon as Count d'Estaing's departure Made My Presence Unnecessary, I Had a Permission to Return to France[3] Where, Among other things, I Endeavoured to Impress this Court With the Propriety to Send a Naval force, and An Auxiliary Army to Serve Under the orders of General Washington.[4] The Plan of a descent in England Lengthened My Negotiation, the Succour was at Last Sent,[5] and

2. Anty engaged several other people to write on his behalf to BF. Charles-Joseph-Alexandre-Marie-Marcelin d'Alsace, prince d'Hénin (*DBF* under Alsace), wrote on Nov. 25, saying that Anty would deliver the letter. Two days after Anty came to Passy, WTF wrote to the chevalier de Chabanon (whose letter of recommendation is missing) that BF had assured Anty of his support with Congress. On Dec. 3 the chevalier replied to WTF, thanking BF for his help. On Feb. 18, 1783, Anty's daughter wrote to an unnamed recipient (perhaps one of the Chaumont daughters) that BF had given her father a letter of recommendation (now missing). Finally, Anty himself wrote a claim against the state of Virginia, mentioning both Vergennes and BF. All these documents are in French and at the APS; WTF's to the chevalier de Chabanon is an undated draft.
3. See XXVIII, 288–9.
4. See XXIX, 623.
5. Rochambeau's army and Ternay's squadron, sent to Newport in 1780, a year after the abortive invasion attempt.

Arrived at a Critical Period. It Prevented Evils, But did not Produce Any great Immediate Good Untill that Naval Superiority Which I Had Been Promised Was Sent to Cooperate With us, and Helped us in the Capture of Lord Cornwallis.

This Event Ended the Campaign in Virginia, and the Army I Had Commanded Was of Course Separated. Congress Gave me Leave to Go to France, and to Return at Such time as I should think Proper. I Had it in Command to Make Some Representations at this Court, and the General's Particular Instructions Were By all Means to Bring a Naval and Land Assistance to Operate in our America.[6]

Count de Grasse's defeat Having Ruined our Plans, I Now was despairing to fulfill the Intentions of Congress and the orders of My General, When it Was Proposed to me to Serve in the Army Under the direction of Count d'Estaing.[7] This Has Appeared to me the only Way I Had to Serve My Views, I Had the Honor to Consult you About it, and Upon Your Approbation of the Measure, I Consented to Accompagny Count d'Estaing in His Expeditions, Provided it Was in My Capacity, and Even Under the Uniform of an American officer, Who Being for a time Borrowed from the United States, Will obey the first order or take the first Opportunity to Rejoin His Colours.

Had I not Been detained By You, Gentlemen, Upon Political Accounts Which You Have Been Pleased to Communicate to Congress, I Would Have Long Ago Returned to America.[8] But I Was With You of Opinion, that My Presence Here Might Be

6. In a Nov. 15, 1781, letter to Lafayette, Washington asked for French naval aid, but refused to discuss the question of reinforcements for Rochambeau's army: Idzerda, *Lafayette Papers*, IV, 435–7.

7. Apparently d'Estaing requested the services of Lafayette for the planned attack on Jamaica and treated him as his chief of staff: Louis Gottschalk, *Lafayette and the Close of the American Revolution* (Chicago, 1942), pp. 379, 388. Lafayette does not seem to have been aware that d'Estaing also had a diplomatic mission, that of convincing Spain to make peace rather than attempt the attack. He traveled to Cadiz by land, visiting the Spanish court, while Lafayette traveled by sea: Dull, *French Navy*, pp. 317–18, 324; Idzerda, *Lafayette Papers*, V, 74–6.

8. According to JA, this comment "nettled" BF and Jay: Butterfield, *John Adams Diary*, III, 71.

Useful, and Since it Appears Matters are not Ripe for a treaty, My first Wish is Now to Return to America With such force as May Expell the Enemy from the United States, Serve the Views of Congress, and Assist Your Political Operations.[9] When, or How this May Be Offered I am Not Yet Able to determine, or I Would not Be at Liberty to Mention, But, However Certain I Have Been of Your Opinion, I think it A Mark of Respect to Congress not to depart Untill I Have Your Official Approbation of the Measure.

With the Highest Respect I Have the Honor to Be, Gentlemen, Your Obedient Humble Servant   LAFAYETTE

Their Excellencies Mrs franklin, Adams

Endorsed by John Jay: marq. Fayette to Comrs 21 Nov 1782

From Robert R. Livingston

Two LS and L: University of Pennsylvania Library; transcript:[1] National Archives

Sir   Philadelphia 21st. Novr. 1782

Congress a few days since passed the enclosed Resolution No. 1. by which they have added Mr Jefferson to the Commission for concluding a peace;[2] the established character of this Gentleman gives me reason to hope, that his appointment will be very acceptable to you, and the other Gentlemen in the Commission, I have not yet learned, whether he will take the task upon him, but I have reason to beleive he will, the death of his Wife having lessened in the opinion of his friends the reluctance which he has

9. Lafayette hoped that once Jamaica had been captured, attacks would be mounted against New York and possibly even Canada: Idzerda, *Lafayette Papers*, V, 89; Gottschalk, *Lafayette*, p. 388.

1. Which indicates that the two LS (the original and duplicate) and the L (marked triplicate) accompanied, respectively, the original, duplicate, and triplicate of Livingston's Nov. 9 letter, above.

2. A resolution of Nov. 12, made on the motion of James Madison: *JCC*, XXIII, 720–1; *Jefferson Papers*, VI, 202. Two copies of it are among BF's papers at the APS.

hitherto manifested to going abroad—[3] I think it would be proper to make a formal anunciation of this Resolution to the Court of France. You will naturally give such a representation of Mr. Jefferson's character as will secure to him there, that esteem and confidence which he justly merrits— The Resolution No. 2. needs no comment, or if it does Mr Morris will prove the abler Commentator, I resign the task to him.[4]

For what end is the shew of Negotiation kept up by England, when peace upon the only terms he can possible expect to obtain it is far from her heart— Her Ministers I suppose, like some ministers of the Gospel, who are unwilling to quit the pulpit, when they have tired out their hearers, expect to keep the People together by calling out at every period "now to conclude" while they continue the same dull tale for want of skill to wind it up. The French Army are at Providence at a loss which Way to move 'till they receive further orders from home: all of them seem prepared to embark except the Legion which is to remain for the present. The fleet are still at Boston.[5] By accounts from Jamaica we learn that the British have recovered most of their settlements on the Bay[6]—some attention will I hope be paid in the treaty of peace to secure to us the share we formerly had in the Logwood Trade it was a valuable remittance to us, and the low price at which we were enabled to sell renders it important to other nations that we should not be excluded from furnishing it as usual— You will find by the enclosed paper, that Mr. Burgess

3. Jefferson wrote Livingston on Nov. 26, accepting the post. Jefferson's wife, Martha, had died on Sept. 6: *Jefferson Papers,* VI, 196n, 199–200n, 206.

4. Probably a reference to the Nov. 18 selection of Thomas Barclay to liquidate the accounts of Americans in Europe entrusted with the expenditure of public money: *JCC,* XXIII, 728–30.

5. The preceding two sentences were written in code, which BF decoded on the original. Rochambeau's army began leaving Providence on Nov. 16 after a week's stay and began arriving in Boston three days later. Except for Lauzun's Legion and a few smaller detachments, it sailed with Vaudreuil for the Caribbean on Dec. 24 (in preparation for the invasion of Jamaica): Rice and Brown, eds., *Rochambeau's Army,* I, 76n, 81, 256; II, 192.

6. The Gulf of Honduras. Governor-General of Jamaica Archibald Campbell recently had sent an expedition to the Black River on its southern shore: Mark Mayo Boatner III, *Encyclopedia of the American Revolution* (New York, 1966), p. 510.

an English Merchant was not permitted to settle at Boston and obtain the rights of Citizenship upon the principles which must be alarming to England, it shews at the same time the respect that is paid to the resolutions of Congress notwithstanding all that has been said and written to prove the contrary—[7] I am, Sir with great Respect and Esteem your most obedt. humble Servant

ROBT R LIVINGSTON

PS I forgot to mention that I am solicited by Mr. Barlow to transmit you proposals for printing a work of his, which you will find described in the enclosed proposals, as they are accompanied with a specimen of his poetry which is as much as I have seen of it[8]—you will judge yourself how far it deserves the patronage he wishes you to give it.

The Honorable Benjn. Franklin

No. 21.

7. According to Samuel Adams, the Mass. General Court refused the petition for naturalization of William Burgess (XXXVII, 702) even before learning of Congress' recommendation that the states admit no British subjects: Smith, *Letters*, XIX, 640n. Some years later, however, Burgess was successful: Harold C. Syrett *et al.*, eds., *The Papers of Alexander Hamilton* (27 vols., New York and London, 1961–87), VII, 194.

8. Among BF's papers at the APS are two copies of Joel Barlow's undated manuscript description of his work in progress, "The Vision of Columbus, A Poem in Nine Books," with selections from it. Barlow had gone to Philadelphia to secure subscribers for this long poem: Charles Burr Todd, *Life and Letters of Joel Barlow, LL.D.* . . . . (New York and London, 1886), p. 40. Published in 1787 (with BF among its subscribers), it made Barlow famous: *DAB; ANB.*

From George Washington

ALS: reproduced in Lion Heart Autographs, Catalogue No. 22 (1991), item 98; draft[9] and transcript: Library of Congress

Sir,   Head Qrs. Newburgh 21st. Novr 1782.

The Credentials with which Mr. Wheelock is furnished are so ample, and so fully set forth the benevolent purposes of the Institution over which he presides, that I am confident nothing more is necessary for me, than barely to introduce him to you and to recommend him to your Patronage and Friendship—[1] Under them, he will be sure to meet with a favorable reception among the Wise and Good.—

I have the honor to be with profound respect Sir Yr. most Obt Hble Ser   GO WASHINGTON

From Jonathan Williams, Jr.   Copy: Yale University Library

Dr & Hond Sir   Nantes Novr 21—1782

I arrived here safe the day before yesterday and found that the Ship Marquis de la Fayette Capt Buffington had arrived to my address from Salem with a prize which was bound from New-york to London with 50 hhds of Tobacco.[2] In this Ship are several Brittish Officers some of whom were in Cornwallis's Army & are under parole from Genl Washington. Some others are prisoners but we have given them their Parole in Town till you

9. In the hand of his aide Tench Tilghman and dated Nov. 20. This text is published in Fitzpatrick, *Writings of Washington*, XXV, 355.

1. For John Wheelock's mission see the Board of Trustees of Dartmouth College to BF, Sept. 24. Wheelock ended his military service (1777–79) as a lieutenant colonel on the staff of Horatio Gates, and claimed to have enjoyed Washington's "particular notice and friendship": *ANB;* [John Wheelock], *Sketches of the History of Dartmouth College . . .* ([Newburyport, Mass., 1815]), p. 28.

2. The prize was the *Tartar*, which JW later purchased: JW to Capt. Stephen Webb, Jan. 20, 1783 (Yale University Library). For Capt. John Buffington of Salem, who took command of the *Marquis de Lafayette* on March 13, see Claghorn, *Naval Officers*, p. 41; Allen, *Mass. Privateers*, pp. 138, 216, 264, 306–7.

please to extend it, they were all bound home on private Business & were Passengers in the ship
these last mentioned are
Capt Macintosh—71 Regt
Capt Campbell 71— do with his Lady
Lieut— Campbell 71— do
Mr Burnes Surgeon Mate 71 do
Capt Meggs—60— do—³ with a Lady—
I told these Gentlemen that as the Treatment of Prisoners in England was on a more liberal & humane footing than formerly I did not doubt you would grant their Paroles to go to England— they engaging not to Serve in any military capacity till duely exchanged. As there are several neutral Ships going hence to Ostend they wish to take that mode on account of their Baggage, but nothing can be done without your answer which I request you to give me as early as possible and if you consent I will take from them the proper Paroles & transmit them to you.—

I hope your are now quite recovered— My Father who talks of paying me a visit in the Spring writes me that Aunt Mecom is well tho' much depressed on acct of the loss of her Grand Daughter.

I am as ever dutifully & affectionately yours—

His Excellency Doctor Franklin Passy

From Lafayette

AL: Library of Congress

[on or before November 22, 1782]⁴
Mis. [Marquis] de Lafayette's Best Respects Waït Upon Mr franklin and Would Be Much obliged to His Excellency for a Copy of

3. Capt. Æneas Mackintosh, Capt. Lawrence Robert Campbell, Lt. Archibald Campbell, and Capt. George Meggs are listed in Steven M. Baule and Stephen Gilbert, comps., *British Army Officers Who Served in the American Revolution, 1775–1783* (Westminster, Md., 2004), pp. 28–9, 32, 114, 126. All five of these men, including surgeon's mate David Burns, signed paroles at Passy on Dec. 6 and 7; see our annotation of the parole granted Capt. Campbell, Dec. 7.

4. The date of Lafayette's letter to Vergennes which he says here he intends to write. For that letter see Lafayette to BF, [Nov. 26].

His Memorial to the french Court[5] As He Intends Pressing Upon this Subject in a Letter to Count de Vergennes.

The Mis. de Lafayette Begs Also to know at What time Captain Barnay Has Set out for L'orient, and When His Courier is Expected Back—[6] Count de Vergennes Appears Unwilling to Decide Any thing Before Chev de la Luzerne's dispatches Have Been Received.

What is the day and Hour Which Mr franklin Has Appointed for a Meeting of the three Ministers Agreable to what He was pleased to say on Tuesday last.[7]

5. BF to Vergennes, Nov. 8, above.

6. Barney was still in Paris on the evening of Nov. 17: Butterfield, *John Adams Diary*, III, 58. He arrived at Lorient on Nov. 22 and wrote BF the following day (below).

7. Probably Tuesday, Nov. 19, the day Lafayette took leave of the King and attended a dinner hosted by Vergennes for the diplomatic corps. (On this occasion Lafayette told JA that he had learned from Vergennes about Rayneval's new trip to England.) JA reports having traveled to Versailles in Jay's coach, but does not mention BF's having been in attendance: Butterfield, *John Adams Diary*, III, 62. The meeting with the American commissioners took place on Nov. 23 at Passy; see our annotation of Lafayette to BF, [Nov. 26].

To François Steinsky[8]

LS:[9] National Museum, Prague

Passy le 23. Novembre 1782.

J'ai reçu, Monsieur, la Lettre très obligeante que vous m'avez fait l'honneur de m'écrire le 12. Septembre 1781, par la quelle je suis charmé d'apprendre que vous étez arrivé en bonne Santé chez vous. Une longue et pénible Indisposition m'a privé du plaisir de vous repondre plustôt et de vous remercier de l'élégant et beau Présent de la Nape à Caffé que vous avez eu la bonté de m'envoyer. J'en admire beaucoup le Travail ingenieux, et pense que les Manufacturiers de votre Pays ont porté leur art à une grande Perfection. Les seules Nouvelles en Physique dans ce Pays icy depuis votre Depart, sont la Chaleur violente produite en souflant de l'air dephologistiqué sur du Charbon de bois, qui a fondu la platine en peu de minutes, et qu'on regarde comme le Feu le plus chaud que l'art ait encore pu produire.[1] Et la Méthode pour alumer une Chandelle en cassant un Tube de Verre; dont vous verrez les Descriptions dans le Journal de Physique de l'Abbé

---

8. In reply to Steinsky's letter of Sept. 12, 1781: XXXV, 468–70. We said there that we would publish in vol. 38 BF's undated notes for a reply, which were drafted on Steinsky's letter but could not have been written before October, 1782. In the meantime, we located this LS. We nonetheless offer BF's notes here, because they will allow readers a rare opportunity to compare an English draft by BF to a polished French text that was probably composed by L'Air de Lamotte:

That I have receiv'd his very obliging Letter of the 12th 7bre. That a long Indisposition has prevented my answering sooner, and thanking him for his kind & elegant Present of the Nape a Caffé. I admire much the Ingenuity of the Workmanship, and think the Manufacturers of his Country have arriv'd at great Perfection in their Art. That I am glad to hear of his safe Return after so long a Voyage. That the only Novelties in *Physics* since his being here, are the violent Heat produc'd by blowing with dephlogisticated Air on Charcoal, which melted Platina in a few minutes, and is thought the hottest Fire Art has yet been able to make. And the Method of lighting a Candle by breaking a small Glass Tube. You will see the Descriptions in Rosier's Journal de Physique. That I wish him Health & Prosperity, and shall be glad to learn from him any new Discoveries made in his Country that are useful. &c

9. In the hand of L'Air de Lamotte.

1. On June 5, 1782, Lavoisier demonstrated this experiment to the Académie des sciences. BF reported it to both Priestley (XXXVII, 446) and Ingenhousz (XXXV, 551).

Rosier.[2] La Corde sans fin du Sr. Verra pour élever l'eau a aussi attiré l'attention et l'Etonnement des Physiciens.[3] Vous m'obligeriez infiniment en m'informant des nouvelles Decouvertes utiles faites en votre Pays, et Je serai fort aise de recevoir de tems en tems de vos Nouvelles. J'ai l'honneur de vous souhaiter une bonne Santé et toutes Sortes de Prosperités, et vous prie de me croire avec beaucoup de Consideration, Monsieur, Votre très humble et très obeissant Serviteur./.   B Franklin

Mr. Steinsky.

From Joshua Barney

ALS: Historical Society of Pennsylvania

Sir,   L Orient Novr. 23d. 1782.
I have the honor to inform you that I only arrived last night owing to My carriage having broke down on the Road. I have found the Dispatches[4] and According to Your orders have Dispatched a Courier with them to You. Your not having Given any

2. See Bettally & Noseda, Oct. 1, above.
3. The "corde sans fin" was a deceptively simple device, operated by a crank, that could raise water to surprising heights by means of a rope that ran between two pulleys, one submerged in a vat of water and the other directly above it. The inventor, a postal employee named Charles Vincent Vera, had observed that water molecules would adhere to the saturated rope and form a "column" that could travel vertically; the spray that issued from the rope as it turned around the upper pulley was collected in a hood that drained into a vat. The Académie des sciences appointed Le Roy and Bossut to investigate these claims (XXXVI, 352n). They confirmed Vera's findings and publicly announced their results: a rope of esparto, the width of a finger, yielded 250 pints of water in 7 minutes, 45 seconds, at a height of 63 feet. *Jour. de Paris*, issues of Oct. 20 and 23, and Dec. 29, 1781. Pilatre de Rozier described this invention in the August, 1782, *Jour. de Physique*, pp. 132–43, and plate III. Vera received a government pension for this invention in 1784: Shelby T. McCoy, *French Inventions of the Eighteenth Century* ([Lexington, Ky.], 1952), p. 116.
4. Vergennes' dispatches from La Luzerne, for which see BF to Vergennes, Nov. 10. Barney was sent to see if they had been left on the *General Washington* when La Forest arrived from Lorient without them: Hulbert Footner, *Sailor of Fortune: the Life and Adventures of Commodore Barney, U.S.N.* (New York and London, 1940), p. 133.

338

Directions to Mr. Barclay concerning the Dispatches he De-
clines having any thing to do with them except providing me
With the person who brings them. Therefore you will plan to
Settle with the Courier on that head.[5] My ship is at present Ready
for Sea and hope I shall not be Detain'd any time And Am Your
Most Obt. And Hble Servt   JOSHUA BARNEY

Excellency B Franklin

Addressed: His Excellency / B. Franklin / Passy / Nr. Paris

Notation: Joshua Barney Nov. 23 1782.

From Castries   Copy: Archives de la Marine

A Versailles le 23. 9bre. 1782.

Jai recû, Monsieur, la lettre que vous m'avez fait l'honneur de
mecrire le 17 de ce mois[6] pour m'informer que vous avez fait
connoître à M Barclay qui est actuellement à l'orient quelles sont
celles des munitions deposées à Brest et appt. au Congrés qui
doivent etre embarquées de preference. En consequence de ce
que vous m'avez marqué, je donne mes ordres á Brest pour qu'on
satisfasse aux demandes qu'il Sera dans le cas de faire pour remplir Sa commission.[7]

J'ai l'honneur d'etre avec une parfaite consideration, Monsieur, Votre &c

M franklin

5. On Dec. 3 Grand paid a courier from Lorient 240 *l.t.:* Account XXVII
(XXXII, 4).

6. Missing, but obviously written in answer to Castries' letter of Nov. 15,
above.

7. Barclay had the goods sent to Nantes and Lorient; see his Dec. 16 letter.

From Nathaniel Fanning[8] ALS: American Philosophical Society

Dunkerque Goal 23d:
May it Please your Excellency   Novr: 1782

That nothing could have enduced me to have troubled your Excellency with these lines, but the way, and manner of my being committed to this loathsome Goal, & the little hopes I have, (as a Stranger) of recovering my Liberty; notwithstanding my Perfect innocence of the Charge laid to my Crew which runs as follows (Viz)

Louis Jean Marie de Bourbon Duc de Penthievre Amiral de France a tous ceux qui ces presentes lettre Verront Salut Savoir faisons que vû les Charge et information fait a la requete du procureur du Roy le dix huit November Present mois a loccasion d'un pillage commis abord du Navire d'anois L'Anegard[9] par les Equipage du Corsaire L'Eclipse Capt: Fanning de ce port &c.[1]

---

8. Fanning (1755–1805) had been a midshipman on the *Bonhomme Richard* (XXX, 630) and subsequently sailed on French privateers. In June, 1782, he was given command of the French privateer *Eclipse* for a cruise that lasted from June 5 to Aug. 12. During that cruise he raised English colors and gave orders to board and search the *Emiliard*, a vessel flying the Danish flag that in fact was neutral. Regardless, the boarding party looted the passengers, some of whom were French, stealing all the effects of the wealthiest and (to their later regret) most influential of them, the marquis de Ségur-Bouzely, the *lieutenant du roi* of Grande Terre, Guadeloupe, who was returning to France. The *Emiliard* proceeded directly to Copenhagen, and the French passengers had to make their own way home. One of them was approached six weeks later in Dunkirk by a crew member of the *Eclipse*, who told him that the privateer and its captain were in port. The passenger filed a complaint with M. d'Anglemont, *commissaire de la marine* at Dunkirk (XXIX, 173n). D'Anglemont initially dismissed the complaint, but when Ségur got involved, and a number of the *Eclipse*'s crew came forward to testify, the affair came to the attention of the highest government officials and became something of a *cause célèbre*. All crew members of the *Eclipse* were arrested pending a thorough investigation, and Fanning found himself—as he writes here—in a Dunkirk prison. The information in this and the following notes is drawn from Henri Malo, "American Privateers at Dunkerque," trans. Stewart L. Mims, United States Naval Institute *Proc.*, XXXVII (1911), 973–83.

9. The *Emiliard*.

1. Castries, minister of the marine, sent orders on Nov. 5 for d'Anglemont to seize Fanning and his crew. They were imprisoned at their own expense. On Nov. 10 Castries complained sharply to the judges of the Admiralty at

Now as your Excellency is well known for administerg: Justice on this Side of the Atlantic to your Countrymen, so I myself (as being Born of a very Reputable Family in New London) most ardently beg your Excellency's Protection, & that your Excellency would be pleased to take such necessary Steps with the French, Court as may be the means of my Enlargement.

The Crews of Privateers from this Place in general, are composed of, Dutch, Swedes, Danes, English, Portuguese, Turks, &C &C. Therefore I leave your Excellency to Judge, how difficult it must be for a Capt: to prevent such People from Plundering if they are bent upon it; nay I even defy any Capt: out of this place with a Crew composed of such men as Afforesaid, to avoid such unlawful Proceedings.[2]

I have now lodged at the Publick Notary of this place a Certificate Signed by my Principal Officers & men, which purports that my Orders were always very Strict against plundering Neutral Vessels; even at every time my Boat was man'd, in order to Board any Vessel, during my Cruise in the Eclipse. I can take my affidavit that if ever my People took any thing out of any Neu-

---

Dunkirk that they had not given him an account of "a crime of such gravity." He demanded that they inform him of the investigation, trial, and punishment. On Nov. 24 the King himself intervened and transferred the case to the *conseil du roi:* Malo, "American Privateers at Dunkerque," p. 978.

2. Fanning's second in command, the man who led the boarding party and who instigated the plundering, was in fact an American, Thomas Potter. Potter had led two mutiny attempts during the cruise, and after looting the *Emiliard* forced Fanning to bring the *Eclipse* back to Dunkirk. Potter then made his way to Passy, received 120 *l.t.* from BF (see the Editorial Note on Promissory Notes), and on Oct. 23 shipped out again aboard the Philadelphia-bound *Renette*, thereby eluding prosecution: Malo, "American Privateers at Dunkerque," p. 979.

After a complex investigation that lasted seven months, the judges rendered their verdict on June 21, 1783. Potter and four other crew members (all French) were convicted of robbery. Potter was condemned to hang; the others received lesser punishments. Fanning was convicted of not being able to maintain discipline, and he was forbidden to command a vessel for three years. The Dunkirk outfitters of the *Eclipse*, Peychiers and Torris, had failed to respond to their summons and were consequently forced to pay all legal expenses, which amounted to twice what the cruise had earned them. Malo, "American Privateers at Dunkerque," pp. 982–3.

tral Vessel, which I always Strove, as much as lay in Power to avoid, that it never came within my Knowledge.[3]

Therefore I think it very hard as I have not been the agressor, to make me Suffer for the Faults of my People, in lying in this prison; having been but just released from an English one; I think I have had my Share of imprisonment this War, having been at one time better than twelve Months, in Forton Prison, at Portsmouth.[4]

I most humbly implore your Excellency not to reject the prayers of him. Who has the honor to be Your Excellency's Humble Petitioner & most Obdt: Servant   NATHANIEL FANNING

P.S. I am most certainly very peculiarly situated; for I have wrote a Letter in English to the French Minister, but cannot get any Friend in this place to translate it into French, nor any one here to speak in my bhalf. I was committed to this Prison by the Order of Mr: Donglemo [D'Anglemont] commissary of the Marine, & have since been ordered by the Admiralty to appear before them in order to justify my innocence but as the former & the latter are at variance so I see nothing else but I shall be Obliged to continue here.

Having been decended from a very reputable Family which I can prove, as I had, when I left America two Uncles Field Offi-

---

3. Fanning was stretching the truth. Crew members later testified that he had indeed known about the plunder—and had even tried on one of the marquis de Ségur-Bouzely's crimson costumes, under the influence of drink— but was powerless to stop Potter and his followers, whom he had previously lectured against committing acts of piracy. Malo, "American Privateers at Dunkerque," pp. 981–2.

4. According to a fictionalized memoir written by Fanning late in life and published posthumously in a limited edition, he spent from June, 1778, to June, 1779, in Forton, was loosely confined at Falmouth for six weeks in 1781, and was captured twice more: John S. Barnes, ed., *Fanning's Narrative: Being the Memoirs of Nathaniel Fanning, an Officer of the Revolutionary Navy, 1778–1783* (New York, 1912), pp. 20, 139–44, 217–24. He was briefly in British custody in October, 1782, just before assuming command of the *Eclipse:* Malo, "American Privateers at Dunkerque," p. 977. Fanning's narrative rewrites the present incident as a matter of a few days' imprisonment, after which he was compensated with 1,500 *l.t.* and a "very handsome apology" from the commandant: Barnes, ed., *Fanning's Narrative*, p. 228.

cers under his Excellency Genl: Washington & one a Member of Congress;[5] when I consider this I feel my Character much hurt by this imprisonment as your Excellency may reasonably Judge.

N. F.

His Excellency Benjamin Franklin Esqr:

Notation: Fannel 23 Nov. 1782.—

From Juliana Penn[6]   ALS: American Philosophical Society

Sir   Spring Garden London. November 23d: 1782.

In consequence of Your obliging Permission, I loose no time in begging Your Assistance & Protection, in the recovery of the rights and Possessions of an unfortunate Family,[7] who have so heavily felt the Misfortunes of this War,[8] and who are likely still to be dreadful Sufferers, if They are not properly consider'd.

You, Sir, are so well acquainted with our losses, that it would be unnecessary to take up your time with relating them: I therefore Earnestly Entreat You to take them into consideration, and by restoring us to our rights and Fortune, confirm the great

5. Fanning was the son of Gilbert Fanning and Huldah Palmer of Stonington, Conn. We have been unable to find any uncles answering this description. He had three maternal uncles who were either privateer or militia captains, and several Loyalist uncles on the Fanning side, including Edmund Fanning, colonel of the King's American Regiment of N.Y. Walter F. Brooks, *History of the Fanning Family* (2 vols., Worcester, Mass., 1905), I, 135–66; Norman F. Boas, *Stonington during the American Revolution* (Mystic, Conn., 1990), pp. 75, 145; Emily W. Leavitt, comp., *Palmer Groups . . .* (Boston, 1901–05), pp. 129–30.

6. Lady Juliana Fermor Penn (IV, 320n) was the widow of Pennsylvania Proprietor Thomas Penn. She also wrote an appeal to Jay the same day: Morris, *Jay: Peace,* pp. 424–5.

7. She had three surviving children, John (1760–1834), Granville (1761–1844), and Sophia Margaretta (1764–1847): *DNB* under Thomas, John, and Granville Penn; Howard M. Jenkins, "The Family of William Penn," *PMHB,* XXI (1897), 346, 421, 439–42, 444.

8. The Penn family's proprietary holdings (but not their private estates) had been sequestered by the Commonwealth of Pennsylvania in 1779: XXIX, 56n; *Morris Papers,* VII, 549n; Jenkins, "Family of William Penn," p. 425.

Character You have so justly merited; and to wch: I shall be proud to owe my Prosperity, and that of my Children and Family.

I know that Lord Shelburne has authorised Mr: Vaughan to back my application to You;[9] but I flatter myself that the justice of my Cause alone will be sufficient recommendation to You. It is then to your feelings that I address myself; and in confidence of your well known Wisdom & Humanity, I adopt You for the Guardian of William Penn's Grand Children, and remain with respect, Sir, Your Excellency's Oblig'd and Obedient Humble Servant   JULIANA PENN

From John Jay   ALS: Library of Congress

Dr Sir   Sunday Morng [November 24, 1782]

Mr Oswald expressed his Desire to me last Evening that we would meet him, at any Time & place that might be convenient to us. As Mr Strachey is confined by a swelled Face, at Mr Oswalds; I promised the latter to propose to you our meeting there at 11 OClk. Tomorrow.[1]

I am Dear Sir Sincerely Yours &c   JOHN JAY

Endorsed: recd Nov. 24. 82

9. Benjamin Vaughan wrote Shelburne on Dec. 10 that her affair would be "taken up" and that his interest in the matter was understood: Charles C. Smith, "Letters of Benjamin Vaughan," Mass. Hist. Soc. *Proc.*, 2nd ser., XVII (1903), 428. See also Samuel Vaughan's letter of introduction, Dec. 16, below.

1. For this meeting, which opened the final round of negotiations leading to the provisional peace agreement, see Strachey's Remarks to the American Peace Commissioners, Nov. 25.

From Jonathan Williams, Jr.

ALS: American Philosophical Society; copy: Yale University Library

Dear & hond Sir.   Nantes 24. 9bre. 1782.

Since writing you about the Prisoners on Parole and others who wanted their Parole,[2] I am informed by the Officer of the Garrison here that if I will add these Prisonners to those now in Rochelle a Cartel may be immediately procured to send them off together, specifying the Distinctions of the Flags under which they were taken & carried account to each Nation according-ly.— As this will save much Expence & Time, & relieve a number of poor Fellows the keeping of whom is of no use, I beg you will give me authority to conform, and I will take Care to have the proper Returns made of Rank Quality &ca. The Paroles I asked your permission for I will take as proper but the common men will go in Accot with the Board of Sick & hurt as is usual.

As I shall be obliged very soon to be in L'Orient, so request as early an Answer as possible, more especialy as there are Ladies in the Question & I know you are as little inclined as myself to make them suffer the Delays & Hardships incident to War.

I am with the highest Respect Your dutifull & affectionate

JONA WILLIAMS J

I have spoken to Mr Dobré & he told me you had written to send these people to Morlaix,[3] but as there is no Cartel there & as the present proposed mode will save both Time & Expence we shall wait your answer.

I find since writing that the Ladies and some of the officers wish to go home by Paris, these I shall take Paroles from as far as passy & then leave them to your future Disposal. JWJ

Doctor Franklin.

Notation: Jona. Williams Nantes 24: 9bre 1782

2. In his letter of Nov. 21, above.
3. BF had sent such directions to Dobrée's late partner Jean-Daniel Schweighauser in 1781 (XXXV, 253), but we have no record of more recent instructions.

Henry Strachey's Remarks to the American Peace Commissioners

Transcript:[4] New York Public Library

Strachey's return to Paris opened a new round of intensive negotiations which culminated in the signing of a provisional peace treaty on November 30. The present document is Strachey's recollection of what he said to the American peace commissioners when he presented them with the British counterproposal to their second draft treaty.[5] This meeting was held at 11 A.M. on Monday, November 25, at Richard Oswald's residence.[6]

The only one of the American commissioners to keep a daily record of these negotiations was John Adams. His diary records the prolonged arguments over the fisheries article, in which he played the lead role. The debate over the fisheries began as soon as Strachey presented the British proposal, and consumed the first day's session. The following day, the American commissioners summoned Fitzherbert to discuss the parallel negotiations with Vergennes concerning French fishing rights. After having been "discussed and turned in every Light," the fisheries article was finally settled on November 29.[7]

The other major source of contention was the Loyalists. Among the American commissioners, Franklin held the strongest views and his contributions were key. Over breakfast on the second day of negotiations, the Americans agreed to reject the proposed article about the refugees. Franklin read his colleagues the letter he had written to Oswald on the subject, published below under November 26, which they approved of his sending as a personal statement. Much of that day "was spent in endless Discussions about the Tories," wrote Adams. "Dr. F. is very staunch against the Tories, more decided a

---

4. Made by Edward Bancroft and, according to his notation, based on the original in Strachey's hand.

5. The British counterproposal is described above, [Nov. 19].

6. Strachey also brought Oswald a new set of private instructions from Townshend. These emphasized that Strachey was privy to the sentiments of the King's ministers and would oversee Oswald's actions. Oswald was authorized to sign a treaty, but only after consultation with Strachey and Fitzherbert. Townshend strongly urged Oswald to insist on this proposal which had the unanimous approval of the cabinet and which gave "full satisfaction ... to the Americans in the principal points of the Controversy, and what any impartial Man must imagine the only ones worth their dispute." Townshend to Oswald, Nov. 19, in Giunta, *Emerging Nation*, 1, 678–9.

7. JA's account of Nov. 26 through 30 is in Butterfield, *John Adams Diary*, III, 75–85.

great deal on this Point than Mr. Jay or my self."[8] For Franklin's role in breaking the deadlock over this issue, see his Proposed Article of November 29, below.

Henry Laurens arrived in Paris just in time to participate in the last day of negotiations. Approving of what his colleagues had achieved and were still fighting for, Laurens added to Article 7 a clause concerning slaves.[9]

25th. Novr. 1782

Since I was here last, I have seen, and conversed with, almost every one of the King's Council. They are unanimous in the desire of concluding the Peace. But they are also unanimous in declaring that they think You unreasonable in refusing a general Amnesty and Restoration of Property, to the Refugees. They are unanimous in declaring that those Two Points must be insisted upon, and that every thing ought to be risqued, rather than submit to Terms highly dishonorable to the British Government. And I must add that those of His Majesty's Ministers, who have been the most zealous Advocates for the Independence of America, are the most forward (if there is the least difference) in condemning America for making a moment's hesitation upon these Points, which seem to affect equally the Honor, the Justice, and even the Policy of America, as of Great Britain.

The Article of the Fishery is another Point. They were determined to resist the Proposition I carried over. They are apprehensive of future Quarels— To obviate which as much as possible, they have expunged that part of the Article, which proposed the Privilege of drying on Cape Sables, and upon the Shores of Nova Scotia, but have left to You what is conceived will be amply sufficient for Your Accommodation.

Objections were made to almost the whole of the Paper I carried from hence, as deficient in point of Form and Precision. The King's Ministers have therefore drawn out the Articles as they wish them to stand, and in Form similar to all other Treaties— They have left out several Preambles, as unnecessary, and unusual. The Point regarding the Debts, though somewhat altered

8. Butterfield, *John Adams Diary*, III, 77.
9. *Laurens Papers*, XVI, pp. 79–80. See also Butterfield, *John Adams Diary*, III, 82–3.

in the Forms of Expression, is exactly as You put it, in respect to Substance. The Article of Independence, is adopted precisely in the Words dictated by Yourselves. The Boundaries, they are not satisfied with; and they hope upon a little more Consideration of the real Rights of the Crown, You will have no Objection to admit of the Extention of Nova Scotia to Penobscot—That is left open for amicable Discussion. But I will acknowledge, (depending upon your not taking Advantage of what I say) that they are not disposed to break off the Treaty absolutely, upon that Article.

The Restitution of the Property of the Loyalists, is the grand Point upon which a final Settlement depends— If the Treaty breaks off now, the whole Business must go loose, and take it's Chance in Parliament, where I am confident the warmest Friends of American Independence, will not support the Idea of the Confiscation of private Property.

Here is the Treaty in such shape as Mr. Oswald can immediately sign—and the War is—for ever I hope, at an end— By this Treaty, You have your Independence confirmed, and in Your own identical mode of Expression. By this Treaty You acquire that vast Extent of Territory You have claimed— New York, with all Your Artillery there, is ceded to You— You will consider well whether You will reject these great Objects for which You have so long and bravely fought, merely upon the Non-admission of a Demand the most humiliating and degrading to Great Britain, and clearly repugnant to the Honor, the Justice, and even the good Policy of America herself.

It is necessary I should apprise You, that in the Article of Restitution, the Words *Rights and Properties* are added to the Word *Estates,* in the view of securing the Proprietary Interests, derived from ancient and solemn Charters—

25th. Novr. 1782. As much as I could recollect of my opening to the Commissrs. at Paris—

348

From John Jay

ALS: Library of Congress

Dr Sir   Monday afternoon [November 25, 1782][1]
The Marquis de la Fayette is about to depart, & wishes for a
speedy answer to his Letter— The enclosed Draft of one, meets
with Mr Adam's approbation, & if it also meets with your's, be
pleased to sign a Copy of it, and send it by the Bearer—[2]
I am Dr Sir sincerely Yours &.   J. JAY

His Exy Dr Franklin

Addressed: His Exy. / Doctr. Franklin / Passy

From François-Pierre de Séqueville

Printed announcement with MS insertions: American Philosophical Society

[November 25, 1782]
Le Roi ne verra pas demain mardi 26. Messieurs les Ambassadeurs
et ministres Étrangers.

La Cour prendra le Deuil le *27* de ce mois, à l'occasion de la mort
de *la Psse Charlotte Amelie, de Dannemk.* Sa Majesté le portera
cinq jours.[3]   DE SEQUEVILLE
                              Secrétaire ordinaire du Roi, à la conduite
                              de Mrs. les Ambassadeurs.

Addressed: a Monsieur, / Monsieur francklin ministre / Plenipre. des Etats unis de / l'amerique septentrionale / a Passy De
sequeville

1. The date of Lafayette's departure for Brest; see our annotation of Lafayette to BF, [Nov. 26].
2. The commissioners' letter to Lafayette is below, [Nov. 27].
3. Princess Charlotte Amalie (1706–1782), sister of Christian VI of Denmark (1699–1746), died on Oct. 28: *Dansk Biografisk Leksikon* (16 vols.,
Copenhagen, 1979–84). BF observed the mourning period, wearing his black
suit (XXXI, 105n) when he signed the preliminary articles on Nov. 30: W. A. S.
Hewins, *The Whitefoord Papers* (Oxford, 1898), pp. 200–1n.

To Richard Oswald[4]

LS:[5] William L. Clements Library; copies: Library of Congress (two), Massachusetts Historical Society (two), National Archives, New-York Historical Society, William L. Clements Library, Ohio State Archaeological and Historical Society; transcript: National Archives

Sir,   Passy, Nov. 26. 1782.

You may well remember that in the Beginning of our Conferences,[6] before the other Commissioners arriv'd, on your mentioning to me a Retribution for the Loyalists whose Estates had been forfeited, I acquainted you that nothing of that Kind, could be stipulated by us, the Confiscations being made by Virtue of Laws of Particular States, which the Congress had no Power to contravene or dispense with, and therefore could give us no such authority in our Commission. And I gave it as my Opinion and Advice honestly and cordially, that if a Reconciliation was intended, no mention should be made in our Negociations of those

---

4. This letter was ostensibly written in response to Article 5 of the British counterproposal, which the American commissioners saw on Nov. 25; see the headnote to that counterproposal, published under [Nov. 19]. However, we suspect that BF drafted parts of it during the previous round of negotiations in early November. Before Strachey left Paris on Nov. 5, and before he and Oswald received answers to their letters urging compromise on the Loyalist question (Nov. 5 and 4, respectively), Oswald saw a draft of the intended answer, "which was that the Refugees should have Compensation, provided Great Britain would compensate for all the Towns, Houses, Barns etc. destroyed during the War!": Strachey to Townshend, Nov. 8, in Giunta, *Emerging Nation*, I, 651. That phrase did not appear in the commissioners' joint answer of Nov. 7, but does echo the language BF uses in the first paragraph of the present letter.

   BF read this letter to JA and Jay on the morning of Nov. 26. They agreed that he should read it to Oswald as "containing his private Sentiments": Butterfield, *John Adams Diary*, III, 75. Jay sent a copy to Livingston on Dec. 12, saying how useful BF's "firmness and exertions" on the subject had been. This letter "had much weight, and is written with a degree of acuteness and spirit seldom to be met with in persons of his age": Wharton, *Diplomatic Correspondence*, VI, 130.

   5. In L'Air de Lamotte's hand with corrections and additions by BF as noted below. BF also wrote the complimentary close, the name of the addressee, and the notations.

   6. In a conversation of June 3: XXXVII, 326. See also BF's April 19 comments to Oswald: XXXVII, 177–8, 295–6.

People; for they having done infinite Mischief to our Properties by wantonly burning and destroying Farmhouses, Villages, and Towns, if Compensation for their Losses were insisted on, we should certainly exhibit against it, an Account of all the Ravages they had Committed which would necessarily recall to View Scenes of Barbarity that must inflame instead of conciliating, and tend to perpetuate an Enmity that we all profess a Desire of extinguishing. Understanding however from you, that this was a Point your Ministry had at Heart; I wrote concerning it to Congress;[7] and have lately received the following Resolution.[8] Viz—

"By the United States in Congress assembled.

"Resolved,

"That the Secretary for Foreign affairs be and he is hereby directed to obtain as speedily as possible authentic Returns of the Slaves and other Property which have been carried off or destroyed in the Course of the War by the Enemy and to Transmit the same to the Minister Plenipotentiary for negociating Peace.

"Resolved,

"That in the mean time the Secretary for Foreign affairs inform the said Ministers, that many Thousands of Slaves and other Property to a very great Amount have been carried off or destroyed by the Enemy; and that in the Opinion of Congress the great Loss of Property which the Citizens of the United States have sustained by the Enemy, will be considered by the several States, as an insuperable Bar to their making Restitution or Indemnification to the former Owners of Property which has been or may be forfeited to, or confiscated by any of the States."

In consequence of those Resolutions and the circular Letters of the Secretary the assembly of Pensylvania then sitting passed the following Act, viz,

"State of Pennsylvania, in General Assembly.

Wednesday, September 18. 1782.

"The Bill intitled. 'An Act, for procuring an Estimate of the Damages sustained by the Inhabitants of Pennsylvania, from the

7. BF to Livingston, Oct. 14, above.
8. Enclosed with the first Sept. 13 letter from Livingston, above, which Barney delivered on Nov. 5.

Troops & Adherents of the King of Great Britain, during the present War,' was read a second time,

"Ordered to be transcribed and printed for the public Consideration.

Extract from the Minutes,
(signed) PETER Z LLOYD.
Clark of the General assembly.

"Bill intitled, An Act, for procuring an Estimate of the Damages sustained by the Inhabitants of Pennsylvania, from the Troops and Adherents of the King of Great Britain, during the Present War.

"Whereas great Damages of the most wanton nature, have been committed by the Armies of the King of Great Britain, or their Adherents, within the Territory of the United States of North America, unwarranted by the Practice of civilized Nations, and only to be accounted for, from the vindictive Spirit of the said King and his Officers; and whereas an accurate Account and Estimate of such Damages, more especially the waste and Destruction of Property, may be very useful to the People of the United States of America, informing a future Treaty of Peace; and in the mean time may serve to exhibit in a true Light to the Nations of Europe, the Conduct of the said King, his Ministers, officers and adherents; to the End, therefore, that proper measures be taken to ascertain the Damages aforesaid, which have been done to the Citizens and Inhabitants of Pennsylvania, in the Course of the present War, with this State:

"Be it enacted by the representatives of the Freemen of the Commonwealth of Pennsylvania, in general assembly met, and by the Authority of the same, that in every County of this State, which has been invaded by the Armies, Soldiers or Adherents of the King of Great Britain, the Commissioners of every such County, shall immediately meet together, each within their County, and issue Directions to the assessors of the Respective Townships, Districts and Places within such County, to call upon the Inhabitants of every Township and Place, to furnish Accounts & Estimates of the Damages, Waste & Destruction, which hath been done & committed as aforesaid, upon the Property real or personal, within the same Township or place since

the first Day of [*blank in MS*] which was in the Year of our Lord
177 , and the same Accounts and Estimates to transmit to the
said Commissioners without Delay. And if any Person or Persons, shall refuse or neglect to make out such Accounts and Estimates, the said assessors of the Township or Place, shall from
their own Knowledge and by other reasonable & lawful Methods, take and render such an Account and Estimate of all Damage done or committed as aforesaid.

"Provided always, that all such Accounts and Estimates, to be
made out and transmitted as aforesaid, shall contain a Narrative
of the time and Circumstances, and if in the Power of the Person aggrieved, the Names of the General or other officer, or Adherent of the Enemy, by whom the Damage in any Case was
done, or under whose Orders the Army, detachment, Party or
Persons committing the same acted at that time, and also the
Name and Condition of the Person or Persons, whose Property
was so damaged or destroyed; and that all such Accounts and Estimates, be made in current Money upon Oath or Affirmation of
the Sufferer or of others having Knowledge concerning the
same; and that in every Case it be set forth, whether the Party injured hath received any Satisfaction for his Losses, and by whom
the same was given.

"And be it further enacted by the Authority aforesaid, that the
said Commissioners having obtained the said Accounts and Estimates from the assessor of the several Townships & Places,
shall proceed to inspect and register the same in a Book to be
provided for that Purpose, distingushing the districts and Townships, and entering those of each Place together; and if any Account and Estimate be imperfect or not sufficiently verified and
established, the said Commissioners shall have power, and they
or any two of them are hereby authorised to summon and compel any Person, whose Evidence they shall think necessary, to
appear before them at a Day & Place appointed, to be examined
upon Oath or Affirmation concerning any damage or Injury as
aforesaid; and the said Commissioners shall upon the Call and
Demand of the President or Vice-President of the Supreme Executive Council, deliver or send to the Secretary of the said
Council, all or any of the original Accounts and Estimates aforesaid and shall also deliver or send to the said Secretary, Copies

of the Book aforesaid, or any Part or Parts thereof upon reasonable Notice.

"And be it farther enacted by the Authority aforesaid, that all Losses of Negro or Mulatto Slaves and Servants, who have been deluded and carried away by the Enemies of the United States, and which have not been recovered or recompenced, shall be comprehended within the Accounts and Estimates aforesaid and that the Commissioners and assessors of any County which had not been invaded as aforesaid, shall nevertheless inquire after and procure Accounts and Estimates of any Damages suffered by the Losses of such Servants and Slaves, as herein before directed as to other Property.

"And be it further enacted by the Authority aforesaid, that the Charges and Expences of executing the Act, as to the Pay of the said Commissioners and Assessors, shall be as in other Cases; and that Witnesses shall be rewarded for their Loss of time and Trouble, as Witnesses summoned to appear in the Courts of Quarter Sessions of the Peace; and the said Charges and Expences shall be defrayed by the Commonwelth, but paid in the first Instance out of the Monies in the hands of the Treasurer of the County rates and Levies upon orders drawn by the Commissioners of the proper County."

It appears by subsequent Newspapers that this Bill passed into an Act.[9]

We have not yet had time to hear what has been done by the other assemblies; but I have no doubt that similar Acts will be made by all of them; and that the Mass of Evidence produced by the Execution of those Acts, not only of the Enormities committed by those People (the Royalists)[1] under the Direction of British Generals, but of those committed by the British Troops themselves, will form a Record that must render the British Name odious in America to the latest Generations. In that Authentic Record will be found the burning of the fine Towns of Charlestown near Boston; of Falmouth just before Winter when

9. This sentence is in BF's hand. The bill was enacted into law on Sept. 21: *Laws Enacted in the Third Sitting of the Sixth General Assembly of the Commonwealth of Pennsylvania* . . . (Philadelphia, 1782), pp. 108–9.

1. This parenthetical phrase was interlined by BF.

the Sick, the Aged, the Women and Children were driven to seek Shelter where they could hardly find it; of Norfolk in the midst of Winter; Of New London; of Fairfield; of Esopus; &c. &c. besides near a hundred and fifty miles of well settled Country laid waste, every House and Barn burnt, and many hundreds of Farmers with their Wives and Children butchered and scalped.[2]

The present British Ministers when they reflect a little will certainly be too equitable to suppose that their Nation has a right to make an *unjust* War (which they have always allowed this against us to be) and to do all Sorts of unnecessary mischief un-justifiable by the Practice of any civilized People, which those they make War with are to suffer, without claiming any Satis-faction; but that if Britons or their Adherents are in return de-prived of any Property it is to be restored to them, or they are to be indemnified! The British Troops can never excuse their Bar-barities. They were unprovoked. The Loyalists say in Excuse of theirs, that they were exasperated by the Loss of their Estates, & it was Revenge. They have then had their Revenge. Is it right they should have both?

Some of those People may have a Merit with regard to Brit-ain; those who espoused her Cause from affection; these it may become you to reward. But there are many of them who were Waverers, and were only determined to engage in it by some occasional Circumstances or Appearances; these have not much of either Merit or demerit; and there are others who have Abun-dance of Demerit, respecting your Country, having by their Falshoods & Misrepresentations brought on and encouraged the Continuance of the War. These instead of being recompenced should be punished.

It is usual among Christian People at War to profess always a Desire of Peace. But if the Ministers of one of the Parties chuse to insist particularly on a certain Article which they have known the others are not and cannot be empower'd to agree to, what Credit can they expect should be given to such Professions?

2. See also XXIX, 590–3. The last item probably refers to the 1778 attacks on the settlements of the Wyoming Valley of the Susquehanna River: Max M. Mintz, *Seeds of Empire: the American Revolutionary Conquest of the Iro-quois* (New York and London, 1999), pp. 54–63.

Your Ministers require that we should receive again into our Bosom those who have been our bitterest Enemies, and restore their Properties who have destroy'd ours: and this while the Wounds they have given us are still bleeding. It is many Years since your Nation expell'd the Stuarts and their Adherents, and confiscated their Estates. Much of your Resentment against them may by this time be abated. Yet if we should propose it and insist as an Article of our Treaty with you, that that Family should be recalled and the forfeited Estates of its Friends restored, would you think us serious in our Professions of earnestly desiring Peace?

I must repeat my Opinion, that it is best for you to drop all mention of the Refugees. We have proposed indeed nothing but what we think best for you as well as ourselves. But if you will have them mentioned, let it be in an Article which may provide; that they shall exhibit Accounts of their Losses, to Commissioners hereafter to be appointed, who shall examine the same, together with the Accounts now preparing in America of the Damages done by them, and state the Account, and that if a Ballance appears in their Favour it shall be paid by us to you, and by you divided among them as you shall think proper. And if the Ballance is found due to us, it shall be paid by you.

Give me leave however to advise you to prevent the Necessity of so dreadful a Discussion, by droping the Article; that we may write to America, to stop the Enquiry.

With great Esteem & Respect, I am, Sir, Your most obedient & most humble Servant   B FRANKLIN

Richard Oswald Esqe.

Copy

Notations by Franklin: Read to the Commissioners at Paris, the same Day / Honble. R. Oswald Esqr[3]

Endorsed: Refugees & Loyalists

---

3. At some time the "Honble." was crossed out.

To the Earl of Shelburne

ALS: Reprinted from Christie's auction catalogue "Important Auto-graph Letters from the Historical Archives of Bowood House" (London, Oct. 12, 1994), p. 35.

My Lord,   Passy, Nov. 26. 1782
  Mr Vaughan brought me some time since from your Lordship a Remedy you were so kind as to send me for my Gravel.[4] I intended to thank you by him. He staid here much longer than I expected, and when he went it was so suddenly that I had not time to write. I was nevertheless extreamly sensible of your Goodness towards me in this fresh Instance, and I beg you to accept my thankful Acknowledgements, and to be assur'd that I shall ever retain a grateful Remembrance of it. With great and sincere Esteem and Respect, I have the honour to be, My Lord, Your Lordship's most obedient and most humble Servant[5]
                                                              B Franklin

Rt Honble. the Earl of Shelburne

From Lafayette   ALS: Library of Congress

                                     Rambouïllet Tuesday Morning
Dear Sir   [November 26, 1782][6]
  Having Waïted some time for Mr. jay, I Was told By doctor Bancroft that the two other Ministers Now Agreed With You in

4. See Vaughan to BF, Sept. 23. The abbé Morellet had written to Shelburne on Oct. 27 that BF was grateful for "le specifique contre la goutte": Medlin, *Morellet*, I, 468.
5. During this period Shelburne also sent a message to WTF, who later described it to his aunt: "Lord Shelburne sent me a very polite Message—by an Under Secy. of State [Strachey]—that if I had any desire of making my Father a Visit, he would Favour the interview—This was before the Preliminaries were signed—I need not tell you I did not accept it." WTF to SB, Dec. 26, 1782, APS.
6. Lafayette left Versailles on Nov. 25, after meeting with Vergennes, and reached Rambouillet the following day. He arrived in Brest on Dec. 1, in time to sail to Cadiz with the expeditionary force destined for Jamaica: Louis Gottschalk, *Lafayette and the Close of the American Revolution* (Chicago, 1942), pp. 385–8.

357

Opinion that After What I Had done in the Affair of Monney, it was Better for me Immediately to join the Convoy— However I Waïted once More Upon Count de Vergennes on My Passage at Versaïlles, and Had a long Conversation With Him— Let the dispatches Arrive or Not,[7] He will to Morrow see M. de fleury— The six Millions, *Betwen us*, I think We Will Have— As to the Remainder, I do not know What May Be decided— Inclosed I Have the Honor to Send You a Copy of My Last Letter to Count de Vergennes and His Answer—[8] You Will oblige me to Make these Communications to Mon. jay and Adams, as well as News of My Last Conversation, Because I want them to see that Nothing More on My Part Remains to Be done— I will also thank You for Your Answer which Has not Yet Come to Hand.[9]

With the Highest Regard and Warmest Affection Yours

LAFAYETTE

P.S. My Secretary Has not Copied My letter— I Will send it By the Next opportunity

From Richard Oswald

ALS: Library of Congress

Paris 26 Novr 1782

By a Letter from Mr Dundass, Lord Advocate of Scotland, dated 12th Novemr, he writes that a Nephew of his, Son of the Lord presedent of the Court of Session, Francis Dundas a Captain of the 1st Regimt of Guards is now at London a Prisoner upon his

7. *I.e.*, the missing dispatches from La Luzerne, which Barney had just found at Lorient; see Barney to BF, Nov. 23.

8. Lafayette's Nov. 22 letter to Vergennes (Idzerda, *Lafayette Papers*, V, 69–72, 368–70) was a lengthy and self-important plea for continued assistance to America. He showed it to the commissioners on Nov. 23, when he also delivered his letter to them of Nov. 21. According to JA, BF regarded it as an attempt to claim credit if the loan was approved; JA was irritated at Lafayette's "unlimited Ambition": Butterfield, *John Adams Diary*, III, 49, 71. The copy Lafayette here encloses and Vergennes' response have not been located.

9. The peace commissioners answered Lafayette's Nov. 21 letter on Nov. [27], below.

Parole, having Served in Lord Cornwallis Army.[1] And wishes much to be discharged under any Obligations or Conditions of Exchange that may be thought proper, & may in the Interim Restore him to his freedom in his Rank of Service— I should consider this as a particular Obligation on my part   RO

From Robert Pigott   ALS: American Philosophical Society

Hond. Sir   Geneva 26 Novemr 1782
I ought in duty to have wrote before this time to express the Satisfaction I Receivd at Paris from the honour of your Acquaintance,[2] & also to acknowledge your very many Civilitys, and If I have been guilty of an Omission in this particular, The cause arose from an apprehension of being troublesome. No Person can have a greater respect & more sincere regard for Dr: Franklyn than myself. Your Name is Immortal, yes Sir What Man who prizes Humanity will not have pride honor & Pleasure in giving Praise to so venerable a Character. I hope the Battle is finally fought & won, & that the Civil Crown(?) so honorably obtained will long be enjoyed in Peace & happyness.

I had the pleasure of seeing Yesterday your Grandson & his Companion Jeanet.[3] They were both in perfect Health, and I consider as two Young Plants which will produce good fruit when transplanted into their native Soil. They appear of Character so different yet each good in their Kind. As I propose to pass the Next succeeding months in Geneva I hope to see them often, if you have any Instructions to give concerning them I

1. Francis Dundas' father was Robert Dundas, Lord Arniston (1713–1787), lord president of the court of session since 1760. Francis' uncle Henry Dundas (later Viscount Melville) became lord advocate of Scotland in 1775. Francis' maternal grandfather William Grant, Lord Prestongrange, also had been lord advocate, serving from 1746 to 1754. See the *DNB* (under Dundas and Grant) and E. B. Fryde *et al.*, eds., *Handbook of British Chronology* (3rd ed., London, 1986), pp. 199, 202.

2. Pigott was in Paris early in 1782: XXXVI, 322–3.

3. Johonnot. BFB noted in his journal a visit to Pigott's on Sunday, Nov. 23, when he went ice skating.

shall have much pleasure in receiving Them. I take the Liberty
to inclose your Excellence a Letter which is destined for Boston.
The Young Man to whom it is addressed is said to be a great Genius & full of Talents. His Parents are very worthy People &
greatly respected.[4] They sollicit me to intreat your Excellence to
say a word in his favour to some friend at Boston, & also his itin-
erant Companion by name Serre. These two young Men formed
a Project to establish themselves in America animated with the
Ideea of the new World where they might have a better opportunity to distinguish Themselves than in the old.

Mrs Pigott desires to present her best Respects which concludes me with all possible regard Honorable Sir Your very devoted Servt.   ROBERT PIGOTT

Notation: Pigott 26 Nov. 1782.

The American Peace Commissioners to Lafayette

AL (draft):[5] Columbia University Library; copies: Library of Congress
(two), Massachusetts Historical Society

Sir   [November 27, 1782][6]
We have recd. the Letter you did us the Honor to write on the
25th. Inst.[7]

Our Country has had early & repeated Proofs both of your
Readiness and abilities to do her Service. The Prospect of an in-
active Campaign in america, induced us to adopt the opinion,

4. Albert Gallatin had left Geneva with his friend Henri Serre in 1780.
Though orphaned at the age of nine, he was from a prominent Geneva family and was brought up by a relative of his father's: XXXVI, 555n; Henry
Adams, *The Life of Albert Gallatin* (Philadelphia and London, 1879), pp. 2–
3, 5–6, 10–11.
5. In the hand of John Jay, and sent to BF for approval on Nov. 25, above.
6. Lafayette, when leaving Paris, asked his wife to procure the present letter. She wrote to Jay on Nov. 27, and he answered on Nov. 28 that the letter
had been sent the previous day: Morris, *Jay: Peace,* pp. 510, 511–12. A now-
missing copy of the present letter, published in Wharton, *Diplomatic Correspondence,* VI, 89, gives its date as Nov. 28.
7. Actually, Nov. 21; the letter is above.

that you might be more useful here than there—especially in Case the Negotiation for peace on the Part of France & England, should be committed to your managemt;[8] for Your Knowledge of our affairs, & attachment to our Interests, might have been very advantageous to us on such an occasion. But as an opportunity now offers of your being instrumental in producing a Co-operation, which would probably put a glorious and speedy Termination to the War in america, we for our part, perfectly approve of your going with Count D'Estaing in the Manner proposed.

We have the Honor to be &c.

Marqs. de la Fayette

Dr. of joint Letter to Marqs. Fayette Appd. verb [Approved verbally]

Franklin: Order for the Release of Captain Francis Dundas

DS:[9] University of Pennsylvania Library; AD (draft) and press copy of DS: Library of Congress; copies: Public Record Office, National Maritime Museum

[November 27, 1782]

A Request being made to me by his Excellency Richard Oswald Esquire,[1] Minister Plenipotentiary of his Britannic Majesty for treating of Peace, in favour of Captain Francis Dundas, of the first Regiment of Guards, Nephew of the Lord Advocate of Scotland & Son of the Lord President, now at London a Prisoner on his Parole, having served in Lord Cornwallis's Army, and desirous of being restored to his Freedom in his Rank of Service; I the underwritten, Minister Plenipotentiary of the United States, being persuaded that the Congress will not disapprove a Compliance with such a Request, do hereby, as far it may

8. Jay here drafted but deleted, "(as there was Reason to hope)".
9. In the hand of L'Air de Lamotte.
1. Above, Nov. 26.

be in my Power, discharge and annul the Parole given by the said Captain Dundas, on this Condition, that Sir James Jay, a member of the honourable Senate of New-York, now a prisoner on his Parole in London, be in Return fully discharged from his said Parole. Given at Passy, this 27th. Day of November 1782.

B FRANKLIN

Notation: Discharge of Capt. Dundas from Parole recd. from Dr. Franklin 27th Novr. 1782.

From Richard Bache: Three Letters

(I), (II), and (III) ALS: American Philosophical Society

I.

Dear & Hond: Sir   Philadelphia Novr. 27th. 1782.

Give me leave to introduce to you Mr. Stuart, Brother to my particular Friend Colonel Walter Stuart;[2] this young Gentleman has resided some time in America, and has gained the esteem of all his Acquaintanc; as a Person deserving your Notice & Civilities, I therefore recommend him to you.

I am Dear Sir Your affectionate Son   RICH BACHE

Dr. Franklin

Addressed: His Excellency / Dr. Benjamin Franklin / Minister Plenipoy: from the United / States of No: America / at / Passy / Favored by Mr. Stuart

Notation: Richd. Bache Nov. 27. 1782.

---

2. Col. Stewart (*c.* 1756–1796), born in Londonderry, Ireland, began serving in the American army in 1776. Appointed inspector for the northern army in early 1782, Stewart was breveted brigadier general the following year and after retirement became a prominent Philadelphia merchant: John H. Campbell, *History of the Friendly Sons of St. Patrick* . . . (Philadelphia, 1892), pp. 134–5; W. W. Abbot *et al.*, eds., *The Papers of George Washington*, Revolutionary War Series (14 vols. to date, Charlottesville, Va., and London, 1985–), IV, 448n.

II.

Dear & Hond: Sir   Philadelphia Novr. 27h. 1782

Permit me to introduce to your acquaintance, Mr. Moses Miers who having resided for some time here, is now going to join his establishment at Amsterdam—[3] He is generally esteemed here as a Gentleman of Probity & Honor; as such I recommend him to your Notice & Civilities. I am Dear Sir Your affectionate Son   RICH BACHE

Dr. Franklin

Addressed: His Excellency / Dr. Benjamin Franklin / Minister Plenipoy: from the United / States of No. America / at / Passy / Favored by Mr. Miers

Notation: Richd. Bache Nov. 27. 1782.

III.

Dear & Hond: Sir   Philadelphia Novr. 27th. 1782.

I have lately wrote you by a variety of opportunities,—since my last, I have the pleasure to inform you a small part of the three Hhhds [hogsheads] of Claret, you were so kind to order me, came safe to hand, and proves of excellent Quality; Mr. Bonfield has done ample justice to his Commission— I wish I may be fortunate enough to get the remaining twenty Boxes; ten of which were sent to L'Orient & ten to Rochfort—[4] Sally has packed up in the Box that contains Squirrel Skins for Temple,[5] all the Newspapers, except a few of yesterday & this day's date, which you will receive herewith— We are all in good Health, & join in Love & Duty to you.

---

3. Moses Myers (XXXIV, 238n) and his brother Samuel were partners in a merchant firm which had recently agreed to ship some of the supplies left in Holland by Alexander Gillon; the ship, however, was lost: XXXVII, 643–4, 663. Their New York partner was Isaac Moses: *Morris Papers,* II, 110n; VI, 215n.

4. BF had ordered the wine from John Bondfield a year earlier: XXXVII, 715n.

5. John Vaughan reported to WTF on Nov. 12 and 15 that SB had packed ten dozen squirrel skins. On Dec. 3, SB wrote WTF that she was sending three skins (plus nine dog pelts) by way of Moses Myers. APS.

I am, Dear sir, ever Yours affecly.   RICH BACHE

Dr. Franklin

Addressed: Dr. Franklin

From Ingenhousz   ALS: American Philosophical Society

Dear Sir   Vienna Nov. 27 1782.

I have at last recieved the German American newspapers as far as august 6th. they have diverted me and many of my friends. I wish to have some more, if you have recieved some of a later date. The almanac is not arrived.[6]

I hope mr. wharton will send me soon an answer after having recieved your admonitory note, you was so good as to join to my lettre. I can not but be anxious about the principels of that Gentleman, after he brooke his word of honour, by which he promish'd me as well by writing as by words, that he will make it his first duty to write to me. Instead of writing to me, he writes to mr. Coffyn, who is interested but for a small part in the trade, and that gentleman divides the provenue between him and Dr. Bankroft, without my Consent, and without my having any intelligence of their acting according to the will of mr. wharton but what mr. Coffyn himself writes me. Indeed I have not the least Sus'picion of mr. Coffyn's honesty. The fault lies in the negligence of mr. wharton, which however unaccountable in a man of his quality, can not be taken by me as yet for a want of integrity. But Dr. Bankroft's unwillingless of giving me any account of the transaction, tho requested repeatedly to doe so by mr. Coffyn by you and by my Self,[7] can not but inspire me with unfavourable ideas of that gentleman. If I was to be treated with such an abominable behaviour as every body, but me, would suspect by the proceeding of mr. S. Wharton towards me, it would

6. BF had promised to send the almanack and newspapers in the letter he began on Oct. 2, 1781, but did not do so until June 21, 1782: XXXV, 547.

7. At BF's request, Bancroft did write Ingenhousz *c.* Oct. 21. He sent that response to WTF, asking him to forward the letter: Bancroft to WTF, Oct. 21, 1782 (Hist. Soc. of Pa.).

hurt me materialy in my moderate circumstances, the more so, as I loose about one hundred pound St. a jear by a reform which the emperour has made, in taking away the right of a free longing [lodging] from every one who belongs to the Court. This reform, of which nobody understands the reason, I could never have exspected to touch me, as I was engaged to settle here under express promiss that I should enjoy Constantly the benefits, which the court granted me without my making the least Step to obtain them, and which is les that the Empress offred me.[8] I could exspect so much the less this harm from that Souverain, as he him Self gave me his hand, shaked it, and toll'd me *Monsieur Ingen Housz je suis bien aise d'apprendre que vous restez avec nous, je vous reconnois pour un parfaitement honnete homme; Comptez sur moi, je serai toujours votre ami.* I wrote him a lettre upon it, repeating him his own promiss and telling him very respectfully, that I have the greatest confidence in Such gracious expressions and that I would doe an injury to his Majesty and magnanimity, if I should permit me to harbour in my breast the least fear of loosing at my age a part of the emoluments which I accepted after having been sollicited during 4 months to accept of them. All has been to no purpos; I doubt even, whether my reluctant submission to be a looser has not done me more harm than good. This makes me sometimes low spirited and unfit for business. If mr. wharton's behaviour had been such as I had a right to expect from him, it would have kept up my spirits by having gained by trade what I lost by having too much Confidence in Courts. You remember I did live quieter in the small Northumberland court[9] than at the most August Court of the world.

I should wish you would ask to mr. Bankroft the original lettres of mr. Wharton and runn them over, or, as this would not suit your business, let them be red over by your grandson or clerk, who could give me a short account of what mr. Wharton may have wrote about my share in the trade. This would, I think, discover at once, whether those gentleman have conspired to

8. Ingenhousz was appointed imperial physician by Empress Maria Theresa: XXVII, 505n.
9. His former residence in London: XXVII, 505.

cheat me or not; tho it will not exculpate Dr. Bankroft of his un-
willingness of giving me a propre account of my own affaires,
which he has in hands. Be So kind as to quiet me on these accounts. *Nusquam tuta fides!*[1]

The polemical piece of the german translator[2] will not be in
the frensh Edition. I hear from a friend of Dr. Priestley, he is
some what in peine about his manner of acting with me. His
friend, now here, Sees the Revd. Dr. is mistaken in his doctrine
by not knowing my decisive experiments.

I sent a paper about it to the R. Society,[3] by which, as I have
understood, every body has been convinced I am perfectly in the
right.

I will follow your good advise by abstaining from polemics,
not to loose time or be vexed.[4]

Mr. le Begue, who has the M.S. a long while, doe not goe on
with the printing. I wish I could come over my Self.

I am respectfuly your obedient humble Servant and faithfull
friend   J. INGEN HOUSZ

I refer farther to my former lettres.

Addressed: a Son Excellence / Mr. B. Franklin, Ministre Plenip.
/ des Etats unis de l'Amerique / septentrionale &c &c. / a
Passy

Endorsed: Nov. 27. 82

1. "Trust is nowhere safe!"
Bancroft was indignant at this request of Ingenhousz', evidently communicated to him by WTF. Replying on Dec. 28 that it would take him a day or
two to find Wharton's letter, he sent it to WTF on Jan. 1 after calling at Passy
and finding no one at home, "not . . . *even a servant*, who could receive a Message." Bancroft insisted that he had already shown this letter to BF. He gave
WTF permission to extract the relevant sections and send them to Ingenhousz,
and strongly suggested that Ingenhousz apologize to him for this "distrust of
my veracity": Bancroft to WTF, Dec. 28, 1782, and Jan. 1, 1783 (APS). A brief,
undated note from Bancroft to WTF (APS), which may or may not be related,
indicates that Bancroft is returning Wharton's bill and his own receipt.
2. Niklas-Karl Molitor: XXXV, 549–50n; XXXVII, 211–12.
3. "Some Farther Considerations on the Influence of the Vegetable Kingdom on the Animal Creation," *Phil. Trans.*, LXXII (1782), 426–39.
4. XXXV, 550.

From Robert R. Livingston

LS:[5] University of Pennsylvania Library; AL (draft): New-York Historical Society; transcript: National Archives

Sir   Philadelphia 27th. Novr. 1782

An opportunity offering from this port to write directly to you, I do not chuse to hazard anything by the Post which carries this to Boston, particularly as I did not hear till just now that a frigate was to sail from thence, and it is uncertain whether this will arrive in time to go by her— This then only accompanies the newspapers which contain all the public information now in circulation—

The Memorial of Messrs. Lé Marque and Fabre are transmitted to South Carolina, as it is a matter in which the United States are not concerned— It is to be hoped that the State will do justice to the Claimants if as is asserted Gillon acted under authority from them—[6] He just left this with his Ship not in the most honorable manner having as I am informed been arrested by order of the proprietor of the Ship for his proportion of the prize money.— The Sherif stands in the gap—[7]

The Swiss Officer mentioned in yours I have sent to Edenton to get information about, you shall have the result of my enquiries in my next—[8]

As your Grandson will probably chuse to continue in the line he is in, I cannot but think he might find important advantages from opening a correspondence with this Office— His dilli-

---

5. According to a note on the transcript this duplicate was carried by Matthias Ogden, who did not reach Paris until July 12, 1783: *Morris Papers,* VII, 761n. The original was sent to Boston, and the triplicate was sent by the *General Washington;* both are missing.

6. For Lamarque & Fabre's claims against Gillon see their letter of Sept. 10.

7. When La Luzerne's secretary Marbois obtained an arrest warrant against him, Gillon handed over command of the frigate *South Carolina* to Capt. John Joyner and departed for Charleston: James A. Lewis, *Neptune's Militia: the Frigate* South Carolina *during the American Revolution* (Kent, Ohio, and London, 1999), pp. 83–4.

8. On June 25, BF forwarded to Livingston the request of Jean-Jacques Vallier for a valid death certificate, his late brother Jean Vallier le cadet having died in Edenton, N.C.: XXXVII, 180–1, 539.

gence and accuracy in collecting and transmitting intelligence would procure him friends here—my attatchment to you will render me desireous to place them in the best light.

I am Sir, with great Respect and Esteem your most obedt. humble servt.   ROBT R LIVINGSTON

No 22. 2plicate

From Benjamin Vaughan[9]

> Reprinted from William Temple Franklin, ed., *Memoirs of the Life and Writings of Benjamin Franklin* . . . (3 vols., 4to, London, 1817–18), II, 412–13.

My Dearest Sir,   Paris, Nov. 27, 1782.

I am so agitated with the present crisis, that I cannot help writing you, to beseech you again and again to meditate upon some mild expedient about the refugees, or to give a favourable ear, and helping hand to such as may turn up.[1]

Both sides agree that the matter of expence is nothing; and the matter of honour in my opinion is least to *that* side, which has most sense and most justice on its side. It seems to me that the matter of present *peace*, and *future happiness*, are the only points of true concern to either.

If I can judge of favourable moments, the present is of all others most favourable to our views of *reconciliation*. We have liberal American Commissioners at Paris, a liberal English Commissioner, and a liberal first minister for England. All these circumstances may vanish to-morrow, if this treaty blows over.

If you wanted to break off your treaty, I am perfectly sensible that you could not do it on grounds in which America would

---

9. Vaughan had just returned from a ten-day trip to London for which he had volunteered on Nov. 16; see his letter above, under Nov. 5. His political mission accomplished little: Morris, *Jay: Peace*, pp. 422–3.

1. Strachey had recently suggested that the Americans allow the Loyalists to repurchase their property at the last price for which it had been sold, as a solution "to save the Kings Honor in respect to those who had adhered to him": Klingelhofer, "Matthew Ridley's Diary," entry of Nov. 27, p. 132.

more join with you, than this of the refugees. On the other hand, if *England* wanted to break, she could not wish for better ground on *her* side. You do not break; and therefore I conclude you *both* sincere. But in this way, I see the treaty is likely of *itself* to break. I pray then, my dearest, dearest Sir, that you would a little take this matter to heart.

If the refugees are not silenced, you must be sensible what constant prompters to evil measures you leave us, what perpetual sources of bad information. If the minister is able, on the other hand, to hold up his head on this *one* point, you must see how much easier it will be for you both to carry on the great work of reunion, as far as relates to prince and people. We are not well *informed* about the deeds of the refugees in England; and we can only *now* be well informed by publications that would do irreparable mischief.

Besides, you are the most magnanimous nation; and can excuse things to your people, which *we* can less excuse to *ours*. Not to mention, that when Congress sent you her last resolutions,[2] she was not aware that you would be so near a settlement, as you are at present. To judge which is the hardest task, yours, or England's, put yourself in Lord Shelburne's place. The only marks of confidence shown him at Paris, are such as he *dares not name;* and the only marks promised him, are *future* national ones. England has given much ground of confidence to America. In my opinion England will do HER business in the way of RECONCILIATION, very much in proportion, as you do your business generously at the present peace. England is to be won, as well as America is to be won; and I beg you would think with yourself and your colleagues about the means. Excuse this freedom, my dearest Sir; it is the result of a very warm heart, that thinks a little property *nothing*, to much happiness. I do not however ask you to do a dishonourable thing, but simply to save England; and to give our English ministry the means of saying on the 5th De-

2. Possibly a report approved by Congress on Aug. 20, which included the recommendation that the peace commissioners inform George III that Congress had instructed them to oppose "strenuously" the return of Loyalists and exiles: *JCC*, XXIII, 479–80, 524.

cember[3] we have done *more* than the last ministry have done. I hope you will not think this zeal persecution; for I shall not mention this subject to you again, of my own accord.[4]

I know you have justice on your side; I know you may talk of precedents; but there is such a thing as forgiveness, as generosity, and as a manly policy, that can share a small *loss* rather than miss a greater *good*. Yours, my dearest Sir, most devotedly, most gratefully, most affectionately,   BENJAMIN VAUGHAN.

From Jonathan Williams, Jr.

ALS: American Philosophical Society; copy: Yale University Library

Dear & Hond Sir   Nantes November 27—1782

The Bearer is Capt George Meggs of the 71st Regiment taken in his Passage from N york to London by the Ship Marquis de la Fayette, arrived here to my Address. As this Gentleman has some pressing Business in London & wishes to return thither as soon as possible, I have taken the Liberty of giving him his Parole as far as Paris, & then he will be considered still a Prisoner unless you consent to grant his Parole & permission to go to England. He has a Lady under his escorte who accompanys him—[5]

I am as ever Your most Dutiful & affectionate Nephew.

JONA WILLIAMS J

3. The Shelburne government had postponed the opening of Parliament until Dec. 5 in order to give itself an extra nine days to negotiate unimpeded: Dull, *French Navy*, p. 322.

4. Vaughan met with each of the three commissioners on Nov. 27 to urge concessions to the Loyalists. One (Jay?) supposedly said he would give "acre for acre, with England, to the refugees." Another (JA?) said he would be inclined to give a tract of land, provided he could justify it to Congress by obtaining a satisfactory solution of the fisheries issue. A third (BF?) said "he would consent to let the land, ceded on the Florida side, be placed expressly to the refugee account": Vaughan to Shelburne, Nov. 27, 1782 (APS). None of these proposals was adopted.

5. JW had written to BF on Nov. 21, above, about Meggs and four of his fellow passengers now in custody. All five were granted parole at Passy; see our annotation of the parole granted Lawrence Robert Campbell, Dec. 7.

Addressed: His Excellency / Doctor Franklin / Minister Plenipotentiary to the United States / Passy

Notation: Jona. Williams Nantes Novr. 27th. 1782

To David Hartley

ALS: D.A.F.H.H. Hartley Russell (1955) on deposit in the Berkshire
County Record Office

Dear Friend   Passy, Nov. 28, 82
   I received your very kind Letters of Oct. 29, 31, & Nov. 8.[6] I
thank you much for the Receipt you send me. It may be of use
hereafter, tho' at present the Gravel has left me. I shall send the
Book you desire[7] by Mr Vaughan. And you may depend on my
doing every thing in my Power to serve the Person you recommend.[8] I have only time to add that I am ever Yours most affectionately   B FRANKLIN

David Hartley Esqr

Addressed: To / David Hartley Esqe. / Member of Parliament,
Golden / Squire, / London.

Notation:[9] Mr. Fox [*torn*] himself the Honor of waiting upon
[*torn:* Mr. Ha]rtly—but not being fortunate enough [to find] him
at home will take the Liberty of waiting upon him another day
[?]to know whether the Letter may have been delivered him

To James Jay   ALS: John Carter Brown Library

Sir,   Passy, Nov. 28. 1782.
   I received the Letter you did me the Honour of writing to me
the 27th past. I have no direct Powers from Congress to transact

6. The second of these letters is missing; the others are above.
7. Which Hartley requested on Oct. 29.
8. Above, Nov. 8.
9. In the hand of Charles James Fox. It is written on the address sheet.

Exchanges, but have taken the Liberty in your Case, to absolve the Parole of Captain Francis Dundas, of the first Regiment, now a Prisoner on Parole in London, on Condition that yours be also fully discharged.[1] You will know whether this Condition is comply'd with by applying to the Lord Advocate of Scotland, who is his Uncle. I have the honour to be, Sir, Your most obedient and most humble Servant[2]   B FRANKLIN

Sir James Jay.

Addressed: To / Sir James Jay / London

Endorsed: from Doctr: Franklin Novr: 28. 1782

From Francis Dana   AL:[3] Massachusetts Historical Society

Sir   St: Petersbourg Novr. 17/28[4] 1782.

I wrote to Mr: Livingston in Augt: last:[5] to advise Congress of a custom established at this Court by order of Her Majesty, That every Power entering into any Treaty with her, shou'd pay Six Thousand Roubles to Four of her Ministers (making in the whole Twenty four Thousand) upon the signing of the Treaty: And that if any occasion shou'd offer for me to make a Treaty on the part of the United-States, it wou'd be indispensably necessary Congress shou'd enable me to advance that sum. I have lately written to him upon that subject again, and acquainted him. "If the present negotiations for a Peace shou'd happily

1. BF's order releasing Dundas from his parole is above, Nov. 27.
2. Acting on the assumption that he had been exchanged, Jay came to Paris in early December. He called on BF to express his appreciation and, not finding him at home, wrote a letter (dated "Friday Evening") thanking him for his intervention. Library of Congress. For Jay's activities in Paris see Morris, *Jay: Peace,* pp. 498–506.
3. A retained copy.
4. We print under the New Style date used in western Europe.
5. Dana to Livingston, Aug. 25/Sept. 5, 1782: Wharton, *Diplomatic Correspondence,* V, 700–2; Nina N. Bashkina *et al.,* eds., *The United States and Russia: the Beginning of Relations, 1765–1815* (Washington, D.C., 1980), pp. 160–3.

suceede, I shall have occasion for the money mentioned in that letter, before I can expect an answer from Congress; and shall apply to Doctr: Franklin and Mr: Adams to advance it between them."[6] I accordingly wrote to Mr: Adams by the last post,[7] and desired to know of him if he wou'd agree to advance one moiety of the sum (which will be somewhere about Twenty three to Twenty five hundred pounds sterlg: as the Course of Exchange may be) if the supposed case shou'd happen. I told him I shou'd make the same application to you by this post; which I have thought it my duty to do, to the end I may be prepared as far as possible, to meet that event. You will judge whether it is consistent with yours to grant it in case it shou'd become necessary before I shall receive an answer from Congress upon the subject. As Mr: Adams is now near you, and as it wou'd be useless to obtain the consent of one of you only, I suppose you will consult together upon the matter, which I am sensible is not without its difficulties on your parts.[8] Shou'd you see your way clear to answer each for one Moiety of the money, it wou'd be sufficient to authorise me to draw upon you for it in the very moment when it shall be indispensably necessary for me to advance it.

I am, Sir, with the greatest Respect and Esteem Your most obedient humble Servant

His Excellency Benja: Franklin Minister Plenipotentiary &c By the Post of the 18th. thro' Mr. W.

---

6. Dana to Livingston, Nov. 7 / 18, 1782: Wharton, *Diplomatic Correspondence*, VI, 54–6.

7. Dana to JA, Nov. 14 / 25, 1782 (Mass. Hist. Soc.)

8. When JA received his letter from Dana, he took it to BF. They agreed to remit Dana the money: Butterfield, *John Adams Diary*, III, 97. On Jan. 14, Grand recorded a payment to Dana of 60,000 *l.t.* (£2,500): Account XXVII (XXXII, 4).

From Jonathan Williams, Jr.: Two Letters

(I) and (II) Copy: Yale University Library

I.

Dear & hond. sir,   Nantes le 28: 9bre 1782:

This will be delivered you by Capt. Archd. Balneavis, Lieut Archd. MacLean, Mr. Ochiltree & Capt. Wm. Hamilton all paroled at York town the 26 Oct 1781. & taken on their Passage from NYork to London by the Ship Marquis de la Fayette arrived here to my address[9] as they have pressing business in London they prefer going by land & on their way will wait on you. I will transmit you a Copy of their Paroles by the next post & the Originals they will shew you / .[1]

I am &

II.

Dr. & hond sir,   Nantes Nov 28. 82

Inclosed you have the Paroles I have taken—the Copy of the Paroles already given Genl. Washington, and the names of the Officers in Question. These Gentlemen will wait on you & shew you Copies certified by me which I request may be destroyed when these are annulled / .

I am &

Dr. Franklin

9. These are most likely the British officers paroled by Washington whom jw mentioned in his letter of Nov. 21, above. Archibald Balneaves, Archibald McLean, and Duncan Ochiltree all served in the 71st regiment, of which Ochiltree was the quartermaster: Steven M. Baule and Stephen Gilbert, comps., *British Army Officers who Served in the American Revolution, 1775–1783* (Westminster, Md., 2004), pp. 9, 123, 138.

1. jw had written a version of this letter on Nov. 27, copied it into his letterbook (Yale University Library), and then crossed it out. It named one other officer in the group—John Kennedy of the 43rd regiment—who may have decided against traveling with the others to Paris. It also contained the following information about Mackintosh, Lt. Campbell, and Burns, three of the five prisoners named in jw's Nov. 21 letter: that they "are paroled no further than Passy & then they will be considered still as Prisoners unless you think proper to grant them their Paroles & permission to go to England." These three men obtained a parole at Passy on Dec. 6; see our annotation of the parole granted Lawrence Robert Campbell, Dec. 7.

Franklin's Proposed Article 5

Copy:[2] American Philosophical Society; copy and transcript: National Archives; copies: Library of Congress (five), Massachusetts Historical Society (three)

The final day of negotiations was held at Jay's residence at the Hôtel d'Orléans. In attendance were Oswald, Strachey, Fitzherbert, Franklin, Adams, Jay, and Henry Laurens (who had just arrived from London). They spent the day wrangling over the British ultimatum about the fisheries and the issue of compensation for the Loyalists. For most of the day, the success of the negotiations was in doubt.[3]

While Adams argued about the fisheries, Franklin brought up the issue of compensation for American citizens who had suffered in the war. He took from his pocket the present document and proposed it as a substitute for Article 5 of the British counterproposal.[4] All four American commissioners elaborated on its contents: Adams explained the history of Gage's doublecrossing the citizens of Boston; Franklin testified to the goods confiscated in Philadelphia, including his own library; Laurens described the plunder of slaves and silver in the Carolinas; and Jay offered other examples. The British commissioners "retired for some time." When they returned, they agreed to drop the offensive terms of both articles. The Americans reciprocated by offering more favorable terms in Article 4, regarding creditors.[5] The en-

2. In the hand of L'Air de Lamotte. This copy was at one time in Oswald's possession (as witnessed by his notation) but ended up with Benjamin Vaughan, who wrote notes of his own identifying BF's handwriting and mistakenly claiming that the text was in the hand of WTF.

Most of the other copies are entitled "Article proposed & read to the Commissioners before signing the preliminary Articles." The one at the National Archives, mistakenly filed with the first draft treaty, is in WTF's hand and is entitled "Article 5. (Proposed)".

3. Strachey wrote Townshend at 11:00 that night that "A very few hours ago we thought it impossible that any Treaty could be made." He went on to explain the modifications they had agreed to, emphasizing that unless they adopted the fisheries article as it now stood, "there could have been no Treaty at all." Oswald and Fitzherbert wrote similar statements: Giunta, *Emerging Nation*, 1, 690–1, 695, 701.

4. BF may have drafted this paper at an earlier date and shown it to Oswald at the end of the discussions of Oct. 30–Nov. 4 (for which see BF to Townshend, Nov. 4). See Strachey's Nov. 8 report to Townshend, quoted above on p. 350, footnote 4. The British counterproposal is above, under Nov. 19.

5. They authorized the repayment of all debts, not just those incurred be-

tire treaty was reviewed and corrected, and the commissioners agreed to sign and seal fair copies the following day.[6] That evening Strachey wrote to a British official that he was "half dead from perpetual anxiety" and would not rest until he knew how these compromises would be viewed. "If this is not as good a Peace as was expected," he continued, "I am confident it is the best that could have been made."[7] The American commissioners justified their own compromises in their letter to Livingston of December 14.

[November 29, 1782]

Article proposed

It is agreed that his Britannic Majesty will earnestly recommend it to his Parliament to provide for and make Compensation to the Merchants and Shopkeepers of Boston whose Goods and Merchandise were seized and taken out of their Stores, Warehouses and Shops, by Order of General Gage and others of his Commanders or officers there; and also to the Inhabitants of Philadelphia for the Goods taken away by his Army there. And to make Compensation also for the Tobacco, Rice, Indigo and Negroes &c. seized and carried off by his Armies under Generals Arnold, Cornwallis and others from the States of Virginia, North and South Carolina, and Georgia; and also for all Vessels and Cargoes belonging to the Inhabitants of the said United States, which were stopt, seized or taken, either in the Ports, or on the Seas by his Governors or by his Ships of War, before the Declaration of War against the said States.

And it is further agreed that his Britannic Majesty will also earnestly recommend it to his Parliament to make Compensation for all the Towns, Villages and Farms, burnt and destroyed by his Troops or Adherents in the said United States.

---

fore 1775. (Both Strachey and Oswald stressed this concession in their letters to Townshend quoted above.) In return they obtained a British concession: "British creditors" was changed to "Creditors on either side."

6. Butterfield, *John Adams Diary*, III, 79–81. See also BF to Livingston, Dec. 5.

7. Strachey to Evan Nepean, Nov. 29, 1782, in Giunta, *Emerging Nation*, I, 690.

Facts.

There existed a free Commerce upon mutual Faith between Great Britain and America. The Merchants of the former Credited the Merchants and Planters of the latter with great Quantities of Goods on the common Expectation that the Merchants having sold the Goods would make the accustomed Remittances; that the Planters would do the same by the Labour of their Negroes and the Produce of that Labour, Tobacco, Rice, Indigo, &c.

England before the Goods were sold in America, sends an armed Force, seizes the Goods in the Stores, some even in the Ships that brought them and carries them off. Seizes also and carries off the Tobacco Rice and Indigo, provided by the Planters to make Returns, and even the Negroes from whose Labour they might hope to raise other Produce for that Purpose.

Britain now demands that the Debts shall nevertheless be paid.

Will She, can She justly refuse making Compensation for such Seizures?

If a Draper who had sold a Piece of Linnen to a Neighbour on Credit, should follow him, take the Linnen from him by Force, and then send a Bailiff to arrest him for the Debt, would any Court of Law or Equity award the Payment of the Debt, without ordering a Restitution of the Cloth?

Will not the Debtors in America cry out that if this Compensation be not made, they were betray'd by the pretended Credit; and are now doubly ruined, first by the Enemy, and then by the Negociators at Paris, the Goods and Negroes sold them being taken from them with all they had besides, and they are now to be obliged to pay for what they have been robb'd of?

In Franklin's hand: Read to the Commissioners Nov. 29. 82

Notation by Richard Oswald: Reparation of Damages, Devastations, Plunder—&ca—

To Vergennes
ALS: Archives du Ministère des affaires étrangères

Sir,   Passy, Nov. 29. 1782
 I have the honour to acquaint your Excellency, that the Commissioners of the United States, have agreed with Mr Oswald on the Preliminary Articles of the Peace between those States & Great Britain. To-morrow I hope we shall be able to communicate to your Excellency a Copy of them.[8] With great Respect I have the honour to be, Sir, Your Excellency's most obedient and most humble Servant   B FRANKLIN

Comte de Vergennes.

From Ingenhousz
ALS: American Philosophical Society

Dear Friend   Vienna Nov. 29th. 1782.
 Yesterday I was favoured with your kind lettre dated Nov. 12.,[9] which gave me the greatest satisfaction, as the defection of the colonies from their alleys is entirely Contradicted by your lettre as well as by the papers inclosed. That for some English people here so flattering news was still so much credited among them a few days ago, that a gentleman of note say'd in full compagnie, that it was true, indeed, America has taken a Frensh instead of an English husband, but that she did not like her spouse and was determin'd to kukhol him very soon, grow rid of him and mary a good one. I told him, that, if his prediction should proove true, America Could never place her herself among the venerable matrons, the other republicks, without blushing, as beyng an adulteress and vile prostitute.

8. That copy is unlocated, but Vergennes sent a translation to Rayneval on Dec. 4. In his cover letter he commented that the English were not so much making a peace as buying it. Their concessions exceeded anything that he had thought possible. But as he had observed to BF, even though the preliminary articles would only go into effect when a peace was concluded between France and England, "La Signature n'en est pas moins prématurée": AAE; trans. in Giunta, *Emerging Nation*, I, 706.

9. Not found. BF was responding to Ingenhousz' Oct. 2 plea (above) to send information that would contradict rumors that a majority of American states were ready to return to British rule.

I red the article of your american Constancy to the first Lord of the Bedchambre and gave him a translation of it in Frensh for the Emperour. He was much pleased with it. The Duch envoye was allso highly delighted with the news; and principaly with the Pensylvania packet of august 27.[1]

I found inclosed Six german news papers, who amuse me and my friends very much. I hope you will continue to send me some more when you have done with them. The lettre of Dr. Bankroft[2] does not clear up the matter; and mr. S. wharton can not excuse himself of his not writing to me. One circumstance, joined by the rest, should make any one Suspect of Som evil intention in that Gentleman; which is, that, when at orient, he wrote me three letters, in which he referrs tho a third one which I never recieved, tho that third one was sent of after the first and before the last, and what makes the suspicion still greater, is that justly that middel lettre contained the whole account of the Cargo, name of the ship, of the master, add to this that this particular adventure regarded only him and me. So that, by this lettre being never come to hand, and perhaps never having existed, I am quite left in the dark about the whole affair; nay I could even not discover whether the Ship in which the goods were put, is arrived, if mr. wharton should make me believe it was perish'd or taken. For that reason I requested a copy of that lettre from him, without telling him the reason of this demand.

However suspicious all these circonstances may be, I can not think that a man of so much personnal dignity, a membre of the souverainty of America should commit such mean action as to sheat a man who placed the greatest confidence in him.

I Send you a wire folded up in a spiral, which you must arrange as you see the wire on the figure I join to it.[3] Leave at the end of it the bit of *agaric*. When you have a bottle of white glas of about a pint or more filled with good dephlogisticated air, take

1. That issue reported the Pa. Assembly's unanimous resolution of Aug. 23 reaffirming the alliance with France and rejecting the possibility of a separate peace. The Dutch minister was Carel Georg van Wassenaer tot Wassenaer.

2. Which Bancroft had asked WTF to forward on Oct. 21. See our annotation of Ingenhousz to BF, Nov. 27.

3. The enclosure is missing.

away the curk and clasp your thumb of the left hand on the orifice. In the mean time turn for a moment the bit of agaric in the flame of a candle till you see it is every were kindled. Hold the wire in the right hand till you see that the piece of agaric gives no more any Smoak but is become quite a red hot coal. Then thrust it immediately in the bottle to above the half of its depth and keep it there till it is consumed. The coal of the agaric will increase in heat so as to set fire to the end of the wire. The flame will slowly run up and the melted metal will now and than fall d to the bottom of the glass, and will Crack it, if even you leave water in the bottle. You will be highly delighted with the experiment. My bottles for that purpose have a metal bottom. You only want to send an empty bottle of flint glass with a good kurk stopper upon it, to mr. *Sigau de la fond* who lives in the *rue S. Jaques maison de l'université*, in the neighbourhood of mr. le Begue. He has allways a good deal of dephlogisticated air ready, and will be glad to let you have as much as you please. He is a good friend of Dr. le Begue. You must recommand not to leave more water in the bottle than is sufficient to keep the curck moist, for the motion of water with this air spoils the air.

I think you aught to be more cautious not to take medicines without the greatest necessity, than to take them at all. For in your age the principal thing is not to hurt the stomach. The most part of medicines destroy the appetite, and therefore harm as much, if not more, in one regard as they may do good in the other. I think opening the pores by bathing, rubbing, and exercising the body are the savest precautions against a relaps.

I am very respectfully your obedient humble servant and affectionat friend   J. INGEN HOUSZ

In the figure the wire is tapered to a very sharp point, when it kindles with a jarr of a quart, or even less in fire; because it is only required to set fire to one end of it.

Addressed: a Son Excellence / Mr. B. Franklin / Ministre Plenipot. des Etats / de l'Amerique &. &. / a Passy

Endorsed: Nov. 29. 82

From Jacques-Christophe Valmont de Bomare

ALS: University of Pennsylvania Library

Monsieur   Paris ce Vendredi 29 9bre. 1782.

L'eloignement et une multitude d'affaires, m'ont empêché d'aller vous temoigner moi même, la part que j'ai prise à votre maladie et à votre retablissement— Je n'ai pû envoyer chez vous que mon domestique— Je vous supplie de ne pas douter du vif interêt que je prens à votre conservation et prosperité. Je vous prie aussi de presenter mes civilitez à monsieur votre fils qui a eu la complaisance de me temoigner beaucoup d'honnêtetéz.

J'ose vous inviter à me faire l'honneur d'entendre mon discours d'ouverture de mes cours,[4] que je prononcerai le jeudi cinq decembre prochain à onze heures un quart précises du matin. Mandez moi, s'il vous plait, et en langue françoise, si je puis compter sur cet avantage, afin de vous destiner votre place. Vous obligerez sensiblement Monsieur Votre très humble et très obeissant serviteur[5]   VALMONT DE BOMARE

rue de la Verrerie, vis à vis celle des deux portes

Addressed: à monsieur / Monsieur Franklin / ministre plénipotentiaire / des Etats unis de l'Amerique / en son Hotel à Passy

Notation: Valmont de Beaumare 29. Novr. 1782.

---

4. The *Jour. de Paris* announced the course on Nov. 23 and described it in terms similar to those of his earlier ones: XXXIV, 58n; XXXVI, 169n.

5. This is Valmont's last extant letter to BF. His course continued with equal success into 1788: Yves Laissus, "Les Cabinets d'histoire naturelle," in *Enseignement et diffusion des sciences en France au XVIIIe siècle,* ed. René Taton (Paris, 1964), p. 665.

Preliminary Articles of Peace[6]

DS: Public Record Office; copies: National Archives (six), Library of Congress (three), Massachusetts Historical Society (two), William L. Clements Library; press copies of copies: American Philosophical Society (two); transcripts: National Archives (four)

[November 30, 1782]

Articles agreed upon, by and between Richard Oswald Esquire, the Commissioner of his Britannic Majesty, for treating of Peace with the Commissioners of the United States of America, in behalf of his said Majesty, on the one part; and John Adams, Benjamin Franklin, John Jay, and Henry Laurens, four of the Commissioners of the said States, for treating of Peace with the Commissioner of his said Majesty, on their Behalf, on the other part. To be inserted in, and to constitute the Treaty of Peace, proposed to be concluded, between the Crown of Great Britain, and the said United States; but which Treaty is not to be concluded, untill Terms of a Peace shall be agreed upon, between Great Britain and France; and his Britannic Majesty shall be ready to conclude such Treaty accordingly.

Whereas reciprocal Advantages, and mutual Convenience are found by Experience, to form the only permanent foundation of Peace and Friendship between States; It is agreed to form the Articles of the proposed Treaty, on such Principles of liberal Equity, and Reciprocity, as that partial Advantages, (those Seeds of Discord!) being excluded, such a beneficial and satisfactory Intercourse between the two Countries, may be establish'd, as to promise and secure to both perpetual Peace and Harmony.

6. On Nov. 30, the American commissioners convened at Jay's residence, then proceeded to Oswald's to examine the fair copies of the preliminary articles. They discovered that Strachey had omitted, in Article 5, the twelve-month limitation for Loyalists who wanted to reside in the United States to pursue restitution of their property. They insisted that this clause be reinstated. Laurens added, in Article 7, a stipulation against British troops carrying off slaves or other American property during their withdrawal; Oswald agreed. With this, the documents were signed. BF, as Whitefoord later noted, was dressed in black, in accordance with the mourning period announced by the French court; see Séqueville's notice, Nov. 25. After the signing, the company repaired to Passy for dinner.

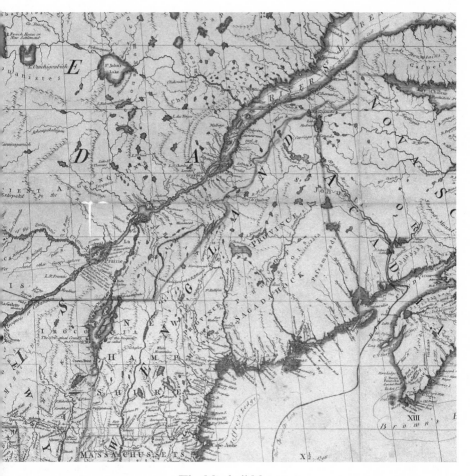

The Mitchell Map

Article 1st.

His Britannic Majesty acknowledges the said United States, Vizt. New Hampshire, Massachusetts Bay, Rhode Island and Providence Plantations, Connecticut, New York, New Jersey, Pennsylvania, Delaware, Maryland, Virginia, North Carolina, South Carolina and Georgia, to be free Sovereign and independent States; That he treats with them as such; And for himself, his Heirs and Successors, relinquishes all Claims to the Government, Propriety, and territorial Rights of the same, and every part thereof; and that all Disputes which might arise in future, on the Subject of the Boundaries of the said United States, may be prevented, It is hereby agreed and declared that the following are, and shall be their Boundaries Vizt.

Article 2d.

From the north west Angle of Nova Scotia, Vizt. that Angle which is form'd by a Line drawn due north, from the Source of St. Croix River to the Highlands, along the said Highlands which divide those Rivers that empty themselves into the River St. Laurence, from those which fall into the Atlantic Ocean, to the northwesternmost Head of Connecticut River; thence down along the middle of that River to the 45th. Degree of North Latitude; from thence by a Line due West on said Latitude, untill it strikes the River Iroquois, or Cataraquy; thence along the middle of said River into Lake Ontario; through the middle of said Lake, untill it strikes the Communication by Water between that Lake and Lake Erie; thence along the middle of said Communication into Lake Erie, through the middle of said Lake, untill it arrives at the Water Communication between that Lake and Lake Huron; thence along the middle of said water communication into the Lake Huron; thence through the middle of said Lake to the Water Communication between that Lake and Lake Superior; thence through Lake Superior northward of the Isles Royal & Phelipeaux, to the Long Lake; thence through the middle of said Long Lake, and the water Communication between it and the Lake of the Woods, to the said Lake of the Woods, thence through the said Lake to the most Northwestern point thereof, and from thence on a due west Course to the River Mis-

383

sisippi; thence by a Line to be drawn along the middle of the said River Missisippi, untill it shall intersect the northernmost part of the 31st. Degree of North Latitude.[7] South, by a Line to be drawn due East, from the Determination of the Line last mentioned, in the Latitude of 31 Degrees North of the Equator, to the middle of the River Apalachicola or Catahouche; thence along the middle thereof, to its junction with the Flint River; thence strait to the Head of St. Mary's River, and thence down along the middle of St. Mary's River to the Atlantic Ocean. East, by a Line to be drawn along the middle of the River St. Croix, from its Mouth in the Bay of Fundy to its Source; and from its Source directly North, to the aforesaid Highlands which divide the Rivers that fall into the Atlantic Ocean, from those which fall into the River St. Laurence; comprehending all Islands within twenty Leagues of any part of the Shores of the united States, and lying between Lines to be drawn due East from the points where the aforesaid Boundaries between Nova Scotia on the one part and East Florida on the other shall respectively touch the Bay of Fundy, and the Atlantic Ocean; excepting such Islands as now are, or heretofore have been within the Limits of the said Province of Nova Scotia.

Article 3d.[8]

It is agreed, that the People of the United States shall continue to enjoy unmolested the Right to take Fish of every kind on the Grand Bank, and on all the other Banks of Newfoundland; Also in the Gulph of St. Laurence, and at all other Places in the Sea where the Inhabitants of both Countries used at any time heretofore to fish. And also that the Inhabitants of the united States shall have Liberty to take Fish of every kind on such part of the

---

7. A precise demarcation of the largely unexplored border between the United States and Canada proved so difficult that the matter was not resolved until the Webster-Ashburton Treaty of Aug. 9, 1842: Bruce W. Jentleson and Thomas G. Paterson, eds., *Encyclopedia of U.S. Foreign Relations* (4 vols., New York and Oxford, 1997), IV, 314–15.

8. This article gave rise to numerous disputes. The subject of American fishing rights finally was submitted to arbitration, which in 1910 resolved most of the issues: *ibid.*, II, 138–9.

Coast of Newfoundland, as British Fishermen shall use, (but not to dry or cure the same on that Island,) and also on the Coasts, Bays, and Creeks of all other of his Britannic Majesty's Dominions in America, and that the American Fishermen shall have Liberty to dry and cure Fish in any of the unsettled Bays Harbours and Creeks of Nova Scotia, Magdalen Islands, and Labrador, so long as the same shall remain unsettled; but so soon as the same or either of them shall be settled, it shall not be lawful for the said Fishermen to dry or cure Fish at such Settlement, without a previous Agreement for that purpose with the Inhabitants Proprietors or Possessors of the Ground.

Article 4th.

It is agreed that Creditors on either side, shall meet with no lawful Impediment to the Recovery of the full value in Sterling Money of all bonâ fide Debts heretofore contracted.

Article 5th.

It is agreed that the Congress shall earnestly recommend it to the Legislatures of the respective States, to provide for the Restitution of all Estates, Rights, and Properties which have been confiscated, belonging to real British Subjects; and also of the Estates Rights and Properties of Persons resident in Districts in the Possession of his Majesty's Arms; and who have not borne Arms against the said United States: And that Persons of any other Description shall have free Liberty to go to any part or parts of any of the thirteen United States, and therein to remain twelve months unmolested in their Endeavours to obtain the Restitution of such of their Estates, Rights and Properties as may have been confiscated; And that Congress shall also earnestly recommend to the several States a Reconsideration and Revision of all Acts or Laws regarding the premises, so as to render the said Laws or Acts perfectly consistent not only with Justice and Equity, but with that spirit of Conciliation which on the Return of the Blessings of Peace should universaly prevail. And that Congress shall also earnestly recommend to the several States, that the Estates Rights and Properties of such last mention'd Persons shall be restored to them; they refunding to any Persons who may be now in Possession the bonâ fide Price, (where any has been given,) which such Persons may have paid on purchasing any of the said Lands, Rights, or Properties since the Confiscation.

And it is agreed that all Persons who have any Interest in confiscated Lands, either by Debts, Marriage Settlements or otherwise, shall meet with no lawful Impediment in the prosecution of their just Rights.

Article 6th.

That there shall be no future Confiscations made, nor any prosecutions commenced against any Person or Persons, for or by reason of the Part which he or they may have taken in the present War, and that no person shall on that account suffer any future Loss or Damage either in his Person, Liberty or Property; and that those who may be in confinement on such charges, at the time of the Ratification of the Treaty in America, shall be immediately set at Liberty, and the Prosecutions so commenced be discontinued.

Article 7th.

There shall be a firm and perpetual Peace, between his Britannic Majesty and the said States, and between the Subjects of the one and the Citizens of the other, Wherefore all Hostilities both by Sea and Land shall then immediately cease: All Prisoners on both sides shall be set at Liberty, & his Britannic Majesty shall, with all convenient Speed, & without causing any Destruction or carrying away any Negroes, or other Property of the American Inhabitants withdraw all his Armies Garrisons and Fleets from the said United States, and from every Port, Place, and Harbour within the same;[9] leaving in all Fortifications the American Artillery that may be therein: And shall also order and cause all Archives, Records, Deeds and Papers belonging to any of the said States, or their Citizens, which in the Course of the War may have fallen into the hands of his Officers to be forthwith restored and delivered to the proper States & Persons to whom they belong.

9. Claiming American noncompliance with treaty provisions, the British did not evacuate their posts in the interior of the United States until after the so-called Jay's Treaty of Nov. 19, 1794: *ibid.*, II, 460–1.

Article 8th.

The Navigation of the River Mississippi from its Source to the Ocean, shall for ever remain free and open to the Subjects of Great Britain and the Citizens of the United States.[1]

Article 9th.

In case it should so happen that any Place or Territory belonging to Great Britain, or to the United States, should be conquered by the Arms of either, from the other, before the Arrival of these Articles in America, It is agreed that the same shall be restored, without Difficulty, and without requiring any Compensation.

Done at Paris, the thirtieth day of November, in the year One thousand Seven hundred Eighty Two

RICHARD OSWALD	[seal]
JOHN ADAMS	[seal]
B FRANKLIN	[seal]
JOHN JAY	[seal]
HENRY LAURENS.	[seal]

Witness

The Words [and Henry Laurens][2] between the fifth and sixth Lines of the first Page; and the Words [or carrying away any Negroes, or other Property of the American Inhabitants] between the seventh and eighth Lines of the eighth Page, being first interlined   CALEB WHITEFOORD
Secretary to the British Commission.
W. T. FRANKLIN
Secy to the American Commission

---

1. Implementation of this article required the cooperation of Spain, which subsequently was awarded control of the lower portion of the Mississippi (when Britain accepted Spanish retention of West Florida). Spain did not grant the United States the right of navigation until the Treaty of San Lorenzo of Oct. 27, 1795 (better known as Pinckney's Treaty): *ibid.*, III, 397–8.
2. The two sets of brackets in this paragraph appear in the manuscript.

Separate Article.

It is hereby understood and agreed, that in case Great Britain at the Conclusion of the present War, shall recover, or be put in possession of West Florida, the Line of North Boundary between the said Province and the United States, shall be a Line drawn from the Mouth of the River Yassous where it unites with the Mississippi due East to the River Apalachicola.

Done at Paris the thirtieth day of November, in the year One thousand Seven hundred and Eighty Two.

Attest
CALEB WHITEFOORD
Secy. to the British Commission.   } RICHARD OSWALD [seal]

Attest
W. T. FRANKLIN
Secy. to the American Commission. }

JOHN ADAMS   [seal]
B FRANKLIN   [seal]
JOHN JAY   [seal]
HENRY LAURENS   [seal]

From Benjamin Putnam   ALS: American Philosophical Society

Honble Sir   Bordeaux 30th. Nov. 1782.
    Having this day negociated to Mr. John Augustus Byrne of this City the four Bills as undermentioned[3] the first & second of which I have heretofore transmitted to you,[4] & not being advisd by your Excellency of their Acceptance or payment I think it proper to mention the 1sts. of sd. Bills are accepted in your hands. Mr Byrne remitts them to his Banker Mr. Julian of Paris[5] who is to recieve their Amount.
    I am your Excellency's most Hble Sert.   BENJA. PUTNAM.

3. The list of bills is missing.
4. Probably those sent in December, 1781: XXXVI, 239.
5. Louis Julien & fils: Lüthy, *Banque protestante*, II, 280, 458, 699.

Addressed: A Monsieur / Monsieur Franklin / Ministre Plenipotentiaire des états unis de / L'amerique / prés Paris / A Passy

From Gilles de Lavallée[6] and Other Offerers of Goods and Schemes[7]

News of the peace negotiations inspires a number of merchants, manufacturers, and schemers to make offers to Franklin during the period
of this volume. In November, Gilles de Lavallée outlines his plan to
establish in the 13 "Colonies Unies" factories for making ribbons,
yarns, and thread as well as textiles, coverlets, and sheets. His letter is
published below.

On September 26, Petit, a *bénéficier* of the Church of Paris, wants
Franklin to meet his relative Villiers, a horologer who wishes to present the watch he has invented, based on new principles. The watch
has been praised in the *Journal des savants* and admired by other
watchmakers.

The firm of Destombes frères[8] writes on November 15 requesting
Franklin to forward to Matthew Ridley a list of articles which they
manufacture in Roubaix, a center of the wool trade, not far from Lille.
Should American merchants ask Franklin to recommend a commercial house, they enclose a note for him describing their goods.[9]

On November 26, M. Arnauld, director of a *maison d'éducation et
école de mathématiques* in Belleville, describes his school in the hope
that Franklin will recommend it to those Americans considering a foreign education for their children. The school caters to the nobility and
enrolls students from different parts of the world. The enclosed
prospectus notes that the school is under the authority and jurisdiction
of the cantor of the Eglise de Paris and strives to inculcate a love for
Christian wisdom and piety. It is located in the suburbs of Paris[1] and

6. Who had made an earlier offer to supply goods to the Americans in
1777: XXIII, 314–15n.

7. Except where indicated the letters discussed in this headnote are in
French, are at the APS, and elicited no response.

8. *Almanach des marchands,* p. 274.

9. The enclosed note has not been found. Their letter is at the University
of Pa. Library.

1. As were most of these establishments: Pierre-Thomas-Nicolas Hurtaut,
Dictionnaire historique de la ville de Paris et de ses environs (4 vols., Paris, 1779),

draws on teachers from the city for instruction in music, dance, and fencing.

Another educational project is that sent by the Nouvelle Librairie de la Cour et de l'Académie of Mannheim, on December 24.[2] Believing that the study of the Greeks and Romans alone can form one's taste for knowledge and that the sciences and the arts make a nation foster progress, greatness, and happiness, they have undertaken to publish Roman writers of the Golden Age at a price everyone can afford. Currently 37 volumes have appeared, representing 18 authors, and this collection may be had for 39 *l.t.* They hope that Franklin, wishing to cultivate the talents of American youth, will take several copies of each to sell and distribute in his native land. Surely this is a goal worthy of a patriot.

In their studies two correspondents claim to have uncovered the secret workings of nature. Mamboumel de Saradin, writing from Lévigny, near Mâcon, on December 19, is not known as a physicist but has been performing experiments for the past 40 years and has perfected his discovery of the system of nature. The implications for agriculture are extensive. He hopes that Franklin can stop by his house in Burgundy to see some of his experiments and wishes him every success in negotiating the independence of the United States.

On January 1, Godefroi Roi fils takes up the pen for his father, J. J. Roi, a Protestant pastor at Chaux-de-Fonds in Neuchâtel, who had written a year earlier offering to dedicate to Franklin his work *Texte de la Nature rétabli,* the result of 20 years of close observation.[3] He hopes that Franklin can examine the work when he has the time or submit it to the "accadémie de Massacusetts" to test the truth of his theories. What better occasion to announce the restoration of nature's origins than that of the rebirth of America under the laws of virtuous liberty? Over the space of 28 pages he offers samples of his ideas and projects on underwater exploration, agriculture, irrigation, and education. If Franklin does not see any way to favor his projects, could he

---

IV, 5–7; "Pensions d'Education pour les jeunes gens," in Luc-Vincent Thiery, *Le Voyageur à Paris* (8th ed., Paris, 1790), part two, pp. 149–50.

2. Karl Theodor, the Elector Palatine (*ADB*), had founded the Grosse Hofbibliothek and the affiliated Akademie der Wissenschaften at Mannheim in 1763: Stefan Mörz, *Haupt- und Residenzstadt: Carl Theodor, sein Hof und Mannheim* (Mannheim, 1998), p. 58.

Earlier, BF had received publications from the Academy: XXVII, 457; XXXIII, 206n.

3. This information is contained in the first four pages of the 1782 letter which were missing when we described it earlier: XXXVI, 314.

recommend them to His Prussian Majesty through one of the Prussian commercial agents at Paris?[4]

With peace near at hand, L. Lanoix writes on December 10 from Bordeaux to offer Franklin half his ship, the *Grand d'Estaing*, to carry goods to Congress. In return he would like letters of recommendation for merchants at Philadelphia to whom he might address his own cargo. He will need a passport also.[5]

M. Antheaume, director of the royal hat factory at Rennes, writes from that city on December 12. Like his parents before him, he has suffered financial reversals, and recently a shipment of hats to the Philadelphia firm of Lacaze & Mallet has been refused because the hats were found to be unfashionable. The Philadelphia firm proposes instead that he send textiles and other articles.[6] This is an opportunity to expand his business, but he requires 30,000 *livres* as an initial investment and hopes that Franklin will intercede. As proof of his reliability he encloses an account of his assets and the proposal from Lacaze & Mallet.

Erdmann Frédéric Senff, inspector of the saltworks at Dürrenberg, Saxony, has read that the English have destroyed many saltworks in the United States and proposes in a letter of December 21 to go over to help remedy the loss. Five or six thousand pounds sterling would serve to launch the project. He can send certificates attesting to his expertise.[7]

On January 12, Daniel Alfons von Sandoz-Rollin, secretary to the Prussian ambassador,[8] sends an undated memoir from the Société du commerce maritime de Prusse proposing trade on a scale greater than has hitherto been possible. The society will fill orders for textiles and

---

4. This letter is at the Hist. Soc. of Pa.

5. His letter is at the University of Pa. Library. On Feb. 15, he writes again: though peace has now been declared, he is not certain what the terms of France's commercial relations are with the United States and whether or not he can expect to be received favorably at Philadelphia. Would BF also tell him what formalities his captain will need to observe and if he will need an English passport? The ship will be ready to sail in a month at the latest. APS.

6. Lacaze & Mallet to Antheaume, June 22 (APS). For this firm see XXX, 88n; XXXV, 484n.

7. Senff (1741–1813) was saline inspector at Dürrenberg, Artern, and Kösen. He published several works related to the salt industry as well as some technical and economic works: J. C. Poggendorff, *Biographisch-Literarisches Handwörterbuch zur Geschichte der exacten Wissenschaften* (2 vols., Leipzig, 1863), II, 906.

8. *Repertorium der diplomatischen Vertreter*, III, 327.

articles of clothing manufactured in the region and will arrange for transportation by ship. Franklin will know what is needed and will be able to recommend reliable merchants in America.

D: Historical Society of Pennsylvania

[*c.* November, 1782][9]
Mémoire

Le Jour que J'ai eu l'honneur d'offrir verbalement mes Services à vôtre Excellence pour former divers Etablissemens de Manufactures dans les 13. Colonies Unies de l'amérique Elle eû la bonté de me demander Si Je n'avais pas un Mémoire à lui présenter à ce Sujet; Je n'en avais pas alors, J'eû L'honneur de vous le dire.

Je Crois qu'il est de mon devoir de le faire aujourdhui et Je viens Suplier vôtre Excellence de vouloir bien l'éxaminer.

Je puis faire, et faire Etablir partout ou je me trouverai sans avoir besoin de Modêle.

1°. Des Metiers grande Mécanique propre à faire par un Seul ouvrier toute Sorte de Rubans, soit en fil, Laine, Soye, Cotton &ca. depuis 10. pièces à la fois Jusques à 30. et de toute Largeur par un seul et même metier, unis, Croisés ou faconnés.

2°. Des Moulins à monter, retordre et mettre en Echevaux par la même Machine toutes Sortes de Matières filées au dégré de Serré que l'on désirera Sans aucun apprantissage.

3°. Des Rouets mécaniques pour faire filer par une Seule Personne depuis 2. brins Jusques à Six à la fois Soit Laine ou Cotton.

4°. Une Navette roulante propre à faire par un ouvrier toute Sorte de toiles, des Couvertures de Lits, du Drap &ca. de la plus grande Largeur.

Non seulement Je puis faire Ces Machines, mais Je puis aussi former Les ouvriers pour travailler avec.

J'ai Chez moi et qui travaillent Journellement Les metiers Mecaniques à Rubans, Le Moulin à retordre et mettre en Echevaux toute Sorte de matière filée, La navette roulante pour faire des Etoffes de la plus grande Largeur; J'aurai quand il me plaira

9. Lavallée alluded to this memoir having been written "about two years ago" in a letter to BF of Nov. 1, 1784 (APS).

les Rouets mécaniques à filer ainsi que Les ouvriers faits & occupés à ces divers ouvrages dont la majeure partie sont mes apprentis, on peut Les venir voir travailler pour en mieux Juger.

Comme Je ne Suis pas pressé et que rien ne me force de quitter ma Patrie, Je desirerais qu'il plaise à Vôtre Excellence de vouloir bien m'instruire, aprés avoir pris les plus éxactes Informations et Vérifié par les faits et Sur Les Lieux, La vérité de ce que J'avance, Qu'elle serait La Protection, Le Secour que Je pourrais obtenir du Congrés pour m'aider à former Ces Etablissemens.

Je desire il est vrai de porter mes Talents Chez un Peuple Brave, Sage & Libre, que J'aime et que Je respecte et à qui Je voudrais de tout mon Coeur être utile, Mais si le Zêle & L'amour propre m'engagent à faire cette Démarche, La Raison m'ordonne de ne La faire qu'aprés que Je Serai assuré d'une Subsistance au moins Egale à Celle que J'ai maintenuë dans ma Patrie et dans ma famille par mon travail &ca. &ca.

Ma Résidence est à Ercuis en Picardie prés de Beaumont sur Oize Distance de Paris de 10. Lieües Et me nomme Gille de Lavallée[1] fabricant en grande Mécanique./.

From the Comtesse de Golowkin

ALS: American Philosophical Society

[after November, 1782][2]

J'ai une grace à vous demander, mon Papa, j'ai demain Jeudi une petite Course à faire à la Campagne, ma Voiture ordinaire est caseè, je me trouve dans L'embarras— N'aurès vous pas la

1. Lavallée signed his other letters "Gilles".
2. The month in which the Passy household evidently acquired a second carriage, which seems to have been for WTF's use. This was a cabriolet, a two-person carriage, open in the front, with two or four wheels. Its earliest mention is in a letter from J. Frank to WTF, Nov. 18, recommending a boy with experience driving a cabriolet (APS). WTF corresponded in the spring of 1783 with a *sellier* (a saddler-carriage maker) who was making repairs to the cabriolet: Madlin to WTF, March 6, May 12, 13, and 25, 1783 (APS).

bontè extrême pour moi de me prêter votre Diligence[3] (rien que la Voiture sans chevaux:) J'ose vous faire cette demande parceque comme vous avès aussi une Berline[4] il vous seras peut-être ègal de vous en servir un jour, et de me rendre Le service essentiel de me prêter l'autre dont je vous promets d'avoir soin comme de moi-même— Adieu, mon Papa, si je ne savois que vous êtes la bontè et L'obligeance même, je n'ôserois pas vous faire cette demande mais jusqu'à prèsent vous n'avès existè que pour faire du bien aux autres. Je vous embrasse aussi tendrement que je vous aime.   C. GOLOFKIN

Addressed: à Monsieur / Monsieur le Docteur Francklin / à Passÿ

Notation: Golofkin

From John Taylor[5]

ALS: American Philosophical Society

Dear Sir   Circus, Bath 1st. Decr. 1782.

The great friendship you have ever shewn me, produces a liberty which I trust you will forgive, as the subject is a matter of the utmost importance to me, and my family— I see in Freemans Philada. Journal of the 27th. february 1782[6] among the names of those who have forfeited their Estates, *two John Taylors,* and as

---

3. While this term often refers to a large coach for travelers, the *diligence de Lyon*, there was also a *diligence à cul de singe,* which resembled a cabriolet in that it was a small carriage open in the front. These different carriages, as well as the berlin mentioned below, are illustrated under "Sellier" in the plates of Diderot's *Encyclopédie* . . . and discussed in Don H. Berkebile, *Carriage Terminology: an Historical Dictionary* ([Washington, D.C.], 1978).

4. A larger, enclosed carriage with face-to-face seating. BF had been leasing a carriage from Mlle Chaumont for many years; see XXVII, 4n. That arrangement continued until July, 1783, when he purchased a carriage: Account XVII (XVI, 3), entry of July 26, 1783.

5. Landscape painter and etcher (*c.* 1745–1806): XIV, 172n; XXXI, 439–42; Lewis, *Walpole Correspondence,* XXIX, 112n.

6. *The Freeman's Journal, or, The North-American Intelligencer,* Feb. 27, 1782, under the heading "Forfeited Estates."

I have not heard from my Agent Wm. West[7] nor from any other person in Philada. since Decr. 1775 I am under the greatest anxiety least my property shoud fall under one of them— Pray tell me Sir is that unfortunately the case? If it is! what have I done to incur so heavy a punishment!—is my residing here the cause?— I did it to take care of a sickly wife, six small children, and an aged Mother. Or shou'd I have quitted all these tender Concerns and have gone an *Individual* to America? Surely that cou'd never be expected— I quitted it Sir with my good father[8] in 1762 long before the beginning of the unhappy dispute— He was ever their warm friend and they told him he and his, shou'd ever have their love; and be assur'd good Sir not a thought ever enter'd my heart which cou'd give a shadow to suspect my warmest attachment and sincerest good wishes to that Country—but I need not take up your time with declarations of this kind— No man knows me and my family better than yourself; and may I add Dr Sir! my hopes that you will in consequence of it, think me worthy of your friendship and assistance in this distressfull business; and by your interest or advice point out to me such methods as I shou'd pursue, to reverse the forfeiture, if it has taken place, or prevent it at any future time.[9]

I shou'd have taken a Journey to intreat this great favor in Person; was not my wife in so precarious a state of health that I cannot think of leaving her. She desires and my Mother joins in most respectful Compliments to You and I am most truly and respectfully Dear Sir Your very obliged & obedt Servt.[1]

JOHN TAYLOR

7. This is probably one of the William Wests, uncle and nephew, of Philadelphia: IX, 291n.

8. Abraham Taylor: III, 428n; XXXI, 440n.

9. Taylor apparently retained his properties in Philadelphia. In May, 1783, he granted power of attorney over those estates to Francis Hopkinson and George Clymer, who presided over the auction of ten lots in early 1784. Taylor quarreled with both men over what he claimed was their mismanagement, and later published his grievances in a pamphlet: John Taylor, *A Narrative of the Dispute between John Taylor, Esquire, and George Clymer & Francis Hopkinson, Esqrs. . . .* ([Bristol], 1787); *Pa. Gaz.*, Feb. 11, 1784.

1. An undated fragment of a letter from John Taylor is among BF's papers at the APS. It inquires about "restitution or reimbursement" to people who

Endorsed: Answer'd by Mr Laurens—[2]

Notation: Tailor Mr. John, 1st. Decr. 1782.

From George Walker[3]   ALS: American Philosophical Society

Dear Sir,   Calais 1st December 1782.

An old friend will excuse this familiarity of address to the Minister.

I found by Mr. Wharton of Philadelphia, when he did me the honour of a visit at Calais,[4] that I was still alive in your memory and good opinion; and that you were content with the excuses I had made you thorough him for my silence. Circumstances however seem now to be approaching, which call upon me to trouble a friend. Publick fame announces the prospect of a speedy peace. It may be so. Sore experience is a mistress that will teach men wisdom, who would not learn it from Dr. Franklin.

Suppose therefore a Peace! Or suppose the war to continue!

In either case is there any way in which your advice and assistance can be of service to an old and honest fellow-labourer in the same cause? You know my history; you know the history of Barbadoes. I fall a sacrifice to the accursed politicks of the British ministry, and the vengeance of their Secretary for America.[5] The hurrican followed and compleated the ruin.[6] Creditors had no mercy, because my wife's separate property had been settled for her separate use. I now subsist upon the kindness of Mrs. Walker, whom I refused to drag down with me in my fall. Sufficient to her is a share of the calamities upon all estates in England.

---

sustained losses by their trade with the Indians. As Taylor has been "a very considerable sufferer," he asks how his claims should be pursued.

2. Laurens left Paris for London and Bath on or about Jan. 11, 1783: *Laurens Papers,* XVI, 129n.

3. A former Barbados planter and colonial agent: XXV, 162n; XXIX, 8n.

4. Samuel Wharton, who probably visited Calais at the end of 1779: XXXI, 205.

5. George Germain, Viscount Sackville.

6. A hurricane had swept through the West Indies in October, 1780, causing much damage in Barbados and the surrounding islands: XXXIV, 174n.

I had proposed that the common misfortune should have been born in common by all parties concerned; but neither the Publick of England, nor the Publick of Barbadoes, was disposed to apply an adequate remedy: indeed Barbadoes could not without the approbation of England, and England satisfied itself with an act of charity, like a wealthy man to a poor beggar, instead of some wise political regulations becoming a great people.

I have found in France more than I expected. From the national character, I expected civility from all individuals in the class of gentlemen; and from government an azylum and personal liberty; even that was denied me in all places to which the British dominion extends. But I have found too what I was not to have expected. I have had the good fortune to be distinguished by the notice of several persons of rank and consequence: particularly I am honoured with the favour of the Duc de Croÿ, and the Prince his Son.[7] The Duc is so kind as to say he will see you, and hopes to interest M. de Vergennes in my behalf. With such friends in conjunction with Dr. Franklin, I must no longer look upon myself as quite unfortunate.

I have seen Mr. Laurens on his return to Paris; but his stay was short; and as his voyage had been tiresome, and himself seemed indisposed in body and mind, we had but little conversation. I could have wished for much. I only mentioned my intention of writing to you, he offered to be the bearer of the letter; but it was not then written. If you see him inclined to co-operate with you in any thing for my advantage, perhaps this is an opening to be improved.

I will not waste your valuable time in compliments or excuses, but believe me as formerly, Dear Sir, Your very affectionate and respectful humble servant   GEORGE WALKER

7. The duc de Croÿ spoke to BF about Walker in 1779: XXIX, 8. His son Anne-Emmanuel-Ferdinand-François (1743–1803) took the title of duc de Croÿ after his father's death in 1783: Croÿ, *Journal,* I, xxiii; *DBF.*

From Jonathan Williams, Jr.

ALS: Historical Society of Pennsylvania; copy: Yale University Library

Dear & hond Sir   Nantes Decemr. 1. 1782.

The Ship Nonesuch[8] is just arrived in 22 Days from Philadelphia. Thinking it of great Importance that the public Dispatches[9] should go forward with the utmost Expedition, and the Post not going out for two Days to come, I thought it my Duty to send off this Express which I hope will be agreeable.

I have given the Courier eight Louis which please to reimburse with sufficient for his Return and such allowance for his Trouble as you may think he merits: The account of his Expences he will give you.

Inclosed is a Letter for Mrs Williams which contains a miniature Picture belonging to her please to give it to Billy to forward by some safe private Hand.

I am as ever yours most dutifully & affectionately

JONA WILLIAMS J

From Filangieri

Translation from ALS in Italian:[1] Historical Society of Pennsylvania

Most respectable Sir,   Naples, December 2, 1782

I don't know whether you received my previous letter[2] in which I alluded to what I am now obliged today to explain with greater clarity. I awaited your answer with impatience; but four months have already gone by and up to now I have not had the

---

8. The *Nonsuch* was built at Nantes by Joshua Johnson. Her captain was Charles Wells of Philadelphia and Baltimore: *Morris Papers*, VI, 660n; Claghorn, *Naval Officers*, p. 331.

9. These included Livingston's letters of Sept. 5, 13, and 18, and probably Morris' of Oct. 27, all of which are above.

1. Translated by the late Robert S. Lopez, Sterling Professor of History, Yale University. Readers wishing to consult the original Italian will find it printed in Antonio Pace, *Benjamin Franklin and Italy* (Philadelphia, 1958), pp. 399–401, and in Eugenio Lo Sardo, ed., *Il mondo nuovo e le virtù civili: L'epistolario di Gaetano Filangieri (1772–1785)* (Naples, 1999), pp. 236–8.

2. Above, Aug. 24.

pleasure of seeing your writing. I flatter myself that this second letter will meet a happier fate. I write to you with the trust worthy of you and of myself. My happiness depends on you, and the depiction of my circumstances and situation will show you the ease with which you could procure it to me.

I am the youngest in my family,[3] whose fame is much greater than its financial resources. The barbarous system of primogeniture, of seniority and of feudal obligations makes me even poorer than the rest of our family. My annual budget is 2000 *l.t.* My position at Court is very honorable but does not fit my character.[4] The presence of a King and the contact with courtiers embarrasses and torments me. I don't know how to obtain the favors of Number One and I despise the others too much to make them my friends, or at least indifferent. It won't be hard for you to understand that I am not securely in my right place and that all my wishes aspire towards a position more in keeping with my nature and more peaceful. Ever since I was a boy, Philadelphia has attracted my attention. I fell into such a habit of considering it as the only place where I could be happy that my imagination cannot let go of that idea. A recent reason, equally powerful, is now added to the ancient ones to make me desire to move to Pennsylvania with still greater impatience. A Lady of whom I am excessively enamored and who loves me in return, a lady whose virtues would bring her distinction right in Pennsylvania, has decided to marry me.[5] The only obstacle to such a desirable union is my poverty. I could not live with her in my own country without exposing myself to the scorn that opulence so often shows to misery. A pension of 3,600 *l.t.* that the King has granted me, joined to the 2,000 *l.t.* of my budget will suffice, I hope, to

3. Perhaps the youngest son. He was the third of eleven children born to Cesare Filangieri, prince of Arianello, and Marianna Montalto, duchess of Fragnito: Marcello Maestro, *Gaetano Filangieri and His* Science of Legislation (Philadelphia, 1976), p. 7.

4. He held the posts of majordomo of the week and gentleman of the King's bedchamber at the court of Ferdinand IV: Larousse; Maestro, *Filangieri*, p. 9.

5. In the summer of 1783 he married the Hungarian-born Charlotte (Carolina) Frendel, governess of Ferdinand's second daughter: Pace, *Benjamin Franklin and Italy*, pp. 147, 150; Maestro, *Filangieri*, pp. 26, 28.

let us lead in Philadelphia a life equally removed from luxury and from indigence. But how can one abandon one's own country without producing a reasonable cause? How could I leave the service of my own Prince without a motivation to justify such a resolution? Dear and respectable Franklin, who better than you would be able to facilitate that enterprise of mine? Would it be possible for my works on legislation to convince you to invite me to collaborate to the great code of laws now in preparation in the United Provinces of America? Those laws will decide not only the fate of those provinces but that of the entire New Hemisphere. What better reason could I offer for my departure than that one? At the beginning I could ask my Court only for a temporary leave in order not to displease it, but, once in America, who could bring me back to Europe? Once in the asylum of virtue, the fatherland of heroes, the city of brotherly love, could I wish to return to a country corrupted by vice and degraded by servitude? Could my soul, once accustomed to the delights of a budding freedom, readapt itself to the spectacle of omnipotent authority vested in the hands of a single man? After having known and appreciated the society of citizens, could I possibly wish to consort with courtesans and slaves? No, please do not refuse, oh respected Sir, to give your help toward my happiness. If you succeed, you will be giving one more family to your country, you will be giving me a wife whom I adore, and you will withdraw a useless slave from a court to turn him into a virtuous citizen who will always see in you his benefactor, his friend, and his redeemer.

I beg you not to communicate my project to anybody and to give me some answer about it so that I'll be able to take the right steps. I also want you to know that two more volumes of my work are already at the press. They deal with criminal legislation.[6] I have tried to deepen and completely cover that subject. I

6. These were the third and fourth books of his *La scienza della legislazione*, excerpts of which are in Maestro, *Filangieri*, pp. 35–9. Among other topics in the fourth book, Filangieri expressed dismay at the use of the death penalty in America: Franco Venturi, *The End of the Old Regime in Europe, 1776–1789. The Great States of the West*, trans. R. Burr Litchfield (Princeton, 1991), pp. 30–1.

have been diligent and indefatigable but the novelty of my ideas always leaves me with certain doubts. You will be the first to judge, and I hope you will also be the first to accept the feelings of the profound esteem and veneration with which I declare myself your most devoted and obliged true servant,[7]

GAETANO FILANGIERI

From Jean de Neufville & fils

LS: Historical Society of Pennsylvania

Sir   Amsterdam 2d. Decr. 1782

We had the honour of Addressing your Excellcy. on the 24th. Octr. last on the subject of 4 Small Continl. Bills endors'd by Mr. Wm. Foster for The Honble. R R Livingston, on Which we have no reply.

We now are to give you advice of having Endorsed 2 Continl. Bills No. 279 & 280—in date of 31st Jany. 1782 for 300 Dollrs. pble. to George putnam—which we hereby accordingly do agreable to the directions by said Mr. Putnam's Endorsement—[8] There remains only for us to add the respectful Sentiments With Which we have the honour to be Your Excellency's Most Obedt. Humble Servants   JOHN DE NEUFVILLE SON

His Excellency Dr. B Franklin Ministr. plenipo: for the States of Amca. at the Court of Versailles

From John Adams

ALS: Library of Congress; copy: Massachusetts Historical Society

Sir   Paris Decr 3. 1782

The Moments we live in, are critical and may be improved, perhaps to advantage, for which purpose I beg Leave to propose

---

7. This letter was forwarded to BF by Luigi Pio on Jan. 9, along with a brief covering note (APS).

8. According to the ledger of loan office bills kept by WTF (XXXVII, 439n) these two bills were accepted by Ferdinand Grand on Dec. 6.

to your Consideration, whether it is not proper for Us to write to Mr Dana at Petersbourg, acquaint him with the Signature of the Preliminaries, inclose to him an authentic Copy of them and advise him to communicate it to the Ministers of the Empress, and to all the Ministers of the neutral Powers at her Court, together with a Copy of his Commission to Subscribe to the Principles of the armed Neutrality. The present Seems to me, the most proper Time for this Step.

The United States are as much interested in the Marine Treaty as any Power,[9] and if We take this Step We may with Propriety, propose, if not insist upon an Article in the definitive Treaty respecting this matter, which will be as agreable to France And Spain as to the United Provinces.[1]

I have heretofore mentioned to Mr Jay a Similar proposal, who approved it, and I will propose it again to day to him and Mr Laurens.[2] If you approve the measure, you will be so good as to order an authentic Copy to be made of the Preliminary Treaty, that We may prepare a Letter the first Time We meet.

I have the Honour to be, Sir, your most obedient   J. ADAMS

His Exy. B. Franklin Esqr

9. The "Marine Treaty" was Empress Catherine II's League of Armed Neutrality, designed to further the rights of neutrals to carry noncontraband items to belligerents. In sending Dana to Catherine's court, Congress hoped she would not only recognize the independence of the United States, but also admit it to the League: XXXIV, 188n.

1. After sending this letter, JA met with Dutch Minister Brantsen. JA observed to him that the peace commissioners intended to send Dana a copy of the preliminary treaty "that he might commence his Negotiations with the neutral Powers, and if he succeeded We could then make common Cause with Holland, and insist on an Article [in the final peace treaty] to secure the Freedom of Navigation. This Idea he received with great Pleasure, and said he would write about it to the States [General]": Butterfield, *John Adams Diary*, III, 87. The insertions are ours.

2. He met with each of them while awaiting BF's response: Butterfield, *John Adams Diary*, III, 88.

To John Adams[3] ALS: Massachusetts Historical Society

Sir Passy, Nov. [*i.e.*, December] 3. 1782

I am perfectly of your Opinion respecting the Copy to be sent to Mr Dana, and shall have one prepared directly for that purpose.[4]

Is it not also a proper time for you to propose the Quadruple Alliance offensive and defensive, or at least defensive, which I think you once mentioned to me?[5] For I apprehend this Peace may be so humiliating to England, that on the first Occasion, she will fall upon one or other of the Powers at present engag'd against her; and it may then be difficult for us to unite again.[6]

I have the honour to be, Sir, Your most obedient and most humble Servant B Franklin

His Excelly. John Adams Esqr

---

3. In answer to the preceding letter, and sent on the afternoon of Dec. 3: Butterfield, *John Adams Diary*, III, 88.

4. WTF brought the copy later that day, with the "separate article" on a separate sheet in case JA wanted to send this copy to the Dutch minister: WTF to JA, Dec. 3, 1782, Mass. Hist. Soc.

5. On Aug. 20, 1781, John Jay suggested to BF a quadruple alliance between France, Spain, the Netherlands, and the United States: XXXV, 384–5. JA mentioned the idea of a triple or quadruple alliance on Dec. 6, 1781 and May 2, 1782: XXXVI, 200; XXXVII, 263. Congress had specified that such an alliance must be solely for the duration of the present war: *JCC*, XXI, 877–8.

6. BF expressed similar fears to Vergennes in a June 11 interview and suggested that the various parties to a treaty with Britain make an alliance for their mutual protection: XXXVII, 335. JA also feared postwar diplomatic involvements, confiding to his diary on Nov. 11 that "[America] had been a Football between contending Nations from the Beginning, and it was easy to foresee that France and England both would endeavour to involve Us in their future Wars." Butterfield, *John Adams Diary*, III, 52. By Article 11 of the Franco-American Treaty of Alliance, the United States agreed to guarantee "forever" the present French possessions "in America" as well as those she acquired at the peace, while France guaranteed American liberty, sovereignty, and independence: XXV, 590–1.

From Sarah Bache

ALS: American Philosophical Society

Dear & Honoured Sir   Philadelphia. December 3d 1782

By this Vessel you will receive a tin and a Wooden box; both with grafts of the best new town Pippins which Mr Powell[7] was obliging enough to procure, each of the grafts has a peice of the Old wood remaining to it, the wooden [*torn:* box] was put up by him in a particular manner with wax and tallow, the other by Mr Bache according to your directions,[8] Mr Powel advises that the grafts should be placed in the earth as soon as they arrive till it is time to use them, and desires to be informed which succeeds the best—the Family at present are all well and join in the sincerest Love to you with your Afectionate Daughter   S BACHE

Addressed: His Excelly. / Dr: Franklin / Minister Plenipoy: from the / United States of No: America / at / Passy. / favored by Mr. Miers / [*In Myers' hand:*] L.Orient Jany. 13th. 1783 Forwarded by—Yr. Excellency's Mo Obedient & very Hble Servt. MOSES MYERS[9]

From George Holt

ALS: American Philosophical Society

Sir   Bolbec. 3 Decr. 1782

The Libty. I take in writing is, to solicit your Friendship; to gain me a pass or an exchange for me to go to England. I have done myself the honor to write to the Secretary of the Marine Department craving his generous release of me— I am from Hudsons Bay the Vessell Calld the Charlotte[1] which circum-

7. Probably Samuel Powel, former mayor of Philadelphia: XII, 203n; XXXVI, 166n.

8. In 1780, BF recommended that the grafts be sent "in a Tin Case solder'd up tight." BF's requests for Newton pippin grafts and apples go back to his years in London: XXXII, 609.

9. Also on the address sheet, someone (possibly BF) has written "E" forward and backward and "B Franklin" backward.

1. Which was captured by a French privateer on Nov. 17 and sent into Le Havre: Anatole, marquis de Granges de Surgères, *Prises des corsaires français pendant la guerre de l'independance (1778–1783)* (Paris and Nantes, 1900), p. 55.

stances you may in all Probality be well acquainted with—my rud'ness of writing to you in this free Maner, I hope you will excuse as I have the Honor to be well acquainted with the worthy Lady Mrs. Bromfield of Islington near London Wife to a Gentleman of America.[2] (I beleive the same Lady and one Mrs. Savidge.) with A Gentleman, had the honor to be in your Company at a Tavern in Paris about the Months, of October, & November, 1776.[3] Therefore hope your goodness will use your Friendship, with Monsieur Le Marquis de Castries, having been Four Years almost from Home. I am Married a Long time . . . Your serving me in this respect will claim the service of your ever obliged Friend and humble Servant   GEORGE HOLT

P.S. hope as Indisposition is the Case your goodness will excuse the rough errasements— G.H.

Addressed: A Monsieur / Monsieur Franklin / Ministre des Etats unis de l'amérique, / en son hôtel / Paris

Notation: Holt Mr. George, Bolbec 3. Decr. 1782.

From Robert R. Livingston

ALS, LS and L:[4] University of Pennsylvania Library; ALS (draft): New-York Historical Society; transcript: National Archives

Sir   Philadelphia 3d Decr. 1782
    I have just now recd the certificates required by Mr. Vallier,[5] the vessel which carries my dispatches having been detained I embrace the opportunity to forward them— Nothing new since my last,[6] except that by a Gent who left Charles town the 4th.

    2. Thomas Bromfield: XXI, 157n; XXII, 161n.
    3. BF did not reach Paris until Dec. 21, 1776: XXIII, lviii.
    4. The LS (marked duplicate) and the L (marked triplicate) both omit the words between "cannon &" and "were upon the point." A note on the transcript indicates that these MSS went by the same conveyances as the three versions of Livingston's Nov. 9 letter (above). The last sentence before the complimentary close was in code; on the original it was decoded by BF.
    5. See Livingston to BF, Nov. 27.
    6. Livingston does not mention that on Dec. 2 he had offered his resigna-

Ult. we learn that the British had dismounted their cannon & embarked the greatest part of their troops he seems to make no doubt that they were upon the point of leaving it—[7] The French Troops embark next Monday, their fleet will sail in a few days.[8] I am Sir with great respect & esteem Your Most Obt hum: Servt

R R LIVINGSTON

From Gurdon S. Mumford   ALS: American Philosophical Society

Respected Sir,   Nantes Dec 3 1782

Inclosed is a letter recd. by the Ship Nonsuch in 22 days from Philadelphia, it would have been sent on by the Express but by some unaccountabe means it was left behind & Mr. Williams now desires me to forward it to your Excellency—[9] I ask a thousand pardons for having thus long delayed acknowledging the many kindnesses your Excellency was pleased to shew me at Passy & I beg you will accept my hearty thanks for the same. I should certainly not have delayed doing this long before had I not known your excellency's time was taken up in more important matters. Thefore I have only to hope you will be pleased to excuse this & believe me to be with the highest Respect & Esteem Your Excellencys most Obliged humble Servt

G. S. MUMFORD

My most respectfull Compliments wait on your Grandson & to Mr. de la Motte

His Exy. Dr. Franklin

Notation: Mumford Decr. 3. 1782

---

tion as secretary for foreign affairs. He soon agreed, however, to serve until the following spring and did not leave office until early June, 1783: Wharton, *Diplomatic Correspondence,* VI, 100–1; *JCC,* XXIII, 823–4; XXIV, 382. Among BF's papers at the APS is a copy of a Dec. 3 congressional resolution (*JCC,* XXIII, 759) authorizing Livingston to perform his duties until a replacement was elected and scheduling a vote (which was not held).

7. The city was evacuated on Dec. 14.
8. Vaudreuil's fleet was not able to sail until Dec. 24.
9. JW sent dispatches by express on Dec. 1, above.

To Robert R. Livingston

LS,[1] press copy of LS, and transcript: National Archives

Sir,   Passy, Decr. 4. 1782.

We detain the Washington a little longer expecting an English Passport for her in a few Days; and as possibly some Vessel bound for North America may sail before her, I write this Line to inform you that the French Preliminaries with England are not yet signed, tho' we hope they may be very soon. Of ours, I enclose a Copy.[2] The Dutch & Spain have yet made but little Progress,[3] and as no definitive Treaty will be signed till all are agreed, there may be Time for Congress to give us farther Instructions if they think proper. We hope the Terms we have obtained will be satisfactory, tho' to secure our main Points we may have yielded too much in favour of the Royalists.— The Quantity of Aid to be afforded us remains undecided, I suppose something depends on the Event of the Treaty.— By the Washington you will be fully informed of every thing.

With great Regard, I have the honour to be, Sir, Your most obedient & most humble Servant.   B Franklin

R. R. Livingston Esqr.

From Lafayette   ALS: Library of Congress

Dear Sir   On Board the *Censeur* December the 4th 1782
   To My Very Great Concern, I Have not Yet Received Your Answer to My letter,[4] Nor the Account of What Has officially

---

1. In WTF's hand.
2. JA also wrote to Livingston on Dec. 4, enclosing a copy of the Nov. 30 preliminary articles. His letter included a request (which may not have been entirely sincere) for permission to return to America: Wharton, *Diplomatic Correspondence*, VI, 106; James H. Hutson, *John Adams and the Diplomacy of the American Revolution* (Lexington, Ky., 1980), pp. 128–9.
3. BF here displays his lack of knowledge about the progress of the other negotiations, which the American-British provisional treaty completely disrupted; see our annotation of his letter to Livingston of Dec. 5[–14].
4. Lafayette's Nov. 21 letter to the peace commissioners, above.

DECEMBER 4, 1782

Past in Monney Matters— But Your Opinion Has Been I should
Go, and I Am Pursuing an object that May I Hope prove Useful
to America— Upon Your Opinion therefore, I Determine My
Going— We are Under sails With 9 ships of the line, And about
6000 Men Recruits Included—[5] Your letters I Beg You Will
send to Mis. [Marquis] de Castries Who Will forward them. My
Best Respects Waït Upon Mis. jay Adams and T. franklin With
the Most tender Affection and Regard I am My dear sir Yours

LAFAYETTE

From Thomas Percival[6]   ALS: American Philosophical Society

Manchester Decemb. 4. 1782.
Messrs. James and Charles Hill, are the Sons of Mr. John Hill,
late a very considerable Tradesman in Manchester, and have left
their Native Country in consequence of the Bankruptcy of their
Father.—[7]   THO. PERCIVAL.

5. The French eventually collected 24 ships of the line and 12,000 men at
Cadiz, but they and a Spanish contingent were unable to sail for Jamaica before France and Spain reached a preliminary peace agreement with Britain
(much to the relief of the French government): Dull, *French Navy,* pp. 318–
19, 333–5; Louis Gottschalk, *Lafayette and the Close of the American Revolution* (Chicago, 1942), p. 399.

6. This testament to the identity of James and Charles Hill—brothers
who were in France awaiting passage to America—was procured so that BF
might write them a letter of recommendation; see their letter of Jan. 7, below, which enclosed the present document. A third brother, Joseph Hill, obtained this letter on their behalf. He informed his brothers on Dec. 4 that Percival wrote these lines "with great Chearfullness" and would have written
more fully but for fear that if the letter miscarried it would be said that "Dr
P. was Carrying on a Correspondence with those whom some people call our
Enemies." As BF knew his handwriting, Percival felt sure that this sentence
would be sufficient. APS. Percival (XVIII, 104–5n) had recently renewed his
acquaintance with BF by sending him books: XXXVII, 361.

7. John Hill and his partner Joshua Marriott, merchants of Manchester, appear on a list of bankrupts for January, 1783: *Gent. Mag.,* LIII (1783), 95.

To Joshua Barney

LS:[8] United States Naval Academy Museum

Sir,   Passy, Dec. 5. 1782.

I receiv'd your Letter of the 23d. past duly by the Express. I was very glad to see the Minister's Dispatches, as the Want of them had much delay'd our affairs. I have kept the Express hoping to have sent by him our final Letters. But the Answer of the Court[9] being not yet obtained, & the time when we may expect it being from some present Circumstances very uncertain, I dismiss him, and shall send another when we are ready. In the mean time, it may be agreable, and of some use to you to know, that tho' Peace between us & England is not concluded, (and will not be till France & England are agreed) yet the Preliminary Articles are Signed, and you will have an English Passport. I acquaint you with this in Friendship, that if you have any little Adventure on your own Account you may save the Insurance:[1] but you will keep it to yourself for the present. Hold your Ship ready, as we know not how soon we may be ready to dismiss you. With great regard, I have the honour to be, Sir, Your most obedient and most humble Servant   B Franklin

P.S. Let me know what Vessels are at L'Orient bound to America, and when they sail.—

[*In Franklin's hand:*] If any Vessel for North America Sails before you, send with her the enclos'd for Mr Livingston[2] & let me know by whom it goes—

Capt. Barney.

---

8. In L'Air de Lamotte's hand, except for the last seven words of the complimentary close, which are in BF's hand.

9. To BF's request for financial aid for Congress.

1. Barney informed Capt. Barry of the *Alliance* and they both purchased goods in Lorient to ship aboard the *General Washington:* Hulbert Footner, *Sailor of Fortune: the Life and Adventures of Commodore Barney, U.S.N.* (New York and London, 1940), p. 134.

2. Presumably BF to Livingston, Dec. 4 (above).

To Robert R. Livingston LS[3] and transcript: National Archives

Sir, Passy, Decr. 5th.[−14] 1782.

I am honoured by your several Letters No 16. 17. 18. & 19. dated Sept. 5. 13. 13. & 18. I believe the Complaints you make in some of them of my not Writing, may ere now have appear'd less necessary, as many of my Letters written before those Complaints must have since come to hand:[4] I will nevertheless mention some of the Difficulties your Ministers meet with in keeping up a regular and punctual Correspondence. We are far from the Seaports, not well informed, and often misinformed about the sailing of Vessels. Frequently we are told they are to sail in a Week or two, and often they lie in Port for Months after, with our Letters on board, either waiting for Convoy, or for other Reasons. The Post Office here is an unsafe Conveyance, many of the Letters we receive by it have evidently been opened, and doubtless the same happens to those we send. And at this Time particularly there is so violent a Curiosity in all trading People to know something relating to the Negociations, and whether Peace may be expected or a Continuation of the War, that there are few Private Hands or Travellers that we can Trust with carrying our Dispatches to the Sea Coast; and I imagine they may be sometimes opened, & destroy'd because they cannot be well sealed again. The Observation you make that the Congress Ministers in Europe seem to form themselves into a Privy Council, transacting Affairs without the Privity or Concurrence of the Sovereign,[5] may be in some Respects just; but it should be consider'd, that if they do not write as frequently as other Ministers here do to their respective Courts, or if when they write, their Letters are not regularly received, the greater Distance, the War, and the extream Irregularity of Conveyances, may be the Causes, and not a Desire of acting without the Knowledge or Orders of their Constituents. There is no European Court to which an Express cannot be sent from Paris in 10 or 15 Days, and from most of them Answers may be obtained in that Time.

3. In WTF's hand.
4. BF wrote on Aug. 12 (XXXVII, 730–4) and Sept. 3 (above).
5. Above, Sept. 5.

There is I imagine no Minister who would not think it safer to act by Orders than from his own Discretion: And yet unless you leave more to the Discretion of your Ministers, than European Courts usually do, your Affairs may sometimes suffer extreamly from the Distance, which in time of War especially may make it 5 or 6 Months before the Ansr. to a Letter shall be received.

I suppose the Minister from this Court will acquaint Congress with the Kings Sentiments respecting their very handsome Present of a Ship of the Line.[6] People in general here are much pleased with it.

I communicated together with my Memoir demanding a Supply of Money,[7] Copies of every Paragraph in your late Letters, which express so strongly the Necessity of it. I have been constant in my Sollicitations, both directly and thro' the Marquis de la Fayette, who has employ'd himself diligently and warmly in the Business. The Negociations for Peace are I imagine one Cause of the great Delay & Indecision on this Occasion, beyond what has been usual, as the Quantum may be different if those Negociations do or do not succeed. We have not yet learnt what we may expect. We have been told that we shall be aided, but it cannot be to the extent demanded. Six Millions[8] has been mentioned, but not as a Sum fixed. The Minister tells me still that he is working upon the Subject, but cannot yet give a determinative Answer. I know his good Will to do the best for us that is possible. It is in vain for me to repeat again what I have so often written, and what I find taken so little Notice of, that there are bounds to every thing, and that the Faculties of this Nation are limited, like those of all other Nations.[9] Some among you seem to have established as Maxims, the Suppositions that France has Money enough for all her Occasions and all ours besides; and that if she does not supply us, it is owing to her Want of Will, or to my Negligence. As to the First, I am sure it is not true, and to the second, I can only say I should rejoice as much as any Man in be-

6. The *America*. La Luzerne conveyed Louis XVI's gratitude for the gift in March, 1783: Giunta, *Emerging Nation*, 1, 803.
7. The "Memoir" was BF's Nov. 8 letter to Vergennes, above.
8. *I.e.*, 6,000,000 *l.t.* The minister in the next sentence is Vergennes.
9. For a recent example of BF's warnings see XXXVII, 535–6.

ing able to obtain more, and I shall also rejoice in the greater Success of those who may take my Place.

You desire to be "very particularly acquainted with every Step which tends to a Negociation." I am therefore encouraged to send you the first Part of a Journal, which Accidents and a long severe Illness interrupted, but which from Notes I have by me may be continued, if thought proper.[1] In its present State it is hardly fit for the Inspection of Congress, certainly not for Public View; I confide it therefore to your Prudence.

The Arrival of Mr Jay, Mr Adams and Mr. Lawrens has relieved me from much Anxiety, which must have continued if I had been left to finish the Treaty alone; and it has given me the more Satisfaction, as I am sure the Business has profited by their Assistance.

Much of the Summer was taken up in objecting to the Powers given by G. Britain, and in removing those Objections. The using any Expressions that might imply an Acknowledgement of our Independence seem'd at first industriously to be avoided. But our refusing otherwise to treat, at length induced them to get over that Difficulty; and then we came to the Point of making Propositions. Those made by Mr Jay and me before the Arrival of the other Gentlemen, you will find in the Paper No 1. which was sent by the British Plenipotentiary to London for the Kings Consideration.[2] After some Weeks, an under Secretary, Mr Strachy, arriv'd with whom we had much Contestation about the Boundaries and other Articles which he proposed; we settled some which he carried to London, and returned with the Propositions, some adopted, others omitted or alter'd, and new Ones added; which you will see in Paper No. 2.[3] We spent many Days in disputing, and at length agreed on and signed the Preliminaries, which you will receive by this Conveyance.[4] The British

1. XXXVII, 291–346, and see XXXVII, 536. The copy that accompanied the present letter is no longer extant: XXXVII, 291–2n. BF never completed the journal.

2. The first draft treaty: above, [c. Oct. 5].

3. The British Counterproposal: above, [Nov. 19].

4. BF also said in his Dec. 4 letter (above) that he was enclosing a copy of the agreement; the packet *General Washington*, which was to carry it, had not yet sailed.

Ministers struggled hard for two Points, that the Favours granted to the Royalists should be extended, and our Fishery contracted. We silenc'd them on the first, by threatning to produce an Account of the Mischiefs done by those People; and as to the second, when they told us they could not possibly agree to it as we required it, and must refer it to the Ministry in London, we produced a new Article to be referr'd at the same time, with a Note of Facts in support of it, which you have No 3.[5] Aparently it seem'd that to avoid the Discussion of this they suddenly changed their Minds, dropt the Design of recurring to London, and agreed to allow the Fishery as demanded.

You will find in the Preliminaries some Inaccurate and Ambiguous Expressions that want Explanation, and which may be explained in the definitive Treaty. And as the British Ministry excluded our Proposition relating to Commerce,[6] and the American Prohibition of that with England, may not be understood to cease merely by our concluding a Treaty of Peace, perhaps we may then, if the Congress shall think fit to direct it, obtain some Compensation for the Injuries done us, as a Condition of our opening again the Trade. Every one of the present British Ministry has while in the Minority declared the War against us unjust, and nothing is clearer in Reason than that those who injure others by an unjust War, should make full Reparation. They have stipulated too in these Preliminaries, that in Evacuating our Towns they shall carry off no Plunder; which is a kind of Acknowledgement, that they ought not to have done it before.

The Reason given us for dropping the Article relating to Commerce, was that some Statutes were in the Way, which must be repealed before a Treaty of that kind could well be formed; and that this was a Matter to be consider'd in Parliament.

They wanted to bring their Boundary down to the Ohio, and to settle their Loyalists in the Ilinois Country. We did not chuse such Neighbours.[7]

5. BF's proposed article 5, Nov. 29.
6. The proposition relating to commerce formed the bulk of the fourth article of the first draft treaty.
7. According to Harlow, *Second British Empire*, I, 301, the British government believed it would have French support if it demanded a territorial set-

We communicated all the Articles as soon as they were signed to Mr. le Comte de Vergennes, (except the separate one) who thinks we have manag'd well, and told me that we had settled what was most apprehended as a Difficulty in the Work of a General Peace, by obtaining the Declaration of our Independency.[8]

Decr 14th. I have this Day learnt, that the Principal Preliminaries between France and England, are agreed on, Viz:

1. France is to enjoy the Right of fishing and drying on all the West Coast of newfoundland, down to Cape Ray. Miquelon and St Pierre to be restored and may be fortified.

2. Senegal remains to France, & Goree to be restored. The River Gambia entirely to England.

3. All the Places taken from France in the East Indies to be restored, with a certain Quantity of Territory round them.

4 In the West Indies, Grenada and the Grenadines, St Christophers, Nevis & Monserat to be restored to England; St Lucia to France, Dominique to remain with France, and St Vincents to be neutraliz'd.

5. No Commissioner at Dunkirk.

The Points not yet quite settled are, the Territory round the Places in the Indies, and the Neutralization of St Vincents. Apparently these will not create much Difficulty.[9]

Holland has yet done hardly any thing in her Negotiation.

Spain offers for Gibralter to restore W. Florida and the Bahamas. An Addition is talked of, the Island of Guadaloupe which France will cede to Spain in exchange for the other half of Hispaniola, and Spain to England: but England it is said chuses rather Porto Rico. Nothing yet concluded.[1]

---

tlement in Maine or in the Old Northwest for the Loyalists. (Gérard de Rayneval had responded with some sympathy to Shelburne's complaints about American territorial claims: Doniol, *Histoire*, v, 132–3.) It could not ask for support, however, without risk of revealing how close it was to a settlement with the Americans.

8. Vergennes later would be more critical; see Vergennes to BF, Dec. 15.

9. The preliminary Franco-British peace agreement of Jan. 20, 1783, roughly followed these provisions, except that the Caribbean islands of Dominica and St. Vincent were assigned to Britain, while France received instead the island of Tobago: Doniol, *Histoire*, v (sup.), 288–94.

1. On Nov. 28, Spanish Ambassador Aranda had agreed to a complex series of exchanges: Spain returning Minorca and the Bahamas to Britain and

As soon as I received the Commission and Instructions for treating with Sweden,[2] I waited on its Ambassador here: who told me he daily expected a Courier on that Subject. Yesterday he wrote a Note to acquaint me, that he would call on me to Day having something to communicate to me.[3] Being obliged to go to Paris, I waited on him, when he shewed me the full Powers he had just received, and I shew'd him mine. We agreed to meet on Wednesday next,[4] exchange Copies, and proceed to Business. His Commission has some polite Expressions in it, Viz: "That his Majesty thought it for the Good of his Subjects to enter into a Treaty of Amity and Commerce with the United States of America, who had established their Independence, so justly merited by their Courage and Constancy"; or to that Effect. I imagine this Treaty will soon be compleated. If any Difficulty should arise, I shall take the Advice of my Colleagues.

I thank you for the Copies of Mr. Paynes Letter to Abbé Raynal, which I have distributed into good Hands.[5] The Errors we see in Histories of our own Times and Affairs, weaken our Faith in antient History. M. Hilliard D'Auberteuil has here written another History of our Revolution, which however he modestly

---

giving Santo Domingo to France, France giving Dominica and Guadeloupe to Britain, and Britain giving Gibraltar to Spain. (Gérard de Rayneval, just returned from England, helped Vergennes persuade Aranda; the fate of West Florida was left unresolved.) This arrangement collapsed in the face of the anger of the British public about the concessions granted to the Americans. It was not until Dec. 11 that Rayneval (who had returned to England a third time) was able to secure British consent to a new settlement giving Minorca, West Florida, and East Florida to Spain in exchange for the Bahamas and an acknowledgment of British timber-cutting rights in Central America. It was questionable, however, whether Spain would agree to a peace without obtaining Gibraltar: Dull, *French Navy*, pp. 321–5, 329–31; Andrew Stockley, *Britain and France at the Birth of America: the European Powers and the Peace Negotiations of 1782–1783* (Exeter, 2001), pp. 117–21.

2. Above, Sept. 28.

3. Creutz's note is below, [Dec. 13].

4. Dec. 18. The following day Creutz reported to King Gustavus III that BF's draft treaty differed in several points from the one sent by the King: Amandus Johnson, *Swedish Contributions to American Freedom, 1776–1783* (2 vols., Philadelphia, 1953–57), I, 576–7.

5. See Livingston's Sept. 13 letter.

calls *an Essay:*[6] and fearing that there may be Errors, and wishing to have them corrected, that his second Edition may be more perfect, he has brought me Six Setts which he desires me to put into such Hands in America as may be good enough to render him and the Public that Service. I send them to you for that Purpose by Capt. Barney, desiring that one Set may be given to Mr Payne, and the rest where you please. There is a Quarto Set in the Parcel which please to accept from me.

I have never learnt whether the Box of Books I sent to you, and the Press to Mr Thomson were put on board the Eagle, or one of the Transports.[7] If the former perhaps you might easily purchase them at New-York. If the latter you may still receive them among the Goods for Congress now shipping by Mr. Barclay. If they are quite lost let me know it that I may replace them.

I have received several Letters from your Office with Bills to pay Ministers Salaries. Nothing has yet been done with those Bills; but I have paid Mr. Lawrens 20,000 Livres.[8]

I have this Day signed a common Letter to you drawn up by my Colleagues which you will receive herewith.[9] We have kept this Vessel longer for two things, a Pass-port promised us from England, and a Sum to send in her; but she is likely to depart without both, being all of us impatient that Congress should receive early Intelligence of our Proceedings; and for the Money, we may probably borrow a Frigate.

I am now entering my 78th. Year. Public Business has engross'd fifty of them. I wish now to be, for the little time I have left, my own Master. If I live to see this Peace concluded, I shall beg leave to remind the Congress of their Promise then to dismiss me,[1] I shall be happy to sing with Old Simeon, *Now lettest*

6. Michel-René Hilliard d'Auberteuil, *Essais historiques et politiques sur les Anglo-Américains* (2 vols., Brussels, 1781–82). See xxxvii, 133n.

7. For the books sent to Livingston see xxxvi, 401–2 and xxxvii, 4n, 71, 214–15. The copy press was for Secretary of Congress Charles Thomson: xxxiii, 115–18; xxxiv, 371n; xxxv, 174, 250, 476; WTF to RB, Sept. 13, 1781 (Library of Congress).

8. This payment is recorded under the date of Dec. 20 in Account XXVII (xxxii, 4).

9. American Peace Commissioners to Livingston, Dec. 14, below.

1. A promise made in June, 1781: xxxv, 175.

thou thy Servant Depart in Peace, for mine Eyes have seen thy Salvation.[2]

With great Esteem, I have the honour to be, Sir, Your most obedient & most humble Servant.   B FRANKLIN

To the honble. Robt. R. Livingston Esqr: Secretary for Foreign Affairs

From Catharine Greene   ALS: American Philosophical Society

My Very Dear Friend   Warwick Decbr. the 5th 1782

Have been favord with your letter by Count Segar, which he forwarded from Philadelphia[3] he Came to Providence with the Army we Sent for him but was gone to Newport[4] on his Return to Providence Ray[5] was at home and waited on him he Sat a day to Come with Count Rhoshambow but it was a heavy Rain for three days, after that the first Coll went to Boston and he Said it was imposible to Come, for they are extreem attentive to there Duty— Yr Curious friend went to Providence to See the Novelty—and Sent for the Count to See her was Very much Pleasd with him and lamented not haveing an oppertunity of a farther acquantance and Shewing him every Civility in our Power he Says his Wife[6] Visits you and Plays Chex but yr So Galant you Never beat her the officers Say; they are the happiest Couple in

2. William Hodgson had asked BF on Oct. 14 (above) not to sing the verse until he had completed his work.

3. BF's recommendation of the comte de Ségur, son of the marquis: XXXVII, 107.

4. When Rochambeau's army left Hartford for Providence on Nov. 4, Ségur and the prince de Broglie obtained permission to detour by themselves through New London and Newport. They arrived in Providence after overstaying their leave by several days. Ségur's regiment subsequently departed for Boston on Dec. 2: Louis-Philippe, comte de Ségur, *Mémoires ou souvenirs et anecdotes* (3 vols., Paris, 1827), I, 379–85; Rice and Brown, eds., *Rochambeau's Army*, II, 192.

5. Her son, a student at Yale College: XXXIV, 218n.

6. Antoinette-Elisabeth-Marie d'Aguesseau (1756–1828), whom Ségur married in 1777: Bodinier, *Dictionnaire*, under Ségur; Idzerda, *Lafayette Papers*, I, xliv–xlv.

France Pray my Regards to her being one of her Spoues admirer he is So Sensible Sociable and Polite but all this you know— Yr Dear Sister is gone to Boston to Spend the Winter She grows infirm Mrs. Greenes[7] Death and not haveing a letter from you a long time makes her low Spirited I Comfort her all I Can Remembering her of your Six Reasons in a former letter[8] our family are all well and Joyn me in the tenderest Regards and Best Wishes for yr health and happiness Ray is at College learning as fast as he Can that he may Come to France when he Comes out of Colege he has enterd his 3d year he is Spoke highly of by the Presedent[9] and Tutors hope he will make a good man the Count Speaks highly of yr Grandson I want a Peice of Beneys Drawing is he Still at Genevea are you well when do you Come to New England and make all our hearts Glad We long for Peice for the inhabitants of this State are and have been exceedingly Distrest and loosing Most all our Vesels are Very Poor but the French troops have greatly Releavd us from haveing the Militia on the Shore we are greatly indebted to them— Old uncle Tuthill has an Heir in his old age— Thomey lives to Torment Sukey and mrs. Partridg are living but not to there Brothers Children[1] this from your affectionate Friend   CATY GREENE

Spoues and Daugters[2] love you Dearly believe every body does

Doctr Franklin

Addressed: Doctr. Franklin

7. Jane Flagg Greene.
8. See XXXV, 158.
9. Ezra Stiles.
1. The Hubbart siblings—Tuthill, Thomas, Susannah ("Sukey"), and Elizabeth (here Mrs. Partridge)—were BF's stepnephews and stepnieces. We find no other record of an heir born to Tuthill, and he eventually left his estate to his nieces and nephews: I, lviii–lix; XXXVI, 204n.
2. Husband William and daughters Phebe Ward and Celia Greene: XXXVI, 202n. The Greenes had a third daughter, Anne, who died before 1787: X, 191n; Catharine Greene to BF, Nov. 8, 1787 (APS).

From Ségur

AL: American Philosophical Society

Vlles. Le 5. Xbre. 1782.
M de segur a l'honneur de faire à Monsieur franklin ses sinceres remerciments de ce qu'il a bien voulu prendre le soin de lui faire parvenir un Paquet venant de nantes par un exprès;[3] il le prie de recevoir les assurances de son parfait attachement. / .

To Vergennes

LS:[4] Archives du Ministère des affaires étrangères

Sir,   Passy, 6 Decr 1782
I have the honour of returning herewith the Map your Excellency sent me Yesterday. I have marked with a strong Red Line, according to your desire, the Limits of the thirteen United States, as settled in the Preliminaries between the British & American Plenipotentiarys.[5]

With great Respect, I am Sir, Your Excellency's most obedt & most humble Servant   B FRANKLIN

His Exy. Count de Vergennes

---

3. Presumably dispatches from America; see JW to BF, Dec. 1.
4. In WTF's hand.
5. In 1842 Jared Sparks located a map in the AAE that he thought might have been the one discussed in this letter: a small (18 inches square) 1746 map of North America by d'Anville on which the American boundary was drawn with a bold line in red ink. The significance of this discovery was debated in the ongoing controversy over the Maine border. All Sparks claimed was that the location and appearance of this map were suggestive; neither he nor anyone since has been able to prove a link to BF. See Herbert B. Adams, *The Life and Writings of Jared Sparks* (2 vols., Boston and New York, 1893), II, 392–411; Henry S. Burrage, *Maine in the Northeastern Boundary Controversy* (Portland, Maine, 1919), pp. 323–4, 370–1.

From Lafayette

ALS: American Philosophical Society

On Board the *Censeur* Brest Road
Dear Sir December the 6th 1782

After Having Been two days out of the Road, a S. o. [SW] Wind Obliges us to Come Back Again, and I fear it Will Give time for Lord Howe to Embarass our Passage—[6] No Letter from You Has Yet Come to Hand, Which I am Very sorry for, as I Impatiently Waït for Information Upon our Monney Affairs— I Have not Yet Received Your Answer to My Consulting Letter— But I know the Opinion of the three Gentlemen in the Commission, and You Have Also thought that I ought not to detain the fleet on My Account— And as I am still More Anxious to do the Best, than to Appear to Have done so, My Conscience is Easy, and I Would Willingly loose the Credit of past Exertions, Rather than to Neglect an Opportunity of Making New Ones. M. de Rayneval's speedy Return Makes me Hope that Peace is not far at a distance—[7] I Would Be Much Obliged to You for Your Opinion— In Case Men of some Rank Are sent By france, I do not know Who Will Be the person— If it is Not the One We spoke About together, it Will Be the Usual Ambassador, My uncle the Mquis. de Noaïlles—[8] This if You please (Entre Nous) Unless You think Useful to Communicate it, Under secrecy, to Your Colleagues.

As to My Part, if Matters Were so Ripe as to Admit of My Return, Nothing Would More Highly please me than the Happiness, Any How, to serve America, and More Particularly in the Capacity of a Man Honoured With Her Confidence.

An Express is sent to Versaïlles, By Whose Return I Hope to

6. Adm. Richard Howe's fleet of 35 ships of the line had returned to England three weeks earlier after a successful mission to replenish the British garrison at Gibraltar. It did not sail again: David Syrett, *The Royal Navy in European Waters during the American Revolutionary War* (Columbia, S.C., 1998), pp. 161–2.

7. For Rayneval's return see our annotation of BF to Livingston, Dec. 5[–14].

8. The marquis de Noailles was the uncle of Lafayette's wife. He represented France at the British court from 1776 to 1778: XXVIII, 188n; Idzerda, *Lafayette Papers,* I, xliv–xlv; *Repertorium der diplomatischen Vertreter,* III, 118.

Hear from You, and I do not think the Weather Will Permit us to set out Before that time.

Requesting My Compliments to Be Presented to Your Grandson I Have the Honor to Be With Every sentiment of Affection and Respect Your Excellency's Most obedient Humble servant

LAFAYETTE

His Excelleny B. franklin

Notation: Lafayette 6. Decr. 1782.

From Robert R. Livingston[9]

AL (draft): New-York Historical Society

Sir   Philadelphia 6th. Decr 1782

The College of Dartmouth in New Hampshire having suffered materialy in its funds since the war by the loss of those contributions which it till then recd. from England—Docr. Wheelock son of the worthy first founder proposes to solicit a subscription in France & Holland for its support— He flatters himself that the charity of an institution whose chief object is to christianize the Savages & the success which has hitherto attended it will recommend it to the liberal in Europe who are sufficeintly Citizens of the world to attend to the morals or religion of the natives of America. I wish his expectation may be answered— And have at his request furnish'd him with the letter of induction to you— He hopes for much from your favour & patronage— I have the honor &c:

Dr Letter to Docr Franklin introducing Docr Wheelock 6th. Decr 1782

9. For background on this letter of introduction for John Wheelock see the Board of Trustees of Dartmouth College to BF, Sept. 24. Wheelock procured from La Luzerne, also in Philadelphia, a letter of introduction to Vergennes: [John Wheelock], *Sketches of the History of Dartmouth College . . .* ([Newburyport, Mass., 1815]), p. 28.

From Jonathan Williams, Jr.

ALS: Historical Society of Pennsylvania

Dear & hond Sir   Nantes Decemr 6. 1782.

The Day before yesterday there were a number of Letters in Town announcing a Peace.[1] The News came from the secretary of the Duc d'orleans who 'tis said informed that the King had announced it to the Duc. Such respectable Information prevented every Doubt and I among the Rest believed it. I immediately set myself to work to get a little fast sailing Brig I have here ready to sail at 24 Hours Notice, supposing you wanted an Express Boat. The foolish Public always think I am in the Secret when anything happens that regards America, and immediately on this news one cried out "M. Williams doit savoir cela". "Oui" says another "& *peut être* il a reçu un express de M. Franklin"— the third left the *peut être* out of the Question, & it was established as a Fact that an Express had arrived to me in 36 hours, nay some knew the matter so well as to describe whether the Expres wore a green or a blue Jacket.— The next Post la nouvelle *meritait* Confirmation how it will be tomorrow I cannot tell, but if it be true, and if you wish to convey it to America, here is the Brig at your Service. I only ask you to give her a protection from the English Plenipotentiaries, or in any other way you judge proper, Paying me for the Brig & outfitts exactly what she cost & no more, & returning me the Vessell in America at her estimated Value when she may arrive; this will be making the public pay what I should otherways lose, & what no Man can think unreasonable. As my only motive is to be usefull it is (as a matter of Interest) perfectly indifferent whether you accept the proposition or not, you have therefore only to say yes or no & your orders shall be punctualy obeyed or the matter will be as if it had never been, if I have not an answer in 10 Days I shall conclude that you have not occasion for my Vessell.

---

1. On Dec. 5 JW wrote to WTF that there were "above 50 Letters" circulating the previous day. He asked WTF to tell BF that he could have a fast brig ready to sail for America within 24 hours. APS. News of the provisional treaty reached England around 2 p.m. on Dec. 3; Townshend immediately informed the Lord Mayor of London, and his letter was published in the *London Courant and Daily Advertiser* on Dec. 4.

I am as ever most dutifully & affectionately Yours.

JONA WILLIAMS J

It is proper to inform you that my Brig has a Cargo on board her & she was intended to wait to fill up on Freight. I suppose there can be no objection to her having on board enough to ballast her & whether this be Brandy or Stones is of no Consequence, I mention this because if there be the usual Restriction of Flags of Truce she must be unloaded & Ballasted again, which would lose time & defeat the Object.[2]

Addressed: His Excellency / Doctor Franklin

Notation: J. Williams 6. Decr. 1782.

Parole for Lawrence Robert Campbell[3]

ADS: American Philosophical Society

On December 6 and 7 Temple and Franklin were faced with an unusual situation: writing paroles for five British army officers who had been captured at sea. Jonathan Williams, Jr., had taken their paroles at Nantes, where they landed, and authorized them to travel to Paris, where they would have to obtain permission from Franklin to continue to England. Four of the officers arrived at the hôtel Valentinois on December 6. Temple wrote paroles for these four, which they signed.[4] He faithfully copied the language of the paroles issued by George Washington at Yorktown, copies of which Jonathan Wil-

2. We have no record of BF's having answered this letter. WTF answered on Dec. 11 (missing), inquiring about the brig. JW replied on Dec. 20, informing him that it could be outfitted for less than 40,000 *l.t.* He also thanked WTF for his hint about "Barney's safety" and assured him that he would keep the secret, though it was already circulating from other sources. APS. BF had promised Barney an English passport on Dec. 5, above.

3. Campbell was traveling with his wife; see JW to BF, Nov. 21.

4. George Meggs carried an individual letter of introduction from JW dated Nov. 27 (above). He signed his own parole. The other three—Æneas Mackintosh, Lt. Archibald Campbell, and David Burns—seem to have been traveling together; see our annotation of JW to BF, Nov. 28, letter (I). WTF wrote for them a single parole, identical in wording to Meggs's (except for the change from singular to plural). Both paroles are at the Hist. Soc. of Pa.

liams, Jr., had recently sent to Franklin.[5] Temple's only alteration was to substitute Franklin's name for Washington's:

I the underwritten . . . do acknowledge myself a Prisoner of War to the United States of America; And having Permission from the honble. Benjamin Franklin Esqre. Minister Plenipotentiary from the said United States at the Court of France, to proceed to any Part of Great Britain, Do pledge my Faith & Word of honour that I will not do or say any thing injurious to the said United States or Armies thereof, or their Allies untill duly exchanged.

I do further Promise that whenever required by the Commander in Chief of the American Army, or the Commissary of Prisoners for the same, I will repair to such Place or Places, as they or either of them may require.

On December 7 the fifth officer, Lawrence Robert Campbell, arrived in Passy. This time, Franklin himself wrote the parole (the present document), adapting it to reflect the circumstances of a prisoner in France and rendering the language more straightforward.

[December 7, 1782]

I the underwritten Captain in the 71st British Regiment, having been taken Prisoner by the American Privateer the Marquis de la Fayette, Capt. Buffington, and brought into France; and being desirous of going immediately to England; do hereby promise on my Word of Honour, that I will not bear Arms against the United States of America, nor do or say any thing to their Prejudice until I shall be exchanged or absolved from this Parole. And I farther promise to render my self at such place as shall be required by any Person vested with Authority for that purpose by the Congress. Witness my hand this seventh Day of December, 1782, at Passy near Paris.— LAW ROBT CAMPBELL
Captn. 71 Regimt

Parole given to me
B FRANKLIN[6]

5. JW sent the paroles (now missing) with his letter (II) of Nov. 28. The one example we have located of a parole issued at Yorktown is the one signed by Cornwallis on Oct. 28, 1781: Lee Family Papers, University of Virginia.

6. The back of this sheet is entirely filled with sketches that appear to have been made by BF and, though we cannot identify them, seem scientific in nature.

From Henry Laurens

L:[7] American Philosophical Society

Hotel d'York Saturday 7th. Decemr: 1782.
Mr: Laurens presents his Compliments to Mr. Franklin, and requests the honor of his Company to dinner on Wednesday next
at 3 oClock.[8]

From Abel James[9]

Copy:[1] Library of Congress

This letter—or at least the first part of it—is well known to readers
of Franklin's autobiography. James announced that he had found a
manuscript in Franklin's hand that appeared to be an unfinished account of his life, as well as a set of "notes" for that account. He enclosed a copy of those notes and urged Franklin to complete the project. When Franklin did resume work on the autobiography in 1784,
he indicated that both this letter and Benjamin Vaughan's of January
31, 1783, should be inserted at the beginning of Part II along with a
statement that explained his continuing the narrative.[2] William Temple Franklin followed those directions when he published the autobiography (through Part III) in his 1818 edition of Franklin's writings.
He printed only the relevant opening section of James's letter, however, presumably following his grandfather's marks on the now-missing ALS.[3] Subsequent editors have followed suit.

7. In the hand of Henry Laurens, Jr.
8. JA attended the dinner: Butterfield, *John Adams Diary*, III, 95.
9. For this Quaker merchant, with whom BF had not corresponded for
nearly a decade, see XI, 436n; *Autobiog.*, p. 287; Whitfield J. Bell, Jr., *Patriot-
Improvers: Biographical Sketches of Members of the American Philosophical
Society* (2 vols. to date, Philadelphia, 1997–), II, 5–9.
1. Made by William Short for Thomas Jefferson in 1786, from a now-missing copy in Le Veillard's possession: *Jefferson Papers*, IX, 483–8; and see the
note below.
2. BF's draft reads, "Thus far was written with the Intention express'd in
the Beginning and therefore contains several little family Anecdotes of no
Importance to others. What follows was written many Years after in compliance with the Advice contain'd in these Letters, and accordingly intended
for the Publick. The Affairs of the Revolution occasion'd the Interruption.
"Letter from Mr. Abel James with Notes of my Life, to be here inserted.
Also Letter from Mr. Vaughan to the same purpose": *Autobiog.*, p. 133.
3. WTF, *Memoirs*, I, 58–63.

Though James's autograph letter has been lost, its enclosure—the copy of Franklin's notes—is still extant. We do not print that so-called outline here, as our predecessors included the text in *The Autobiography of Benjamin Franklin*, pp. 267–72. J. A. Leo Lemay and Paul M. Zall identified the copyist as Henry Drinker (IX, 436n), James's business partner.[4] The outline consists of single words and clipped phrases, ending with, "Writing for Jersey Assembly." After receiving it Franklin made several emendations and added in red ink about fifteen more items, bringing his life up to the present. The new entries begin with "Hutchinson's Letters," cover his return from England to America, and end with the briefest of summaries of his life since December, 1776: "To France, Treaty, &c."[5]

My dear & honored Friend.   [before December 8, 1782][6]
I have often been desirous of writing to thee, but could not be reconciled to the Thoughts that the Letter might fall into the

4. J. A. Leo Lemay and P. M. Zall, eds., *The Autobiography of Benjamin Franklin: a Genetic Text* (Knoxville, Tenn., 1981), p. 196.

5. Drinker's copy of the outline with BF's additions is at the Pierpont Morgan Library; as BF's original has been lost, this copy is of particular importance. Before leaving France BF permitted Le Veillard to copy it along with Abel James's letter. Thomas Jefferson borrowed both texts from Le Veillard in 1786 and had his secretary William Short make copies of them (Library of Congress). As we noted above, Short's copy of the James letter is the only MS version extant. His copy of the outline has been shown to have errors as compared to the Drinker copy; whether these were introduced by Short or Le Veillard is not clear. For a history and analysis of these versions, as well as annotated texts, see *Jefferson Papers*, IX, 486–95; Lemay and Zall, *Genetic Text*, pp. 196–211.

The Drinker copy bears three notations in French at the top of the sheet, squeezed into what little white space existed above and below the first line of text. These were obviously added at a later date. We differ from Lemay and Zall in our identifications of two of the handwritings. We speculate that the first notation, "Autographe très curieux de Bn. Franklin—1ere Esquisse/memorandum de ses mémoires" was made by Le Veillard's son. Le Veillard crossed out the word "Autographe" and wrote over it, "Copie d'un Projet," as Lemay and Zall assert. The third notation, "Les additions à l'encre rouge sont de la main de Franklin," is in the hand of the abbé de La Roche.

6. The first reference in BF's papers to this undated letter is on Dec. 8, when Benjamin Vaughan wrote to WTF, "I wish you would give my extreme respects to your grandfather, and inform him that I have a note to send him, in favor of the papers which his quaker American friend lately sent him." APS. Vaughan's promised "note" turned into the lengthy letter he finally sent on

Hands of the British, lest some Printer or busy Body should publish some Part of the Contents & give our Friends Pain & myself Censure.[7]

Some Time since there fell into my Hands to my great Joy about 23 Sheets in thy own hand-writing containing an Account of the Parentage & Life of thyself, directed to thy Son ending in the Year 1730 with which there were Notes likewise in thy writing,[8] a Copy of which I inclose in Hopes it may be a means if thou continuedst it up to a later period, that the first & latter part may be put together, & if it is not yet continued, I hope thou wilt not delay it, Life is uncertain as the Preacher tells us, and what will the World say if kind, humane & benevolent Ben Franklin should leave his Friends & the World deprived of so pleasing & profitable a Work, a Work which would be useful & entertaining not only to a few, but to millions.

The Influence Writings under that Class have on the Minds of Youth is very great, & has no where appeared so plain as in our public Friend's Journal.[9] It almost insensibly leads the Youth

---

Jan. 31, 1783, detailing all the reasons why BF should complete and publish the account of his life. As we remarked in the headnote, BF specified that this letter be published at the beginning of Part II of the autobiography: *Autobiog.*, pp. 135–40.

7. The British blockade of Philadelphia ended in early August; see XXXVII, 715. We suspect that James would only have felt free to write this letter as of that time.

8. These MSS were among the papers BF entrusted to Joseph Galloway before sailing to France. Galloway, who defected to the British and eventually went into exile in England, evidently separated them from the rest of BF's papers and seems to have left them to the care of his wife Grace Growden Galloway, who stayed behind to protect the family's American properties. (The rest of BF's papers were subsequently raided by the British during the occupation of Philadelphia, causing BF much concern: XXXII, 610; XXXV, 471.) After Grace Galloway died on Feb. 6, 1782, James, one of two executors of her estate, discovered these papers among her possessions: *Autobiog.*, 22–5; Lemay and Zall, *Genetic Text*, pp. xxxvii, xxxix, 182; Raymond C. Werner, ed., "Diary of Grace Growden Galloway," *PMHB*, LV (1931), 32–94.

9. "Public Friend" was the Quaker term for a self-appointed minister. James is probably referring here to the journal of his father-in-law Thomas Chalkley (1675–1741), which he helped edit for publication and which Franklin and Hall printed: *A Collection of the Works of Thomas Chalkley* (Philadelphia, 1749). A second edition was issued in Philadelphia in 1754, and

into the Resolution of endeavouring to become as good and as eminent as the Journalist. Should thine for Instance when published, and I think it could not fail of it, lead the Youth to equal the Industry & Temperance of thy early Youth, what a Blessing with that Class would such a Work be. I know of no Character living nor many of them put together, who has so much in his Power as thyself to promote a greater Spirit of Industry & early Attention to Business, Frugality and Temperance with the American Youth. Not that I think the Work would have no other Merit & Use in the World, far from it, but the first is of such vast Importance, that I know nothing that can equal it.

The inclosed Letters are of much Importance to our mutual worthy Friend John Strettell & myself as Executors of our deceased Friend Amos Strettell Esqr. decd. as well as his Children &c.[1] which with that directed to Frederick Pigon,[2] I shall be obliged to thee to forward in such Way as will be likely to reach them in Safety & charge the Expence of Postage to me. The Balance resting with thee in Payment of Stringfellow's Right will serve for such Purpose,[3] at same Time I acknowlege the many Obligations I am under, & present my best Respects to thy

---

four London editions appeared between 1751 and 1766: George T. Willauer, Jr., "Editorial Practices in Eighteenth-Century Philadelphia: the Journal of Thomas Chalkley in Manuscript and Print," *PMHB*, CVII (1983), pp. 217, 220, 223–4, 232–3; C. William Miller, *Benjamin Franklin's Philadelphia Printing, 1728-1766* (Philadelphia, 1974), pp. 251–2.

1. The enclosures have not been located. Amos Strettel, who campaigned against BF's slate and had opposed him in the Pa. Assembly (XI, 390, 407), died on Jan. 13, 1780. His brother John (1721–1786) was a merchant in London: Lemay and Zall, *Genetic Text*, p. 184; *PMHB*, XIV (1890), 444. Strettel had three children, a son who was mentally incompetent to manage his own affairs, and two daughters: *PMHB*, II (1878), 115; Elaine F. Crane *et al.*, eds., *The Diary of Elizabeth Drinker* (3 vols., Boston, 1991), II, 1415n.

2. Frederick Pigou, Sr., was one of the directors of the Bank of England and the East India Company: *Walpole Correspondence*, XII, 36n. His son Frederick Pigou, Jr., established himself as a merchant in New York, but returned to England after the war broke out. He recommended Drinker and James to the East India Company: Katharine A. Kellock, "London Merchants and the Pre-1776 American Debts," *Guildhall Studies in London History*, I (1973–74), 140.

3. An allusion to a land transaction involving James and BF. John Stringfellow had held the rights to the land: XIX, 97–9, 168–9.

Grandsons, particularly Temple. I am not much in Trade yet have been very attentive to the Goods imported here from France, in examining the spining & weaving & the Quality of the Materials from which they are manufactured, & with Pleasure I can assure thee, that not only in Silks, but Cottons & Linens, say every Kind manufactured in & about Manchester, I think the spinning & weaving rather excel & the Dyes are equal. England to be sure has the Advantage in woollen & worsted as well as Iron & Steel Wares, but the latter we can easily help ourselves in, if Industry & Oeconomy prevails as I wish it. My Partner & self have brought the casting of almost all Kind of Iron ware to acknowledged great Perfection, to the Benefit of ourselves & the public at a large Work we have between this & little Egg-harbour, which could Hands be obtained at reasonable Wages, might be carried to great Extent in other Branches, I think with the Assistance of two Potters and Founders from New England we made last Year & sold near 2000 neat Tea-kettles very pleasing at this Time to the People.

I trust I need make no Apology to my good Friend for mentioning to him these Matters, believing he continues a Relish for every Exertion of the Sort, in Confidence of which I rest with great Truth & perfect Esteem his very affectionate Friend

(signed) ABEL JAMES

Dr Franklin

From Lafayette
ALS: Library of Congress

On Board the Censeur Under sails

My Dear Sir   December the 8th 1782

However Certain it Appears that Peace is Near at Hand, I Have thought that Personal Considerations ought to Give Way to Motives of Public Utility— I am therefore sailing With the fleet, and Untill Peace is Ascertained, Will Continüe in Promoting the Views Which You Have Decided to Be the Most Advantageous to America— in this Affair, it is Useless to observe that My Personal Interest Has Been By me Entirely Given Up— God Grant this May prove of some service to our Noble Cause.

In Case My Return to Paris, in a few Weeks, Might Be of Use, pray, Give Your letter to Count de Vergennes, and to Marquis De Castries With a Particular Recommendation.

My Best Respects Waït Upon Your Colleagues Whom I Beg You Will Acquaint With My departure and the Motives of it— My Compliments to Your Grand son and Doctor Bancroft.

Most Respectfully and Affectionately I Have the Honor to Be Your obedient Humble servant   LAFAYETTE

His Excellency dr franklin

From the Marquis de Saint-Auban

ALS: American Philosophical Society

paris le 8 xbre. 1782

Si la communiquation Monsieur relativement a la saison etoit plus comode jaurais deja eu lhoneur de vous aler voir, ce nets que depuis quatre jours que nous somes arivés de la campagne, mde de st. auban et moy nous flattons, que vous voudres bien nous demender a diner avec monsieur votre fils, en voulant bien aussi par la petite [*poste*] nous faire informer du jours afin que nous ayons peu de monde, et seulement les gens que nous scavons vous convenir, il ny auroit mesme persone ce jours, mde de st. auban etant incomodée dun rhumatisme qui luy fait garder sa chambre, come nous vivons un peu a lanciene mode, vous voudrés bien venir a deux heures.

Lors de mon depart au mois de 7bre vous eties incomodé faites moy donc [*savoir*] je vous suplie si vous etes parfaitement retabli, je me flatte que vous ne douteres jamais de la verite, et de la sincerite de tous les sentiments que vous nous inspirés et avec les quels jauray toujours lhonur detre Monsieur votre très humble et tres obeissant serviteur   ST. AUBAN

Addressed: A Monsieur / Monsieur de frankclin ministre / plenipotentiaire des provinces / unies de lamérique, a passy / pres de paris / a passy

Notation: St Auban 8 Decembre 1782 A Paris

430

From Joshua Barney

ALS: American Philosophical Society

Sir   LOrient Decr. 9th. 1782

I recd. Yours[4] by Express and have to thank You for Your Early advice in respect to Saving any Insurance on My own Adventure, we had a rumour of the kind the day before I recd. Yours by Way of Nantes, but coming from You has cleared every Doubt.

The Vessells that are at this place are the Ships, Revolution, Capt. Webb, Buccaneer Capt. Prearson, Cicero, Hill, America Caldwell, St. James, Cain, Washington, Josiah, Queen of France, Deal,[5] but when they Sail is Very uncertain, on Acct. of Late change of Affairs, but not untill the Middle of Jany. at all events. Capt. Barry Left this place Yesterday On a Cruise,[6] My Ship is ready at a Moments Warning and hope not to Wait Long for Your Orders.

I sincerly Congratulate You on the Conclusion of a War which must tirminate so much in favor of our Country, and Assure You Nothing can be a Greater Satisfaction than Carrying News of Freedom to an Opress'd Country, Wishing you health And happiness I am Sir Your Most Obt. And Very Hble Servt.

                                              JOSHUA BARNEY

My Compts. to Mr. W T. Franklin

Addressed: A Monsieur / Monsieur Franklin / Ministree planipotentiaire / des Etats unis de L'Amerique / à la Cour de France / a Passy preès Paris

Notation: Barney Mr. Joshua L'Orient Decr. 9 1782

---

4. Of Dec. 5, above.

5. For the first three ships and their captains see Williams, Moore & Co.'s Sept. 11 letter. The *America* was commanded by Robert Caldwell: Thomas Barclay to BF, Jan. 29, 1783 (APS). This may be the Robert Caldwell of Boston described in Claghorn, *Naval Officers,* p. 47. For the *St. James, Washington,* and *Queen of France* and their captains see Jonathan Nesbitt to BF, Sept. 23.

6. In fact, Barry sailed to Martinique; see our annotation of his Oct. 31 letter.

From Rodolphe-Ferdinand Grand

ALS: American Philosophical Society

Ferdinand Grand's resources were stretched to their limit. He was besieged by demands from the various American peace commissioners to pay loan office certificates and other expenses,[7] and by requests from Robert Morris to pay bills of exchange.[8] Moreover, an interest payment on the 1781 Dutch loan arranged by France had come due on November 5.[9] In mid-December Grand drafted for Franklin's signature two letters regarding financial assistance from France and the Netherlands, which he hoped the American minister would send. Franklin sent neither.

The first one, intended for Vergennes, was enclosed with the present letter.[1] In it, Franklin acknowledges receipt of a letter from Vergennes (now missing) that promised to apprise Finance Minister Joly de Fleury of Franklin's request for 1,000,000 l.t. Franklin specifies that Fleury should pay Grand half that sum on December 15 and the remainder at the end of the month. He thanks Vergennes for assuring him that he will no longer have to rely on new funds to satisfy Congress' drafts as regards the loan office. He will inform Congress of this arrangement at the first opportunity, and requests a memorandum that he could send to Congress regarding the 6,000,000 l.t. that Vergennes granted "dans le temps."

We have found no trace of either Franklin's having asked for one million *livres* (presumably an advance on the loan he requested on November 8) or anything resembling a commitment from Vergennes. Franklin did visit Vergennes "a few days" after the preliminaries were signed; whether the two discussed the loan at that time is not known.[2] The second draft letter that Grand provided to Franklin was writ-

---

7. In August, 1782, Grand recorded payments of 946,470 l.t. for "Bills of Exchange drawn on the Commissioners for Interest of Money": Account XXVII (XXXII, 4).

8. For recent examples see *Morris Papers*, VI, 473–4, 522–3, 663.

9. XXXVII, 638. See also Morris to BF, Sept. 30. Grand used part of JA's loan raised in the Netherlands to pay it: BF to Morris, Dec. 14, below.

1. Two pages in length, it was undated and written in a secretarial hand.

2. BF was joined by Laurens on that occasion, which Vergennes described in a Dec. 19 letter to La Luzerne: Giunta, *Emerging Nation*, I, 728. Vergennes criticized them for having broken their promise to sign the preliminaries conjointly with France, but their conversation nonetheless "passed amiably." See also Vergennes to BF, Dec. 15, below.

ten on December 13 and evidently was intended for the consortium of bankers in the Netherlands who were handling the loan being raised by John Adams.[3] In it Franklin acknowledges the consortium's letter of December 2 (now missing) and expresses confidence that they will not refuse the American commissioners' request for whatever funds might remain from that loan, once Morris' drafts have been deducted. Repayment is assured. He then lists the Americans' obligations, which exceed their credit by 28,695 *l.t.* 4 *s.*, not including the 1,567,000 *l.t.* they will have to pay for anticipated bills from Morris.

Monsieur   Paris ce 9 De 82

Vous mavés permis de vous donner mes idées, notre derniere conversation ma fait naitre celle que vous trouverés dans le projet de Lettre dautre part pour mr De Vergennes, & que je vous Soumet monsieur persuadé que Si vous n'en faites pas usage vous demanderés Cependant a ce ministre Les payements que jindique puis quils Sont indispensables. Jay Lhonneur d'etre plus que persone monsieur votre tres humble & tres obeisst servitr

GRAND

Franklin's Sketch of Articles of Peace

Copy: South Carolina Historical Society

[between December 10 and 13, 1782?][4]

That there shall be a firm & perpetual Peace &ca.
A Renunciation on the Part of the K. of G. B. of all Claim or

---

3. This two-page draft is in the hand of Henry Grand (Hist. Soc. of Pa.). The three firms involved were those of Wilhem & Jan Willink, Nicolaas & Jacob van Staphorst, and De la Lande & Fynje: Butterfield, *John Adams Diary*, III, 9n.

4. On Dec. 10, according to JA's diary, BF and JA visited Oswald and discussed the British reaction to the preliminary articles as well as Britain's ongoing negotiations with the other warring powers. At the end of the conversation BF told JA that "he was for beginning early to think about the Articles of the difinitive Treaty. We had been so happy as to be the first in the Preliminaries, and he wished to be so in the definitive Articles." JA then listed in his diary five articles that he wanted to see included: Butterfield, *John Adams Diary*, III, 94–5.

Within the next few days JA thought of four additional items and drew up

Pretention to the Government or Territory of all or any of the United States, ceding all Claim to the Lands, or to the Right of Preemption of any of them from the Natives, included in the Boundaries, Viz.

That all his Troops shall be withdrawn from the Continent, and the Provinces of Canada & Nova Scotia declared free & Independent States, and at Liberty to join the Confederacy or remain separate.

That the Island of Bermudas shall likewise be left at Liberty.

That Ships belonging to any of the Subjects of G. B. shall and may enter freely into any of the Ports of the United States, and expose their Merchandize there to Sale, subject to no other Restrictions, Duties &c. than the most favoured Nations are or shall be subject to.

That the Vessels belonging to any Subjects of the said States may enter as freely all the Ports of Great Britain, Ireland, or any of its Dependencies, as they might have done in the Year 1750, liable to no other Duties &c than the most favoured Nation— or than they were subject to at that time.

That the Subjects of the United States and those of the King of Great Britain shall not be deemed Aliens in the Dominions of either, but enjoy the same Rights of Citizenship, as at the time above mentioned.

That the Right of Fishery shall remain the same & be enjoyed

---

a sketch of nine "Articles to be proposed in the definitive Treaty" (Mass. Hist. Soc.). One of the new items reads: "Dr Franklin desired to draw an Article respecting exempting Husbandmen Fishermen and Merchants as much as possible from the Calamities of War, in any future War." BF drafted that article by Dec. 13, when he showed it to JA; it is published below, under that date.

The present document certainly predates BF's draft of that proposed article, many of whose well-organized elements are listed here in a scattershot fashion among other ideas that seem to have been jotted down as they came to mind. We speculate that BF drew up this list after his Dec. 10 meeting with JA, and possibly after a subsequent conversation during which they discussed the idea that Canada, Nova Scotia, and Bermuda should be free to join the United States: both men's lists contain articles to that effect, and the coincidence is striking. To the best of our knowledge, this idea was never actually proposed. This copy is in the hand of L'Air de Lamotte.

in common by the Subjects of both Nations under such Regulations only as were in Force in 1750.

Damages.

In Case of future War, no Privateers.

All Merchant Vessels unarmed to pass freely with their Cargoes.

Any Merchandize taken out of them because wanted, to be paid for.

No Goods contraband.

Military Stores may be detain'd paying for the delay, or taken paying the Price.

Landing, Farmers & Inhabitants of open Towns not to be molested.

Fishermen free.

Notation in Henry Laurens' hand: Dr. Franklin's sketch of Articles of Peace./
Copy of a sketch of Articles for a Treaty of Peace between Great Britain & America proposed by Doctor Franklin & delivered by him to Mr. Jay to be extended, as appears by Mr. Jay's endorsement in the words contained in the two first Lines above-written which I have seen in Mr. Jay's own hand writing & carefully compared this Copy with the original. Paris 5th. Novr. 1783. H L.

From Charles-Dominique de Vyssery de Bois-Valée[5]

ALS: American Philosophical Society

Monsieur   a st: omer le 10 xbre: 1782

Pourroit t'on s'imaginer qu'en imitant ce que vous faite de si admirable pour le bien de l'humanité; je me serois fait une affaire

---

5. A lawyer and amateur *physicien* whose installation of an elaborate lightning rod in May, 1780, caused an uproar in his village and led to a highly publicized, three-year legal battle. The incident is described and analyzed in Jessica Riskin, *Science in the Age of Sensibility: the Sentimental Empiricists of the French Enlightenment* (Chicago and London, 2002), pp. 139–87. There his name is spelled Vissery, as it was in some of the memorials published at the time.

serieuse avec mes concitoyens, avec mes voisins, avec nos juges
de police enfin, qui m'ont condamné rigoureusement a detruire
mon para-tonnerre dans les 24. heures pour tout delai, comme
une invention des plus dangereuse.[6]

Sentence frapante, qui a causée une fermentation extraordi-
naire parmi le bas peuple; qui a exposé ma personne et ma maison a des insultes inattendues, et outrageantes; comme vous
pourrez le voir dans le Memoire que mon Avocat d'Arras se
charge de vous faire parvenir.[7] C'est un hommage que je crois
devoir a l'Auteur d'une invention si célébre par toute la terre, et
cependant jadis si redoutée a st: omer, mais maintenant adoptée
par les personnes instruites.— Vous ne serez peut être pas faché

6. Vyssery's construction was inspired by Barbier de Tinan's 1779 translation of the abbé Toaldo's memoir on the design of conductors (XXXII, 373–
4). It was a gilt swordblade mounted atop a weathervane in the image of a
globe that had been struck by lightning and was emitting burning rays. The
weathervane was hoisted 16 feet above the chimney by an iron bar; the bar
was set in a stoppered funnel attached to a 57-foot tin tube that ran down the
wall of a neighboring house, over to a well, and was there attached to a rod
and chain, which dropped into the water. The terrified neighbors petitioned
the aldermen, who delivered the verdict described here on June 14, 1780.
Vyssery appealed, but agreed to remove the blade while awaiting the final decision: Riskin, *Science in the Age of Sensibility,* pp. 139–40, 149–50.

7. In the fall of 1780 Antoine-Joseph Buissart (*DBF*) agreed to take Vyssery's case on appeal to the Conseil d'Artois in Arras. Buissart, like Vyssery,
was also an inventor and *physicien,* with a strong interest in lightning rods;
he was a member of the academies of Arras and Dijon and of the Société
royale de médecine, and was a regular contributor to the *Journal de physique.*
(His April 24, 1781, article on the advantages of multiple lightning rods was
published there in 1782: *Jour. de physique,* XXI, 140–8.) In drafting his brief
in the spring of 1781, he consulted Le Roy, Condorcet, and Bertholon, among
others. The brief and consultation were published in Arras in November,
1782, as *Mémoire signifié pour Me. Charles-Dominique de Vyssery de Bois-
Valé, Avocat en Parlement, demeurant en Ville de Saint-Omer, Défendeur et Ap-
pellant . . . .* Buissart sent copies to his scientific consultants, who debated its
contents and recommended taking out certain exaggerated claims. Le Roy,
for example, pointed out that there was no lightning rod on the King's residence at La Muette. In fact, the first lightning rod was not installed in Paris
until December, 1783: Riskin, *Science in the Age of Sensibility,* pp. 156–74,
292. The press reported on the case and recommended the memorial as a scientific treatise: *Jour. politique, ou Gaz. des gazettes* for the second half of December, 1782, pp. 58–9; Bachaumont, *Mémoires secrets,* XXII, 55–6.

Monsieur que je vous retrasse ici un abregé, de ce qui a donné lieu a tant de peinnes et de tracasseries que l'on m'a fait essuier a ce sujet.

Ce fut d'abord une voisine qui m'a chicanee ci devant plusieurs fois, pour une muraille de separation, de nos jardins reciproques, laquelle dans un conseil feminin, a exagerée le peril de cette invention insinuant que la lame d'Epée êtoit aimantée et Electrisée et que par ce moyen j'allois attirer le Tonnerre des 4. coins de la ville, et par ainsi les exposer a être brulées, et Ecrasées dans leurs maisons. D'ou on conclud qu'il faloit presenter une Requeste au Magistrat a effet de faire detruire une machine si dangereuse.

Le petit et tendre mary d'une voisine en fut le colporteur secret, pour obtenir des signatures: 7. ou 8. personnes l'ont fait par complaisance ou par importunitées, tandis que des Dames, et meme deux de ses oncles l'ont refusé constamment.— La plus proche voisine ajant un frere Echevin aussi peureux qu'elle, secondé par un bruyant faiseur d'ordonnances de vie et de mort, disant que des femmes auroient avortées &c ils firent pancher la balance de Themis, avec d'autres peureux pour la destruction de tout l'appareil: sentence memorable! qui fut prononcée contre l'avis des meilleures têtes qui font toujours le plus petit nombre dans les assemblées.

M'étant rendu opposant a cette sentence par defaut, elle fut cependant confirmée malgré les autoritées respectables comme la vôtre Monsieur, citées dans la playdoirie, attendu est-il dit, *qu'il s'agist de police, de tranquilité, et de seureté publique.*

Une sentence aussi foudroyante renversa la cervelle a la multitude ignare, on s'est attroupé, on a menacé & comme le dit le Memoire:—dans cette crise abandonné ici de tout le monde, j'Ecrivis a plusieurs Academies et a de bons physiciens, pour savoir à quoi m'en tenir,—je reçus des consolations de tout côté, et surtout de Dijon (quoi qu'inconnu) comme le prouve l'avis honorable de cette savante Académie.

Plusieurs bons Ecrivins, se sont offerts genereusement pour faire le Memoire et surtout Mr: Buissart, qui regardant cette affaire comme la sienne propre, s'en est acquité avec honneur.— Pour d'autant mieux appuier la chose, on a voulut une consultation de cèlèbres Avocats de paris, cette consultation mieux raisonnée au Commencement qu'a la fin puis-ce que les craintes du peuple n'existoient plus, s'est fait attendre pendant un an.— M.M. les Avocats d'Arras par leur consultation posterieure, ont rectifiés cette fin qui n'etoit pas de mon goût.

Ce Memoire enfin etant imprimé, fut signifié a la partie publique au commencement de novembre *1782*.— Un des plus Eloquent plaideur d'Arras s'est chargé de la plaider,[8] j'en attend le *resultat* avec une sorte d'impatience, et voila a quoi les choses en sont.

Compatissant comme vous este Monsieur pour les opprimés, vôtre indulgence excusera j'espere la longueur de cette Epitre qui detaille en bref les peinnes, et les tracasseries d'un pauvre martir de la chicane qui a l'honneur de se dire avec non moins de confiance, d'admiration de vos talents superieurs que de respect, Monsieur Votre tres humble et tres obeisant serviteur

DE VYSSERY DE BOIS-VALÉE
demeurant marché aux herbes.

Addressed: a Monsieur / Monsieur franklin, Ministre / plénipotentiaire Des états unis De / L'Amérique, Membre De l'Académie Des / Sciences De paris / A Paris

From Isaac-Jean-Georges-Jonas Grand

AL: American Philosophical Society

Rüe Poissonniere le 11. Xbre. 1782.

Le Cher. Grand prie Son Excellençe Monsieur Le Docteur Francklin & Monsieur Son Fils de luy faire l'honneur de Diner chez luy Lundy prochain 16 de ce mois, avec M. Le Duc De La Vauguyon.[9]

R.S.V.P.

---

8. Maximilien Robespierre, Buissart's junior partner, would plead the case the following spring: Riskin, *Science in the Age of Sensibility,* pp. 140–2, 176–84.

9. The duc de La Vauguyon had returned to Versailles with his wife on account of her ill health: La Vauguyon to Vergennes, Nov. 8, 1782; Laurent Bérenger to Vergennes, Nov. 29, 1782 (AAE).

The American Peace Commissioners to Francis Dana

ALS, AL (draft), and copy:[1] Massachusetts Historical Society; two copies: Library of Congress

Sir   Paris Decr. 12 1782

We have the Honour to congratulate you, on the Signature of the preliminary Treaty of Peace, between his Britannic Majesty and the United States of America, to be inserted in the definitive Treaty, when France and Britain[2] Shall have agreed upon their Terms. The Articles, of which We do ourselves the honour to inclose you a Copy, were compleated, on the thirtieth of last Month.

To Us, at this Distance, the present opportunity, appears to be the most favourable for you to communicate your mission to the Ministers of the Empress of Russia, and to the Ministers of the other neutral Powers residing at her Court, and if you have no Objections, We presume you will wish to be furnished with the inclosed Paper,[3] to communicate at the Same Time.

We heartily wish you Success, and if you Should inform Us of a fair prospect of it, We Shall propose an Article in the definitive Treaty, to Secure the Freedom of Navigation according to the Principles of the late marine Treaty between the neutral Powers.[4]

With great Respect, We have the Honour to be, Sir, your most obedient and most humble Servants   JOHN ADAMS
                                                       B FRANKLIN
                                                       JOHN JAY
                                                       HENRY LAURENS

1. Both the ALS and the AL (draft) are in JA's hand. The commissioners agreed to send this letter on Dec. 3; see the exchange between JA and BF on that date.

2. JA's draft originally read, "when the other belligerent powers". This change implies that the American agreement would become effective even if Spain and / or the Netherlands failed to make peace with Britain.

3. JA's draft here includes the phrase "for that Purpose". We assume that the enclosed paper was related to Dana's appointment as minister to the Russian court.

4. The League of Armed Neutrality, to which by now Denmark, Sweden, the Netherlands, Prussia, Austria, and Portugal had acceded: Sir Francis Piggott and G. W. T. Omond, eds., *Documentary History of the Armed Neutralities, 1780 and 1800* ... (London, 1919), pp. 198–278.

The Honourable Francis Dana Esq.

Endorsed: Letter from J. Adams & other Commissioners of the U. States Dated Paris Decr: 12th. 1782 Recd. Jany: 1st. 1783— O. Stile[5]

From John Adams   L:[6] American Philosophical Society

Hotel du Roy, au Carrouzel, Decemr: 12th. 1782 Mr: Adams presents his Compliments to his Excellency Dr: Franklin, & requests the honor of his Company to dinner on Monday the 16th. inst. at 3. oClock.[7]

Addressed: Son Excellence / Monsieur Franklin. / Passy

From Alleyne Fitzherbert   AL: American Philosophical Society

Hotel du Parc Royal Decr. 12th Mr Fitz-Herbert presents his Compliments to Dr Franklin and Mr Franklin and desires the honour of their Company to dinner on Tuesday next, the 17th, at 3 o'clock.[8]

Addressed: A Monsieur / Monsieur Franklin / à Passy.

Notation: Mr. Fitzherbert Decr. 12th

5. By the New Style calendar the date of receipt was Jan. 12.
6. In the hand of Charles Storer. JA issued a nearly identical invitation to WTF (APS).
7. Fitzherbert, Oswald, and Laurens attended JA's dinner, among unspecified others: Butterfield, *John Adams Diary*, III, 96. BF and WTF received an invitation from Georges Grand for the same day (above, Dec. 11).
8. On Dec. 19 Fitzherbert wrote to Strachey that Townshend had advised him to "cultivate" the American commissioners, and that this "great dinner" for 20 guests was part of his attempt. It "went off very cheerfully," he wrote, "and Dr. Franklin in particular was (in his usual oracular & sententious strain) uncommonly full of conversation." New York Public Library. JA noted in his diary that the guests included all four commissioners, along with Baron Mountnorris, a member of the Irish House of Lords, and "several English gentlemen": Butterfield, *John Adams Diary*, III, 96.

From William Hodgson   ALS: American Philosophical Society

Dear Sir   London 12 Decemr. 1782

I have the pleasure to acquaint you that we arrived safe here after a quick passage, but not Time enough I fear to undo what had been done wrong in consequence of premature advice, however still much depends upon future contingent Events, if the final arrangement takes place, all may yet be well, shou'd it happen otherwise, without previous information the conclusion may be severely calamitous, yr Sentiments upon the probability or otherwise of the final Issue it will lay me under very great obligations.[9]

A few days ago I wrote to the Secretarys of State Office respecting the exchange that had been so long promised & so long delayed, I yesterday recd a Note & was desired to attend, which I did this day & was very much surprised & mortifyed to find that advices had been recd from N york that Congress absolutely refused to comply with the Agreement made here relative to the exchange of Prisoners,[1] but as I was at same Time informed that all the papers relative thereto had been transmitted to Paris to be laid before you I need not enter further into it— I hope for the honor of Congress that the Affair is not as they represent, I shall be glad however to receive your Explanation for my Goverment. At first they appeared very angry & said they woud not send away the Prisoners now here however they recalled their words & promised a Ship shoud be sent to LOrient very soon & desired I woud request you to have all the English Prisoners assembled at LOrient from the different places of their Confinement, in order that they may all come home to gether— Under the Cir-

9. All we know about Hodgson's visit is that on Nov. 29 he received from Grand 360 *l.t.* "on Account of American Prisoners": Account XXVII (XXXII, 4).

1. On Oct. 6 Carleton reported that a meeting to arrange a general prisoner cartel had failed: K. G. Davies, ed., *Documents of the American Revolution, 1770–1783 (Colonial Office Series)* (21 vols., Shannon and Dublin, Ire., 1972–81), XIX, 333–6. Ten days later Congress resolved that it would not consent to any partial exchange of prisoners, but would wait until "a general cartel on liberal and national principles be agreed to and established": *JCC*, XXIII, 661. See also Livingston to BF, Nov. 9.

cumstances of things at present they again have requested me to write you to release from their Paroles Lt Col Tarleton & Col Simcoe[2] & they seem to ground their claim the more to this Indulgence on Acc't of the Demurr that exists in America relative to the Exchange of the Prisoners who went from hence. Mr Wren has sent me a Bill for 36 Dollars or 180 Livres which a Prisoner has given him & he has advanced some money upon please to Credit me in Acct for the same if the Bill be good advising me for how much Sterling I am to Debit you in Acc't,[3] I am with great & sincere Respect Dr sr yr most oblged Hble servt

WILLIAM HODGSON

His Excellency B Franklin Esqr

From Kéralio   AL: American Philosophical Society

Forbach, le 12e. Xbre. 1782.

La Celeste amie de Monsieur Franklin[4] n'a pas le temps de lui écrire; mais elle lui fait les plus tendres amitiés et l'embrasse de tout son cœur; elle recommande à ses bontés ordinaires le paquet ci-joint pour son fils ainé.[5]

Le courier de Demain est attendu avec bien de l'impatience; nous esperons qu'il nous apportera la paix. Et qui aura joué Le premier role? L'illustre Mr. Franklin que le secretaire Keralio assure de son tendre respect./.

Mille amitiés à Mr. son fils.

Notation: Chevr. de Keraglio Forbach 12 Decr. 1782

2. John Graves Simcoe, colonel of the Queen's Rangers (*DNB*).

3. Hodgson was indeed credited with 180 *l.t.*, according to an undated letter from Henry Grand to WTF (APS).

4. The duchesse douairière de Deux-Ponts.

5. Comte Christian de Forbach de Deux-Ponts, whose regiment, Royal Deux-Ponts, was serving with Rochambeau. He accompanied the regiment when it sailed to the Caribbean: Rice and Brown, eds., *Rochambeau's Army*, I, 300.

From the Comte de Lacepède

ALS: American Philosophical Society

Monsieur   à agen en guienne le 12 déc 1782

Pendant que vous achevez de fonder un nouvel empire, permettez à un de vos plus profonds admirateurs, de vous parler de tous les sentimens que vous lui avez inspirés. On a du, Monsieur, faire hommage de ma part à vôtre excellence, du premier volume de la physique générale et particulière, que je viens de publier:[6] puissiez vous avoir agréé cet hommage, et puisse-t-il vous avoir engagé à m'honorer toujours de vos bontés! Il me tarde bien que mon retour à paris me mette à portée de vous rendre tous mes devoirs; et que je puisse aller dire au grand homme que je vénère, que ce n'est pas seulement à la fin ou au commencement des années que je fais des voeux ardens pour la gloire des sciences et le bonheur de l'amérique septentrionale, en en faisant pour vous. Ne me répondez point; vous avez mieux à faire: mais, si vous voulez me flatter infiniment, ayez la complaisance de dire à m. le roi, ou à ceux de mes autres amis qui ont le bonheur de vous voir, que vous daignez avoir quelque bonté pour moi. Je suis avec toute vénération et tout respect Monsieur de vôtre excellence le très humble et très obéissant serviteur   LE CTE. DE LA CEPÈDE

From Joseph Priestley: Extract

Translation of extract:[7] American Philosophical Society

Extrait d'une Lettre de Mr. Priestley,
datée de le 12. Xbre. 1782.

Je n'ai eu que peu de *Soleil;* mais j'en ai profité pour faire plusieurs Observations nouvelles: Je ne vous rendrai Compte main-

---

6. Promised in his letter of May 23: XXXVII, 403–4. The *Jour. de Paris* announced the work in its Nov. 9 issue. This is his last extant letter to BF.

7. In the hand of L'Air de Lamotte (with one phrase by WTF), and made perhaps for submission to a scientific society. The paragraphs translated here are nearly identical to those in Priestley's letters to Jean-André Deluc (XX, 78n) and Arthur Young, dated Dec. 11 and 12, respectively: Robert E. Schofield, *A Scientific Biography of Joseph Priestley (1733–1804)* (Cam-

tenant que de la derniere qui est assèz remarquable, et qui pourra vous donner quelque plaisir ainsi qu'à vos Amis.

Je convertis en peu de temps l'*Eau pure* en *Air permanent,* Poids pour Poids, en la combinant d'abord avec la Chaux vive et en l'exposant ensuite à une forte chaleur. Aucune Portion ne s'en dégage sous la Forme de *Vapeur,* Et un Ballon de Verre que je place entre la Retorte et le Recipient pour l'air, demeure entierement *Sec* et *froid* jusqu'à la fin de l'Operation.

L'air que je me procure par ce moyen contient une Portion d'air fixe, mais dans un Proportion telle qu'une Chandelle peut bruler dedans; Et qu'il seroit, à mon Avis, le meilleur pour les Plantes, qui le purifieroient et le rendroient propre à la Resperiation. Comme les Volcans fourniroient cette Espece d'Air en grande Abondance, dès matieres calcaires que la Terre renferme; Il est peut-être probable que cette Espece d'air formoit la premiere Atmosphére de la Terre qui, selon Moïse, eut des Plantes avant qu'il y eût des animaux Terrestres.

Franklin: Proposed Article for the Definitive Treaty[8]

Copy:[9] Library of Congress

[on or before December 13, 1782]
Article proposed for Consideration.

If War should hereafter arise between Great Britain and the United States, which God forbid, the Merchants of either Coun-

---

bridge, Mass., and London), pp. 215–18. Priestley later doubted his conclusions; see Benjamin Vaughan to BF, Dec. 31, below.

8. In this proposed article, BF seeks to codify the ideas he had expressed in a July 10 letter to Benjamin Vaughan and in two related essays: XXXVII, 610, 617–20. He showed the article to JA on Dec. 13, when JA came to Passy to review with him the draft of the commissioners' joint letter to Livingston (signed on Dec. 14, below). JA's private comment was, "This is a good Lesson to Mankind at least": Butterfield, *John Adams Diary,* III, 96. BF enclosed a copy of this article in his letter to Oswald of Jan. 14 (below). It was incorporated *verbatim* into the drafts of the definitive treaty that the American commissioners presented to David Hartley in the summer of 1783. Though those drafts were not adopted, a version of this article did get incorporated into the 1785 Treaty of Amity and Commerce with Prussia, signed by BF just before he left France: Giunta, *Emerging Nation,* I, 872, 910; II, 711, 810.

9. Made under Oswald's direction from the texts enclosed in BF's letter to

try then residing in the other, shall be allowed to remain 9 Months[1] to collect their Debts and settle their Affairs, and may depart freely carrying off all their Effects without Molestation or Hinderance. And all Fishermen, all Cultivators of the Earth, and all Artizans, or Manufacturers unarmed & inhabiting unfortified Towns, Villages or Places, who labour for the common Subsistence and Benefit of Mankind, & peaceably follow their respective Employments, shall be allowed to continue the same, and shall not be molested by the Armed Force of the Enemy in whose Power by the Events of [the][2] War they may happen to fall; but if any thing is necessary to be taken from them for the use of such Armed Force, the same shall be paid for at a reasonable Price. And all Merchants or Traders with their unarmed Vessels, employed in Commerce, exchanging the Products of different Places & thereby rendering the Necessaries, Conveniences & Comforts of human Life more easy to obtain and more general shall be allowed to pass freely unmolested. And neither of the Powers, Parties to this Treaty, shall grant or issue any Commission to any private armed Vessels empowering them to take or destroy such trading Ships, or interrupt such Commerce.

---

him of Jan. 14, 1783. It closely resembles the version WTF printed in *Memoirs*, II, 422.

1. This first sentence was an adaptation of Article 22 of the 1778 Franco-American Treaty of Amity and Commerce (XXV, 615), and the analogous Article 18 of the Dutch-American Treaty of Amity and Commerce (Giunta, *Emerging Nation*, II, 978–9), which JA had signed in October. The major difference between them was in the length of time the merchants would be allowed; the French treaty provided for a six-month term, but the Dutch treaty provided for nine months. BF followed what JA had just negotiated.

2. This word is missing in the MS but present in subsequent versions of the article and in WTF, *Memoirs*.

From the Comte Creutz[3]   AL: American Philosophical Society

A Paris le 14. [*i.e.*, 13][4] Dec. 1782.
Monsieur L'Ambassadeur de Suède à L'honneur de faire bien des Complimens à Monsieur francklin et de le prevenir qu'il aura L'honneur demain Samedy avant midy de l'aller voir pour lui communiquer des affaires de consequences. Il le prie de vouloir bien lui faire L'honneur de luy faire sçavoir s'il pourra avoir celui de le trouver.

Notation: L'Ambassadeur de Suede A Paris 14 Decembre 1782

To [Creutz][5]   Draft:[6] American Philosophical Society

[December 13, 1782]
M. Franklin etant obligé d'etre demain Matin à Paris pour Affaire ne pourra pas avoir l'honneur de recevoir chez lui M. l'Ambassadeur de Suede— Mais il aura celui de lui faire sa Cour sur les 11 heures—si toutefois cela est agreable à M. l'Ambassadeur.

Madame F. Pechigny[7] to Franklin or William Temple Franklin   AL: American Philosophical Society

a passy ce 13. xbre. 1782
Mde. Pechigny supplie monsieur franklin de vouloir bien lui permettre le 26. du present, de lui presenter lhommage de sa vive re-

3. Gustaf Philip, graf Creutz, the Swedish ambassador to the French court.
4. Since Creutz mentions the next day as being a Saturday, this has to have been written on Friday, Dec. 13. On Dec. 14, moreover, BF described his meeting with Creutz, saying that he had received this note the day before: BF to Livingston, Dec. 5[–14].
5. In answer to the preceding document: BF described this meeting in the Dec. 14 portion of his letter to Livingston begun on Dec. 5.
6. In WTF's hand.
7. Mme Pechigny and her husband ran a local pension, where Robert Morris, Jr., and his brother Thomas were enrolled: XXXV, 51n; XXXVI, 80–1n.

connoissance en lui remettant les 300 l.t. que noblement il lui a preté et dagréer les regret de limpossibilité ou elle a èté de ne les lui avoir pas remis plûtot.[8]

Si monsieur franklin a un protegé qui enseigne langlois mde. pechigny le prie de lui procurer, étant dans lintention de n'en prendre dautre part que de la sienne pour le premier janvier prochain.[9]

Addressed: A Monsieur / Monsieur franklin / en son hotel / A Passy

Notation: Mde. Pechiny 13 Dec. 1782.

Notes for a Reply to ——— Stockar zur Sonnenbourg[1]

AL (draft): Historical Society of Pennsylvania

[before December 14, 1782][2]

Different Men who have been present and Witnesses of a Transaction, often give different and inconsistent Accounts of it thro'

8. Mme Pechigny received this loan on Feb. 27: Account XVII (XXVI, 3), entry of Feb. 28, 1782.

9. An undated letter from Mme Pechigny to WTF (University of Pa. Library) suggests that he recommended a teacher to her at a time when she had only one student. She says she can offer WTF's protégé room, board, and one *louis d'or* a month; once she has other students she will offer the teacher a regular salary and the freedom to give lessons in Passy. She signs herself Devillier Pechigny.

1. BF drafted these notes on a duplicate of Stockar's Dec. 6, 1781, letter, sent on Aug. 3, 1782: XXXVI, 204n; XXXVII, 701–2. They responded to the question Stockar posed in the earlier letter about the reliability of the abbé Raynal's *Révolution de l'Amérique* (London, 1781), a pamphlet issued in both French and English: XXXVI, 205.

2. The day BF acknowledged having received copies of Thomas Paine's *Letter Addressed to the Abbe Raynal on the Affairs of North-America, in which the Mistakes in the Abbe's Account of the Revolution of America are Corrected and Cleared Up* (Philadelphia, 1782): BF to Livingston, Dec. 5[–14], above. This is undoubtedly the pamphlet BF mentions below. Paine's criticism of Raynal centered on the causes of the revolution and the legitimacy of American independence. See Edoardo Tortarolo, "La réception de l'Histoire des deux Indes aux Etats-Unis," in *Lectures de Raynal: l'*Histoire des deux Indes

Defaults in their Observation or Memory. It is still more difficult for a Historian who writes of Affairs distant either in Time or Place, to come at the exact Truth. It is therefore no Wonder if some Errors have escaped the Abbé Raynall's Care in his History of the American Revolution which this Pamphlet points out.[3] It is nevertheless upon the whole an excellent Work. Tho' There are some other Errors, such as that European Animals degenerate in America.[4] That Men are shorter liv'd. That they have

---

en Europe et en Amérique au XVIIIe siècle, Actes du Colloque de Wolfenbüttel, ed. Hans-Jürgen Lüsebrink and Manfred Tietz, Studies on Voltaire 286 (Oxford, 1991), pp. 319–20.

3. This sentence, alluding to Paine's pamphlet, and the statements that follow lead us to wonder if BF was not speaking generally about views Raynal had expressed in earlier editions of Histoire philosophique et politique . . . des Européens dans les deux Indes (known by the short title Histoire des deux Indes), the multi-volume work from which Révolution de l'Amérique had been extracted. Some of the errors BF lists are not in Révolution de l'Amérique. At least one of them, the theory of degeneracy discussed in the following note, had been present in earlier editions of Histoire des deux Indes but was dropped in the 1780 edition that BF owned: XXXV, 343. We claimed in XXXV, 343n, that BF owned a copy of Révolution de l'Amérique; this was based on a mistaken reading of an abbreviated title on one of BF's book lists, and our correction is in XXXVI, 339–40n. We are no longer certain that BF had a copy of that pamphlet in his possession.

4. In the first two editions of his work (1770 and 1774), Raynal had adopted Cornelius de Pauw's thesis of degeneracy (XIX, 197n) and had argued that English settlers degenerated intellectually in North America. His acquaintance with BF and other Americans convinced him otherwise, and he retracted the claims in the 1780 edition, citing BF as a counterexample: Durand Echeverria, Mirage in the West: a History of the French Image of American Society to 1815 (Princeton, 1957), pp. 7–14, 29–30, 64–6.

Two stories survive about BF's demonstrating the absurdity of the theory. William Carmichael wrote to Thomas Jefferson about a dinner he attended in Paris at which a guest asked BF his opinion of de Pauw's thesis. Looking at the five Americans seated at the table, BF asked his interrogator to judge for himself whether "the human race had degenerated by being transplanted to another section of the Globe." Any one of those Americans, Carmichael reported, could have "tost out of the Windows any one or perhaps two of the rest of the Company, if this Effort depended merely on muscular force." Carmichael to Jefferson, Oct. 15, 1787, in Jefferson Papers, XII, 240–1. In 1818 Jefferson recounted that BF had told him of a dinner at which Raynal himself was arguing "his favorite theory of the degeneracy of animals and even of man, in America." Of the twelve guests, half were American, the other half

448

a bad Method of Inticing Inhabitants. That the People of Massachusetts Bay preserve their Fanaticism. That the Soil is bad and has grown worse. With others of less Importance.[5]

The American Peace Commissioners to Robert R. Livingston

LS:[6] National Archives; AL (draft):[7] Massachusetts Historical Society; copies: American Philosophical Society, Library of Congress, Massachusetts Historical Society; transcript: National Archives

Sir,   Paris, Decr. 14. 1782.

We have the honour to congratulate Congress on the Signature of the Preliminaries of a Peace between the Crown of Great Britain & the United States of America, to be inscribed, in a definitive Treaty so soon as the Terms between the Crowns of France & Great Britain shall be agreed on. A Copy of the Articles is here inclosed, and we cannot but flatter ourselves that they will appear to Congress as they do to all of us, to be consistent with the honour and Interest of the United States, and we are

---

French, and they were seated at opposite sides of the table. BF challenged the assembly to rise, so that the "remarkably diminutive" Frenchmen (the abbé himself was a "mere shrimp") would be gazing up at the strapping Americans: Paul Leicester Ford, ed., *Works of Thomas Jefferson* (12 vols., New York, 1904–05), XII, 110–11n. These two stories are often assumed to be interchangeable, though Jefferson's secondhand version, recalled decades after he heard it, suffers from at least one major inaccuracy: the three American guests he identifies by name—Carmichael, Josiah Harmar, and David Humphreys—were never in Paris at the same time, and the latter two never overlapped with Raynal, who fled the country in 1781.

5. Even in the recent edition of *Histoire des deux Indes,* Raynal retained his views about the poor American soil; they appear in *Révolution de l'Amérique,* pp. 175–7. BF and Silas Deane had told the abbé Raynal in late 1777 or early 1778 about many of the errors in the first edition of *Histoire des deux Indes,* one of them being his reporting the story of Polly Baker; see III, 121–2, and Ford, *Works,* XII, 110–11n.

6. In WTF's hand.

7. Dated Dec. 13 and primarily in JA's hand. He incorporated suggestions from the other commissioners: Butterfield, *John Adams Diary,* III, 95–6.

persuaded Congress would be more fully of that Opinion if they were apprized of all the Circumstances and Reasons which have influenced the Negotiation. Although it is impossible for us to go into that Detail, we think it necessary nevertheless to make a few Remarks on such of the Articles, as appear most to require Elucidation.

Remarks on Article 2d. relative to Boundaries.

The Court of Great Britain, insisted on retaining all the Territories comprehended within the Province of Quebec, by the Act of Parliament respecting it. They contended that Nova Scotia should extend to the River Kennebeck; and they claimed not only all the Lands in the Western Country, and on the Missisippi, which were not expressly included in our Charter and Governments, but also all such Lands within them as remained ungranted by the King of Great Britain: It would be endless to enumerate all the Discussions and Arguments, on the Subject. We know this Court and Spain to be against our Claims to the Western Country, and having no Reason to think that Lines more favourable could ever have been obtained, we finally agreed to those described in this Article: indeed they appear to leave us little to complain of, and not much to desire. Congress will observe that although our Northern Line, is in a certain Part below the Latitude of Forty five, yet in others it extends above it, divides the Lake Superior, and gives us Access to its Western & Southern Waters, from which a Line in that Latitude would have excluded us.

Remarks on Article 4th. respecting Creditors.

We had been informed that some of the States, had confiscated British Debts, but although each State has a Right to bind its own Citizens, yet in our Opinion, it appertains solely to Congress, in whom exclusively are vested the Rights of making War and Peace, to pass Acts against the Subjects of a Power with which the Confederacy may be at War. It therefore only remained for us to consider whether, this Article is founded in Justice & good Policy.

In our Opinion no Acts of Government could dissolve the Obligations of Good Faith, resulting from lawfull Contracts between Individuals of the two Countries, prior to the War. We know that some of the British Creditors were making common Cause with the Refugees, and other Adversaries of our Independence: besides, sacrificing private Justice to Reasons of State and political Convenience, is always an odious Measure, and the Purity of our Reputation in this Respect in all foreign Commercial Countries, is of infinitely more Importance to us, than all the Sums in question. It may also be remarked, that American and British Creditors, are placed on an equal footing.

Remarks on Articles 5 & 6: respecting Refugees.

These Articles were among the first discussed, and the last agreed to. And had not the Conclusion of this Business at the Time of its Date, been particularly important to the British Administration the Respect, which both in London and Versailles, is supposed to be due to the honour Dignity and Interests of Royalty, would probably have forever prevented our bringing this Article so near to the Views of Congress and the sovereign Rights of the States as it now stands. When it is considered that it was utterly impossible to render this Article perfectly consistent, both with American and British Laws of Honour, we presume that the middle Line adopted by this Article, is as little unfavourable to the former, as any that could in Reason be expected.[8]

As to the Separate Article,[9] We beg leave to observe, that it was our Policy to render the Navigation of the River Missisippi

8. On Dec. 7, Vaughan wrote to Shelburne about a discussion he had had that morning with BF concerning the peace terms. BF expressed regret that the British had not agreed to reciprocity of commerce (fearing so favorable an opportunity would not recur), and discussed the concessions the commissioners had made concerning the refugees. He told Vaughan (as had JA and Jay) that the commissioners had exceeded their instructions and expected to be reprimanded by Congress; had they granted what the British wished, Congress either would not have ratified the treaty or would not have had the power to enforce it. Vaughan claimed that BF had moderated his conduct "after the communications I made to him upon my return from London": Mass. Hist. Soc. *Proc*, 2nd ser., XVII (1903), 423–4.

9. This paragraph is missing from the draft. The following paragraph was drafted by Jay, while a variant of the paragraph following it was drafted by Laurens; see Morris, *Jay: Peace*, pp. 440–3.

so important to Britain, as that their Views might correspond with ours on that Subject. Their possessing the Country on the River, North of the Line from the Lake of the Woods, affords a Foundation for their claiming such Navigation: and as the Importance of West Florida to Britain was for the same Reason rather to be strengthen'd than otherwise, we thought it adviseable to allow them the Extent contained in the Separate Article, especially as before the War it had been annex'd by Britain to W. Florida, and would operate as an additional Inducement to their joining with us in agreeing, that the Navigation of the River should forever remain open to both. The Map used in the Course of our Negotiations was Mitchells.

As we had reason to imagine that the Articles respecting the Boundaries, the Refugees & Fisheries did not correspond with the Policy of this Court, we did not Communicate the Preliminaries to the Minister, until after they were signed; and not even then the Separate Article. We hope that these Considerations will excuse our having so far deviated from the Spirit of our Instructions. The Count de Vergennes on perusing the Articles appear'd surprized, but not displeased, at their being so favourable to us.

We beg leave to add our Advice that Copies be sent us of the Accounts directed to be taken by the different States, of the unnecessary Devastations and Sufferings sustained by them from the Enemy in the Course of the War:[1]—should they arrive before the Signature of the definitive Treaty they might possibly answer very good purposes.—

With great Respect, We have the honour to be, Sir, Your most obedient, & most humble Servants.   JOHN ADAMS.
B FRANKLIN
JOHN JAY
HENRY LAURENS.

Enter'd on the Minutes. W. T. Franklin secy:

The honble. Robert R. Livingston Esqr. Secretary for Foreign Affairs.

1. Livingston tried without success to obtain such an accounting for BF: XXXVI, 128–9, 645; XXXVII, 718.

To Robert Morris

Copies:[2] Connecticut State Library, New Jersey State Library, New Hampshire Division of Records Management and Archives, Delaware Public Archives Commission, National Archives

Sir,   Passy, Decr. 14th. 1782.

I received duly your several Letters of Septr. 25th. 27th. 28th. and 30th. October 1st. 5th. 7th. all by Capt. Barney, and October 27th. since. I immediately made the Application so strongly pressed by the Congress for a Loan of four Millions of Dollars.[3] I annex'd to my memoir the Resolves of Congress, with Copies and Extracts of your several Letters and those of Mr. Livingston upon the Subject, all of which appear'd to me extreamly well written for enforcing the Request. I was at first told that it would be a difficult thing to furnish such a Sum at present, but it should be considered. It was much wondered that no Letters were brought by the Washington for M. le Comte de Vergennes, as several were come to the Secretary of War, M. de Segur, and to the Marquis de Castries Secretary of the Marine; and the next time I waited on the Minister, I was told that nothing could be done till the Dispatches from M. de la Luzerne were received. I enquired of Capt. Barney, who told me he believ'd M. de Forest[4] had them, who left him to go for Paris by way of Nantes. M. de Forest was a week or ten Days before he arriv'd; at Paris; and he had not the Dispatches. After a Fortnight had thus pass'd, I sent Capt. Barney down to search for them in his Ship; he there found them, and in about eight Days more they arriv'd and were delivered.— I have since continually press'd for a favorable Answer; The Marquis de la Fayette has likewise been importunate; but we could only learn that there was yet no Decision. The Negociations for Peace were going on, and I ascribed the Delay partly to the uncertainty of the Event, which might make a less Sum Sufficient if it succeeded, or a greater necessary if the War was still to be continued. I believe too, that the new Loan medi-

---

2. Morris sent either copies or extracts of both the present letter and BF's Dec. 23 letter (below) to all the state governors on March 25, 1783: *Morris Papers*, VII, 205n, 232n, 593, 596n, 632n.

3. See BF to Vergennes, Nov. 8.

4. Antoine-René-Charles-Mathurin de La Forest.

tated for this Government, but not ascertain'd, might occasion some Suspension. But whatever are the Causes, the Fact is, that, tho' I understand we are to be aided, I am still ignorant what the Quantum will be, or when it can be obtained. I have detain'd Capt. Barney, hoping he might carry a part of it, but seeing that so very uncertain, the Commissioners for the Treaty here, urge me to send him away with the Preliminary Articles, and take some other opportunity of sending Money when we get it. Perhaps we can make use of the Alliance, who is now out upon a Cruize.

Of the Amount of Mr. Adams's Loan in Holland, I have no certain account. He thinks it may be between 15 and 1,700,000 florins.[5] Mr. Grand has obtain'd a Part of it to pay the Interest of the Dutch Loan,[6] which is done, But he will acquaint you better with the state of his Funds than I can do. He tells me he will restate his Accounts as you desire.

The Shipping of the Stores from Brest is wholly in the Hands of Mr. Barclay.[7] He will likewise take Care of those which are unloaded out of the three Transports at Rochefort, that were to have gone with Convoy in May last, and have ever since been detained there unaccountably, which I did not know till lately.[8] The four Jamaica Ships brought in by the Alliance will furnish him with Money for paying Charges.—[9]

The Accounts of Goods bought to replace the Fayette's Cargo, having been sent you by several Opportunities, I hope you have them before this time.[1]

5. By this time 1,625,000 f. (more than $650,000) had been subscribed: Ferguson, *Power of the Purse*, p. 128.

6. *I.e.*, the funds obtained in the Netherlands by the French government and then provided to the United States. The first interest payment on the loan had been due Nov. 5: XXXVII, 638. See JA's Nov. 1 letter for his concerns about paying the interest.

7. In a now-missing letter of Oct. 19, BF had placed management of the supplies at Brest entirely in Barclay's hands: Barclay to John Hanson, Oct. 23, 1782 (National Archives).

8. For these three ships see Palteau de Veimerange's Sept. 6 letter.

9. BF had condemned the prizes on Nov. 24; see our annotation of JW to BF, Oct. 18.

1. BF sent the now-missing accounts on Aug. 12: XXXVII, 736–7.

I am extreamly glad to be freed from your Money Accounts, and the Payment of Bills. And I hope this will be the last Application I shall be charg'd with to borrow. In a former Letter I requested you to be my Atterney, to receive and remit my Salary, which I now repeat.[2] The Friends of the Duc de Lauzun, who is an Officer in the French Army, having Occasion to send him some Money, requested me to furnish Bills. To oblige them I gave a Draft on you for Six thousand Livres,[3] which I request you would honor, and deduct the same out of my Salary. Me thinks Mr. Grand should have some general Order to defray the contigent Expences of your Ministers. I am concern'd that the Resolution of appointing a Person to settle all our Accounts in Europe has not yet been carried into Execution.[4] They certainly cannot so well be settled in America; and I shall think it hard, after I am out of Place, to be detain'd here on that Account for Years like poor unhappy Deane, who by the way is I think in that Respect hardly dealt with. Settlement of Accounts and Payment of just Balances, is due even between Enemies.

I know not where the Virginia Stores lie. I will enquire, and acquaint Mr. Barclay with your Resolution concerning them, which I think very prudent.[5]

Penet, who was employed by that State as an Agent to borrow Money here, is broke and absconded. His Creditors are all worrying me with their Complaints, who have nothing to do with his Affairs. I have long since mentioned the Inconvenience of the Attempts of seperate States to borrow Money in Europe.[6] They have hurt our Credit, and produc'd nothing. We have put Faith in every Adventurer who pretended to have Influence here, and

---

2. XXXVII, 738.

3. Armand-Louis de Gontaut, duc de Lauzun (XXXVI, 175–6n), commanded Lauzun's Legion, as well as other units which Rochambeau left behind in America: Rice and Brown, eds., *Rochambeau's Army*, I, 76n, 168n. A rough version of the draft mentioned here, dated Dec. 4, is at the APS. BF later modified it for use as the model for a bill drawn on Gabriel Johonnot (for which see BF to Johonnot, Dec. 20).

4. Four weeks earlier Congress had chosen Thomas Barclay to settle the accounts; see our annotation of Livingston to BF, Nov. 21.

5. See Morris' letters of Oct. 27 and Jan. 19.

6. See, for example, XXIX, 557–8.

who when he arriv'd had none but what our appointment gave
him.[7]

I congratulate on the Tokens of approaching Peace. I wish
nothing may happen to prevent it.

With sincere and great Esteem, I am, Sir, your most obedient
& most humble Servant   (Sign'd) B: FRANKLIN

Honble. Robt: Morris, Esqr.

No. 5

Notation: 14th Decemr. 1782 Dr B Franklin To Office of Finance
Copy recd 7th April seq.

From ———— Le Baron[8]   ALS: American Philosophical Society

Monsieur   A Dieppe ce 14. Xbre. 1782.
Je ne puis m'empêcher de vous exprimer le plaisir que j'ay
ressenti lorsque j'ai appris que l'Angleterre venoit de reconoitre
l'Indépendance des 13. Provinces unies de l'Amérique; je partage
bien sincérement celui que doit vous causer un événement aussi
glorieux, et qui termine touttes vos peines et vos inquiétudes. Je

7. One of the French merchants Penet had ruined was the subject of Vergennes to BF, Nov. 20, and other letters described in annotation there. On
Nov. 22, Cohin & Cie., merchants of the cloth manufacturing town of Bel-
lême (near Alençon), informed BF that they had been taken in by Penet and
had yet to be paid for the nine bales of *toile* they had supplied. They assumed,
from Penet's title, that his word would be guaranteed by the state of Virginia.
Another of Penet's creditors sent BF an undated and unsigned letter announcing his intention of going to Virginia to seek redress and asking BF's
advice. Both these letters are at the APS. On Oct. 11, M. Coulougnac, a
Nantes merchant, wrote from his hotel in Paris reminding BF of his promise
(made both times Coulougnac obtained an audience) to write on his behalf
to the governor of Virginia. Since he was about to leave Paris, he begged BF
not to delay (University of Pa. Library). Coulougnac & Cie. (XXXI, 289n;
XXXII, 31–2) wrote on Feb. 3, 1783, thanking BF for his letter of recommendation to the governor of Virginia, asking him to intervene with Barclay, and
enclosing a memoir discussing their losses of 85,788 *l.t.* 14 *s.* 9 *d.* APS. See
also the annotation of Amelia Barry to BF, Sept. 20, where a note left by
Coulougnac at Passy is quoted.
8. A Dieppe merchant: XXVIII, 130n.

prie le seigneur qu'il daigne conserver de longs jours au respectable Ministre qui vient d'avoir un succés aussi éclatant, afin qu'il
joüisse longtemps du fruit de ses travaux.

Si vous pouviez disposer d'un instant, faittes moy la grace de
me répondre en deux mots, si le Pavillon Impérial[9] peut se
présenter sans crainte devant vos ports comme Boston, Philadelphie, avec des chargements pour compte d'Ostendois, comme
sel et eaux de vies de france, si on peut y faire la vente et la traitte
avec des Marchandises du pays, cela est du plus grand intérêt
pour la maison de mon fils qui est à Ostende, et dont l'établissement a eu tout le succès que je pouvois desirer pour le peu de
temps qu'il est fait.[1] J'attends de vous cette complaisance, comme
celle de me croire avec la plus respectueuse considération Monsieur Votre très humble et très Obéissant serviteur[2]

LeBaron

Endorsed: Baron 14 Dec. 1782.

From Pierres   ALS: University of Pennsylvania Library

Monsieur,   Paris 14 Xbre. 1782.

J'ai l'honneur de vous adresser le sr. saudot auquel vous pouvez remettre les deux alphabets que vous voulez bien me prêter.
Je me ferai un grand plaisir de vous offrir ce que j'ai de mieux en
vignettes mais Je desirerois savoir de quel genre & de quelle
grandeur.[3]

9. The colors of the Holy Roman Empire, of which the Austrian Netherlands was a part.

1. Insufficient work and the continuing war had caused Le Baron to open
a branch at Ostend that spring under his son's name: Le Baron to WTF, June
8, 1782. APS.

2. WTF replied on Dec. 17 that the ships were free to enter any American
port and engage in commerce without interference from the Americans. Because the war was still not over, however, British ships along the coast might
not accord them the same respect. APS.

3. Pierres may have been borrowing type from BF in order to print for him
Barbeu-Dubourg's *Petit Code de la raison humaine.* For that work see our annotation of BF to Mary Hewson, Jan. 8.

Si vous pouvez, monsieur, être utile à l'honnête infortuné que je vous adresse vous ferez une bien bonne action. Il est chargé de famille & ses enfans sont tous nuds. Je fais de mon côté Ce que je puis mais je ne puis pas faire tout ce que je voudrois.

Agréez, monsieur, les sentimens de la sincere vénération de l'Inviolable attachement & du respect avec lequel je suis, Monsieur, Votre très humble & très obeissant servîteur   PIERRES

M. Franklin.

Notation: Pierre, 14 Decr. 1782

From the Baron de Thun[4] ALS: University of Pennsylvania Library

Monsieur   a Paris ce 14 Dec: 1782

En conséquence de votre conseil, le Sr. Schneider habitant de Germantaun, a payé au Sr. Richard Bache votre gendre 200 *l.t.* en especes, faisants la valeur de 1200 florins, et celui-ci en a délivré la quittance, ci-jointe en copie.[5]

Le Sr. Auer Ministre de l'église d'Ebingen dans le Wirtemberg, a eu l'honneur Monsieur de vous en donner avis, dès le mois d'Octobre dernier,[6] en vous priant de vouloir bien, par la voie qu'il vous plairoit, faire passer cette somme pour le compte de la veuve Hoecklin, demeurant au dit Ebingen.

N'ayant point eu de reponse de votre part, il m'a prié Monsieur de vous demander les éclaircissemens et conseils ulterieurs que le cas éxige, et de vous offrir mon canal pour la transmise de cette somme.

Connoissant vos sentimens charitables et bienfaisants, j'ose attendre cette complaisance de votre part, et j'ai l'honneur d'être

---

4. Who had been involved in this attempt to secure money for the widow Höklin since 1781: XXXV, 274–5n.

5. The baron had received a German translation of RB's April 2 receipt; he copied this for BF. For that receipt see XXXVII, 90.

6. Oct. 21, above.

avec les sentimens les plus sincers et les plus distingués Monsieur
votre très humble et trés obeissant serviteur[7]

LE BARON DE THUN
Ministre Plénipre. de Wirtemberg

Notation: Le Baron de Thun Paris 4 Decr. 1782.

To Vergennes   ALS: Archives du Ministère des affaires étrangères

Sir   Passy, Dec. 15. 1782

I have the honour to acquaint your Excellency, that our
Courier is to set out to-morrow at Ten aClock, with the Dispatches we send to Congress by the Washington, Capt. Barney,
for which Ship we have got a Passport from the King of England.[8] If you would make any Use of this Conveyance, the
Courier shall wait upon you to-morrow at Versailles, and receive
your Orders.

I hoped I might have been able to send part of the Aids we
have asked, by this safe Vessel. I beg that your Excellency would
at least inform me what Expectations I may give in my Letters. I
fear the Congress will be reduc'd to Despair, when they find that
nothing is yet obtained.

With the greatest and most sincere Respect, I am, Sir, Your
Excellency's most obedient and most humble Servant

B FRANKLIN

7. The baron presented a "reçu" to Ferdinand Grand on Dec. 19, and received 3,200 *l.t.:* Account XVII (XXVI, 3).

8. The passport was dated Dec. 10. Issued on the part of George III, "King
of Great Britain, France and Ireland," it permitted the *General Washington*
(called, as in the present letter, simply the *Washington*), "belonging to the
United States of North America, to sail from either of the Ports of France to
any Port or Place in North America, without any Lett, Hindrance or Molestation whatsoever, but on the Contrary affording the said Vessel all such
Aid and Assistance as may be necessary." The passport is published in WTF,
Memoirs, II, 417, and in Hulbert Footner, *Sailor of Fortune: the Life and Adventures of Commodore Barney, U.S.N.* (New York and London, 1940), p. 137.
Copies are in the American commissioners' letterbooks at the Mass. Hist.
Soc. and the Library of Congress, and also among Morris' papers at the Na-
tional Archives.

Excelly. M. le Comte de Vergennes

From Edward Bancroft

ALS: American Philosophical Society

Dear Sir   Chaillot 15 Decr. 1782

I went again yesterday to Mr. de Beaumarchais but found, what had not been told me before, that he is at Bourdeaux, & therefore it will be impossible for me to obtain the Certificate Mr. Deane desires until his return—[9] I must therefore write Mr. Deane to day & wish to inclose in my Letter a Line or two from you importing something, or so much as you may think proper, of the paper, I had the honor of Leaving with you on thursday Evening—[1] I would be obliged to you also to inform me when you think of sending away your Dispatches for America. I have the honor to be very truely Dear Sir Your respectful & affectionate Humble Servant,   EDWD. BANCROFT

Addressed: A Monsieur / Monsieur Franklin / Minister Plenipotentiaire / des Etats Unis &c / a Passy

Notation: Ed: Bancroft Chaillot 15th. Decr. 1782

9. Deane had written to Bancroft on Nov. 17, asking him to procure certificates from BF, Jay, and Beaumarchais that would absolve him of the charges made against him in the *London Evening Post* and *St. James Chronicle.* The accusation was that he had grossly overcharged Congress for the repair of old arms. Deane sought a general statement from BF and Jay saying that they knew these charges to be false. From Beaumarchais, he wanted a certificate of the price of the arms and the amount that was charged to Congress' account. (Jay Papers, Columbia University Library.) Deane and Bancroft had been business partners and, unknown to BF, fellow stockjobbers: XXIII, 25, 202n; XXV, 417n.

Not hearing from Bancroft, Deane wrote Jay on Dec. 1 (Columbia University Library). Jay did not respond: *Deane Papers,* V, 122–5, 131–2.

1. Doubtless the certificate that Bancroft had drafted for BF's signature; see below, Dec. 18.

From John Holker

ALS: American Philosophical Society

My Respectable friend   Rouen 15 of Decr 1782

It is hoigh time that I make you my Complements on your having obtaind Peas, & puting your Contery at Liberty; to which wee may Justley say, your Manly Conduct, & Supereor Judgment, has don the Business.

May you long Live my Good friend, to Injoy the Sweets of it, which is what I wish from my very Soule being most sincearly attached to you, & the Causes you have so Bravely susstaind.

My best Complements attend your Son, & Live in hopes that youl keep your Promis, & spend som days with us here before you Returne to the Land of Promis, it is what my wife desiers & Joyns with me in Beging youl not faile doeing us that Pleaseur.

I ever am with Respects & Sincerety My Dear friend your Most Obedt & affectionet Servant   J HOLKER

Notation: Holker, Rouen 15 Decr. 1782.

From Vergennes[2]

AL (draft): Archives du Ministère des affaires étrangères

Versailles le 15 Xbre 1782

Je puis etre surpris, Monsieur, après l'Explication que j'ai eue avec vous et la promesse que vous m'aviez faite que vous ne presseriez pas l'obtention d'un Passeport Anglois pour l'expedition du Paquet bot le Wasington,[3] que vous me fassiez part que vous avez reçu ce meme passeport et que demain a dix heures du

---

2. In answer to BF's of the same date, above.

3. A "few days" after the signing of the provisional articles BF and Laurens visited Vergennes, who told them that their hastening to sign the articles had not been very obliging to Louis XVI. BF informed Vergennes that the peace commissioners wished to send the articles to Congress and had agreed to exchange passports with the British. Vergennes warned that this would be dangerous because the articles were provisional and the remaining negotiations uncertain. According to Vergennes, BF and Laurens promised to do what he desired: Vergennes to La Luzerne, Dec. 19, in Giunta, *Emerging Nation,* I, 728.

matin votre courier partira pour porter vos Depeches. Je suis assés embarrassé, M, a expliquer votre conduite et celle de vos collegues a notre egard. Vous avez arreté vos articles préliminaires
sans nous en faire part quoique les instructions du Congrés vous
prescrivissent de ne rien faire sans la participation du Roi.[4] Vous
allez faire luire un Espoir certain de paix en Amerique sans meme
vous informer de l'Etat de notre negociation.[5] Vous etes sage et
avisé, M, vous connoïssez les bienseances vous avez rempli toute
votre vie vos devoirs. Croyez vous satisfaire a ceux qui vous lient
au Roi? Je ne veux pas porter plus loin ces reflexions, je les abandonne a votre honneteté.[6] Quand vous aurez bien voulu satisfaire a mes doutes je prierai le Roi de me mettre en Etat de repondre a vos demandes.

J'ai l'honneur d'etre avec une veritable Consideration, M, Ve.
&a.

4. Congress gave the peace commissioners these instructions on June 15,
1781: XXXV, 166–7.

5. Vergennes had made the same point in his conversation with BF and
Laurens. In fact, when Joshua Barney arrived in Philadelphia on March 12
with news of the preliminary treaty, Americans in general considered it to
mean the end of hostilities. Had France been forced by its alliance with Spain
to continue the war, the United States would have been nearly worthless as
an ally, and the huge British garrison at New York could have been used to
attack the French and Spaniards in the Caribbean: William C. Stinchcombe,
The American Revolution and the French Alliance (Syracuse, 1969), pp. 195–
9. Fitzherbert told Grantham on Nov. 30 that the commissioners had pro-
claimed that they would not continue fighting to satisfy the demands of Spain
or Holland: Andrew Stockley, *Britain and France at the Birth of America: the
European Powers and the Peace Negotiations of 1782–1783* (Exeter, 2001),
p. 87.

6. In the letter to La Luzerne cited above, Vergennes asked him to inform
the most influential members of Congress of the irregular conduct of their
commissioners. Vergennes did not blame BF personally; he suspected BF's
colleagues of influencing him: Giunta, *Emerging Nation*, 1, 728–9. He had
reason to be upset. Should negotiations between Spain and Britain fail,
France, already in dire economic and military circumstances, was committed
to participating in an almost hopeless Franco-Spanish attack on Jamaica.
This danger was reduced, however, when on Dec. 16 Ambassador Aranda
on his own authority indicated Spain's willingness to accept the British offer
of Minorca and Florida in lieu of Gibraltar: Dull, *French Navy*, pp. 317–19,
330–5. This doubtless made it easier for Vergennes to accept BF's apology of
Dec. 17 (below).

From Thomas Barclay

LS: American Philosophical Society

Sir   L'Orient 16 decembr. 1782

Captain Casson of the Ship Washington arrived here last night from Philadelphia, which place he left the 20th November.[7] He brought the Inclosed Packet for you Just in the Condition which I send it. I do not hear that he brings any News of consequence, except a report of the Evacuation of Charlestown.

All the Public Goods that were at Brest are now on their way to Nantes, and L'Orient, but I shall wait a little longer to see what the Event of the present negotiations will prove, before they go forward, as the difference of a War, and Peace freight and risk, is a matter of great consequence. The Ships St. James, America and Washington are now in this Harbour, loading for Philadelphia, they are all Arm'd, fast Sailing Vessels, but the Freight demanded for Carrying the Public Goods, is in my opinion extravagantly high, and which I will not comply with— I shall however, I expect, get all those that go to Nantes, or come here ship'd in good time, and I intend setting out for Rochfort, as soon as Captain Barneys dispatches come from Paris, when probably I may be able to form a better Judgement of what will be proper to do, than I can at present.

I have the honour to remain respectfully Sir Your Excellencys Most Obedient Most Huml. Servt.   THOS BARCLAY

His Excellency Benjamin Franklin Esqr.

From Samuel Vaughan[8]

ALS: American Philosophical Society

My dear Sir,   London 16th. Decemr 1782

Altho no person occupies so much of my thoughts or after whom I make so frequent enquiries as your self, yet knowing the importance & weight of public affairs on Your hands, I purposly avoid troubling You with uninteresting correspondence, but I now take the liberty of introducing to Your acquaintance Lady

7. We have found no further record of either this ship or its captain.
8. Benjamin Vaughan's father: XXI, 441.

Juliana Penn, whose character in every point of view, is truly amiable & to whose case I doubt not you paying due attention.[9]

I congratulate you on the provisional steps taken towards a peace, which I hope will give us the happiness of seeing you once more in England and in America, for which place my Family embarkes, so soon as that valuable & desireable end is obtained. I am with perfect regard & esteem, Dear Sir, Yours most affectionately   SAML VAUGHAN

Benjamen Franklin Esqr.

To Vergennes[1]   ALS: Archives du Ministère des affaires étrangères

Sir   Passy, Decr. 17. 1782

I received the Letter your Excellency did me the Honour of writing to me the 15th. Instant. The Proposal of having a Passport from England was agreed to by me the more willingly, as I at that time had Hopes of obtaining some Money to send in the Washington, and the Passport would have made its Transportation safer, with that of our Dispatches, and of yours also if you had thought fit to make use of the Occasion. Your Excellency objected, as I understood it, that the English Ministers by their Letters sent in the same Ship might create inconvenient Expectations in America. It was therefore I propos'd not to press for the Passport till your Preliminaries were also agreed to. They have sent the Passport without being press'd to do it; and they have sent no Letters to go under it; and ours will prevent the Inconvenience apprehended. In a subsequent Conversation, your

9. See her letter above, Nov. 23. Lady Juliana left Dover for France on Dec. 31: *Morning Herald and Daily Advertiser,* Jan. 3, 1783. Neither BF nor the other American commissioners were impressed by her arguments about the Penn family claims against the government of Pennsylvania: BF to Jan Ingenhousz, April 29, 1785 (Smyth, *Writings,* IX, 26, 309–10); JA to Juliana Penn, Jan. 14, 1783 (Mass. Hist. Soc.); Morris, *Jay: Peace,* pp. 403, 424–5.

1. BF showed to his colleagues Vergennes' letter of Dec. 15 and a draft of the present letter at a meeting he called for eleven o'clock on the morning of Dec. 17, at Laurens' residence. JA, Laurens, and Jay unanimously advised him to send it: Butterfield, *John Adams Diary,* III, 96.

Excellency mention'd your Intention of sending some of the King's Cutters; from whence I imagin'd that Detaining the Washington was no longer necessary; And it was certainly very incumbent on us to give Congress as early an Account as possible of our Proceedings, who must think it extremely strange to hear of them by other means without a Line from us. I acquainted your Excellency however with our Intention of dispatching that Ship, supposing you might possibly have something to send by her.

Nothing has been agreed in the Preliminaries contrary to the Interests of France; and no Peace is to take Place between us and England till you have concluded yours. Your Observation is however apparently just, that in not consulting you before they were signed, we have been guilty of neglecting a Point of Bienséance. But as this was not from Want of Respect for the King whom we all love and honour, we hope it may be excused; and that the great Work which has hitherto been so happily conducted, is so nearly brought to Perfection, and is so glorious to his Reign, will not be ruined by a single Indiscretion of ours. And certainly the whole Edifice falls to the ground immediately, if you refuse on that Account to give us any farther Assistance. I have not yet dispatch'd the Ship, and shall beg leave to wait upon you on Friday[2] for your final Answer.

It is not possible for any one to be more sensible than I am, of what I, and every American, owe to the King, for the many & great Benefits & Favours he has bestow'd upon us. All my Letters to America are Proofs of this; all tending to make the same Impressions on the Minds of my Countrymen, that I felt in my own. And I believe that no Prince was ever more belov'd and respected by his own Subjects, than the King is by the People of the United States. The English, I just now learn, flatter themselves they have already divided us. I hope this little Misunderstanding will therefore be kept a perfect Secret, and that they will find themselves totally mistaken.[3]

2. Dec. 20.

3. In his negotiations with the British, BF himself had given them reason to believe that his allegiance to the alliance was not unconditional; see XXXVII, 320.

With great and sincere Respect, I am, Sir, Your Excellency's most obedient and most humble Servant   B FRANKLIN

le Comte de Vergennes.

Endorsed: M. de R[4]

From Chalut and Arnoux   AL:[5] American Philosophical Society

paris mardi 17 Xbre 1782

Nous assurons notre respectable ami de notre estime et de notre amitié et nous lui envoyons un exemplaire de l'ouvrage que M. l'abbé de Mably[6] vient de donner au public. L'auteur en fait hommage au patriarche de la raison et de la liberté.[7]

Il nous tarde d'aller Celebrer le retour de la paix et l'independence de l'amerique avec notre ami. Nous faisons des voeux pour cet heureux moment.

Les amitiés des abbés de chalut et arnoux au cher petit fils.

4. Rayneval.

5. In the hand of Arnoux.

6. BF had met Mably years earlier, through the abbé Chalut, and owned many of his works: XXVI, 504; XXVII, 388.

7. Mably was offering to BF his *De la manière d'écrire l'histoire* (Paris, 1783), which was approved for release (receiving its *privilège du roi*) on Dec. 7, 1782. A highly opinionated and controversial book, it covered all aspects of writing history, from the requisite scholarly preparation to points of style that would keep a work from being flat and lifeless. For Mably the primary purpose of history was to inspire a love of virtue. In his view the works of most Enlightenment historians lacked the clear sense of moral purpose he found in those of the ancient Greek and Roman historians. Some contemporary reviews of *De la manière* ridiculed Mably's summary judgment of Voltaire that for all his erudition "[il] ne voyait pas au bout de son nez" (*De la manière,* p. 40): Tourneux, *Correspondance littéraire,* XIII, 225–9 (December, 1782); *Jour. de Paris,* Feb. 17, 1783.

On Dec. 19, and again on Jan. 5, JA dined with Mably in the company of Chalut and others. Mably discussed with JA his plan to write on the American constitutions; this led to an exchange of letters and the publication of Mably's *Observations sur le gouvernement et les loix des Etats-Unis d'Amérique* (Paris, 1784): Charles Francis Adams, ed., *The Works of John Adams . . .* (10 vols., Boston, 1850–6), V, 491–2; Butterfield, *John Adams Diary,* III, 97, 101–2.

From Williams, Moore & Co.

LS:[8] University of Pennsylvania Library

Honnorable Monsieur   [before December 18, 1782][9]

Nous avons l'honneur de vous remettre cy inclus Les papiers de la mirauté pour la Condamnation de la chambre faite, par le Corsaire ameriquain Le Buccanéer, nous vous suplions aprés l'examen de nous honnorer du renvoy de la piece qui constate La validité de ladite prise.

Nous Sommes avec un profond Respect honnorable Monsieur Vos tres humbles & trés obts Serviteurs.

WILLIAMS MOORE & CO.

Notation: Wm. Moore

---

8. Signed by James Moore.

9. The cargo of the *Chambers,* a prize that was brought into Lorient by the *Buccaneer* in October and that BF is here being asked to condemn, was sold on Dec. 18, 1782: JW to John and Andrew Cabot, Oct. 25, 1782 (Yale University Library); Account between Williams, Moore & Co. and the owners and crew of the *Buccaneer,* attested by BF on Oct. 28, 1784 (University of Pa. Library).

Franklin: Certificate Concerning Silas Deane[1]

Printed in Silas Deane, *An Address to the United States of North-America* ... (New London, Connecticut, 1784), p. 21;[2] draft:[3] American Philosophical Society

[December 18, 1782]

Certain paragraphs having lately appeared in the English newspapers, importing, that Silas Deane, Esqr. formerly Agent and Commissioner Plenipotentiary, of the United States of America, had sometime after his first "arrival in France, purchased in that kingdom, for the use of his countrymen, 30,000 muskets, &c. that he gave three livres for each of them, being old condemned arms; that he had them cleaned and vamped up, which cost near three livres more,[4] & that for each of these, he charged and received a louis d'or." And that he also committed similar frauds, in the purchase of other articles, for the use of his country; and Mr. Deane having represented, that the said paragraphs

1. Deane sent copies of this certificate to British newspapers, paired with a copy of BF's letter to then-president of Congress Laurens, written when Deane was recalled: XXVI, 203–4. These documents, with an introductory statement by Deane, were published in three papers that we know of: the *Whitehall Evening Post* and the *General Evening Post*, issues of Jan. 9–11, 1783, and the *London Courant*, which reprinted them on Jan. 10, reportedly from an evening paper. A slightly variant version, identifying the *London Morning Post* as the source of the recent "libel" and including a final paragraph summarizing Deane's public service, was reprinted from an unnamed source in *The Remembrancer*, XVI (1783, part II), 6–7.

2. Deane wrote this *Address* in mid-1783 and sent it to America for publication; he then had it printed in London. We have chosen the text from this edition, reprinted from a London version, because it most closely resembles the draft that Bancroft prepared for BF. (The draft lacks the signature and dateline, and takes a great deal of punctuation for granted.) The *Address* is published in *Deane Papers*, V, 235–79; see also p. 221.

3. In the hand of Edward Bancroft; see his Dec. 15 letter to BF. BF endorsed it, "Draft of the Certificate I sign'd for Mr Deane". WTF forwarded the signed certificate to Bancroft shortly before Dec. 28, when Bancroft wrote to thank him for it. APS.

4. On arriving in France in 1776, Deane, in association with Beaumarchais, entered into contracts for arms and supplies. The following year Deane, BF, and Arthur Lee purchased a number of muskets: XXIII, 25, 351, 379–80, 450–1; *Deane Papers*, I, 247–9. In May, 1777, the commissioners signed a contract for repairing the muskets: XXIV, 100–1.

are likely to injure him in the opinions of many persons, unacquainted with his conduct, whilst in public service; I think it my duty, in compliance with his request, to certify, and declare, that the paragraphs in question, according to my best knowledge and belief, are entirely false, and that I have never known, or suspected any cause to charge the said Silas Deane with any want of probity, in any purchase, or bargain whatever made by him for the use or account of the United States.

Given at Passy, the 18th December, 1782
　　　　B. FRANKLIN,
　　　　Minister Plenipotentiary from the
　　　　United States of America, at the Court of France.

From Nicholas Geoffroy[5]　ADS: American Philosophical Society

[December 18, 1782]
Le né. [nommé] Bonnefoi[6] a remis à la secretairerie de M Le Comte De Vergennes la Lettre de Monsieur francklin[7] aujourd'hui 18 Xbre. 1782 à sept heures et demie du Soir. GEOFFROY Secretre de M. Le Cte. De Vergennes./.

Notation: Comte de Vergennes 18th. Decr. 1782 Versailles

From ——— Parent de Bellehache and Other Favor
Seekers　ALS: University of Pennsylvania Library

Requests for recommendations or positions in France or America continue to arrive on Franklin's desk during the five months covered by

5. A *sous-commis* under Vergennes and later Montmorin, Geoffroy was the only member of their staff to desert the royalty during the Revolution. After he joined the Jacobins, his career prospered. He rose to first secretary, then *chef du bureau*, and finally head of the *dépôt des archives:* Frédéric Masson, *Le Département des affaires étrangères pendant la Révolution, 1787–1804* (Paris, 1877), pp. 35, 140n, 166, 255–6.
6. Jean-Nicolas Bonnefoÿ, BF's gardener, occasionally ran errands: XXXIV, 5; XXXVII, 4.
7. Doubtless BF's letter of the previous day to Vergennes, above.

this volume.[8] Sometimes the supplicant frames his request as a response to an offer Franklin has made, as Parent de Bellehache suggests in his letter, printed below.

Another of these supplicants is Frère Frederic, a Capuchin friar and former naval chaplain with Ternay's fleet. He was sent by Ternay and members of the Boston Council to persuade the Indians of St. John River to rejoin the French and Americans, in particular a group of 500 who had sided with the British when the British promised to send them a Catholic priest.[9] During the year he spent on this mission[1] he had suffered so from the cold and a diet of unsalted meat and water that now, at the age of 56, he is unable to take up again the religious duties of his order. He has petitioned the King to serve as chaplain in one of the royal chapels or castles. That petition has gone unanswered, but since Franklin promised a few days ago to add a note of support to a second petition, he presents it now.

One petitioner, Jean-Baptiste de Loose, a merchant at Ghent,[2] sends

8. Unless otherwise indicated, all the documents discussed here are in French and at the APS.

9. The Micmacs and Malecites of the St. John River in Nova Scotia had been converted to Catholicism under French rule, and retained a strong Catholic identity long after the British assumed control. Getting a priest was one of the tribes' highest priorities, and it was widely known that they would side with whichever group would send them one. The priest the British sent to live among the Indians in 1768 left on account of the severe winters. His replacements lived at some remove. In July, 1776, the tribes signed a treaty of alliance and friendship with Massachusetts, promising to send some 500 men to join the Continental army and requesting a French priest to live among them. Before the Americans were able to satisfy that request, the British, in 1778, sent out a priest, Father Bourg, who had been authorized by the Bishop of Quebec to excommunicate anyone who acted against the British authorities. Leslie F. S. Upton, *Micmacs and Colonists: Indian-White Relations in the Maritimes, 1713–1867* (Vancouver, B.C., 1979), pp. 67–8, 73–8, 153–4; W. W. Abbot *et al.*, eds., *The Papers of George Washington*, Revolutionary War Series (14 vols. to date, Charlottesville and London, 1985–), v, 270–1, 510–14; Peter Force, ed., *American Archives* (9 vols., Washington, D.C., 1837–53), 5th ser., I, 841–2.

1. Frederic arrived on the *Jason* in 1780, and in the summer of 1781 resumed shipboard duty on the *Sagittaire*, which returned to France in September, 1782: Ministère des affaires étrangères, *Les Combattants français de la guerre américaine, 1778–1783* (Paris, 1903), pp. 147, 200. His letter is undated, but its earliest possible date is after the *Sagittaire* returned in September.

2. De Loose was also a magistrate at that city and was married to a daugh-

a signed memorial about the *Empereur toujours auguste*, a ship he is outfitting at Ostend for a voyage to America. Anticipating the establishment of formal commercial ties, he wishes a permit to enter the port at Philadelphia and, in the event of an emergency, other ports as well. On September 25 he writes again, this time in English, to remind his "Lordship" of his memorial which his father-in-law delivered some time ago. He is certain that a vessel provided with a note from Franklin will "meet generaly with more freedom than those without." Franklin's note for a reply states: "Recd the honour of his Memorial & Letter requesting a Passport for a Vessel to sail from Ostend. That I have no Authority to give such Passports, and that if I had it would be of no Use. Otherwise it would be a Pleasure to oblige him."

Franklin received only three requests for commissions in the army. Cousturier, a former officer of the French *maréchaussée*, writes on August 25 from Saissac, near Carcassonne, a brief but insistent plea "au plus grand ministre de la terre." Given his natural inclination for the military, as well as his desire to see America under the orders of the great "Vaquinston," he begs Franklin to obtain for him a military position and protection in North America.

Gourdeau de Monthigny, a Poitevin from Chantonnay, asks Franklin for a position in the army but will also accept a job in a state-owned company or clearing land on one of the American islands. Should proof of nobility be required for the army, M. d'Hozier de Serigny[3] recently certified the family titles for his brother, a cadet at the École militaire.

One wonders what Franklin made of the last of these requests for an army commission, from Richard Barrington, second son of the late Maj. Gen. John Barrington and nephew of Lord Barrington.[4] His "ex-

---

ter of J. F. X. Dierickx, the tax councillor there: Piet Lenders, *Gent: Een stad tussen traditie en verlichting (1750–1787)* (Kortrijk-Heule, Belgium, 1990), pp. 462, 479. This letter, undated, is at the University of Pa. Library.

3. *Commissaire du Roi pour certifier la noblesse des éleves: état militaire* for 1782, p. 451. A law of 1781 required officers and cadets to document their nobility before the royal genealogist: François-André Isambert *et al.*, *Recueil général des anciennes lois françaises* (29 vols., Paris, 1821–33), XXVII, 29–31.

Gourdeau did not date his letter, but it is unlikely that he wrote after the cessation of hostilities in early 1783.

4. The Barringtons were an illustrious family. When Richard's father, Gen. John Barrington, died in 1764, his uncle William Wildman, 2nd Viscount Barrington (1717–1793) in the Irish peerage, became guardian to his three nephews, bought Richard his military commission but also paid secret agents to shadow him, and, eventually, paid him to stay out of England:

travagance and dissipation," he writes in English on January 16, forced him to resign his commission in the 3rd Foot Guards and join the troops of the East India Company. Ill health compelled him to return to England, and, as his mother lived in France, he sought refuge there from his creditors.[5] He has lived in France since last March. His health reestablished, he is now determined to settle in America, as "the cause of Liberty has always had my best and sincerest wishes, and happy I am that it has succeeded so well." His annuity allows him to maintain his gentlemanly appearance, and if employed in the American Army, "I shall think Myself bound by Gratitude as well as inclination to exert my poor abilities for their service." If Franklin hasn't the power to appoint officers, will he recommend him to the commander-in-chief? Barrington assures Franklin that he has "seen the errors and folly of my former conduct and have too severely suffered, ever to be guilty of the like again."[6]

The surgeon Marcel, who says Franklin promised to aid him when he stopped at Passy on his way back from England in 1780, writes from Le Blanc in Berry on September 29.[7] He refers Franklin to M. de La Martiniére[8] or his secretary for references. Marcel was released five months ago from his imprisonment on the "ne Kerre" [Necker?]. Whatever position Franklin wishes to have him fill, Marcel is ready.

Writing in Latin from Leopoli (Lemberg or L'viv), the capital of Galicia, on January 12, Josephus Corabita de Laskowski begs Franklin to obtain for him a suitable and remunerative position in America.

Franklin also receives a good number of requests to forward mail. On August 25 Madame Sorin,[9] just returned to Passy from Spa, inquires after his health and sends four packets which she wishes him to forward by four different ships.

Alphonse Leroy, signing himself "docteur et professeur de mede-

---

DNB; Namier and Brooke, *House of Commons,* II, 55–9; G. E. Cokayne *et al., The Complete Peerage . . .* (13 vols., London, 1910–40), I, 433–4.

5. Barrington notes that his mother, Elizabeth Vassal Barrington, has for the past six years been married to a Mr. Browne and has lived at Montreuil-sur-Mer. Barrington writes from Abbeville, where he is visiting.

6. Barrington sailed to Philadelphia, probably without a recommendation from BF, and married Susan Budden, daughter of William Budden of that city, in 1783: Cokayne, *Complete Peerage,* I, 434.

7. University of Pa. Library.

8. The King's principal surgeon, Germain Pichault de La Martinière: XXXVI, 313n.

9. Mme Sorin de Bonne: XXXVI, 131n.

cine de la faculté de paris,"[1] writes on September 16. He has received correspondence from one of John Hancock's closest relatives[2] with instructions to address his reply care of Franklin to ensure its prompt delivery. Leroy is happy to have this occasion to express his esteem and veneration.

Two days later, H. Adolph Hoffmeister writes a one-sentence note from Heidelberg, asking Franklin to forward an enclosed letter to America. This was undoubtedly addressed to his brother-in-law in New York.[3]

The comtesse de La Brosse writes from the château d'Hérouville near Void, Lorraine, on December 4, to ask whether Franklin will accept letters to be forwarded to her brother in America. After serving with Rochambeau's army for two years, her brother retired in August as captain of the Saintonge Regiment. He has written to her from his home near Williamsburg, but neglected to indicate how she might reach him. She in turn neglects to give Franklin her brother's name, and there is no one in the Saintonge Regiment who goes by either of the names she gives for herself.[4]

On December 27, J. Tahon, a Premonstratensian,[5] writes from Ar-

1. Alphonse-Vincent-Louis-Antoine Leroy (1742–1816) was a professor of physiology and obstetrics at the University of Paris. He published extensively on obstetrics, the care of premature infants, and related topics: Larousse; Quérard, *France littéraire*. This letter is at the University of Pa. Library.

2. Most likely Joseph (Jean) Dupas de Iden de Valnais (1748–1826), who went to America as a cavalry officer; he served as French consul at Boston from 1779 to 1781, was given an honorary doctorate by Harvard, and married Hancock's niece Eunice Quincy in the spring of 1781. The couple had their first child on Sept. 10, 1782, and moved to Paris in the summer of 1783, carrying a letter of introduction from Hancock to BF. BF saw them socially thereafter. *Sibley's Harvard Graduates*, XIV, 667–70; Hancock to BF, June 30, 1783 (Hist. Soc. of Pa.).

3. Hoffmeister had asked BF to forward a letter to his brother-in-law George Jacob Leonhard Doll the year before (XXXVI, 309), and would ask for a third and final time on March 31, 1783 (APS).

4. She signs herself "du Trembley, comtesse de La Brosse." The Saintonge officers are listed in Ministère des affaires étrangères, *Les Combattants français*, pp. 253–4.

5. Also called Norbertines, an order of Augustinian Canons Regular founded by St. Norbert in the twelfth century at Prémontré, near Laon: *France ecclésiastique* for 1779, pp. 399, 401; *New Catholic Encyclopedia* (19 vols., New York, St. Louis, and San Francisco, 1967–96) under "Premonstratensians."

mentières, near Lille, to ask Franklin to forward a letter to his brother, a resident of Boston for 12 years now. Earlier attempts to send letters to him have failed, but Tahon is certain that under Franklin's auspices the letter he encloses will reach his brother.

The next day, a Saturday, M. Enouf, general agent of the King's brother, the comte de Provence,[6] writes about a packet of eighteen bills of exchange he sent Franklin on December 7. As the people who gave him these bills are in extreme need of the money, he asks Franklin to forward them to M. Grand by Monday morning.

On the first day of the new year, Wilhelm Augustine von Steuben, General von Steuben's father, writes in German entreating Franklin to forward an enclosed letter to Congress. He adds his wishes for continued victories in the new year and an enduring peace.[7]

On January 2 Moreau-Dufourneau, *avocat* and magistrate,[8] writes from Saint-Florentin in Burgundy to ask "Millord Docteur" to forward a letter to George Fox in answer to one he has received. "Millord fox," who had lived with his family for a year, did not include his return address. The writer has heard that Fox is living in England.[9]

Many people turned to Franklin for help with money owed to them. A longstanding debt prompts M. Bucaille, writing from Saint-Omer on September 10, to solicit Franklin's intervention. In 1775 he lent 3,000 *l.t.* to M. de Monneron, an officer of engineers then garrisoned

6. Enouf is listed with the officers of Monsieur's chancellery in the *Almanach royal* for 1782, p. 129. His letter is at the University of Pa. Library.

7. For the writer see XXX, 617n. BF wrote at the top of the first sheet, "Mr Franklin wishes to know the purport of this letter." An English summary, in an unknown hand, is at the APS.

8. Probably Jacob Moreau-Dufourneau, *avocat au Parlement* in 1787, and nephew of the anti-philosophe pamphleteer and historiographer Jacob-Nicolas Moreau (for whom see Larousse): Dieter Gembicki, *Histoire et politique à la fin de l'Ancien Régime: Jacob-Nicolas Moreau (1717–1803)* (Paris, 1979), pp. 59, 261; Xavier Charmes, *Le Comité des travaux historiques et scientifiques (histoire et documents)* (3 vols., Paris, 1886), I, lxvii, 409–12n, 417, 486; *Almanach royal* for 1788, p. 383.

9. WTF's friend Fox (XXXII, 313n), fearing that he would never learn French if he remained in Paris among his American friends, left for St. Florentin in the summer of 1780, with plans to board with the Fontaine family: Fox to WTF, Aug. 19, 1780. He wrote WTF on July 28, 1781, that he was soon to leave St. Florentin for Paris and thence to Holland. On Aug. 17, 1782, he wrote WTF from Lyon that he planned a tour of Languedoc before returning to Paris. Fox left for America in the spring of 1783: Fox to WTF, May 15, 1783. All these letters are at the APS.

in his city but who has since left for service in the United States.[1] Bucaille encloses copies of notes Monneron signed promising to repay half of the loan by February, 1776, and the other half by March, 1776.

Writing from Lorient on September 12, the widow Dubois,[2] now joined by Mlle La Morlon, renews her request for help in obtaining reimbursement for money owed them these past three years by officers in Jones's squadron. They have applied more than once to Messrs. Montigny and Moylan, merchants at Lorient in charge of distributing prize funds; they have written the comtesse de Maillé;[3] and they have even obtained orders from M. de Castries that they be paid. According to James Moylan, the only thing that will ensure their reimbursement is a note from Franklin. With their creditors about to carry off their furniture and their many children languishing in the worst misery, they hope that Franklin will take pity on them.

Charles Quentin Racine "dit picard," as he signs himself, writes on November 14, claiming to have served under John Paul Jones on the *Bonhomme Richard*, and to have risen to the rank of corporal. He has heard from other French volunteers that they have received 450 *l.t.* He asks Franklin to send his share as soon as possible. He adds that the prize ship they captured was named "La Serapisse une frégate du premier Rang."[4]

Alexis Bremont, a native of Pau, addresses an undated letter which we believe could only have been written as of 1782.[5] He requests an audience, and encloses a petition to "Son Altesse Royale D'amérique" in which he explains that he embarked on the frigate "La Bostonnoise" at Bordeaux in 1778[6] and cruised for eight months before landing at

1. Paul Mérault (Paul-Méraud) de Monneron had intended to go to the United States but evidently never got there: XXVI, 274n. He is listed in Anne Blanchard, comp., *Dictionnaire des ingénieurs militaires 1691–1791* (Montpellier, 1981), p. 544.

2. Jeanne Dubois already had written twice about this same matter: XXXVI, 306–7. The present letter is at the University of Pa. Library.

3. Maillé (XXXIII, 438n) married Madeleine-Angélique-Charlotte de Bréhan, his second wife, in 1769: *Dictionnaire de la noblesse*, IV, 46; XII, 822–3.

4. Racine's name does not appear on the roster of the *Bonhomme Richard*, and in any case, prize payments were not made until 1784. Augustus C. Buell, *Paul Jones, Founder of the American Navy: a History* (2 vols., New York, 1906), II, 407–13.

5. This is based on our calculations of his stated years of service and captivities.

6. The *Boston* reached Bordeaux on April 1, 1778, and departed on May 17: XXVI, 216–17, 594n.

Boston, where he began three years of service under Colonel Armand. With General "Guethz"[7] in command of Armand's troops, he was captured by Cornwallis and taken to Charleston. Later he "repassa en Amerique" with a "certificat de prisonnier" from General "Haô" and "Mr. Le Barron Destebingue" and embarked on a series of cruises on the privateer "Le poptor," the frigate "Ladine," and the privateer "General Pecrine,"[8] ending with his capture and imprisonment at New York. Despite all his years of service, he has never received any payment. He is now at Paris, ill and without any support. Franklin is his last hope.

Another undated letter from a Frenchman imprisoned in America, most likely written in 1782, comes from Mathieu Martinet, a native of Marseille. In 1778 he embarked on the *Marie Marguerite Toucher*, which was captured outside Boston and sent in to New York. Following his imprisonment and exchange, he served on several more ships, the most recent being the *Protector*. When it was captured, he was sent to England where he says he remained from May 4, 1781, until last September 25.[9] He asks Franklin to help him obtain his share of the prize money and encloses his certificate and passport.[1]

A German merchant of Nantes who signs himself "D'ron" writes on January 11, to enlist Franklin's help in tracking down a Boston saddler named Fritz, who borrowed 2,000 *écus* from him during a stay in Nantes four years earlier. He has heard nothing from him since then.

Many people turn to Franklin for information or advice of one sort or another. On August 26 M. de Ferriere, a former officer of dragoons, writes from Lorient asking for Franklin's wisdom in settling a dispute.[2] Ferriere and his wife were living in Quimper when his wife prevailed upon him to move to Nantes. By great misfortune the boat carrying their furniture and effects was captured by the English, then retaken by an American brig, the *Hambourg*, which carried the prize

7. Gen. Gates had command of Armand's troops at the Battle of Camden, S.C., in 1780: XXXIII, 418n.

8. By the first he may mean the *Protector:* XXXV, 411, 519n. The second was most likely either the privateer frigate or the Continental frigate named *Deane;* for the privateer see Allen, *Mass. Privateers,* p. 109; John A. McManemin, *Captains of the Privateers during the Revolutionary War* (Spring Lake, N.J., 1985), pp. 78–9, 96–7. The third may be the *General Pickering:* Allen, *Mass. Privateers,* pp. 150–1.

9. In fact, the *Protector* was captured on May 5, 1781: XXXV, 411. The captain, John Foster Williams, was committed to Mill Prison on July 21, presumably with his crew: Kaminkow, *Mariners,* p. 208.

1. Not found.

2. His letter is at the University of Pa. Library.

to Lorient where it was consigned to Messrs. Cuming and Macarty.[3] Armed with a letter of recommendation from Jonathan Williams, Jr., Ferriere went to Lorient to buy back his belongings. Initially Cuming and Macarty had promised to let him set his own price for his copy of the *Encyclopédie* and his editions of Voltaire and Raynal. Cuming reneged and is now demanding an exorbitant price for those volumes. Ferriere gives details of what he paid and what he has lost, and promises to abide by Franklin's judgement of the case. As Ferriere will soon return to Nantes, he asks Franklin to reply to an address there.

In a letter of October 12, the firm Frères Camusat et C. Lerouge of Troyes[4] thanks Franklin for recommending their firm to merchants "de votre climat." The resulting business has been significant, but one particular liaison makes them uneasy and only Franklin can put their minds at ease. Mr. Jean André Stockolm et Co., newly established at Nantes, has recently made them a proposal, but all they have been able to learn of the firm is that Franklin knows of its existence in America. Receiving no answer, they write again on October 23.[5]

Also writing on October 12, M. de Castella describes himself as a native of the canton of Fribourg[6] and recalls that city's "petite revolution" of the year before, which the newspapers mentioned briefly.[7]

3. The firm was founded on July 15, 1781: XXXVII, 53n.

4. The firm Camuzat de Bellombe appears in a list of the principal cloth merchants of Troyes: *Almanach des marchands*, p. 474.

5. Both letters are at the University of Pa. Library. We have no direct evidence that BF knew the firm. Stockholm had left Philadelphia in early spring, 1782, was in Bilboa at the beginning of April (whence he forwarded a package from Congress to John Jay), and from there sailed to Bordeaux, arriving by April 14. JW had corresponded with "Messrs. Andrew Stockholm & Co." on their arrival at Bordeaux, and his April 20 letter to them suggests that they intended to proceed to Paris: Henry P. Johnston, ed., *The Correspondence and Public Papers of John Jay* (4 vols., New York and London, 1890–93), II, 293; JW to Stockholm & Co., April 20, 1782, Yale University Library. Stockholm established himself at Nantes, and had emigrated by 1791 to New York, where he became a partner in a Manhattan cotton mill: Harold C. Syrett *et al.*, eds., *The Papers of Alexander Hamilton* (27 vols., New York and London, 1961–87), IX, 440n; XX, 201n.

6. There is a de Castella listed among the captains of the Swiss Guards in the *Etat militaire* for 1782, p. 144. This letter is at the University of Pa. Library.

7. The papers had reported that 10,000 peasants took up arms on May 3, the apparent cause being the abolition of certain festivals. The seigneurie of Bern quickly sent 8,000 militia and the uprising soon subsided: *Courier de l'Europe* of May 15 and June 15, 1781.

He requests a short private interview and asks that Franklin keep secret his name until he has a chance to explain himself.

Captain Niebelschütz,[8] in the Eichmann regiment, writes on October 18 in favor of a distinguished family that is trying to locate one of its members, Frantz Siegfried de Wulfen, formerly in the service of Prussia and thought to have transferred to the American army in 1777 with Franklin's recommendation.[9] Since that time his relatives have had no word of him. Now it is necessary to decide the ownership of land which he inherited, and the family does not know whether he is alive. The family hopes that "le celebre et Vertueux franklin" will help them learn the fate of their relative.

Franklin receives two requests in German for help in settling inheritances. Writing on December 4 is Heinrich Hartmann Zeller, a minister in Nussbaum. He inquires about a local burgher's son, Johann Jakob Höfle, who left home for Philadelphia in 1744 at the age of 19. He wrote his parents in 1750 that he worked for Michel Diel in Philadelphia,[1] the only news they have had of him. At his leisure could Franklin inform them whether or not Höfle is living and what his family situation is? If he has died, the family would like a death certificate so that they might take possession of his inheritance. They will reimburse all expenses.[2]

From Hayn (Grossenhain), in Upper Saxony, on December 16, R. Bingel sends Franklin, as requested, three copies of a legal brief in German, dated October 21 and attested on November 16. He asks Franklin to forward the copies to Johann Friedrich Schmidt, minister

8. Possibly Balthasar Heinrich Rudolf von Niebelschütz, a Prussian officer who received the Ordre pour le Mérite in 1794 when a captain in the Wolfframsdorff regiment: Karl-Friedrich Hildbrand and Christian Zweng, *Die Ritter des Ordens pour le Mérite* (2 vols. to date, Osnabrück, Ger., 1998), I, 148.

9. Most likely the baron Jean Henry de Wulffen (Wolff) who identified himself in one of several letters he exchanged with BF as a native of Magdeburg, a former lieutenant in service to the King of Prussia, and, in 1780, a captain in the American service: XXXII, 457, 486–7, 503–4, 597–8; XXXIII, 43–4. The baron's sister M. A. de Sonnemaens exchanged letters with BF about her brother and his inheritance: XXXII, 111–12, 538.

1. Michael Diel, or Diehl, was a Philadelphia cooper who died c. 1760. In 1750 he was involved in a dispute about the German Reformed Calvinist meetinghouse: *Pa. Gaẓ.*, April 5, 1750, and Feb. 7, 1760.

2. WTF wrote a note in French on the top of this letter to an unknown translator, requesting on BF's behalf a summary of its contents. That two-page summary, in French, is at the APS.

at Germantown.[3] The brief warns that either Schmidt or his legal heirs must appear at Hayn within a year to claim his portion of his father's estate at Frohse.

On January 12, Franklin's neighbor Louis-Guillaume Le Veillard writes on behalf of M. de Boislandry, his relative by marriage and a merchant from L'Aigle (Normandy), who desires a private conversation with Franklin. Le Veillard hopes that what his relative requests may be something Franklin will wish to grant.[4]

In a category all its own is the request from President Pigault de Lepinoy, former mayor of Calais, who writes from that city on September 11. Heroes and great men are usually immortalized by means of reliquaries, paintings, statues, and mausoleums. But what monument could be raised to the man who stole thunder from the sky and the scepter from tyrants? He begs Franklin for some items to serve as devotional objects: an engraving, a pair of his eyeglasses, and a pen used to compose the glory and salvation of America. Such a request from an unknown cannot surprise: whoever has been inspired by the abbé Raynal's depiction of the great man will want to possess some instrument of his immortality.[5]

Monsieur   a paris rüe st. Sauveur no 27. Ce 18 Xbre 1782

L'orsque j'eûs l'honneur cet etè de me recommander a votre bienveillance, implorant a cet effet votre penchant a obliger les infortunès, votre pouvoir a cet egard, et l'estime dont vous aviez honorè mon pere dont je vous appris la mort,[6] vous voulütes bien

3. Schmidt (1746–1812) matriculated at Halle in 1765 and was ordained as a Lutheran minister three years later. He settled in Germantown in 1769 and was the pastor at St. Michael's Church until 1786, when he moved to St. Michael's Church and Zion Church in Philadelphia: Frederick Lewis Weis, "The Colonial Clergy of the Middle Colonies: New York, New Jersey, and Pennsylvania, 1628–1776," *Proc. of the American Antiquarian Soc.*, new ser., LXVI (1956), 308; A. G. Roeber, "J. H. C. Helmuth, Evangelical Charity, and the Public Sphere in Pennsylvania, 1793–1800," *PMHB*, CXXI (1997), 92–3.

4. Louis de Boislandry wrote BF on April 18, 1784, from Paris, mentioning their interview of the previous year at which he sought information about commercial ties with America. APS.

5. In an earlier letter Pigault de Lepinoy had written of the French worship of glory and honor: XXVII, 29.

6. Melchior-François Parent (1716–1782), *avocat au Parlement*, was named *conseiller* and, in 1775, *président* of the Cour des monnaies. He was also intendant of the porcelain manufactory at Sèvres and, in 1780, was prosecuted for mismanagement and imprisoned first in the Bastille and then at the Cha-

me promettre de vous ressouvenir de moi dans l'occasion; une telle promesse de votre part est faitte pour inspirer de la confiance, la mienne a etè sans bornes et m'engage aujourd'huy a vous prier de vouloir bien laisser cette lettre sur votre bureau pour remèmorer un infortunè de 27 ans qui après avoir servi dans la cavalerie, est actuellement sans aucune ressource quelconque portè d'une bonne volontè, etaÿè de quelques connoissances qui le rendent propres a plusieurs emplois, et müni de la recommandation de personnes de merite et de consideration. La multitude de vos affaires me feroit regarder comme une indiscretion d'aller vous presenter mes respects en un moment Comme Celui-çi. Je me borne a vous prier de m'accorder la presente faveur.

Je suis avec respect Monsieur De votre excellence Votre tres humble et tres obeissant serviteur

PARENT DE BELLEHACHE

anc. [ancien] off. de Cavalerie au reg. de M. Le Cte D'artois 2eme fils de feu le president Parent reduit au tombeau par le vol d'une femme nommèe Rogè.[7]

Notation: Parent de Belle Hache 18. Decr. 1782.

From Jean-Frédéric Perregaux[8]

AL: American Philosophical Society

Rue st Sauveur 18th. / . Decr 1782

Mr: Perregaux has the honour to enclose to His Excellency Mr Franklin a Packet Just received for him from London & recomended to his Care.

---

renton asylum, where he died on July 12, 1782: François Bluche, *Les Magistrats de la Cour des monnaies de Paris au XVIIIe siècle, 1715–1790* (Paris, 1966), p. 65; *Almanach royal* for 1779, pp. 295 and 493 *bis.*

7. The troubles of Parent père evidently were the outcome of his affair with a Mme Rogé or Roger in whose name he placed large sums in dubious investments in his native city of Lyon. She in turn absconded with the money, leaving him to face the creditors and a lengthy legal process, which despite the assistance of his fellow Lyonnais Prost de Royer, resulted in his imprisonment. Bachaumont, *Mémoires secrets,* XIV, 303; XV, 95; XVIII, 28–9.

8. The banker who had forwarded letters to BF before: XXXV, 556n. We have confirmed his identity, as he is listed at this address in the *Almanach royal* for 1782, p. 468.

He will be obliged to him to let him know he received it.

From Vergennes

Copies: Library of Congress, Massachusetts Historical Society

Versailles le 19 Decembre 1782

Je vous recevrai demain, Monsieur, avec bien du plaisir et J'espere que vous voudrez bien me faire l'honneur de venir diner avec moi.[9] J'ai celui d'etre avec une parfaite Consideration, Monsieur, votre tres humble et tres obeissant Serviteur.

(signé) DE VERGENNES.

A Monsieur Franklin.

The American Peace Commissioners to Robert R. Livingston

ALS:[1] National Archives

Sir

Paris December 20. 1782

The Proposal inclosed, has been transmitted to us by Mr Bridgen, a Gentleman in London, who has been uniformly a Friend to America, and in a Variety of Ways, and at a great Expence has Served her Cause. It is a Project for introducing Copper Coins into the United States, and Seems to Us to merit the early Attention of Congress, to whom We have the Honour to recommend it.[2]

---

9. For this meeting, at which Vergennes granted the loan of six million *livres,* see BF to Morris, Dec. 23.

1. In JA's hand.

2. Bridgen had sent the enclosed proposal to BF on Oct. 23; two days later he asked BF not to forward it. (Both letters are above.) Bridgen also sent a copy of the proposal to JA on Oct. 23, with a similar request to forward it. After the preliminaries were signed Laurens suggested to JA that the commissioners might now send Bridgen's proposal. JA surprised him and the other commissioners by acting on his own and sending his copy to Livingston with a cover letter of Dec. 14 (National Archives). His explanation to Laurens was that BF would never agree to sign a joint letter. On Dec. 19

With the greatest Respect, We have the Honour to be, Sir, your most obedient and most humble Servants

JOHN ADAMS
B FRANKLIN
JOHN JAY
HENRY LAURENS.

Robert R. Livingston Esqr Secretary of State for the Department of foreign Affairs.

To Gabriel Johonnot

Press copy of ALS: American Philosophical Society

Sir,   Passy, Dec. 20. 1782

I have this Day drawn on you for 1026 Livres 3 Sols & 6 deniers, being what I have lately paid for your Son's Education to the 5th of October last. Another Quarter will be soon due. He is a fine Youth, and I make no doubt but his Improvements are more than equal to the Expense. You will be pleas'd to honour the Bill,[3] and transmit a Fund for defraying future Charges, which will oblige.

Sir, Your most obedient & most humble Servt   B FRANKLIN

Col. Johonnot

Laurens ascertained from BF that this was far from true; he then persuaded JA to draft the present letter, which all the commissioners willingly signed: Laurens to Bridgen, Dec. 18[–21], *Laurens Papers*, XVI, 88–90.

3. The bill of exchange was dated Dec. 20 and was payable to Jane Mecom at 30 days' sight. While none of the four copies has survived, the contents are clear from BF's alterations to a draft bill of exchange he had drawn up on Dec. 4 (for which see the annotation of BF to Robert Morris, Dec. 14). APS.

From Francesco Favi ALS: American Philosophical Society

Monsieur   Paris ce. 20. Xbe. 1782
J'ai L'honneur de vous envoyer un portrait qui a etè adressè de Vienne à M. Le Comte de Mercy.[4]

Ce Ministre m'ayant chargè de vous Le faire passer de sa part je m'empresse de remplir cette commission, qui me procure L'honneur de me dire avec Le plus grand respect Monsieur Votre très humble, et très Obeissant Serviteur   FAVI

Notation: Favi 20 xbre. 1782.

From the Conde de Sousa Coutinho[5]

L: Historical Society of Pennsylvania

Paris ce 20 Decembre 1782.
L'Ambassadeur de Portugal a l'honneur de faire ses compliments à Monsieur Francklin, et de rapeler à son souvenir le passeport et lettre de recommendation en faveur du Pere Patrice Ôcleary qui se dispose a passer en Amerique relativement à la succession dont il lui a parlé il y a quelque tems:[6] L'Ambassadeur de Portugal auroit été voir lui même Monsieur Francklin si la foîblesse qu'il eprouve encore des suites d'une serieuse maladie ne l'empechoit dans le moment: il compte sur ses bontés, pour pouvoir remettre à Lisbonne le dit passeport et lettre lundi prochain, s'il

---

4. We cannot be sure which portrait was being sent, but it may have been a plaster profile of Ingenhousz. On April 8, 1783, complaining that he had not heard from BF in a long time, Ingenhousz asked whether BF had received the "new cast of my profil framed" (APS). BF replied on May 16 that he had, and inquired about the method of manufacture (Library of Congress). As Ingenhousz explained on June 23, the plaster was varnished, sprinkled with silver dust, and burnished (APS).

5. Portuguese representative at the French court from 1763 to 1792: XXIII, 611–13; Jules Flammermont, *Rapport à M. le ministre de l'instruction publique sur les correspondances des agents diplomatiques étrangers en France avant la révolution* (Paris, 1896), pp. 488–91.

6. Patrick Cleary had written from Lisbon four years earlier to ask BF's assistance; his subsequent undated memorandum was given to BF by Sousa Coutinho: XXVII, 195–7.

est possible;[7] et le prie de recevoir les hommages de sa reconnoissance, et de son inviolable attachement.

From Samuel Cooper

ALS: Henry E. Huntington Library

My dear Sir,   Boston Decr 21. 1782

I know not how to express my Obligations to you for introducing me to the Acquaintance & Friendship of Count Segurs.[8]
I have known him but a few days and yet he has induldged me
wth an Intimacy. So many shining, so many amiable Qualities we
seldom see united in one Man. He has inspired me with an Esteem, a Respect, and a Love coexistent with myself. Think, my
dear Sir, what I must feel at this Moment when I am called to part
with him and so many Noble Men and Gentlemen of the Kings
Army and Fleet, who allow me to call them my Friends, whose
great and good Qualities have seized my heart & f'm whom I
have received the most obliging Attentions. I know not wch is
greatest, either the Honor & pleasure they have given me in their
acquaintance, or the Regret I feel at parting wth them.[9] It is no
small Distinction to the Cause of our Country that such men approve it; but that they ardently love it & have so chearfully exposed themselves to such Toils & Dangers in it's Defence, while
it raises us in the Estimation of the world[1] must captivate all our
Work. In the Field they have honor'd their own Nation & saved
our's. May Heaven defend and bless them, and crown them with
fresh Glories. My warmest good Wishes are particularly due to

7. BF did send the passport and letter to the governor of North Carolina,
though neither is extant: XXVII, 197n; BF to Mme Bertin, [after March 1, 1783],
Library of Congress.

8. BF gave the comte de Ségur a letter of introduction on April 7: XXXVII,
105–6. Cooper and Ségur continued to correspond. Ségur later praised
Cooper's talents, characterizing his religious and political speeches as bold
and profound: Louis-Philippe, comte de Ségur, *Mémoires ou souvenirs et anecdotes* (3 vols., Paris, 1827), I, 406–7.

9. Ségur accompanied the French army to the Caribbean: Rice and Brown,
eds., *Rochambeau's Army*, I, 263–6, 269.

1. Cooper used here his customary symbol for "world," a circle with a dot
in its center. Information kindly provided by Professor Charles W. Akers.

the Count Segurs, whose Conversation has so much enlightened & charmed me. May he soon have an happy Meeting with his Family and Friends, and the Pleasure of embracing you. With an ardent & constant Friendship I am my dr Sir, Your's   S. C.

Copy to Dr Franklin.

From Penet[2]   ALS: University of Pennsylvania Library

21 Dbre 1782./.

Je viens d'Etre informmé que votre Exelance est Continuellement assailli de la part de mes Creantiers qui nont ny pretantions ny droits meme de L'interompre a Ce Sujet.

Cette Conduite Est ausi enprutande que mechante puisque je les ài prevennuë que mes engagements nav'oient rien de Comun avec Votre Exelance, et que Ceux a quis il est Düe pour L'Etat de virginie m'ayant mis en meme de justifier leurs Comptes je l'arretteréz et en Sollisiteréz le rempourscement.

Mais Sans Egarres a mes raisons tous me menassent de Sonne Exelance de la justisce de la quelle ainsi que de lEquité de ma Conduite je nest rien a Craindre.

Jay lhonneur dEtre avec un profond respect de votre Exelance le plus Soumis Serviteur   ./.P. PENET./.

Notation: Penet 21. Decr. 1782

2. This is BF's last extant letter from Penet. Fleeing from his creditors, he took refuge in Hamburg, emigrated to New York State in 1783, and later went to St. Domingue. He died around 1812: Giunta, *Emerging Nation,* II, 78; Thomas J. Schaeper, "Pierre Penet: French Adventurer in the American Revolution," *Daughters of the American Revolution Mag.,* CXVII (1983), 856.

Receipt for John Adams   DS:[3] Massachusetts Historical Society

ce Dimanche 22 Decembre [1782]
Reçu le Pacquet que m'a envoyé son Exe. M. Adams addressée a
M. Livingston[4]   B FRANKLIN

Notation: Receipt Dr. Franklin. for a Packet addressed to Mr.
Livingston 22. Decr. 1782.

Charles-Etienne Gaucher to William Temple Franklin

Printed invitation, signed, with MS insertions:[5] American Philosophical
Society

[before December 23, 1782]
VERITE∴ UNION∴ FORCE∴

T∴ C∴ F∴[6]

L∴ R∴ L∴ des Neuf Sœurs, Est convoquée pour le *Lundi 23
du 10e mois* D∴ L∴ D∴ L∴ V∴ L∴ 5782, en son local, rue Co-
quéron, à 5 heures précises. *On traitera des Lectures et autres objets relatifs à la solemnité de la fête St. jean et à celle de la prochaine
loge de rentrée qui, aura lieu le même jour.*[7]

3. WTF drafted the basic statement; BF added "addressée a M. Livingston"
and "22 Decembre".
4. This packet contained JA's journal of the peace negotiations as well as
several letters for Livingston. It was carried by Capt. Barney: Butterfield,
John Adams Diary, III, 41–3n.
5. This invitation presumably was accompanied by one to BF; see XXXII,
330n.
6. Très Cher Frère. The two abbreviations in the next paragraph stand for
La Respectable Loge and De L'année De La Vraie Lumière. The masonic
year began in March.
7. The freemasons celebrated the Feast of St. John the Evangelist on Dec.
27. The *rentrée* usually occurred on Nov. 21 to mark the end of the vacation
of September and October: Louis Amiable, *Une Loge maçonnique d'avant
1789* . . . (Paris, 1897), pp. 35–6; Daniel Ligou, *Dictionnaire de la franc-
maçonnerie* (Paris, 1991), pp. 1083–6.
The combined *fête* was set for Jan. 13, 1783. WTF's invitation (BF's is missing) announced that there would be a banquet preceded by readings by the
marquis de La Salle (XXXIV, 470n), Venerable, the comte de Milly (XXIII,
128n), Le Changeux (XXXI, 372n), La Dixmerie (XXIX, 529n), and three mem-

Vous êtes prié d'y venir augmenter les douceurs de l'union Fraternelle.

Je suis par les N∴ C∴ D∴ V∴ M∴ V∴ T∴ H∴[8] & affectionné Frere.   GAUCHER

2eme. Secretaire de la R∴ L∴ des IX. Sœurs.

L'adresse de la Loge est à M. Gaucher, des Académies de Londres, &c. rue S. Jacques, porte cochère, vis-à-vis Saint-Yves.

Addressed: A Monsieur / Monsieur franklin fils / A Passy / N∴ S∴../.

To Robert Morris

Copies:[9] Connecticut State Library, New Jersey State Library, Virginia State Library, New Hampshire Division of Records Management and Archives, Delaware Public Archives Commission, National Archives

Sir,   Passy Decemr 23rd: 1782

When I wrote to you on the 14th: I expected to have dispatch'd the Washington immediately, tho' without any Money. A little misunderstanding prevented it. That was after some Days happily got over, and Friday last, Order was given to furnish me with six hundred thousand Livres immediately to send in that Ship, and I was answered by Mr. de Vergennes that the Rest of the Six Millions should be paid us quarterly in the Course of the Year 1783.[1] If your Drafts make it necessary, I believe we can

---

bers not mentioned in earlier correspondence. Jean-Pierre-Louis-Laurent Houël (1735–1813) was a painter and engraver: *DBF.* Louis-Vincent Marcadé was an interpreter of Oriental languages: Le Bihan, *Franc-maçons parisiens,* p. 338. Claude-Emmanuel-Joseph-Pierre, marquis de Pastoret (1755–1840), was a *conseiller* in the *Cour des aides:* Ligou, *Dictionnaire,* pp. 902–3; Amiable, *Une Loge,* pp. 155, 176–80, 238–43, 247, 351.

8. Probably "Nombres Connus Des Vénérables Maîtres Vôtre Très Humble."

9. These were copies Morris sent to governors of various states; see our annotation of BF to Morris, Dec. 14.

1. On "Friday last," Dec. 20, BF met with Vergennes. The following day JA wrote in his journal that BF had been to Versailles "and was assured of the Six millions, and all is fair Weather—all friendly and good humoured": But-

have it advanced, at least on paying Discount. Mr. Grand has been ever since busy collecting the proper Species to send it in, and it will go I suppose to morrow or next Day. I am glad to make use of this Opportunity, and wish the Sum could have been larger, as we have got a Pasport from England for the Ship Washington, Capt: Barney, sign'd by the King's own hand, the more curious as it acknowledges us by our Title of the *United States of America*.[2] We should not however, imagine ourselves already in Peace. The other Powers are not yet agreed, and the War may still continue longer than we expect. Our Preliminaries have not yet been communicated to Parliment, and I apprehend there will be great Clamours against them when they appear. Hints are already thrown out that the King has gone beyond his Powers, and if the new Ministry do not stand their Ground perhaps the Ratification may be prevented. A little more Success in the W. Indies this Winter may totally turn the Heads of that giddy Nation.

I pressed hard therefore for the whole Sum demanded; but was told it was impossible; the great Efforts to be made this Campaign in the East & West Indies, (the Armies for which are now afloat)[3] and the enormous Expence engaged in, having much embarrass'd the Finances.

Our People certainly ought to do more for themselves. It is absurd the pretending to be Lovers of Liberty while they grudge paying for the Defence of it. It is said here, that an Impost of 5 per Cent on all Goods imported, tho' a most reasonable Proposition

---

terfield, *John Adams Diary*, III, 98. Vergennes wrote to La Luzerne on Dec. 21 about the meeting, saying that it had been amiable. BF told him that both Congress and the American commissioners would prefer to renounce peace rather than neglect their obligations and their gratitude to the King; they would be "inconsolable" if their conduct had displeased him. Vergennes informed La Luzerne of the decision to grant a new loan, emphasizing that it would be the last one. He noted that the departure of the *General Washington* had been delayed, and he predicted that France would know the success of her peace negotiations by the end of the following week: Giunta, *Emerging Nation*, I, 731–2.

2. For the King's passport see our annotation of BF to Vergennes, Dec. 15.

3. The Brest squadron for the Jamaica attack was still on its way to Cadiz. French forces in the East Indies were outnumbered during the 1783 campaign, which continued until June, when news of peace arrived from Europe: Dull, *French Navy*, pp. 319, 334.

had not been agreed to by all the States; and was therefore frustrated;[4] and that your News Papers acquaint the World with this, with the Non Payment of Taxes by the People, and with the Non Payment of Interest to the Creditors of the Public.[5] The Knowledge of these things have hurt our Credit & the Loan in Holland, and would prevent our getting any thing here but from the Government. The Foundation for Credit abroad should be laid at home; and certain Funds should be prepared and established before hand, for the Regular Payment at least of the Interest.

With sincere Esteem and Respect, I am, Sir, Your most Obedient and most Humble Servant   (signed) B FRANKLIN

Honble: Robt: Morris Esqr.

Notation: No. 5. 23d— Decemr 1782 Dr B Franklin To Office of Finance— Copy recd— 7th— April, seqe

From Matthew Ridley   AL: American Philosophical Society

Rue de Clery. Monday Evening [December 23, 1782][6] Mr. Ridley presents his Respects to Dr. Franklin & begs the honor of his Company at Dinner on Wednesday the 25. Currt.— M R begs Leave to inform Dr. Franklin it will be a Christmas dinner &, the principal dainty a Round, of Beef[7]

Addressed:[8] A Son Excellence / Son Excellence Monr. Franklin / a Passy

4. The impost, needing the consent of all the states, was blocked by Rhode Island: Ferguson, *Power of the Purse,* pp. 152–3.

5. Congress on Sept. 9 had stopped the issuance of bills of exchange drawn on American ministers abroad to pay interest on loan office certificates; see our annotation of Morris to BF, Oct. 5. For a sample of the public outcry over the decision see *Morris Papers,* VI, 53–4.

6. The only year that Dec. 25 fell on a Wednesday during Ridley's stay in France was 1782.

7. BF evidently did not attend. Ridley's diary (entry of Dec. 25) indicates that the guests were JA, John and Sarah Jay, Henry Laurens and his son Henry Laurens, Jr., John Thaxter, Jr., Charles Storer, Edward Bancroft, and Edmund Jenings (Mass. Hist. Soc.).

8. Written on the address leaf are the following notes in an unknown hand:

To Francis Hopkinson[9]

ALS (draft): Library of Congress

Mr Hopkinson, My Dear Friend,   Passy, Dec. 24. 1782

I received your very kind Letter of Oct. 18. I am glad you have at length got the Battery from Mr Coombe. He had had it long enough in his Possession to believe it his own, it being lent to him in 1756.— He had also of me a nine Inch Glass Globe, well mounted; and a Vol. of the Philosophic Transactions. If they still exist I wish you could recover them also.

I have subscribed for two Sets of the new Encyclopedia, one for you,[1] the other I intend a Present to our Philosophic Society.— I have forwarded to you in this Ship what is already publish'd.

I thank you for your ingenious Paper in favour of the Trees.[2] I own I wish we had two Rows of them in every one of our Streets. The comfortable Shelter they would afford us, when walking, from our burning Summer Suns, and the greater Coolness of our Walls & Pavements, would I conceive in the improv'd Health of the Inhabitants, amply compensate the Loss of a House now and then, by Fire, if such should be the Consequence: But a Tree is soon fell'd; and as Axes are at hand in every Neighbourhood, may be down before the Engines arrive.—

You do well to avoid being concern'd in the Pieces of Personal Abuse, so scandalously common in our Newspapers that I am afraid to lend any of them here, till I have examined & laid aside such as would disgrace us; and subject us among Strangers to a Reflection like that us'd by a Gentleman in a Coffee-house, to two Quarrellers, who after a mutually free Use of the Words Rogue, Villain, Rascal, Scoundrel, &c seemed as if they would refer their Dispute to him:—I know nothing of you or your

---

"Thomas Spencer taken prisoner on board the Ship Commerce of Liverpool by the Buccaneer private Ship of War. & carried into Port L'Orient. / James McTeer master of the Commerce". For the capture of the *Commerce* and BF's condemnation of the prize see our annotation of Williams, Moore & Co. to BF, Oct. 9.

9. Sent via Joshua Barney: Hopkinson to BF, [March 27, 1783]. APS.

1. Hopkinson had requested the subscription in his letters of April 29 and Oct. 18.

2. See Hopkinson's letter of Oct. 18.

490

Affair, says he; I only perceive *that you know one another.*

The Conductor of a Newspaper, should, methinks, consider himself as in some degree the Guardian of his Country's Reputation, and refuse to insert such Writings as may hurt it. If People will print their Abuses of one another, let them do it in little Pamphlets, and distribute them where they think proper. It is absurd to trouble all the World with them; and unjust to Subscribers in distant Places, to stuff their Papers with Matters so unprofitable & so disagreable.

With sincere Esteem & Affection, I am, my dear Friend, Ever yours   B FRANKLIN

From Henry Laurens

AL: American Philosophical Society; copy: South Carolina Historical Society

Hotel d Yorke 24th. Decemr 1782—
Mr. Laurens presents his Compliments to Doctor Franklin & requests him to give a place to the Inclosed Letter for Robt. R. Livingston Esqr[3] among his dispatches for the Ship Washington & to inform him whether he will be in time for saving the Courier with other Letters any time to day.

Addressed: His Excellency / Benja. Franklin Esquire / &c & / Passy—

Notation: H. Laurens Paris 24. xbre 1782

To Henry Laurens   L:[4] South Carolina Historical Society

Passy, 24 Decr. 82
Dr Franklin presents his Compliments to Mr Lawrens, has recd his Packet for Mr Livingston, and will forward it by the Courier,

---

3. Laurens wrote Livingston on Dec. 24: *Laurens Papers,* XVI, 97–100.
4. In WTF's hand.

who will not leave Paris 'till Thursday,[5] being to wait for Count de Vergennes Dispatches: so that any thing else that Mr. Lawrens may wish to send, will be time enough if it is here by Tomorrow Night.

Addressed: His Excellency / Henry Lawrens Esqr / &c &ca. / Paris.

Notation: Note from Dr. Franklin Passy 24th December 1782

To Robert R. Livingston

LS[6] and transcript: National Archives

Sir,   Passy, Decr. 24.[–25] 1782.

Sundry Circumstances occurring since mine of the 5th & 14th. have hitherto retarded the Departure of our Dispatches. They will now go under the Security of a British Passport, be accompanied by a Sum of Money, and by some farther Intelligence from England, which show the still unsettled State of Minds there, and, together with the Difficulties and small Progress in the Dutch and Spanish Negociations, make the speedy Conclusion of Peace still uncertain.

The Swedish Ambassador has exchanged full Powers with me. I send a Copy of his herewith.[7] We have had some Conference on the proposed Plan of our Treaty, and he has dispatched a Courier for farther Instructions, respecting some of the Articles.[8]

5. Dec. 26. L'Air de Lamotte advanced 288 *l.t.* to a courier going to Lorient around this time, and was reimbursed on Dec. 28: Account XXVII (XXXII, 4).

6. In L'Air de Lamotte's hand, except for the last seven words of the complimentary close, which are in BF's hand.

7. The copy of Creutz's powers (in French) is in L'Air de Lamotte's hand, with an attestation by WTF that it was a true copy, and that the original was signed by Gustavus.

8. The conference was held on Dec. 18. The following day Creutz informed Gustavus that BF's draft treaty differed on several points from the one the King had sent. Creutz would endeavor to have BF accept unconditionally the King's version; if unsuccessful he would send the American version by courier: Amandus Johnson, *Swedish Contributions to American Freedom, 1776–1783* (2 vols., Philadelphia, 1953–57), I, 576–7.

The Commissioners have join'd in a Letter to you, recommending the Consideration of a Proposal from Mr. Bridgen relating to Coper Coin. With this you have a Copy of that Proposal, and some Samples of the Copper.[9] If it should be accepted, I conceive the Weight and Value of the Pieces (Charge of Coinage deducted) should be such, as that they may be aliquot Parts of a Spanish Dollar.[1] By the Copy enclosed of an old Letter of mine to Mr. Bridgen, you will see the Ideas I had of the additional Utility such a Coinage might be of in communicating Instruction.[2]

Dec. 25. Inclosed is a Copy of a Letter just received from M. le Comte de Vergennes upon the present State of their Negociation with England.[3] With great Regard, I have the honour to be, Sir, Your most obedient and most humble Servant B FRANKLIN

Honble. Robt. R. Livingston Esqr.

From Edward Bridgen   ALS: American Philosophical Society

My Dear Sir   Decr: 24 1782

As I don't know Mr Ls: particular address I take the Liberty to inclose a Letter for him to your care and at the same time to embrace this opportunity to return you my best thanks for the attention you were so good to pay to the proposal he was so kind to charge himself with he accquainted me with the reception it met with from the concerned to whom also I beg leave to charge you with my respectful thanks.[4] May your days be many and

9. The commissioners' Dec. 20 letter is above. Bridgen had sent two sample copper blanks in September, 1779: XXX, 355–6.

1. In 1775 perhaps half of the coins in the American colonies were Spanish dollars (also called "pesos" or "pieces of eight"): John J. McCusker, *Money and Exchange in Europe and America, 1660–1775: a Handbook* (Chapel Hill, N.C., 1978), p. 4. For Robert Morris' recent proposed exchange rates for various coins see *Morris Papers*, VII, 197.

2. See XXX, 429–31.

3. Vergennes to BF, Dec. 25, below.

4. See our annotation of American Peace Commissioners to Livingston, Dec. 20.

happy is the sincere wish of my Dear Sir Yr: Excellency's Affect
& faithful   EDWD: BRIDGEN

His Excellency Benjn: Franklin

Addressed: His Excellency / Benjn: Franklin / Passy

Notation: Bridgen Mr. Edward Decr. 24 1782

From Joseph Hirigoyen   ALS: American Philosophical Society

Monseigneur   Nantes le 24 xbre. 1782.

Comme super Cargue du navire Le Camberwell cape. Silas
Ewers armé de dix Canons & pret a partir pour le dit lieu[5] au premier tems favorable, j'ai crû devoir retarder mon depart de
quelques jours dans l'espoir d'une heureuse paix prochaine & ne
pas exposer les interets de ceux qui m'ont accordé leur Confiance
avant d'en avoir la Certitude;

Nous trouvant Monseigneur en cette Ville sans consulat des
Etats Unis de L'amerique septentrionale, ni de personne qui en
fasse les fonctions, je prends la liberté de supplier Votre Excellence, de m'accorder un passeport pour le dit navire afin que je
puisse proffiter sans perte de tems, de la Securitté que nous donne
une heureuse paix;[6] je ne Cesse de faire des Vœux au ciel pour la
Conservation des jours de Votre Excellence.

Je suis avec un profond Respect Monseigneur De Votre Excellence Le tres humble & tres obeissant Serviteur
                                        JOSEPH HIRIGOYEN

Son Excellence Monseigneur De Franklin

Endorsed: LPh hirigoyen 24 Xbre. 1782.

5. Probably Boston, home port of the *Camberwell:* Charles H. Lincoln,
comp., *Naval Records of the American Revolution, 1775–1785* (Washington,
D.C., 1906), p. 245; Claghorn, *Naval Officers,* p. 103.

6. Neither Britain nor America issued passports to protect the other's shipping until after the general peace was signed by France and Britain on Jan.
20, 1783. Hirigoyen's confusion about the impact of the preliminary articles
between America and Britain was shared by many Americans; see our annotation of Vergennes to BF, Dec. 15.

From Valltravers   ALS: American Philosophical Society

Honorable Sir! Vienna, Christmas Daÿ, Décr. 24th. 1782./.

Still ignorant of the Fate of mÿ several Letters to Your Excellency, written in the Year 1778; and lately, on the 2d. of Octr., conveÿed by Monsr. Lieutaud, a french Man of Letters, who had visited this Capital; And not conscious of ever having forfeited the Honor of your invaluable Esteem, and antient Friendship: I still attribute your Silence, rather to the daily increasing Extent and Weight of your exalted, and important, public Functions, than to any other Impediment, or Cause whatever.——

The Occasion of this Letter, is furnished me by a verÿ ingenious Gentleman, Mr. Kampl, Counsellor of his Impl. Majesty's Finances, for the Kingdom of Hungaria,[7] who, on a Furlow obtained for two Years, is ready to Set out for Paris, Brusselles, Holland, and England, attended with his whole Family, his Ladÿ, 2. sons, and 2. Daughters;[8] not only to satisfÿ his own Curiosity, but, also, in great measure, that of the Public Endowed with a peculiar Taste and Genius for mechanical Inventions and Improvements, of which he sees no Manner of Encouragemt. in these Parts, he means to impart several of his most important Discoveries and Experiments, wherever theÿ shall be best re-

7. Wolfgang von Kempelen (1734–1804), trained in philosophy and law, was also gifted in linguistics, science, and mechanics. He served the Austrian court in many capacities over his lifetime, most notably as an engineer and later a councillor in the Hungarian chancellery. As a 21-year-old, he was appointed councillor to the imperial court by Empress Maria Theresa and rewarded so handsomely that he equipped himself with a scientific workshop: *Neue Deutsche Biographie* (21 vols. to date, Berlin, 1953–); Tom Standage, *The Mechanical Turk: the True Story of the Chess-Playing Machine That Fooled the World* (London, 2002), pp. 13–20, 36.

8. In 1769 Kempelen had boasted to the court that he could invent an automaton more impressive than one they had just witnessed. Maria Theresa granted him a six-month leave to make good on that claim. The result was the mechanical chess player described below. In 1781 her successor, Joseph II, ordered Kempelen to resurrect the machine for the visiting Grand Duke Paul of Russia; he then directed Kempelen to take the machine on a two-year tour of Europe. Despite his reluctance to leave his serious pursuits, Kempelen prepared the automaton for travel. He arrived in Paris in April, 1783, accompanied by his wife, Anna Maria, their children, Theresa and Carl, and an assistant: Standage, *Mechanical Turk*, pp. 18–20, 40–6.

cieved and rewarded.— As an amusing specimen of his Skill in Mechaniks; and, as a Means, at the same Time, of supporting his travelling Charges, he intends to exhibit the Figure of a Turk, as big as Life, plaÿing at Chess with anÿ Plaÿer; and answering bÿ pointing at the Letters of an alphabet, any Questions made to him. I saw him plaÿ twice, without discovering his intelligent Director anÿ where, in, or about him. Was there nothing, but the organisation of his Arm, Hand, and Fingers, besides the motions of his Head, that alone would entitle him to no Small Admiration.—[9]

Besides his Chess-Plaÿer, he amuses himself with forming a Child, of 4. or 5. Years of Age, uttering the first articulated Sounds of Elocution. Of these, I have heared him pronounce, distinctly, upwards of 30. Words, and Phrases. There remain but 5. or 6. Letters of the Alphabet, to express, which he proposes to compleate at Paris.—[1]

Apprised of your eminent Merit, in this, as well as manÿ other Branches of usefull Knowledge, Mr. Kampl is verÿ desirous of the Honor of your Acquaintance. And as I presume the Same Satisfaction on the Part of yr. Excellcÿ., I esteem mÿself happÿ, in being instrumental to yr. mutual personal Aquaintance & Regard.

9. The wooden figure of a Turk was seated at a large cabinet which contained an elaborate mechanism; doors opened on every side to reveal the intricate workings to an amazed public. Much of this machinery was a decoy. The cabinet was ingeniously designed to hide an adult who could follow an opponent's moves by means of magnets and operate the Turk's arm by means of sophisticated mechanical equipment. The Turk was a sensation, but an accurate explanation of the hoax was not offered until the nineteenth century: Standage, *Mechanical Turk*, pp. 194–204.

1. Known today as the father of experimental phonetics, Kempelen invented the first machine that could imitate both vowels and consonants and form them into short sentences. Based on Kempelen's study of human physiology, the machine was "played" like a musical instrument and could be made to "speak" several languages. Kempelen had considered placing the device in the form of a child, which might have made its stilted speech more believable, but opted instead to leave it undisguised. His improvements in the machine went hand in hand with his evolving understanding of speech production, resulting in an important treatise, *Le Méchanisme de la parole, suivi de la déscription d'une machine parlante* (Vienna, 1791): Thomas L. Hankins and Robert J. Silverman, *Instruments and the Imagination* (Princeton, N.J., 1995), pp. 190–7; Standage, *Mechanical Turk*, pp. 76–81.

I wish Yr. Excellcy. Joÿ on the final Success of ÿour own, and yr. Fellow-Laborers, glorious struggle, for the Liberties of ÿour own Countrÿ, now the peaceable Asÿlum of oppressed Industrÿ.

Stript of mÿ All, persecuted & demolished bÿ those I have faithfullÿ & liberally served, deprived of House and home, without Emploÿ, unprotected, and unsupported: how happÿ shd. I esteem mÿself, could those few abilities, I have endeavored to aquire and to treasure up in the Course of an Active, as well as studious Life, render me Subservient to the Introduction and Increase of the Arts of Peace under ÿour philanthropic American Government! This, your Excy. knows, has long been mÿ fondest Wish. Nor have I been wanting in offering Several Means, within the small sphere of mÿ Power, to several of yr. Patriots. Who knows, but yr. consolidated Independance and Peace maÿ prove favorable to my Zeal, & Suggest Yr. Excÿ, & yr. Friends some Opportunity of saving and emploÿing— Your Excellcy's. old Admirer, and Suffering Friend: RODH. VALLTRAVERS.

My adresse is, under Cover, a monsr. de Fichtl, Agent du St. Empire romain—á Vienne, En Autriche.

P.S. Mr. Kampl will hardly be able to reach Paris before the month of February. I therefore send this Letter off bÿ the Poste, & shall give Mr. Kampl another Line of Introduction.[2]

Notation: Valltravers Dec. 24. 1782

From the Comte d'Albon[3]   ALS: American Philosophical Society

franconville La garenne ce 25 Xbre 1782.
C'est avec empressement, Monsieur, que jai l'honneur de vous envoier mon ouvrage. L'hommage que je vous en fais vous est

2. Valltravers wrote that recommendation on Dec. 30. He added nothing to his letter of Dec. 24, he said, because Kempelen's "great Ingenuity pleads far better for him to yr. Excellency, than any Thing, I could saÿ in his Favour." APS.

3. Claude-Camille-François d'Albon (1753–1789), who had ties to François Quesnay and Court de Gébelin (who later was buried at the comte's

dû mieux qu'à toute autre personne. Je m'y suis attaché à défendre Les intêréts d'un peuple opprimé dont vous êtes aujourdhui le representant, comme vous en fûtes le créateur, car, le vrai créateur d'un peuple est celui qui lui donne de sages loix. Si une mauvaise santé ne me retenoit à la campagne, je me serois fait un véritable plaisir d'aller vous assurer moi même des sentiments profonds avec les quels je suis, Monsieur, votre très humble et très obeissant serviteur   Le comte d'Albon

Endorsed: Rue de Grenelle, Hotel du Castellain.[4] answer'd Dec. 27.

Notation: Le Comte D'Albon Franconville la garrenne 25 Decembre 82

From James Carr   ALS: American Philosophical Society

Honoured Sr.   cherburg Decr. the 25 1782

I James carr Late Second mate & carpenter of the Brigantine active Capt John Hodge in the Service of the united States was taken Prisoner on our Passage from Philadelphia to the Havana by one of his Britanick Majestys Ships & sent to England where with a Large number of others I have Lain some time[5] & have-

---

country estate), was a writer and member of many academies. His most recent work, *Discours sur l'histoire, le gouvernement, les usages, la littérature et les arts, de plusieurs nations de l'Europe* (4 vols., Geneva and Paris, 1782), was announced in the *Jour. de Paris* on Nov. 15. The work was a new edition of an earlier title and included a discussion of the origin of the American Revolution: *DBF; Nouvelle biographie;* Quérard, *France littéraire; Jour. de Paris,* issue of March 3, 1783.

4. Probably the residence of the marquis and marquise de Castellane, who lived on this street: Charles Lefeuve, *Les Anciennes Maisons de Paris, par Lefeuve. Histoire de Paris, rue par rue, maison par maison* (5 vols., 5th ed., Paris, 1875), IV, 87. The comtesse d'Albon and the marquise were both ladies in waiting to Madame Victoire, the King's aunt: *Almanach royal* for 1782, p. 139.

5. The Continental packet *Active* was captured in early 1782 and sent into Jamaica. Capt. Hodge sailed to America, arriving there by early August; the crew, sent to Forton Prison, must have arrived there after the cartels carry-

ing with five others made our escape in a small sloop & it being a matter of Doubt weather She will be condemd would be glad if your Honour would Speak in behalf of us & order some assistence for to help us to some Port in France that we may gett a Passage to our native homes[6] in so Doing you will greatley Oblige Sr. yours to Serve[7] JAMES CARR

Addressed: To / Doctor Benjamin Franklin / Pleinopotentary to the United / States of America at Paris

Notation: Carr M. James Decr. 25. 1782.

---

ing American prisoners departed in early June: XXXVII, 447; *Morris Papers,* VI, 136–7.

6. The sailors engaged a French official on Dec. 30 to draft a petition to BF describing this "circonstance assez rare": six Americans escaped from Forton Prison on Dec. 11 and talked their way onto a small fishing vessel manned by three crew members that was preparing to ferry a British marine, a sailmaker, and four women to a large ship moored off shore. Before arriving at the ship the Americans seized control of the shallop and sailed it to Cherbourg; they arrived on Dec. 19 and were greeted with great astonishment and public admiration. These brave Americans now request that BF condemn the shallop as a prize; the proceeds from a sale would be meager, especially when split six ways, but it would ease their situation. The petition is unsigned. BF, confused as to the number of prisoners cited (the correct number, "9," was written over "11"), endorsed it, "Petition in favour of Six Americans who brought an English Shallop and 19 Prisoners into France 1782." APS.

7. Among BF's papers at the APS is a general letter from Thomas Wren to "whom it may concern" regarding James Carr and dated Portsmouth, Dec. 5. It certifies that Carr was a carpenter on the *Active,* was taken by the ship *Proserpine,* and was imprisoned at Forton for "many months" where he conducted himself with "great propriety and good behavior." Carr may have forwarded this to Passy along with the present letter. As his name does not appear on the "List of Escaped Prisoners" and he never signed a promissory note, we assume that he did not come to Passy in person. No trace of a response from BF has been located.

From Vergennes

Copies: National Archives,[8] Library of Congress, Massachusetts Historical Society; transcript: National Archives

Versailles 25 Xbre. 1782

J'ai l'honneur de vous envoyer, Monsieur, mes Depeches pour Mr. le Chevr de la Luzerne. Le pacquet est volumineux mais il renferme beaucoup de Duplicata.[9]

Je voudrois pouvoir lui mander que notre Negociation est au meme point que la Votre, mais elle en est encore fort eloignée.[1] Je ne puis meme prevoir quelle en sera l'issue, car les Difficultés naissent des facilités aux quelles nous nous sommes pretés. Il sera bon Monsieur, que vous en preveniez le Congrès pour le premunir contre tout ce qui peut arriver. Je ne desespere pas, j'espere plutot, mais tout est encore incertain.

J'ai l'honneur d'etre avec une parfaite Consideration M.

(signed) DE VERGENNES.

Copy of a Letter from his Excy. Count de Vergennes to B. Franklin Esqr.

8. In WTF's hand.

9. These dispatches included a Dec. 24 letter in which Vergennes asked La Luzerne to inform Congress that the outcome of the French negotiations with Britain was uncertain. He speculated that they might have proceeded more rapidly if the American peace commissioners had been less hasty in signing their own provisional articles with Britain: Giunta, *Emerging Nation*, I, 733.

1. The remaining difficulties included the territorial settlements in the West Indies and India: Doniol, *Histoire*, v, 264–75; Giunta, *Emerging Nation*, I, 734–6; Dull, *French Navy*, pp. 332–3.

Benjamin Franklin's Suit of Clothes

Elkanah Watson, Jr.,[2] to William Temple Franklin

LS:[3] American Philosophical Society

Dear Sir   Nantes 25 December 1782

I write this principally to acquaint you that I find the Unfortunate Captn. Hardy sick in my Appartments—but is determined if possible to go out with Captn. All who waits the Event of Peace or War. His Situation is really distressing; & I beg you'll make a little Exertion to accomplish what I assured him last Septr. would be done through your Influence. If you can make up the Sum between you & Mr. Jay to about 15 Guineas, I have the best Reasons to assure you, that I am fully persuaded, you will be reimbursed by Captn. Hardy immediately after his Arrival in America.[4] After this I have another favour to beg for myself—no less singular than impertinent, however when you have made full Allowance for my Whim—I beg you'll say nothing upon the Matter, whether it be practicable or not. In short, I mean to beg a suit, of your Grand fathers Old Cloaths, that never can be of any Service to him, or any Body else—to be plain—Madam Wright, has fabricated (I think) a most striking Likeness of him in Wax in my Possession—which I wish to sett up in my study—dressed in his own Cloaths.[5] If I can be grati-

2. Watson had returned to Paris on Dec. 15 from his three-month-long trip to England (for which see the annotation of Watson & Cossoul to BF, Aug. 20). He dined with the peace commissioners the following evening. At Passy he gave BF a recent London paper containing a detailed account of BF's death and funeral. BF was "very much amused," and told Watson that this was the third time during his French mission that the London papers had "buried him alive." Watson continued on to Nantes, where he arrived on Dec. 23 and stayed until the following March: Winslow C. Watson, ed., *Men and Times of the Revolution; or, Memoirs of Elkanah Watson* ... (New York, 1856), pp. 180–1; Watson to Joseph Green, Jan. 11, 1783, Elkanah Watson Papers, Journal no. 5 (1781–83), New York State Library.

3. The postscript is in Watson's hand.

4. Watson tried to aid Joseph Hardy in August: Hardy to BF, Aug. 19, and Watson & Cossoul to BF, Aug. 20, both above. Isaac All's departure was delayed until the spring of 1783: All to BF, Sept. 3, above; Joseph Mayo to WTF, April 30, 1783 (APS).

5. Watson intended to refine the trick he had recently played in England. There, he had placed the wax head of BF sculpted for him by Patience Wright (xxxv, lix) on a figure dressed in a morning gown with slippers and a night-

501

DECEMBER 25, 1782

fyed in this, pray be so polite as to write me, as I will take the necessary Means of having them conveyed forward—[6]
I am with Esteem Sir Yr. very Hum: Sert.

ELKH. WATSON JR:

Mr. Willm. Franklin Passy.

We have taken the liberty to Inclose you a packett—the postage
for wch. you'l please to note to me—& I beg you'l be so good
as to forward it by the first messenger for England—

Addressed: A Monsieur / Monsr. Wm. Franklin / a Passy / prés
Paris

Notation: E Watson 25 Dec. 82

---

cap. This mannequin fooled a stream of visitors including Frederick Reynolds, an 18-year-old Englishman who had accompanied Watson on his journey from Paris to Calais disguised as his servant, and John Reynolds, his
father (XXVI, 291). Frederick Reynolds had been in France illegally. He attached himself to Watson in September after having been apprehended by
the Paris police. BF evidently signed a statement allowing him to stay in Paris
another week. Not being able to procure his own passport, he persuaded
Watson to protect him, and the two traveled together: *DNB;* Frederick
Reynolds, *The Life and Times of Frederick Reynolds* (London, 1826), pp. 222–
6, 242–4 of first pagination; Watson, *Men and Times of the Revolution,*
pp. 143–4. For more on this incident, including Reynolds' lively account of
Watson's hoax, see Charles Coleman Sellers, *Patience Wright: an American
Artist and Spy in George III's London* (Middletown, Conn., 1976), pp. 165–
72.
   6. WTF complied with Watson's request, sending a suit of silk clothes that
BF supposedly wore in 1778. With this, Watson fashioned a dummy figure of
BF and placed it in the corner of a large room, seated behind a table on which
was set an open atlas and some mathematical instruments. He threw a hand-
kerchief over the cuffs to disguise the missing hands, and rigged wires into a
nearby closet from which the body could be raised and lowered. "Thus
arranged," he wrote, "some ladies and gentlemen were invited to pay their
respects to Dr. Franklin by candle-light." The gulled guests kept the secret,
and more visitors soon arrived, including the mayor of Nantes: Watson,
Men and Times of the Revolution, pp. 120–2.

To Richard Bache: Extract[7]

Copy: Historical Society of Pennsylvania

Dear Son   Passy Dec 26 1782

You will hear of the progress made towards a Peace from various quarters. It is not yet concluded, and perhaps it may be some time first. But as soon as it is, I hope to be permitted to return home, there being nothing that I more desire, than to spend my last days with my family & lay my bones to rest in America.

To Samuel Cooper

Copy: Archives du Ministère des affaires étrangères; extract: Library of Congress[8]

My dear Friend,   Dated, Passy, Decer. 26. 1782.

I have received several kind Letters from you, which I have not now before me, and which I shall answer more particularly hereafter.[9]

Your Grandson[1] was well not long since, & I hear good Account of him. I hope his Improvements will answer your Expectations.

We have taken some good Steps here towards a Peace. Our Independence is acknowledged, our Boundaries as good & extensive as we demanded; and our Fishery more so than the Congress expected. I hope the whole Preliminaries will be approv'd and with the Definitive Treaty, when made, give entire Satisfaction to our Country. But there are so many Interests to be con-

---

7. Written on what is presumed to be the address sheet from BF's letter to RB of May 14, 1781. (The sheet is filed with sections of that letter, and the address, in BF's hand, specifies that the letter is being sent by Col. Laurens. Col. John Laurens did deliver that letter to the Baches upon his return to America: XXXV, 58n, 421, 560.)

8. The copy, probably prepared for Vergennes, omitted the penultimate paragraph concerning America's "true political interest." The extract, made for inclusion in WTF's edition of BF's writings, omitted the salutation and the first two paragraphs but included the penultimate paragraph, which we quote below in footnote 4.

9. The extant letters from 1782 that BF had so far received are dated March 6, June 15, July 22, and Sept. 6. Cooper wrote most recently on Dec. 21.

1. Samuel Cooper Johonnot.

sidered between Five Nations;[2] & so many Claims to adjust, that I can hardly flatter myself to see the Peace soon concluded, tho' I wish and pray for it, and use my best Endeavours to promote it.

I am extreamly sorry to hear Langage from Americans on this side the Water, and to hear of such Language from your Side, as tends to hurt the good Understanding that has hitherto so happily subsisted between this Court and ours. There seems to be a Party with you that wish to destroy it.[3] If they could succeed, they would do us irreparable Injury. It is our firm Connection with France that gives us Weight with England, and Respect throughout Europe. If we were to break our Faith with this Nation *on whatever Pretence;* England would again trample on us, and every other Nation despise us. We cannot therefore be too much on our guard how we permit the private Resentments of particular Persons to enter into our public Counsels. You will hear much of an interrupted Letter communicated to us by the British Ministry. The Channel ought to be suspected. It may have received Additions and Alterations. But supposing it all genuine, the forward mistaken zeal of an Undersecretary, should not be imputed to the King who has in so many ways provided himself our faithful and firm Friend and Ally.——[4]

I long to see you and my Country once more before I die, being ever, my dear Friend, Yours most affectionately.

(signed) B. FRANKLIN

Copy of a Letter from Benjn. Franklin Esqr. To Dr. Cooper.

2. Great Britain, the United States, France, Spain, and the Netherlands.

3. As Robert Morris had warned on Sept. 27 (above, Letter I), the American public became more suspicious of France once peace negotiations began. This suspicion was strongest in Massachusetts because of concern about sharing with Britain and France in the Newfoundland fisheries: William C. Stinchcombe, *The American Revolution and the French Alliance* (Syracuse, 1969), pp. 189–91.

4. On the extract, WTF corrected "Undersecretary" to "Secretary of Legation." This is more accurate, as it refers to the intercepted letter of Barbé de Marbois discussed in our annotation of BF to Livingston, Oct. 14.

The paragraph deleted from this copy, but present in the extract, reads: "In my opinion the true political interest of America, consists in observing and fulfilling with the greatest exactitude the engagements of our alliance with France; and behaving at the same time towards England so as not entirely to extinguish her hopes of a reconciliation."

From Catharine Greene   ALS: Historical Society of Pennsylvania

My Very Dear Friend   Warwick Decbr the 26th 1782
  I did my Self the Pleasure to write you A few days Since[5] by
Count Segar by his Request, was exceedingly Pleasd with him
and wisht him to Spend a good deal of time with us but they are
So attentive to there Duty that they allow them Selves but little
time to Ramble he Says his wife is Neighbour to you and She
Visets you often you Play Chex with her but you are so gallant
you will not beat the Ladies She Seams to me like an acquaint-
ence as She loves & Visets My good friend me thinks She is like
a Daugter to you we hear the French troops are on board we Pity
them as it must be Very Disagreeable being on board So many
together this Disagreeable Weather but the more they Suffer the
higher our obligation they have been So Polite to the inhabitants
that there Departure is generally Lamented.[6]
  We are happy to hear you injoy So great a Share of health
Pray heaven to Continue it to you and every Blessing—our
family is well except our Daughter Ward who is a bed a week
with a third Son the Branches of that family are well that are left
and Samy makes a good Husband and Son.[7]
  Yr Dear Sister Spends the Winter with her Daugter[8] She has
I hope before this been made happy in a letter from you we heard
of one on the Rhode here but a Persen forwarded it to her She
has long wisht for that Pleasure Mr Willms[9] who Suppose with
you by this will tell you of her health &c when do you Return to
New England.
  Your Friends love for Learning and her anxciety for the Rise-
ing Generation makes her wish that the Bearer Mr President

---

5. On Dec. 5, above.
6. The regiments embarked on Vaudreuil's ships during the first week of
December, but the fleet did not depart Boston until Dec. 24: Rice and Brown,
eds., *Rochambeau's Army,* II, 193.
7. On Dec. 15, Phebe gave birth to Henry, who died the following September. Phebe's husband was Samuel Ward: XXXVI, 202n; John Ward, *A
Memoir of Lieut.-Colonel Samuel Ward . . . with a Genealogy of the Ward
Family* (New York, 1875), p. 17.
8. See Jane Mecom's letter, immediately following.
9. Jonathan Williams, Sr.; see Jane Mecom's letter, below.

Whelock may Succeed in the Business he is upon, he is a Person Universally esteemd and his heart and Soul is in the Semenery he now applies to you for Doubt not he will meet with yr freendship and assistance.[1] Ray is at College Doctr Stiles was to Viset us with his Bride[2] we talk of you and all love you if love would keep People alive what a monstous age would our friend live too.

Do when you have leisure write a few lines to us and any friend that you think would be Pleasd with our Plane manner we Shall be happy to have an oppertunity to Shew every Civility too this from your affectionate and obligd freend   CATY GREENE

Doctr Franklin

Addressed: Doctr. Franklin / Passy Near Paris / France / Hond by Presedent Wheelock

From Jane Mecom   ALS: Historical Society of Pennsylvania

Dear Brother   Cambridge Decr. 26—1782

I wrot to you two months ago From Warwick, which cousen Williams has yet to carry,[3] Afterwards I concluded to come Hither & spend the Winter as most agreable by being more Retiered, & Less Exposed to Doers opening on me which in cold wether Increeces my cough & is very Tedious to me, but on my Arival at Boston I had the maloncholy acount of a Distressing fitt of Illness you have had tho something beter when the mesenger came Away, I am Freequently Reflecting on the Paine you Enduered & the Danger of the Freequent Returns of the disor-

1. John Wheelock, accompanied by his brother James, was en route from Philadelphia (where on Dec. 6 he received a letter of recommendation from Livingston to BF, above) to Boston. They sailed to France from Boston on Jan. 3: Leon B. Richardson, *History of Dartmouth College* (2 vols., Hanover, N.H., 1932), I, 205.

2. On Oct. 17, Ezra Stiles married Mary Checkley. They visited the Greenes around Oct. 28: Edmund S. Morgan, *The Gentle Puritan: a Life of Ezra Stiles, 1727–1795* (New Haven and London, 1962), p. 439.

3. She wrote on Oct. 6. Jonathan Williams, Sr., departed for Europe around Jan. 6: Williams to BF, Jan. 26, 1782 [*i.e.,* 1783], APS.

der you are Liable to; & fearing they may be too hard for you, may God who has hitherto given you so much Health Prevent it, & Restore you to Perfect Health again, if that may not be I hope you will be Endowed with all the submition nesesary on so Trying an ocation.

It was mrs Writes son[4] who tould me of your sickness & of what mortified me very much besides the condition & behavour of that, I had almost sade worthles Litle Anemil Thare, I sinsearly ask your Pardon for Introduscing him to you,[5] & have no other Excuse to make but to Tell you He took me In by being the first that Informed me of a Book that contain'd all your Philosophical & Political Papers,[6] & Runing on so Pritily on won thing & another contained in them that I thought he must be cleaver, Tell me you forgive me this & I will take more care for the future by the way I have never been able to come at a sight of the Book yet, tho I am Tould Dr. Cooper[7] has it, & have sent times without Number after it & have been Put off with some Frivolus Excuse; I would gladly bye won if it were to be Purchased but can't find that it is, I wish my Brother would do me the favour to send me won & I may be so Lucky as to Recive it, I would be a grat Amusement to me & that is the most I have to seek after at Present. My son Collas & Daughter[8] who is all the child I have Left & Jenny mecom (won of my son Benjamin's children)[9] do all in there Power to make me comfortable & I go some times to Boston where I am kindly Entertained by Cousen Williams & famely and see a few other Friends, I have won of

4. Joseph Wright (XXXVI, 223n), son of Patience Wright, left Europe in September and arrived safely in America on Nov. 21, even though his ship foundered off the coast: Monroe H. Fabian, *Joseph Wright: American Artist, 1756–1793* (Washington, D.C., 1985), pp. 41–2.

5. Mecom had recommended John Thayer in October, 1781. BF bought him a suit: XXXV, 642; XXXVI, 272.

6. Probably *Political, Miscellaneous, and Philosophical Pieces* (London, 1779): XXXI, 210–18.

7. Rev. Samuel Cooper.

8. The unlucky seafarer Peter Collas, back from Halifax where he had been captured the preceding year, and Jane Mecom Collas: XXXV, 642.

9. This Jane Mecom, now about seventeen, had been living with the Collases since 1780: I, lxi; XXXIV, 202–3.

my Deceasd Grand Daughters children[1] with me & Expect to Return with it in the spring as there I Live very Pleasantly all the warm wether & can do a number of things nesesary for Him & the children Exept He should git Him a nother wife which I beleve there is no grat Likelihood of.[2] He is so sensable it is Imposable to make up his Lose, she was Indeed an Extroydenary wife. Mr Williams will be able to Ansure you any questions you shall think fitt to Ask concerning me which might have been Tedious for you to have Read had I thought of any thing more to write, my children Joyn in Love an duty with your Affectionat sister JANE MECOM

Addressed: His Excellency Doctr Franklin / Paris

From David Barclay   ALS: University of Pennsylvania Library

Respected Friend.   Youngsbury[3] 27th: of 12th: mo: 1782.

Had it pleased the wise disposer of Events to have permited our inestimable Friend & Colleague, to have lived until this day; I should have been spared the *melancholy,* 'tho *pleasing* reflections of that good man's multiplied great Actions— Doctor Lyttsom a physician of London, has undertaken, & I think has well executed, the Biography of our late dear Friend, in a manner, that, will transmit to Posterity—the *Virtues*—the *Sentiments,* & many of the *Actions* of that Friend to Mankind,[4] nearer to the original than Stewart has his Person on Canvas, 'tho, that, is not esteemed a bad Likeness:[5]

1. Probably Sarah, daughter of Jane Flagg Greene: Van Doren, *Franklin-Mecom*, p. 217.
2. Elihu Greene never remarried: Carl Van Doren, *Jane Mecom: the Favorite Sister of Benjamin Franklin* . . . (New York, 1950), p. 160.
3. Barclay's estate in Hertfordshire: XXI, 364.
4. John Fothergill died on Dec. 26, 1780: XXXIV, 260. John Coakley Lettsom's biography was soon published as *Some Account of the Late John Fothergill, M.D.* (London, 1783). Lettsom, a long-time acquaintance of BF's, had written in 1781 about his larger project, Fothergill's collected works: XXXV, 478–9.
5. Gilbert Stuart's portrait of Fothergill, painted from memory after the doctor's death, is reproduced in XXI, facing p. 365.

I have now the M:S: before me for Correction as one well acquainted with anecdotes of the deceased, & in some instances more intimately than any other person now living— I therefore wish for thy opinion how far it might be proper, at *this juncture*, to let the World see, how much two great Men had laboured to prevent what has happen'd (keeping their Colleague intirely out of view, the *propriety* of which must forceable strike Thee, on *his* own account) I allude to the propriety or impropriety of inserting in the Work, *Hints* for a Conversation, or the paper drawn therefrom, intituled the *Basis* of a *plan* of Reconciliation &c.[6] The favour of thy Opinion speedily on the Subject will oblige me, as the press will [*not*], I fear stand still for a determination. As it is proposed to insert in the work a *few* of Doctor Fothergill's Letters on great or peculiarly useful Subjects, I request to know whether Thou couldst furnish one or two suitable for publick view, if inclined so to do?

I have only to add on *this* Subject, that the pamphlet sent herewith, will be inserted at large, having been compiled by an intimate Friend of Dr. F.s from materials *furnished* by the Dr. but unfortunately so near his end, that, he could not correct the press, nevertheless the work is compiled so much in the very *words* of our deceased Friend, that, those who knew him must acknowledge it to have been *his* performance.[7]

Before I close, I cannot omit this opportunity of telling Thee,

6. In 1774–75, BF, Fothergill, and Barclay engaged in secret negotiations with the British government to avoid war. To that end, BF drew up a list of "Hints" for a conversation about terms likely to produce a durable union: XXI, 360–8. Barclay's revision of the "Hints" was ultimately included in Lettsom's biography: Lettsom, *Some Account of the Late John Fothergill, M.D.*, pp. clviii–clxi. We cannot identify the paper here called "Basis of a plan of Reconciliation," but for the series of documents that grew out of the initial "Hints" see XXI, 378–86; Fox, *Dr. John Fothergill and his Friends . . .*, pp. 393–407.

7. The pamphlet, *An English Freeholder's Address to his Countrymen* (London, 1780), called for Britain to make peace with America. It does not appear in the biography of Fothergill but was included in Lettsom's edition of *The Works of John Fothergill, M.D. . . .* (3 vols., London, 1783–84), III, 31–57, where it is introduced as "the substance of various letters" between Fothergill and Henry Zouch, the "intimate Friend" mentioned here. Zouch was a social reformer and the vicar of Sandal Magna: *DNB*.

that, I trust, it will be unnecessary for me to advocate the cause of any of my Friends on this, or the otherside of the Atlantick who have *Justice* on their side— I have troubled Thee with a few lines in testimoney of my veneration of William Penn;[8] & did I think it necessary, I should not say less on the subject of *Friends* in Pensylvania, but when I consider what our Society have done toward founding a mighty Empire, I have not a doubt but that the *Body* will be consider'd as desireable Subjects, however some among them may have intemperately acted to their own hurt— consequently our known Conscientious Scruples against Oaths, paying Tythes, serving in the Militia or finding substitutes will be made as easy to them, at least as in this Country.

I am respectfully Thy affectionate Friend   DAVID BARCLAY.

From David Barclay

ALS: American Philosophical Society

Youngsbury Herts: [Hertfordshire] 28th:
Respected Friend.   of 12th: mo: 1782

Having been informed of the intention of Lady Juliana Penn to go to Paris, as an *Advocate* for the Representatives of the *Founder* of Pensilvania,[9] I feel my self impress'd with a desire to cast in my Mite, unsolicited, & I trust, unnecessary, because that family have better Advocates—*Justice,* on their side, & my honourable Friend so large a share in the dispensing thereof— I shall add only, that, could I have believed my presence at Passy would have added one tittle to the advantage of the Descendants of William Penn, I should chearfully have offer'd my personal Service.

I am respectfully Thy affectionate Friend.   DAVID BARCLAY.

P.S. I expect this will be delivered by my intimate & worthy Penn Richard Penn, who, I think, has the amplitude of heart & the nobility of Sentiment of his great Ancestor, whose memory he venerates.[1] I trust, & hope we may live to meet on *this* spot to-

8. See Barclay's letter of Dec. 28.
9. See Samuel Vaughan to BF, Dec. 16.
1. Richard was the grandson of William Penn, as was his cousin John, the son of Juliana Penn.

gether & to brighten the Chain—[2] Be assured my fattest Calf shall be killed, & my oldest Mutton produced—   D. B.

Youngsbury 27/12 mo. 82.

Benjamin Franklin

From Le Couteulx & Cie. ᴸˢ: Historical Society of Pennsylvania

Monsieur   Paris le 28: Xbre. 1782.

Nous avons Eu L'honneur de vous écrire le 6 novembre pour vous communiquer la Lettre que nous avions reçu de Monsieur Morris portant ordre de vous demander Si vous aviez la possibilité de remettre en nos mains une somme de 2,500,000. *l.t.* tournois pour en Suivre les dispositions que le dit sieur Morris nous avoit ordonné pour Compte des Etats unis de L'amérique; vous nous avez fait l'honneur de nous répondre que les circonstances ne vous permettoient pas de prendre un parti à cet égard, et que vous nous feriez celui de nous prévenir dès que vous seriez dans le cas de nous donner une résolution affirmative ou négative.[3]

Comme il S'est passé près de deux mois depuis cette Epoque, que d'ailleurs les ordres qui nous ont été confiés par Mr. Morris Sont de nature a ne pouvoir être effectués Si les espérances de paix Se réalisent nous avons cru, Monsieur, devoir vous remettre cette affaire Sous les yeux et vous demander de nouveau S'il vous sera possible de tenir à notre disposition tout ou partie de la Susditte somme de 2,500,000. *l.t.* afin de pouvoir d'après votre réponse donner des ordres en Espagne, et qu'ils y arrivent avant que La paix en empêche l'exécution.[4]

2. A favorite expression of Barclay's friend John Fothergill and of ʙꜰ; the chain was the chain of friendship: xxxi, 124n.

3. Both the Nov. 6 letter and ʙꜰ's response are missing. The firm was responding to the letter they received from Morris dated Sept. 27 (*Morris Papers*, vi, 452–3); see Morris' letter to ʙꜰ of the same date, telling him to pay the firm $500,000 (roughly equivalent to the figure they quote in *livres tournois*).

4. ʙꜰ's Dec. 31 reply, acknowledged in Le Couteulx & Cie.'s letter of Jan. 1, 1783, is missing. Eventually more than 2,000,000 *l.t.* from ᴊᴀ's Dutch loan

Nous avons L'honneur d'être avec respect Monsieur Vos très humbles obt. serv.   Le Couteulx &c

From Benjamin Putnam   ALS: American Philosophical Society

                          Paris, l'hotel Danemark, Rué Jacob.
Honble. Sir,   Decr. 28th. 1782.

I feel hurt at the thought of troubling you so immediately—my forgetfulness of yesterday & Engagements today, must be my Appology for the Occasion & Mode. I am bound for North Carolina; in my Passage, I shall take the Circuit of New-Providence from Expectations of procuring by Purchase, or Address a Clearance of a Cargo of Tobacco from that Island to Europe; and which Papers, I shall take into Carolina with me; & which, as the Gulph Stream Sweeps that Shore, will Effectually protect my Vessel, she being under the Imperial Flag, in her Return to France. Any Assistance Sir, you'll please to give me to facilitate my Success in this, should it be but a bear Certificate to the Governor, of my being a Subject of the United States, will be acknowledged with warm gratitude.

Should I not be able to see Mr. Chardon, Mr. Ridley has very politely offer'd to take my Affairs into his Charge, & carry on any necessary Prosecution which their nature may require: Permit me Sir, in this Case, to entreat your Excellency's Counsel & Protection; as thro you, alone, neither Mr. Ridley or myself can only be known, in the *one Case*, in which, *Congress has interfer'd.* And which appears to me only to be necessary to be regularly laid before the French Court in order to obtain Decision; & restore to me, my Property.[5]

---

was transferred to the company for Morris' use: *Morris Papers*, VII, 23–4, 403–4n, 698.

5. WTF had recently introduced Putnam to Daniel-Marc-Antoine Chardon, the *procureur général* of the *conseil des finances pour les prises en mer* (XXIX, 164). Putnam wished to rebut testimony given by French naval officers to the *conseil des prises* on the legal ownership of the schooner *Terrible* and to appeal a decision of the Guadeloupe Admiralty Court. Congress had supported this appeal in a resolve passed in September, 1779. Ridley agreed to repre-

I am Sir, with every Duty & Respect Your Excellency's most Obedient and most Humble Servant[6]   BENJAMIN PUTNAM.

His Excellency Doct. Franklin

Addressed: His Excellency Doctor Franklin, / Minister Plenipotentiary to the / Court of France, / Passey

Notation: Benj. Putnam Paris Decr 28. 1782

From Vergennes
AL: Library of Congress

Lundi 30. December 1782.

M. de Vergennes prie Monsieur francklin si sa santé peut le Lui permettre de vouloir bien se rendre demain mardi a Versailles a lheure qui Lui sera la plus Commode, si Ce pouvoit Etre a neuf heures du matin, il y auroit moins de risque dEtre interrompû. M. de Vergennes auroit a entretenir Monsieur francklin dun objet tres interressant pour la Cause Commune. M. de Vergennes a lhonneur de renouveller a Monsieur francklin, lassurance de son sincere attachement.

To Vergennes
AL (draft):[7] Library of Congress

Passy Dec. 30. 82

Mr Franklin will have the Honour of Waiting upon M. le Comte de Vergennes, tomorrow Morning at 9 oClock, agreable to the Notice just received. He begs leave to assure M. le Comte of his most sincere Respect

---

sent Putnam's interest in the matter of the *Terrible:* XXXIV, 369–70; WTF to Chardon, December, [1782] (APS); Putnam to WTF, [Jan.] 7, 1783 (APS).

6. Putnam sailed from Bordeaux in January, intending to return to settle his affairs once the papers for his claim could be sent from Guadeloupe. He told WTF that the comte d'Estaing had promised to support his case if the *conseil des prises* ruled against him: Putnam to WTF, [Jan.] 7, 1783 (APS).

7. Written on the bottom of Vergennes' letter, the preceding document.

513

From Richard Bache

ALS: American Philosophical Society

Dear & Hond: Sir   Philadelphia Decr. 30th. 1782.

The Bearer of this, Mr. Benjamin Morris, is the youngest Son of your old Friend Mr. Samuel Morris, lately deceased;[8] he visits Europe upon a plan of Business; I believe him to be a deserving young Man; as such, and from the regard I have for his Family Connections here, I beg leave to introduce him to your Friendship & Civilities,—I am ever Dear Sir Your affectionate Son

RICH: BACHE

Dr. Franklin

Addressed: The Honble. / Dr. Benjamin Franklin / Minister Plenipoy: from the United / States of No: America / at / Passy / Favored by Mr. Morris

From John Dickinson[9]

ALS: American Philosophical Society

Sir,   Philadelphia Decr. 30th—1782

I cannot deny Myself the Pleasure of introducing to the Honor of your Acquaintance Mr. Benjamin Morris, the youngest son of your Friend Mr. Samuel Morris.

Your Regard for the Memory of his Father, and his own Merit, will, I am persuaded, place him before You in that Light, which his Relations desire.

I am with perfect Esteem sir, your most obedient & hble servt.

JOHN DICKINSON

His Excellency Benjamin Franklin Esquire

---

8. Samuel Morris (II, 376n) died on March 31, 1782, and was interred in Quaker's Burial Ground on Arch Street: Robert C. Moon, *The Morris Family of Philadelphia* . . . (3 vols., Philadelphia, 1898), I, 260. Benjamin (1760–1841) was in France by the following February, but was soon urged by his brother to return to the Charleston merchant house of Thomas Morris & Co. He would later serve in the Pa. legislature, own an iron mine and works, and sit as an associate judge of Berks County, Pa.: *ibid.*, II, 441, 452–4.

9. Dickinson had recently been elected president of the Pa. Supreme Executive Council: *ANB.*

Addressed: His Excellency / Benjamin Franklin Esqr / Minister Plenipotentiary / for the United States / of America / Passy. / per Mr. B. Morris

Notation: John Dickinson Dec. 30. 1782.

From Henry Laurens
L:[1] University of Pennsylvania Library

Hotel d'York Monday 30th. Decemr: 1782.[2]
Mr. Laurens presents his Compliments to Doctor Franklin and requests the honor of his company at dinner on thursday next at 3 oClock.

From Benjamin Vaughan
ALS: American Philosophical Society

My Dear sir,   Paris, Decr 31, 1782.
I inclose you an extract of a letter from Dr. Priestley to my brother William, on the subject of his late supposed discovery.[3]

At the same time I inform you that I have procured a small glass jar, for the purpose of observing the cause of the phœnomenon of the small bits of tea-leaves, which you find whirled to the *centre* of the bottom of your breakfast cup, when you stir your tea.

I had told you "at a hazard", that as there were different velocities in the different ringlets of fluid that moved about the axis of your cup, if at any time the motion of your bitt of tea-leaf was checked, the different ringlets of fluid I thought might have an opportunity of exhibiting their difference of force, and that the outer ones might have balance enough in their favor to enable

1. In the hand of Henry Laurens, Jr.
2. Laurens sent a separate invitation to WTF on the same day (APS). He was still in ill health, and on Jan. 9 he asked WTF to procure passports for himself, his son, and a servant to return to Bath. They left on Jan. 11: *Laurens Papers*, XVI, xlv, 126–7.
3. The extract is undated. In it, Priestley expresses doubt about his calculation of "the weight of water in air." For his description of the experiment to convert purified water into "permanent air" see the extract of his letter to BF of Dec. 12.

them to incline the tea-leaf inwards, towards the axis of the cup.— You then bid me observe bodies in the situation you described, and see whether my explanation would suit the fact.

I have accordingly made some observations by means of my small glass jar, as follows.— First, bodies whirling at the *surface* of a fluid, seem to move as carelessly as the fluid itself; generally proceeding circularly, sometimes where the motion is very slow yielding to the attraction of the glass at the side, and perhaps at other times after a long continued motion inclining to the axis of the jar. I observed a similar indifference in the motion of the particles whirling about, *lower down,* in the body of the fluid. Particles however which are *heavier* than the fluid, and which if stopped at the surface or watched in the course of their descent, appear indifferent in all their horizontal movements; yet, when they descend, and come to touch the bottom of the vessel, soon begin to shew an inclination to the centre.

This pretty *sand* of a blue color, which I inclose for you, will shew two of the cases which I allude to. Upon throwing it into the fluid which I had moved briskly round with the feather of a quill, a part of it remained at the top, where it moved round like a portion of the fluid; while that which descended, soon tended to the axis at the bottom of the jar. As the jar which I use, has a very steep bottom pointed upwards, this tendency to the centre lasts only while the whirl of the fluid is considerable; for afterwards & long before the fluid has lost its motion, the particles of sand will slide down the ascent and fall to the sides of the vessel, except in parts where it lodges.— To vary the experiment, I threw in pieces of a breakfast roll. The crusty parts will swim at the top, some pieces of the crum will descend, and a mixture of both will take any level of the water at pleasure, or change that level slowly enough for the purpose of observation. At the bottom I saw a great deal of your phœnomenon of the tea leaves; but it is only at the bottom.— At the bottom, when the water is first agitated, the crums and sand together, make an amusing appearance; for while some particles of the sand cover the apex of the bottom of the vessel, the rest of the sand flies about and above the apex, and the crums of bread fly round the whole, like birds darting and skimming round a little mountain that is laboring under some commotion.

On the whole, I am inclined to think that the principles which I guessed at, may turn out to be the right principles, for explaining all the appearances at the bottom of my jar.— If a boat is put in motion, and the moving power is made to act more on one side than the other, the boat will decline from the stronger moving power; that is, when the rudder by being turned to one side of the boat, clogs that side, and suffers the other side to move quicker, the boat in this situation declining from the greater force, turns inwards towards the retarded side.— Again. If I cut a round slice of cork, and place it on the surface of any fluid; and if I place a ruler in the direction of a tangent to the side of the round piece of cork, and draw a lancet swiftly along the edge of that ruler, the consequence will be, that the lancet striking the edge of the cork will drive it off nearly at right angles from the ruler.

A short application will shew perhaps, the action of these principles, in the case in question.— When the *heavy* body once touches the bottom of the jar, it loses some of that whirl, which it once had in equal degree with the fluid; and is therefore left liable to the impulse of the fluid which is still whirling. The blow it receives on its outer side, being greater than that which it receives on the inner side, its motion begins to acquire a tendency inwards, towards the center of the bottom. Being by its weight often sunk and rubbed against the bottom, the effect of this impulse is often repeated; and therefore if the impulse is strongly enough applied, the body will distinctly approach the axis, in spite of the slope upwards in the bottom.— Where the body is only a *little* heavier than the fluid, as in the case of the crum of a roll, the approach to the centre is less decided; because the body having a great tendency to swim while the water is moving swiftly, it touches seldomer, and with less force, than if it were heavier.

The *form* of the particles in question may likewise have great influence, as well as their weight; as in the case of your tea-leaves; which, being usually oblong, afford a powerful lever to the action of the fluid.— It is also not to be forgotten, that the effect will always seem increased by the *smallness of the vessel;* because in small concentric circles taken at a given distance from each other, the *difference* of velocity will be much greater, than in large concentric circles, placed at a similar distance from each other.

At the *surface* of the fluid, there are yet two farther circumstances worthy of remark. First; if the swimming body projects out of the fluid, the resistance it will meet with from the air will a little retard its motion and when this motion is revived by the impulse of fluid placed at different distances from the axis, it may be seen to tend some little towards the axis, even at the surface. And next; at the surface, we see the operation of two other principles; namely attraction to the sides, and attraction between the swimming bodies respecting each other.— Perhaps there is a little attraction subsisting between the particles at the bottom; but it is less than at the top, where at best it is very feeble. The intangling of the particles one with another, may be of more consequence; for they may assume the form & nature of a lever, and in consequence become much more seriously acted upon, than when they are separate.

So much at present for these tea-leaves.— When we were talking on the subject of them, I remember some one stated an assertion that the heaviest bodies had always most disposition to quit the centre, in the case of centrifugal forces. I mention it by the by, that I suspect this position was not truly understood in the quarter whence it came. The heavy body does not *tend* to quit the centre with more velocity than the light body; but, in consequence of having more force to overcome obstacles, it eventually moves more effectually, & therefore faster.— If I tie one end of a string to the centre of a board and move that board swiftly round its centre, the momentum given to the particles of the string will not be sufficient to keep it stretched; but if I fasten a bullet to the other end of the string, the momentum of a heavy bullet not being to be put in comparison with the disposition of the string to remain curled & crooked, the string will become both straightened and stretched. In this situation however, every particle in the string gets as far from the centre, *as its circumstances permit;* but the bullet having most momentum from its contents, and most sphere of action from the parts of the string to which it is fastened, takes the most circuit in its motion.

There was another fact suggested in the conversation, not more difficult to explain than the above. If water and lead are supposed to be put into different tubes which have each one of their ends joined in a common centre, if the whole is put in motion from that centre, we expect that the lead will be found at the farther extremities of the tubes, instead of the water; and very properly so; for the bullet without tending to have a swifter motion than the water has nevertheless power to *displace* the water when the water becomes stationary, and to put itself in its stead at the farther end of the tube. If the tubes were indefinitely prolonged, the water or even a piece of cork in the water, would go on just as fast as the bullet, other things being equal; but the moment a stop is put to their progression, then the bullet, adding its force to that column of water of which it makes a part, overcomes all the other columns, and drives on to the obstacle, as the only way of securing its own rest.— In this, the bullet acts precisely as it would in a case of gravity. Where there is no resistance, it moves no faster than a feather towards the earth. But when resistance occurs, though it is only from a medium as thin as the air, a difference is immediately perceived in favor of the motion of the bullet. And the moment a bullet is put upon the surface of water at rest, though the bullet begins with being stationary, like the water, yet it will penetrate and displace the water, as long as it finds water and passage left for its motion.

As to a third supposed fact, which I think was mentioned, namely that of separating bodies of different gravities spread through a fluid, by including them in a vessel to which a centrifugal force is given, it seems only another consequence of these principles. The heaviest bodies without tending faster from the centre in their origin than the lighter ones, yet by moving more powerfully, will always (where fair play is given them) be found at the bottom of the vessel; that is, as far as possible from the centre of motion. And as the centrifugal force may easily be made more violent than the force of gravity, separations of the particles may possibly be made in this way, which gravity in the common way of its operation cannot effect.

None of these principles, I apprehend, will be found at all inconsistent with the fact of our tea-leaves. Originally, these leaves set out (not with a centrifugal force resembling the other cases,) but with much the same force that belonged to that *precise ringlet of fluid in which it stood*, when the parts received their first motion; and this force, as soon as gravity carried them to the bottom and exposed them to friction, they soon lost. The inclination they afterwards acquired towards the centre, depended on principles still more different from the common centrifugal force, than the first motion they had.— It is easy however to imagine this force combined with a centrifugal force, by supposing a whirling motion given to a fluid that has light and heavy particles immersed in it; and, when the phœnomenon of the tea-leaves &c. has begun to work, then to suppose the vessel and its contents swiftly swung round a common centre. The whirling and centrifugal motions will then be exhibited on the same bodies.

As I have seldom found any of these questions fail to yield, sooner or later, to a little patience and thinking, I should now turn to the discussion of the cause of the agitation attending the surfaces of oil & water, when they are in contact with each other in any quantity, and affected by a vibrating motion; but at present, the time of both of us is, I hope, better occupied. At some future moment of your leisure, and when you are less fatigued than at present, I shall beg to call your attention to this & other subjects, which you have started in your writings and conversation. In the mean time, I am, my dearest sir, your most devoted, affectionate, & grateful,   BENJA: VAUGHAN

Franklin: Proposed New Version of the Bible

Reprinted from William Temple Franklin, ed., *Memoirs of the Life and Writings of Benjamin Franklin* . . . (3 vols., 4to, London, 1817–18), III, 308–9.

[1782 or after][4]

PROPOSED NEW VERSION OF THE BIBLE.

To the Printer of * * * *

SIR,

IT is now more than 170 years since the translation of our common English Bible. The language in that time is much

4. Dated on the basis of the first sentence. The King James Bible was first printed in 1611; 1782 is more than 170 years later.

changed, and the stile being obsolete, and thence less agreeable, is perhaps one reason why the reading of that excellent book is of late much neglected. I have therefore thought it would be well to procure a new version, in which, preserving the sense, the turn of phrase and manner of expression should be modern. I do not pretend to have the necessary abilities for such a work myself; I throw out the hint for the consideration of the learned: and only venture to send you a few verses of the first chapter of Job, which may serve as a sample of the kind of version I would recommend.   A. B.

PART OF THE FIRST CHAPTER OF JOB MODERNIZED.

OLD TEXT.

Verse 6 Now there was a day when the sons of God came to present themselves before the Lord, and Satan came also among them.

7 And the Lord said unto Satan, Whence comest thou? Then Satan answered the Lord, and said, From going to and fro in the earth, and from walking up and down in it.

8 And the Lord said unto Satan, Hast thou considered my servant Job, that there is none like him in the earth, a perfect and an upright man, one that feareth God, and escheweth evil?

9 Then Satan answered the Lord, and said, Doth Job fear God for nought?

NEW VERSION.

Verse 6 And it being *levée* day in heaven, all God's nobility came to court, to present themselves before him; and Satan also appeared in the circle, as one of the ministry.

7 And God said to Satan, You have been some time absent; where was you? And Satan answered, I have been at my country-seat, and in different places visiting my friends.

8 And God said, Well, what think you of Lord Job? You see he is my best friend, a perfectly honest man, full of respect for me, and avoiding every thing that might offend me.

9 And Satan answered, Does your Majesty imagine that his good conduct is the effect of mere personal attachment and affection?

10 Hast thou not made an hedge about his house, and about all that he hath on every side? Thou hast blessed the work of his hands, and his substance is increased in the land:

11 But put forth thine hand now, and touch all that he hath, and he will curse thee to thy face.

10 Have you not protected him, and heaped your benefits upon him, till he is grown enormously rich?

11 Try him; only withdraw your favor, turn him out of his places, and with-hold his pensions; and you will soon find him in the opposition.

Passport for Cartel Ships[5]

Passy, printed by Benjamin Franklin, 1782. Printed form and AD (draft):[6] American Philosophical Society

To all Captains and Commanders of Vessels of War, Privateers, and Letters of Marque, belonging to the United States of America. [1782]
WHEREAS an Act of the Parliament of Great Britain has been lately passed for the Exchange of American Prisoners;[7] and in pursuance thereof, sundry Vessels are by that Government engaged as Transports to convey to America those Prisoners of War who have been confined in the Goals of England and Ireland; of which Vessels the [*blank*] is one, commanded by [*blank*] mounting [*blank*] Guns, navigated by [*blank*] Men, and bound for the Port of [*blank*]
THIS is therefore to require of you, or any of you who may

5. William Hodgson informed BF on April 14 that transport ships for exchanged American prisoners would soon be ready, and requested BF to send passports. BF did so by April 20: XXXVII, 153, 181–2. This blank form, the only example of the passport that has been located, must have been printed before April 20 and should have been included in vol. 37.

6. The form is reproduced in Luther S. Livingston, *Franklin and His Press at Passy* (New York, 1914), facing p. 91. It differs slightly in wording and punctuation from the draft.

7. Burke's bill: XXXVII, 32n.

meet with the said Vessel, either in her Voyage from England to America, or in her Passage from thence to any Port in the British Dominions, that you do not detain or molest her, or suffer any Injury to be done to her, or to the People belonging to her, or to their Effects; but that, on the contrary, you afford the said Vessel and People belonging to her, every friendly Aid or Assistance they may stand in Need of. And the same is requested of the Commanders of armed Vessels belonging to any of the Allies or Friends of the said United States.

GIVEN at Passy, this [*blank*] Day of [*blank*] 1782.

> *Minister Plenipotentiary of the United States*
> *of America to the Court of France.*

Notation by William Temple Franklin: Pass-port for the Cartel

From Samuel Cooper

AL: American Philosophical Society

Sir,   [1782?]

Before you left America, I believe I mention'd to you the great Losses I had sustain'd from the Enemy, in my Household Furniture, Books, Debts from Persons who took Refuge in Howe's Army &c.[8] so that take all together, I am perhaps, as large a Sufferer, in Proportion to what I possess'd, as any one in this Town; nor would two thousand Pounds Lawf: Money make me Whole.[9] I had before full little enough to make me easy in my usual Manner of living, which was not excessive, and this Loss is the heavier in advancing Age. I have made no Application to any on this Side the Water, knowing the many Calls upon them for public Services & private Wants in this Time of great Exertion & common Distress. Many of my former Friends I honorably lost by my through, undisguis'd Attachment to the Rights of my Country & those who espous'd them. If they are establish'd I am still

---

8. XXII, 387–8.

9. Cooper was permitted, however, to purchase on favorable terms furniture sequestered from the houses of Loyalists: Charles W. Akers, *The Divine Politician: Samuel Cooper and the American Revolution in Boston* (Boston, 1982), p. 214.

happy. But as you will have a principal Hand in Negotiations, Should Britain come to Terms with us, I hope she will be induc'd to make some Compensation to American Sufferers; On that or some similar honorable Occasion you may be of particular Service to your Friend.— This in Confidence.

From ———— Favier[1]   ALS: University of Pennsylvania Library

Bon Maître   [1782?][2]

Mes malheurs ne vous Sont pas connus, et si l'on vous en a dit quelque chose, ce ne peut être que sous un paliatif. J'ai regret de ne vous en avoir rien dit dans le temps où je le pouvois, ou vous l'avoir donné par écrit et bien détaillé, ce tissu de miseres! Aujourd'hui on débite que vous m'avez renvoyé parce que je vous ai fait des torts, et cette calomnie m'a atteint à Senlis, où je travaillois paisiblement en attendant une paix prochaine. Je vous prie très-humblement de me donner un certificat qui démente une telle accusation, laquelle ne manqueroit pas de me faire un tort irréparable. Je Suis encore Sans ouvrage et manquant de tout; ma misere est telle, que j'ai cherché à m'engager, mais on n'a pas voulu de moi à cause de mon âge. On dit plus, on dit que je Suis un espion de police; mais qui est-ce qui me donne de Si mauvais noms? Des coquins et des espions eux-mêmes, payés pour ça. Pourquoi cherche-t-on à vous nuire de la Sorte? C'est ce que j'ignore; mais mr. Pierres, imprimeur de la police,[3] n'est pas de mes amis; il protege l'auteur de cette calomnie, contre

1. The *compagnon imprimeur* recommended to BF the year before for his work on the *Histoire générale de la Chine:* XXXV, 305n. The work was published by the firm of Philippe-Denis Pierres.

2. In the absence of other clues, we place this in 1782 because of Favier's reference to waiting for the peace. He had long hoped to emigrate to America: XXXV, 305n.

3. Philippe-Denis Pierres (XXXV, 635n) was named official printer of the police in 1778, at the request of the former printer, Louis-François de la Tour: George B. Watts, *Philippe-Denis Pierres, First Printer Ordinary of Louis XVI* (Charlotte, N.C., [1966]), p. 11. Watts based much of his account on Pierres's "Autobiographie, 1741–An VI," an unpublished manuscript at the Bibliothèque du Cercle de la Librairie, Paris.

lequel je donna un placet, le 10 mars de cette même année, au Lieutenant de police,[4] duquel je n'ai eu aucune réponse. Cette histoire diabolique est dans ma tête, Sans qu'il y manque une Syllabe, et elle Contient au moins Six feuilles in-40. de Saint-Augustin. J'ai l'honneur d'être, avec le plus profond respect, du meilleur des Maîtres, le plus humble et le plus obéissant et le plus zélé de Ses Serviteurs   FAVIER

Addressed: A Monsieur / Monsieur le Docteur franklin, / Ministre Plénipotentiaire des Etat-Unis / de l'Amérique Septentrionale, à la Cour / de france, à Passy, en Son hôtel. / A Passy-les-Paris

Notation: Favier.

From Anne-Catherine de Ligniville Helvétius

AL: American Philosophical Society

ce lundi [1782?][5]

Mon cher, ami je Comte vous avoire adiné mecredi, avec votre enfant, jespere avoire Mr. le Comte destin [d'Estaing] bonjour je vous embrasee de toute mes force, elle sont bien grande pour vous.

Proposé a Mr. de chaumon de venire je ne lui donnerai que du rie, et de la gelée.

Addressed: a Monsieur / Monsieur franklin

4. Lenoir, head of the Paris police, was related to Pierres: Watts, *Philippe-Denis Pierres . . .* , p. 11.

5. I. Minis Hays catalogued this letter as [1782] and we leave it tentatively under that date, although we now realize that it could have been written earlier. The dating hinges on when d'Estaing was in Paris. He returned to France in January, 1781, and stayed until early November, 1782, when he left for Spain. He was back by the end of April, 1783; if the "enfant" mentioned in the present letter refers to BFB rather than WTF, this letter would date from after BFB's return from Geneva in July, 1783.

From Mademoiselle ——— Juppin[6]

AL: American Philosophical Society

[1782 or after][7]

Mon papa lon ma priée de vous demander, si les papiers que je vous envoyes ont quelque valeur, si la personne a qui ils appartiennent peut esperer en tirer quelque argent, et sil ne faut pas ladresser a Mr Jay.

Je vous presente mon papa, mes civilites, et amities et mes compliments a Mr votre petit fils.

From Le Roy: Two Letters

(I) and (II) ALS: American Philosophical Society

I.

ce Lundy [1782?][8]

J'ai vu hier Mon Illustre Docteur a Versailles de belles Dames qui s'ont desoleès d'avoir èté Si Long-tems Sans avoir eu lhonneur de vous voir ce sont Made. Dangiviller[9] et Made. De Flahaut[1] cette jolie personne qui parle si Joliment anglois. Elles

---

6. The Brillons' former governess: XXVIII, 8n.

7. Dated on the basis of our tentative reading of the name she gives at the end of the first paragraph. While "Jay" is the only name that makes sense to us, the initial letter looks almost identical to both her lowercase *l* and *s*.

8. After Mme d'Angiviller's marriage; see the following note.

9. Elisabeth-Josèphe de La Borde (1725–1808). In 1781 (the month given variously as August, September, or December) she left her first husband (an arranged marriage) to marry her longtime *ami intime*, Charles-Claude Flahaut de La Billarderie, comte d'Angiviller (Angivilliers) (XXXV, 529n). With this marriage her salon, already a rendezvous for the physiocrats, became "un bureau d'esprit" for the *philosophes*, with Diderot and d'Alembert in attendance: *DBF* under Angiviller, both husband and wife; Jacques Silvestre de Sacy, *Le Comte d'Angiviller, dernier directeur général des batiments du roi* ([Paris, 1953]), pp. 22–32, 157–63; Mathurin-François-Adolphe de Lescure, ed., *Correspondance secrète inédite sur Louis XVI, Marie-Antoinette: la cour et la ville de 1777 à 1792* (2 vols., Paris, 1866), I, 431.

1. Adélaïde-Marie-Emile Filleul (1761–1836) married in 1779 Charles-François Flahaut de La Billarderie, comte de Flahaut (1728–1793?), a general and later intendant of the royal gardens. She and the comtesse d'An-

ont fait la partie d'aller vous demander du Thé Vendredy prochain à cinq heures du soir Et comme vous avez dans ce moment cy plus d'une chose à faire J'ai lhonneur de vous prévenir de leur projet afin que Si elles avoient mal pris leur tems vous ayez la bonté de me le mander pour que je le leur fasse Savoir. J'espere mon Illustre Docteur qu'on vous aura dit que J'ai été vous voir Vendredy dernier dans la Matinée on me dit que vous etiez allè à Versailles adieu Mon Illustre Docteur vous savez combien Je vous suis bien Véritablement et bien Sincèrement attaché pour la Vie   LE ROY

Addressed: a Monsieur / Monsieur Franklin Ministre / Plenipotentiaire des Etats Unis / de LAmèrique Septentrionale / a Passy / LR maison du Notaire

Notation: Le Roy

II.

                                        ce Vendredy matin [1782?]
Nos Dames viennent dapprendre mon Illustre docteur que vous allez dîner en ville elles craignent en conséquence que cela ne vous dérange de revenir aussi promtement chez vous pour leur donner du Thé avant cinq heures elles me chargent ainsi, sil est vrai, qu'elles n'ayent pas reçu un faux avis, de vous prier de ne pas vous gêner par elles elles attendront un autre jour où elles pourront prendre du Thé chez Vous sans vous déranger. Vous savez mon Illustre Docteur combien Je vous suis passionnément attaché   LE ROY

Addressed: A Monsieur / Monsieur le Docteur Franklin

---

giviller were sisters-in-law as well as good friends and neighbors in Paris. She was the mistress of Talleyrand, by whom she had a son in 1785. She became a novelist of some repute, publishing her first book in 1794. In 1802, she married José-Maria de Souza-Botelho (1758–1825), the Portuguese minister to France (1802–1805): *DBF* under Flahaut de La Billarderie; Sacy, *Le Comte d'Angiviller . . .*, pp. 7, 159–60; Catherine M. Bearne, *Four Fascinating French Women . . .* (London, 1910), 23–141; Quérard, *France littéraire* under Souza and Souza-Botelho.

From the Abbé Gabriel Bonnot de Mably[2]

AL: American Philosophical Society

[1782][3]

La personne dont l'abbé de Mably a eu l'honneur de parler à Monsieur jay, et qu'il vouloit aussi avoir l'honneur de recommander à monsieur franklyn, s'appelle Rochas, c'est un jeune homme âgé de vingt quatre ans, il est bien né d'une famille de riches marchands de Romans en dauphiné. Il y a trois ans qu'il est à Marseille pour s'instruire et se former au Commerce de Droguiste-Epicier. Sa conduite a toujours été tres bonne, et ce qui donne à l'abbé de mably une tres bonne idée de son coeur et de son esprit, c'est l'envie extrême qu'il a d'aller s'etablir à Boston, et d'y porter une pacotille qui servira de fondement à son commerce. La recommandation de Monsieur franklyn et de Monsieur jay est du plus grand prix pour lui, et l'abbé de Mably sera penetré de la plus vive reconnoissance pour les bontés dont ces Messieurs voudront bien honorer le sieur Rochas.

Notation: l'abbé de Mably

From the Abbesse Marie du Saint Esprit[4]

ALS: American Philosophical Society

De notre Pauvre monastre De L'avé

Monsieur   Maria de paris 1782

Le respect et La reconnoissance nous font également un Devoir de vous offrir nos vœux fasse Le Ciel que vous Jouissiez D'une santé aussy parfaite que nous Le Desirons. Nous Le Demandons avec ardeur. Daigné monsieur être persuadé De L'interest que nous y prenons. La Confiance que nous avons en votre

2. The only extant letter from the abbé who in December sent BF his most recent publication care of Chalut and Arnoux; see their letter of Dec. 17, above.

3. The allusion to John Jay places this letter sometime after the Jays' arrival in Paris on June 23 (XXXVII, 343).

4. The abbesse here renews an annual appeal on behalf of her community of Franciscan nuns; see XXXVI, 353.

Charité nous fait espérer La Continuation de vos bienfaits. Nous vous supplions d'agréer Le profond respect avec Lequel nous avons L'honneur dêtre Monsieur Votre tres humble et tres obeissante servante   SŒUR MARIE DU ST ESPRIT ABBESSE

From Balthazar-Georges Sage

AL: American Philosophical Society

[c. 1782?]

Sage salue et Embrasse Monsieur francklin, auquel il envoye un ouvrage D'un de ses amis qui l'a prié de Lui offrir. La personne qui lui remettra Ce Billet est un medecin de ses amis qui accompagne Les princes de Carlath[5] qui desirent avoir Lhonneur De Voir Monsieur francklin.

Addressed: A Monsieur / Monsieur francklin / De Lacademie des / sciences

The Abbé Alessandro (Agostino) Beliardi's Account of Franklin's Remedy for a Cold[6]   AD: Bibliothèque nationale

[1782 or after]

M. Holcker a appris du docteur francklin qu'une petite cuiellerée à café de quinquinà jettée dans le fond d'un goblet où l'on verse

5. It is impossible to say with any certainty which of the Carlaths or Kolowrats (Kolowraths), aristocrats of Bohemia, are meant here. In the fall and winter of 1782, Franz-Joseph Kolowrath-Liebstensky (-Liebsteinsky), chamberlain to Joseph II and then Grand Chancellor of Bohemia, was in Paris where he was inducted into the *Amis réunis:* Charles Porset, *Les Philalèthes et les Convents de Paris: Une politique de la folie* (Paris, 1996), pp. 13–14, 568–9, 632–5; René Le Forestier, *La Franc-Maçonnerie templière et occultiste aux XVIIIe et XIXe siècles* (Paris and Leuven, 1970), pp. 733–4. Léopold de Kolowrath-Krakowski (1726–1809) was also in Paris in the last months of 1782: Gustave Bord, *La Franc-Maçonnerie en France des origines à 1815* (Paris, 1908), pp. 351–2.

6. Born in Italy, the abbé (1723–1803) began his career in service to the Spanish ambassador to the Vatican. He became *agent général du commerce et*

un peu de lait pour Les bien meler ensemble, ensuitte remplissant le reste du goblet avec du lait, et en avalant un verre le matin à jeune, un autre en se mettant à table pour dinner, et un troisieme en se couchant, que çest un excellant remede pour guerir un gròs rhume en trois jours.

Franklin and Jacques Finck: Agreement[7]

D:[8] American Philosophical Society

[before January 1, 1783]

Le Mtre. d'Hotel entreroit le 1r. Janvr. 83. et agiroit en cette Qualité de concert avec le Cuisinier actuel[9] pendant 2 ou 3 Mois pour se mettre au fait de la maniere de vivre de M. Franklin, ainsi que de la Depense que cette vie exige. Il aura des Gages à raison

---

de la marine for France in Spain, and during several trips to Paris worked closely with Choiseul on Franco-Spanish trade. He was one of several supporters who joined the minister in exile at Chanteloup: *Dizionario Biografico degli Italiani* (60 vols. to date, Rome, 1960–); *Repertorium der diplomatischen Vertreter*, II, 266–7.

This account of BF's remedy appears in the abbé's notes and journals, which are described in Pierre Muret, "Les papiers de l'abbé Béliardi et les relations commerciales de la France et de l'Espagne au milieu du XVIIIe siècle (1757–1770)," in *Revue d'histoire moderne et contemporaine* IV (1902–03), 657–72. We tentatively place it in 1782 because of a reference elsewhere on the same page to the influenza of that year.

7. Though this agreement predates the new year, Jacques Finck did not take over as maître d'hôtel until Jan. 15, the day Daniel Duchemin (XXXIV, 266, 287n) submitted his final bill: Account XVII. Finck remained in charge of BF's household for the duration of BF's stay in France. His itemized accounts have survived for the first year of his employment. They are described as Account XXXI in the Editorial Note on Accounts at the beginning of this volume. Duchemin seems to have departed on account of illness; see Millet to BF, Jan. 20.

8. In L'Air de Lamotte's hand.

9. Coimet, who had been in BF's employ since Dec. 15, 1778: Account XXIII (XXIX, 3), entry of July 7, 1779; and see the Editorial Notes on Accounts in vols. 31–37. "Actuel" or not, Coimet seems to vanish from BF's household the moment Finck takes over as maître d'hôtel. According to Finck's records, the cook as of Jan. 15 was a certain M. La Marque: Account XXXI, entry of Feb. 15, 1783.

de 600 lt. par an.[1] On lui donnera en outre une Gratification, Si on a lieu d'être content de lui, tant par rapport à sa maniere de faire l'office,[2] que par les Epargnes qu'il pourra introduire dans la Maison.

Au bout de 3 mois voici l'Arrangement qu'on propose.

Le Mtre. d'Hotel prendra sur son Compte le Linge, Batterie de Cuisine, Fayance &ca. après Estimation faite des dit Articles.—

Alors il n'aura plus de Gages, Mais Mr. Franklin lui donnera 6 lt. par Tête pour lui ainsi que pour chaque personne qui dinera à sa Table, et le Mtre. d'Hotel fera toutes les Depenses du Diner et du Dessert tant par rapport au manger que pr. le Bois de Cuisine, Charbon et Eau et generalement tout ce qui concerne le Repas. Le Mtre. d'Hotel fournira en outre, sans augmenter de Prix, tout le Pain, beurre, Sucre, Thé, Caffé &ca. qui pourront être consommés au Dejeuné de M. Franklin.— Les Gens auront leur argent à depenser. Le Cuisinier et Garçon de Cuisine deront aux Gages du Mtre. d'Hotel.[3]

Par cet Arrangement M. Franklin n'aura a fournir dans sa maison que les articles suivants, savoir,

Les Vins et Liqueurs

Le Bois pour les Chambres,

Bougies et Chandelles pour les Appartements

& L'huile à bruler.

Si au bout d'un an on a raison d'être tres content du Mtre. d'Hotel par rapport à l'abondance et Bonté des provisions qu'il aura fournies—On lui donnera encore une Gratification.

<hr>

1. The same wages BF had offered Duchemin two years before: XXXIV, 266.

2. Separate from the kitchen, the *office* was traditionally overseen by the *officier* who was responsible for the household's bread, wine, silver, and linen, and the preparation of its preserves and desserts: Cissie Fairchilds, *Domestic Enemies: Servants & Their Masters in Old Regime France* (Baltimore and London, 1984), p. 30.

3. Finck's proposal is a marked change from the practice in BF's household. Up to this point BF had rented much of his kitchen furniture, relied on outside suppliers for fuel and other provisions, and paid the cook and his helper directly.

From Sarah Bache

ALS and copy: University of Pennsylvania Library

Dear and Honoured Sir   Philadelphia Jan 1st.[–2] 1783

I do not know how I could employ myself more agreeably on the beginning of the new Year, than by writing to my dear Papa, wishing him many happy returns of it, and that I may live to begin and end many of them with him is my sincere prayer, who knows what a Peace may produce— In Mr Bache's letter you desire I would continue my histories of the Children,[4] you could not have given me a more pleasing task, the Copies of my letters are filled with accounts of them, but when I come to write them fair I frequently leave a great deal about them out, in my last Copy "The Family are all well and love you as much as ever, little Deby sings dances and talks tho she does not walk yet, You are already acquainted with all the Clever things, that the rest of the little runabouts do" and I now can add with truth that I do not think there is a finer family of little Children in America, Will grows very handsome if I may judge by my own eyes, and my ears, he is a good english Scollar, he is now learning to dance which he likes very much, no boy ever posess'd a better memory, and I hope with a good education he will make a very clever fellow— Betsy goes to the same Miss Nancy Mash[5] that I went too when a Child and hems pocket Handkerchiefs as well as any girl of her highth in Philadelphia, she shall send you one of her making very soon, her passion at present is dress, she loves fine waveing Plumes, and smart Sashes, and wishes for a Carriage, if it was only big enough to hold her Sister Deby, she says she should be satisfied, she desired me a few minutes ago, when I bid her hold her tongue that I was writing to her Grandpapa, Oh do tell him, if you wont take me to france to see him, that my little Mittins are almost worn out that he sent me and that I want a little fan, now I have got a Carolina hat to go to Church, Mrs Read ask'd her the other day where she got such Beautiful mitins, where do you think I should get them but from my dear Grand Papa, they dont make such beautifull Mittins any where but in

4. We cannot identify this letter.
5. Nancy Marsh.

France, I wish you could see her with all my heart, there is not a more brilliant pair of eyes in Philadelphia, Deby and Louis, are just Betty and Willy over again,

Januy 2d.
General Chataleux will bring you this, I spent last evening with him at Mr Morri's who gave an Eligant Ball, I hope he will get safe, he is a very Valuable Man, and has a sincere regard for you, we were in hopes he was going to stay the Winter with us, and had no Idea he was going till last night—[6] Mr Bache join in duty and Love with Your afectionate and dutiful Daughter
S BACHE

Addressed: The Honble. / Doctor Benjamin Franklin / Minister Plenipoy: from the United States / of No America—at the Court of / Versailes / Favored by General Chastellux

From Samuel Cooper Johonnot

ALS: American Philosophical Society

Respected Sir   Geneva 1st Jan 1783
Among your political Occupations I take the Liberty of troubling you with a french Letter wrote in English. Peace has been made this long time in the Mouths of Politicians, tho' unhappily for Humanity it does not actually exist any where else.
We however in this Part of the World have a calm after all our Storms & are pursuing quietly thoug with Ardour our Studies. Our Endeavours have been crown'd with Success & in a few Days Benny & I shall each of Us receive a Prize from the Hands of the President of the College.[7] I have the first of the 2d Band, & Benny has the 3d of the same. I am to be put in the 1st after the Delivery of the Prizes, & then we are to apply ourselves to

6. The chevalier de Chastellux, assigned to Rochambeau's army, first met the Baches when he visited Philadelphia two years earlier: XXXII, 135n; XXXIV, 283. Now concluding his travels in America, he greeted the new year at Robert Morris' and left Philadelphia on Jan. 3; see Morris to BF, Jan. 2.
7. The distribution of prizes took place on Saturday, Jan. 11: BFB's journal entry for that day.

have others at the Promotions. If I gain another my Ambition will be satisfied & shall hope that a speedy Peace may facilitate, according to my Friends Desire my Return to my native Country. In the mean Time I beg my venerable Friend to accept of the Tribute of Gratitude & of the sincere Wishes of your Prosperity Haelth & Happiness for many succeeding Years that are offer'd You by Your most humble Servant

SAML. COOPER JOHONNOT

His Exellency Dr Franklin

Addressed: A Monsieur / Monsieur Franklin / Ministre plenipotentiare des Etats unis / de l'Amerique auprés sa Majesté / trés chrétienne A Passy / pres Paris

Notation: S. Cooper Johonnot 1er. Janvr. 1783.

From Le Couteulx & Cie. LS: Historical Society of Pennsylvania

Monsieur   Paris le 1er. Janvier 1783.

Nous répondons à la lettre que vous nous avez fait l'honneur de nous écrire le 31. Xbre. der.[8] L'opération qui nous avoit été confiée par Monsieur Morris consiste a acheter en Espagne des Piastres fortes livrables à la havanne.[9] Nous avons pu l'exécuter a 33 Pr% de bénéfice en faveur des Etats unis, nous la croyons encore possible dans ce moment quoique plus difficile, et nous ne devons pas vous dissimuler que la publication de la paix en Espagne, n'enleve absolument tout espoir à cet égard.

Quant aux debours réels et effectifs Ils auront lieu a peu près trois mois après l'execution des ordres que nous pourrons donner, et Si pour vos arrangemens particuliers il vous convenoit de nous donner des effets a plus longue echéance nous ne ferions aucune difficulté de les recevoir, ne désirant rien tant que de donner aux Etats unis des preuves de notre desir de leur être utiles et notre unique demande dans cette occasion tombant sur cet objet

8. Missing.
9. Morris' attempts to obtain specie via Havana were only partially successful: *Morris Papers*, VI, 425–6n; VII, 403–4n.

nécessaire pour un engagement aussi considerable que celui que nous allons prendre, nous voulons dire une assignation quelconque libre entre nos mains, et dont la disposition ne puisse être changée.

L'Importance de la somme dont nous avons besoin est réglée par Mr. Morris à 2,500000, *l.t.*—montant des ordres qu'il nous avoit donné. Elle est Susceptible d'augmentation ou de diminution suivant que vous Le Jugerez convenable.

Nous avons L'honneur d'être avec respect Monsieur Vos très humbles et très obéissans Serviteurs   LE COUTEULX &c

Mr. B. franklin Ministre plenipotentiaire des Etats unis de l'amerique à Passy

From Sarah Bache

ALS: American Philosophical Society

Dear and Honoured Sir   Philadelphia Jan. 2d 1783
    Mr Restiff called to let me know he was going to France,[1] I allways promiss'd him a letter when he return'd: he is an exceeding good Young Man, has been often at our House and can tell you how we all look—as I have just wrote you a long letter,[2] and shall write you again in a few days by Coll Cambray,[3] shall only add the Love and duty of an Afectionate Daughter   S BACHE

Addressed: The Honble. / Doctor Benjamin Franklin / Minister Plenipoy: from the United / States of No: America / at / Passy / favored by Monsr. Restife

1. Restif de La Serve returned to France around April, 1783, after four years as second secretary to the French legation. He wrote an article about the 1782 fire at the legation's residence, caused by lightning (XXXVII, 462): William E. O'Donnell, *The Chevalier de La Luzerne: French Minister to the United States 1779–1784* (Bruges and Louvain, 1938), p. 45; Abraham P. Nasatir and Gary E. Monell, comps., *French Consuls in the United States: a Calendar of their Correspondence in the Archives Nationales* (Washington, D.C., 1967), pp. 147–8.

2. Dated Jan. 1[–2], above.

3. Louis-Antoine-Jean-Baptiste, chevalier de Cambray-Digny, whom BF had recommended to George Washington in 1777: XXIV, 526. Recently freed in a prisoner exchange, the chevalier returned to France in June: XXXIV, 65n.

From Dominique-Louis Ethis de Corny

ALS: American Philosophical Society

Dear Sir,   Paris the 2d. january 1783.
  I Would be acquainted if the *Washington* american Ship has already sailed for its destination. Mr. De Veimerange Who goes to morrow at versailles desires some Knouledge about it, Before his departure.[4] I Was Disposed to Wait on your Excellency in this after noon, in order of Renewing my Best Wishes for the happiness and good health of your Excellency, during this new year. But I am told that it Was not certain that you must Spend the Evening at home; consequently I chuse the Way of Writting on this matter. Be so Kind, Excellency, as answer me a single Word concerning the Departure of this ship, the Washington, Which advice I may send Directly, to Mr. De Veimerange.
  I am With the most Everlasting, faith full attachment and Respect Dear sir your Excellency's the most obedient and humble servant   DE CORNY

Mrs de Corny[5] Desires you Will agree thousand compliments. She shall be Extremly pleased, if your Excellency Will chuse a Day, to Drink tea, and make some Music. Mrs. De Corny, and Mr. De Corny too, present his Best compliments to his Excellency's son

Notation: De Corny Paris 2nd January 1783

---

4. Corny had worked with Palteau de Veimerange to collect supplies for the American army: XXXV, 524.
5. Anne Mangeot: *DBF* under Ethis de Corny.

From Robert R. Livingston

Two LS and L:[6] University of Pennsylvania Library; AL (draft): New-York Historical Society; transcript: National Archives

Sir   Philadelphia 2d Jany. 1783

I was honored with your Letters by the Danae—[7] I congratulate you upon the promising State of our negotiations, since peace begins to be no less desirable here than elsewhere.— But I will not enter into that subject at present as I mean to write very fully both to Mr Jay & you by Mr Jefferson who will sail in company with this frigate in the Romulus, a ship of 44 guns—[8] Lest however any accident should prevent his arriving so soon as the Emerald,[9] I enclose a resolution of Congress, which was suggested by the proposition you mention to have been made by Mr Oswald on the subject of commerce—[1] For my own part I pre-

6. A note on the transcript indicates that the LS from which we print, the original, was carried by the *Emeraude;* the other LS (marked "2plicate"), by Col. Ogden; and the L (marked "duplicate" and signed by a secretary), by the packet *Washington.*

7. The *Danaé,* 26, sailed from France on Nov. 8 and reached Philadelphia by Dec. 28; she carried BF's Oct. 14 letters to Livingston and Morris (above): *Morris Papers,* VII, 223n, 229n. Her arrival was reported in the Jan. 1 *Pa. Gaz.*

8. The French frigate *Romulus* was trapped by ice in the Delaware and was unable to sail before news arrived of the impending peace. This led Congress to excuse Jefferson from joining the other peace commissioners and he returned to Virginia: *Jefferson Papers,* VI, 210–11, 228–31, 236–7, 245–6, 253–4, 259–60.

9. The *Emeraude,* 26, then at Annapolis, which soon carried the comte and vicomte de Rochambeau, Chastellux, and other French officers to France: Rice and Brown, eds., *Rochambeau's Army,* I, 84n.

1. The Dec. 31 congressional resolution ordered the commissioners "to endeavour to obtain for the citizens and inhabitants of the United States a direct commerce to all parts of the British dominions and possessions, in like manner as all parts of the United States may be opened to a direct commerce of British subjects, or at least that such direct commerce be extended to all parts of the British dominions and possessions in Europe and the West Indies, and the said ministers are informed that this stipulation will be particularly expected by Congress, in case the citizens and subjects of each party are to be admitted to an equality in matters of commerce with natives of the other party": *JCC,* XXIII, 838. The resolution was sent to BF in cipher; one copy is at the University of Pa. Library, and another, deciphered by either BF or WTF, is at the APS.

Livingston may have meant "to Mr Oswald" rather than "by Mr Oswald."

sume that it is already included in your propositions, but as we
have yet been favoured only with that short note of them which
has been transmitted by you, we can form no accurate judgment
on the subject; you can hardly conceive the embarrassments that
the want of more minute details subjects us to.

You will learn from the Count de Rochambeau that the french
Army sailed the 24th ulto. perhaps it were to be wished that they
had remained here at least till New York or Charlestown were
evacuated, or rather till the peace— Congress have however
given them a good word at parting as you will see by the enclosed
resolves—[2] Not being consulted, they could interpose no objections to their departure, tho' they were not without many reasons for wishing to detain them— Our finances are still in great
distress, if the war continues, a foreign loan in addition to those
already received will be essential— A plan for ascertaining what
shall be called contingent expences is under the consideration of
Congress, as well as the objections you have stated with respect
to the mode of paying your salaries, which will, I believe, be altered.[3] The allowance to Mr T. Franklin has been confirmed, &
your moderation & his upon this point have done you both
honor in the opinion of Congress—[4] I have the honor to be, sir
With great respect & esteem Your most obedt. humble servant
ROBT R LIVINGSTON

No. 24

BF's letter of Oct. 14 (above) reported that Oswald had approved and forwarded the preliminary draft treaty that the Americans had drawn up.

2. On Jan. 1, Congress approved two resolutions thanking Louis XVI and
Rochambeau and praising the conduct of Rochambeau and his troops: *JCC,*
XXIV, 1–2. One of the copies Livingston enclosed has survived; it is at
the APS. A draft French translation by L'Air de Lamotte is at the Hist. Soc.
of Pa.; BF endorsed it "Minute of Congress respecting the Departe. of the
French Army / Jan. 1. 1783".

3. BF's objections were in his Oct. 14 letter.

4. BF had informed Livingston on Sept. 3 (above) that he was allowing WTF
300 *louis* (7,200 *l.t.*) per annum. On Dec. 27 Congress approved continuation of that allowance: *JCC,* XXIII, 832.

From Robert Morris

Sir,   Office of Finance 2 January. 1783.

—Circular—[5]

The Bearer of this Letter is the Chevalier de Chattelleux who sets off to Morrow Morning, for France.[6] There are many Things which I am desirous of communicating to you but which I have not now sufficient Time to commit to Paper and still less to put in Cypher. I have therefore entered very much into the Detail of our Situation with Genl. Chattelleux and requested him to communicate to you the Result. His attentive Observation in this Country will also enable him to place before you a more complete State of it than could easily be written as he will be able to Answer Questions which might not even suggest themselves to me.

I am Sir with sincere Respect and Esteem Your most obedient and humble Servant   RM

His Excelly. Benja. Franklin and John Jay Esqr.

5. A duplicate was sent to John Jay.
6. Chastellux embarked aboard the frigate *Emeraude* at Baltimore on Jan. 8 and arrived at Nantes on Feb. 13: *Morris Papers*, VII, 264n. For details of the voyage see Rice and Brown, eds., *Rochambeau's Army*, I, 84n.

Draft of a Declaration to Be Made by the American Peace Commissioners[7]

Two D:[8] Archives du Ministère des affaires étrangères

1783. Janr. 2

Projet de Declaration

Nous soussignés Ministres Plenipres. des Etats unis &a. Déclarons qu'en agréant et consentant a fixer par notre signature des articles qui avoient été discutés entre nous et M. Oswald muni de pleins pouvoirs a cet effet par S. M. le R. [Sa Majesté le Roi] de la grande Bretagne pour être inserés dans le futur traite de paix, nous n'avons eu pour objet que de faciliter et de con-

---

7. A statement drafted by the French foreign ministry for the commissioners to sign. We strongly suspect that Vergennes never presented it to BF, as there are no extant copies other than the unsigned drafts in the AAE and there are no mentions of it in the papers of any of the American commissioners. We include it here for the following reasons: (1) it is a striking expression of the court's concern over the American signing of the preliminary articles, especially as their own negotiations with Great Britain were still not concluded, and (2) it has been misunderstood by historians who thought a final version was dated Jan. 20, for reasons explained in the following note. Jan. 20 makes no sense; this declaration reaffirms what the Americans had written in the preamble to the preliminary articles, that the articles would not take effect until an Anglo-French treaty was signed. On the day of that signing, the declaration was obsolete. It was also, in any case, redundant, which is why Vergennes may not have given it to the Americans. An English translation is in Giunta, *Emerging Nation,* I, 757–8; Richard B. Morris puzzles over it in *The Peacemakers: the Great Powers and American Independence* (New York, Evanston, and London, 1965), pp. 384–5.

8. We print the earlier draft, where the date of composition, placed at the upper left corner, is unambiguous. The second D is a fair copy of the first (with accent marks added and minor variations in abbreviations); this must have been the copy that was to have been offered to the Americans for consideration. The title is simply "Declaration," and, as in the first draft, the dateline "a Passy ce" was left blank. A different hand, however, misled contemporary eyes by filling in the dateline with "20. Jer. 1783." This handwriting matches that of the clerk who wrote a notation in the upper left corner of the first page, summarizing the contents and again dating it Jan. 20. This clerk, seeing that the undated document concerned the French peace treaty, made an erroneous assumption and took the liberty of inserting the incorrect date in the text.

stater la negociation dans laquelle les interets de nos souverains devoient etre préalablemt. Traités. Quoique le preambule de ces articles stipule positivement qu'ils n'auront d'effet que dans le cas ou le Traite de paix entre S. M. T. C. [Sa Majesté très Chretienne] et S. M. Brite. [Britannique] sera conclu, nous croyons devoir manifester *plus spécialement* les intentions de nos souverains a cet egard parceque nous appercevons que le titre de *Traité preliminaire* dont on qualifie ces articles soit en Angleterre soit dans les papiers publics de l'Europe peut induire en erreur sur la nature de l'acte que nous avons signé le 30. du mois dernier.[9]

Les Etats unis de l'amérique septe. jaloux de faire connoitre leur fidelité à remplir leurs engagemens et leur reconnoissance pour S. M. T. C. regardent leur cause comme inseparablement unie a celle de S. de. [dite] M. c'est la base des instructions qu'ils nous ont données[1] et aucune de nos demarches ne peut s'ecarter de ce principe. Nous remplissons donc un de nos plus pretieux devoirs en declarant que les articles arretés et signès entre nous et le Plenipre. de S. M. Brite. ne changeront rien a la position des Etats unis envers l'Angleterre tant que la paix entre S. M. T. C. et s. M. Brite. ne sera pas conclue, et que nous rejettons toute interpretation des ds. [dits] articles toute induction de la signature que nous y avons apposée qui seroient contraires a cette assertion. Nous esperons que ces verites bien connues dissiperont tous les soupcons qu'on pourroit chercher a repandre sur les sentimens d'une Republique naissante dont l'honneur et les interets

9. The British papers published Townshend's Dec. 3 letter containing an accurate description of the preliminary articles and their provisional nature; see the annotation of jw to bf, Dec. 6. The Dec. 13 issue of the *Gaʒ. de Leyde*, however, reported that Oswald had concluded a "Traité de Paix" with the American commissioners. They corrected this rumor in that day's supplement, quoting from Townshend's Dec. 3 letter (which they had just received). The next issue, Dec. 17, printed a full translation of that letter and described the British concessions.

1. xxxv, 166–7. The commissioners' fidelity to their instructions, particularly relative to their responsibilities to the alliance, was questioned by some delegates to Congress (and criticized by La Luzerne) when Barney arrived with the preliminary agreement: William T. Hutchinson *et al.*, eds., *The Papers of James Madison*, First Series (17 vols., Chicago, London, and Charlottesville, 1962–91), vi, 328, 358–61, 375.

demandent égalemt. qu'elle s'etablisse dans l'opinion generale comme mettant au dessus de tout la fidelite et la constance dans ses engagemens.

Fait a Passy ce

From Michel-Guillaume St. John de Crèvecœur

ALS: American Philosophical Society

Chès Mr. Le Marquis de Blangy[2] Lieutt. Gènéral Caën—
Normandie 3d. Jany 1783.—
I have been Wittness whilst I was in America of a Cir Constance which I think it Imports Your Excellency to Know; my Good Intention will I hope, apologyse for the Liberty I am taking, if your Excellency is acquainted With it; if unknown, it is Certainly my duty as a good Cytysen of that Country to Inform you of what Follows—

In the Year 1775 Samuel Bayard Junior dèputy Sècretary of, the then Province of New York, was ordered by the Convention to the house of Nicholas Bayard a Mile out of Town, in order to watch over the records of the Province, then under the Guard of a Capt. & 30 Men; Some Time after, they were Transported to Kingston on the North River, Vulgarily Called *Eusopus;* under the Guard of the Same Person, & the Same Military Party;—18 Months after the Said Samuel Bayard, Contrary to the oath he had Taken to the Convention, found Means of Sending that part of those Records which Contained the Grant of Lands &ca. to Govr. Tryon then on board the Dutchess of Gordon; Since that, they have been Conveyed to the Tower of London, Where they now are;—those papers, fortunately become useless to Gr. Britain; at the return of the Peace must be of the Greatest Consèquence to that State; because, as you well know, they contains not only the Title of Lands but the Copy of Wills &ca.[3]

2. Maximilien-Pierre-Marie, vicomte de Blangy (1718–1791): *DBF.*

3. Crèvecœur's story was basically correct, except for one essential detail, the current whereabouts of the documents. In November, 1775, Gov. William Tryon ordered Samuel Bayard, Jr., to secretly withdraw 25 volumes of

I cannot Terminate this Letter Without taking the Liberty of Congratulating your Excellency, non only as a Man, an European, or Gaul, but as an American Cytisen, on the happy, Thrice happy rèvolution, which you have began Conducted & Terminated with So much Wisdom; hence forth Will begin a new Era in the annals of Mankind, far more Intèresting than those absurd rèvolutions which have hitherto Stained the Earth with Blood Without meliorating it; May nature Extend your days to the utmost Verge, to the End you may See the Misfortunes of War repaired, the Energy of this new people, the Wisdom of their Laws the Industry of those new States admired & respected by all nations.— Permit me to add that I am the Person who under the name of St. Jean de Crèvecoeur had the honor of dining with your Excellency Last March, with the Contesse de Houdetot & who last July Sent you, by the hands of Mr. Target a Book Intitled, Letters of An Américan Farmer.[4]

I am with the most unfeigned Respect Your Excellency's Most Obedient Humble Servant   H. St. John

Notations in different hands: H. St. John Caen Normandie 3rd. January 1783 / De Crevecoeur

New York records—land grants, records of commissions and charters under the Great Seal of Great Britain, Indian cessions, and minutes of council—and place them on the *Duchess of Gordon,* a British ship in New York Harbor. Sealed in two boxes, these volumes were unknowingly transferred from ship to ship over the next few years, finally sailing to Portsmouth on the *Eagle* and unloaded. When the boxes were opened in the fall of 1781 and their nature discovered, they were placed aboard the *Warwick* and returned to New York, where they were delivered to Gen. James Robertson, the military governor. All but one volume survived the adventure; the rest were damp and mildewed, but legible: William Smith, *Historical Memoirs,* ed. William H. W. Sabine (2 vols., New York, 1969–71), II, 72–3, 449–50; Hugh Hastings *et al.,* eds., *Public Papers of George Clinton* (10 vols., Albany, 1899–1914), I, 9–11.

4. XXXVI, 691; XXXVII, 628–9, 693–4.

From Ferdinand Grand

LS:[5] Historical Society of Pennsylvania

Monsieur   Paris ce Trois Janvier 1783

L'Idée de Mr. Rt. Morris de se procurer des Piastres de la Havanne[6] est bien bonne, mais je ne puis en dire autant de ses dispositions pour les faire payer ici. Je présume qu'il comptoit alors sur les fonds qu'il esperoit que vous obtiendriez, mais come ils se reduisent à Six Millions qui suffiront à peine pour faire face au courant des payemens ordinaires, je ne pense pas qu'on puisse rien détourner de cette somme, sans courrir risque de se mettre dans des Embarras dont le moindre Seroit de compromettre la signature de Mr. Rt. Morris & la confiance publique. Voilà, Monsieur ce qu'un examen refléchi de vôtre position financiere actuelle me dicte; mais en refléchissant sur l'Idée de Mr. Morris je me suis rappellé que nôtre administration achetta pareillement l'année précedente de la Cour d'Espagne des Piastres prises à la Havanne, par le canal d'un Négocient qui consentit à recevoir en payement des Valleurs de finance à 12 Mois de terme & qui en fit son Affaire avec la Cour d'Espagne. Je suis si ignorant sur les secrets politiques qu'il peut m'être permis de faire des sillogismes sur cette matiere; mais si vous pensiez qu'il put convenir aux Interrets politiques de vous aider & quil n'y eut que la rareté de l'argent qui y mit obstacle on pourroit le lever par ce moyen puisqu'avec de pareilles valleurs de finance jespererois pouvoir procurer à Mr. Morris des Piastres à la Havanne, si comme j'en suis persuadé la Cour d'Espagne ne se refuse pas d'en vendre.

Je vous soumet, Monsieur, cette Idée pour en faire l'usage que vous croirez convenable, n'aiant pas besoin de vous faire observer que par ce moyen la Cour vous aideroit, sans dèbourser pendant une Année & que vous pourriez remplir par là les besoins de Mr. Morris.

Je suis avec un profond Respect Monsieur Vôtre très humble & très obeissant Serviteur   GRAND

5. In the hand of his son Henry.
6. For which see Le Couteulx & Cie. to BF, Jan. 1.

544

From Thomas Jefferson

ALS: American Philosophical Society; AL (draft): Library of Congress

Sir   Philadelphia Jan. 3. 1783.

I arrived at this place a few days ago[7] expecting to have proceeded to Europe in the vessel which carries Count Rochambaud
& the Chevalr. de Chastellux;[8] but it sails before I can be ready.
I shall follow however in a very few days, & may possibly be
with you as soon as this. Conscious that I can add no good to the
commission, it shall be my endeavor to do it no injury. I understand that I am to be the bearer of something new to you, but not
of a nature to embarrass your operations.[9] I expect so shortly after your receipt of this to have the pleasure of paying my respects to you in person, that I shall only add those expressions of
respect & esteem with which I have the honor to be Sir Your
most obedient & most humble servt   TH: JEFFERSON

From Le Roy   ALS: University of Pennsylvania Library

De Paris ruë de Seine ce Vendredy 3 Janvier 1783

Voulez vous bien Mon Illustre Docteur que J'aye Lhonneur de
vous recommander M. Envier de Dunkerque que j'ai deja eu
l'honneur de vous présenter L'annee derniere et qui Souhaite
prendre vos ordres pour Nantes, et M. Williams qu'il compte
voir dans cette Ville sous peu de Jours. Je vous Souhaite, Mon
Illustre Docteur, et de grand coeur la meilleure Santé dans
cette année cy, et qu'elle vous mette à portée de Jouïr, pleinement
de vos Succès, et de vos triomphes. Il n'y a plus de Souhaits à
vous faire pour L'indépendance reconnuë, et la liberté de L'Amèrique. Cette Grande affaire est terminée aux Yeux de ceux qui
Savent lire dans l'avenir, au milieu de tous les delais des Negociations, et de tous les nuages dont une politique peu eclairée
pourroit l'envelopper.

7. On Dec. 27: *Jefferson Papers*, VI, 211, 217n.
8. The frigate *Émeraude*.
9. Probably the Dec. 31 resolution quoted in our annotation of Livingston
to BF, Jan. 2.

J'ai l'honneur dêtre Monsieur et Illustre Docteur avec les Sentimens de L'attachement le plus vrai et le plus Sincère et pour la
vie Votre très humble et très obeïssant Serviteur   LE ROY

Notation: Le Roy, 3 Janr. 1783

From Robert Morris

LS: American Philosophical Society; draft: Yale University Library

Sir   Office of Finance 3rd. January 1783.
    I do myself the Honor to enclose to your Excellency under
flying Seal a Letter to Mr Grand which I pray you to peruse.[1] To
what is said in that Letter I need add but little. The Bill to Messrs.
Wadsworth and Carter is in Payment of what our Army have
eaten during the last two Months and an half,[2] and you will see
by the Correspondence on that Subject which will be transmitted in my next Letter[3] what a Situation I was drawn to. Be assured my dear Sir that nothing but extreme Necessity shall induce me to distress you but be also assured that unless a
considerable Sum of Money is obtained for us in Europe we are
inevitably ruined and that too whether a Peace takes Place or not
for we must keep our Army together and we must prepare for
war or we do Justice neither to ourselves nor our Allies. The Expence therefore is inevitable and I have no means of defraying it

1. Dated Jan. 2[–4], it enclosed a list of bills amounting to about 1.3 million *l.t.*, drawn by Morris in 1782 and the first days of 1783, and apologized
for continuing to draw on Grand "without the Certainty of Funds": *Morris
Papers,* VII, 264–7.
    2. Connecticut merchant Jeremiah Wadsworth (1743–1804), formerly the
commissary general of the American army, served as commissary for Rochambeau's army from 1780 to 1782: *ANB.* His business partner was "John
Carter" (an alias for John Barker Church), an Englishman who in 1777 had
married Gen. Philip Schuyler's daughter Angelica. Wadsworth and Carter
had supplied the American army when Morris could no longer keep up the
payments with the former contractors. They agreed to accept payment in
bills on France. The bill Morris issued them, drawn on Grand at 100 days'
sight, was for 1,038,000 *l.t.*: *Morris Papers,* VI, 538n, 565–73; VII, 261, 262n,
267.
    3. Dated Jan. 11, below.

but the Sales of Bills. I shall write you more particularly as soon as my Leisure will admit and only repeat for the Present once more that money is indispensible.

I am Sir With Esteem and affection Your most obedient & humble Servant.   ROBT MORRIS

His Excellency. Benjamin Franklin.

From John Sargent   ALS: American Philosophical Society

My Dear Doctor   London 3d Jan 1783.

The Moment is come when I may safely assure You of my constant Esteem, affection & Veneration for Your Character, & may congratulate You on the Services You have renderd Mankind—!

I dared not write You before,—some Officious Sycophants had represented me to the late Ministry as an Active Instrument of America,—&, if I had written You but a single Line, by virtue of the Suspension of the Habeas Corpus, regarding Those that should hold Correspondence with That Country, or any *belonging to it*, I was informed, I might be shut up, & distressed by the vile Miscreants that have brought on all the late Calamities to each Country— So I desisted addressing You— my Innocence being a poor Shield against Power in such Hands— For you know, I afforded nothing to America but my Good Wishes—nor was more in my Power but a little private Relief to the Distressed not worth mentioning—[4]

My Wife & The Old Lady Her mother[5] ardently pray for Your Health, & still many happy Years to You— Hardly a day

---

4. BF's last extant correspondence with his old friend, the former director of the Bank of England (VII, 322n), was in 1775. For the act suspending the Habeas Corpus Act see XXIII, 322n. Though Sargent would not correspond with BF during the war, his wife broke the silence in early 1782 and explained her husband's reluctance: XXXVI, 551–2.

5. Rosamond Sargent and her mother, Elizabeth Greenwood Chambers: XXXVI, 551; David Hancock, *Citizens of the World: London Merchants and the Integration of the British Atlantic Community, 1735–1785* (Cambridge, New York, and Melbourne, 1995), p. 405.

has passed since We parted, We have not thought & talked of
You— My Sons are in the same Sentiments— The Eldest single
yet,[6] with me at Halsted— The Youngest Father of Four Boys—
Two Living—marryed to a Lady of Family & Fortune in Sus-
sex[7]—turned Country Gentleman, residing wholy there—improving His Estate by the Study of Country affairs, Planting &c
& endeavouring to mend & improve His Nieghbours by the acting a Justice's Part,—which He is happy to be highly approved
by Them in— I who am upon my *Save-All*, near the last Bitt of
Candle left,—and only fit to save a better from being expended
to the Purpose, remain in The Track You ever knew me,—being among the greatest Sufferer's in point of Fortune by the unhappy Breach with America—to try what I can save from the
Ship wrecks.

But I will not enter farther into that disagreable Subject— Let
me embrace You, & wish You all Happiness, having but just
Time to seize the opportunity offerd, & assure You once more I
am Dear Sir Most unalterably & affectly Yours   J SARGENT.

From Antoinette-Thérèse Melin Dutartre[8]

ALS: University of Pennsylvania Library

ce 4 janvier 1783

Mon papa, voila encore mon abbé, pour qui vous avez eu des
bontés; voulez vous en avoir encore? Et à ma consideration,
écouter ses demandes? Voulez vous aussi recevoir l'assurance de
mon amitié? Et voulez vous bien aussi ne me pas oublier en 83,

6. George Arnold Sargent (1748–1805): Henry Wagner, "Pedigree of Sargent, Afterwards Arnold, and Sargent," *Genealogist*, 2nd ser., XXXIII (1917),
189.

7. The future M.P. John Sargent (1750–1831), who had married Charlotte
Bettsworth, the heiress of Woolavington, on Dec. 21, 1778: X, 365n; R. G.
Thorne, ed., *The History of Parliament: the House of Commons, 1790–1820*
(5 vols., London, 1986), V, 95–6.

8. Mme Brillon's cousin, who had written to BF about a young Irish abbé
in 1781: XXXVI, 47.

comme vous avez fait en 82? Car ce pauvre arbaletre ne vous a pas vû! Je ne Suis pas en bonne santé, j'ai été une fois à passy, et des affaires que vous aviez, m'ont empechée d'avoir le plaisir de vous voir: venez dont me dedomager de cette perte, en venant diner avec moy? Car je vous aime toujours: et j'aurrai grand plaisir a vous le dire   MELIN DUTARTRE

Comment va vôtre enfant?

Addressed: A monsieur / monsieur franklin / à Passy

Notation: Dutartre.

From Jonathan Williams, Jr.

ALS: Historical Society of Pennsylvania

Dear & hond sir.   Nantes Jan. 4. 1783.

I beg leave to reccommend to your kind Notice Mr Purviance son to a Respectable Merchant in Maryland.[9] This young Gentleman proposes to make a Tour to Ireland with a View of reestablishing his Health & visiting some Relations. I shall be much obliged by your giving him the necessary passport, and whatever Civilities you may think proper to show him you may depend he will be worthy of, & I shall esteem them as a favour done to me.

My Friend Mr Nikson [Nilson?], an Irish Gentn but an american in his Heart, goes with Mr Purviance, & I equaly reccommend him to your notice. I am as ever most dutifully & affectionately Yours   JONA WILLIAMS J

His Excelly Doctor Franklin.

---

9. Perhaps John H. Purviance (d. 1820), son of Samuel Purviance, Jr. (XXII, 606n). Samuel and his brother Robert were natives of Donegal who emigrated to Philadelphia with their father in the mid-1750s and became partners in a Baltimore mercantile firm. We have found no record of Robert's children. Samuel's son John served as secretary and interpreter for James Monroe during his tenure as U.S. minister to France. Edward C. Papenfuse *et al.*, eds., *A Biographical Dictionary of the Maryland Legislature, 1635–1789* (2 vols., Baltimore and London, 1979–85), II, 667–9.

From Ferdinand Grand LS:[1] Historical Society of Pennsylvania

Monsieur   Paris ce 5 Janvr. 1783

La lettre dont vous m'avez honoré me demande mon Opinion sur celle qu'elle renfermoit de Mrs. Lecouteulx &c qui desirent scavoir si vous pouvez vous engager de leur fournir jusqu'à Deux Millions & demi pour les Achats de Piastres quils ont à faire pour M. Morris.[2] Je ne puis ni ne dois avoir d'Opinion à ce sujet, mais pour fixer la vôtre, Monsieur, je dois vous éclairer sur la situation des Finances du Congrès en mes mains en conséquence & Suivant la situation actuelle de ce compte chez moi, Il resulte que mes payemens ou mes acceptations à ce Jour Sans y comprendre celles des votres dont je n'ai pas la Notte montent à L5.720/m.[3] & que le crédit n'est que de 4,548,880 *l.t.* 15 *s.* 4 *d.* & qu'à ce deficit d'environ 1200/m *l.t.* Il faut ajouter les dépenses courantes qui, quoique peu considerables, etant repetées font un objet. Vous voyez par là, Monsieur, que le premier Quartier de L1500/m qui echoit au premier d'Avril prochain, réduit à 900/m *l.t.* à cause des L600,000 reçues & envoiées à L'Orient,[4] est plus qu'absorbé & que je Serai obligé d'y Supléer de ma caisse. Il faut même que je me premunisse d'avance en conséquence, puisque dans l'Etat ci dessus je ne comprends que les traites de M. Rt. Morris avisées qui vont jusques à N 429[5] & qu'il m'en a deja été presenté sous le N 602 puisqu' etant sans avis de cette suite de Numéros je ne peux en evaluer l'objet. Si d'après cette situation il m'est permis d'avoir une Opinion elle me porteroit à me refuser à la demande de Mrs. Lecouteulx &ce.

---

1. In the hand of his son Henry.

2. BF's letter is missing, but it concerned the Jan. 1 letter he received from Le Couteulx & Cie.

3. Grand is using *L* to indicate *l.t.* and *m* to indicate 1,000. The amount in question is 5,720,000 *l.t.*

4. As BF had told Morris on Dec. 23 (above), the new 6,000,000 *l.t.* loan from the French government was to be paid in quarterly installments with 600,000 *l.t.* in specie to be deducted from the first payment. This money was sent to Lorient to be carried to America by the *General Washington*.

5. On Oct. 7 and 25 Morris had sent Grand bills of exchange numbered 362 to 429 inclusive (worth in total 590,450 *l.t.* 8 *s.*). On Nov. 23 he sent those numbered 430 to 623 inclusive (worth in total 1,336,958 *l.t.* 10 *s.* 8 *d.*): *Morris Papers*, VI, 663; VII, 114.

& je la fonderois Sur ce que ces Messieurs ont deja tiré de Hollande & pourront tirer encore de l'Emprunt qui y est ouvert; Sur ce qu'il me paroit que l'acceuil des traites de M. Rt. Morris doit être preferé à tout, & Sur ce qu'enfin nous pourrions ègalement lui procurer des Piastres si la suite offre le même avantage & nous laisse des fonds libres, aiant pour cela tous les moyens possibles par mes relations intimes à la Cour de Madrid— Voila, Monsieur, mes reflexions puisque vous les avez Souhaitées, je les subordonne avec plus de confiance encore aux vôtres. J'ajouterai qu'avant de faire une réponse à M M. Lecouteulx il conviendroit peut être davoir celle de M. de Vergennes sur ma lettre que vous vous proposiez de lui communiquer parceque s'il goutoit mon Idée M. Morris ne manqueroit pas de Piastres & plus convenablement que par tout autre Voye.

Je suis avec un profond Respect Monsieur Vôtre très humble & très obeissant Serviteur   GRAND

Depuis cette Lettre Ecritte je recois une remise de Mrs Willink & Van Staphorst d'amstd[6] de 360/m *l.t.* qui figurent bien dans L'Etat de situation cydessus.

Son Excellence M. Bn. Franklin Passy.

From Michael Hillegas   ALS: American Philosophical Society

May it please your Excellency   Philada: January 6th. 1783
  The Bearer hereof Mr. William Wood of a reputable Family connected with your old Friend my Uncle Mr. Thomas Boude and the Newbolds in the Jerseys whom you have frequently heard of if not personally known to you—[7] having an inclina-

6. Part of the consortium of bankers handling JA's loan in the Netherlands; see the American peace commissioners' letter to them, Dec. 13.
  7. Thomas Boude (1, 233n) and BF had both been members of St. John's Masonic Lodge. Hillegas was married to Henrietta Boude; Thomas Boude must have been her father Samuel's brother. Thomas married Sarah Newbold, from a prominent family of Burlington County in New Jersey: *DAB* under Hillegas; George DeCou, *Burlington: a Provincial Capital* . . . (Philadelphia, 1945), pp. 207–9; Whitfield J. Bell, Jr., *Patriot-Improvers: Bio-*

tion to see the World as well as to do something with reputation to himself by endeavouring in the Commercial Way to increase his fortune, has thro his good Friend Mr. Matthew Clarkson whom you well know[8] prevailed on me to trouble you with a few lines and to introduce him to your Acquaintance as a sober & discreet person; the pleasure we all know you have in encouraging Youth leaves us no doubt but you will shew him every favour your great avocations will admit of.— I wrote you sometime since[9] at the request of the said Mr. Clarkson, to request you would please to enquire Whether a Compleat set of the Encyclopedia (as first published) is to be had, and what the price will be— You know him to be a man of genius and such we delight to encourage.—

I am with the greatest esteem imaginable Your Excellencys most Obedt. Servt,   M. HILLEGAS

His Excelleny B Franklin Esqr. &c. &c.

Notation: Mac Hillegas, Philada. Jany. 6. 1783.

From Robert R. Livingston

LS and copy:[1] University of Pennsylvania Library; AL (draft): New-York Historical Society; transcript: National Archives

Sir   Philadelphia 6th. January 1783
I have before me your Letters of the 25th. & 29th. of June, 12th. August 3d. and 26th. September and 14th. October last —[2] several matters contained in them have already been an-

---

graphical Sketches of Members of the American Philosophical Society (2 vols. to date, Philadelphia, 1997–), II, 305.

8. Clarkson was a member of the APS and the Library Company and had speculated in Nova Scotia lands with BF. He was married to Thomas Boude's daughter Mary: XVIII, 263n; Whitfield J. Bell, Jr., *Patriot-Improvers*, II, 305–11.

9. On April 29, 1782: XXXVII, 239–40.

1. According to a note on the transcript, the LS was carried by Col. Ogden and the copy (marked "2plicate") by the packet *Washington*.

2. For the first three of these letters see XXXVII, 535–9, 565–7, 730–4; the final three are above.

swered—and some others I am unable to reply to till Congress have decided on such propositions as I have submitted to their consideration— The convention relative to Consuls has been objected to by Mr. Barclay on accounts of its prohibiting the Consuls from trading— As the funds of Congress leaves them no means of affording an adequate support to Persons who are properly qualified, they fear that the only inducement to accept the appointment will be taken away by this prohibition— Mr. Barclay's letter on that subject is under consideration.[3]

I see the force of your objections to solicit the additional twelve Millions—[4] and feel very sensibly the weight of our obligations to France— But every sentiment of this kind must give way to our necessities, it is not for the interest of Allies to loose the benefit of all they have done by refusing to make a small addition to it, or at least to see the returns that our Commerce will make them suspended by new convulsions in this Country— The Army have chosen Committees—a very respectable one is now with Congress—they demand with importunity their arrears of pay.—[5] The Treasury is empty, no adequate means of filling it presents itself— The People pant for peace— Should contributions be exacted, as they have heretofore been at the point of the Sword—the consequences may be more dreadful than is at present apprehended— I do not pretend to justify the negligence of the States in not providing greater supplies— some of them might do more than they have done—none of them all that is required— It is my duty to confide to you that if the war is continued in this Country it must be in a great measure at the expence of France, if peace is made a loan will be absolutely necessary to enable us to discharge an Army, that will not easily separate without pay— I am sorry that neither Mr Jay

3. Asked by BF for his comments about the proposed convention concerning consuls (XXXVI, 484–5; XXXVII, 535), Barclay expressed objections about its restrictions and then informed Congress. In response, a congressional committee recommended suspending the convention: Barclay to BF, Sept. 3 (above); Barclay to President of Congress John Hanson, Oct. 23, 1782 (National Archives); *JCC*, XXIV, 3–4.

4. XXXVII, 535–6.

5. A committee headed by Maj. Gen. Alexander McDougall had arrived in Philadelphia at the end of December: *Morris Papers*, VII, 247–50.

or you sent me the propositions at large as you have made them, since we differ in opinion about the construction to be put on your commercial article, as you will find by the resolution enclosed in my letter No. 24.—[6] I wish the concession made of our trade may be *on condition* of similar priviledges on the part of Great Britain. You will see that without this precaution every Ally we have that is to be treated as the most favoured Nation may be entitled to the same priviledges, even tho' they do not purchase them by a reciprocal grant.

As to confiscated property it is at present in such a state, that the restoration of it is become impossible— English Debts have not that I know of been forfieted unless it be in one State, and I should be extremely sorry to see so little integrity in my Countrymen as to render the Idea of withholding them a general one—[7] however it would be well to say nothing about them if it can conveniently be done.

I am more and more convinced that every means in your power must be used to secure the Fisheries—they are essential to some States—and we cannot but hate the Nation that keeps us from using this common favor of Providence— It was one of the direct objects for carrying on the war— While I am upon this subject—I cannot but express my hope that every means will be used to gaurd against any distrusts or jealousies between you and France the United States having shewn their confidence in her by their instructions—[8] She has repeatedly promised to procure for us *all we ask,* as far as it lies in her power— Let our conduct leave her without appollogy if she acts otherwise which I am far from suspecting—

With respect to the Seamen you mention[9] I wish if any farther order is necessary than that Mr Barclay already has, that you

6. His letter of Jan. 2 (above).

7. See BF's Oct. 14 letter. Livingston is not accurate. British creditors faced numerous problems in collecting debts from Americans. Maryland and Virginia, for example, permitted debtors to use depreciated American currency: Charles R. Ritcheson, *Aftermath of Revolution: British Policy towards the United States, 1783–1795* (Dallas, 1969), pp. 63–4.

8. The congressional instructions to the peace commissioners: xxxv, 166–7.

9. XXXVII, 538–9.

would give it so far as to enable him to state their accounts and
transmit them to Mr Morris— As the Treaty with Holland is
concluded—I hope you have made some progress in that with
Sweden—a plan of which has been transmitted,[1] another Copy
will go by Mr Jefferson—

I am glad to find you have some prospect of obtaining what is
due on the Bon Homme Richard's prize money[2] that matter has
been much spoken of, and occasioned some reflections, As it is
alledged that Mr. Chamont was imposed on the Officers as their
Agent by the Court, and of course that they should be answer-
able for his conduct, which certainly has been very exceptionable.

Congress have come to no determination as to the size or expence of the pillar they propose to erect at York Town—[3] What
I wished of you was to send me one or two plans with estimates
of the expence in order to take their sense thereon.

As to the designs of Spain they are pretty well known,[4] and
Mr. Jay and Congress concur so exactly in sentiment with respect to them, that I hope we have now nothing to fear from that
quarter—

Congress have it now under consideration to determine what
should be allowed as contingent expences— I beleive house-
rent will not be allowed as such— I mentioned in my last[5] what
respected your Grandson to which I have nothing to add— I
agree with you in sentiment, that your Salaries should not depend on the fluctuation of the exchange and have submitted that
part of your Letter to Congress— I beleive they will direct a
stated sum to be paid waiting for their determination. I am prevented from drawing Bills at this time— As for the money received from me you will be pleased to replace with it the two
quarters Salary you had drawn before it came to hand—you will
have Bills for a third quarter which have been sent on some time
since—

1. See the commission and instructions of Sept. 28.
2. See XXXVII, 731–2.
3. See XXXVI, 262–3, 644; XXXVII, 732–3.
4. BF had written Livingston of his conjectures that Spain wished to "coop
up" the United States "within the Allegheny Mountains": XXXVII, 733.
5. Above, Jan. 2.

Several important political events have taken place here lately — The evacuation of Charles town— The Sailing of the French Fleet and army—the decision of the great cause between Connecticut and Pensilvania in favor of the latter—⁶ The State of the Army &c. all of which I should enlarge upon if this was not to be delivered by Mr. Jefferson, who will be able to inform you fully on all these points, and many others that you will deem important to a right knowledge of the present state of this Country.

I enclose a state of the trade between these States and the West Indies as brought in by a Committee of Congress and referred to me,⁷ it may possibly afford you some hints, and will serve to shew how earnestly we wish to have this market open to us.

I have the honor to be sir—with great Respect and Esteem your most obedt. humble Servant   ROBT R LIVINGSTON

The Honorable Benjamin Franklin

No. 25

To Benjamin Franklin Bache

ALS: Chapin Library, Williams College; press copy of ALS: American Philosophical Society

My dear Child,   Passy, Jany. 7. 1783.
I received some time since, and sent to your Father, the Samples you had sent to me of your Drawing, particularly the Copy of the Print of your Grand Father, which appear'd to be well done.⁸

6. On Dec. 30, a court of commissioners appointed by Congress had disallowed Connecticut's claims to land within the state of Pennsylvania: *JCC*, XXIII, 533–6; XXIV, 6–32.
7. On Nov. 21, a congressional committee had recommended transmitting to American ministers abroad copies of a paper entitled "Thoughts on the West India trade": *JCC*, XXIII, 747. This paper (National Archives) urged France to grant American merchants free access to the French West Indies. A copy is with BF's papers at the APS.
8. Enclosed in BFB's letter of [on or after Oct. 3], above.

I have also just now receiv'd your Letter written to wish me a happy New Year;[9] but you should nevertheless have put a Date to it, and to all your Letters. It was accompanied with several to your other Friends, all without Dates.[1] I shall forward them by the first Opportunity.

You should also, when you write, acknowledge the Receipt of Letters that have come to your Hands, mentioning their Dates. I sent you some time ago a Parcel containing several English Books, and I have not yet heard that you receiv'd them.

I am glad to learn that you have obtain'd another Prize.[2] Present my best Respects to Madam Cramer, & to Mr & Made. Marignac. I am ever, Your affectionate Grandfather

B FRANKLIN

Mr. Benja. F. Bache

Addressed: A Monsieur / Monsieur B. F. Bache / chez M. Marignac / à Genéve

Endorsed: Grandpapa Passy Jan 7 1783 Benjamn. Franklin Geneva 16 Jan 1783[3]

Notation: Benjamin Franklin 7 Jany 1783

To Samuel Cooper Johonnot

Press copy of ALS: Historical Society of Pennsylvania

My dear young Friend   Passy, Jany. 7. 1782 [*i.e.,* 1783]

I received your kind good Wishes of a Number of happy Years for me.[4] I have already enjoy'd and consum'd nearly the whole of those allotted me, being now within a few Days of my

---

9. Not found.

1. The one BFB wrote to WTF is at the APS. He told his cousin, "I now [know] the begening schal be agreable for me because I shall go to a party of dance and because I shall have 1 Prize."

2. See Johonnot to BF, Jan. 1.

3. On the address sheet BFB also wrote, in pencil, "3 Chemises [5] Mouchoirs 1 P de bas."

4. Johonnot's letter of Jan. 1 is above.

78th.——[5] You have a great many before you; and their being happy or otherwise will depend much on your own Conduct. If by diligent Study now, you improve your Mind, and practice carefully hereafter the Prompts of Religion & Virtue, you will have in your favour the Promise respecting the Life that now is, as well as that which is to come. You will possess true Wisdom, which is nearly allied to Happiness; *Length of Days are in her right hand, and in her left hand Riches & Honours; all her Ways are Ways of Pleasantness, and all her Paths are Peace!*[6]

I am glad to hear that you are intitled to a Prize. It will be pleasing News to your Friends in New England, that you have behav'd so as to deserve it. I pray God to bless you, and render you a Comfort to them and an Honour to your Country. I am, Your affectionate Friend   B FRANKLIN

Mr. S. C. Johonnot

From Sarah Bache   ALS: Yale University Library

Dear & Honoured Sir   Philadelphia Jan 7th: 1783

Yesterday which was your birthday[7]—and which I allways keep in the most festive Manner in my power—Willy & Eliza invited their Friends to a little dance, and made about sixty young folks, as happy as twas possible for People to be in this World. My children quite in an extacy, even little Deby had her share in the beginning of the evening— I have not the least doubt but they wish Grandpa's birth day would happen once a week— This will be delivered to you by Major Franks, whom I recommended to you last Year,[8] I have given him a memoran-

5. BF began his 78th year on Jan. 17, 1783.
6. Prov. 3:16–17.
7. BF was born on Jan. 6 (Old Style), which became Jan. 17 when the calendar was adjusted: I, 3n.
8. XXXV, 255. After David Franks returned to America in July, 1782, he was appointed secretary to Jefferson's mission to France. In late January he accompanied Jefferson from Philadelphia to Baltimore, to await passage, but when Jefferson's mission was canceled neither one made the voyage. The dispatches they had been given were either distributed back to the writers or

dom of some things I want, which Mr Bache has desired Mr Williams to pay for,[9] if there is any thing that he cannot get in Nantz, I have desired him to call on You. I gave last year a small Memorandom to Mrs Barkly which I requested her to give Mr W: or You, but she went to LOrient. I hear she is to spend the Winter in Paris, I hope you will see her often, she was a real Friend to me, and Mr Barkly as good a little Man as ever lived. I shall write to them by this opportunity—

Last Assembly[1] I introduced a God daughter of mine Miss Deby Donaldson,[2] she bids fair to be one of our greatest Beauties. Mr Bache would tell you she was one already— I am going this afternoon to sitt with Mrs Francis, who has lost her darling Sister Dolly Stirling, whom you knew and loved.[3] Of all my

---

given to other couriers: XXXVI, 551n; *Morris Papers*, VI, 136; VII, 263n, 689; *Jefferson Papers*, VI, 225–6.

On their trip to Baltimore Franks told Jefferson a story BF had told him about his dealings with "Mr. Z" (Ralph Izard) in Paris. Izard had repeatedly pressed BF to communicate information about the alliance negotiations. BF put him off "as decently as he could." Finally there came a stream of "intemperate" letters, which BF consigned to a pigeonhole. When Izard arrived in person to angrily demand an answer, BF replied, "I can no more answer this conversation of yours than the several impatient letters you have written me [*taking them down from the pigeonhole*]. Call on me when you are cool and goodly humoured and I will justify myself to you." Izard never came again: *Jefferson Papers*, VI, 226.

9. Mariamne Williams assembled the articles during the summer, valued at just over 1,581 *l.t.*, and JW shipped them in mid-August. RB acknowledged receiving the goods on March 7, 1784: JW to RB, July 7 *and* Aug. 16, 1783; May 7, 1784 (Yale University Library).

1. A subscription ball: V, 235. The chevalier de Chastellux described one in his *Travels in North America in the Years 1780, 1781 and 1782*, ed. and trans. Howard C. Rice, Jr. (2 vols., Chapel Hill, N.C., 1963), I, 176–7.

2. A Deborah Donaldson married Philip Nicolin in Christ Church in 1785, but we know nothing of her family: "Marriage Record of Christ Church, Philadelphia," in *Pa. Arch.*, 2nd series, VIII (1890), 82.

3. Anne Willing Francis (1733–1812) was the wife of Tench Francis, Jr., a merchant serving as first cashier of the Bank of North America (XIV, 137n, 160n). Her sister Dorothy (Dolly) Willing Stirling (d. 1782) was married to British Navy captain Sir Walter Stirling (IV, 324n). According to their brother Thomas Willing, first president of the Bank of North America, Dolly died in Glasgow, Scotland, having left her London home to visit her daughter. XXXVI, 405n; W. A. Newman Dorland, "The Second Troop Phil-

Friends Mrs Francis, is the most attentive when any thing is the matter, in ones gay moments every body is ready and Willing to come, she is not a common acquaintance and I would not neglect her for the world, and have this day refused two very agreable engagements to go to her— Since I began to write I have had the pleasure of a Visit from you—a French Man from on Board the Danie Frigate,[4] brought me a minature picture, which he said was drawn by a Lady in Paris from a large one, and sent a Venture by him, he asked eight Gunies, I am no great judge of painting, but I did not think the likeness good, not half so strong as the one the Minister gave me, done with a black lead pencl, by the Young Man who was kill'd by litening—[5] You will not I think find fault of the scaricetty or length of my letters, I have began the Year a meer scribler— Mr Bache and the Children join in love with your Afectionate daughter   S BACHE

From Joshua Barney   ALS: American Philosophical Society

Dr Sir   LOrient Jany. 7th. 83
    I recd. your Dispatches last night Accompanied with the Money,[6] which is all onbd & Shall Sail in the Morning if the Wind is fair, as it is at present—[7] I am Sorry I could not carry

---

adelphia City Cavalry," *PMHB*, XLIX (1925), 82; *Morris Papers*, I, 109n; *DNB* under Sir Walter Stirling; Thomas Willing, "Autobiography of Thomas Willing," in Thomas W. Balch, *Willing Letters and Papers* . . . (Philadelphia, 1922), p. 121.
    4. The *Danaé*.
    5. Lt. Albert-Rémy de Meaux was killed by lightning the previous spring while convalescing at La Luzerne's residence in Philadelphia: XXXVII, 462; Bodinier, *Dictionnaire*, under Meaux. We know nothing further about this portrait.
    6. The 600,000 *l.t.* in specie which the *General Washington* brought to America.
    7. Barney did not sail until Jan. 17 or 18. His passage was difficult, and he did not arrive in Philadelphia until March 12: Thomas Barclay to WTF, Jan. 24, 1783 (APS); Hulbert Footner, *Sailor of Fortune: the Life and Adventures of Commodore Barney, U.S.N.* (New York and London, 1940), pp. 137–8; *Morris Papers*, VII, 557.

the News of Peace as expected,[8] But console Myself with its being effected very soon. I cannot help observing as you mention the Curosity of my pasport, the Name of the Ship and the Bitter pill of United States, however it is what we have Been long Struggling for, Wishing You health and happiness am Sir Your Most Obt Servt JOSHUA BARNEY

Addressed: His Excellency Benn. Franklin Esqr. / Passy, near / Paris

Notation: Jos. Barney, L'orient Jany. 7. 1783.

From the Marquis de Grammont[9]

ALS: American Philosophical Society

Monsieur paris ce 7 janvier 1783.
Je vous prie instament de maccorder un quart d'heure daudiance particuliere au jour et a l'heure quil vous plaira mindiquer vous obligerez infiniment celui qui a lhonneur detre avec une respectueuse Consideration Monsieur Votre tres humble et tres obeissant Serviteur LE MIS DE GRAMMONT

Notation: Marquis de Grammont Paris 7 Janvier 1783

From James and Charles Hill

ALS: American Philosophical Society

Sir, Bourdeaux the 7th Janry. 1783
When we were at Paris we took the Freedom to Call on your Excellency at Passe to request your Kind Assistance in giving us

8. He carried the preliminary agreement of Nov. 30, 1782 (*Morris Papers,* VII, 558n), but the general peace was not concluded until Jan. 20.
9. This Grammont may be the *président* of the parlement of Toulouse who was to have represented BF at an academic ceremony in that city the previous spring: XXXVII, 396–7. Another possibility is Ferdinand, marquis de Grammont (1709–1797), a retired lieutenant general in the French army (*DBF*).

a letter of Recommendation to some Friends of yours in Philadelphia or Boston; and your Excellency was Kind Enough to
Promise us; Provided you receiv'd a Letter from Doctor Percival of Manchester Certifying that we were the Men we Seem'd
to be.

Inclos'd you'l receive the Letter of Doctor Percival's as well
as the Letter from my Brother[1] which hope will be Satisfactory
Enough for your Excellency to Assist us; as at this Time we are
in very great Need of Friends; and are going into a Strange
Country with a very little Money and not one Acquaintance; We
have took our Passage in an American Ship Call'd the Minerva,
of 12 Guns and about 50 Men we Part from here in about 12 or
14 Days at the Farthest, for Philadelphia must therefore Solicit
your Excellency's Letter as Soon as Possible for fear of its Coming too late and your Excellency will Confer a lasting Obligation
on us, who begs leave to Subscribe Ourselves Your Excellency's
most Obedient and most Devoted Hum Se[2]

JAMES & CHAS: HILL

NB Please to direct for us at Messrs. Jacobs & Stevens a lHotel
d'Angleterre a Bourdeaux

Addressed: A Son Excellency / Benjn. Franklin M. D / Ministre
Plenipotentaire / Des Etats Unis / a Passe. / pres / Paris

Notation: Hill, Mess. James & Charles, Bordeaux 7. Jany. 1783.

From Antoine-François Prost de Royer[3]

ALS: American Philosophical Society

Monsieur   Lyon 7e. Janvier 1783
     Je n'ai point oublié le bonheur que J'ai eu de vous voir à Paris
et l'accueil que vous m'avez fait. J'ai lu avec transport les pre-

---

1. Both were dated Dec. 4, 1782. Thomas Percival's letter is above, and
Joseph Hill's letter is described in annotation there.
2. No letter from BF has been located.
3. For whom see XXXII, 274–5.

mieres loix que vous avez donné à La Pensilvanie, et c'est à ce double titre que j'ai l'honneur de vous faire hommage des deux premiers volumes du *Dictionnaire de Jurisprudence et des arrets.*[4]

Je ne vous propose point, Monsieur, de lire en entier ces deux tomes: Les tables placées a la fin, vous indiqueront les matieres. Mais Il est des articles qui peuvent des à présent fixer votre curiosité.

Tels Sont en général l'article *administration,* qui n'avoit eté fait par aucun Juris consulte, et l'article *accusation* qui renferme tout le droit criminel.[5]

Dans cet article accusation Il y a une notice interesante et neuve de la procedure criminelle de tous les etats de l'Europe et même de l'amerique unie.

Tome 2 page 414 vous trouverez la procedure criminelle de l'angleterre et page 419 la procedure de l'amerique unie dont la base est votre ouvrage.[6] Vous y verrez de suite le proces de Zinger libraire de New york si bien deffendu par votre compatriote hamilton.[7] Ce morceau ma paru d'autant plus interessant qu'il renferme un des germes de la revolution actuelle et de l'independance americaine. Je desire beaucoup que vous Soyez content de la traduction et de l'extraite, et de ce que J'ai dit de votre confederation.[8]

---

4. Prost de Royer had enclosed a prospectus for this work in the letter cited above, where he asked for BF's advice on the section concerning the United States. BF may have directed him to La Rochefoucauld's translation of the Pennsylvania Constitution, published in the *Affaires de l'Angleterre et de l'Amérique,* IV, cahier XVII, lx–cxxi. That translation also included a document announcing BF as the chief signer; this gave way to the common and erroneous belief in Europe that BF was its author: XXII, 514.

5. Both these articles were in volume II, which ended with the entry "Administration."

6. Prost de Royer quoted La Rochefoucauld's translation of Chapter I, Article 9 of the Pennsylvania Constitution on p. 419 of volume 2.

7. Andrew Hamilton's successful defense of John Peter Zenger, New York printer and journalist, in a libel suit in 1735 set an early precedent for freedom of the press. BF sold many copies of Zenger's *Narrative* of the trial (1736): II, 127, 189.

8. BF had also brought to France the draft Articles of Confederation, which La Rochefoucauld promptly translated and published in the *Affaires de l'Angleterre et de l'Amérique:* XXIII, 118n, 214.

Les mots *acte* et *action* me paroissent pouvoir encore fixer vos regards en ce qui concerne la Jurisprudence angloise page 662 et 693 du To. 2. J'y ai parlé avec franchise de la procedure civile angloise, qui certes ne vaut pas la criminelle.

Si Je desire une aprobation, Monsieur, c'est la votre. Vous avez donné a votre patrie la liberté et des Loix. Vous avez plus de droit que qui que ce soit de juger celles de tous les peuples, et les Juris consultes, qui, comme moi, rendent le service penible et delicat de les rassembler, de les comparer et de les évaluer.

S'il m'etoit permis de former encore un vœu, ce seroit celui de voir passer mon ouvrage à Philadelphie, de l'y voir accueilli et recherché par raport aux bons principes que J'ai taché d'y jetter sur la liberté, la sureté, la tranquillité et toutes les parties qui constituent la félicité publique dans la societé politique.

Je ne borne point, Monsieur, ma lettre à l'hommage de mon livre, permettez moi le desir de vous etre utile ici, d'avoir avec vous une correspondance suivie, et d'etre en quelque sorte a vos ordres pour tout ce qui peut dependre de mon personnel, de mon zele, et du desir que J'ai de mériter votre estime.

Je Suis avec respect Monsieur Votre tres humble et tres obeissant Serviteur   DE ROYER
                        general des monnoïes, ancien Lieutenant
                        general de police, des academies de
                        Lyon et de Bordeaux et de Rome.

M. Franklin

Endorsed: De Royer 1783

To David Barclay

Reprinted from William Temple Franklin, ed., *The Private Correspondence of Benjamin Franklin* . . . (3d ed., 2 vols., London, 1818), I, 123–4.

Dear Sir,   Passy, Jan. 8, 1783.

I received yesterday your favor of the 27th past, which I immediately answer, as you desire to know soon my opinion respecting the publication of a certain paper. I see no objection, and leave it entirely to your discretion. I have had several letters from our inestimable friend that would do him honor, as they generally contained some schemes and plans for the public good; but they were left among my papers in America, and I know not how those have fared in our troubles. If I live to get home, I will send you what I can find; they may perhaps serve in a second edition of the work, which I am much pleased to hear is undertaken by so good a hand, and that it will have the benefit of your inspection. I thank you for the pamphlet you sent me. It is full of good sense, and I doubt not had great effect, as the sentiments it contains soon after became general. Your friends on both sides the Atlantic may be assured of whatever justice or favor I may be able to procure for them. My veneration for William Penn is not less than yours; and I have always had great esteem for the body of your people. With great and sincere respect, I am, Dear Sir, your most obedient and most humble servant,

B. FRANKLIN.

p.s. As possibly your wet harvest may have in some places produced a quantity of what is called *grown corn*, I send you enclosed a pamphlet published here on that subject, which may contain some useful hints.[9]

---

9. The autumn of 1782 had been particularly wet in France, delaying the harvest and causing some of the grain to sprout while still in the ear or after having been cut; this was the condition known in English as "grown corn." The French government asked a committee of the Ecole gratuite de boulangerie (XXXII, 481–2) to investigate the problem and its implications for breadmaking. Cadet de Vaux submitted their report on Oct. 31, and the government soon sponsored the publication of their pamphlet, *Avis sur les blés germés.* Their experiments dispelled the myth that sprouted wheat itself was harmful, and they recommended that public ovens be established so that the grain could be dried before fermenting: *Jour. de Paris*, Nov. 19, 1782; Bachaumont, *Mémoires secrets*, XXI, 197. The committee's report, "Observations sur les blés germés," was published in the December issue of Rozier's *Jour. de physique*, XX (1782), 444–50. BF's copy of the pamphlet is at the Hist. Soc. of Pa.

To Mary Hewson   ALS: American Philosophical Society

My dear dear Friend,   Passy, Jany. 8. 1783

I sent you sometime since 11 Pamphlets of the same kind with the enclos'd, supposing, as I had heard them well spoken of, that you who are so laudably attentive to the Education of your Children, might possibly find in them some Hints worth your Notice. I find the Work is to go on, and I will send you what comes out for the present Year, if you desire it.[1]

I receiv'd a Letter last Summer from my excellent old Friend your good Mother.[2] I was soon after taken ill with the Gravel & Sciatica, which together harrass'd & confin'd me till very lately. I am now, Thanks to God, freed from both; but the Sciatica has left me Weak on the left Side, so that I go up & down Stairs with Difficulty. I am in other respects at present well & hearty.— Present my sincere Love to her. Nothing would give me greater Pleasure than to see you both once more, well & happy. But you, who are truly sagacious, & honest, & can give good Advice, tell me frankly your Sentiments, whether, in case of a Peace, it will be prudent in me to visit England before I return to America. I have no other Call there, but the Pleasure of seeing my Friends of whom I must again soon take leave; and my Appearing may perhaps exasperate my Enemies. If you think this not of serious Consequence, tell me whether I may come right through London to Kensington, with the View of finding Room in your House; or whether I should take a Lodging in the City, to return to. Don't let me in the least incommode you.

I forget whether I ever acknowledg'd the Receipt of the Prints of Mr Hewson.[3] I have one of them fram'd in my Study. I think it very like. I believe I acquainted you with good M. Dubourg's

1. These were monthly installments of *L'ami des enfants* (Paris, 1782) by Arnaud Berquin (*DBF*). The work was announced in several issues of the *Jour. de Paris* (*e.g.*, see that of Dec. 6, 1782) and consisted of fables, stories, dialogues, and short plays for children: Mary Hewson to BF, April 2, 1784 (James S. Bradford, Philadelphia, 1956); Quérard, *France littéraire;* Tourneux, *Correspondance littéraire*, XIII, 45.

2. Margaret Stevenson wrote on July 24: XXXVII, 675–6.

3. In December, 1780, BF thanked her for sending prints of her late husband, William: XXXIII, 14; XXXIV, 134.

PETIT CODE

DE LA

RAISON HUMAINE,

O U

EXPOSITION SUCCINTE

DE CE QUE

LA RAISON DICTE A TOUS LES HOMMES,

POUR éclairer leur conduite &
aſſurer leur bonheur.

Par M. B. D.

par mr Barbeu du Bourg. D.M.

M. DCC. LXXXII.

Title page of Jacques Barbeu-Dubourg,
Petit Code de la raison humaine

Death. He had enlarg'd his little Piece which you translated; and in respect for his Memory, I have had it printed. I enclose a Copy.[4]

I am sorry to learn the still unsettled State of Mr. Wilkes's Family.[5] Mrs Wilkes is undoubtedly well qualified to teach English here, but I cannot think it would be worth her while to come hither for that purpose. It is true that our Language is in vogue here, and many learn a little of it. But the Instructors are poorly paid, & the Employ precarious and uncertain: the Observation is so general as to have given Rise to a Proverb, *Pauvre comme un Maitre de Langue.*

I have not yet quite determin'd about sending Bache to England. If I do, he will certainly be plac'd under your Care; for I am much pleas'd and oblig'd by the Readiness with which you kindly undertake to inspect his Education.[6]

I am concern'd to hear of poor Peirce's Misfortunes.[7] People are rarely fortunate that quit the Profession they were bred to. I believe he was an excellent Farmer, and I think it a pity that he quitted that Calling. I intend sending him Ten Guineas, by a Friend who talks of going soon to London.[8] They shall be left

4. BF's close friend and editor Jacques Barbeu-Dubourg died in December, 1779. In 1770 Hewson translated his *Petit Code de la raison humaine* for publication in England, as it had been denied permission for publication in France: XV, 115n; XVII, 185–6, 291; XXXI, 237n, 361n. Dubourg continued to revise and enlarge the work up to the time of his death. A French text consisting of 91 sections was published in England in 1773 and 1774. The manuscript BF inherited consisted of 102 sections, substantially rearranged and to some degree revised from the earlier publication. BF, as he says here, "had it printed." The question is, when and by whom? As the imprint date is 1782, we speculate that the book was printed in December, shortly before BF wrote the present letter. The type is unquestionably BF's, but the printing need not have been done at Passy. Pierres's letter of Dec. 14, discussing fonts that BF is lending him, suggests that Pierres could have taken BF's type and printed the work clandestinely on his own press.

5. Israel and Elizabeth Wilkes and their two sons were struggling to find gainful employment: XXXVII, 651–2.

6. BF was considering sending BFB to study with Hewson's sons at the Cheam school: XXXVII, 471–2, 652–3.

7. See James Pearce's letter of Oct. 29.

8. Probably Benjamin Vaughan, who returned to England the following month; he wrote BF from London on Feb. 25 (APS).

with you, so that if his Necessities should press before my Friend arrives, you may safely advance & afterwards deduct such part as you judge proper. I know not how otherwise to help him.

You know how much I love you, and that I am ever, My dear Friend, Yours most sincerely　　　　　　　　　B FRANKLIN

Mrs Hewson

From William Hodgson　　　ALS: American Philosophical Society

Dear sir　　　　　　　　　　　London 8 Jany—*1783*—

I did myself the pleasure of writing you some time ago per a friend in which I informed you how much I was hurt to find that Congress had refused to comply with the agreement made here for the Exchange of Prisoners,[9] I have not since then been favored with any of yours. This day I have been at the Secretarys Office[1] again relative to the Exchange of Prisoners— The admiralty have now absolutely ordered Vessells to depart immediately with all the American Prisoners, & they are to be sent to Morlaix, to which place they desire you wou'd be pleased to order all the English Prisoners to be sent in order that they may be ready to embrace the Opportunity of returning per the same Vessells— The Ministry say they send away these Prisoners to convince you that notwithstanding the disappointment in America, they wish to continue to shew every disposition on their Parts to promote Cordiality & I hope yet, that something will appear that shall clear up that Cloud relative to the Exchange in America. The Secretary of State pressed me again relative to Lt Col. Tarleton & Simcoe & added the Name of another Officer taken at york Town Capt. Maclean of the 43d Regt[2]—they wish

9. Above, Dec. 12.
1. The office of either Undersecretary of State Nepean or Secretary of the Admiralty Philip Stephens (*DNB;* Namier and Brooke, *House of Commons,* III, 475).
2. For the first two see Hodgson's Dec. 12 letter. The additional officer was Capt. Charles McLean: Steven M. Baule and Stephen Gilbert, comps., *British Army Officers Who Served in the American Revolution, 1775–1783* (Westminster, Md., 2004), p. 124. BF discharged him from his parole on Jan. 14. The

very much that you woud oblige them with the Exchange of
these three Gentlemen, for whom they wou'd release any Officers at New York that might be named— I informed them that I
had recd from you an Answer purporting that you did not conceive yourself authorised by your Instructions to grant the Indulgence required, however they seemed to wish me to renew
the Application, which is the Occasion of the present Letter. I
beg the favor of you to oblige me with an Answer, that I may
communicate to them in course. I am very sorry to find by what
dropped to day at the Office that Things are in such a very precarious State as to the final Issue. New Claims & new Explana-
tions seem rather to portend a breach than a Conclusion— I am
in a Cleft Stick & Know not which way to turn for Safety, for tis
Safety alone that I now look to— If your Friendship can lend
me a little light to guide me out of the Wilderness, you will do
me an infinite Kindness, Any Letter of Yours will come to me
per the Messengers that I suppose will return with the Ultimatum, or per any other quick mode of Conveyance you shall judge
prudent I am with the greatest respect Dr Sr yours most Sincerely   WILLIAM HODGSON

To His Excellency Benj. Franklin Esqr

Addressed: To / His Excellency / Benj. Franklin Esqr

Notation: Hogdson 8 Janr. 1783.

From Francis Coffyn   ALS: American Philosophical Society

Monsieur   Dunkerque ce 9 Janvr 1783.
    J'ai l'honneur de vous ecrire la presente laquelle vous Sera
remise par le Sieur Thomas Connoly Americain Lequel a eu le
malheur d'Etre pris dans le navire Le Blear Mc Clanaghan a Son
Passage de L'orient a Philadelphie par un corsaire de Guernsey

---

statement, written by WTF and signed by BF, is similar to what Capt. Fage received on Oct. 1 (above), except that here the request comes from the British
government through Hodgson: New England Hist. Geneal. Soc.

auquel endroit il a été conduit prisonnier.[3] Il a trouvé le moyen de S'echaper & de Se rendre ici, & Comme il s'est trouvé dans le cas d'avoir besoin de quelques Secours, Je lui ai payé pour le Compte de votre Excellence une somme de £96.[4] contre son double récépicé pour l'aider a payer les frais de sa route.

J'ai l'honneur d'etre tres respectueusement Monsieur Votre tres humble & tres obéissant Serviteur   F. COFFYN

Addressed: A Son / Excellence Monsieur Bin. Franklin / Ministre plenipotentiare des Etats unis de / L'amerique Septentrionale a la cour de france / a Passi pres Paris

Notation: Coffyn Dunkerque 9 Janv 1783

Endorsed: give 5 Louis to this Gentleman taking his Notes &c with Directions to go via Orleans

From Jonathan Williams, Jr.[5]

ALS: American Philosophical Society; copy: Yale University Library

Dear & hond sir.   Nantes Jan. 9. 1783

Please to read the inclosed Letters to Lord shelburne & Mr Vaughan then please to deliver them to Mr Vaughan if with you or forward them to him if not.—[6] The subject appears to me

3. Probably the brigantine *McClenachan*, 6, commanded by Thomas Houston and owned by Blair McClenachan and others. The ship was captured sometime prior to September by the *Guernsey*, doubtless a privateer: Claghorn, *Naval Officers*, p. 157; Kaminkow, *Mariners*, p. 229; Charles H. Lincoln, comp., *Naval Records of the American Revolution, 1775–1788* (Washington, D.C., 1906), p. 381.

4. 96 *l.t.* Connoly reached Passy a few days later and on Jan. 13 signed a promissory note for 5 *louis* (120 *l.t.*): Editorial Note on Promissory Notes, above.

5. JW sent this letter and its enclosures to WTF on Jan. 9 with a covering letter asking him to treat this with "the utmost dispatch" (APS). WTF's now-missing response of Jan. 15 enclosed a copy of BF's Jan. 15 note to Shelburne, below: JW to WTF, Jan. 21, 1783 (APS).

6. JW's letter to Shelburne, dated Jan. 9, was an appeal for the restoration of his brig *Trio*, an unarmed vessel that had sailed from the Loire on Dec. 7—after the preliminary peace agreement had been signed, he pointed out.

worth a national Claim if you think so please to add a Line to my
Letter to Lord shelburne, if you think an official Claim not con-
sistent & you in your private name can with propriety add a
Word to enforce my Representation I know you will do it.[7]

I beg you will accept my sincere Wishes for as many Returns
of the season as you yourself desire.

I am most respectfully Dutifully & affectionately Yours

JONA WILLIAMS J

His Excelly Dr Franklin.

Notation: Williams M. Jona. Nantes 9. Jany 1783.

To Filangieri   LS:[8] Museo Civico Gaetano Filangieri

Sir,   Passy, Jany. 11. 1783

The Letter you did me the Honour of writing to me in August last,[9] came to my Hands when I lay ill of two painful Disorders, which confin'd me near three Months, and with the Mul-
tiplicity of Business that follow'd oblig'd me to postpone much
of my Correspondence. I have yesterday receiv'd a second Letter from you,[1] and I now without farther Delay sit down to answer them both.

The crew mutinied and brought the ship into Kinsale, where they were hoping to sell the cargo. JW blamed a "Negro Lad" for instigating the mutiny;
this was Jean Montague, former slave of Capt. Robeson (XXXIII, 96–7), who
owed JW money and whom JW mistrusted. The British press, however, credited the success of the mutiny to the four English sailors on board, former
prisoners of war who had recently been released from a Nantes prison in order to fill out the crew. They conspired with the mate and locked the captain
in his cabin: JW to Shelburne, Jan. 9, 1783; JW to Capt. Birrell, Nov. 22, 1782
(both at Yale University Library); *The General Evening Post*, issue of Jan.
2–4; *Morning Herald and Daily Advertiser*, issue of Jan. 3, 1783.

JW's letter to Benjamin Vaughan, dated Jan. 8, asked him to deliver Shelburne's letter, either to obtain a passport allowing the *Trio* to return to France
or else to remit to JW the proceeds of the sale of the cargo, and to assist the
captain in returning to France: Yale University Library.

7. See BF to Shelburne, Jan. 15.
8. In L'Air de Lamotte's hand.
9. Above, Aug. 24.
1. Above, Dec. 2.

The two first Volumes of your excellent Work,[2] which were put into my hands by M. Pio, I perus'd with great Pleasure. They are also much esteem'd by some very judicious Persons to whom I have lent them. I should have been glad of another Copy for one of those Friends, who is very desirous of procuring it, but I suppose those you mention to have sent to M. Pio did not arrive. I was glad to learn, that you were proceeding to consider the criminal Laws. None have more need of Reformation. They are every where in so great Disorder, and so much Injustice is committed in the Execution of them, that I have been sometimes inclin'd to imagine, less would exist in the World if there were no such Laws, and the Punishment of Injuries were left to private Resentment. I am glad therefore that you have not suffered yourself to be discouraged by any Objections or Apprehensions, and that we may soon expect the Satisfaction of seeing the two Volumes on that Subject which you have now under the Press.

With regard to your Project of removing to America, tho' I am sure that a Person of your Knowledge, just Sentiments, and useful Talents would be a valuable Acquisition for our Country, I cannot encourage you to undertake hastily such a Voyage; because for a Man to expatriate himself is a serious Business, and should be well considered, especially where the Distance is so great, and the Expence of removing thither with a Family, & of returning if the Country should not suit you, will be so heavy. I have no Orders or Authority of any kind to encourage Strangers with Expectations of Employment by our Government, nor am I impower'd to be at any Expence in transporting them, tho' our Country is open, and Strangers may establish themselves there, where they soon become Citizens and are respected according to their Conduct. Men know, because they feel the Inconveniencies of their *present* Situation; but they do not know those that may, if they change, attend the *new one*. I wish therefore you could see that Country by your self, before you carry thither the Lady with whom you propose to be united in marriage. You will then be able to form a good Judgment how far the Removal is likely to be advantageous, and may proceed on surer Grounds. England

2. *La scienza della legislazione.*

has now acknowledged our Independence, and the Sovereignty of our Government; and several States of Europe who think a Commerce with us may be beneficial to them are preparing to send Ministers to reside near the Congress. It is possible to establish a profitable Trade between the Kingdoms of Naples and America. Should your Court be of that Opinion, and think fit to employ some one to visit our several States, and take Information of our Productions and Wants, the Nature of our Commerce &c. &c. perhaps it could not find a fitter Person than yourself for such a Mission: I would afford you all the assistance in my Power towards its due Execution; and by this means your Voyage would not only be without Expence to you, but might afford you some Profit.

With great & sincere Esteem I have the honour to be, Sir, Your most obedient and most humble Servant,   B FRANKLIN

Endorsed: 1783 Franklin 11. Geñajo

From John Bondfield   ALS: American Philosophical Society

Sir   Bordeaux 11 Januy 1782 [*i.e.* 1783][3]
The Don Galva[4] of and from Salem arrivd at this Port Yesterday he saild from Salem the 1 December Mons De Vaudrieul with the Fleet remain at Boston and from the report of the Captain would not sail before the later end of the month the french Troops were arrivd at Boston to embark on board the Fleet.

The Indians have committed some fresh Crueltys on the back settlements near Sunbery[5] otherway all is quiet in America.

I have the Honor to be with due respect Sir Your most Obedient Humble Servant   JOHN BONDFIELD

3. The year is based on the reference to Vaudreuil's fleet in Boston.
4. Either the brig *Don Galvez*, 6, or the ship *General Galvez*, 18: Allen, *Mass. Privateers*, pp. 119, 144. The latter arrived at Bordeaux sometime in January: Vergennes to BF, Feb. 7 (APS).
5. Sunbury (or Fort Augusta), Pa. Indian raids on the Pa. frontier gradually subsided after mid-1782: Jack M. Sosin, *The Revolutionary Frontier, 1763–1783* (New York, Chicago, and San Francisco, 1967), p. 137; Barbara Graymont, *The Iroquois in the American Revolution* (Syracuse, 1972), p. 255.

Addressed: A Son Excélance / Benjmn. Franklin / Ministre Plenre. des Etats / Unis de Lamerique. / à Paris

Notation: Bondfiel 11 June 1782.

From Robert Morris

LS: American Philosophical Society, Library of Congress; copy: Library of Congress

Sir   Office of Finance 11th. January 1783

On the ninth Instant, from an Investigation of Mr. Grands Accounts, then lately received,[6] I found that after making due Allowance for Loan Office Bills &ca. which might still come upon him, my Drafts (and those which I have directed) would exceed, by Something more than six Millions (exclusive of the Interest payable by him in November on the Dutch Loan) any Funds which he could be possessed of. It appeared also by indirect Information so late as in the Month of September, that the Loan opened by Mr. Adams had not produced above three Millions,[7] so that unless he had met with further Success, there would be a Deficiency of three Millions. Had the Court granted us twelve Millions in the first Instance, Had Mr. Adams' Loan produced six Millions, had Mr de Beaumarchais Bills been provided for, without Recurrence to the American Banker, or finally had the heavy Deduction made by those Bills been replaced,[8] this disagreeable Thing would not have happened. Presuming that

---

6. Grand's accounts, now-missing, arrived in December: *Morris Papers,* VII, 265n.

7. All these sums are in *livres tournois.* 3,000,000 *l.t.* is equivalent to about 1,320,000 *f.* (or guilders); see XXXVI, 190n. The "indirect information" Morris alludes to was probably the communication he received from Lewis Morris on behalf of Livingston, dated Sept. 11, which included JA's July 5 letter to Livingston announcing the opening of a subscription for the Dutch loan. JA warned that of the 5,000,000 guilders he was seeking, Congress should expect no more than 1,500,000 "by Christmas." By January, 1783, the Dutch banks had raised about 1,800,000 guilders: *Morris Papers,* VI, 352; VII, 24n; Wharton, *Diplomatic Correspondence,* V, 594.

8. For Beaumarchais' bills see Robert Morris to BF, Sept. 30.

the Loan of the last Year was exclusively at my Disposition, I drew during the Year to the Amount of it, and I am convinced that all my Bills, and those drawn by my Authority will have been paid. Rely on it, that as I told you in a former Letter,[9] I have acted under the Influence of dire Necessity, and this you will be convinced of by a few out of many Circumstances. Enclosed you have a general State of the public Account, until the end of 1781:[1] On which you will observe, that the Army was fed principally (tho scantily) by the specific Supplies called for at different previous Periods; and that there remained in the Treasury near three hundred thousand Dollars, being Part of the Money which Colo. Laurens brought with him from France. I also enclose you the Copy of a Letter written to Congress, on the twenty first of October, and of its several Enclosures[2] whch. will need no Commentary, or if it did, I would only add that I have been obliged to sell part of the Goods which arrived here from Holland, in Order to raise so much Money as would save my sinking Credit from Destruction.[3] I would go into a Detail of the various Measures pursued to stimulate the Exertions of the States, but to do this with Accuracy would be to give a tedious History of my whole Administration. Whatever Expedient could suggest itself which might have that desirable Effect, I have tried: and

9. Of Jan. 3, above.

1. This printed statement prepared under Morris' supervision is reproduced in *Morris Papers*, VII, 62–3.

2. Morris' Oct. 21 letter to President of Congress John Hanson and its 14 enclosures concerned the lack of funds to pay the contractors for supplying the army and the replacement of the existing contract with the firm of Wadsworth and Carter. The enclosures (APS), all from 1782, include: Morris to George Washington, Aug. 29, 30, and Sept. 9; Comfort Sands, Walter Livingston, William Duer, and Daniel Parker to Morris, Sept. 11; Morris to Ezekiel Cornell, Sept. 20, 23, and Oct. 10; Cornell to Sands, Livingston, Duer, and Parker, Sept. 30; Sands, Livingston, Duer, and Parker to Cornell, Oct. 1; Cornell to Morris, Oct. 5; Tench Tilghman to Morris, Oct. 5; Morris to the Contractors for West Point and the Moving Army, Oct. 10; Robert Morris, Jeremiah Wadsworth, John Carter: Contract for Military Food and Stores, Oct. 12; Morris to the Governors of the States, Oct. 21. They are in *Morris Papers*, VI, 282–3, 286, 345–6, 356–64, 408–9, 419–20, 501–4, 508–9, 544–5, 545–6, 551–3, 553, 565–73, 631–4, 635–8.

3. Morris had to sell part of the cargo of the *Heer Adams: Morris Papers*, VI, 372–3, 429, 600–1; VII, 295n.

I do assure you that when I look back at the Scenes I have passed thro, they strike my own Mind with Astonishment. As soon as I can get the Accounts made up, I will transmit you the Total of our Expenditures,[4] but to transmit, or even relate, our Hazards and Difficulties would be impossible.

Even at this Moment I am making farther Exertions to bring our unwieldy System into Form, and Ward off impending Evils, but what the Success may be Heaven knows. Imagine the Situation of a Man who is to direct the Finances of a Country, almost without Revenue (for such you will perceive this to be) surrounded by Creditors whose Distresses, while they encrease their Clamors, render it more difficult to appease them. An Army ready to disband or Mutiny. A Government whose sole Authority consists in the Power of framing Recommendations. Surely it is not necessary to add any Colouring to such a Piece, and yet Truth would justify more than Fancy could paint. The Settlement of Accounts, long and intricate beyond Comprehension, becomes next to impossible, from the Want of that Authority which is on the Verge of Annihilation from those Confusions which nothing can disipate except the complete Settlement of Accounts, and an honest Provision for Payment.

Upon Discovering the Situation of our Affairs, in the manner already mentioned, I laid them before Congress. You will know the Result. The Secretary of foreign Affairs will doubtless transmit their Act,[5] to which I must add this farther Communication, that I expect my Bills will amot. to a Million, within a Month from this Date. There are Cases where Nothing worse can be apprehended from a Measure, than what would inevitably happen without it, and our present Position is one of them. An immedi-

4. For the 1782 statement of receipts and expenditures, dated Jan. 31, 1783, see *Morris Papers*, VII, 386 and facing page.

5. Given the vastness of the shortfall, Morris had asked Congress on Jan. 9 to convene a secret advisory committee and sanction his drawing of bills of exchange on the credit of contingent loans in Europe. On Jan. 10, Congress passed a secret resolution authorizing him to do so: *JCC*, XXIV, 43–4; *Morris Papers*, VII, 266n, 286–8. Two copies of that resolution, written entirely in code, were sent to BF (APS; Hist. Soc. of Pa.), though we cannot determine when or by whom. The one at the Hist. Soc. of Pa. was endorsed by BF, "Resolution of Congress Jan. 10. 83 Money."

ate Command of Money is alike necessary to our present Existence and future Prospects. In Europe, when this Letter arrives,
you will know decidedly whether we are to expect Peace or War,
but in America we must prepare for the latter; for by so doing we
may forward Negotiations for Peace, and at the worst will only
have incurred some additional Expence whereas by neglecting
it, we risk the Chance of being taken unawares, and paying very
dearly the Penalties of Neglect.

But Sir, notwithstanding these Reasons and many others
which will justify every Counsel and every Act (however irregular in other Respects) I would not draw one more Bill, and I
would boldly hazard every Consequence of the Omission, if I
were not persuaded that they would be paid. On this Occasion
your Sovereign will expect your most vigorous Exertions, and
your Country will, I trust, be indebted to you in a Degree for her
political Existence.

I am Sir your most obedient and humble Servant

ROBT MORRIS

His Excellency Benjamin Franklin Esquire

1st.

Endorsed: Mr Morris Jan. 11. 83 Money— Money—

From Antoine-Alexis-François Cadet de Vaux

ALS: American Philosophical Society

Monsieur,   ce 13 Jer 1783

M. Brongniart de l'académie Royale d'architecture a fait tirer
Empreinte de la médaille destinée à consacrer l'union des Etats
unis avec la france; il desire avoir l'honneur d'en présenter
l'Epreuve à monsieur franklin.[6] Je desire de mon coté avoir

---

6. See Brongniart to BF, Sept. 22. By Jan. 23, the date of Brongniart's next
letter (APS), Dupré had made two new impressions, one of which showed
the reverse side of the medal, the head of a woman representing Liberty. The
medal became known by the inscription above the head, "Libertas Americana."

577

l'honneur de lui rendre mes devoirs, mais comme M. Brongniart et moi avons beaucoup d'occupations, chacun de notre coté, et que nous ne Voudrions pas courir les risques de ne point trouver Monsieur franklin, Je me Suis chargé d'avoir l'honneur de vous Ecrire et de vous prier de me mander Si nous pouvons nous rendre *jeudi* à Passy et à quelle heure pour la plus grande commodité de Monsieur franklin.

J'ai l'honneur d'Etre avec un respectueux attachement Monsieur, Votre très humble et très obeissant Serviteur

CADET DE VAUX
censeur royal, rue des Gravilliers

Notation: Cadet de Veaux 13. Sept. 1783 Paris

From Richard Grubb   AL: American Philosophical Society

Hotel de Valois Monday Morng. 13 Jany. 1783

Mr. Grubb presents his respectful Compliments to his Excellency Dr. Franklin, & requests him to grant him a passport for England via Callais.

Mr. G. ill state of Health is the cause of the demand, & hopes his Excellency will in consequence, order one to be made out

Addressed: His Excellency / Benjamin Franklin. / Passy

Notation: Mr. Grubb Paris 13th. Jany. 1783

From Mary Hewson   ALS: American Philosophical Society

Dear Sir.   Kensington Jan. 13. 1783

I received eleven little books for which I thank you.[7] But why was there not one line with them? My poor mother was much disappointed, and I believe imagined that I did not speak truth when I told her there was no letter in the parcel. I know you will pay the tribute of a sigh for the loss of one who loved you with the most ardent affection. She lingered under a most painful dis-

7. See BF to Hewson, Jan. 8.

order many weeks, and departed the first day of this year. I have the satisfaction to think she had every alleviation her illness could admit, and more than she could have had if I had not come to this place, therefore I am well recompensed for moving. My dear Children[8] are all well. My boys are at home now for their holidays.

I have heard that you are out of health. I wish you would give me a line, and if you can contradict that report I shall rejoice. Believe me Dear Sir Your affectionate humble Servant

MARY HEWSON

In the last letter my mother received from you,[9] you desired to be informed of the Pearces. Poor Sally died above a year ago, and left four children. The Grandfather Franklin has taken the boy. The three girls remain at Richmond, very poorly supported, for the Father has not succeeded in his business, and is now out of employ. The old folks were obliged to give up their Farm. I wish we could have made up a Peace, for I think James might do in America. But I suppose till hostilities cease there can be no opening for him & his family.[1]

Addressed: A Monsieur / Monsieur franklin Ministre / plenipotentiaire des Etats unis / d'amerique, / A Passy.

From William and R. Macarty[2]

AL: American Philosophical Society

Monday 13 Jany [1783][3] 9 oClock. Morn
Mr & Mrs. Macarty present thier most Respectfull Compliments to Doctr. Franklin, and are Sorry they cannot have the honor of

8. William, Thomas, and Elizabeth: XXXIV, 524n.

9. XXXVII, 624–5.

1. See James Pearce to BF, Oct. 29. "Grandfather Franklin" was Thomas Franklin, Sally Pearce's father and BF's first cousin once removed: I, li–lii. The Pearce farm had been at Ewell: XX, 277.

2. William Macarty's wife joined him in Lorient in September, 1781: XXXV, 482.

3. The only year since Mrs. Macarty's arrival in which Jan. 13 fell on a Monday.

Dining with him to Day, being Engage'd; having only this moment Recieved Doctr Franklins polite Invitation of the 11th.

Addressed: Monsieur / Monsieur Franklin / Passy

From Robert Morris

LS: American Philosophical Society, Independence National Historical Park; copy: Library of Congress

Dear Sir   Office of Finance 13th January 1783,

I have received, in Addition to those already acknowledged, your Letters of the twelfth of August, twenty sixth of September, and fourteenth of October. I should therefore, regularly, have received two Copies of the Contract entered into on the sixteenth of July between you and the Count de Vergennes; but I suppose it has been omitted, thro' Mistake, in both the Letters which refer to it.[4] I lament this the more, as no one Copy of it has yet arrived, and consequently the Congress cannot do what I am perswaded they would, on the Occasion. But altho' they (from this Circumstance) do not make Professions, yet as far as I know the Sentiments of that Body, they are penetrated with Gratitude. And you hazard Nothing in making to the King the fullest Assurances of their Desire to repay the Obligations they have received, and gratify their Affection for his Person and Family, by Services and Benefits. You will oblige me much if (together with the Contract in Question) you will send a State of the farmers-generals Account, and of the Agreement with them.

You tell me that the Losses in the West Indies prevent you from obtaining farther Aid.[5] It is therefore to Us a double Loss. As to the Caution you give me about my Banker, you will find that before the Receipt of Mr. Grand's Accounts, I had valued on him beyond his Funds.[6] I have this Day entered into an Ex-

4. The contract (XXXVII, 633–9) was enclosed in BF's letters of Aug. 12 and Sept. 26. A duplicate of the latter with its enclosure arrived by Jan. 19; see Morris to BF of that date.

5. Here, and in the rest of the letter, Morris is responding to BF's letter of Aug. 12.

6. See Morris to BF, Jan. 11.

planation with the Minister on that Subject, and I inclose you the
Copy of my Letter, as also of another Paper deliverd him which
may be worth your Attention.[7] In my Turn, I rely on your Promise of Exertion to pay my Drafts. If one Bill should be protested,
I could no longer serve the United States.

With Respect to the Apprehension you express as to my Bills,
I do not perceive the Matter in the same Point of Light with you.
The Lists of my Bills are transmitted to Mr. Grand, by various
Opportunities, and *they* will check any which might be forged or
altered.

I shall take due Notice of what you say about your Salary,[8]
and will enclose the Bills to you, the Amount will depend on the
Course of Exchange: during the War you will be a Gainer, and
after the Peace you may perhaps loose some Trifle but not much,
because Remittances might then be made in Specie should the
Exchange be extravagantly high. You will readily perceive, that
altho the Fluctuations of Exchange are in themselves of very little Consequence to the Individuals who may be connected with
Government, they become Important at the Treasury, partly
from the Number of Payments and consequent Amount, but
more so because they would introduce a Degree of Intricacy and
Perplexity in the public Accounts, which are generally either the
Effect or the Cause of Fraud and Peculation. Besides, there is no
other Way of adjusting Salaries than by a Payment of so much
at the Treasury, unless by rating them in the Currency of every
different Country, as Livres, Dollars Guilders, Rubles &c. The
late Mode of rating them, in Pounds Sterling, required a double
Exchange. For Instance, the Number of Livres to be given in

7. The letter to La Luzerne was dated Jan. 13; BF endorsed it, "Mr Morris
to the Minister of France" (APS). The other paper was probably the Office
of Finance's "Observations on the Present State of Affairs," composed
around this time and almost certainly presented to the French minister. The
only known copy is at the AAE. For both texts see *Morris Papers*, VII, 300–
4, 304–7.

8. On Aug. 12, in response to a congressional resolution designating Morris to handle the salaries of American diplomats serving overseas, BF had authorized Morris to receive and remit his salary: XXXVII, 738. Congress, however, changed its mind and returned the authority to Robert R. Livingston;
see our annotation of BF to Livingston, Oct. 14.

Payment of one hundred Pounds Sterling, at Paris, on any given Day, depends on the then Rate of Exchange between Paris and London, and the Value of those Livres here, depends on the Exchange between Paris and Philada.

I pray you, Sir, to accept my sincere Thanks for the kind Interest you take in the Success of my Administration. The only Return which I can make to your Goodness, is by assuring you that all my Measures shall be honestly directed towards the good of that Cause which you have so long, so faithfully, and so honorably served.

I am with the Sincerest Respect & Esteem Sir Your most obedient & humble Servant   ROBT MORRIS

His Excellency Benjamin Franklin Minister plenipotentiary of the United States of America

Endorsed: Mr Morris Jan 13. 1783 Salaries

From Servin   ALS: American Philosophical Society

Monsieur   a Rouen 13 Janvier 1783

Je n'ai reçû qu'avant hier La Lettre Que Vous avez bien Voulû m'Ecrire le 16 novembre dernier.[9] Ce retardement etonnant a fait Que mon libraire n'a pû Vous Envoier de Basle l'Exemplaire Que Je Vous ai prié d'Agréer.[1] Mais j'irai a paris dans Quelques Semaines et j'aurai l'honneur de Vous presenter en personne Mon hommage. Je desire d'autant plus Qu'il Vous Soit Agréable Que Je releve dans Mon Ouvrage les Vices de La Législation Criminelle d'angleterre Que Vous Connoissez Mieux que tout Autre.

Je Suis Avec Respect, De Votre Excellence Monsieur Le Trés humble & Trés obéissant Serviteur   SERVIN
avt au parl.

9. BF's notes for this now-missing reply were drafted on Servin's earlier letter of Sept. 16, above.

1. Servin's publisher was Johannes Schweighauser (1738–1806), printer and bookseller at Basel: Marcel Godet *et al.*, eds., *Dictionnaire historique et biographique de la Suisse* (7 vols., Neuchâtel, 1921–33); Antoine Perrin, *Almanach de la librairie* (Paris, 1781; reprinted, Aubel, Belgium, 1984), p. 85.

Notation: Servin, Rouen 13 Janvr. 1783

To William Hodgson: Extract and Note[2]

(I) Press copy of copy:[3] American Philosophical Society; (II) press copy
of AL: American Philosophical Society

I.

[January 14, 1783]
It was in the Beginning of October that you inform'd me, the
Prisoners would be immediately sent over hither to be exchang'd.[4] There were then in the French Ports several American
Vessels in which I could have sent them. I fear that I shall now
be obliged to send a Vessel with them, which I must hire for that
purpose. I therefore request you would procure for me a Passport with a Blank for the Captain and Vessel's Name. Mr. Oswald will assist you in the Application if necessary. If the Vessels still here can take them I shall not make use of it; but
methinks the Prisoners should be furnish'd with some kind of
Protection to serve them till they get home.—

Extract of a Letter from B Franklin Esq to W. Hodgson Esqr.
dated Passy Jan. 14 1783

II.

Jany. 14. 1783
I heartily wish it were in my Power, my dear Friend, to give you
the Information you desire: But I am afraid of misleading you,
being as much in the dark as you can possibly be.— The Mo-

2. Though the recipient's name does not appear on the note, we conjec-
ture that BF added this paragraph, written on a separate sheet, to the now-
missing letter from which the extract was made. Hodgson had asked BF on
Dec. 12 about the "probability" of a peace settlement. He repeated that inquiry, in equally veiled but pointed terms, in his letter of Jan. 8.
3. The text is in L'Air de Lamotte's hand. The notation was written by
WTF.
4. Above, Oct. 14.

ment I learn any thing that can be depended on, and may [*be*] of Use to you, it shall be sent you. But I hope you may obtain earlier Intelligence nearer home.—

To Richard Oswald

ALS: William L. Clements Library; copies: Library of Congress (two), Massachusetts Historical Society, Ohio State Archaeological and Historical Society

Sir,   Passy, Jany. 14. 1783.

I am much oblig'd by your Information of your intended Trip to England.[5] I heartily wish you a good Journey, and a Speedy Return; & request your kind Care of a Pacquet for Mr Hodgson.

I enclose two Papers that were read at different times by me to the Commissioners; they may serve to show if you should have Occasion, what was urg'd on the part of America on certain Points; or they may help to refresh your Memory.[6] I send you also another Paper which I once read to you separately. It contains a Proposition for improving the Law of Nations, by prohibiting the Plundering of unarm'd & usefully-employ'd People. I rather wish than expect that it will be adopted. But I think it may be offer'd with a better Grace by a Country that is likely to suffer least & gain most by continuing the antient Practice, which is our Case, as the American Ships laden only with the Gross Productions of the Earth, cannot be so valuable as yours

5. Oswald left on Jan. 15, taking the present letter with him. In a Jan. 15 letter to Shelburne, Fitzherbert commented on it. He complained of the "monstrous injustice of introducing fresh articles in the treaty," although he doubted BF would insist on them: Giunta, *Emerging Nation*, 1, 752–3. Oswald had told Fitzherbert a month earlier that the American commissioners were talking about inserting new commercial stipulations in the final treaty, and Fitzherbert expressed his outrage in a letter to Strachey of Dec. 19: Giunta, *Emerging Nation*, 1, 725–7.

6. The enclosures were probably BF's letter to Oswald of Nov. 26, which he read to the commissioners the same day (according to his own notation), and BF's proposed Article 5, published above under the day he read it to the commissioners, Nov. 29. Both concern the question of compensation for Loyalists.

fill'd with Sugars or with Manufactures.— It has not yet been consider'd by my Colleagues; but if you should think or find that it might be acceptable on your side, I would try to get it inserted in the General Treaty.[7] I think it will do honour to the Nations that establish it.

With great & sincere Esteem, I am, Sir, Your most obedient & most humble Servant   B Franklin

R. Oswald Esqr.

Francis Dana to the American Peace Commissioners

Copy:[8] Massachusetts Historical Society

Gentlemen   St: Petersbourg Jany: 3 / 14 1783.

I was honoured with your favour of the 12th. of Decr: by the last post, enclosing a Copy of the preliminary Treaty of Peace between his Britannic Majesty and the United-States. I most heartily congratulate with you upon this great event, in which you have had the honour of so distinguished a part. I think that we ought to be, and shall be satisfied with the terms of peace. But we are here wholly at a loss whether the other belligerant parties will be able to adjust their several pretensions, and of Course whether our Treaty will take effect. The prevailing opinion here among the best informed, is that we shall have a general peace. However this may be, we shall see a war break out on the other side of Europe.[9] Some of the Powers which will be engaged in it, do not wish to see *all* the present belligerant Powers at peace, for reasons which will readily occur to you. I thank you, Gen-

7. When WTF published this letter, he printed as the enclosure BF's "thoughts" on privateering and the Sugar Islands—the two short essays (run together as one piece) that we published in XXXVII, 617–20—and the article that BF proposed for the final treaty that summarized those thoughts (above, under Dec. 13): WTF, *Memoirs*, II, 420–2.

8. In Dana's hand. As usual, we publish under the New Style date.

9. Russia annexed the Crimea the following April, but this did not lead to the war with the Ottoman Empire that many had expected: Alan W. Fisher, *The Russian Annexation of the Crimea, 1772–1783* (Cambridge, 1970), pp. 135–8.

585

tlemen, for your opinions respecting the communication of my Mission to the Ministers of Her Imperial Majesty, and of the other Neutral Powers, residing at this Court. But, "absolute certainty of success" are strong words,[1] and will bind me down to a state of inaction till the conclusion of the present War; unless I shou'd receive positive assurances that things are prepared for my reception; of which I have no expectation. I have yesterday consulted the French Minister[2] upon this matter, and acquainted him at the same time with your opinions, as well as communicated to him the preliminary Treaty. He thinks that tho' in this moment I might not meet with a refusal, yet my admission wou'd be upon various pretences, postponed, till advice shou'd be received here, whether we are to have peace or war: a question which it is expected will be decided at furthest in the course of a fortn'night, and that if the War shou'd be continued, I shou'd *not* be received. Thus I am doubly bound down as above, during the War. If unfortunately the negotiations shou'd be broken off, it is my present determination to retire from this Court, without communicating my Mission, and to return by the first opportunity to America. I cannot think it for the honour or interest of the United-States, after what has already taken place between them and his Britannic Majesty, that I shou'd wait the issue of another campaign. I am persuaded we have nothing to fear from this quarter in any event. If they will not improve a fair occasion which is presented to them, to promote the mutual Interests of both Empires, they may hereafter repent it.

I am, Gentleman, with the greatest respect and esteem, Your most obedient & most humble Servant.

The Commissioners of the United States, at Paris, By the post of the same day thro' Mr: W. to Mr: G. under cover to Mr: *A*.[3]

The Commissioners of the United States, at Paris.

1. Dana's March 2, 1782, instructions from Livingston had forbidden him to present his credentials unless he had "absolute certainty" he would be received: Wharton, *Diplomatic Correspondence*, v, 209.

2. Minister Plenipotentiary Charles-Olivier de Saint-Georges, marquis de Vérac: xxxvi, 259; *Repertorium der diplomatischen Vertreter*, III, 133.

3. *W* probably stands for the banker Wolff, *G* for Grand, and *A* for Adams.

From Sidney Lee[4]   ALS: American Philosophical Society

Sr   Newgate Street Chester January 14th. 1783.
   I hope the enclosed will meet with your Excellency's approbation, and that I am not guilty of an impropriety in requesting
of you the favor of transmitting it to his Excellency General
Washington. I am Sr with great respect your most obedient humble Servant   SIDNEY LEE

Addressed: His Excellency Benjamn Franklin

To the Earl of Shelburne
                    ALS: G. T. Mandl-Trust, Nestal, Switzerland (2001)

As Jonathan Williams, Jr., requested on January 9, Franklin appended
this note to the letter Williams wrote to Shelburne regarding the muti-
nous seizure of his merchantman *Trio.* The vessel had been brought
into Kinsale and was awaiting condemnation as a prize.
   The British government's encouragement of mutinies on Ameri-
can-owned ships had long enraged Franklin. His writings on the subject were expressed in language so strong, however, that they were not
made public in the early years of the war. When Congress passed a
resolution on privateering in response to the Prohibitory Act, Franklin drafted a strongly worded preamble; this was never entered into
the record, either because Franklin himself held it back or because
Congress voted it down. After the first cases of mutinies were reported in August, 1776, and the British rewarded the captors by allowing them the full value of the cargo, Franklin was appointed to a
congressional committee to investigate the reports. Once in France in

---

4. Sister and principal heir of Maj.-Gen. Charles Lee (XXII, 292), who had
served in the American army, was court-martialed in 1778 and suspended,
and died in Philadelphia on Oct. 2, 1782. The letter to Washington she enclosed, dated Jan. 14, asked for a copy of her brother's will and advice on how
she ought to proceed. Washington agreed to assist her: *ANB;* W. W. Abbot
and Dorothy Twohig *et al.*, eds., *The Papers of George Washington,* Confederation Series (6 vols., Charlottesville, Va., and London, 1992–97), I,
115n. For Lee's will and his sister's disposition of her inheritance see *The Lee
Papers, 1754–1782* (4 vols.; New-York Hist. Soc. *Collections,* IV–VII, New
York, 1872–75), IV, 29–33, 346.

early 1777, Franklin and Silas Deane drafted a stern memorial to Lord George Germain declaring the policy a "violation of all moral obligation" and threatening to retaliate. This they did not send. In 1782, he finally did publicize his true feelings on the subject, though not under his own name. His letter, purportedly from John Paul Jones to Sir Joseph Yorke, was published in the London press at the end of September.[5]

Franklin sent the present note to Benjamin Vaughan along with Williams' papers on January 15. That evening Vaughan rushed to Passy to discuss the matter. Vaughan recounted their conversation in his cover letter to Shelburne, written the next day. Franklin had told him about the Prohibitory Act and about the "strong paper" he had been prepared to send to London in 1777 (which he had held back because Vergennes advised him that it would do no good), and then discussed the general issue of "treachery." It was, said Franklin,

a shocking thing to encourage for the world; it went into people's families and houses; and good men should try to render it detested. Force was the proper implement of war; and that was bad enough; but bringing in fraud over and above force, was making things worse and worse for the world, instead of mending them. He then gave a deep sigh, and an exclamation marking some anxiety.— They talk said he, of man's growing better: I wish he may not be growing worse, and I do not know how it should be accounted for; but you see said he, one thing, How the ties of religion are every day wearing out.[6]

Passy, Jan. 15. 1783

Mariners are the hired Servants of Merchants, entrusted with their Property.

The corrupting of Servants, & hiring them to betray the Trust reposed in them, & rob their Masters of the Property con-

5. For the Prohibitory Act and BF's draft preamble to the congressional resolution on privateering see XXII, 268n, 388–9. His appointment in August, 1776, to the congressional committee investigating mutinies is in *JCC*, V, 692. The 1777 proposed memorial to Lord Germain is in XXIII, 294–5. BF's hoax, the purported letter from Jones, was part of his "Supplement to the Boston Independent Chronicle"; see XXXVII, 190–5, and for his discussion of the Prohibitory Act, which is echoed in the present note, see p. 192.

6. A typescript of Vaughan to Shelburne, Jan. 16, 1783, is at the APS. The section of the letter describing Vaughan's conversation with BF is quoted in the Christie's sales catalogue of Oct. 12, 1994, "Important Autograph Letters from the Historical Archives of Bowood House," p. 36.

fided to them, by sharing the Plunder among them, was one of the infamous Modes of making War against America adopted by the late Administration,[7] which ought to render them for ever detestable among good Men, who wish to see the Mischiefs of War diminished, and not augmented.   B F.

Endorsed: Dr. Franklin *note* on the Case of his Nephew Jonathan Williams respecting the Brig *Trio.*

From Léonard Appée   ALS: American Philosophical Society

Ce 16 jenvier De la presente anée 1783
Monsieur   De la tournelle[8] à paris
Les Bonté que vous faite regallire [rejaillir] Sur un umbre [nombre] infinie De malhureux Et la justice Du congrés donc vous En nette [êtes] le digne réprésentant me fait prendre la liberté de vous adressé la présante pour imploré Votre protections, de plus Monsieur la justice de ma Cause me fait tout Esperé De Votre imtegrittée je reclâme dont monsieur 3 mois de gage quil mest dus pour mon Service En Callité [qualité] de Vonlontaire Sur la frégate amériquaine nommé la providence a raison de dix Ecus par mois En narmement [armement] á pinbœuf [Paimbœuf] avec la frégate la Bostonne toute deux destinée pour Boston ou nous arrivame a la fin dotobre De la née [l'année] 1778 lescadre francaise alors muilliée En rade de Boston manquaÿ de monde, Et monsieur le Comte Destainstg optin [obtint] la permisions du Congrés de prendre toute les francois qui estoit abort de la fregate ámériquaine. Cest alors que je me Vie forcé de quitté une nation de quï javais recut mille Bienfait pour Servire a ma patrie je fut my abort du languedoc Vaisseaux amiral. Lors ce que je fut á bort je demanda a monsieur le comte destin ce quil pouvais me revénire de mon Service a vec les ameriquin ausy

7. BF expressed this sentiment to Vergennes in 1779, in similar language: XXIX, 388–9.
8. The château de la Tournelle, a staging point for convicts about to be dispatched to French naval ports to fulfill terms of enforced labor as galley slaves: Hillairet, *Rues de Paris,* II, 567.

Bien que ma pard des 3 prise[9] faite dans notre traversé consistant En une Caiche corsaire portant 12 canon un Bric Et un Brigantin chargé de Vain Et autre marchandise. Monsieur le comte D'estainstg promis de me faire payé Et man Voÿat [m'envoyat] a mr. de Bordat[1] major de lescadre mais les affaire qui Survinre [survinrent] tant a la grénades qua Savannat[2] ou il recut plusieur Blessure lon pechat [l'empêchat] de pansé a moy nous Somme revenut a Brest ou ont [on] me delivrat un Congés pour revénire á paris ce quil fut mon malheur par un differant que Jut [j'eus] avec un de mes Suppérieurs Et je fut Condamné á 5 ans de gallere mon triste Sort ma Enpéché de pouvoir Vous adresseé mes representations plutot.

Jose donc Ésperré que Vous aurés Egard a mes representations Et que touché Du deplorable Etât de mon Sort Vous Voudre Bien ma cordér ma demandes. Je joint a la presante lettre une autre que jay recut Du Commissaire ordonnateur De la marine de pinbœuf[3] qui Vous Convaincra Monsieur de la réallité De mes juste representa[*tions*.] Jose tout esperré Monsieur De votre justice Et Suis de Monsieur le tres humble tres obéisant Serviteur[4]

LÉONARD APPÉE

Notation: Jan. 16. 1783

9. The *Providence* sailed from France in company with the *Boston* and the *Ranger* around the beginning of August, 1778, and first touched at Portsmouth, N.H., with her prizes: XXVII, 186–7, 213n, 358; XXVIII, 186n.

1. Jean-Charles Borda (1733–1799), a celebrated scientist as well as naval officer: *DBF*.

2. D'Estaing's squadron fought in 1779 at Grenada and Savannah.

3. Appée enclosed an undated letter from Louvel, *commissaire des classes,* who advised him to contact the *intendant de la marine* at Brest.

4. On Feb. 6 Appée renewed his plea, fearing that BF had not received his first appeal (APS).

From Samuel Curson[5]

ALS: American Philosophical Society

Sir   Marseilles 16th. January 1783

I have some time had in veiw the intention of fixing myself in Lisbon, for the purpose of transacting business for my country-men,— This seems a favourable moment, if credit is to be given to the report, of that place being lately opend, to American ves-sels,— Am induced to think your Excellency will be acquainted with the truth of this; my reason for troubling you with this let-ter;—at same time to ask your opinion, whether an American will be permitted to establish a house, where an English factory[6] has so much influence.— If you think Sir! I might be assisted in my object, by the French Ambassador,[7] dare say you will not deem it too much trouble to give me a line to him on the subject, with a passport, which propose to make immediate use of.—

A few days ago the Ship Hawk, Ca. Bull[8] arrived here from Phil-adelphia,—she saild the 21t. Novr. but brings nothing new.—

I beg my best comps. to your grandson and remain with per-fect respect.—Sir Your most humble and obedient servant

SAM. CURSON

His Excel. Ben. Franklin Esqr. Minister Plenipoy.

Notation: Curson Saml. 16 Janvr. 1783.

5. The story of Curson's capture by the British, imprisonment, and release in March, 1782, is told in vols. 35 and 36.

6. A trading station for merchants. The Portuguese were long-standing al-lies of Great Britain.

7. Jacques-Bernard O'Dunne: *Repertorium der diplomatischen Vertreter,* III, 130.

8. John Bull was from Maryland. On the return voyage his was the first American ship to call at Gibraltar since the beginning of the war: Claghorn, *Naval Officers,* p. 42; *Pa. Gaz.,* May 7, 1783.

From Vergennes

LS: American Philosophical Society; copy: Archives du Ministère des affaires étrangères

A Versailles le 16. Janver. 1783

J'ai l'honneur, Monsieur, de vous envoyer la copie d'un Mémoire qui m'a été adressé par les Srs. faure Donneau et Compagnie de Marseille propriétaire du Senaut l'Elégante.[9] Vous avez déjà connoissance de cette affaire, puisque ces Négociants vous ont transmis leurs représentations sur cet objet, et vous avez été à portée de juger combien est juste la réclamation qu'ils font de la Somme effective de cent mille livres, argent de France, qui leur a été allouée par le Conseil de Williamsbourg en dédommagement de la perte de leur Navire et de sa cargaison.

Je vous prie, Monsieur, de prendre cette affaire en considération et de vouloir bien employer vos bons offices les plus efficaces pour procurer aux Srs. faure Donneau et Compagnie l'entiere satisfaction qui leur est düe. Les faits tels qu'ils sont exposés vous convaincront surement de la légitimité de cette demande, et vous sentirez, Monsieur, combien il seroit injuste et contraire au droit des gens que nos Négociants fussent les malheureuses victimes d'une conduite aussi repréhensible que celle dont le Commandant de la milice à Carterscreek[1] s'est rendu coupable envers eux.

J'ai l'honneur d'être très sinceremt. Monsieur, votre très humble et très obéissant serviteur   DE VERGENNES

M. Franklin.

---

9. The memorial is missing. For the case of the snow *Elégante* see XXVI, 502–4; XXIX, 510–11; XXXI, 516–17; XXXV, 327–9.

1. Carter's Creek is near the mouth of the Rappahannock, where the *Elégante* was captured.

Bill of Exchange Drawn on Robert Morris[2]

DS:[3] American Philosophical Society

Passy, 16. Jany. 1783

Exchange for £4000. Tournois.

At thirty Days Sight of this my first of Exchange, Second, Third and Fourth not paid, Pay to the Count de Langeron[4] or order, the Value of Four Thousand Livres Tournois, in the current Specie of the United States, according to the then common Rate of Exchange, with or without Advice from, Sir, Your humble Servant[5]   [*torn:* B FRANKLIN]

To Robt. Morris Esqr. Superintendant of the Finances. Philadelphia

2. We publish the first of a set of four bills in L'Air de Lamotte's hand (APS). On the verso of this bill is written in pencil, "What think the chosen Judges?"

3. The signatures on all four bills have been cut off. The pen strokes that are still visible suggest that the signature was BF's.

4. This was most likely Louis-Alexandre Andrault, comte de Langeron, who was *sous-lieutenant* in the Bourbonnais regiment. He sailed to America aboard the *Aigle* in May, 1782, arriving in September. He served under Antoine-Charles du Houx, baron de Vioménil (XXXII, 144n, 150n), commander-in-chief of the French forces in North America, and probably went to the West Indies and South America before returning to France in June, 1783: Bodinier, *Dictionnaire* under Andrault; *DBF* under Langeron; Rice and Brown, eds., *Rochambeau's Army,* I, 81n, 84, 100; Dull, *French Navy,* p. 333.

5. We know nothing more about this bill except that someone evidently called on BF to discuss the matter. On the wrapper sheet of Damboix to BF, Jan. 7, is written "Le Comte de Langeron" in an unknown hand. Elsewhere on the sheet BF has divided 4,000 by 24, and performed other calculations.

From the Comtesse d'Houdetot

LS:[6] American Philosophical Society

paris Le 17. jer 1783.

J'ay Eté Bien affligée de voir hier a ma porte Le nom de Mon Cher Et Respectable Docteur, je le prie D'Estre persuadé de mes Regrets Et Du Desir que j'ay depuis Longtems de le Voir Et de le feliciter De L'heureuse paix qui Va Couronner sy heureusement Et sy Glorieusement ses Voeux Et Ses traveaux; puisqu'il Vient quelques fois a paris je puis me flatter De L'Esperance De L'y Voir Et je luy propose De Venir Entendre De la Musique Chez moy avec Monsieur Son fils Le jeudy trante de Ce Mois Depuis un peu avant huit heures jusqu'a dix; je Scay qu'il a du Goust pour Ce Genre D'amusement Et je ne puis me Consoller De ne M'Estre pas trouvée Chez moy hier ou je l'aurais Retenu a ma Musique qui a lieu tous Les quinze jours; je Voudrais Scavoir L'heure Et Le moment ou je pourrais trouver Chez luy Mon Cher Docteur Et Luy porter mes hommages Et mes plus tendres Sentimens   LA CTESSE DHOUDETOT

Addressed: A Monsieur / Monsieur franklin / Ministre Plenipotentiaire / Des Etâts Unis D'Amerique / A Passy / pres paris

Notation: D'Houdetot la Cesse. 17 Janr. 1783

From Le Roy

ALS: American Philosophical Society

De Paris ce 17 Janvier 1783

Il y a des siécles Mon Illustre Docteur que je n'ai eu lhonneur et le plaisir de vous voir et je m'en ennuye beaucoup. Tous ces jours cy Jai voulu Aller à Passy mais incertain de vous y trouver j'ai differré Jusqu'a ce que ce tems des visites fut passé. Enfin pour etre plus sur de passer quelques momens avec vous jai cru qu'il etoit mieux de vous demander à dîner le Jour qui vous conviendra, de Dimanche, lundy ou mardy, car Mde Le Roy desire également d'avoir Lhonneur de vous voir faites moi donc le plaisir

---

6. In the hand of M. Girard, Mme d'Houdetot's close friend: XXXVI, 583n.

mon Illustre Docteur de mander par un mot si vous acceptez ma proposition et pour quel Jour. Je suis bien impatient de vous renouveller dans cette nouvelle année tous mes Voeux pour votre santé et pour tout ce qui peut vous être agreable.

Je me flatte que je n'ai pas besoin de vous dire Mon Illustre Docteur combien je vous suis sincèrement et veritablement attaché pour la Vie   LE ROY

Addressed: a Monsieur / Monsieur Franklin Ministre / Plenipotentiaire des Etats unis de / L'amèrique auprès de la Cour de France / en Son hôtel / à Passy

Notation: Le Roy 17 Janvr. 1783.

From Vergennes

Copies:[7] Library of Congress (two), Massachusetts Historical Society

Versailles le samedy Soir 18. Janr. 1783[8]

Il est essentiel, Monsieur, que Je puisse avoir l'honneur de conferer avec vous, avec M. Adams et avec ceux de Mrs. [Messieurs] Vos Collegues qui peuvent se trouver à Paris. Je vous prie en consequence, Monsieur, de vouloir bien inviter ces Mrs. à se rendre a Versailles avec vous Lundi avant dix heures du Matin. Il seroit bon que vous amenassiez M. votre Petit fils avec vous, il pourra nous être necessaire pour rendre plusieurs choses d'Anglois en François et même pour écrire. L'objet dont J'ai à vous entretenir est très interressant pour les Etats unis vos maitres.[9]

7. All three copies are from the peace commissioners' letterbooks.

8. The day that French and Spanish negotiations with Great Britain were concluded, and plans were made for the signing of a preliminary peace agreement and armistice. Vergennes gave particular credit to Aranda for the services he had rendered the common cause: Vergennes to Montmorin, Jan. 18, 1783, AAE. An agreement between the Netherlands and Britain had not yet been reached, but Fitzherbert and Vergennes had decided on the terms the Dutch would have to accept, and they were included in the armistice: Dull, *French Navy,* pp. 332–3; Doniol, *Histoire,* v, 275, 278.

9. Vergennes wished to formalize the preliminary American peace agreement with Great Britain and thereby reaffirm the continuation of the Franco-American alliance: Doniol, *Histoire,* v, 276–7. On Monday, Jan. 20, at Ver-

J'ai l'honneur d'être avec une parfaite Consideration, Monsieur, votre tres humble et tres obeissant Serviteur.

(signé) DE VERGENNES.

à M. Franklin

To Vergennes

ALS: Archives du Ministère des affaires étrangères; copies: Library of Congress (two), Massachusetts Historical Society

Sir,   Passy, Jany. 18. 1783 at 10 P.M.

Agreable to the Notice just receiv'd from your Excellency, I shall acquaint Mr Adams with your Desire to see us on Monday before 10 aClock, at Versailles; and we shall endeavour to be punctual. My other Colleagues are absent: Mr Laurens being gone to Bath in England to recover his Health; and Mr. Jay into Normandy.[1] With great Respect I have the honour to be, Sir, Your Excellency's most obedient & most humble Servant

B FRANKLIN

I shall bring my Grandson as you direct.

M. le Comte de Vergennes.

From Benjamin Vaughan

Reprinted from William Temple Franklin, ed., *Memoirs of the Life and Writings of Benjamin Franklin* . . . (3 vols., 4to, London, 1817–18), II, 423–4.

My dearest sir,   Paris, Jan. 18, 1783.

I cannot but in the most earnest manner and from *recent* circumstances, press your going *early* to Versailles to-morrow; and

---

sailles, the American commissioners signed a declaration of the cessation of hostilities, in accordance with Vergennes' wishes (below). They had never informed him about the secret article of the treaty, which was now rendered moot because Florida was returned to Spain.

1. Jay visited Normandy in company with Matthew Ridley. They left Paris on Jan. 7 and returned on Jan. 23: Morris, *Jay: Peace,* pp. 487–8.

I have considerable reason to think, that your appearance there will not displease the person whom you address. I am of opinion that it is very likely that you will have the glory of having concluded the peace, by this visit; at least I am sure if the deliberations of to-morrow evening end unfavourably, that there is the strongest appearance of war; and if they end favourably, perhaps little difficulty may attend the rest.[2]

After all, the peace will have as much that is conceded in it, as England can in any shape be made just now to relish; owing to the stubborn demands principally of Spain, who would not I believe upon any motive recede from her conquests. What I wrote about Gibraltar, arrived after the subject as I understand was canvassed, and when it of course must have appeared impolitic eagerly and immediately to revive it.[3]

You reproved me, or rather reproved a political scheme yesterday, of which I have heard more said favourably by your *friends* at *Paris,* than by any persons whatever in London. But do you, my dear sir, make *this* peace, and trust our common sense respecting another war. England, said a man of sense to me the

2. Vaughan, believing that there was a crisis in the French and Spanish negotiations with Great Britain, had urged BF to visit Vergennes and intervene if necessary. After receiving Vergennes' summons of Jan. 18, however, BF did not make this separate journey to Versailles; see his Jan. 19 letter to Vaughan. Vaughan recounted in a letter to Shelburne a conversation he and BF had around this time: BF expressed the view that war "was made according to the mistaken imaginations of the people, and peace, according to their real necessities as seen by the peace makers; and hence the frequent idea that they were bribed. He added that England was ruined by her great places, and though it was not a thing likely perhaps to be reformed, yet no reform was more necessary than what respected places. He said that the king's being obliged to provide for a party prevented great persons from agreeing, and that it seemed to him as if the love of quarrelling was so great on account of those places, that there were those who wished the minister just now to make a bad peace, in order to abuse him for it when it was concluded." Charles C. Smith, ed., "Letters of Benjamin Vaughan," Mass. Hist. Soc. *Proc.,* 2nd ser., XVII (1903), 435–8. Vaughan had no idea that the peace discussions were successfully completed by the evening of Jan. 18.

3. In a Dec. 4 letter to Shelburne, Vaughan had encouraged the exchange of Gibraltar. Vaughan said that BF had suggested that, as an equivalent to it, Spain surrender Florida, Puerto Rico, and all claims to Jamaica: Smith, "Letters of Vaughan," pp. 421–2.

other day, will come out of the war like a convalescent out of a disease, and must be re-established by some physic and much regimen. I cannot easily tell in what shape a bankruptcy would come upon England, and still less easily in what mode and degree it would affect us; but if your confederacy mean to bankrupt us now, I am sure we shall lose the great *fear* that would deter us from another war. Your allies therefore for policy, and for humanity's sake, will I hope stop short of this extremity; especially as we should do some mischief first to others, as well as to ourselves. I am, my dearest Sir, your ever devoted, ever affectionate, and ever obliged,   B. VAUGHAN.

(Private)

To John Adams

ALS and copy: Massachusetts Historical Society; copy: Library of Congress

Sir,   Passy, Jany. 19. 1783

Late last Night I received a Note from M. de Vergennes, acquainting me that it is very essential he should have a Conference with us, and requesting I would inform my Colleagues.[4] He desires that we may be with him before Ten on Monday Morning. If it will suit you to call here, we may go together in my Carriage. With great Regard, I have the honour to be, Sir, Your most obedient & most humble Servant[5]   B FRANKLIN

We should be on the Road by 8.——

His Excelly. J. Adams Esqr

---

4. Vergennes to BF, Jan. 18, above.

5. JA went to Passy after receiving this letter. He told BF that he had been told the previous evening that Vergennes was "uneasy" at Oswald's departure, as "he expected to sign the Preliminaries in a day or two." Butterfield, *John Adams Diary*, III, 106.

To Benjamin Vaughan

ALS: William L. Clements Library

My dear Friend,   Passy. Sunday morng. Jan. 19. 83.

I should have been at Versailles this Morning as you desired,[6] tho' I had no clear Conception, from what you said to me, how my going could be of Use; but late last Night I received a Note from M. de V. [Vergennes] which postpones the Interview till tomorrow at 10 aClock. Your Brother[7] tells me that you would have come out here to day if you had not imagined I should be at Versailles. I dine at home without Company, and shall be glad of yours; being ever Yours most affectionately   B FRANKLIN

B Vaughan Esqr

From René-Georges Gastellier[8]

ALS: American Philosophical Society

Monsieur et trés illustre docteur   Montargis 19 janvier 1783.

Recevés, je vous supplie, mes actions de Graces trés humbles de l'honneur que vous voulés bien me faire en recevant la dédicace d'un ouvrage qui vient d'être orné du sceau de la societé royale de médecine à la quelle j'ai l'avantage d'appartenir, votre nom à son frontispice sera un témoignage aussi flatteur qu'honorable pour l'auteur.[9]

6. See Vaughan to BF, Jan. 18.
7. Samuel Vaughan, Jr. (1762–1802), who had been in Paris with his brother since at least Oct. 17: John H. Sheppard, *Reminiscences of the Vaughan Family* . . . (Boston, 1865), p. 26; Klingelhofer, *Matthew Ridley's Diary*, p. 121.
8. This letter was enclosed in one from Mlle Defay of Feb. 6, 1783 (APS). She had written on Gastellier's behalf a year earlier, when the author sent BF copies of two of his works: XXXVI, 547–8; XXXVII, 30.
9. We have no record of when BF might have agreed to this request. The work in question was *Des spécifiques en médecine* (Paris, 1783), written in answer to the question posed by the Académie des sciences, arts et belles lettres de Dijon, "Are there specific remedies in medicine?" Gastellier's negative conclusion, that there was not a one-to-one correspondence between a drug and a disease, deprived him of the Academy's prize: Quérard, *France littéraire*. Nevertheless, as he says here, the Académie royale de médecine ap-

Mademoiselle de fay vient de me faire part des entraves que votre modestie m'impose, et Conformement à vos désirs je viens de changer l'épitre dédicatoire que vous trouverés cy incluse.[1] J'ose me flatter que celleci n'affectera point votre délicatesse, car il n'est pas possible de dire moins à quelqu'un qui merite autant. Au surplus j'obeis à vos ordres qui ne font qu'accroître mon admiration et le respect avec lequel je suis Monsieur et trés illustre docteur votre trés humble trés obeissant serviteur   GASTELLIER

P.S. Comme l'impression du petit ouvrage que j'ai l'honneur de vous presenter, est absolument finie, je vous serai infiniment obligé, Monsieur, de vouloir bien me faire parvenir au plutôt votre acceptation et de me faire part de vos observations sur vos titres, si j'en ai omis quelques uns.[2]

Notation: Gastellier. 19 Jan 83

From Robert Morris

LS: American Philosophical Society; copy: Library of Congress

Sir,   Office of Finance 19th. Janry. 1783
His Excellency the Governor and the Honorable the Delagates of Virginia have applied to me for my Assistance in ob-

---

proved the treatise, which argued in favor of medical observation and judgment. The work was favorably reviewed in the *Jour. de Paris,* issue of March 23, 1783.

1. The dedicatory epistle was addressed "A Monsieur franklin," followed by a long list of BF's titles (APS). A second manuscript version of the dedication, minus the titles, is also at the APS; this one has a few alterations in wording that make it nearly identical to the version eventually printed. We surmise that Gastellier included it with a later letter, after having received BF's changes to the list of titles that he requests below, in the postscript.

2. Gastellier's account of BF's titles reads: "docteur en médecine, deputé du Congrès près la Cour de france; président de la société de philadelphie; de la société royale de londres, de l'academie royale des sciences de paris, de la societé royale de médecine de la même ville, etc." When the dedication appeared in print, the second element was moved to the first position and was corrected to read, "Ministre Plénipotentiaire des Etats-Unis de l'Amérique Septentrionale à la Cour de France." Whether BF intentionally left in this allusion to his non-existent medical degree, or whether Gastellier or the printer ignored his deletion mark, is an unanswerable question.

taining from France certain Arms and Ammunition said to have
been furnished by the Court for that State according to an
Agreement entered into between Mr. Harrison a special Agent
appointed by the Legislature and Monsr. de la luzerne the King's
Minister.[3] These Articles wheresoever they may be deposited
are (according to my Informants) in the Care and Custody and
Subject to the Direction of Mr. Thomas Barclay the Consul[4]
General of the United States who is also the agent of the State
of Virginia in France. I have accordingly written to the Consul
directing him to cause those Goods to be shipped along with
those belonging to the United States and at the repeated Instance
of those Gentlemen I am now to address your Excellency upon
the same Subject. Going upon the Supposition that the Arms &c.
may still be in Europe I take the Liberty to mention that if the
War continues the necessity of a Convoy necessarily continuing
with it Monsr. de Ville Brun[5] who has long been in the Chesapeak and is well acquainted with the Coast would not only feel
himself happy in being charged with that Business but has even
assured me that he would gladly take them on Board of his own
Ship and at the same Time act as Convoy to the Trade which
might be bound to the Chesapeak. Your Excellency will undoubtedly obtain every Information which may be useful on this
Subject and your Zeal and Talents will prompt and direct to what
is best. I can only add that I shall be happy if you can render any
Service on this occasion to the State of Virginia and shall esteem
as a Favor the Efforts which you may make—

3. In late November, 1782, Morris had agreed to help Gov. Benjamin Harrison convey arms and ammunition from France to Virginia, after the governor warned that he would be forced to use state revenues to purchase arms if
those in France did not arrive: *Morris Papers*, VI, 421, 651; VII, 55–6, 133. For
the February, 1781, agreement between La Luzerne and Harrison (then serving as agent for Virginia), which covered both arms and clothing, see *Morris
Papers*, V, 74–5n. In late October, Morris had reported to BF that Virginia no
longer needed the clothing purchased for it: Morris to BF, Oct. 27, above.
    4. On Nov. 29, 1782: *Morris Papers*, VII, 135.
    5. Jacques-René Le Saige, chevalier de La Villesbrunne, captain of the *Ro-
mulus*, who was asked to convoy trade from Baltimore to France: *Morris Papers*, VII, 250–1, 267; Christian de La Jonquière, *Les Marins français sous
Louis XVI: guerre d'indépendance américaine* (Issy-les-Moulineaux, France,
1996), p. 187.

Before I close this Letter it is well to observe that I have received another Copy of your Letter of the twenty sixth of September in which I find a Copy of the agreement entered into between you and Monsr. de Vergenes.[6]

I have the Honor to be Sir Your most obedient & humble Servant   ROBT MORRIS

His Excellency Benjamin Franklin Esqr. Minister plenipotentiary of the United States of America.

Copy[7]

From Barthélemy Faujas de Saint-Fond[8]

ALS: American Philosophical Society

Monsieur   a paris le 19 janvier 1783

Mr vaughan, m'ayant dit que vous seriés Curieux de voir le nouveau métal qu'on vient de proposer au gouvernement, pour doubler les vaisseaux, je m'empresse de vous envoyer avec grand plaisir, le petit echantillon que j'en possède, que mr douët de la Boulaye intendant Géneral des mines[9] a eu la Bonté de me donner, ainsi q'un des cloux qui doivent Servir a fixer les feuilles de métal Contre le vaisseau.

Les cloux sont fondus. Leur forme en coin est des plus favorable et des plus solide, et le métal dont ils Sont Composés les met à l'abri de la rouille qu'occasione le sel marin sur le fer; ils me paroissent être faits d'un mélange de Zinc, de Bismut, et peut-être d'un peu d'etain. Au reste il seroit facile de Connoitre

6. See Morris' letter of Jan. 13.
7. This word is in Morris' hand.
8. The important geologist and paleontologist (1741–1819): *DBF*. Faujas obtained a position at the Jardin du roi in 1778, the same year he published *Recherches sur la pouzzolane* and *Recherches sur les volcans éteints* . . . , to which BF subscribed: XXVIII, 341.
9. Gabriel-Isaac Douet de La Boullaye had been named to this position on Nov. 23, 1782: *DBF;* Michel Antoine, *Le Gouvernement et l'administration sous Louis XV: dictionnaire biographique* (Paris, 1978), p. 88.

lespece et la quantité des matieres quils Contiennent, par la voye de l'analyse. Vous pouvés garder Ces échantillons.[1]

Voila aussi un morceau d'une pierre très Curieuse, q'un de mes amis, le Commandeur de *dolomieu*, chevalier de malthe, m'a apporté d'un voyage qu'il vient de faire en sicile.[2] Cette pierre qui est Calcaire, Contient une très grande quantité de Bitume, les habitans de raguse en sicile, voisins des Carieres, en font des Carraux pour leurs appartements et particulierement pour les Sales de Bain, parce quelle prend un Beau poli, et quelle ne Craint point l'humidité l'on en Bâti des maisons, et lorsque les

1. This new pliable metal, which came in the form of a paste, would soon be announced in the press as available from the *Manufacture Royale du Doublage des Vaisseaux de la Marine*, a factory in Nantes that received its patent letters and royal imprimatur in March, 1782. One of the principals of the factory, and most likely the inventor of the unnamed alloy, was Fabre du Bosquet, who had been introduced to BF by John Paul Jones in 1780 and had shown him a prototype of the metal at that time. Both the metal and the varnish described here were an attempt to solve the poorly understood problem of galvanic action, the corrosion that occurred in the presence of salt water when the copper sheathing being affixed to ships' hulls interacted with iron nails or the iron bolts beneath the sheathing that held fast the hull itself. Iron bolts with a diameter of an inch and a quarter were being reduced to "the size of a quill" in just a couple of years, according to a 1779 British report. In 1782, the loss of several ships of the line during a severe storm (for which see our annotation of Williams, Moore & Co., Oct. 9) was attributed to this corrosion, and Parliament debated whether to forbid the coppering of ships' bottoms. Manufacturers in Britain and France raced to find a solution to the problem. The metal alloy produced in this Nantes manufactory did not prove to be effective, and the operation was shut down in 1786: *Courier de L'Europe*, Jan. 28, 1783; Bachaumont, *Mémoires secrets*, Feb. 4, 1783 (XXII, 66) and Jan. 19, 1787 (XXXIV, 46); Fabre du Bosquet to BF, July 2, 1783 (APS); Fabre du Bosquet *et al.*, Memoir of the Manufacture Royale de Nantes [1784] (Hist. Soc. of Pa.). Background information in this note is from J. R. Harris, "Copper and Shipping in the Eighteenth Century," *The Economic History Review*, New Series, XIX, no. 3 (1966), 550–60 (quotation about iron bolts on p. 555n); and J. R. Harris, *Industrial Espionage and Technology Transfer: Britain and France in the Eighteenth Century* (Aldershot, Eng., Brookfield, Vt., and Singapore, 1998), pp. 262–7.

2. Dieudonné-Sylvain-Guy-Tancrède, *dit* Déodat de Gratet de Dolomieu (1750–1801), was another talented geologist. He became a corresponding member of the Académie des sciences in 1778, and carried out important geological explorations of Sicily and the Pyrenees in the early 1780s which he described in subsequent publications. *DBF*.

murs Sont Construit, on y met le feu, tout le Batiment s'en-
flamme, et la maison Brule jusqu'a Ceque tout le Bitume soit
Consummé, la pierre de noire qu'elle etoit devient Blanche alors,
et acquiert plus de durete, et Comme elle S'etoit dilatée pendant
l'incandescence Les molécules se resserent par le refroidisse-
ment, et l'ensemble des pierres Se rejoint de maniere à ne faire
presque q'un Seul et même Corps. Je n'ai pas eu le tems d'etudier
encore Cette pierre Comme je le desire; je vous prie de vouloir
en accepter Ces deux petits morceaux.

J'avois eu l'honneur dans le tems de vous offrir un exemplaire
du dernier traité que jai publié sur la *pouzzolane*,[3] mais la multitude de vos travaux, ne vous a Certainement pas permis d'y jetter un Coup d'oeil. Cependant Comme il se fait dans Ce moment
differents envois de Cette terre dans plusieurs parties de l'europe, et quelle est à très Bon marché dans les ports de la medi-
terannèe ou il y en a de Grands magazins, et ou elle ne Coute que
18 sols le quintal, elle pourroit être de la plus grande utilité pour
l'amerique; je joins donc ici un second exemplaire de Cette
Brochure que vous pourriés envoyer, à la personne chargée du
département des ports et des ouvrages publics en amérique. J'ai
l'honneur d'etre avec le plus respectueux attachement Monsieur
votre très humble et très obeissant serviteur

    FAUJAS DE SAINT FOND
    logé ches Mr le Duc de chaulnes rue de Bondy à paris

Notation: Faujas de St. fond. Paris 19 Janr. 1783.

3. *Mémoire sur la manière de reconnoître les différentes espèces de pouzzolane,
et de les employer dans les constructions sous l'eau et hors de l'eau* (Amsterdam
and Paris, 1780), a supplement to his earlier work mentioned above. Poz-
zuolana was a kind of volcanic ash that made cement. At some time BF also
received a memoir in an unknown hand entitled "Pouzzolanes du Vivarais,"
citing Faujas' work and offering BF advantageous terms to furnish the substance to the United States for construction. In Paris BF could apply to either
M. Renard, architect, or M. Guillomot, *intendant des bâtiments du roi;* in Marseille, to either M. Hugues fils, merchant, or M. Dupouget, *lieutenant de
l'amirauté.* Hist. Soc. of Pa.

From Benjamin Vaughan

AL: Library of Congress

Paris, Jany 19, 1783.

B V: presents his most affectionate respects to Dr. Franklin, and is unfortunately so engaged to day, as not to be able to accept of his kind welcome.[4] B V's brother acted for the best, but not being privy to circumstances, misunderstood him.— Tomorrow evening B V will however call at Passy, unless inconvenient to his friend, and directed otherwise.

Addressed: A Monsr / Monsr Franklin, / a Passy.

The American Peace Commissioners: Acceptance of the British Declaration of the Cessation of Hostilities

Copies: Massachusetts Historical Society (three),[5] National Archives (three), Library of Congress (two), Public Record Office, Archives du Ministère des affaires étrangères; press copy of copy: National Archives; transcripts: National Archives (three)

When Franklin, Adams, and William Temple Franklin arrived at Vergennes' office at ten o'clock on the morning of January 20, they learned that Fitzherbert and Aranda would arrive at eleven to conclude the preliminary peace agreements between France and Great Britain, and Great Britain and Spain.[6] After examining and signing those documents, Fitzherbert (in lieu of Oswald, who had been called back to England) presented Franklin and Adams with a declaration of an armistice. Their reciprocal declaration, the present document, incorporated his text.[7] The two documents were signed, sealed, and ex-

4. BF's invitation of Jan. 19, above.

5. We print the one in WTF's hand. He made one slip of the pen that we have silently corrected, in the date of Fitzherbert's declaration.

6. For the texts of these treaties see Clive Parry, comp., *The Consolidated Treaty Series* (243 vols., Dobbs Ferry, N.Y., 1969–86), XLVIII, 231–42, 249–52. They were published along with the British/American Preliminary Articles in the *Public Advertiser* on Jan. 30, and the *Courier de l'Europe* on Jan. 31.

7. Copies of the British declaration in the original French and in English translation are in the American commissioners' legation letterbooks at the Mass. Hist. Soc. and Library of Congress; translations of both the British

changed. Adams commented in his diary, "Thus was this mighty System terminated with as little Ceremony, and in as short a Time as a Marriage Settlement."[8]

The Americans returned to Paris, where they dined with the duchesse d'Enville and the duc de La Rochefoucauld. The latter recalled Franklin telling him as they embraced, "Pouvois-je espérer, à mon âge, de jouir d'un pareil bonheur?"[9]

Vergennes related the news to Lenoir at three o'clock in the afternoon, and the *lieutenant général de police* saw to it that the information was disseminated in cafés and theaters. That evening at the Théâtre-Français, the renowned comedian Molé announced that the company would perform *L'Anglois à Bordeaux* the following Saturday, in honor of the peace. This one-act play by Charles-Simon Favart had been composed in March, 1763, in honor of the signing of the Treaty of Paris; its allusions were updated for this reprise.[1]

[January 20, 1783]

Nous soussignés Ministres Plenipotentiaires des États-Unis de l'Amerique Septentrionale, aïant reçu de la Part de M. Fitzherbert Ministre Plenipotentiaire de sa Majesté Britanique une Declaration relative a une suspension d'Armes a établir entre sa de. [dite] Majesté et les dits Etats dont la teneur s'ensuit.

---

and American declarations are in Giunta, *Emerging Nation*, I, 756–7. See also Wharton, *Diplomatic Correspondence*, VI, 223–4.

8. Butterfield, *John Adams Diary*, III, 106.

9. We assume that BF and WTF were present at that dinner, which JA mentions in his diary; La Rochefoucauld wrote that BF had uttered those words to him on the day the peace was signed, with an "air de satisfaction douce et complète": Butterfield, *John Adams Diary*, III, 107; Eulogy by La Rochefoucauld, June 13, 1790, in Gilbert Chinard, *L'Apothéose de Benjamin Franklin* (Paris, 1955), p. 97.

1. As it happened, the theater's featured performance on Jan. 20 was the premiere of a French adaptation of a British play, *King Lear;* the duc de Croÿ was delighted by the symbolism and cheered this display of *anglomanie.* Ducis' *Le Roi Léar*, however, was a radical revision of Shakespeare's play. Not wanting to portray a monarch gone mad (as he explained in the *avertissement*), and wanting to reward filial gratitude (the *avertissement* urged parents to bring their children), Ducis arranged it so that both Lear and Cordelia (Helmonde) survive, and Lear regains his sanity and his throne. Emmanuel-Henri, vicomte de Grouchy, and Paul Cottin, eds., *Journal inédit du duc de Croÿ, 1718–1784* (4 vols., Paris, 1906–07), IV, 266–7; *Jour. de Paris*, issues of Jan. 20, 21, and 26; Bachaumont, *Mémoires secrets*, XXII, 42–4; Jean-François Ducis, *Le Roi Léar* (Paris, 1783).

"Comme les Articles Preliminaires arrettés et signés aujourd'hui entre sa Majesté le Roi de la Grande Bretagne et sa Majesté le Roi très Chretien[2] d'une Part, et aussi entre sa dite Majesté Britanique et sa Majesté Catholique[3] d'autre Part, renferment la Stipulation de la Cessation des Hostilités entre ces trois Puissances; laquelle doit commencer après l'Echange des Ratifications des dits Articles Préliminaires; Et comme par le Traité Provisionel signé le trente Novembre dernier, entre sa Majesté Britanique et les Etats Unis de l'Amerique Septentrionale; il a été stipulé, que ce Traité sortiroit son Effet aussitot que la Paix entre les des. [dites] Couronnes seroit retablie, Le sousigné, Ministre Plenipotentiaire de sa Majesté Britanique, declare au Nom et par Ordre exprès du Roi son Maitre, que les dits Etats Unis de l'Amerique Septentrionale, leurs Sujets et leurs Possessions seront compris dans la Suspension d'Armes susmentionée, et qu'ils jouiront en Consequence du Benéfice de la Cessation des Hostilités aux mêmes Epoques, et de la meme maniere que les trois Couronnes susdites leurs Sujets et leurs Possessions respectives, le tout a Condition, que de la Part et au Nom des dits Etats Unis de l'Amerique Septentrionale il soit delivré une Declaration semblable qui constate leur Assentiment a la presente Suspension d'Armes et renferme l'Assurance de la plus parfaite Reciprocité de leur Part.

"En foi de quoi, Nous Ministres Plenipotentiaire de sa Majesté Britanique, avons signé la presente Declaration, et y avons fait aposer le Cachet de nos Armes.

A Versailles le 20 Janr. 1783. (signé) ALLEYNE FITZ-HERBERT"

L.S.

Avons au Nom des dits Etats Unis de l'Amerique septentrionale, et en Vertu des Pouvoirs dont ils nous ont munis, accepté la Declaration ci dessus; l'acceptons par ces Presentes purement et simplement, et declarons reciproquement que les dits Etats feront cesser toutes hostilités contre sa Majesté Britanique ses Sujets et ses Possessions aux Termes et aux Epoques convenus entre sa de. [dite] Majesté le Roi de la Grande Bretagne sa Ma-

2. Louis XVI.
3. Charles III of Spain.

jesté le Roi de France et sa Majesté le Roi d'Espagne, ainsi et de la meme maniere qu'il a été convenu entre ces trois Couronnes, et pour produire le meme Effet.

En foi de quoi Nous Ministres Plenipotentiaires des Etats-Unis de l'Amerique septentrionale avons signé la Presente Declaration et y avons apposé les Cachets des nos Armes. A Versailles le Vingt Janvier mil sept Cent quatre vingt trois.

JOHN ADAMS} signé {B. FRANKLIN
L.S.   L.S.

From Louis-Julien Garos[4]   ALS: American Philosophical Society

Monseigneur   à fontenay Le comte Le 20. Janvier 1783.

Quil me Soit permis d'implorer votre protection pour un particulier françois d'origine Résidant depuis très Long-tems à philadelphie. Je vais, Monseigneur, vous mettre Sous les yeux les faits tels quils Se Sont passés, afin que vous puissiez Juger Si ce particulier peut tirer de la position où Il Se trouve tous les avantages quil paroit S'en promettre. Voicy ce dont Il S'agit.

Le Sr. françois Geay originaire des Environs de cette ville, Servoit Il y a plus de quarante ans dans les troupes de france, Il y Etoit Encore En 1743, car au mois de Juin de la même année Il fut Blessé dangéreusement à la Bataille d'ettingen.[5] Fatigué du Service, Il déserta. Il le fit même, Si Je ne me trompe avec armes Et Bagage. Il passa En hollande, L'à Il S'embarqua Et fut fixer Son Sejour à philadelphie, où Il a toujours Résidé depuis. Il S'y Est même marié. Il ne luy Reste plus icy qu'une Soeur. Tous Ses autres freres Sont morts depuis Son passage à L'amerique. Ces morts Successives ont ouvert differentes Successions aux quelles

4. Garos (1739–1808) became *conseiller du roi* in 1767. He subsequently served as justice of the peace and in 1792 was elected to represent the Vendée at the Convention. He voted for the execution of Louis XVI: *DBF;* Adolphe Robert and Gaston Cougny, *Dictionnaire des parlementaires français . . .* (5 vols., Paris, 1889–91; reprinted, Geneva, 2000), III, 118.

5. The Battle of Dettingen, during the War of the Austrian Succession. Geay served in a regiment of dragoons: Garos to BF, May 1, 1783 (APS).

aujourdhuy comme ainé Il auroit la meilleure part. Sa Soeur S'est mise En possession de la totalité de ces Successions, quoyquelle ne veuille point, Monseigneur, l'en priver S'il y a droit. Elle veut cependant Etre assurée avant de luy En faire l'abandon, Sil Est fondé à les Reclamer ou non. C'est moy, Monseigneur, qui ay Instruit le dit Sr. Geay des Evénemens arrivés dans Sa famille. Il m'a fait passer Ses pouvoirs, pour que j'eusse à toucher pour luy les portions qui pouvoient luy Revenir.[6] Je les ay demandées, mais on m'objecte quil Est inhabile à Succeder En france au moyen de Sa désertion Et de ce quil n'a pas profité des differentes amnisties quil a plû aux Roix d'accorder.

Comme je ne veux point que Mr. Geay puisse me Reprocher de n'avoir pas Repondu autant quil Etoit En moy à Sa confiance, les difficultés qui S'elevent En ce moment à Son Égard, m'ont fait prendre la liberté, Monseigneur, de vous adresser celle cy, pour Vous Supplier, En cas que vous Jugiez que la désertion du Sr. Geay le Rend Inhabile à Succéder En france, D'employer vos Bons offices auprès du gouvernement pour obtenir Son pardon, Et luy procurer les moyens de Rentrer En possession des héritages, qui, Sans Cette Raison, luy Sont Incontestablement acquis par les Loix de la nature.

Je ne vous terrai pas, Monseigneur, que Monsieur Livingston m'a fait L'honneur de Répondre à une lettre que J'avois adressée à Nos Seigneurs du congrès à ce Sujet. Il a Eû la complaisance de Menvoyer L'art. 13. du traité d'alliance fait Entre la france Et les Etats unis de L'amerique.[7] Cet article a bien quelque Relation à

6. Garos wrote a letter to the President of Congress on April 28, 1781. He explained Geay's situation and asked two questions: could Geay collect his inheritance by submitting a power of attorney rather than going to France, and secondly, if Geay were no longer alive, would his American-born children stand to inherit his French estate? He enclosed instructions for Geay. (Garos' letter and a duplicate dated May 9 are at the National Archives.) Garos' inquiry was forwarded to Livingston, who did not reply until the following April, when Anthony Benezet pressed him to intervene on Geay's behalf. It was Benezet who sent the powers of attorney that Garos mentions here: Livingston to Garos, April 17, 1782, and to Thomas Barclay, April 19, 1782 (both at the National Archives); Benezet to BF, May 5, 1783 (APS).

7. Livingston to Garos, April 17, 1782, mentioned above. Livingston wrote Garos that the 13th article of the Treaty of Amity and Commerce would answer his questions. He assured Garos that his letter of instructions

la question que J'ay L'honneur de vous proposer, mais Il ne l'a decide pas. Il Est même En quelque Sorte contraire à la prétention de Mr. Geay, car Il y Est dit à la fin: *Mais Est convenû En même tems que Son contenû n'apportera nulle atteinte aux loix promulguées En france contre les Émigrations où qui pouront Etre promulguées dans la Suite, les quelles demeureront dans toute Leur force Et vigueur.*[8]

Deignez, Monseigneur, donner quelque attention, à ceque Je prens La liberté de vous marquer. C'est la grace que vous demande au nom du Sr. Geay, celuy qui à L'honneur d'etre avec un très profond Respect Monseigneur Votre très humble Et très obeissant Serviteur   Garos

Conseiller du Roy Elû à fontenay le comte

Notation: Garos, 20 Janvr. 1783.

From ———— Millet   als: American Philosophical Society

Monsieur   paris ce 20 Janvier 1783

J'ai lhonneur de Vous adressér cy joint Le Mémoire des Marchandises d'Epicéries que je Vous ait fournie,[9] jespere que Vous Vouderez bien Employer Votre autorité pour Scavoir ce qu'est devenus Le S. duchemin[1] Votre Me. d'hotel ne le connoissant point jaurais crû Manquer Si jeû refuses crédit Sachant que Les Marchandises etoient pour Votre consommation, et La justice dont Vous êtes Le Modêle me rassure que je ne perderez

---

would be forwarded to Geay, and promised to assist Geay in prosecuting his claim. Livingston's letter to Thomas Barclay, cited above, asked him to assist Geay's attorneys in France should they apply to him.

8. "But it is at the same Time agreed that its Contents shall not affect the Laws made or that may be made hereafter in France against Emigrations, which shall remain in all their Force and Vigour": xxv, 606–7.

9. Millet's two-page bill covered the period Nov. 20 through Jan. 7. He had supplied sugar (*fin*, *très fin*, and *royal*, that is, double refined), capers, pickles, tarragon, olive oil, mocha coffee, pepper, rice, almonds, figs, grapes, and prunes.

1. Daniel Duchemin submitted his final bill as bf's maître d'hôtel on Jan. 15, 1783; see our annotation of Jacques Finck's agreement, [before Jan. 1, 1783].

point cette Somme. Jai vû m Sude auquel Vous aviez recomandé
le S. duchemin pour le faire entrer a La charité[2] mais il ne La
point Vu et est tres faché d'avoir manqué cet occasion de Vous
prouver son Sincere Attachement.

Jai lhonneur dêtre avec Un Tres profond respect Monsieur
Votre tres humble et tres obeissant serviteur
MILLET
Epicier droguiste rue betizy [Béthisy] a paris

Par les recherches que jai faites jai Scû que le nommé jourdain
Votre porteur d'Eau, et qui reste au Nouvelle Eau[3] avait conduit
ses malles a La Villette. Il est partie pour compiegne et est Surement chez son frere a lhotel Barillet rue du Vieux pont A Compiegne.

Jai tout Lieu desperer Monsieur que Voulant employer Votre
crédit il ne balencera point a payer.

2. The Hôpital de la charité, on the rue des Saints-Pères, was open to men
with curable, noncontagious diseases and was the best-kept hospital in the
city: Hillairet, *Rues de Paris*, II, 499–500; Pierre-Thomas-Nicolas Hurtaut,
Dictionnaire historique de la ville de Paris et de ses environs (4 vols., Paris, 1779),
III, 226–7.

3. The Nouvelles Eaux de Passy, a resort developed by Mme Le Veillard's
father around a spring whose waters were believed to be curative. The waters were bottled at the estate for sale, but it was considered more therapeutic to drink the water at the source where one could exercise by strolling in
the gardens, or relax by reading in the library or enjoying conversation in the
drawing rooms of the estate. There were games, refreshments, and, occasionally in the evening, balls, concerts, and plays: XXIII, 542; Louis Batave,
"Les Eaux de Passy au XVIIIe siècle," *Revue du Dix-huitième siècle*, II (1914),
119–21.

Index

Compiled by Jonathan R. Dull.

(Semicolons separate subentries; colons separate divisions within subentries. A volume and page reference in parentheses following a main entry refers to an individual's first identification in this edition.)

Franklin, Benjamin (*continued*)
197n; and money owed W. Lee, 200–1, 236, 300: French decision to debit U.S. for state debts, 251n; Livingston inquires about salary he pays his secretary, other expenses, 299; Congress sets salary of, 299n: to ascertain contingent expenses of, 538, 555; asked for lists of merchants, letters of recommendation to merchants, 391–2; draws on Morris in order to provide money to Lauzun, 455: G. Johonnot to pay for S. Johonnot's education, 482: Morris to pay Langeron, 593; has L'Air de Lamotte advance money to courier, 492n; offers recommendations on coinage, 493; advised not to send money to Le Couteulx & Cie., 550–1; land speculations of, 552n
—character and reputation: Turgot poem about, quoted, 39; vigor, judgement of praised by Wright, 45; claims never to have solicited or refused office, 60–1; testimonies to kindness of, 92–3, 282n; compared to Socrates, 130; accusations of Lee, others against, 155, 171; world cannot part with him yet, says Hodgson, 224; JA criticizes, praises, 257–8; James, Vaughan believe his autobiography will be example to others, 426–7n, 427–8; called oracular and sententious by Fitzherbert, 440n; credited with writing Pa. constitution, 563n; believed to have a medical degree, 600n
—earlier political and diplomatic career: and Hutchinson letters, 77–8; earnest endeavors of, to prevent war, 85; undertakes 1776 mission to Canada, 107n; as commissioner to France, 142–3, 223, 460n, 468n, 559n, 580; appointed to congressional committee to design Great Seal, 152n: congressional committee investigating mutinies, 587, 588n; works for repeal of Stamp Act, 275n: with Barclay, Fothergill to avert war, 509; hinted to British that his allegiance to French alliance not unconditional, 465n
—family: writes on behalf of JW to Castries, 53: Shelburne, 571; praises character of WTF, 59–60; gives Courtauld introduction to RB, 110; informed by RB of BFB's age, 170; promises to visit BFB in Geneva, 186; has G. Johonnot pay J. Mecom, 482n; tells RB that he would like to spend his last days with his family, 503; sends congratulations to BFB, 557; considers sending BFB to study at Cheam school, 567n
—health: suffers severe attack of bladder or kidney stones, lvii, 30–4, 39–40, 67n, 87n, 90, 112, 113, 164: earlier, later attacks of bladder or kidney stones, 31–2: recurrent attacks of gout, 54n, 253: lameness, 117n; recuperation of, lviii, 32, 101, 117n, 122n, 179, 224, 257, 371; remains mentally agile but is shaken by his illness, longs to see his American friends before he dies, lxiv–lxv; says he has little time, wishes to depart in peace, lxv, 416–17: he has consumed most of years allotted him, 557–8; reports himself as hearty as can be expected, 12: still in pain, 112: free of kidney stones, 371, 566; feared to be dying, 30, 113n; illness of, attributed to stroke, apoplexy, 30: gout, 30–1, 54, 87n, 92n, 112, 114, 117n: sciatica, 30n, 566; MacMahon prescribes medication for, 30–4, 105–6; sent various remedies for kidney stones, 31, 41–2, 132, 133n, 253, 357, 371; uses warm baths, poultices, 31: honey, 31–2; writes his own medical history, 31, 32n; Withering prepares essay on bladder, kidney stones for, offers to recommend treatment, 39–41; friends, colleagues inquire about, offer wishes for recovery, 42, 54, 56, 67, 88, 98, 101, 122, 132, 133, 157, 163, 198, 205, 207, 208, 214, 218–19, 230, 247, 261, 291, 311, 319, 579; harmed by lack of exercise, 60, 101; is too unwell to travel, 66n, 92, 164, 185n, 209: attend meeting of Société royale de médecine, 81: attend negotiating sessions, 190n: communicate regularly with JA, 226: write Steinsky, 337: write Filangieri, 571; Oswald fears disturbing, 73–4; has difficulty sleeping, 92n, 101: going up and down stairs, but is otherwise well and hearty, 566; describes situation as

New York (city): as potential source of troops for West Indies, lx, 36–7n, 70, 75, 232, 462n; troops embark at, 36–7, 75–6n; future British evacuation of, 70, 348; Loyalists at, distressed by Carleton's announcement, 75; arrival of British squadron at, 76n, 232; Carleton arrives in, 145; departure of British squadron from, 232n; Lafayette hopes to attack after capturing Jamaica, 331n; goods from *Aigle* taken to, 416; prize sent to, 476; Livingston concerned at Rochambeau's departure before evacuation of, 538; American prisoners at, 569
New York (province): records of, sent to Britain, 542
Nicolin, Philip, 559n
Niebelschütz, Capt. [Balthasar Heinrich Rudolf von?], 478
Nikson (Nilson?), ———, 549
Nipissing line: as boundary between U.S., Canada, lix, 192, 268, 271n
Nivière, sieur ——— (consulship seeker), 316
Noailles, Emmanuel-Marie-Louis, marquis de, 420
Nonsuch (ship), 68n, 102n, 117n, 251n, 398
Norfolk, Va.: burning of, 354–5
North, Frederick, Lord, 77
Northampton (prize), 242n
N. C.: confiscates Bridgen's property, 243n; Putnam plans voyage to, 512
Noseda, ———: forms partnership with Bettally, 174n
Nossa Senhora da Soledade São Miguel é Almas (Portuguese ship), 185n
Nostitz, Ludwig, graf von (Prussian minister at Spanish court), 23
Nouvelle Librairie de la Cour et de l'Académie (Mannheim), 390
Nouvelles experiences et observations sur divers objets de physique . . . (Ingenhousz), 28, 366
Nova Scotia: boundaries of, are issue in peace negotiations, 192, 194n, 219n, 220, 265–8, 271, 272n, 348, 450; drying of fish in unsettled bays of, 267–8, 273, 323n, 347, 385; should be declared independent and allowed to join U.S., pro-

pose BF, JA, 434; Clarkson's, BF's land speculations in, 552n
Nunc Dimittis (prayer), lxv, 224, 416–17
Nyon aîné, ——— (bookseller), 4, 284n

O', Miguel do, 185n
Observations on Reversionary Payments . . . (Price), 320
"Observations on the Present State of Affairs" (Office of Finance), 581n
Observations sur le gouvernement et les loix des Etats-Unis d'Amérique (Mably), 466n
"Observations sur les blés germés," 565n
Ochiltree, Duncan (quartermaster), 374
O'Dunne, Jacques-Bernard (French minister in Lisbon), 591
Offerers of goods and schemes: collectively described, 389–93
Ogden, Matthias (former army officer), 292n, 367n, 537n, 552n
Oglethorpe, James, 184
Ohio River: as possible boundary of United States, 413
Olavide y Jáuregui, Pablo Antonio José de (statesman), 126n
"On Calculus Complaints" (Withering), 40–1
Ontario: future boundaries of, affected by peace negotiations, lix, 192n, 271n
Opium poppies: syrup from, prescribed for BF, 33n
Orations against Catilina (Cicero), 52
Orléans, Louis-Philippe, duc d', 128n, 422
Osgood, Samuel (congressional delegate), 223
Ostend: military supplies sent from, 156n; merchants from, wish to trade in American ports, 457, 470–1
Oswald, Richard (diplomatic representative, xxxvii, 103n): refuses to sit for West painting, xxix; portrait of, as a young man, xxx; map shows boundary line proposed by, xxx; BF conducts discussions with, before arrival of other commissioners, lvi, lxii–lxiii: does not share optimism of, 219: gives letter opposing retribution to Loyalists, 346, 350–6, 584: sends congressional, state

Russia (*continued*)
by recognizing U.S., 95; threatens Turks, 98n, 585n; Dana requests, receives money to pay ministers of, 372–3: should communicate his mission to ministers of, suggest commissioners, 439, 585–6; Congress hopes will recognize American independence, admit to League of Armed Neutrality, 402n. *See also* St. Petersburg; Treaty of Commerce, proposed American-Russian

Rutledge, John (congressional delegate), 223

Ryan, Luke (privateer captain), 99–101

Sage, Balthazar-Georges (mineralogist, xxv, 356n, 678n): recommends physician, 529; letter from, 529

Saggi di naturali esperienʒe (Accademia del Cimento), 137n

Sagittaire (French 50-gun ship), 470n

St. Asaph (Anglican diocese in Wales), 129

Saint-Auban, Geneviève Gruyn, marquise de (xxxvi, 257n), 316n, 430

Saint-Auban, Jacques-Antoine Baratier, marquis de (army officer, xxxvi, 257n): and wife extend dinner invitation, 430; letter from, 430

St. Christopher (St. Kitts), W.I., 210, 414

St. Clair, ———: recounts captivity in Dunkirk, asks for assistance, 90–1; asks WTF's intervention with BF, 90n, 91n; letter from, 90–1

St. Croix River: as proposed border of Maine, 267, 271; unclear whether equivalent to Magaguadivic or Schoodiac, 271n

St. Domingue, W.I.: *Flora* arrives from, 12n, 214–15. *See also* Cap-Français

Saint Esprit, Sœur Marie, abbesse du: asks for continuation of BF's generosity, 528–9; letter from, 528–9

St. Germain: JW, Mariamne Williams visit Alexander family at, 233n, 261

St. James (privateer), 131, 157, 206, 208, 215–16n, 431, 463

St. James Chronicle (newspaper), 460n

St. John River: as proposed border of Maine, 192, 266–7; Frère Frederic's

mission to Micmacs and Malecites of, 470

St. John's Masonic Lodge, 551n

St. Lucia, W.I., 414

St. Petersburg: Dana's mission to, 94–5, 166–7

St. Pierre (island), 414

St. Thomas, W. I., 215

St. Vincent, W.I., 414

Sainte Virginie. *See* Virginie

Saintes, Battle of the, 16n, 75, 330

Salisbury, Diocese of, 130n

Sallust (Roman historian), 52

Sandoz-Rollin, Daniel Alfons von (secretary to Goltz), 391–2

Sandy Hook. *See* New York

San Lorenzo, Treaty of (Pickney's Treaty), 387n

Santo Domingo (Spanish colony), 414

Saratoga, Battle of, xxx, lxiv, 128n

Sargent, George Arnold (John and Rosamond's son), 548

Sargent, John (banker): sends greetings, family news, 547–8; letter from, 547–8

Sargent, John (John and Rosamond's son), 548

Sargent, Rosamond (John's wife), 547–8

Sarsfield, Guy-Claude, comte de (army officer, xiv, 205n), 112, 253

Sartine, Antoine-Raymond-Gualbert-Gabriel de (former French naval minister, xxii, 453n), 11n

Saudot, ——— (printer), 109n, 457

Savannah: British evacuate, 69–70, 75, 226n, 283n; 1779 French attack on, 590

Savidge, Mrs. ———, 405

Schmidt, Johann Friedrich (minister), 478–9

Schneider, Christian, 237, 458

Schofield, William (textile worker), 107n

Schoodiac River, 271n

Schuyler, Angelica (Philip's daughter), 546n

Schuyler, Maj. Gen. Philip, 546n

Schwediauer (Swediaur), Francis Xavier (physician and scientist): identified, 116n; accompanies Ingenhousz to England, 116; wishes to communicate work by Bentham, 116–17; reports on

Townshend, Thomas (*continued*)
Hartley to assist, 9n; informs Oswald that King consents to American independence as first article of treaty, 65, 66, 73n, 82; authorizes Oswald to offer BF's necessary articles, 65n; acknowledges letters, 74n; Oswald sends Jay's alteration of Oswald's commission to, 83n, 132n, 133n: information on BF's health to, 185n: first draft treaty to, 190n, 194n: commissioners' letter to, 286n; approves Laurens visiting England, 87n: exchange of James Jay, 250; revises Oswald's commission, 132n, 133n, 142n; and Oswald arrange exchange for Fage, 168n; and Strachey, 244–5, 268, 275, 278–9n, 346n, 375n, 376n: Hodgson, prisoners, 305, 441–2, 568–9: Nepean, 305: Fitzherbert, 440n; proclaims aversion to the war and desire for peace, 245, 275; works for repeal of Stamp Act, Tea Act, 275n; Vaughan to carry BF letter to, 280; delivers counter proposal to King, 321; tells King which articles of counter proposal Oswald to insist on, 323; sent accounts by Fitzherbert, Oswald, Strachey of final day of negotiations, 375n, 376n; announces signing of preliminary articles of peace, 422n, 541n; letter from, 244–5; letter to, 275–6
Trade: American, desired by France, 35: with Britain, opening of, suggested as negotiating tool, 413: with France, is endangered, 553: with Kingdom of Two Sicilies, should be possible, 573; with West Indies, desired by Americans, 71–2, 556; Irish, Newenham fears effects of peace treaty on, 301; Prussian, with U.S. proposed, 391–2
Treatise on the nature and properties of Air . . . , A (Cavallo), 57–8
Treaty of Alliance, American-French, 112, 216n, 379n, 403n, 465, 595n, 609–10
Treaty of Amity and Commerce, American-Dutch, 151n, 445n, 555
Treaty of Amity and Commerce, American-French, 216n, 293n, 445n
Treaty of Amity and Commerce, American-Prussian, lxiii, 444n

Treaty of Amity and Commerce, proposed American-Swedish, 118n, 151–3, 292–3, 415, 492, 555
Treaty of Commerce, proposed American-British, 6, 220n, 265, 413
Treaty of Commerce, proposed American-Russian, 372
Treaty of Peace, American-British. *See* Cessation of Arms, Declarations of; Peace Treaty, Definitive American-British; Peace negotiations, American-British; Preliminary Articles of Peace, American-British
Treaty of Peace, Preliminary British-French, lxii, 408n, 494n, 540n, 541, 595n, 605, 607–8
Treaty of Peace, Preliminary British-Spanish, lxii, 387n, 408n, 595n, 605, 607–8
Treaty of Peace and Armistice, Preliminary General, lxii, 561n, 595n, 605–8
Trees: Hopkinson's paper on, 229–30, 490; BF discusses utility of, 490
Trevitt, Samuel R. (commander of *Argo*), 51n
Trio (brig), 570–1n, 587, 589
Troye, François-Antoine de (officer in American Army), 288
Trumbull, Jonathan (gov. of Conn.): Hermelin introduced to, 288n; recommends Wheelock, 296; letter from, 295–6
Tryon, William (former governor of N.Y.), 542
"Turk, mechanical" (supposed chess-playing automaton), lxiv, 495n, 496
Turks. *See* Ottoman Empire
Two Brothers (prize), 212n, 285
Two Sicilies, Kingdom of: might appoint Filangieri to explore possibilities of trade with America, suggests BF, 573

Ulster Volunteers, 188n
Uniforms: shipped aboard the *South Carolina*, 85n: *Sukey*, 207; listed on invoice sent by Morris, 141n; purchased in U.S. by Morris, 160, 251
United States: American peace commissioners offer British choice of northern boundary for, lix, 268, 271n, 322, 450,

United States (*continued*)

452; boundaries of, delineated in preliminary articles of peace, lx, 191–2, 194, 271–2, 275, 322, 383–4, 388: resolved by Webster-Ashburton Treaty, 384n: are as good and extensive as demanded, says BF, 503–4; people of, consider preliminary articles mean the end of hostilities, lx, 462n: hold Rochambeau's army in high esteem, 139: are described as estranged from Britain, attached to France, 144–7: are reluctant to pay taxes, 147, 488–9: are most striking for their knavery, says George III, 321: love Louis XVI, claims BF, 465: are suspicious, critical of France, 504; if withdraws from war, France and Spain would be threatened, lx, 402n; citizens of Britain and, should enjoy reciprocal citizenship, commercial rights, suggests BF, lxiii, 434; possible federal connection between Britain and, 27, 145; economic effects of independence of, feared by Filangieri, 37n; talent, valor highest recommendation in, claims Chaumont, 56n; proposed consular convention between France and, 63, 553: post-war alliance of France, Spain, Netherlands with, 403; importance of logwood cutting to, 71, 332: West Indies trade to merchants, farmers in, 71: fisheries to, 554; BF wishes reconciliation between Britain and, 85; is not recognized by Russia, 95; is represented as Hercules on Libertas Americana medal, 128–9n; federal constitution of, will be completed within 20 years, predicts Morris, 146; great seal of, 152; Morris fears lethargy in, if war continues, 162; will abide by engagements with France, proclaims commissioners, 191; back country of, as possible compensation to Loyalists, 219n, 265, 413: is disputed with Spain, France, 220n, 450: is claimed by British, 450; diplomatic representatives not exchanged between Sweden and, 287n; Hermelin reports on mining in, 287n; deficiency in taxes raised by, necessitates new loan says BF, 289–90;

British refuse to evacuate posts in interior of, 386n; fails to comply with treaty provisions concerning Loyalists, 386n; Lavallée wishes to establish factories in, 389, 392–3; Senff proposes to establish saltworks in, 391; Filangieri wishes to work on code of laws for, opposes use of death penalty in, 400–1; and Russia, League of Armed Neutrality, 402n; ports of, are closed to British shipping, 413; map showing borders of, is sent to Vergennes, 419; Canada, Nova Scotia, Bermuda should be free to join, propose BF, JA, 434; inquiry if ports of, are open to ships from Austrian Netherlands, 457; will not continue war to satisfy Spanish, Dutch demands, say commissioners, 462n; firm connection with France gives it weight with England, respect throughout Europe, says BF, 504; Congress wishes to obtain commercial reciprocity between Britain and, 537n; cause of, is inseparably linked with Louis XVI, says draft declaration, 541; Livingston urges importance of mutual trust between France and, 554; must prepare for continuation of war, says Morris, 577. *See also* Army, American; Continental Congress; Peace negotiations, British-American; States, American

Urgent Necessity of an Immediate Repeal of the Whole Penal Code . . . , The, 326–7

Vallier (Wallier), Jean, le cadet, 367n, 405
Vallier (Wallier), Jean-Jacques, 367n, 405
Valltravers, Johann Rodolph (Rodolphe) (journalist, xiv, 24n): introduces Kempelen, lxiv, 495–7; complains letters not answered, 183, 495; sends letter via Rauquil-Lieutaud, 183, 495; recounts difficulties, volunteers services, 183–5; claims to have acquired land in N. Y., Ga., 184; and Ingenhousz, 185; wishes to emigrate to U.S., 497; letters from, 183–5, 495–7
Valmont de Bomare, Jacques-Christophe (naturalist, xxviii, 142n): announces opening of courses, sends greetings to WTF, 381; letter from, 381